Third Edition

Business Law and the Legal Environment of Business

Victor D. López, J.D., Esq.
*Professor of Legal Studies in Business
Hofstra University
Frank G. Zarb School of Business*

**The Quality Instructors Expect.
At Prices Students Can Afford.**

Replacing Oligarch Textbooks since 2004

Business Law and the Legal Environment of Business, 3rd Edition
Copyright © 2017 Victor D. Lopez.

ISBN-13: 978-0-9969962-2-8
ISBN-10: 0-9969962-2-2

All rights reserved. No part of this book may be reproduced or transmitted in any form or by any means, electronic or mechanical, including photocopying and recording, or by any information storage or retrieval system without the prior written permission of the publisher.

Printed in the United States of America by Textbook Media Press.

Dedication

*For my wife, Alice Z. López,
my mom, Manuela (Lita) López, and my dad,
Felipe López, with all my love and gratitude.*

Brief Contents

Preface xxi
Acknowledgments xxi
About the Author xxiii

UNIT 1 — THE FOUNDATION OF LAW AND ETHICS — 1

1	The Civil Law and Common Law Traditions	3
2	Constitutional Law	11
3	The Court System	21
4	Ethics and Its Impact on Law and Government	29
5	Administrative Law	35
6	Criminal Law	39
7	Intentional Torts	55
8	Negligence and Strict Liability	65

UNIT 2 — CONTRACTS — 75

9	General Introduction to Contracts	77
10	Offer and Acceptance	81
11	Consideration	87
12	Capacity	93
13	Genuine Assent	97
14	Legality	103
15	Statute of Frauds	107
16	Assignment of Contracts and Third-Party Beneficiaries	113
17	Performance and Breach	119
18	Remedies	123

UNIT 3 — SALES, LEASES, COMMERCIAL PAPER, AND SECURED TRANSACTIONS UNDER THE UNIFORM COMMERCIAL CODE — 137

19	Introduction to UCC Article 2 (Sales) and Article 2A (Leases)	139
20	Rights and Duties of Parties in the Performance and Breach of Sales and Lease Contracts	147
21	Warranties	155
22	Remedies for Breach of Sales and Lease Contracts	161
23	Introduction to UCC Article 3 (Commercial Paper)	167
24	Transfer and Negotiation of Commercial Paper and Rights of Holders	175
25	Liability of Parties to Commercial Paper and Warranties of Transfer and of Presentment	181
26	Introduction to UCC Article 9 (Secured Transactions)	187

UNIT 4 — BANKRUPTCY — 199

27	Liquidation, Reorganization, and Adjustment of Debts	201

UNIT 5 — PROPERTY AND INSURANCE — 219

28	Personal Property	221
29	Intellectual Property	229
30	Bailments	237
31	Real Property	243
32	Creation and Transfer of Interests in Real Property	251
33	Landlords' and Tenants' Rights and Responsibilities	259
34	Insurance	265
35	Wills	271
36	Trusts	281

UNIT 6 — AGENCY — 301

37	Agency	303

UNIT 7	GOVERNMENT REGULATION OF BUSINESS	317
38	Employment Relations	319
39	Federal Securities Acts	331
40	Federal Antitrust Law	337

UNIT 8	BUSINESS ORGANIZATIONS	353
41	Sole Proprietorship	355
42	Partnership	359
43	Limited Partnership	369
44	Corporations	375
45	Limited Liability Companies	383

Appendix A: U.S. Constitution 399
Appendix B: Uniform Commercial Code (UCC) 413
Index 555

Contents

Preface xxi
Acknowledgments xxi
About the Author xxiii

UNIT 1 THE FOUNDATION OF LAW AND ETHICS 1

1 The Civil Law and Common Law Traditions 3

Civil Law Systems 3
Common Law Systems 4
Sources of American Law 5

Questions 9 ■ *Hypothetical Cases 9*

2 Constitutional Law 11

The Commerce Clause 12
The Bill of Rights 13
The Scope of Constitutional Protection 18

Questions 19 ■ *Hypothetical Cases 19*

3 The Court System 21

Jurisdiction 21
The Federal Court System 23
The State Court System 25

Questions 27 ■ *Hypothetical Cases 27*

4 Ethics and Its Impact on Law and Government 29

Ethical Philosophies 29
Ethics and Public Policy 31

Problem Areas 32
The Regulatory Environment of Business 32

Questions 34 ■ Hypothetical Cases 34

5 Administrative Law — 35

Administrative Agencies 35
Purpose of Federal Agencies 35
Independent Federal Agencies 35
Executive Agencies 36
State Agencies 36
The Administrative Procedure Act 36

Questions 37 ■ Hypothetical Cases 38

6 Criminal Law — 39

Elements of a Crime 39
Classification of Crimes 41
Specific Crimes 41
Crimes against Persons 41
Crimes against Property 43
Bribery, Extortion, and Crimes against the Judicial Process 45
Attempted Crimes and Criminal Conspiracy 47
Defenses to Criminal Liability 47

Questions 52 ■ Hypothetical Cases 52 ■ Ethics and the Law: Questions for Further Study 52

7 Intentional Torts — 55

Breach of Duty as a Prerequisite to Tort Liability 55
Intentional Torts against Persons 56
Intentional Torts against Property 60

Questions 62 ■ Hypothetical Cases 62 ■ Ethics and the Law: Questions for Further Study 63

8 Negligence and Strict Liability — 65

Negligence 65
Defenses to Negligence 66
Strict Liability 68

Questions 70 ■ *Hypothetical Cases 70* ■ *Ethics and the Law: Questions for Further Study 70*

Unit I—Cases for Further Study 71

UNIT 2 CONTRACTS — 75

9 General Introduction to Contracts — 77

Classification of Contracts 78

Questions 80 ■ *Hypothetical Cases 80*

10 Offer and Acceptance — 81

Requirements of a Valid Offer 81
Revocation of an Offer 82
Acceptance 82
Modes of Acceptance 83

Questions 84 ■ *Hypothetical Cases 84*

11 Consideration — 87

Illusory Promises 88
Past Consideration 89
Pre-existing Duty 89

Questions 90 ■ *Hypothetical Cases 90* ■ *Ethics and the Law: Questions for Further Study 91*

12 Capacity — 93

Definition of Capacity 93

Questions 95 ■ *Hypothetical Cases 96* ■ *Ethics and the Law: Questions for Further Study 96*

13 Genuine Assent 97

Mutual Mistake 97
Duress 98
Fraud in the Inducement 98
Fraud in the Execution 99
Undue Influence 100

Questions 100 ■ Hypothetical Cases 100

14 Legality 103

Contracts Involving the Commission of a Tort or a Crime 103
Restraint of Trade 103
Gambling Contracts 104
Usurious Contracts 104
Contracts Contrary to Public Policy 104

Questions 105 ■ Hypothetical Cases 105 ■ Ethics and the Law: Questions for Further Study 106

15 Statute of Frauds 107

Definition of a Signed Writing 108
Contracts That by Their Terms Cannot Be Performed within One Year 108
Contracts Transferring an Interest in Real Estate 108
Contracts for the Sale of Goods for $500 or More 109
Contracts Promising to Answer for the Debt of Another 109
Contracts of Executors and Administrators 109
Contracts in Consideration of Marriage 109

Questions 110 ■ Hypothetical Cases 110

16 Assignment of Contracts and Third-Party Beneficiaries 113

Assignment of Contract Rights 113
Novation 115
Rights of Third-Party Beneficiaries to Contracts 115

Questions 116 ■ Hypothetical Cases 116 ■ Ethics and the Law: Questions for Further Study 117

17 Performance and Breach — 119

Discharge through Performance 119
Discharge through Substantial Performance 119
Discharge through Impossibility of Performance 120
Discharge through Commercial Impracticability of Performance 120
Discharge through Frustration of Purpose 121
Discharge through Release 121
Discharge through Novation 121
Breach of Contract 122

Questions 122 ■ Hypothetical Cases 122

18 Remedies — 123

Legal Remedies 123
Equitable Remedies 125
Election of Remedies 126
Mitigation of Damages 127

Questions 127 ■ Hypothetical Cases 128 ■ Ethics and the Law: Questions for Further Study 128

Unit II—Cases for Further Study 130

UNIT 3 SALES, LEASES, COMMERCIAL PAPER, AND SECURED TRANSACTIONS UNDER THE UNIFORM COMMERCIAL CODE 137

19 Introduction to UCC Article 2 (Sales) and Article 2A (Leases) — 139

Applicability of Article 2 139
Applicability of Article 2A 140
Formal Requirements and Rules of Construction 140
Statute of Frauds [§ 2-201(1), § 2A-201(1)] 140
Parol Evidence Rule [§ 2-202, § 2A-202] 140
Inapplicability of Seals [§ 2-203, § 2A-203] 141
Contract Formation 141
Contracts for International Sale of Goods 143

Questions 144 ■ Hypothetical Cases 144

20 Rights and Duties of Parties in the Performance and Breach of Sales and Lease Contracts — 147

Delivery of Goods [§ 2-308] 147
Time Frame for Delivery of Goods and Notice of Termination [§ 2-309] 147
Contract Options and Duty of Cooperation [§ 2-311] 147
Shipment by Common Carrier [§ 2-311] 148
F.O.B. and F.A.S. Shipment Terms and Risk of Loss [§ 2-319] 148
C. I. F. and C. & F. Terms [§ 2-320] 148
Sale on Approval, Sale or Return, and Consignment Sales [§ 2-326] 148
Risk of Loss with Regard to Sale on Approval and Sale or Return [§ 2-327] 149
Passing of Title to Goods [§ 2-401] 149
Insurable Interest on Goods [§ 2-501] 149
Seller's Tender of Delivery [§ 2-503] 149
Shipment by Seller [§ 2-504] 150
Effect of Seller's Tender of Delivery [§ 2-507] 150
Risk of Loss [§ 2-509] 150
Buyer's Right to Inspect Goods [§ 2-507] 151
Buyer's Rights on Improper Delivery [§ 2-601] 151
Merchant Buyer's Duties as to Rightfully Rejected Goods [§ 2-603] 152
Anticipatory Repudiation [§ 2-610] 152
Casualty to Identified Goods [§ 2-613] 152
Substituted Performance [§ 2-614] 153

Questions 153 ■ Hypothetical Cases 153

21 Warranties — 155

Express Warranties [§ 2-313, § 2A-210)] 155
Implied Warranties 156
Third-Party Beneficiaries of Warranties Express or Implied [§ 2-318, § 2A-216] 158

Questions 158 ■ Hypothetical Cases 158

22 Remedies for Breach of Sales and Lease Contracts — 161

Seller's and Lessor's Remedies 161
Seller's Remedies 161

Buyer's Remedies 162
Lessee's Remedies 164
General Rules Affecting Buyers, Sellers, Lessees, and Lessors 164
Liquidation of Damages [§ 2-718, § 2A-504)] 165
Contractual Modification or Limitation of Remedies [§ 2-719, § 2A-503] 165
Statute of Limitations [§ 2-725, § 2A-506] 165

Questions 165 ■ Hypothetical Cases 165

23 Introduction to UCC Article 3 (Commercial Paper) 167

Parties to Commercial Paper 168
Form of Negotiable Instruments [§ 3-104] 168
Type of Negotiable Instruments 168
Requirements for Negotiability 170
General Rules Applicable to Commercial Paper 172

Questions 173 ■ Hypothetical Cases 174

24 Transfer and Negotiation of Commercial Paper and Rights of Holders 175

Transfer of Negotiable Instruments and the Transferee's Right to an Indorsement 175
Negotiation [§ 3-201] 175
Indorsement [§ 3-204] 175
Rights of a Holder 177
Rights of a Holder in Due Course 177

Questions 178 ■ Hypothetical Cases 178

25 Liability of Parties to Commercial Paper and Warranties of Transfer and of Presentment 181

Liability of Parties to Commercial Paper 181
Warranties on Presentment and Transfer 183
Presentment and Notice of Dishonor 184

Questions 184 ■ Hypothetical Cases 185

26 Introduction to UCC Article 9 (Secured Transactions) 187

Applicability 187
Basic Terminology 188
Creating a Security Interest 188
Perfecting a Security Interest 189
Duration of a Perfected Security Interest 189
Priorities among Conflicting Security Interests in the Same Collateral 190
Default 190

Questions 190 ■ *Hypothetical Cases 191*

Unit III—Cases for Further Study 192

UNIT 4 BANKRUPTCY 199

27 Liquidation, Reorganization, and Adjustment of Debts 201

Introduction 201
Chapter 7: Liquidation 201
Chapter 11: Reorganization 205
Chapter 13: Adjustment of Debts of an Individual with Regular Income 207

Questions 213 ■ *Hypothetical Cases 213*

Unit IV—Cases for Further Study 214

UNIT 5 PROPERTY AND INSURANCE 219

28 Personal Property 221

Acquiring Title to Personal Property through Possession 221
Acquiring Title to Property through Purchase 222
Acquiring Title to Personal Property through Manufacturing 223
Acquiring Title to Personal Property through Accession 224
Acquiring Title to Personal Property through a Gift 225

Questions 226 ■ *Hypothetical Cases 226* ■ *Ethics and the Law: Questions for Further Study 227*

29 Intellectual Property 229

Patents 229
Copyrights 230
Trademarks 231
Service Marks, Collective Marks, and Certification Marks 231
Remedies for Infringement of a Registered Mark 232
Trade Secrets 232
Intellectual Property in the International Arena 233

Questions 234 ■ Hypothetical Cases 234

30 Bailments 237

Introduction to Bailments 237

Questions 240 ■ Hypothetical Cases 241

31 Real Property 243

Estates in Land 243
Freehold Estates 244
Nonfreehold Estates 245
Future Interests 245
Nonpossessory Interests in Land 246
Easements 246
Profits à Prendre 247
Licenses 248

Questions 248 ■ Hypothetical Cases 248

32 Creation and Transfer of Interests in Real Property 251

Transfer by Deed 251
Title through *Inter Vivos* and Testamentary Gifts 252
Title through Eminent Domain 252
Recording Statutes 253
Title through Adverse Possession 253
Concurrent Ownership 254
Public and Private Restrictions on Land Use 255

Questions 256 ■ Hypothetical Cases 256 ■ Ethics and the Law: Questions for Further Study 257

33 Landlords' and Tenants' Rights and Responsibilities — 259

Creation of the Landlord-Tenant Relationship 259
Termination of the Landlord-Tenant Relationship 259
Unlawful Termination of the Landlord-Tenant Relationship 259
Tenant's Rights and Responsibilities 262
Landlord's Remedies Upon Breach of the Rental Agreement 262
Tenant's Remedies Upon Breach of a Rental Agreement 263

Questions 264 ■ Hypothetical Cases 264 ■ Ethics and the Law: Questions for Further Study 264

34 Insurance — 265

The Insurance Contract 265
Types of Insurance Contracts 267

Questions 269 ■ Hypothetical Cases 269

35 Wills — 271

An Introduction to Wills 271
Requirements of a Valid Will 274
Holographic and Nuncupative Wills 276
Revocation of a Will 276
Disinheritance of Spouses and Children 277
Intestacy 277

Questions 278 ■ Hypothetical Cases 278 ■ Ethics and the Law: Questions for Further Study 279

36 Trusts — 281

Creation of Express Trusts 282
Requirements, Rights, and Responsibilities of Trustees 282
Irrevocable and Revocable Trusts 282
Totten Trusts 284
Creation of Testamentary Trusts 286
Creation of a Resulting Trust 287

Creation of a Constructive Trust 287
Termination of Trusts 287

Questions 287 ■ Hypothetical Cases 287

Unit V—Cases for Further Study 289

UNIT 6 AGENCY 301

37 Agency 303

Introduction 303
Creation of an Agency 303
Agent's Authority 304
Agent's Apparent Authority 304
Agency by Estoppel 305
Termination of an Agency 306
Principal's Duties in an Agency Agreement 306
Agent's Duties in an Agency Agreement 307
Liability of Principal for Agent's Torts 308
Liability of Agents for Contracts Entered Into on the Principal's Behalf 309
Agent's Unauthorized Contracts 309
Agent's Authorized Contracts on Behalf of a Fully Disclosed Principal 309
Agent's Authorized Contracts on Behalf of a Partially Disclosed Principal 309
Agent's Authorized Contracts on Behalf of an Undisclosed Principal 310

Questions 310 ■ Hypothetical Cases 310

Unit VI—Cases for Further Study 312

UNIT 7 GOVERNMENT REGULATION OF BUSINESS 317

38 Employment Relations 319

Rights and Responsibilities of Employers and Employees Based on Agency 319
Rights and Responsibilities of Employers and Employees Based on Contract Law 320
Governmental Regulation of Labor-Management Relations 320
Additional Federal Regulation Affecting Employment 323

Questions 328 ■ Hypothetical Cases 329 ■ Ethics and the Law 330

39 Federal Securities Acts — 331

Securities Act of 1933 331
Sanctions under the Securities Act of 1933 333
Securities Exchange Act of 1934 333
Sarbanes–Oxley Act of 2002 334
Securities Regulation by the States 334

Questions 335 ■ *Hypothetical Cases 335*

40 Federal Antitrust Law — 337

The Sherman Antitrust Act of 1890 337
The Clayton Act of 1914 339

Questions 340 ■ *Hypothetical Cases 340* ■ *Ethics and the Law 341*

Unit VII—Cases for Further Study 342

UNIT 8 BUSINESS ORGANIZATIONS — 353

41 Sole Proprietorship — 355

Formation of a Sole Proprietorship 355
Benefits of the Sole Proprietorship 356
Liabilities of the Sole Proprietorship 356
Property Status of the Sole Proprietorship 357
Termination of the Sole Proprietorship 357

Questions 357 ■ *Hypothetical Cases 357*

42 Partnership — 359

Model Partnership Act 359
Formation of a Partnership 359
Relationship of Partners to the Partnership and to One Another 360
Agency Rights and Duties of Partners 360
Contractual Rights and Duties of Partners 360
Limitations on Partners' Ability to Define their Rights and Obligations as Partners 362

Limitation on Partners' Right of Compensation 362
Partners' Capital Contributions 362
Admission of New Partners 362
Partners' Right to Inspect Partnership's Books 362
Partners' Liability for Partnership Debt 362
Purported Partners 363
Partners' Property Rights 363
Partner's Dissociation 364
Dissolution of a Partnership and Winding Up 365
Notice to Third Parties upon Dissolution 365

Questions 366 ■ *Hypothetical Cases 366*

43 Limited Partnership 369

Formation of a Limited Partnership 370
Admission of New Partners 370
Rights and Obligations of General and Limited Partners 370
Sharing of Profits and Losses 371
Withdrawal by General and Limited Partners 371
Assignment of Partnership Interest 372
Dissolution of a Limited Partnership 372
Foreign Limited Partnership 372
Right of Limited Partners to Bring Derivative Actions 373

Questions 373 ■ *Hypothetical Cases 374*

44 Corporations 375

Corporate Formation 375
Articles of Incorporation 375
Corporate Name 376
Corporate Existence 376
Defective Incorporation 376
Promoters' Liability for Preincorporation Contracts 377
First Organizational Meeting of the Corporation 377
Management of the Corporation 378

Shareholders' Derivative Actions 379
Classification of Corporations 379
The Corporation as an Entity 380
Piercing the Corporate Veil 380
Chapter S Corporations 381

Questions 381 ■ *Hypothetical Cases 382*

Limited Liability Companies — 383

Purpose and Duration of a Limited Liability Company 384
Entity Status 384
Name of LLC 384
Operating Agreement 384
Formation of an LLC 384
Annual Report 384
Agency Power of Members 385
Liabilities of Members and Managers 385
Admission of New Members 385
Management 385
Transferable Interest 385
Dissociation 386
Dissolution and Winding Up 386

Questions 386 ■ *Hypothetical Cases 386* ■ *Ethics and the Law 387*

Unit VIII—Cases for Further Study 388

Appendix A: U.S. Constitution 399
Appendix B: Uniform Commercial Code (UCC) 413
Index 555

Preface

I began working on my first textbook for Irwin/Mirror Press, *Business Law: An Introduction*, as a newly minted assistant professor of business at SUNY Delhi. Having served as both a professor and dean for a number of years prior to that posting, I was familiar with the leading textbooks from the major presses and wanted to go in a very different direction to create a textbook that was both affordable and student-centered. At that time, textbooks were too expensive, as they are currently, due to factors that I document in one of my articles, "Legislating Relief for the High Cost of College Textbooks: A Brief Analysis of the Current Law and Its Implication for Students, Faculty and the Publishing Industry" (*Journal of Legal Studies in Business*, Vol. 15 p. 35 [2009]). One contributing reason for the high cost of college textbooks in the legal studies area is the overuse of pedagogical devices such as case studies, sidebars, definitions, case excerpts, and the myriad other devices intended to explain and expand on the ideas in the main text that, in my view, more often distract students than enlighten them and results in bloated, expensive textbooks. My preferred approach is very different: make the material accessible, relevant, and interesting for my students to actively engage them in the learning process. A textbook that students do not read or struggle to understand is of little use. I want students who are assigned my textbooks to want to read them and to successfully master the learning outcomes for the course. But I also want them to be challenged by the ideas they contain, the questions they raise, and the examples they use, and to understand on a personal level the interplay between law, politics, and ethics, and the impact of the regulatory environment on business, on the professions, and its role in helping to attain social justice. I want the experience of reading my textbooks to be memorable for students; I want their eyes to brighten rather than glaze over as they read the main text, answer questions or work on case briefs, and engage in class discussions that build upon their assigned readings. I want them to come to class prepared to ask questions, apply the law to business situations and participate in class discussions, especially when their professor stirs the pot in the devil's advocate role to challenge their assumptions or question established legal precedents.

Portions of this book were originally published in my *Legal Environment of Business* textbook (Prentice Hall, 1997). The original material was significantly edited, updated, and expanded, with numerous chapters excised and added, in the text's second edition. The third edition has once again been significantly revised and expanded to make this new textbook appropriate for one- and two-semester course sequences in business law, introduction to law, and the legal environment of business. Each unit now features select case excerpts suitable for briefing and class discussion: a new chapter on Constitutional Law in direct response to adopters' feedback.

This book is accompanied by an Instructor's Manual and a test-item file in Word. The test items are also available on a test CD-ROM (Diploma software by Blackboard). These materials are available to interested instructors upon request.

Acknowledgments

I would like to gratefully acknowledge the support of the Frank G. Zarb School of Business at Hofstra University for my research, publication, and professional development activities. I would also like to thank the chairs, deans, and provosts with whom I've served as well as my colleagues in the Department of Accounting, Taxation, and Legal Studies in Business and at the Frank G. Zarb School of Business for their strong support and for making me feel welcome in my new academic home. I am especially grateful to my colleague and friend Eugene T. Maccarrone for chairing my tenure committee and for his collaboration on four published articles. Likewise, I am most grateful to Cheryl R. Lehman for chairing my ad hoc promotion committee to full professor as I write this.

It has been two decades since I began writing my first textbook, *Business Law: An Introduction* (Irwin/Mirror Press, 1993), and had the privilege to work with David Helmstadter, the president and publisher of Irwin's Mirror Press division, and Carla Tishler, my editor. I will never forget David's kindness, encouragement, and the time he dedicated to me as a fledgling writer during and after the publication of the book. He is a remarkable human being to whom I will always be grateful, and who is in no small part responsible for my continuing to pursue the writing of textbooks and scholarly books. I am very pleased to have come full circle in working with Ed Laube, the co-founder and publisher of Textbook Media Publishing, whose support and dedication to this project have brought me back to my first experience as a textbook author. I am enormously grateful for his support and that of Tom Doran, president and co-founder of Textbook Media Publishing, for the opportunity to join an enterprise devoted to making high-quality affordable textbooks available to all students. My thanks also to Victoria Putman for her patience and thoroughness during the production of this third edition.

I also need to thank all of my friends and colleagues at the institutions I have served prior to joining the Hofstra University faculty in a variety of roles that included adjunct instructor, professor, consultant, and dean: Plaza Business Institute, LaGuardia Community College, SUNY at Farmingdale, MTI, SUNY at Delhi, Hartwick College, Excelsior College, and SUNY Broome. Among all my exceptional colleagues, I must single out one to whom I am especially grateful for his friendship, counsel, and strong, unconditional support of my academic and personal goals—Dr. William Raynor, Professor at Southern Wesleyan University (Adult & Graduate Studies Division). As I have told others numerous times, when the day comes and St. Peter stops me at the Pearly Gates and asks, "Why should I let you enter?" my best response will be, "Bill Raynor was my friend."

Finally, and perhaps most importantly, I need to thank my students—past, present, and future—in the urban, suburban, and rural colleges I have had the privilege to serve. You have brought me more fulfillment and happiness over the past quarter century than I could ever articulate or gratefully acknowledge. Ultimately, it is all about you.

About the Author

Victor D. López is currently a tenured Professor of Legal Studies in Business at Hofstra University's Frank G. Zarb School of Business. In the past, he has served as an adjunct instructor at LaGuardia Community College, SUNY at Farmingdale, Hartwick College, and SUNY Broome (while serving as Dean of the Business Division there), Academic Dean at MTI, a professor and director of the Extended-day Program at Plaza Business Institute, a tenured Professor of Business at SUNY at Delhi for 12 years, and Dean of Business and Business Information Technologies at SUNY Broome. He also served for a number of years on the consulting faculty of Excelsior College.

Prior law-related published textbooks by Professor López include *Business Law: An Introduction* (Irwin/Mirror Press and McGraw Hill, 1993), *Legal Environment of Business* (Prentice Hall, 1997), *Case and Resource Materials for the Legal Environment of Business* (Prentice Hall, 1997), *Business Law and the Legal Environment of Business,* 2nd edition (Textbook Media Publishing, 2010), and *Business Law: An Introduction,* 2nd edition (Textbook Media Publishing, 2011). He has also published *Intellectual Property Law: A Practical Guide to Copyrights, Patents, Trademarks and Trade Secrets* through Amazon and CreateSpace. His recent published and accepted articles include

- Victor D. López, "When Lenders Can Legally Provide Loans with Effective Annual Interest Rates Above 1,000 Percent, Is It Time for Congress to Consider a Federal Interest Cap on Consumer Loans?" *Notre Dame Journal of Legislation,* 42 J. Legis 101 (2016).
- Eugene T. Maccarrone & Victor D. López, *Medical Malpractice Limitations for New York Infants—Time for a Change of Time?*, 34 Buff. Pub. Int. L.J. 99 (2016).
- Victor D. López and Eugene T. Maccarrone, "Traffic Enforcement by Camera: Privacy and Due Process in the Age of Big Brother," *Law Journal for Social Justice* at Arizona State University (Vol. 5, Spring 2015 at 120).
- Victor D. López and Eugene T. Maccarrone, "Leading the World in the Wrong Direction: Is It Time for the U.S. to Adopt the World Standard Loser Pays Rule in Civil Litigation?" *North East Journal of Legal Studies*, Spring 2014 at 1.
- Victor D. López , "Dealing with Uninvited and Unwelcomed Guests: A Survey of Current State Legislative Efforts to Control Illegal Immigration within Their Borders," *International Journal of Public Law and Policy*, Vol. 3, No. 1 at 43 (2013, Geneva, Switzerland).
- Victor D. López , "Unauthorized Practice of Law in the U.S.: A Survey and Brief Analysis of the Law," *North East Journal of Legal Studies,* Vol. 26 at 60 (Fall 2011).
- Victor D. López, "Principled Leadership: Finding Common Ground among Divergent Philosophies," *University of Botswana Law Journal*, Vol. 11 at 153 (December 2010).
- Victor D. López, "State Homestead Exemptions and Bankruptcy Law: Is It Time for Congress to Close the Loophole?" *Rutgers Business Law Journal*, Vol. 7 at 143 (Spring 2010).

- Victor D. López, "Illegal Immigration: Economic, Social and Ethical Implications," *North East Journal of Legal Studies*, Vol. 22 at 45 (Spring 2009).
- Victor D. López, "Legislating Relief for the High Cost of College Textbooks: A Brief Analysis of the Current Law and Its Implication for Students, Faculty and the Publishing Industry," *Journal of Legal Studies in Business*, Vol. 15 at 35 (2009).

Professor López was admitted to practice in New York State in 1984, is a member of the New York State Bar, the New York State Bar Association, the Academy of Legal Studies in Business (ALSB), and the North East Academy of Legal Studies in Business (NEALSB). He has previously served two terms as vice president and president of the North East Academy of Legal Studies in Business and as the program chair for two NEALSB annual conferences. He has also served as a reviewer for the *American Business Law Journal*, *North East Journal of Legal Studies*, and *Journal of Legal Studies in Business*.

THE FOUNDATION OF LAW AND ETHICS

UNIT 1

Lukas Gojda/Shutterstock

CHAPTER 1
The Civil Law and Common Law Traditions

CHAPTER 2
Constitutional Law

CHAPTER 3
The Court System

CHAPTER 4
Ethics and Its Impact on Law and Government

CHAPTER 5
Administrative Law

CHAPTER 6
Criminal Law

CHAPTER 7
Intentional Torts

CHAPTER 8
Negligence and Strict Liability

Introduction

Throughout the ages, philosophers, jurists, political scientists, political leaders, and common people from all walks of life have defined law in a number of ways. Cicero viewed law as "nothing but a correct principle drawn from the inspiration of the gods, commanding what is honest, and forbidding the contrary." For the eminent British jurist William Blackstone, law could be defined as "a rule of civil conduct, prescribed by the supreme power in a state, commanding what is right and prohibiting what is wrong." Saint Thomas Aquinas, on the other hand, defined law as "an ordinance of reason for the common good, made by him who has care of the community." Whatever our working definition, law is often what Justice Felix Frankfurter described as "all we have standing between us and the tyranny of mere will."

At its simplest, law can be defined as the rules of behavior that a government imposes on its people for the benefit of society as a whole. As such, it represents the governing body's subjective views of what is best for that society. And even though most legal systems attempt to protect society and promote the common good, there can be radical differences in the law from one country to another, and even in different regions within countries; this is inevitable given that, as we will explore further in Chapter 4 on ethics and public policy, such ethereal concepts as fairness, justice, and the public good can have different meanings depending on which ethical system one uses as a point of reference. Thus, for the good of society, the laws of Holland tolerate drug use and prostitution, but those of Iran can exact the death penalty for the same behavior. Likewise, a 10-year-old can drink wine in some countries around the world today, while that behavior is generally limited to 21-year-olds in most U.S. states, and is prohibited to all in Saudi Arabia. Reasonable people can debate (often heatedly) the relative good to society inherent in the diametrically opposed viewpoints expressed in these countries' laws, but philosophical discourse aside, travelers to these jurisdictions had better know the law, for they will most certainly be subject to penalties for its violation, and it is a universal precept that ignorance of the law generally will not excuse its breach.

Businesses have always been faced with the practical problem of conflicting laws in sovereign jurisdictions. This is particularly the case in the United States, where, as we will explore in the next chapter, we have no unified legal system and must contend with separate federal, state, and local laws. When you further consider the realities of global commerce and the trend toward lifting trade barriers through international treaties such as the North American Free Trade Agreement (NAFTA) to encourage international trade, the implications for business are staggering. A company needs to be familiar with the laws in every state and country where it conducts business. Larger companies have in-house legal departments or have access to the expertise of large law firms. Small businesses, on the other hand, often operate with little knowledge of the law and minimal access to legal counsel—a practice somewhat akin to playing Russian roulette. Regardless of size, any business can benefit greatly from employing people at all levels who have at least a basic understanding of the law and a solid grasp of essential legal principles so that they can recognize potential legal problems and refer them to legal counsel before they can become costly catastrophes.

While no textbook can become a comprehensive hands-on guide to American law (the legal encyclopedias that attempt to do so run tens of thousands of pages and do not comprehensively cover all aspects of the law), it is the purpose of this text to provide an accurate, easy-to-understand, useful guide to some areas of the law that have the greatest impact on business. Business law, legal environment of business, and legal studies courses will provide students with the skills to recognize and apply the proverbial ounce of prevention to their business careers and personal lives. This can prove more useful to employers and to themselves than pounds of competent, costly legal advice obtained too late to remedy a problem that could have been avoided.

In this unit, we will begin our excursion into the practical application of the law by examining the sources of American law and the American court system. We will then delve into the role and impact of ethics on law and government and begin an exploration of substantive law in the areas of administrative law, criminal law, intentional torts, negligence, and strict liability.

The Civil Law and Common Law Traditions

CHAPTER 1

Chapter Outline
Civil Law Systems
Common Law Systems
Sources of American Law

While the laws of sovereign states can vary widely, all law can be traced to basic roots in one of two distinct legal traditions: civil law and common law. A brief examination of each system is a useful way to begin our journey through American law and the legal environment of business, for it can give us useful clues as to the basic philosophies that underlie legal systems, and allow us to explore some strengths and weaknesses inherent in the two major competing systems of law.

Civil Law Systems

Civil law is the oldest and by far the most commonly used system of law throughout the world. It traces its roots to a tradition that dates back to the Code of Hammurabi, an ancient Babylonian king who ruled from 1792 B.C. to 1750 B.C. Hammurabi is credited with providing the world with the first comprehensive code of law. A stele containing the code of laws was unearthed in 1901 in what is today Susa, Iran, by a team of French archaeologists. The stele, which was found in three pieces, is made of stone and stands nearly seven and a half feet tall and is more than two feet wide. It was removed to France and restored, and is currently housed at the Louvre in Paris. The Code of Hammurabi, which consists of 282 laws literally written in stone, serves as a metaphor for the stability and slow-changing nature of civil law. It is a basic concept of civil law that all law should be reduced to written codes and made public so that it can be read, understood, and applied by common people. This tradition was continued in the Twelve Tables of Roman law where, in 450 B.C., 12 bronze tablets specifying a code of law applicable in the Roman Empire were attached to the orator's platform on the Roman Forum in an attempt to make the law accessible to all Roman citizens. The tradition of codifying the law found its greatest expression in 533 A.D., when the Byzantine Emperor Justinian I integrated 1,000 years of existing law into a single code that he called *Corpus Juris Civilis*—the body of civil law—and is now commonly referred to as the Justinian Code. The Justinian Code is still widely studied today in civil law jurisdictions as the most important pillar of jurisprudence upon which all modern civil law is based. The most notable attempt in modern times to codify the law into a comprehensive civil code was carried out by a commission appointed by Napoleon Bonaparte in 1800 that resulted in the 1804 Code Civil, more commonly referred to as the Napoleonic Code. Using the Justinian Code as a guide, the Napoleonic Code is divided into three parts. The first part deals with civil rights, marital rights, personal property, and education; the second part deals with real property ownership and the government's rights under eminent domain; the third part of the code concerns *inter vivos* and testamentary gifts, as well as contractual rights.

Between 1807 and 1811 the Code was supplemented by additional codes on civil procedure, commercial law, criminal procedure, and criminal law. Taken together, this extensive body of law forms the basis of many modern legal systems in Europe, Central and South America, and Quebec. The Napoleonic Code was also very influential in Louisiana, where a modified form of the Code is still in effect today as the basis of that state's law.

The defining characteristic of civil law is the attempt at codifying the law—of reducing all law into a written form that ideally can be both understood and applied by the common citizenry. Perhaps the most tangible benefit of civil law is its efficiency and stability. Because civil law leaves little room for judicial interpretation and because trial by jury is usually not an option, the application of the law is highly predictable, the administration of justice relatively swift, and the law itself slow to change. In civil law jurisdictions, a single judge or a panel of judges, depending on the nature and seriousness of the case, decide issues of both fact and law. This greatly speeds up trials and lowers their cost to litigants in civil matters and to the state in criminal and administrative matters. In addition, because judges have relatively little power to interpret the law in civil law jurisdictions, the outcome in many civil and criminal disputes is highly predictable—another factor that results in less litigation in civil law jurisdictions than in common law jurisdictions like Great Britain and the United States. Finally, the nature of civil law as a codified and accessible system reduces the need for attorneys in civil law jurisdictions. Since relatively little expertise is needed to interpret the law, many tasks that can only be performed by licensed attorneys in common law jurisdictions can be performed by lesser trained and less expensive paralegals. In civil law jurisdictions, paralegals (often called notaries) can legally perform routine, uncomplicated legal tasks and give limited legal advice in certain areas, such as will preparation, preparation of affidavits, and execution of powers of attorney. In common law jurisdictions, all of these tasks can only be performed by an attorney or by a paralegal under the direct supervision of an attorney.

Common Law Systems

The common law system has its roots in England. Under the feudal system, the king as supreme authority and landholder granted large tracts of land to favorite barons and lesser nobility, who in turn granted small tracts of land to their knights. Each baron became the arbiter of legal disputes within the boundaries of his domain, subject only to the will of the king. Thus, local law developed based on regional customs and traditions. Not surprisingly, then, there was little uniformity from one manor to another in the application of the law. Due largely to its unique status as an island nation and its isolation from the rest of Europe, the civil law tradition was never imported into England other than under Roman occupation. Even after England became a province at the outer reaches of the Roman Empire, the civil law tradition of Roman law did not take root on English soil in the turmoil that followed the fall of the Roman Empire.

During the Norman Conquest of 1066 A.D., William I attempted to consolidate English law into a single body of law that could be applied throughout England. He established the King's Court (Curia Regis) as an advisory body to the barons. The court had both legislative and judicial powers that eventually led to the development of Parliament and the English court system. By the latter part of the twelfth century, the influence of the King's Court was extended into the local or regional courts by royal justices who visited these courts periodically at set intervals, traveling along a set route or circuit. As these visits from royal judges increased in frequency, the power of the local courts was slowly eroded, and the law in England began to be unified in a single common law that slowly erased regional differences in law and established greater uniformity throughout the realm. The law was still largely based on custom and tradition—largely the custom and tradition held in common by the King's Court judges. It was these judges who first began writing down their decisions to serve as guidelines for local magistrates and themselves in future cases. This tradition of writing down decisions to serve as guidelines, or precedent, for deciding future cases formed the basis for our modern common law system.

While royal judges wielded great power in the shaping of early English common law, the king and Parliament retained the right to overturn court decisions and amend legal precedent by the issuance of statutes—written pronouncements on the law that courts were bound to follow.

After the invention of the printing press in the fifteenth century, it became possible to publish court decisions to serve as resources for lawyers and judges in researching the law. The first truly useful court reporters began appearing in the mid-eighteenth century. The stability of common law is dependent on judges following legal precedent guided by the doctrine of *stare decisis* (to abide or stand by decided cases). Legal precedent is the body of court decisions relating to a legal issue. The system of common law is based on judges following the reasoning in previously decided cases as they decide cases before them. This gives the law its stability and allows legal practitioners to predict how a given case will be decided by examining how similar cases were decided in the past. Precedent can be binding or merely persuasive. The decisions of a state's highest court are binding precedent on that state's lower courts, which must follow it, but only persuasive precedent on the courts of other states, which are free to follow or ignore such precedent. A state's highest court is always free to follow its own established legal precedents or to change them. The doctrine of *stare decisis* states that courts should stand by decided cases and not overrule established precedent lightly. Under the principle of *stare decisis*, a court should follow established legal precedent unless there is a compelling reason not to do so. This principle is crucial to the stability of the common law; if judges did not follow established precedent, there would be little predictability to the law. Attorneys would have no solid guidelines upon which to base the advice they give to clients, and no stable guideposts on which to base legal arguments and chart legal strategies for arguing cases in court. Today, common law is observed in Great Britain and in former British colonies, like the United States, while the rest of the world typically follows the civil law tradition.

Sources of American Law

American law is based on the English common law system. When the early pilgrims immigrated to America, they brought with them their legal system, along with their customs, traditions, and values. It is these that helped to shape our legal system. It is in the nature of common law, however, that it adapts to the local customs, traditions, and needs of a people. Thus, despite its English roots, American law has evolved to fit the needs of our federalist system, and reflects regional differences and values. As a result, law in the United States today more resembles the early English common law system, with its regional differences based on local customs and traditions, than it does the relatively unified law of modern-day Great Britain. We have a splintered system of federal, state, and local laws to contend with, leaving us with separate legal systems that share many similarities but also contain many differences in both substantive and procedural law.

It is a common misconception to think of the law as a set of rules written in dusty rows of books in law libraries. While such an analogy might be somewhat accurate with regard to civil law, it is wholly inaccurate in our common law system. It is true that court reporters and statutes for the 50 states, for the various commonwealths, and for the federal system are collected in thousands of volumes in law libraries and provide an invaluable resource for legal research. But American law is far more than a collection of court decisions and the text of statutes; it is a vibrant, flowing river fed by many tributaries and streams that is neither stagnant nor static, but ever changing (albeit slowly) over time. In addition to the court decisions of the various federal and states' courts, sources of the law include constitutional law, statutory law, and administrative law.

Constitutional Law

A country or state's constitution is the most fundamental source of law. It delineates in general terms the sovereign state's form of government and provides the basic framework for its laws. Article VI, Section 2 of the U.S. Constitution specifically sets the U.S. Constitution as the "supreme law of the land." As such, no other law passed by a state or the federal government can conflict with it; any law that does is unconstitutional and void.

Constitutions are of necessity broad documents. In the United States, the job of interpreting the federal constitution and that of every state is left to the courts. Both state and federal courts have the power to interpret the U.S. Constitution, but the final word on the analysis of the federal constitution is reserved to the U.S. Supreme Court, whose interpretation of the Constitution is final and represents binding precedent for all lower state and federal courts.

But even the U.S. Constitution is not static. Both Congress and the states have the power to amend it in any way they choose. Under Article V of the Constitution, Congress may propose a constitutional amendment by a two-thirds vote by the House of Representatives and the Senate. If a proposed amendment is approved by Congress, it then goes to all the states' legislatures. If three-quarters of the states' legislatures approve the amendment, it becomes part of the Constitution and the preeminent law of the land. States may also propose amendments to the Constitution to Congress on their own initiative by votes for such a proposal in two-thirds of the states' legislatures. If the states make the initiative, Congress must decide whether to allow ratification by constitutional conventions in three-quarters of the states; if the states initiate the amendment, it also becomes law upon its approval by three-quarters of the states' legislatures or by a constitutional convention in three-quarters of the states or by a vote for ratification by three-quarters of the states' legislatures. Other than the right to each state's equal representation in the Senate, there is no limit to what changes can be written into the Constitution. To date, the constitution has been amended 27 times. In the case of the Eighteenth Amendment (1919), which outlawed the manufacture, sale, or transportation of intoxicating liquors in the United States, Congress changed its mind and repealed prohibition in the Twenty-First Amendment (1933), leaving it up to the individual states to prohibit the sale of alcoholic beverages as they saw fit.

The U.S. Constitution serves as an important source of law in the areas of governmental power. It empowers states and the federal government to pass and enforce laws that regulate people's interactions with one another and with their government, while it sets limits on government's ability to legislate in certain areas. (We will continue our discussion of constitutional law in greater detail in Chapter 2.)

Statutory Law

Statutes enacted by federal, state, and local legislative bodies make up another important source of law.

At the federal level, Congress can legislate over a broad range of areas, as we will see in Chapter 2, by relying on its power to regulate interstate commerce, as well as through the exercise of its constitutionally granted powers. Whenever Congress legislates within its area of constitutionally granted power, the resulting legislation has the force of law. The Internal Revenue Code, the Americans with Disabilities Act, and the 1964 and 1991 Civil Rights Acts are examples of statutory law enacted by Congress. The same is true of treaties that are negotiated by the president and ratified by the Senate, such as the North American Free Trade Agreement.

At the state level, every state has its own legislature that is usually patterned after Congress. These legislatures enact state laws in a wide range of areas, including civil and criminal law and procedure, business regulation, and, of course, taxation. The power of state legislatures to regulate both business and private conduct is far greater than that of the federal government, since most states reserve to themselves in their state constitutions broad powers to legislate in all areas touching on the welfare of their citizens. In general, states have the right to regulate all areas of private or public life as long as they do not infringe on any right protected by the U.S. Constitution. State and local legislation that does not infringe on a constitutionally protected right is valid as long as it can pass a relatively flexible rational relationship test, which simply means that any state law that is rationally related to the preservation of a valid societal interest is valid. This litmus test of constitutionality is a simple one to pass, since nearly any law can be rationally justified as serving some valid purpose. The test, however, is somewhat more stringent when a vital interest or suspect classification is involved; in such instances, the state must pass a strict scrutiny test of constitutionality, wherein the courts weigh the state interest against the infringement of protected rights in determining the validity of a statute. For purposes of the strict scrutiny test, a vital interest can be defined as any constitutionally protected right, such as the rights enumerated under the Bill of Rights. A suspect classification would include a law that makes distinctions based on race, sex, color, religion, or national origin. The following examples should illustrate:

- The legislature of the State of Moot enacts a statute that requires all citizens to cover their mouths when they sneeze and subjects violators of the statute to a $50 fine. Since sneezing with one's mouth uncovered is not a constitutionally protected right, the courts would defer to the state's legislature and enforce the statute as long as there is a rational basis for the legislation. Because preventing the spread of germs and viruses that can makes citizens ill is a rational goal and the statute does not infringe on a constitutionally protected right, a rational basis for the statute seems to exist and it would probably be upheld in the courts.
- The State of Moot passes a statute that prohibits the use of the word *God* in public and subjects violators to a $50 fine. This statute would be subject to the strict scrutiny test because it deals with two constitutionally protected rights: free speech and religious expression. It is highly unlikely that the state would be able to show a sufficiently compelling reason for adopting the statute despite its infringement on constitutionally protected rights, so that the statute would almost certainly be struck down as unconstitutional.

Finally, city councils and various town boards and planning commissions also have the power to legislate in areas allowed them by their local charters. These local ordinances also carry the weight of law and form a part of the state's statutory law.

With all of these legislative bodies producing volumes of new statutory law every year, one might well think that the difference between civil law and common law has become blurred. But in reality, it has not. The distinguishing characteristic of common law is the broad power to interpret and invalidate statutes that is reserved to the courts. No matter how clear the language of a statute or how plain its import, it is generally impossible in a common law jurisdiction to interpret a statute, or the federal or state constitutions, at face value. Ultimately, the validity of any statute is determined by the courts, as is its meaning. A case in point is the Second Amendment to the U.S. Constitution, which reads: "A well-regulated militia being necessary to the security of a free state, the right of the people to keep and bear arms shall not be infringed." Any reasonable interpretation of that amendment that looks at the plain meaning of the language used, particularly when viewed from the inherent distrust of government of its revolutionary framers, would lead one to believe that the U.S. Constitution guarantees the right of citizens to own and bear guns. Nevertheless, until recently when the U.S. Supreme Court for the first time ruled in *District of Columbia v. Heller*, 554 U.S. 570 (2008), that the right to bear arms is a personal right that the states can control but not completely abrogate, the amendment had been interpreted to mean only that individual states can raise their own militias (e.g., national guards) if they so choose. Regardless of the wisdom of such an interpretation, one message is clear: any statute, including the U.S. Constitution, means only what the courts ultimately decide it means. This has been the case ever since *Marbury v. Madison*, 5 U.S. 137 (1803), when Chief Justice John Marshall first announced the power of judicial review (the power of courts to declare the acts of legislative bodies, including the U.S. Congress, void if they violate the court's interpretation of the Constitution). In what is arguably the greatest act of judicial activism in the history of U.S. jurisprudence, Chief Justice Marshall argued that, "It is a proposition too plain to be contested that the Constitution controls any legislative act repugnant to it, or that the legislature may not alter the Constitution by an ordinary act...." This novel proposition was not challenged. The power of the courts generally, and ultimately the U.S. Supreme Court in particular, to declare any act of the U.S. Congress or any federal or state law unconstitutional has now been well established by more than 200 years of legal precedent. It should be noted that nothing in the U.S. Constitution itself explicitly reserves this right to the courts, and that the British courts did not historically enjoy a similar privilege (only the king, queen, or Parliament itself could invalidate a royal edict or Act of Parliament). Arguably, the chief justice could have been successfully impeached at the time for overstepping his bounds and infringing on congressional legislative privilege. By not challenging the decision, Congress left the courts as the ultimate authority on the Constitution, empowering the judicial branch of government to curb the actions of the legislative and executive branches when these in its view transgressed on the U.S. Constitution.

Administrative Law

The increase of government regulation of business in the twentieth century, in addition to the increasingly expansive social engineering role of the federal and state governments during the same time period, has given birth to what is often referred to as the fourth branch of government—the administrative agency system. Administrative agencies are empowered either by the executive or legislative branches of the state and federal governments to assist them in carrying out necessary governmental functions that they lack either the time or expertise to carry out themselves. When Congress decided to regulate nuclear energy, for example, it created the Nuclear Regulatory Commission and empowered it with the ability to both create and enforce rules for the safe civil use of nuclear energy. Although Congress could have created and enforced these rules itself, individual members of Congress have neither the necessary expertise nor time to engage in such micromanagement of the regulatory environment. The same holds true for other agencies whose primary purpose is the regulation of business and industry, including the Federal Aviation Administration, the Securities and Exchange Commission, the National Labor Relations Board, the Federal Trade Commission, and the Federal Communications Commission, among many others. At the state level, state legislatures and governors also set up administrative agencies to help them regulate business and carry out other important governmental functions. Taken together, the rules that all federal and state agencies promulgate have the force of law and form the most important component of administrative law. Like statutes, however, most administrative rules and many administrative agency decisions are subject to judicial review, the process whereby statutes, administrative rules, and administrative agency decisions are reviewed by courts when challenged. (See Chapter 5 for a fuller discussion of administrative law.)

Taken together, federal and state court decisions, federal and states' constitutions, federal and states' statutes, and federal and states' administrative agency rules and decisions all represent primary sources of law. To these must be added secondary sources of law, such as legal encyclopedias, model acts, compiled Restatements of Law, legal treatises, law review articles, and articles published in other scholarly journals, as well as textbooks on the law—all of which can offer persuasive but nonbinding authority and insight on the law for lawyers and judges alike. To know what the law is in any given state, then, one must know the legal precedent represented in the state's case law, as well as the state's constitutional, statutory, and administrative law and its interpretation by the courts. The same holds true for federal law. It should come as no surprise, then, that we have more lawyers per capita and more litigation than any other nation on earth; it is an inevitable result given the complexities and uncertainties inherent in what is one of the most complex legal systems any country has ever known. Keep this in mind when you hear absurd comparisons that stress the disparity in the number of lawyers or lawsuits in, say, Japan or France (civil law jurisdictions) and the United States. Even comparisons to Great Britain are misleading, since the U.K. does not need to contend with more than 51 different major court systems, each with its own laws. Ours is a complex legal system by design based on the adversarial system that presupposes legal issues will be resolved by legal experts settling disputes as advocates for their clients in a court of law. Self-help is decidedly discouraged by our system of law, which makes little effort to ensure that law is accessible or understandable to the common citizen and prohibits the uninitiated from providing legal assistance or legal advice to those in need of settling disputes. As long as we wish to preserve the essential nature of our federalist common law system with its guarantees of trial by jury; federal, state, and local laws; emphasis on judge-made law based on precedent and *stare decisis*; and reliance on the adversarial system as a means of obtaining justice, we will continue to need more lawyers per capita than any other nation on earth.

Questions

1. Define the term *law*.
2. What are some potential problems that conflicting state laws pose for businesses?
3. A business with a good legal department does not need employees to be familiar with basic legal principles. Do you agree or disagree with this statement? Why?
4. What are the main sources of law in our common law system?
5. What is the basic difference between common law and civil law?
6. In what way is our system of law based on an adversarial model?
7. What makes our legal system more complex than that of other countries around the world?
8. Why are comparisons between the number of lawyers or lawsuits in Japan and the United States unfair?
9. What is administrative law?
10. Why are administrative agencies created at the state and federal levels?

Hypothetical Cases

1. The legislature of the State of Moot enacts a statute that reads as follows: "In recognition of the spiritual importance of the Sabbath, citizens of the State of Moot are henceforth forbidden from engaging in any work-related activity on Sundays. Any citizen who violates this statute will be subject to a fine not to exceed $500 and/or imprisonment for up to 30 days in the county jail."
    A. If this statute is challenged, will the court use the strict scrutiny or the rational relationship test in reviewing the statute's constitutionality, given its First Amendment implications? Explain.
    B. Should the statute be enforced or struck down as unconstitutional? Explain.
2. Your local state legislature enacts the following statute: "Because of the inherent dangers represented to public health by the smoking of cigarettes, such activity will henceforth be prohibited to everyone under the age of 35."
    A. If this statute is challenged, will the court use the strict scrutiny or the rational relationship test in reviewing the statute's constitutionality? Explain.
    B. Should the statute be enforced or struck down as unconstitutional? Explain.
3. Congress passes a bill prohibiting discrimination in hiring, promotion, or housing based on a person's sexual orientation. The bill is challenged in court on the basis that Congress lacks the power to pass such a bill under the U.S. Constitution.
    A. Does Congress have the power to pass and enforce such a statute? Explain.
    B. Would such a bill be constitutional? Explain.
4. Congress passes a bill that restricts the sale of music that promotes or condones violence to persons under the age of 21. The statute is challenged in court and is ultimately struck down by the U.S. Supreme Court as an unconstitutional infringement of First Amendment free speech rights. What, if anything, can Congress do if it is unhappy with the high court's decision?

Constitutional Law

CHAPTER 2

Chapter Outline

The Commerce Clause
The Bill of Rights
The Scope of Constitutional Protection

Under our constitution, the federal government is one of limited powers. Congress has the power to legislate only in areas that it has been specifically granted the power to regulate by the U.S. Constitution. The powers of Congress are enumerated in Article I, Section 8 and include the power

- To borrow Money on the credit of the United States;
- To regulate Commerce with foreign Nations, and among the several States, and with the Indian Tribes;
- To establish an uniform Rule of Naturalization, and uniform Laws on the subject of Bankruptcies throughout the United States;
- To coin Money, regulate the Value thereof, and of foreign Coin, and fix the Standard of Weights and Measures;
- To provide for the Punishment of counterfeiting the Securities and current Coin of the United States;
- To establish Post Offices and post Roads;
- To promote the Progress of Science and useful Arts, by securing for limited Times to Authors and Inventors the exclusive Right to their respective Writings and Discoveries;
- To constitute Tribunals inferior to the supreme Court;
- To define and punish Piracies and Felonies committed on the high Seas, and Offences against the Law of Nations;
- To declare War, grant Letters of Marque and Reprisal, and make Rules concerning Captures on Land and Water;
- To raise and support Armies, but no Appropriation of Money to that Use shall be for a longer Term than two Years;
- To provide and maintain a Navy;
- To make Rules for the Government and Regulation of the land and naval Forces;
- To provide for calling forth the Militia to execute the Laws of the Union, suppress Insurrections and repel Invasions;
- To provide for organizing, arming, and disciplining, the Militia, and for governing such Part of them as may be employed in the Service of the United States, reserving to the States respectively, the Appointment of the Officers, and the Authority of training the Militia according to the discipline prescribed by Congress;
- To exercise exclusive Legislation in all Cases whatsoever, over such District (not exceeding ten Miles square) as may, by Cession of particular States, and the Acceptance of Congress, become the Seat of the Government of the United States, and to exercise like Authority

> over all Places purchased by the Consent of the Legislature of the State in which the Same shall be, for the Erection of Forts, Magazines, Arsenals, dock-Yards, and other needful Buildings;—And
>
> - To make all Laws which shall be necessary and proper for carrying into Execution the foregoing Powers, and all other Powers vested by this Constitution in the Government of the United States, or in any Department or Officer thereof.
>
> Although the enumerated powers of Congress may seem impressive at first glance, they are, in fact, quite limited by design. The founding fathers were afraid of giving too much power to the federal government and believed that it was the responsibility of the states rather than Congress to create laws for the protection of the health, safety, and general welfare of their citizens. States enjoy very broad police powers that allow them to pass nearly any law intended to promote the general welfare of their citizens. There are only two basic limits to the states' general police powers: (1) They cannot pass laws that violate the U.S. Constitution, the state's own constitution, or valid federal laws; and (2) all laws passed by state and local legislatures must pass a rational basis test. In other words, a state or local legislature cannot pass laws that violate the state's or federal constitutions or any valid federal law. In addition, states cannot pass laws that are irrational (e.g., arbitrary or capricious laws that serve no rational purpose). The founding fathers, however, purposely denied to the federal government the general police powers enjoyed by the states and limited Congress to legislating only in the areas enumerated under Article I, Section 8 above.

The Commerce Clause

Given the constitutional limits on Congressional power, where does Congress get the authority to pass legislation intended to promote the common good such as the various civil rights acts, social safety nets, federal labor laws, and most federal regulation of business? The answer lies primarily in the Commerce Clause, which, as shown previously, provides Congress the right to "regulate Commerce with foreign Nations, and among the several States, and with the Indian Tribes." Through a very broad interpretation of the Commerce Clause, the U.S. Supreme Court has given Congress the power to regulate nearly any activity, including activity that takes place wholly within a single state (intrastate activity) if it has the potential to impact interstate commerce. Most social legislation and federal regulation of business can trace their roots to the Commerce Clause. If Congress can make an argument that an area it wishes to regulate has the potential to affect interstate commerce in some tangible way, then it can generally pass legislation to regulate the area based on its power to regulate interstate commerce under the Commerce Clause. Thus, Congress lacks the power to pass a civil rights act that protects employees from discrimination based on race, color, religion, national origin, or sex simply to protect workers against unlawful discrimination because it lacks general police powers. However, if Congress can make an argument that unlawful discrimination has a negative impact on interstate commerce, then it can pass legislation such as the 1964 and 1991 Civil Rights Acts, as well as other federal acts that protect workers against discrimination based on age or disability, and prohibit employers from paying men and women different wages for the same work.

States can prohibit discrimination against any group on the basis that it is wrong, immoral, and bad for society but Congress can prohibit discrimination only if it can show a nexus exists between discrimination and a negative impact on interstate commerce. That is why most federal acts apply only to businesses that arguably have the potential to impact interstate commerce. The fiction that Congress uses and the U.S. Supreme Court generally accepts is that if an employer hires a certain number of employees for a minimum number of weeks per year, it is large enough to have a potential impact on interstate commerce, and Congress can regulate it. (For the Civil Rights Act of 1964, the magic number that triggers the applicability of the act is 15 employees for at least 20 weeks per year on a part-time or full-time basis.) Thus, a business with 15 employees cannot discriminate in hiring based on race, color, religion, national origin, or sex because Congress believes it is large enough to have a potential impact on interstate commerce. However, a business that hires only 14 employees, or a seasonal business that hires 15 or more employees but for only 10 weeks every year, is not covered by the act and can discriminate at will unless the state law prevents it. Because states have general police powers, they can provide much greater protection without having to show any impact on commerce. New York, for example, generally prohibits employers (even those who hire fewer than 15 workers) from discriminating based on race, color, national origin, religion, or sex and extends protection for discrimination based on sexual orientation, which federal law currently does not.

The Bill of Rights

While the Constitution gives broad regulatory powers to states and, through the liberal judicial interpretations of the Commerce Clause and the necessary and proper clause in Article I, Section 8 of the U.S. Constitution, to the federal government, it also serves to preserve the rights of the individual. The most significant body of constitutional law concerns itself with the prohibitions on governmental powers provided in the Constitution—in particular the guarantees provided to individuals by the Bill of Rights (the first ten amendments to the U.S. Constitution) and the Fourteenth Amendment, and the U.S. Supreme Court's interpretation of the broad language in which they are framed. Much of the constitutional law that flows from the U.S. Supreme Court has centered on the high court's interpretation of several key amendments. It must be noted that the Bill of Rights originally prohibited only Congress from infringing on the enumerated rights and was not applicable to the states. Thus, despite the First Amendment, states were free to pass laws that punished criticizing a sitting governor and, for that matter, could establish a state-supported religion. Through a series of U.S. Supreme Court decisions in the early part of the twentieth century, most of the protections in the Bill of Rights have now been applied to the states as well, incorporated through the equal protection clause in the Fourteenth Amendment. We will briefly examine these next.

First Amendment

The First Amendment reads as follows: "Congress shall make no law respecting an establishment of religion, or prohibiting the free exercise thereof; or abridging the freedom of speech, or of the press; or the right of the people peaceably to assemble, and to petition the government for a redress of grievances." The essence of the amendment is to protect citizens from governmental interference with freedom of speech, religion, and assembly, and to prevent government from establishing a state religion.

The First Amendment has been broadly interpreted to provide very strong protection against governmental interference with free speech. Government may not generally regulate the content of speech, even if the content offends, angers, or even causes mental anguish to others. Governments may regulate the time and place for speech to take place if the regulations are reasonable and intended to protect public safety or other compelling interests. A municipality may require groups who wish to hold rallies, marches, or other public events in order to express their views to apply for a permit; it also may place reasonable restrictions on time and place as a condition to granting the permit. Thus, a municipality may restrict marches or rallies to daylight hours to prevent unreasonable noise at times when people are asleep, and may also require a parade to follow a prearranged route to prevent an unreasonable interference with traffic or public safety. But municipalities may not refuse to grant a permit because the subject matter, content, or ideas of the speakers will be controversial or even hateful to some listeners. Speech extends not only to the written and spoken word but also to actions such as burning the flag as a form of protest. Not all speech is protected, however. Obscenity, fighting words, and incitement to riot, for example, are not protected by the First Amendment, and governmental action to punish or prevent such speech is permissible. In addition, commercial speech is offered less protection than noncommercial speech. Reasonable restrictions on commercial speech by government are permissible if they are reasonably related to promoting a valid governmental purpose, such as public safety or aesthetics. For example, municipalities can place reasonable restrictions on the types, sizes, and placement of business signs. Neon signs can be banned if a local municipality believes they are either aesthetically displeasing or if they are believed to be a public safety hazard (such as by distracting drivers). The same is true of billboards. Banning all lawn signs, including signs with political messages or endorsements, however, would violate the First Amendment unless a municipality could meet a strict scrutiny test and show that the restriction is absolutely necessary to promote a vital state interest and that such an interest could not be safeguarded by a lesser restrictive means than an outright ban.

Second Amendment

The Second Amendment provides: "A well regulated militia, being necessary to the security of a free state, the right of the people to keep and bear arms, shall not be infringed." Advocates for the right to bear arms and gun control advocates have long debated whether the Second Amendment provides a personal right for individuals to own and carry guns or whether it merely protects the right of states to form armed militias (e.g., the National Guard). Some local municipalities like Washington D.C. and New York City have extremely restrictive gun laws that make it nearly impossible for individuals to legally own and use firearms, especially handguns, for self-defense. In 2008, the U.S. Supreme Court weighed in and decided in a 5–4 decision in the case of *District of Columbia v. Heller*, 554 U.S. 570 (2008), that the right to possess firearms for lawful purposes, including self-defense, is a personal right that municipalities cannot abrogate. Municipalities can place reasonable restrictions on the licensing of firearms and can prevent certain types of firearms (such as grenade launchers) from being owned, but they cannot prevent people who are not otherwise disqualified from gun ownership for such reasons as mental disability or prior felony convictions from owning firearms.

Third Amendment

The Third Amendment provides: "No soldier shall, in time of peace be quartered in any house, without the consent of the owner, nor in time of war, but in a manner to be prescribed by law."

Fourth Amendment

The Fourth Amendment reads as follows: "The right of the people to be secure in their persons, houses, papers, and effects, against unreasonable searches and seizures, shall not be violated, and no warrants shall issue, but upon probable cause, supported by oath or affirmation, and particularly describing the place to be searched, and the persons or things to be seized."

The Fourth Amendment offers protection against unreasonable searches and seizures and requires probable cause before a search or arrest warrant is issued. Generally speaking, police are required to obtain a search warrant prior to searching a person's home, automobile, or person. To obtain a warrant, police must convince a judge that probable cause exists to believe that a crime has been committed or that a situation exists that poses a risk to the public health or safety before a warrant is issued. There are exceptions to the general rule, however. For example, police officers do not need a search warrant to seize a handgun in plain sight if they stop a vehicle for a driving infraction. Nor do police officers need a warrant if they chase a suspected criminal avoiding arrest into a home in which illegal substances are in plain sight of the arresting officers who entered in hot pursuit of the fleeing suspect. And police may legally enter a home without a warrant if they reasonably believe that someone inside is facing imminent danger (such as when hearing gunshots or a cry for help from behind a locked door). Moreover, police can search without a warrant if the owner of the property invites them to do so. They also can search an individual after legally arresting the person to ensure that the person is not carrying weapons that may be used against the arresting officers and also to ensure that the person does not destroy evidence in his or her possession on the way to the police station.

Fifth Amendment

The Fifth Amendment provides: "No person shall be held to answer for a capital, or otherwise infamous crime, unless on a presentment or indictment of a grand jury, except in cases arising in the land or naval forces, or in the militia, when in actual service in time of war or public danger; nor shall any person be subject for the same offense to be twice put in jeopardy of life or limb; nor shall be compelled in any criminal case to be a witness against himself, nor be deprived of life, liberty, or property, without due process of law; nor shall private property be taken for public use, without just compensation."

The Fifth Amendment requires a grand jury indictment for capital crimes and most felonies. It also provides protection against double jeopardy; once acquitted of a crime, a defendant may never again be tried for the same crime, even if she subsequently admits to having committed the crime of which she was acquitted. But double jeopardy does not protect a criminal defendant from being tried and convicted in a civil court for the same offense that she was acquitted of in the criminal trial. This may seem unfair, but it is important to remember that an acquittal is not a pronouncement by a jury that the defendant is "innocent"; rather, it is a finding that the prosecutor failed to convince the jury "beyond a reasonable doubt" that the defendant committed the crime with which she was charged. In Chapter 7 we will discuss the burden of proof for criminal offenses further. For now, it is simply worth noting that the burden of proof for criminal offenses is much greater than that required for civil offenses, and that a finding of "not guilty" in a criminal trial does not prevent a defendant from being found guilty of the same offense in a civil trial. That is why O.J. Simpson was found guilty of wrongful death in a civil trial involving the 1994 death of his ex-wife, Nicole Brown Simpson, and Ron Goldman, even though he was acquitted of the criminal charges against him.

The Fifth Amendment also provides a privilege against self-incrimination. A person cannot be compelled to give incriminating testimony in any proceeding. Everyone has the right to refuse to answer questions while giving testimony in court, before Congress, in any deposition, or in any other formal proceeding on the grounds that his testimony may incriminate him. Someone who invokes the Fifth Amendment's protection from self-incrimination can be compelled to testify only if he is offered immunity from prosecution for any incriminating information he may provide in his testimony.

The Fifth Amendment further requires individuals to be provided with due process of law by any governmental authority before being deprived of life, liberty, or property. Both substantive and procedural due process are guaranteed. Procedural due process requires governmental authorities to follow certain procedures before depriving citizens of life, liberty, or property. At the heart of procedural due process is the concept that the government must provide fair and impartial procedures before taking actions that constitute the taking of a person's life, property, or freedom. The Bill of Rights helps to define some of the specific processes, such as the right to counsel for criminal defendants and the right to a speedy trial by an impartial jury, the protection against self-incrimination, the prohibitions against double jeopardy, and the prohibitions against cruel and unusual punishment and excessive bail. Substantive due process, on the other hand, protects persons against arbitrary government actions and actions that deprive them of fundamental rights guaranteed under the Constitution. Arbitrary and inherently unfair government actions violate substantive due process, as does the denial of fundamental rights guaranteed explicitly or implicitly by the Constitution. In the second half of the twentieth century, the U.S. Supreme Court created additional due process protections against certain types of government actions by its interpretation of the Constitution and the Bill of Rights (especially the Third, Fourth, and Ninth Amendments) to provide fundamental privacy rights. The court ruled in *Griswold v. Connecticut*, 381 U.S. 479 (1965), that a ban on contraception violated a fundamental right to privacy implicitly guaranteed in the Constitution; it used similar seasoning in *Roe v. Wade*, 410 U.S. 113 (1973), to find that a woman has an absolute right to an abortion (at least during the first trimester of pregnancy). More recently in *Obergefell v. Hodges* (No. 14–556, decided June 28, 2015), the U.S. Supreme Court inferred a right to same-sex marriage in the Constitution, holding in a 5–4 decision that the equal protection and due process clauses of the Fourteenth Amendment guarantee gays and lesbians the right to marry.

Finally, the Fifth Amendment also guarantees that just compensation must be provided for any property taken for public use by a governmental body exercising its right of eminent domain. The federal and state governments have always had the right to take private property for public use, such as for building roads, airports, or hospitals, but if they exercise that right, the property owner must be paid the market value of the property. In *Kelo v. City of New London*, 545 U.S. 469 (2005), the U.S. Supreme Court ruled in a 5–4 decision that a municipality may also take private property and give it to a private developer for development for either a public or a private use if proper procedures are followed, including having a development plan approved by the appropriate planning council that shows that the development may increase tax rolls for the community, create jobs, or have other local beneficial impact in the view of the local government authorities.

Sixth Amendment

The Sixth Amendment reads as follows: "In all criminal prosecutions, the accused shall enjoy the right to a speedy and public trial, by an impartial jury of the state and district wherein the crime shall have been committed, which district shall have been previously ascertained by law, and to be informed of the nature and cause of the accusation; to be confronted with the witnesses against him; to have compulsory process for obtaining witnesses in his favor, and to have the assistance of counsel for his defense." The amendment guarantees a speedy public trial by jury for criminal offenses, the rights of accused persons to be informed of the charges against them and to confront their accusers, the rights of accused persons to be represented by counsel and to subpoena witnesses.

Seventh Amendment

The Seventh Amendment provides that: "In suits at common law, where the value in controversy shall exceed twenty dollars, the right of trial by jury shall be preserved, and no fact tried by a jury, shall be otherwise reexamined in any court of the United States, than according to the rules of the common law." Thus, the amendment guarantees the right of trial by jury in most civil cases.

Eighth Amendment

The Eighth Amendment provides that: "Excessive bail shall not be required, nor excessive fines imposed, nor cruel and unusual punishments inflicted."

Ninth Amendment

The Ninth Amendment guarantees that: "The enumeration in the Constitution, of certain rights, shall not be construed to deny or disparage others retained by the people."

Along with the Tenth Amendment (see the following discussion), the Ninth Amendment accentuates the fact that the rights of the people are not fully enumerated in nor do they exclusively flow from the Constitution. The Constitution and Bill of Rights do not provide an all-inclusive listing of rights and privileges.

Tenth Amendment

The Tenth Amendment provides that: "The powers not delegated to the United States by the Constitution, nor prohibited by it to the states, are reserved to the states respectively, or to the people."

Along with the Ninth Amendment, this is a reminder that the powers of government, especially the federal government, are limited and that the rights and freedom of the people do not flow exclusively from the U.S. Constitution. The reservoir of residual rights not specifically covered in the Constitution rests not with the federal government, but with the states and the people in which they originate.

Fourteenth Amendment

The Fourteenth Amendment provides as follows:

Section 1

"All persons born or naturalized in the United States, and subject to the jurisdiction thereof, are citizens of the United States and of the state wherein they reside. No state shall make or enforce any law which shall abridge the privileges or immunities of citizens of the United States; nor shall any state deprive any person of life, liberty, or property, without due process of law; nor deny to any person within its jurisdiction the equal protection of the laws."

Section 2

"Representatives shall be apportioned among the several states according to their respective numbers, counting the whole number of persons in each state, excluding Indians not taxed. But when the right to vote at any election for the choice of electors for President and Vice President of the United States, Representatives in Congress, the executive and judicial officers of a state, or the members of the legislature thereof, is denied to any of the male inhabitants of such state, being twenty-one years of age, and citizens of the United States, or in any way abridged, except for participation in rebellion, or other crime, the basis of representation therein shall be reduced in the proportion which the number of such male citizens shall bear to the whole number of male citizens twenty-one years of age in such state."

Section 3

"No person shall be a Senator or Representative in Congress, or elector of President and Vice President, or hold any office, civil or military, under the United States, or under any state, who, having previously taken an oath, as a member of Congress, or as an officer of the United States, or as a member of any state legislature, or as an executive or judicial officer of any state, to support the Constitution of the United States, shall have engaged in insurrection or rebellion against the same, or given aid or comfort to the enemies thereof. But Congress may by a vote of two-thirds of each House, remove such disability."

Section 4

"The validity of the public debt of the United States, authorized by law, including debts incurred for payment of pensions and bounties for services in suppressing insurrection or rebellion, shall not be questioned. But neither the United States nor any state shall assume or pay any debt or obligation incurred in aid of insurrection or rebellion against the United States, or any claim for the loss or emancipation of any slave; but all such debts, obligations and claims shall be held illegal and void."

Section 5

"The Congress shall have power to enforce, by appropriate legislation, the provisions of this article."

The Fourteenth Amendment was passed after the Civil War with the primary purpose of extending citizenship and the protection of the Bill or Rights to former slaves. In a series of decisions starting in the first quarter of the twentieth century, the U.S. Supreme Court interpreted the Fourteenth Amendment to extend the protection of most of the Bill of Rights to the states. In other words, the protections offered to citizens in the Bill of Rights with regard to actions by the federal government were extended to also apply to the states by a broad interpretation of Section 1 of the Fourteenth Amendment. When the amendment was passed in 1866 and ratified in 1868, the protections that the Bill of Rights afforded citizens applied only to the federal government. None of the constitutional protections found in the Bill of Rights applied to the states. Section 1 of the amendment was the first attempt to require all states to accord equal protection under the law to all citizens in the state (e.g., requires citizens of other states to be treated the same as citizens of the state). The amendment also prohibits the states from abridging the privileges and immunities of any citizen of the United States or depriving any citizen of life, liberty, or property without due process of law.

Section 1 of the amendment has generated a great deal of ongoing litigation and spirited debate among justices with conservative and liberal judicial philosophies. They take a very different view on the appropriate role of the courts in shaping and creating law as they decide cases based on broad or narrow interpretations of the Constitution and federal and state statutes. The remaining sections offer little by way of controversy, though it should be noted that Section 2 has been modified by the Nineteenth Amendment, which provides women with the right to vote, and by the Twenty-Sixth Amendment, which lowers the voting age from 21 to 18.

The Scope of Constitutional Protection

As we have already seen, the Bill of Rights protects individuals against infringement of protected rights by the federal government and, through judicial interpretations of the Fourteenth Amendment's privileges and immunities and due process clauses, also prohibits state and local governments from infringing most of the rights accorded citizens under the Bill of Rights. Constitutional protection is offered to individuals against actions by the federal and state governments and all agencies of the federal and state government. The protection extends to the official actions of all government employees. For example, neither the federal government (including all federal agencies) nor any federal employee acting in an official capacity may deny individuals in the United States the right to free speech guaranteed by the First Amendment. The federal government cannot pass a law that prevents individuals from expressing ideas that people find disagreeable or offensive, and neither can any state. A professor employed by a public university also cannot infringe on students' First Amendment rights because he is also an employee of the state. Along similar lines, a state employee cannot be fired from her job without due process of law, which at a minimum would require the person to be given a fair hearing prior to being dismissed. But constitutional protection is not available for private actions by nongovernmental bodies. The Constitution offers no protection and does not require that any due process be afforded individuals with regard to the actions of private individuals, organizations, or companies. Unless a federal or state law prevents it, individuals and private companies are free to infringe on all of the constitutionally provided rights since these apply only to government actions.

If Professor Smith at State University bans a student from his class because he is wearing a "Communists Are Cool" T-shirt, for example, the student will have a good argument that his First Amendment rights were violated. If Professor Jones bans a student wearing the same T-shirt from her class at Private University, however, this student would not be able to allege a violation of his First Amendment right to free speech. In the latter example, the student is probably protected by university policies ensuring free speech and may also have a valid civil action against the university for breach of contract if he is prevented from returning to class or is otherwise penalized for expressing a political view the university finds offensive, but no constitutional protection applies. In a similar vein, if a private company fires an employee because she is overheard saying that she voted for a candidate her supervisor dislikes, no constitutional issue exists because no state action is involved. In fact, the employee can be dismissed on the spot without a reason being given or the opportunity to be heard. Again, no First Amendment issue and no equal protection or due process of law issue exists because no state action is involved. Likewise, a private homeowner's association or condominium board can prevent homeowners from posting political signs on their lawns or religious symbols in their windows, and no constitutional issue is involved. The same would not be true if a state or federally owned housing authority imposed the same rules on residents, however.

Questions

1. Since Article I, Section 8 of the Constitution does not grant to Congress broad police powers to pass legislation for the common good, where does Congress get the authority to create federal labor laws and federal civil rights acts?
2. Which amendment(s) provide(s) the guarantee to criminal defendants of a speedy public trial by jury?
3. Which amendment(s) require(s) government to provide due process of law to individuals before taking their lives, property, or freedom?
4. Which amendment(s) guarantee(s) the right to a jury trial in most civil cases?
5. Which amendment(s) state(s) that all persons born in the United States are citizens of the United States and of the state in which they were born?
6. Which amendment(s) protect(s) individuals from self-incrimination and double jeopardy?
7. Which amendment(s) protect(s) individuals against unreasonable searches and seizures?
8. Which amendment(s) prevent(s) the government from quartering soldiers in private homes in times of peace?
9. What is the commerce clause, and why is it so important today?
10. Why are immigration law and bankruptcy law handled by the federal government rather than by the individual states?

Hypothetical Cases

1. Harry Homeowner buys a condominium unit in Happy Acres, a new private development of townhouses. The condominium association rules prevent owners from posting any signs on their property and also prohibit the placement of holiday lights or decorations of any kind outside the home or on windows that are visible from outside the home. Violations of the rule are subject to a $100 fine for each violation. In October, Harry places a Vote for Senator Smith sign in his front lawn as well as a life-size skeleton hanging from his front door and carved, lighted jack-o'-lanterns in each of his two front windows that are visible from outside. When he is fined $200 for the violations by his condominium association, he goes to court seeking an injunction against the condominium association for violating his First Amendment rights. What is the likely result? Would your answer be the same if Harry rented the townhouse as part of a state-owned public housing project with the same rules? Explain.
2. Martha Motorist is stopped by a police officer for speeding. During the traffic stop, the police officer notices a handgun in Martha's glove compartment when she opens it to retrieve her car's registration. He arrests her when she cannot produce a pistol permit or explain how the gun got in her glove box. After arresting Martha, the police officer hears a faint cry for help from the trunk of the car and opens the trunk to discover a man who has been shot and a kilo of cocaine next to him. Martha is tried for illegal gun possession, attempted murder, and possession of a controlled substance with the intent to distribute. At trial, her attorney tries to have the seized evidence excluded, claiming that the gun, wounded victim, and cocaine were discovered pursuant to an illegal search because the police officer did not have a valid search warrant to search the car when the incriminating objects were discovered. What is the likely result?
3. Shady Town, a village in a cash-strapped state, decides it would be a good idea to improve its economic situation by increasing the number of fines it imposes on motorists and by implementing a toll system on village roads. Not wishing to anger local residents, town officials provide special stickers

that exempt local residents from the town tolls, and police are instructed to ticket only drivers with out-of-state license plates for speeding. Freida, a tourist passing through Shady Town, is stopped for speeding and issued a $300 summons. She also pays a $10 toll for the privilege of passing through town. The summons she is given states that the $300 fine will become a $600 fine if she contests the ticket in court and is found guilty of speeding. She would like to contest both the ticket and the toll on constitutional grounds. Does she have a valid argument that the fine and/or toll violates the U.S. Constitution? Explain fully.

4. Despite the 2015 U.S. Supreme Court decision in *Obergefell v. Hodges* declaring that states may not constitutionally deny same-sex couples the right to marry, various churches, synagogues, and temples refuse to perform same-sex marriages based on religious objections. Could the federal or state governments successfully sue religious institutions that refuse to perform marriage ceremonies? Based on principles of constitutional law, how do you think the issue should or would be resolved in the courts? What options, if any, does the federal government have to force religious institutions to perform religious marriage ceremonies? Explain fully.

The Court System

CHAPTER 3

Chapter Outline

Jurisdiction
The Federal Court System
The State Court System

The court system in the United States is made up of two distinct federal and state systems. There are 50 state court systems and a federal court system made up of 13 federal circuits that share the power and responsibility for the administration of justice. Fortunately, there are more similarities than differences between the federal system and that of each of the 50 sovereign states. This is so because most state court systems are patterned after the federal model that we will explore momentarily. But first, it is important to grasp some basic principles relating to the way our court systems operate.

Jurisdiction

Jurisdiction can be defined as a court's power to hear and decide (or adjudicate) a case. The types of jurisdiction with which you must be familiar include personal jurisdiction, subject matter jurisdiction, original jurisdiction, and appellate jurisdiction.

Personal and Subject Matter Jurisdiction

Personal jurisdiction (also referred to as *in personam* jurisdiction) is the power of a court to decide a case between the specific litigants involved. Subject matter jurisdiction (also referred to as *in rem* jurisdiction) is the power of a court to adjudicate the type of case, or subject matter, before it. To put it another way, personal jurisdiction relates to a court's ability to decide a case between the litigants involved, whereas subject matter jurisdiction relates to a court's power to hear the type of case brought before it.

A court must have both personal jurisdiction over all litigants and subject matter jurisdiction over the type of matter in controversy before it can hear and decide a case. As an example, a family court in a state is empowered to adjudicate issues relating to domestic relations such as divorce and child custody disputes for citizens of the state. It cannot, however, hear a divorce case between citizens of other states or cases relating to traffic violations, breach of contract, or any other matter beyond the scope of its subject matter jurisdiction.

For the federal courts, the limits on subject matter and personal jurisdiction can be found in the U.S. Constitution under Article III, Section 2. The federal courts are limited to hearing cases involving the following criteria:

- cases involving the U.S. Constitution, federal laws, or federal treaties;
- cases involving ambassadors, other public ministers, and consuls;
- cases involving admiralty and maritime law;
- cases in which the United States is a party;

- cases between two or more states, or between a state and the citizens of another state, or between citizens of different states (when the amount in controversy exceeds $75,000 under Title 28 of the U.S. Code); and
- cases between citizens of the same state involving lands under grants by different states, and cases between states or the citizens of states and foreign countries or foreign citizens.

The jurisdiction of state courts is set by the state constitution or other state statutes creating the court system. Generally speaking, access to the state courts is greater than that of the federal courts. The reason is that states have the power to adjudicate all cases and controversies arising out of a state's laws for its citizens and others who have sufficient contacts with the state. State courts can also hear issues relating to federal law unless jurisdiction to hear such cases has been limited to the federal courts, as is the case, for example, with claims against the United States, which must be brought in federal court. Most states impose subject matter jurisdiction limits on their court systems for the sake of expediency by setting up specialized courts with limited subject matter jurisdiction to handle routine matters. (See Illustration 3.1.)

Generally speaking, state courts' personal jurisdiction extends only to persons who have substantial contacts with the state. Although state laws vary somewhat as to what constitutes a substantial contact with the state, in general, litigants who meet any one of the following criteria are deemed to have sufficient contact with a state so as to allow its courts to adjudicate matters in which they are a party:

- being present in the state when they are served with notice that they are being sued;
- living in the state;
- doing business in the state (e.g., working or conducting business in the state on a regular basis);
- committing a crime or tort in the state;
- owning real or personal property in the state, but if property ownership is the only contact with the state, courts in the state may not issue a judgment that extends beyond the value of the property (When personal jurisdiction is based on property ownership in the state, it is referred to as *quasi in rem* jurisdiction, and it is the property itself that is sued rather than the person of its owner. If the property owner chooses not to appear in the state to defend himself, a default judgment can be issued and the property seized and sold to satisfy the judgment.); and

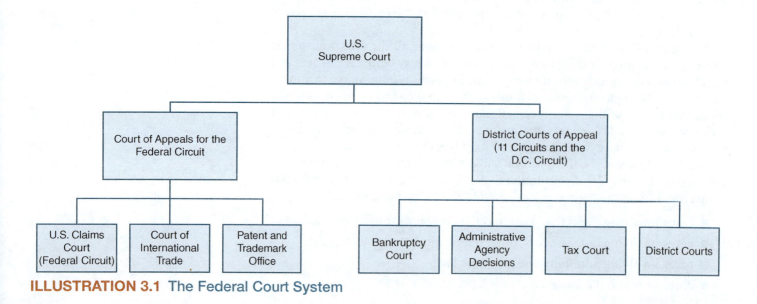

ILLUSTRATION 3.1 The Federal Court System

- voluntarily agreeing to allow the state to exert personal jurisdiction by personally appearing before the court as a plaintiff (one who institutes a lawsuit) or defendant (one who defends herself against a lawsuit initiated by another).

Where the court's jurisdiction is predicated solely on the defendant's property ownership in the state and the defendant appears in the state to defend against the *quasi in rem* action, however, the court's jurisdiction will still be limited to the property itself, and the court will not be able to adjudicate any dispute beyond the value of the property.

States have enacted long-arm statutes that allow them to extend personal jurisdiction to people who do not meet any of the noted jurisdictional criteria. Typically, states' long-arm statutes allow states to exert personal jurisdiction over anyone who commits a crime or a tort in the state or who enters into a contract that is the subject of the lawsuit in the state. Under a state's long-arm statute, for example, a person who drives from Rhode Island to Florida can be forced to appear and defend himself in lawsuits brought by citizens of any East Coast state he drove through on the way for accidents or traffic violations alleged to have been committed by him while driving through those states, even if he has absolutely no other contact with those states. Likewise, a citizen of Nevada who mails a letter bomb to a citizen of California can be sued in California for any civil or criminal damages flowing from that act, even if he has no other contacts with that state.

Most types of cases that can be brought in federal court can also be brought in state court. With few exceptions, such as cases relating to bankruptcy, which can only be brought in the appropriate federal court, state courts are free to hear cases relating to federal laws and the U.S. Constitution. Ultimately, the final word on the interpretation of all federal law, however, rests with the U.S. Supreme Court, which can hear appeals relating to cases involving federal law or the U.S. Constitution from any lower federal court or from any state's highest court.

Original and Appellate Jurisdiction

State and federal courts can be classified into two basic types: those that hear and adjudicate disputes for the first time and those that hear cases only on appeal. Courts with the power to hear cases for the first time have original jurisdiction, whereas courts that can hear cases only on appeal have **appellate jurisdiction**. The U.S. Supreme Court is one of the few courts that has both original and appellate jurisdiction in certain cases. Under Article III, Section 2 of the U.S. Constitution, the U.S. Supreme Court is given original jurisdiction "[i]n all cases affecting ambassadors, other public ministers and consuls, and those in which a State shall be a party." Nevertheless, the highest court is highly unlikely to exercise its original jurisdiction, and the limited types of cases over which it has original jurisdiction are invariably tried in the lower federal courts.

The Federal Court System

The federal courts are organized into a system of four types of courts that include specialized courts with limited original jurisdiction, courts of general original jurisdiction, intermediate appellate courts, and the U.S. Supreme Court. The federal courts of general original jurisdiction and the intermediate appellate courts are divided into 11 judicial circuits, a D.C. Circuit, and a Federal Circuit for a total of 13 distinct judicial circuits with 94 judicial districts (see Table 3.1). There is at least one federal judicial district in each state, the District of Columbia, Puerto Rico, the Virgin Islands, Guam, and the Northern Mariana Islands.

Specialized Courts

A number of federal courts have limited original jurisdiction. They include the U.S. Tax Court (which hears cases relating to federal income tax law), the U.S. Claims Court (in which lawsuits against the U.S. government must be filed), and the U.S. Court of International Trade (which adjudicates matters relating to foreign commerce). Appeals from

TABLE 3.1 The Federal Court System

Circuit Name	Composition
District of Columbia	District of Columbia
First	Maine, Massachusetts, New Hampshire, Puerto Rico, Rhode Island
Second	Connecticut, New York, Vermont
Third	Delaware, New Jersey, Pennsylvania, Virgin Islands
Fourth	Maryland, North Carolina, South Carolina, Virginia, West Virginia
Fifth	Louisiana, Mississippi, Texas
Sixth	Kentucky, Michigan, Ohio, Tennessee
Seventh	Illinois, Indiana, Wisconsin
Eighth	Arkansas, Iowa, Minnesota, Missouri, Nebraska, North Dakota, South Dakota
Ninth	Alaska, Arizona, California, Hawaii, Idaho, Montana, Nevada, Oregon, Washington, Guam, Northern Mariana Islands
Tenth	Colorado, Kansas, New Mexico, Oklahoma, Utah, Wyoming
Eleventh	Alabama, Florida, Georgia
Federal Circuit	Hears appeals from specialized federal courts and some appeals from U.S. District Courts in all federal circuits (includes the U.S. Court of Federal Claims, the U.S. Court of International Trade, and the U.S. Court of Appeals for Veterans' Claims)

these courts may generally be taken to the federal District Court of Appeals that has personal jurisdiction over the litigants.

U.S. District Courts

The U.S. District Courts are the federal courts of original general jurisdiction. They are the federal trial courts that have the power to adjudicate civil and criminal matters relating to federal law subject to the limits of Article III, Section 2 on the federal courts discussed previously. As is true of all trial courts, the purpose of the district courts is to provide a forum for the resolution of civil and criminal disputes. Parties present their cases, and the **trier of fact** (usually a jury, unless the parties agree to waive a jury trial, in which case the judge acts as trier of fact) decides whether the plaintiff (the person bringing the suit) or the defendant (the person being sued) should prevail.

U.S. District Courts of Appeal

The U.S. District Courts of Appeal are the federal intermediate appeals courts. These courts hear appeals from a number of sources, including specialized federal courts, federal agencies, and the district courts. As is the case for all appellate courts, these courts are concerned only with issues of law, not of fact. The losing party in a civil or criminal trial in a federal court of original jurisdiction can appeal to a district court of appeals only if she can show that an error was made in the trial court judge's application of the law. Questions of fact are not reviewable on appeal; only material errors in the application of the law by a trial court are grounds for reversing the judgment of that court. Examples of errors in the application of law that can lead to an appeal would include a judge giving improper instructions to a jury or incorrectly ruling on what evidence could be introduced at trial. A plaintiff or defendant can never appeal simply because he is unhappy with his trial's outcome. With very few exceptions (such as capital convictions that may carry an automatic appeal), the district courts of appeal decide for themselves whether to grant petitions for appeal. When a district court of appeals in exercising its discretion believes there is sufficient evidence of a possible reversible error having been committed in the lower (trial) court, it can grant the petitioner's request to hear oral arguments as to the error or errors allegedly committed by the lower court. Federal district courts of appeals are constituted of three-judge panels selected at random from the available judges in the circuit, who are appointed by the president and confirmed by the Senate. Federal judgeships are lifetime appointments; federal judges serve until retirement, death, or impeachment based on a conviction of treason, bribery, or other high crimes and misdemeanors (U.S. Constitution, Article II, Section 4).

U.S. Supreme Court

The U.S. Supreme Court, the nation's highest court, can hear appeals from all district courts of appeals as well as from the states' highest courts (as long as a question of federal law or the U.S. Constitution is involved). As is the case with the district courts of appeals, the U.S. Supreme Court decides for itself whether or not to hear cases on appeal. The highest court typically receives more than 5,000 requests for appeals each year, and grants *Writs of Certiorari* (demands to lower courts at the state or federal levels to forward to it all transcripts of trials it wishes to review) at its sole discretion. In recent years, the Court has heard oral arguments for fewer than 100 cases each term. The U.S. Supreme Court is made up of nine justices who, like all federal judges, are appointed by the president and serve for life terms.

The State Court System

There are significant differences in the court systems of the 50 states. However, most states' systems are patterned on the federal court system and include specialized courts of limited original jurisdiction, courts of general original jurisdiction, intermediate appellate courts, and the highest appellate court in the state (usually called the State Supreme Court).

Specialized Courts

Most state court systems include some or all of the following courts of limited original jurisdiction (see Illustration 3.2):

- **Small claims court:** This court has broad jurisdiction to try nearly any civil case that does not exceed a set dollar amount. The typical maximum amount that a plaintiff can sue for in a small claims court varies from state to state and can be as little as $2,500 (Kentucky and Rhode Island, as of this writing) or as much as

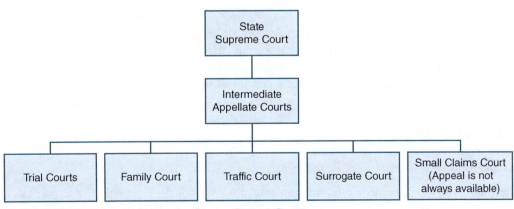

ILLUSTRATION 3.2 Sample State Court System

$25,000 (Tennessee), with 25 states setting the limit at $5,000 or less. The benefit of these courts is that they provide an expeditious and inexpensive means for private individuals and businesses to litigate minor claims in a relatively informal setting in which attorneys are usually not needed and sometimes not allowed to represent litigants. These courts help to channel away some litigation from the states' general trial courts, which are usually overburdened. They provide an important forum for dispute resolution for people who would not otherwise be able to avail themselves of the courts for reasons of time or expense. A small claims judge can hear cases in a matter of weeks, contrasted to the years it takes to litigate civil cases in most states' trial courts. The cost to litigants who represent themselves is a very modest filing fee (typically under $10), contrasted with the many thousands of dollars it takes to adjudicate disputes in the traditional trial courts. The disadvantage of these courts is that there is usually no appeal allowed from them.

- **Traffic court:** Many larger cities provide specialized courts to handle the large volume of litigation that arises out of traffic violations each year. Where these courts are available, they usually share subject matter jurisdiction with the state's general trial courts. Serious criminal traffic-related offenses, such as driving while intoxicated, vehicular manslaughter, or reckless endangerment, and similar offenses that can result in incarceration of more than one year are usually not handled by traffic court but rather by the states' general trial courts.
- **Justice of the peace court:** These tribunals often handle minor offenses that can subject the accused to fines or short prison terms. In many jurisdictions, these courts serve as the criminal analog to the small claims court in handling minor matters that would otherwise exacerbate the overcrowded calendars of states' general trial courts.
- **Surrogate court:** These courts handle matters relating to trusts and estates.
- **Family court:** The subject matter jurisdiction of these courts relates to matters pertaining to marriage and family life. Divorce, child custody, separation agreements, and (often but not always) criminal offenses committed by minors are all subject matters within this court's jurisdiction. In some states, family court jurisdiction is not exclusive; in such states, cases can be brought either before family court or in the state's court of general original jurisdiction (the state's general trial court).

General Trial Courts

The trial courts are a state's courts of general original jurisdiction. Most any civil or criminal case can be adjudicated in these tribunals, which have very broad subject matter jurisdiction. In many states, the trial courts share jurisdiction with specialized courts of limited jurisdiction, so it may be possible for a plaintiff to sue a defendant for redress of a civil wrong in more than one court. For example, a person who wishes to bring a lawsuit for $5,000 in property damages arising out of an automobile accident can sue in the state's small claims court and the state's general trial court in most states. The expense and time needed to gain access to specific courts and the important procedural differences in practicing before different courts are crucial considerations that attorneys weigh in deciding the best tribunal for a specific client's lawsuit to be brought. This is especially true in cases when a variety of federal and state courts may have appropriate jurisdiction to adjudicate a dispute.

Intermediate Courts of Appeals

State court systems typically include an intermediate court of appeal. These courts entertain appeals from losing parties in the state's trial courts who allege that the trial court judge has made one or more significant errors in the application of the law at trial. Common errors by lower court judges that form the basis of successful appeals include misinterpretation of state statutes, improper jury instructions, erroneous rulings on the types of evidence allowed to be presented by parties at trial, improper rulings on attorneys' motions and objections throughout a trial, and any other misapplication of substantive or procedural law at trial that in the appellate court's judgment materially impaired the jury's ability to render a fair verdict.

If the court believes that there is sufficient evidence that a **reversible error** (a mistake by the lower court judge that is serious enough to warrant overruling his decision and ordering a new trial) has occurred, it agrees to listen to oral arguments by the **appellant** (the losing party at trial who now seeks to overturn the lower court's decision) and the **respondent** (the winning person at trial who seeks to defend the lower court's application of the law).

Typically, intermediate appeals courts are composed of three justices, although this number can vary from state to state.

Highest State Court

Every state has a state court of final appeal, usually referred to as the State Supreme Court. This court is analogous to the U.S. Supreme Court and has the final word on the application of state law and the interpretation of state statutes. Losing parties at the level of the intermediate appeals court can seek to have a state's highest court review their cases. In cases in which that court disagrees with the lower appellate court's interpretation of the law, it can reverse that court's judgment and **remand** the case (order the case to be sent back to the trial court to correct the error or for a new trial). The number of justices that sit on a state's highest court varies, but five or seven justices is common.

For most cases, no further appeal is possible after the state's highest court has either ruled on the appeal or refused to hear it. But if the matter in controversy relates to federal law or the U.S. Constitution, then appeal is possible from the highest state courts to the U.S. Supreme Court.

Questions

1. Define the term *jurisdiction* and briefly discuss the different types of jurisdiction available.
2. What kinds of cases may a federal court adjudicate?
3. What is a long-arm statute?
4. What type of jurisdiction may the U.S. Supreme Court exercise?
5. Name at least three state and three federal courts of limited original jurisdiction (also known as specialized courts).
6. What are the federal courts of general original jurisdiction called?
7. What is the highest court in each state usually called?
8. How many justices serve in the federal District Courts of Appeals?
9. How many justices typically serve on a state's highest court?
10. Is appeal possible from a state's highest court? Explain.

Hypothetical Cases

1. Dominic, a resident of Delaware who has no significant ties to Pennsylvania, gets into an automobile accident in Pennsylvania with Paula, a resident of Pennsylvania, and Jenine, a resident of New Jersey also traveling in Pennsylvania.
   A. In which states may Dominic be sued by Paula?
   B. In which states can Jenine, the New Jersey resident, sue Dominic?
   C. If Paula, the Pennsylvania resident, wants to sue Jenine, the New Jersey resident, in which state or states may she do so?
   D. Assume that all three parties decide to sue each other for $100,000 in alleged personal injury and property damage. May this lawsuit be brought in federal court? Would your answer be the same if each party were suing for $10,000 in property damage?

2. Wendy, a resident of New York City, wants to purchase a handgun for personal protection. After doing some research on the subject, she comes to the conclusion that it is nearly impossible for her to legally obtain a gun permit due to New York City's restrictive gun laws. She has also read the U.S. Constitution, and she believes that New York City's laws are unconstitutional since they infringe on her right to keep and bear arms guaranteed by the Second Amendment. Certain of her rights, she purchases a handgun for personal protection from her local illegal gun dealer for $300. The next day, she is arrested when an undercover police officer sees her fending off a mugger with her illegally obtained gun. She is charged with illegal gun possession—a crime that carries a minimum one-year mandatory jail sentence upon conviction in New York City. Her defense is the unconstitutionality of the law under which she was arrested. What is the likely result?
   A. Assume that Wendy is tried and convicted in State Supreme Court—New York's oddly named trial court of general original jurisdiction. (New York's highest court is the Court of Appeals. Its intermediate appellate courts are called the Supreme Court, Appellate Division or Appellate Term.) Can she appeal? Explain.
   B. Assume for the moment that she can appeal. What court should she appeal to?
   C. Assume that she can and does appeal. What court in the state will have the final say on interpreting the U.S. Constitution?
   D. Assume for the sake of the argument that she exhausts her appeals to the state courts and none agrees to hear her case, or, after hearing her case, they rule against her. Is there anything further she can do?
3. Assume that in the last case Wendy loses all her appeals and serves her one-year sentence for illegal gun possession. If she is convinced that the law is unfair and wants to fight it, is there any way she can do so?
4. Veronica suffers minor burns while dining at Richard's restaurant when a waiter trips and drops a plate of hot soup on her dress. Richard agrees to pay for the dry cleaning of the dress but refuses to pay for pain and suffering that Veronica alleges she suffered as a result of the incident. After several discussions, Richard won't budge from his position and Veronica decides to sue. Her uncle is a justice in the intermediate appeals court in her state, so she would like to institute her lawsuit in that court, trusting her uncle to issue a fair verdict.
   A. May she do so? Explain.
   B. Assume that she cannot bring the lawsuit in her uncle's court. Which courts in her state have the appropriate jurisdiction to hear the case?
   C. Under the circumstances, which court do you believe is best suited to hear the case if she decides to sue for $2,500 in damages?

Ethics and Its Impact on Law and Government

CHAPTER 4

Chapter Outline

Ethical Philosophies
Ethics and Public Policy
Problem Areas
The Regulatory Environment of Business

Ethics is the branch of philosophy that concerns itself with the study of morality. Ethical inquiry centers on concepts such as good and evil and right and wrong. Thousands of years of philosophical inquiry into the field of ethics has produced numerous conflicting theories by noted classical and contemporary philosophers. Not surprisingly, however, no consensus has emerged as to which theory is the more valid. While this may not be surprising, it is troubling, since law is closely tied to the fragile, ephemeral principles that are at the heart of ethics. By definition, law concerns itself with issues of right and wrong, good and evil, and the administration of justice, and those who help shape the law need valid ethical reference points in order to steer the law in the direction of the common good. Legislators, judges, presidents, governors, and regular citizens who help to shape the law through their official capacity or at the ballot box may not consciously engage in the study of ethics in shaping their views on what constitutes justice or how to best promote the common good. Nevertheless, most of us act in accordance with certain principles that we may commonly refer to as our "values." Whether we acknowledge it or not, the guiding principles by which we steer our lives and that form the basis for our core ideas about right and wrong are an expression of our ethical philosophy. The names of the ethical systems we adhere to, and the notable philosophers who espouse them, are not as important as the views themselves, which help shape our government and mold our laws. Regardless of what ethical philosophy or value system a government and its laws are based on, it is healthy to examine the validity of those ethical views and values from time to time. Ethics forms the cornerstone of every society, its system of government, and its laws. Any society whose basic values cannot stand up to objective scrutiny and free debate rests on precarious ground.

Ethical Philosophies

The quest to discover ethical truths has led Western philosophers on some very different paths throughout the past 2,500 years. Because law inevitably reflects a society's ethical views, even a brief glimpse at some of the core principles that underlie various systems of ethics can be very useful in enhancing our understanding of the common thread of ethics that runs through every nation's system of jurisprudence.

Ethical Absolutism

Ethical absolutism is an ethical philosophy with many diverse branches all tied in to the central idea that there are certain universal standards by which to measure morality. Under this philosophy, concepts such as good and evil, right and wrong, and justice have a separate objective existence that can be discovered and understood by human beings through philosophical inquiry and introspection. Right and wrong are concepts that stand on their own and do not change based on circumstances or on the outcome of a person's actions. If stealing is wrong, then it is always wrong, regardless of the circumstances surrounding it. Thus, stealing is always morally wrong, whether it is done out of greed, for sport, or to feed a hungry child. Proponents of this broad branch of ethics represent a wide range of schools of thoughts that often include diametrically opposed world views. Plato, St. Thomas Aquinas, and Karl Marx all believed in a form of ethical absolutism, despite the fact that the overall philosophy and world view of each man was quite different.

Religious Fundamentalism

Like ethical absolutism, religious fundamentalism as a theory of ethics relies on the existence of certain immutable truths. Unlike ethical absolutism, however, which requires that these values be discovered through philosophical inquiry and, for Plato and St. Thomas Aquinas, at least, through introspection, ethical norms under religious fundamentalism can be found by studying the lives and writings of prophets or by consulting holy scriptures. Under this philosophy, living a moral life depends on strict adherence to religious principles and values, and its proponents often view theocracy as the most just form of government.

Deontology

Deontology is a duty-based ethical theory whose principal proponent is the German philosopher Immanuel Kant (1724–1804). For Kant, an act's morality depends on the actor's motive, and the only unconditionally good motive is duty. Therefore, for an act to be moral or good, it must be undertaken out of a sense of duty. For Kant, the concept of duty finds it expression in categorical imperatives, a set of rules of behavior derived from practical reason and tested through a filter of universal application. A basic categorical imperative that is arrived at through practical reasoning, such as "you should not steal," is valid if you can justify the whole world living up to the rule. In other words, moral behavior can be defined as acting in accordance with rules that you would be willing to impose on your society (or the whole world) as a valid code of conduct. A person acts morally whenever she follows a categorical imperative out of a sense of duty. Merely engaging in "right" action of itself is not moral. If you refrain from stealing because you feel obligated to honor society's rules that forbid stealing, then you are engaged in moral conduct. But if you refrain from stealing only out of fear of getting caught, then you are not engaged in moral conduct.

Utilitarianism

Utilitarianism assigns ethical value to actions based on their intended outcome. Under utilitarianism, the ultimate good is defined as actions intended to bring about the greatest happiness (or greatest good) for the greatest number of people. Thus, moral action under utilitarianism requires the constant evaluation of actions based on their intended result. Actions that bring about the greatest good to the greatest number of people are ethical, or good, while actions that fall short of that goal are unethical, or wrong. To put it another way, utilitarianism does not recognize an intrinsic value to actions, but rather assigns a positive or negative moral judgment to actions only in view of their intended consequences. The most notable proponents of this philosophy are the British philosophers Jeremy Bentham (1748–1832) and John Stuart Mill (1806–1873).

Ethical Relativism

Like utilitarianism, ethical relativism denies the existence of absolute moral values, and holds that moral judgments cannot be made in a vacuum. Unlike utilitarianism, however, the yardstick by which to measure the morality of an act is not the common good, but rather the circumstances surrounding the person committing an act at the time that an act is committed. It is a precept of this philosophy that a person's actions cannot be judged other than by placing oneself in the same situation that the actor faced in committing the act in question. So, stealing to feed one's hungry child, for example, is not necessarily wrong. On a societal level, ethical relativism acknowledges that there are differences between cultures and that what is considered wrong or even hateful in one culture may be acceptable in another, depending on its particular circumstances. Human sacrifice, cannibalism, infanticide, and ethnic cleansing are all at least arguably justifiable for some cultures. Notable proponents of relativistic theories include W. G. Sumner (1849–1910) in the United States and E. A. Westermarck (1862–1939) in England.

Nihilism

Nihilism denies the existence of any ethical standards. Derived from the Latin word for "nothing," nihilism originated as a movement in Russia, where the term was popularized in 1862 by the writer Ivan Turgenev. Nihilism is central to the political philosophy of anarchists, such as Peter Kropotkin, who reject all centralized authority. It could be argued that nihilism is the final result in a 2,500-year march in Western philosophy away from the ethical absolutism of Plato. He believed in a perfectly ordered universe in which truth, beauty, and justice are attainable; in which individuals should be recognized and rewarded solely on the basis of merit; and in which reason and conscience keep the baser appetites (what Freud would later call the "id," which always threatens to lead us astray) in check. In nihilism we find the ultimate rejection of order, of absolute codes of behavior, or the existence of any transcendent truths. If only each individual's will guided by the individual's conscience can dictate what is right or wrong, then centralized government with its "arbitrary" laws and sanctions represents an illegitimate, oppressive restraint on individual freedom.

Ethics and Public Policy

The political implications that flow from even a brief overview of differing ethical systems should not be ignored. Whether by design or by default, the ethical values held by political leaders and lawmakers invariably become a part of the political system. We need not look far to see examples of the influence of ethical systems on public policy and on the politics of nations. The influence of religious fundamentalism can readily be seen today in a number of countries, particularly in the Middle East, where militant religious fundamentalists are engaged in armed struggles to overthrow what they perceive to be immoral secular governments that are instilling in their people false moral values. If one believes that the only true source of morality is religion, it is logical to believe that the best (or only) form of moral government is a theocracy, a government based on religious principles. Ethical absolutism is also readily observable in its secular form in past and present nonreligious totalitarian regimes. Totalitarian regimes, be they Marxist, Communist, or Fascist in nature, are usually based on principles of ethical absolutism. Taken to their logical conclusion, absolutist ideals can be used to justify totalitarianism; if there are certain knowable, immutable truths that are valid for all time, then the only moral form of government, the argument goes, is one that educates (or indoctrinates) the people to recognize those truths and ensures that they conform to the moral conduct that those truths dictate.

If totalitarian regimes are based on ethical absolutism or religious fundamentalism, it is clear that democratic governments lean toward nonfundamentalist ethical principles. The assumption that a variety of plausible views exist on even essential ethical principles is central to a democratic form of government. The principle of majority rule inevitably leads to the adoption of some type of moral relativism as the guiding ethical principle. The very notion that issues of great import are subject to debate and can ultimately be decided by a vote, and the tolerance for opposing viewpoints that are essential to any democracy worthy of the name, institutionalizes ethical relativism. Issues such as the death penalty, abortion, and pornography, with the strong emotions and endless debate they elicit, illustrate our relativistic ethics. That laws relating to these and other issues are subject to change and do, in fact, undergo change slowly over time underscores that societal definitions of ethical conduct change as well. Individuals in democracies are free to reject ethical relativism, and many do. They can also lobby their government for change, arguing for the adoption of their point of view. But a pluralistic democratic system that completely abandons ethical relativism cannot remain a democracy for long.

It can be argued that the ethical principles of a society are reflected even in the type of legal system it chooses. The civil law system, with its detailed codes that carefully prescribe individual rights and responsibilities in minute detail, its swift administration of justice, and limited power of judicial interpretation, tends toward an absolutist or deontological ethical philosophy. In effect, governments with such systems tend to demand strict adherence to set codes of behavior and leave relatively little room for deviation from the established norm by their citizens. Common law systems such as ours, on the other hand, leave the judiciary with wide latitude for interpreting the governmental edicts found in legislative enactments and provide a multilayered system of appellate courts to further review trial courts' application of the law, with the determinations of fact usually left to the interpretation of juries. In a word, the civil law leaves little room for arguing the validity or meaning of the law, while the common law allows great latitude to litigants to argue both.

Problem Areas

The obvious problem we face when trying to impose an ethical system is in deciding what system to use. While it can be argued that government should not legislate morality, all governments in fact do so. Criminal law is largely based on prohibiting and punishing antisocial behavior; as such, criminal law inevitably reflects society's ethical standards and attempts to discourage behavior that society deems immoral. Ultimately, questions of ethics come down to personal belief. Depending on the philosophical system applied, nearly any moral point of view is defensible; unfortunately, one person's ethical conduct is frequently another's mortal sin. In a political context, ethical debate often hinges on irreconcilable differences. On the abortion issue, for example, the pro choice and pro life groups have philosophical differences that simply cannot be reconciled. The same is true of people on opposite sides of the perpetual debate on the death penalty, gun control, legalization of drugs, animal rights, climate change, gay marriage, and innumerable other issues. Very often, groups on either side of a political controversy believe themselves to be morally right and, by definition, believe that people on the opposite side of the issue are morally wrong. The strength of a democracy is in its ability to incorporate differing points of view and to obtain functional compromise on most issues. But some issues leave no room for compromise, and it is here that the battles for the minds—and votes—of citizens are often fought. Regardless of what group wins and what opinion manages to weave itself into the fiber of the law, issues of ethics cannot be resolved by majority rule for most people, or by the latest decision of the U.S. Supreme Court, and spirited debate continues, sometimes escalating into violence and death, both in this country and abroad.

The Regulatory Environment of Business

One of the areas in which government tries to legislate ethical conduct that has been vigorously debated over the years is the ethical accountability of business. Many people today believe that businesses have a responsibility to society as a whole to act in a responsible manner and to work for the betterment of society as the price for being allowed to do business and make a profit. Others believe that the sole social responsibility of business is to obey the law while turning a profit for investors. Although the issue is by no means settled, the trend over time, especially since the mid-twentieth century, has been to increase the amount of government regulation of business, both at the federal and state levels. Primarily through the establishment of administrative agencies (see Chapter 5), the federal and state governments have put in place wide-reaching regulations in an attempt to ensure that business is conducted in a responsible manner. Some of the more notable areas in which the federal government actively regulates business include antitrust, securities, labor law, and consumer protection. Legislatures and the courts at both the state and federal levels have also addressed ethical concerns about U.S. companies doing business abroad. Conduct that was once seen as acceptable, such as the bribery of foreign officials in the regular course of business in some foreign countries, can now bring criminal penalties. A debate has also been taking place for years about the responsibility of American firms selling products in foreign countries that cannot be sold in the United States due to health and safety regulations but whose sale is not prohibited in foreign countries. This battle is likely to be fought largely in civil courts in the United States and abroad as foreign nationals sue American companies for selling allegedly unsafe products. In the past, such claims have been made with regard to a wide range of products, including baby formula, pharmaceutical products, and pesticides. Where foreign countries do not yet regulate the safety of consumer products or safety in the workplace, what ethical responsibility do American companies have when they do business abroad to their foreign customers and workers?

There is often a chasm between what is legal and what is right. In the wake of the many highly publicized corporate lapses of good ethical judgment by key players at companies like WorldCom, Enron, and Arthur Andersen in recent memory, companies rushed to implement codes of ethics, ethical training, and other processes to help make employees more aware of ethical issues and provide them with some practical tools for resolving potential ethical problems when they arise. These are steps in the right direction but will not in themselves bridge the gap. Perhaps the best way to ensure ethical conduct from our corporate citizens is to hire, promote, and retain ethical leaders. The most effective training model for ethics in any company is to have its leaders, from board of directors to line supervisors, model ethical behavior. In a company where leaders consistently act ethically and make it clear that they expect the same of their subordinates, where individuals are not rewarded for unethical behavior that is profitable or reprimanded for ethical behavior that hurts the bottom line, people will not only consistently act in an ethical manner but will also feel better about themselves and the company for which they work.

As the law reactively seeks to address well-publicized ethical lapses by imposing new and stiffer penalties for the ethical violations and corporate mismanagement of corporate directors and officers, and as corporations struggle to implement processes to show their stakeholders that they are "doing something" about the problem, they might consider whether their existing policies or procedures are encouraging unethical behavior in their employees. They also might consider whether they are appropriately screening current and prospective employees for ethical competency. Are employees who lie on their resumes fired if a lie is discovered? Is adherence to ethical standards a criterion evaluated during periodic performance reviews? Can subordinates trust the word and motives of supervisors and executives at all levels? Are principled leaders who take personal responsibility for the failure of those they lead and share credit for the success that others have made possible promoted and retained? Do people at all levels feel valued for their contributions and proud to go to work every day? If the answer is no to these and similar questions, employees and stakeholders in a company will see ethical training and implementation programs for what they are: a public relations effort or a risk-management scheme to avoid litigation.

Questions

1. Define the term *ethics*.
2. What is the central idea behind ethical absolutism?
3. What defines moral conduct under religious fundamentalism?
4. How does one define ethical conduct under utilitarian principles?
5. "You cannot judge a man until you have walked a mile in his shoes" is a statement that is best linked to which philosophy of ethics?
6. Who is the principal proponent of duty-based (deontological) ethics?
7. What is the basic problem in trying to legislate ethical behavior through the law?
8. What area of law most clearly involves a society's effort to legislate morality?
9. Why do democratic systems tend to reflect ethical relativism?
10. In your view, what is the best way for a company to promote ethical conduct among its employees?

Hypothetical Cases

1. XYZ Pharmaceuticals develops a new drug that causes the abortion of female fetuses up to the first trimester of pregnancy and does not affect male fetuses. The drug has no known side effects for women who take it, and seems perfectly safe to use. While awaiting approval of the drug from the U.S. Food and Drug Administration (FDA), a process that takes several years, the company receives very negative press and numerous groups call for a boycott of the manufacturer. Because of the negative reaction to the drug by the general public, the manufacturer decides to scrap plans to produce the drug in the United States, but wants to market it abroad in a number of countries where it expects the drug to be well received. There is nothing in U.S. law or in the laws of the countries it intends to market the drug to prevent its sale. Make an ethical argument either for or against the drug's sale abroad. Justify your argument with sound reasoning.
2. Most jurisdictions still have on their books laws that make certain kinds of conduct illegal based on religious principles. Such laws, often referred to as blue laws because they were traditionally written on blue paper, commonly prohibit the conducting of business on Sunday, the traditional Christian Sabbath, as well as many kinds of sexual practices, such as sodomy—even between consenting, married, heterosexual adults. Should such laws be enforced or overturned, in your view? Justify your answer through legal or ethical arguments.
3. Some argue that government needs to increase its regulation of business for the good of society as a whole, while others believe that the marketplace is self-regulating and that government intervention through needless regulation places an unfair, costly burden on businesses generally and small businesses in particular. What role do you believe government should play through regulation to ensure ethical conduct by businesses?
4. Large corporations often spend significant amounts of money every year on charitable contributions to a number of causes. While this long-established practice continues, so does the debate as to its ethical value in some quarters. Some people believe it is not just the right, but the social duty of for-profit corporations and other businesses to contribute money to worthy causes as a means of giving back something of tangible value for the profits they reap from society as a whole. Others believe that corporate contributions are an improper use of money that rightfully should be distributed to shareholders as dividends from corporate profits, and that making such charitable gifts without shareholder consent constitutes a misuse of corporate assets. What do you think? Explain your answer fully.

Administrative Law

CHAPTER 5

Administrative Agencies

Administrative law governs and defines the powers of government agencies. A number of political and technological factors have led to a veritable explosion in the growth of government since the turn of the twentieth century, both at the federal and state levels. This growth has given rise to what has come to be commonly referred to as the fourth branch of government: administrative agencies.

Purpose of Federal Agencies

Since the 1930s, the federal government has been steadily expanding its regulatory powers over business and individuals. Although Congress has the power to regulate nearly any matter that has an impact on interstate commerce under the U.S. Supreme Court's broad interpretation of the Commerce Clause, the 535 men and women who make up Congress have neither the time nor expertise to become involved in the specifics of drafting regulatory rules for each federal agency. What Congress does instead is create administrative agencies to oversee or carry out a specific governmental function, and then empowers that agency to create the rules by which it will operate. The same holds true for the executive branch of government, where the president uses administrative agencies to help carry out the responsibilities of the office. When an agency is created, Congress gives the agency the power to draft its own agency rules—the guidelines under which the agency operates and that must be followed by persons over whom the agency is given regulatory powers. When federal agencies enact rules, they must follow the guidelines set forth in the Administrative Procedure Act, which specifies the procedures agencies must follow in promulgating new rules. As long as an agency creates rules in accordance with the Administrative Procedure Act, such rules have the force of law.

Agencies have two main purposes: assisting in carrying out vital government functions and exerting regulatory control. They are the instruments through which Congress and the president act to institute policies and implement government regulation. As both government and government regulation have steadily grown since the first half of the twentieth century, agencies as the instrumentality of that growth have likewise swelled in both size and power. While the titular seat of power may rest with legislative and executive branches of government, it is administrative agencies that carry out the day-to-day operation of governmental regulatory and service functions.

Independent Federal Agencies

Federal agencies fall into two basic categories: independent and executive. Congress created independent agencies to assist it in exerting regulatory control or carrying out governmental administration. Once created, these agencies are headed by a director who is appointed by the president and confirmed by the

Chapter Outline

Administrative Agencies
Purpose of Federal Agencies
Independent Federal Agencies
Executive Agencies
State Agencies
The Administrative Procedure Act

Senate. To distance these agencies from the political process, independent agency directors serve for set terms that are staggered so as to prevent any given administration from having too great an impact on such agencies through presidential appointments of agency heads.

Independent agencies can wield tremendous power. Congress often imbues these agencies with quasi-judicial, quasi-legislative, and quasi-executive powers: They create their own rules (a legislative power), enforce these rules, conduct investigations (executive powers), and adjudicate disputes relating to these rules or their applications in administrative hearings similar to trials (a judicial power).

Agencies perform a vital function in areas where specific expertise is a requirement to perform a governmental function or regulate a specific business. Independent federal agencies include the Central Intelligence Agency, Environmental Protection Agency, Equal Employment Opportunity Commission, Federal Communications Commission, Interstate Commerce Commission, Federal Trade Commission, Nuclear Regulatory Commission, and Securities and Exchange Commission, among many others. While Congress may have the right to regulate aviation (because of its impact on interstate and international commerce), the civilian and military use of nuclear energy, and intelligence gathering, few senators or representatives have the highly specialized knowledge necessary to effectively regulate any of these areas. Rather than regulating these areas directly, Congress can set up agencies staffed with experts who can promulgate rules by relying on their superior knowledge of the fields they regulate or operate in, with appropriate congressional oversight.

Executive Agencies

Federal agencies have also been created to assist the executive branch in carrying out its responsibilities. Notable executive branch agencies include the Federal Bureau of Investigation (Justice Department), U.S. Immigration and Customs Enforcement (Department of Homeland Security), Food and Drug Administration (Health and Human Services Department), Bureau of Indian Affairs (Interior Department), Secret Service (Department of Homeland Security), Federal Aviation Administration (Transportation Department), and Social Security Administration (Health and Human Services Department), to name only a few.

Unlike independent agencies, executive agencies are under the control of the president, who can appoint and remove their directors at will. Executive agency directors, including members of the president's cabinet, serve at the pleasure of the president. These agencies are, therefore, much more responsive to political issues and subject to the winds of political change, at least at the top levels. Nonetheless, most agency workers are civil servants, not political appointees, and enjoy the relative job security that status conveys. Thus, while the heads of executive agencies may come and go with changing administrations, the bureaucracy itself is well entrenched and grows yearly as new agencies are created and existing agencies expanded to help implement government goals and programs.

State Agencies

The appeal of agencies as a means of implementing necessary regulation and providing vital services is not limited to the federal government. States also use agencies to assist with such matters as the administration of workers' compensation, social services, tax collection, and the regulation of business.

As is true for federal agencies, state and local government agencies can be created by the state legislature or the state's chief executive (the governor) as well as by city councils and mayors.

The Administrative Procedure Act

Independent federal agencies are created through an act of Congress that establishes the agency and empowers it to perform whatever duties Congress specifically delegates to the agency. The actual creation of the agency and the scope of its authority are detailed in the enabling legislation—the act of Congress that creates the agency. The details of the agency's operation are left to the agency, which creates its own rules in accordance with the guidelines set out in the 1946 Administrative Procedure Act (APA). The APA gives agencies broad rule-making powers, as long as they act within the guidelines that the APA provides. Federal executive agencies are usually created by presidential order. Like independent agencies, executive agencies are also subject to the guidelines of the APA.

Rulemaking Requirements of the APA

Under the Administrative Procedure Act, agencies have the power to create rules that have the force of law provided that the guidelines of the APA are observed. The basic requirements that all federal agencies must observe in rule making are as follows:

- giving notice to the general public that a new rule or rule change is being considered by publication of the proposed rule in the Federal Register;
- providing an opportunity for all interested parties to participate in the rule-making process by conducting public hearings and giving all interested parties a reasonable opportunity to voice their views on the proposed new rule or rule change; and
- publishing in the Federal Register a draft containing the essential factors relating to the proposed rule and its purpose at least 30 days before the rule is to take effect.

Once the requirements of the APA have been met, the proposed rule takes effect on its proposed effective date and has the force of law.

Limits on Administrative Agencies

As previously noted, federal agencies have far-reaching powers within the areas that they oversee. A congressional grant of authority to an agency often includes the ability to carry out investigations, create rules that are the functional equivalent of statutes, hold hearings to adjudicate alleged violation of agency rules, and assess punishment (usually by way of fines) to those adjudicated to be in violation of the agency's rules. Agencies with such powers, such as the Internal Revenue Service, can act as legislators, police, judge, and jury. While this concentration of power leads to the swift administration of justice, the average citizen facing an administrative hearing may take comfort in the knowledge that both agency rules and most agency decisions are subject to judicial review on any of the following grounds:

- the agency acted beyond the scope of its authority under the agency's enabling act;
- the agency misinterpreted federal law (including its enabling act) in its rule making or in the adjudication of any matter before the agency;
- the agency action violates the U.S. Constitution or any federal law; or
- the agency rules or the findings of administrative law judges are arbitrary or capricious.

Courts uphold agency rules and procedures, as well as the adjudications by administrative law judges of agency hearings conducted as informal trials, as long as they meet the noted requirements.

Questions

1. What is the basic purpose of government agencies?
2. What are the two basic categories of federal agencies?
3. How do directors of independent agencies come to power?
4. What is the purpose of state administrative agencies?
5. What are the basic requirements that the Administrative Procedure Act requires agencies to observe in rule making?

6. What are the grounds for overturning agency action in the courts?
7. Where does one look to find the exact power that Congress has given to an independent federal agency?
8. What agency heads serve at the pleasure of the president?
9. What are the quasi-judicial and quasi-legislative powers that some agencies are given in their enabling legislation?
10. Although agency heads change from time to time as part of the political process, most agency employees are unaffected by changes in political administrations. Why?

Hypothetical Cases

1. The Federal Aviation Administration (FAA) wants to institute new safety regulations relating to the use of drugs and alcohol by pilots in civil aviation. After conducting a study, the agency decides that it would be in the best interest of the general public to begin weekly random drug testing of all airline pilots effective immediately. At the direction of the agency director, the FAA sends out notices to all airlines that a new drug testing program is now in effect. Is this regulation valid under the facts given? Explain.

2. The Nuclear Regulatory Commission (NRC), concerned about safety in the nation's nuclear-power-generating stations, wishes to impose new safety regulations affecting such power-generating plants. After issuing a notice to the general public that it is considering safety rule changes, the agency conducts hearings with interested persons in the industry as well as the general public for a period of 60 days. At the conclusion of these hearings, it decides that it would be in the best interest of the industry to ban the sale of alcoholic beverages in counties where nuclear generating plants are located. It then publishes a copy of the proposed regulation as well as a general statement of the need for such regulation in the Federal Register 30 days before the regulation is to take effect. After the effective date of the regulation, it is challenged in a federal district court of appeals by liquor store owners in affected counties. What is the likely result?

3. In the last example, assume that the NRC followed the same procedure and promulgated a rule that forbade nuclear-generating-plant workers from working with a blood alcohol level of .05%, subjecting violators to a fine of $5,000. Is such a regulation likely to be upheld if it is challenged in court? Explain.

4. The Federal Communications Commission, concerned with the increasing violence and hatred depicted in the popular media, decides to consider new rules affecting the broadcasting of material of a violent, sexual, or hateful nature. After following the established procedures for rule making under the APA, it promulgates the following new rules:
   1. Material of a violent or sexual nature can be broadcast only between the hours of 12:00 AM and 6:00 AM;
   2. Music that advocates physical violence, the degradation of women, or racial bigotry cannot be broadcast at any time.

   Will these two regulations withstand court challenges? Explain.

Criminal Law

CHAPTER 6

Chapter Outline

Elements of a Crime
Classification of Crimes
Specific Crimes
Crimes against Persons
Crimes against Property
Bribery, Extortion, and Crimes against the Judicial Process
Attempted Crimes and Criminal Conspiracy
Defenses to Criminal Liability

Criminal law is the branch of law that concerns itself with the punishment of prohibited behavior seen as harmful to society as a whole. In every society, criminal law is the primary vehicle through which government imposes standards of behavior for its citizens as a means of preventing antisocial behavior and maintaining order. Because criminal law punishes behavior deemed to be damaging to society, it is the branch of law that most clearly reflects a society's ethical values. All crimes are offenses against society, and convicted criminals are punished by having them forfeit their property (by having to pay a fine), their freedom, and even their lives depending on the seriousness of their crime. In a criminal trial, a prosecutor (the government representative who is charged with proving the guilt at trial of individuals accused of committing crimes) sues a person suspected of committing a crime (the criminal defendant) to have that person punished by having to pay a fine, being sentenced to jail, or both. In extreme cases, convicted criminals may also be put to death. Thus, criminal law is punitive in nature, with the intended result of a successful conviction being the punishment of the criminal for having committed the prohibited act.

Although criminal law in both England and the United States developed as common law based on custom and tradition, today all states have extensive criminal codes that enumerate a wide range of prohibited conduct and specify its punishment. As is often the case in our legal system, there are important differences in criminal law statutes at the state and federal levels, in terms of both the kinds of conduct that are prohibited and the kinds of punishment that can be exacted for such conduct. Despite these differences, there are still many similarities in the kinds of conduct that are prohibited in each of the 50 states and by the federal government, since all criminal statutes trace their roots to the common law. Most states today have incorporated at least in part the Model Penal Code promulgated by the American Law Institute in 1962 and revised in 1981. In this chapter, we focus on areas of criminal law that are fairly standard in most states. Keep in mind, however, that the law is fluid and subject to revision and change; this is particularly true in the area of criminal law, where legislatures are constantly making changes both to the types of conduct deemed criminal and to the punishment for such conduct in order to reflect changing societal values.

Elements of a Crime

There are two elements to every crime that the prosecution must prove before a criminal defendant can be found guilty of having committed a crime: (1) a criminal act or omission by the accused, and (2) the existence of a wrongful state of mind, or intent at the time of the commission of the wrongful act or omission. (A criminal omission is a failure to act when the law imposes a duty to act, such as the duty of a parent to care for and protect a minor child.) If a criminal act (or criminal omission) is carried out with the required criminal intent, then a crime is complete; but criminal intent alone or a harmful act that was not committed with the required criminal intent does not rise to the level of a crime. A few examples should help to illustrate:

- Jane hates Josh and wishes he were dead. She spends every waking moment hoping for his demise and imagining ingenious, painful ways of bringing it about. One day, Josh is struck by lightning and dies, much to Jane's delight. Jane is guilty of no crime, since she committed no act to help bring about Josh's death.
- Jane wishes Josh were dead. She takes a butcher knife and plunges it into Josh, intending to kill him. Josh dies. Jane is guilty of a crime (murder) since she undertook a criminal act (plunging the knife into Josh) while possessing the necessary criminal intent (the intent to kill him).
- Jane, while deer hunting, sees the luckless Josh in the woods 100 yards away. He is wearing a tan deerskin-colored coat and hat and crawling on all fours looking for a lost contact lens. Believing Josh to be a deer, Jane shoots and kills him. Jane is not guilty of murder under the facts given, despite the fact that a criminal act was committed (homicide), since she lacked the required criminal intent. (The wrongful act was caused by a mistake rather than the intent to do harm.)

In general, failure to act will not result in criminal liability unless the accused had a duty to act. In our society, individuals are generally free to stand by and do nothing when others are faced with danger unless:

1. there is a special relationship that by its nature requires the bystander to come to the assistance of the person in danger, or
2. the dangerous situation was caused or contributed to by the bystander.

If a special relationship exists that imposes a duty to act on a bystander, or if the bystander contributed through his actions to placing the victim in a dangerous situation, then the bystander will be guilty of criminal omission if he does not render assistance. The following example will illustrate:

- Sam, a sadistic sociopath who enjoys others' suffering, watches as a sightless stranger crosses a busy intersection while a tractor trailer approaches her at a high rate of speed. He does not warn the stranger of the danger or move to assist her. If the truck strikes the sightless woman, Sam will not generally be guilty of any crime. As a stranger, he has no duty to warn or assist another in danger. His failure to do so is clearly morally reprehensible, but since he did not place the woman in the dangerous situation and owed her no legal duty, he is guilty of no crime in failing to assist her through word or deed. Sam would, however, have had an affirmative duty to act to at least warn the woman if he were the woman's husband or father, or if he were a police officer on duty whose responsibility it is to protect and safeguard the welfare of all citizens in his community.

It is possible to be guilty of a crime without having the required criminal intent in a few kinds of special cases. Legislatures want to prevent certain types of behavior regardless of the intent of the person engaging in the behavior, usually because of the inherently dangerous nature of the behavior and the danger it poses to others. Such criminal offenses are termed strict liability crimes. Whenever a strict liability crime is involved, the only issue is whether the act was committed; the mental state of the person committing the act is irrelevant. Typical strict liability offenses include traffic violations and driving while under the influence of alcohol or other drugs. If a person is accused of speeding or running a red light, for example, all that the prosecutor needs to show is that the act occurred. It is irrelevant that the accused did not intend to speed or did not see the red light before crossing it; what is punishable is the act itself. Likewise, with driving while under the influence or driving with ability impaired, that the accused may not have intended the violation or was so intoxicated that she lacked the ability to form criminal intent is irrelevant.

Classification of Crimes

Traditionally, crimes have been classified into three basic categories based on their seriousness: felonies, misdemeanors, and violations. Felonies are the most serious crimes and are punishable by more than one year of imprisonment in a state or federal penitentiary. Misdemeanors are less serious criminal offenses that can carry a maximum penalty of one year of imprisonment. Violations are minor offenses that typically are punishable by a fine or short prison sentence of 30 days or less.

Felonies and misdemeanors are further subdivided into other categories based on the maximum penalty by which they are punishable. The following example is typical, but be aware that, in keeping with our common law system, there is great variation in the criminal statutes among the states, both in the classification and punishment of crimes.

- First-Degree Felony: Punishable by death or imprisonment from 15 years to life, or by a fine of up to $10,000;
- Second-Degree Felony: Punishable by imprisonment of up to 15 years and/or a fine of up to $10,000;
- Third-Degree Felony: Punishable by imprisonment of up to 5 years and/or a fine of up to $5,000;
- Class A Misdemeanor: Punishable by imprisonment of up to 1 year and/or a fine of up to $1,000;
- Class B Misdemeanor: Punishable by imprisonment of up to 6 months and/or a fine of up to $1,000;
- Class C Misdemeanor: Punishable by imprisonment of up to 3 months and/or a fine of up to $1,000.

Violations are also classed by their type and the maximum sentence or fine to which violators can be subjected. Common violations include minor traffic infractions as well as offenses such as littering and spitting on the sidewalk. The maximum fine for each violation is commonly $500 or less.

Specific Crimes

Although a comprehensive study of criminal law is beyond the scope of this text, an examination of conduct punishable as criminal in all states is a useful exercise for two reasons: First, practical knowledge of basic criminal law principles can be important tools to average citizens in their business and private lives, and second, even a cursory examination of criminal law principles can show government efforts at legislating morality and highlight some basic societal values worthy of intellectual inquiry and discussion.

The following sections present a brief examination of specific crimes in three basic categories: crimes against persons, crimes against property, and crimes against judicial process.

Crimes against Persons

The first category of crimes that we examine is crimes against persons. The law recognizes the rights of individuals in our society to be left alone. Undue interference with that right through physical or mental means often leads to criminal liability, as the following types of crimes illustrate.

Murder: The unjustified taking of a human life with malice aforethought constitutes the crime of murder, a first-degree felony. For a homicide to rise to the level of murder, it must be committed on purpose or knowingly. A homicide that occurs under circumstances that demonstrate extreme indifference to human life or any homicide that results from the commission or attempted commission of another felony also constitutes murder.

Manslaughter: The unjustified taking of a human life under circumstances that would constitute murder can result in the lesser crime (second-degree felony) of manslaughter if it is committed under extreme emotional distress. A homicide resulting from reckless conduct also constitutes manslaughter.

- Donna stabs her husband Vince to death immediately after learning he has been unfaithful. She is probably guilty of manslaughter, since the crime is likely to have been committed under extreme emotional distress. (As we'll see shortly, she might be able to avail herself of a valid insanity defense, depending on the circumstances.)
- Jack drives his hotrod in a school zone at 95 mph, not intending to harm anyone but merely seeking to impress the kindergartners. He accidentally kills a crossing guard when he loses control of his car. Despite his lack of intent to commit the homicide, Jack is guilty of manslaughter because a death resulted from his reckless conduct.

Negligent Homicide: The negligent taking of a human life results in the crime of negligent homicide. This type of homicide results from carelessness, or the failure to exercise the care that a reasonably prudent person would exercise under similar circumstances.

- Melinda accidentally fires a handgun while cleaning it, not realizing it was loaded. The bullet strikes and kills a houseguest. She is guilty of criminally negligent homicide.

Aggravated Assault: Both the attempt to cause severe bodily harm to another and the actual causing of such injuries constitute the crime of aggravated assault (a second-degree felony) if such an attempt is made intentionally or with extreme indifference to human life. The attempt to cause any injury through the use of a deadly weapon in itself constitutes aggravated assault.

Simple Assault: Any of the following offenses constitute the crime of simple assault:

1. an attempt to cause or the actual causing of any bodily injury to another either intentionally or recklessly;
2. negligently causing a nonlethal injury to another through the use of a firearm; or
3. an attempt to place another in fear of impending serious physical harm through physical threats. Simple assault is usually a class A or B misdemeanor, or a class C misdemeanor if it results from a physical confrontation voluntarily entered into by the parties involved.

Reckless Endangerment: Engaging in conduct that recklessly places another in danger of death or serious injury constitutes the misdemeanor of reckless endangerment. Under the Model Penal Act, merely pointing a firearm in the general direction of any person constitutes reckless endangerment, whether or not the person pointing the gun believes it to be loaded.

Kidnapping: The unlawful taking of a person or confinement of a person in a place of isolation constitutes the crime of kidnapping if it is done for any of the following purposes:

1. to hold the victim for ransom or as a hostage;
2. to facilitate the commission of any felony or to facilitate escape after a felony is committed;
3. to inflict bodily injury or to place the victim or another in fear of imminent serious bodily injury to the victim; or
4. to interfere with the performance of any governmental or political function.

Kidnapping is a first-degree felony, but it is reduced to a second-degree felony if the victim is voluntarily released alive prior to the kidnapper's trial.

False Imprisonment: The unjustified, intentional interference with the right of another to move about freely constitutes the crime of false imprisonment, a misdemeanor. It is not necessary that the restraint be physical. Threats directed at the victim or at another can constitute a sufficient interference with the person's right to move about freely if the person at whom the threats are directed reasonably believes that they may be carried out.

False imprisonment is a crime of particular concern to retail merchants who hold shoplifting suspects for questioning. A suspected shoplifter can lawfully be restrained for questioning provided that there is sufficient evidence to believe that the person has stolen merchandise belonging to the store. Even when such evidence exists, however, as is the case when a store employee witnesses the shoplifting, the suspect can be restrained only for a reasonable length of time for questioning or until police arrive on the scene.

Rape: The crime of rape is defined both at common law and by the Model Penal Code as sexual intercourse (requiring some anal or vaginal penetration) by a male with a female who is not his wife when such intercourse

1. is compelled by force or by the threat of imminent death, serious injury, extreme pain, or kidnapping directed at the victim or any third party; or
2. is engaged in after the female's resistance was intentionally overcome through the use of drugs or alcohol administered by the male; or
3. involves a female who is unconscious; or
4. involves a female who is under the age of consent in the state (the legal age of consent for sex is usually age 18).

Rape is a second-degree felony but can rise to a first-degree felony if the rapist inflicts serious physical injury during the rape or if the victim was not a social companion of the rapist at the time of the crime and had not had previous sexual relations with the attacker.

Generally, whenever rape is predicated on the age of the victim (statutory rape), that the woman gave her consent freely or that the man might not have reasonably been able to know that the woman was below the legal age of consent is irrelevant. This is in nearly every state a strict liability crime, where the only question is whether the act was committed and whether the woman was below the age of consent.

Note that at common law, a husband cannot be guilty of rape, and in most states as well as under the Model Penal Act, parties who live together as a traditional husband and wife are considered to be husband and wife for purposes of rape. Note, too, that rape is a male-specific crime. At common law, a husband who forces his wife to submit to sexual intercourse is at most guilty of simple assault. Today, many states criminalize marital rape as a separate criminal offense.

Crimes against Property

Crimes against property include offenses that result in the destruction of property or the permanent or temporary deprivation of the owner's right to exclusively use and enjoy real or personal property.

Arson: At common law, arson was defined as the intentional burning of another's home. Today, the definition of arson has been substantially expanded in the criminal law statutes of most jurisdictions to include the intentional burning of another's occupied structure or the intentional burning of any property, including one's own, for the purpose of collecting insurance. For purposes of arson, an occupied structure is usually defined as any personal or real property that is constructed so as to permit overnight accommodation of persons or the conducting of business therein, whether or not the structure is actually occupied at the time that it is burned. Thus, all homes and businesses can be subjected to arson, as can mobile homes and trailers that are set up for human occupancy. Arson is typically a second-degree felony.

Criminal Mischief: Damaging the personal or real property of another purposely, recklessly, or negligently by the use of explosives, fire, or other dangerous means constitutes criminal mischief, which can be either a third-degree felony; a class A, B, or C misdemeanor; or a violation, depending on the nature and extent of the damage caused. (Under Section 220.3, paragraph 2 of the Model Penal Code, for example, it is a third-degree felony if damage in excess of $5,000 is caused, a misdemeanor if more than $100 but less than $5,000 in damages is caused, a petty misdemeanor if more than $25 but less than $100 in damages is caused, and a violation if $25 or less in damages results from the criminal mischief.)

Burglary: At common law, burglary was defined as breaking and entering into the dwelling house of another at night with the intent to commit a serious crime inside. As is the case with arson, modern criminal law statutes have liberalized the definition to be less restrictive. A common definition of burglary today is breaking and entering into any occupied structure with the intent of committing any crime inside. The requirement of a breaking is fulfilled whenever the burglar exerts any amount of force to gain access to a building; turning a doorknob or gently pushing in a door that is unlocked both constitute a sufficient breaking in most states. The requirement of entering is satisfied by the intrusion of any part of a person or any tool in his or her control into the occupied structure. The crime is complete as soon as the breaking and entering is accomplished, provided that the burglar intended to commit a crime inside. The following three examples constitute the crime of burglary:

- Bob Burglar kicks in a door and enters Victoria Victim's home in order to steal her valuables. Once inside, he is scared off by Victoria, who is wielding a shotgun, before he has a chance to take anything of value.
- Belinda Burglar pushes an unlocked door and walks into Vince Victim's apartment to physically assault him.
- Ben Burglar slides open a window to Victoria's home and, using a fishing pole, manages to hook and reel in a purse and a gold chain from her nightstand as she sleeps.

Bob, Belinda, and Ben are all guilty of burglary, since the requirement of breaking and entering with a criminal intent is met in all three cases. Notice that in the third case, Ben never physically enters Victoria's home; nevertheless, when he casts the fishing line through the window, it is the same as if he had entered himself. Notice too, in that example, that sliding up an unlocked window constitutes a sufficient breaking, and the crime is complete as soon as the line is cast through the window with the intent to commit a crime (stealing the purse and chain), even if he fails to snag the personal property after several casts and goes away empty-handed.

Burglary is usually a third-degree felony, but it can be raised to a second-degree felony in many states if the crime is committed at night, if anyone is injured during the commission of the crime, or if the burglar carries a deadly weapon during the burglary.

Criminal Trespass: Anyone who knowingly enters real property owned by another without permission to do so is guilty of criminal trespass, a misdemeanor. Entering any building not open to the general public without permission constitutes criminal trespass, as does the entering into posted land that warns intruders not to trespass, or the entering into land that the trespasser knows or reasonably should have known belongs to another. Failure to leave another's property when instructed to do so also constitutes trespass, even if the trespasser originally was given permission to enter the land by its owner or tenant. Willfully throwing a rock onto another's land is trespass, as is firing a bullet or arrow above another's land—even if the bullet or arrow never touches the ground. On the other hand, if a ball accidentally bounces onto a neighbor's land when children are playing basketball, it would not constitute trespass because the ball was not intentionally thrown there. But the intentional act of retrieving the basketball without consent would constitute trespass.

At common law, property rights extended below one's real property (subsurface rights) to the center of the earth and above one's property (air rights) all the way to the heavens. Today, every jurisdiction limits air rights, typically to a given number of feet above the tallest structure on one's land. Were this not the case, it would be virtually impossible to engage in civil aviation, and even satellites orbiting miles above the earth would be trespassing on landowner's air rights.

Robbery: A theft that is accomplished through either the use of force or the threat of force constitutes the crime of robbery. Robbery is usually a second-degree felony, but it can become a first-degree felony if the perpetrator inflicts or attempts to inflict serious bodily harm during the course of the crime.

Larceny: The intentional taking and carrying away of the property of another with the intent to permanently deprive the owner of its use constitutes the crime of larceny. Larceny can be either a third-degree felony or misdemeanor, depending on the value of the stolen property.

Embezzlement: The misappropriation of property in one's care belonging to another constitutes the crime of embezzlement, which is typically punishable in the same manner as larceny.

Receiving Stolen Property: A person who purchases or otherwise acquires stolen property is guilty of the crime of receiving stolen property, which is usually punishable in exactly the same manner as larceny, provided that the property is received with actual knowledge that it was stolen, or under circumstances that should have made the receiver suspicious that it might be stolen.

Theft of Services: A person who knowingly receives the benefit of services that are available for compensation through the use of deception or any physical means to avoid paying for such services is guilty of theft of services, a crime punishable in the same manner as larceny. Common examples of theft of services include using slugs in public telephones, vending machines, or parking meters, as well as illegal hookups to cable services and the use of illegal descramblers to obtain scrambled satellite broadcasts.

Forgery: The crime of forgery consists of any material alteration to a written document issued by another that is made in order to defraud or mislead anyone. The crime of forgery is a felony or misdemeanor depending on the nature of the offense. Altering government or commercial enterprise instruments that purport to have monetary value, such as currency, stamps, stocks, bonds, and similar instruments, represents a second-degree felony. Alteration of documents that affect legal relationships, such as wills, trusts, deeds, contracts, and claims releases, is a felony in the third degree. Any other forgery, such as the material alteration of the date in a driver's license, is a misdemeanor.

Issuing a Bad Check: It is a misdemeanor to issue a check for which one no longer has an account in the bank on which it is drawn, or to issue a check when one has a valid account but that account lacks sufficient funds for its payment when it is presented within 30 days of the date of issue. A person may avoid criminal liability for bounced checks by promptly paying the due amount in many states (typically within 10 days of the notice of dishonor).

Credit Card Fraud: Using a forged or stolen credit card to obtain goods, services, or cash advances or using a credit card after it has been canceled or recalled constitutes credit card fraud. Credit card fraud is usually a third-degree felony if the amount of the fraudulent charge exceeds $500 or a misdemeanor if the amount is $500 or less.

Bribery, Extortion, and Crimes against the Judicial Process

To ensure fairness in the administration of justice and in the normal conduct of business, the criminal statutes of every state prohibit conduct that seeks to interfere with fair business practices or the impartial administration of justice.

Bribery of a Public Official: At common law, the crime of bribery consisted of promising to give something of value in exchange for a public official's official conduct. The solicitation, acceptance, and promise to give or accept a bribe are all equally punishable as a misdemeanor. The consideration involved need not be monetary; a promise of sexual favors made to a judge, police officer, or housing inspector for favorable official action constitutes bribery as much as does a promise to exchange money or goods for such action.

Commercial Bribery: It is a misdemeanor in most states to solicit, accept, or agree to accept anything of value in exchange for violating a duty of fidelity owed to one's employer, client, or company as an employee, officer of a corporation, partner, trustee, guardian, or member of a profession. Commercial bribery is applicable in a wide variety of settings, and would include each of the following:

- a promise by a parent to pay a little league umpire $100 if he does not call a child out on strikes;
- a promise to give the CEO of XYZ Company an executive position in ABC Company if she discloses trade secrets;
- an offer by a plaintiff's attorney to a defendant's attorney in a civil suit to pay him $100,000 if he loses the case;
- an offer of a new car by an unqualified applicant to Ivy League University to the Director of Admissions if she is accepted as a student; and
- an offer of a designer suit made by Failing Student to Scruffy Professor in exchange for a passing grade.

Threatening a Public Official: Threatening any public official with harm in order to influence official action is a misdemeanor. Making similar threats to influence a judicial or administrative proceeding, however, is a third-degree felony. (Members of a jury are deemed public officials for purposes of this crime.)

Influence Peddling: It is a misdemeanor to solicit, receive, or agree to receive any consideration for the trading of political influence by a public servant. This crime includes the solicitation, giving, or receiving of a political endorsement by a public official in exchange for something of value.

Perjury: Making a material misrepresentation while under oath or through a sworn statement (such as an affidavit) constitutes the crime of perjury, a third-degree felony. A misrepresentation is material if it can affect the course or outcome of a proceeding.

Tampering with Public Records: It is a misdemeanor to knowingly falsify, destroy, or attempt to hide any official government record or document. The crime includes creating or using falsified documentation issued by the government, such as using a false Social Security or Alien Registration card. If the tampering is done to defraud or injure anyone, then the offense is a third-degree felony. Simply carrying a false Social Security card, for example, is a misdemeanor, but using it to attempt to obtain social services that one is not entitled to receive, thereby defrauding the government, is a third-degree felony.

Obstruction of Justice: Any intentional interference with the administration of justice in a person's official or private conduct is a misdemeanor, regardless of whether such interference is obtained through physical force or official action. Physically interfering with an arrest, disrupting courtroom proceedings, and giving false information that misleads police in an investigation are all examples of obstructing justice.

Aiding in the Commission of a Crime: Any assistance rendered to a criminal in the commission of a crime and hiding or converting the proceeds of criminal activity are punishable as a misdemeanor. If the underlying crime was a first- or second-degree felony, however, then facilitating its commission is a third-degree felony.

Attempted Crimes and Criminal Conspiracy

The law punishes not only completed criminal acts but also the attempted commission of a crime that for some reason is not completed. In addition, conspiring to commit a crime, whether or not the crime is ultimately committed, is a separate offense unto itself.

The Crime of Attempt: Under the Model Penal Code and the criminal codes of most states, the attempt to commit a crime that is not ultimately carried out is punishable to the same degree that the crime itself would have been punishable if completed. In general, to convict a criminal defendant for attempting the commission of a crime, all that is necessary is that the defendant takes a substantial step toward committing the criminal act, and that the defendant acts with the required criminal intent. The penalty for attempting a crime is the same as that for committing the crime attempted with the exception that first-degree crimes become second-degree attempted crimes.

For example, attempted murder is second-degree felony because murder is a first-degree felony. But attempted robbery is a second-degree felony because robbery is a second-degree felony, and attempted larceny is either a third-degree felony or a misdemeanor depending on the value of the goods, exactly as is the case with larceny itself.

It must be noted that a defendant can be tried and convicted for either the attempt to commit a crime or the crime itself, but not both.

Criminal Conspiracy: Either planning and agreeing to commit a crime with others or agreeing to assist others in the commission of a crime results in the crime of criminal conspiracy. Criminal conspiracy, like the crime of attempt, is subject to the same punishment as the underlying crime that the conspirators intend to perpetrate. As is the case with the crime of attempt, criminal conspiracies to commit crimes that are first-degree felonies are punished as second-degree felonies, and the punishment for conspiring to commit any second-degree felony or lower crime is exactly the same as for the underlying crime itself.

The crime of conspiracy is a completely separate crime from the underlying crime that the conspirators intend to commit. Therefore, persons found guilty of criminal conspiracy can also be found guilty of the underlying crime that the conspirators perpetrated or its attempt if the crime was not fully carried out. The following example will illustrate:

- Tom, Dick, and Harriet agree to kill Bill Billionaire and to steal the valuables from his home. Tom agrees to buy a gun from a local illegal gun dealer that specializes in untraceable weapons, Dick agrees to drive the car and disable Bill's alarm system, while Harriet agrees to do the actual killing. On the appointed day, the three thugs arrive at Bill's home, break in, and all three stand by as Harriet attempts to shoot Bill several times, but the gun jams and will not fire. The three panic, run out, and are arrested a short time later. They are charged with burglary and criminal conspiracy to commit murder, and Harriet is also charged with attempted murder. Under the facts given, the three are guilty of all counts.

Despite the fact that there was a criminal conspiracy to commit more than one crime in the preceding example (burglary and murder), there can be only a single conviction for any conspiracy that is ongoing. In this case, the conspiracy charge would be based on attempted murder rather than burglary, since it is the more serious offense. Similarly, if a group of bank robbers plans and executes a dozen successful robberies, they can be charged with 12 separate counts of bank robbery but only a single count of conspiracy to commit bank robbery, since the criminal affiliation was ongoing and subject to the same agreement by the parties to commit the crimes.

Defenses to Criminal Liability

As previously noted, the two prerequisites to criminal liability are a criminal act and criminal intent. Unless a prosecutor can establish both beyond a reasonable doubt, the defendant is entitled to an acquittal. It stands to reason, then, that criminal defendants can avoid a conviction by presenting evidence that they did not commit the criminal act (such as an alibi that shows they were not present in the area at the time the crime was committed) or, if the criminal act occurred, that the defendant lacked the required intent for criminal culpability. To put it another way, criminal defense attorneys have two basic avenues on which to base their defense: that the act in question was not committed by the criminal defendant or that if the act was committed, the defendant did not possess the requisite criminal intent. In addition, behavior that is normally criminal may be justifiable under certain circumstances, such as the intentional infliction of bodily harm to another in self-defense.

In a criminal trial, the prosecutor must establish beyond a reasonable doubt both that a criminal act occurred and that the defendant committed the act with the required criminal intent. All that counsel for the defense needs to do in order to be entitled to an acquittal is to inject a reasonable doubt into the minds of jurors as to the defendant having committed the alleged act or as to the defendant having acted with the required criminal intent. Even in situations in which the defense cannot effectively raise a reasonable doubt as to a defendant's guilt, the defense can raise some affirmative defenses to excuse criminal liability. When any one of the affirmative defenses is raised at trial, the burden of proof is on the defendant's attorney to prove the defense by a preponderance of the evidence. The following example will illustrate:

- Andrew Angry runs up to Don Dunderhead, a candidate for political office in his state, yelling "I'm going to punch your lights out, you blundering idiot. I've been listening to your meandering speeches for months and have yet to hear you say a single thing that makes any sense." Andrew then jumps onto the speaker's platform and beats Don silly. At Andrew's trial for aggravated assault, his attorney won't be able to deny either the act or the intent, since both were broadcast for a week over every television news program. But she might be able to assert an affirmative defense, such as insanity or intoxication, to win Andrew's acquittal.

Specific defenses to criminal liability include insanity, intoxication, infancy, self-defense, defense of others, defense of property, and entrapment.

Insanity

The basic premise behind the insanity defense is that a person who due to some mental illness or deficiency commits a criminal act that he or she would not otherwise commit should not be held responsible for such an act. A defendant who effectively raises an insanity defense in fact proves to the satisfaction of the jury that even though he committed the criminal act as charged, the act was committed without the requisite criminal intent. In other words, whenever the insanity defense is successfully used, the defense convinces the jury that although a criminal act was committed, its cause was not criminal intent but rather the defendant's mental infirmity.

Tests for establishing a valid insanity defense vary from state to state, but states commonly apply one of the following four variations:

1. **M'Naughten Rule:** A defendant who suffers from a mental illness that prevents him at the time of committing a criminal act from either knowing the wrongfulness of his actions or understanding the nature of his actions is excused from criminal liability. Under this rule, it is not enough that a defendant may be suffering from mental illness; the test is whether such illness prevented him from understanding the wrongfulness of his actions.
2. **Irresistible Impulse Test:** A person who establishes that he acted as a result of an irresistible impulse due to a mental illness is entitled to acquittal.
3. **The New Hampshire Rule** (also known as the Durham Rule): Under the New Hampshire Rule, a defendant cannot be found criminally liable if she establishes that her crime was a product of a mental defect or disease. For a crime to be the product

of mental illness, it must be shown that the crime would not have been committed but for the mental illness. This is a much broader test than either the M'Naughten or the irresistible impulse tests, and is currently used by very few jurisdictions.
4. **Model Penal Code Test:** The model Penal Code Test adopted by the American Law Institute excuses criminal conduct if the defendant suffers from a mental disease or defect that prevents him from recognizing the wrongfulness of his conduct or prevents him from conforming his conduct to the requirements of the law. This is the most commonly used test of insanity today and essentially combines the M'Naughten and irresistible impulse theories.

Intoxication

The defense of intoxication is very similar to the insanity defense in that it seeks to exculpate criminal behavior by showing that at the time the behavior took place the criminal defendant was incapable of forming criminal intent due to being intoxicated.

If the intoxication is involuntary, the intoxication is treated exactly in the same manner as insanity. If, for example, a state subscribes to the Model Penal Code definition of insanity, then a person who is involuntarily intoxicated cannot be found guilty of a crime if the intoxication prevented the defendant at the time of committing the criminal act from recognizing the wrongfulness of his conduct or from conforming his conduct to the requirements of the law. To qualify for involuntary intoxication, the defendant must establish that he was tricked or forced into taking the intoxicating substance.

In cases of voluntary intoxication, where the defendant took the intoxicating substance freely, the effect on the defense varies depending on the nature of the crime. If the crime is one that requires a finding of willful criminal intent in order to prove culpability, as is the case with such offenses as murder, rape, or robbery, then it makes no difference whether the intoxication was voluntary or involuntary. Voluntary intoxication will not be a valid defense, however, when the crime is one that does not require willful criminal intent, such as a strict liability crime (driving while intoxicated or general traffic offenses, for example) or a crime based on negligence or recklessness, such as reckless endangerment or negligent homicide. The following two examples will illustrate:

- While at a party, Juan eats several cookies that, unknown to him, have been laced with LSD. An hour later, while his world seems to melt about him, Juan burns down his college's administration building and drives away in the college president's car. He then drives the car at 95 mph in a 15-mph school zone, killing a pedestrian. He is charged with arson, vehicular manslaughter, larceny of the automobile, speeding, and driving while intoxicated. In most states, Juan has a valid defense of involuntary intoxication to all charges, since none of the offenses would have been committed but for his unintentional intoxication.
- If Juan committed the preceding offenses after voluntarily drinking a fifth of vodka while at the party and became so drunk as to lose the ability to know what he was doing, however, his voluntary intoxication would be a valid defense in most states to the arson and larceny charges, for they require willful intent, but not to the manslaughter, speeding, or driving while intoxicated charges, since these are offenses based on recklessness and strict liability.

Infancy

At common law, a child under the age of 7 was deemed incapable of forming the necessary criminal intent to commit a crime, and a child between the ages of 7 and 14 was presumed incapable of forming criminal intent, but that presumption could be overcome by a prosecutor. The assumption was that, as a matter of law, a child under 7 years of age could not understand the difference between right and wrong, and a child between 7 and 14 probably did not understand the difference between right and wrong (but a prosecutor could show that a particular child did understand the difference).

Today, most states retain the common law defense of infancy with little change in their criminal statutes but have made provisions for dealing with youthful offenders through other means (such as by setting up juvenile courts or having the state's family court adjudicate offenses committed by minors). The basic assumption is that minors who commit crimes need to be treated differently than adults; the emphasis when dealing with minors is less on punishment and more on rehabilitation, counseling, and education. Many states provide an option for courts to treat violent youthful offenders as adults if they fall within a certain age (such as 14–17) and subject youthful offenders to the same (harsher) punishment as adults when they commit such violent crimes as rape and murder.

Self-Defense

A person is free to use reasonable force in defense to an unprovoked attack. A person may generally use any necessary force to repel a physical attack or the threat of an attack. A person faced with an attack that she reasonably believes may cause death or serious bodily injury may use any physical force to repel such a threat or attack, up to and including deadly physical force. The key to the justification of the use of force is the reasonableness of the perceived danger in the mind of the victim. If, for example, a mugger pulls a realistic-looking toy gun on a victim who shoots him with a real gun in response, the victim would be justified in repelling the attack even if the mugger is killed in the process, provided that he reasonably feared death or serious injury before fending off the attack. If the mugger's gun in the last example is clearly visible to the victim as a neon-green, transparent toy water pistol, the shooting in self-defense would not be justified. In addition, some states require that a victim exhaust all reasonable options, including flight from the scene where practical, before resorting to the use of deadly force. Even in these states, though, victims may generally use deadly force to repel a reasonably perceived threat of death or serious injury within their own homes without first trying to evade the home invader.

Defense of Others

In every state, a person who rushes to the aid of another who is being victimized may use as much force in defending the person as the person could use himself in his own defense. Thus, if Susan, a passerby, sees Sam with his back against a wall being held up by a gunman who is threatening to kill him, she can use any force against the assailant that Sam himself could use (she can injure or even kill the assailant in this example, since Sam is clearly in danger of death or serious bodily injury).

A problem arises for Good Samaritans when, as is often the case, things are not as they seem. Consider the following facts:

- Mohammed, a passerby, notices Carla, who is dressed as a police officer, being held at gunpoint by Frank, whom he hears saying, "If you move, I'll shoot." Mohammed, sure that a police officer is in danger, tackles Frank, wrestles with him for the gun, and shoots him in the scuffle. Later, he learns that Frank was an undercover police officer attempting to arrest Carla, who had held up a convenience store while impersonating a police officer.

Mohammed's fate as a mistaken Good Samaritan depends on the state where the action occurred. In some states, Mohammed's actions would be judged simply on their reasonableness under the circumstances; if a reasonable person would have believed Carla to have been a police officer in danger, then Mohammed's actions would be justified and not subject him to criminal liability. In other states, however, Good Samaritans are held to "stand in the shoes" of persons whom they try to defend; in such states, a person can use only as much force as the perceived victim had a legal right to use against the perceived attacker. In a state with such a rule, Mohammed would be criminally liable for the injury inflicted on Frank (the undercover police officer) since Carla, the person he perceived to be a victim, in fact had no actual right to defend herself under the circumstances.

Defense of Property

All states recognize the right of an individual to protect property from being taken, misused, or damaged by another. Any force short of deadly physical force (force that may reasonably be expected to cause death or life-threatening injury) may generally be used to protect one's property. In other words, you may threaten, restrain, or physically prevent another from harming or taking your property, but you may not kill or seriously wound another merely to protect your property. Keep in mind that you may use deadly physical force if you reasonably feel threatened with death or serious bodily injury. For example, in most states you may use deadly force to protect yourself from a carjacking during the course of which you are threatened with serious injury, but you may not use deadly force to prevent your car from being stolen from your driveway by shooting the thief from inside your home when you are not directly being threatened by him.

Entrapment

A person who is enticed or convinced to commit a crime by law enforcement agents when he or she is not otherwise predisposed to commit such a crime can escape criminal liability by asserting the defense of entrapment. To successfully assert the defense, the criminal defendant must prove two elements:

1. that the commission of the crime was instigated or enticed by a law enforcement agent(s), and
2. that the crime would not have been committed but for the enticement or instigation of the law enforcement agent(s).

It is not enough for a defendant to show that police provided the opportunity for the crime to occur or that police suggested the crime's commission; to successfully assert an entrapment defense, the defendant must also show that he or she was not predisposed to commit the crime. Let's look at two examples for the sake of clarification:

- Lina, an undercover police officer, offers to purchase a vial of crack cocaine from Freddy, a drug dealer. Freddy sells Lina the crack, and Lina immediately arrests him.
- Lyssandra, a special agent for the Drug Enforcement Administration (DEA), offers Rosalie, a state legislator, $20,000 to transport a kilogram of heroin from a contact in Mexico. Rosalie initially refuses, but Lyssandra manages to convince her, wearing down her resistance through the use of hard-sell tactics over a period of several weeks. When Rosalie delivers the drugs, Lyssandra arrests her for drug trafficking.

Freddy, in the first example, will not be able to successfully assert the defense of entrapment. Even though he was approached by a police officer, he was clearly predisposed to commit the crime and was not in any way convinced to do so. In the second example, however, Rosalie will be able to successfully assert the defense of entrapment, since it is clear from the facts given that she was not predisposed to commit the crime but was convinced to do so by Lyssandra. In the real world, the more pressure a police officer needs to exert on a criminal defendant to get the defendant to agree to commit the illegal act, the likelier it is that the defendant will be able to successfully assert the defense of entrapment. A criminal defendant who offers little or no resistance to the suggestion of committing a crime will not be able to successfully assert the defense of entrapment. One of the key elements for prosecutors trying to overcome the defense when it is raised is the criminal predisposition of the defendant to commit the crime. Predisposition is usually shown by a pattern of previous behavior; thus, persons who are enticed by police to commit criminal acts that they are known to have committed in the past have a very difficult time in raising the defense of entrapment, since their previous acts will point to a predisposition to commit the crime they are charged with.

Questions

1. What is the basic concern of criminal law?
2. What are the elements of a crime?
3. Can a failure to act lead to criminal liability? Explain.
4. In general, is there a legal duty for citizens in our society to come to the assistance of those in need? Should there be one, in your opinion? Explain fully.
5. What are the three basic classifications of crimes?
6. What is the difference between a first-degree and a third-degree felony?
7. Define murder, manslaughter, and negligent homicide.
8. What is the difference between simple assault and aggravated assault?
9. What is the difference between larceny and embezzlement?
10. Name the major affirmative defenses to criminal liability covered in this chapter.

Hypothetical Cases

1. Ralph, a 13-year-old boy, mistakenly takes another's bicycle from a bike rack at school, thinking the bike to be his own. He is arrested and tried for larceny. You agree to represent Ralph, having just passed the bar exam in your state. What will be your defense? Be specific and thorough in your arguments.
2. Rowena, a gun collector, jokingly points a gun she believes to be unloaded at her best friend, Mark. The gun accidentally discharges and Mark is instantly killed. What crimes, if any, could Rowena be charged with?
3. Barbara, while shopping at her local department store, absentmindedly walks out of the store holding a folding umbrella she had grabbed a half hour earlier, intending to pay for it on her way out of the store. A store security officer stops her just outside of the store and asks her to accompany him back inside. Barbara, realizing her mistake, apologizes profusely and attempts to pay for the umbrella, but the security guard refuses to release her and accuses her of shoplifting. Barbara becomes enraged and slaps the security guard when he tells her that he will call the police to have her arrested. The security guard then physically restrains her until police arrive by placing her in handcuffs, while Barbara continues to kick him from time to time. When police arrive to arrest her, she resists arrest and demands that the security guard be arrested for false imprisonment. On the way to the police station, she offers the arresting officer $500 to "let her go and forget the whole thing."
    A. What crimes, if any, can Barbara be charged with?
    B. Assuming that she can convince the trier of fact that she intended to pay for the umbrella at her trial for larceny, will she be convicted of the crime? Explain.
    C. What should be the determination of all other criminal charges based on the facts given?
    D. Can she assert the defense of self-defense against any of the charges?
    E. Should the guard be charged with false imprisonment?
4. Ben sets a fire to a grain silo in his neighbor's farm after a heated argument. Fortunately, the silo is not attached to the neighbor's house or barn, so that the damage does not spread beyond the destruction of the silo and its contents. The next day, Ben is arrested and charged with arson. Should he be convicted of the crime if the prosecutor can show that he purposely set the fire? Explain.
5. Spark and Flash, malicious but less than brilliant arsonists, agree to burn down a number of apartment buildings in exchange for a fee from landlords eager to collect insurance on unprofitable rent-controlled apartment buildings. As they arrive at the first site, they slosh several gallons of gasoline only to discover that they neglected to bring matches or a lighter. Housing police arrest the two after observing them go from door to door asking tenants for matches. What crime or crimes, if any, can they be charged with, and what is the maximum penalty they face for each crime?

Ethics and the Law: Questions for Further Study

1. We have seen in this chapter that an attempt to commit a crime, even if unsuccessful, is generally punishable in the same manner as if the crime had been successfully committed. This may seem a bit unfair at first glance. What do you think is the purpose of such a rule? In most cases, is it ethical to sentence someone to a crime he did not complete exactly as if he had completed it? Does the law in this instance promote justice? Explain.
2. The common law differentiation of youthful offenders from adults was largely based on a paternalistic view of children by the courts. The underlying rationale for

treating youthful offenders differently from adults is that children are inherently good, innocent, and incapable of forming criminal intent until they grow into adulthood and are somehow hardened by the "ways of the world." The law tends to view children in an idealistic way reminiscent of William Blake's "Songs of Innocence." It can be argued that Blake's "Songs of Experience," however, is more directly applicable to youthful offenders today, who often begin their criminal careers at a young age, encouraged by the relative small risk of harsh punishment. Statistics today unequivocally show that most violent crime, including murder, rape, and aggravated assault, is committed by young adults and by children under the age of 18. Yet the violent crimes of youthful offenders are usually handled by states' juvenile courts or family courts, with the emphasis on rehabilitation and training, as opposed to punishment. Furthermore, youthful offender convictions are typically sealed and unavailable to establish a pattern of criminal behavior when these young criminals continue to commit crimes as young adults, thereby allowing them to escape the harsher sentences reserved for repeat offenders when they commit criminal offenses after reaching adulthood. What are your views on this issue? What do you think are the causes of juvenile crime? What, if anything, should society do to reverse this troubling trend?

3. Although the emphasis of criminal law is fundamentally on punishment, there has been a gradual shift in the philosophical base of our penal institutions away from punishment and toward rehabilitation as a means of fighting crime. Whether one views crime as resulting primarily from external causes such as poverty, lack of education, bigotry, sexism, or any number of other societal causes, or whether one believes that most crime results from innate human flaws and human weaknesses can have a fundamental impact on the approach one takes to combating it. What do you believe to be the most important cause of crime in society (internal causes, external causes, a combination of the two, or something else entirely)? Based on your view, what do you think is the best way to deal with the issue of crime? How is your answer influenced by your view of ethics? Your political philosophy? Your religious views?

Intentional Torts

CHAPTER 7

Chapter Outline

Breach of Duty as a Prerequisite to Tort Liability

Intentional Torts against Persons

Intentional Torts against Property

Torts, from the Latin *torquere* and *tortus* ("to twist" and "twisted"), is the branch of law that governs civil wrongs, other than breach of contract, for which a court will provide a remedy. The purpose of tort law is to provide just compensation to injured parties for civil injuries inflicted by others.

At first glance, it is easy to confuse tort law with criminal law insofar as both attempt to exact a penalty for wrongful conduct. Such confusion is exacerbated by the fact that many crimes are also torts. What distinguishes a crime from a tort, however, is the nature of the offense. As we saw in the last chapter, criminal law concerns itself with wrongs against society as a whole and is punitive in nature, whereas tort law concerns itself with wrongs against individuals and is primarily compensatory in nature. To put it another way, crimes are wrongs against society, while torts are offenses against individuals.

Tort law is grounded on the principle that individuals have the right to be left alone—to live free of unreasonable interference from others. While not every action that an individual may consider objectionable may rise to the level of an actionable tort (a recognized civil wrong other than breach of contract for which a court may grant civil relief), tort law as it has developed from early common law through today recognizes a large number of specific torts that persons can inflict on one another. This chapter provides an overview of the most common intentional torts against persons and property. Negligence and strict liability torts are the subject of Chapter 8.

Breach of Duty as a Prerequisite to Tort Liability

Tort liability is based on the breach of a civil duty owed by one person to another. The law imposes on all persons in society the responsibility not to cause injury to one another either on purpose or carelessly. Thus, purposely hitting a stranger with a stone thrown at him is a tort (battery), as is carelessly hitting a person's car with a stone thrown from a rooftop without the specific intention of damaging the automobile (negligence). It is also possible to breach a duty of care owed another by failing to act when one has a duty to act. A person who fails to step on the brakes when approaching a red light breaches an affirmative duty to act, as does a parent who fails to stop a minor child from destroying another's property while under his direct care. Automobile drivers have an affirmative duty to observe the rules of the road, and parents have a duty to supervise minor children in their care to prevent them from harming themselves or others.

Where no duty to act exists, individuals are free to act or refuse to act in order to prevent harm to the persons or property of others as they see fit. Thus, a passerby who sees another in a dangerous situation generally has no duty to render assistance and can merely stand by and watch events unfold without incurring criminal or tort liability. The following example will illustrate:

- Mark Meany, a sadistic sociopath, sees a young, lost child playing next to the lion's cage at the zoo just before feeding time. He looks around and notices no other adults in the area. Deciding that this scene has some entertainment potential for him, he sits down and waits as the child plays around the cage, hoping that the toddler will eventually squeeze through the bars. A half hour later, Mark gets his wish as the child slips through the cage and is promptly pounced on by the lion. (Don't worry: the child escapes after suffering only minor scratches.) If the parents of the child want to have Mark arrested for endangering the safety of a minor (a crime) and for the torts of battery, intentional infliction of emotional distress, and negligence, will they succeed?

In the preceding example, Mark is clearly an immoral, monstrous individual. Nevertheless, he has committed no crime or tort in most states, since he was not responsible for placing the child in danger and had no duty to intervene on the child's behalf. If, on the other hand, Mark were a close relative of the child, a police officer, firefighter, or zoo employee, a duty to act would have been imposed on him by nature of his familial ties or the duties of his job. A duty to rescue someone in an emergency situation may exist, however, for emergency workers and for individuals who subject a victim to harm. And a state is free to impose the duty on others under its general police powers.

Intentional Torts against Persons

The first type of tort that we will explore is intentional torts against persons. While we explore the most common torts of this type, keep in mind that each of the following torts comes into existence only if a duty owed by the tort feasor (the person who perpetrates a tort) to the victim is breached. When intentional torts against persons are involved, the duty typically breached is the duty to refrain from undue interference with the right of others to be left alone.

Battery

Battery can be defined as an unconsented-to touching that is either harmful of offensive. Any intentional touching that has not been consented to can give rise to the tort, whether or not serious injury occurs; the extent of the injury is relevant only in determining the monetary damages to which the victim is entitled. For purposes of the tort, a touching is deemed to be offensive if a reasonable person would object to the touching under similar circumstances. Punching someone on the nose without provocation is clearly a battery. But so is kissing or hugging a stranger without permission, since a reasonable person would likely find such an unconsented-to touching objectionable. Consent can be assumed by the nature of the relationship between the parties, so kissing one's spouse or significant other or hugging a friend is not generally a tort. Nor is it a tort to punch a boxer on the nose during a boxing match, no matter the damage that such contact may inflict.

Assault

The tort of assault consists of placing someone in apprehension of an imminent unconsented-to touching (battery). For the tort to be complete, all that is required is that the victim believe that he is about to be battered. It is not necessary that a battery actually take place or that the tort feasor intend to batter the victim. The tort seeks to compensate victims for the apprehension they suffer when they reasonably believe they are about to be battered, and all that is required is that the apprehension be reasonable for the tort to be complete. Thus, the words "I am going to kill you" can constitute an assault if the hearer reasonably believes that he is about to be harmed. Likewise, pointing a gun at someone constitutes the tort of assault if the person at whom the gun is aimed reasonably believes that she may be shot. But pointing a gun at someone's back is not assault unless the person is aware that he is being targeted. Also, persons who learn that they had been placed in danger after the fact are not the victims of assault, since they are not placed in fear of an immediate or imminent battery.

Intentional Infliction of Emotional Distress

Intentionally causing someone to suffer extreme emotional distress by engaging in extremely cruel, outrageous conduct constitutes the tort of intentional infliction of emotional distress. Like assault, this tort attempts to compensate victims for the apprehension that they are subjected to by the willful acts of others.

For this tort to arise, the conduct of the tort feasor must be outrageous and shockingly cruel. Conduct that is merely unkind will not give rise to the tort, regardless of the pain that such conduct causes the person at whom it is directed. Telling someone "You're ugly and stupid," for example, will not give rise to the tort, regardless of the devastation these words may cause for the person hearing them; the statement may be unkind, antisocial, and mean spirited, but it is not sufficiently shocking to constitute intentional infliction of emotional distress. Calling up someone at 4:00 AM every day for a month to say "You're ugly and stupid," however, is probably sufficiently outrageous conduct to give rise to the tort.

False Imprisonment

Intentionally interfering with a person's right to freely move about without just cause constitutes the tort of false imprisonment. The restriction can be physical or psychological in nature. Tying a person to a chair without justification clearly constitutes the tort, but so does threatening a person with recrimination if she leaves—even if no physical restraint is used.

In business, this tort is of particular interest to retailers who frequently question suspected shoplifters. Holding someone for questioning who is reasonably suspected of shoplifting is permissible, as long as the retailer has probable cause to believe that the person has stolen merchandise and the length of time the person's movements are restrained is reasonable. A customer who is unreasonably detained or who is questioned for an unreasonable length of time can successfully sue for false imprisonment.

Invasion of Privacy

Tort law recognizes an individual's fundamental right to privacy and provides four distinct torts under the umbrella of invasion of privacy to compensate persons whose right to privacy is violated.

Appropriation of a Person's Name or Likeness for Commercial Use

It is a tort to use a person's likeness or name for commercial purposes without permission. The law recognizes the right of individuals to profit from the use of their name or likeness, as well as to prevent others from using their name or likeness for commercial purposes without consent. Thus, if Joan Smith, a famous athlete, eats brand X of cereal, the makers of brand X cannot state that fact (even though true) in promotional material without her consent, nor can they use her picture on a cereal box unless she authorizes it. A newspaper, magazine, or television newscast can use her name and likeness without her consent for a newsworthy purpose, however; such use does not constitute a commercial purpose under the law.

Intrusion into Seclusion

It is a tort to willfully observe the private conduct of others under circumstances when an expectation of privacy exists. Before the tort arises, three conditions must be met: (1) the conduct observed must be private, not public; (2) the intrusion must be willful; and (3) the nature of the intrusion must be such that it is objectionable to a reasonable person. A passerby who glances into an open ground-level window from the street is not guilty of invasion of privacy regardless of the private nature of the acts observed inside, since there can be no reasonable expectation of privacy for persons who carry out their private business in plain view. But a passerby who climbs a telephone pole to look into a second-floor window clearly is guilty of invasion of privacy.

False Light

It is a tort to place persons in a false light by publishing true facts about them in such a way that unpopular views or actions are falsely attributed to them. For the tort to arise, the views or actions that are attributed to the victim through false light must be objectionable to a reasonable person. The following example will illustrate:

- Jane Doe, a prominent politician, stops to give assistance to the victims of an automobile accident. She helps to extricate five people from their car and leaves after an ambulance arrives. She later learns that the five individuals, whom she had not previously met, happen to be members of the American Communist Party when she reads the following headline in the next morning's paper: "Doe Seen Driving Away from Accident Scene after a Meeting with Five Communists." If Jane Doe sues, what is the likely result?

Jane wins, of course, since the headline clearly places her in a false light—making it appear she has unlawfully left the scene of an accident, and further making it appear that she had an official meeting with known communists. Leaving the scene of an accident is criminal conduct, and being falsely associated with the Communist Party (or other fringe group) is something that most people (and especially a politician) would find objectionable.

Public Disclosure of Private Facts

Publication of private facts that a reasonable person would find objectionable can also result in a valid invasion of privacy tort derived from a common law breach of confidence tort. For this tort to arise, the facts disclosed must be private in nature, and disclosure must be objectionable to a reasonable person. The disclosure also needs to have been made under circumstances in which the plaintiff had a reasonable expectation that the defendant would keep the matter confidential (e.g., a confidential relationship has to have existed between the parties). Note that truth is not a defense to this tort, as long as the truth disclosed is not generally known and a reasonable person would object to its disclosure.

Defamation

The tort of defamation consists of publishing false statements about a person that damage the person's reputation. Defamation takes two forms: libel, if the false statements are written, and slander, if the false statements are spoken. Oral defamation broadcast over a mass medium such as radio, television, cable, or the Internet constitutes libel rather than slander.

To successfully sue for defamation, one must establish the following three requirements: (1) the statement must be false, (2) it must have a negative effect on the person's reputation, and (3) it must be published (communicated to one or more third persons).

If the person or company suing for defamation is a private person, the only issue remaining once defamation is proven is that of damages—what monetary sum will compensate the person or company for the damage to the reputation made by the false statements. If the person suing is a public figure (a person who has either thrust herself into the public eye or who has been thrust into the limelight by events outside her control), it must also be shown that the false, damaging statements made about the person were made with malice. For purpose of the tort, malice is defined as making a false statement with the actual knowledge that it is false, or with reckless disregard for its truth or falsity. If a newspaper publishes a defamatory story about a public figure, failing to adequately verify the accuracy of printed information or the credibility of sources can fulfill the requirement of malice.

Whether a person is a private or public figure, the tort of defamation requires that damage to the reputation made by the false statement be shown. Merely showing that a false statement was made is generally not enough; the plaintiff must also show actual damage to his reputation. Such damage can include loss of business as a result of the false statement, or simply that the person's stature was tangibly diminished in the eyes of friends, business associates, and the general public, leading to some economic loss. An exception to the requirement of establishing actual damage to one's reputation exists when false statements impugn a person's moral character or falsely accuse the person of having a dreaded disease (such as a sexually transmitted disease) or drug or alcohol addiction. False statements about these matters are deemed harmful in themselves because of the potential for serious harm they pose to a person's reputation and ability to earn a living.

A problem with defamation actions relates to defamation aimed at a group of people. The larger the group, the more difficult it becomes to prove that any individual member is harmed by the statements, regardless of their falsity, maliciousness, or even viciousness. A perfect example is the maligning of entire professions by such statements as "All lawyers are thieves," "All doctors are quacks," or "All accountants are cheats." The mere size of these groups of professionals makes it impossible to show that any one person is harmed by such statements, even though taken together and repeated often enough, they might indeed tend to damage the reputation of the group. If a group is small enough so that its individual members are readily identifiable, such general false statements can be the source of libel actions. Thus, "All lawyers are amoral liars, cheats, and scoundrels" is not actionable, since no one lawyer can show significant damage to her reputation from a statement aimed at an entire profession; but "All lawyers in Smalltown are amoral liars, cheats, and scoundrels" can be the basis of a defamation by any or all lawyers if there is only a handful of legal practitioners in the town.

Disparagement

Disparagement is a tort, closely related to defamation, that relates to willful misrepresentations about the quality of a competitor's goods or services that are untrue or misleading and are made to influence the public not to buy or use the product or services.

Fraud

Fraud occurs whenever one person intentionally misleads another into undertaking an action that causes tangible harm. For this tort to arise, the following five elements must be proven by the defrauded party:

1. an intentional misrepresentation by defendant to the plaintiff;
2. about a material fact;
3. made in order to induce the plaintiff to take some action;
4. reliance by the plaintiff on the misrepresentation; and
5. a loss suffered by the plaintiff as a result of reliance on the defendant's misrepresentation.

Fraud typically arises in the context of contract negotiations, in which one party purposely lies to another about some material fact relating to the contract to induce the defrauded party to enter into the contract. But fraud is not limited to the inducement of a contract. The inducement of any act by a material misrepresentation intended to induce the act can be the basis of a legal action for fraud if the plaintiff suffers a tangible loss. The following examples should illustrate:

- Rose tells Sanji that her 2006 Toyota Corolla has 25,000 miles to induce him to purchase the car. Sanji believes her and agrees to purchase the automobile, which has 125,000 miles on it but has had its odometer tampered with to show only 25,000 miles.

- Bob tells Sandra that he is collecting funds for hurricane relief after yet another bad storm causes extensive damage to the Southeast. Sandra makes a generous cash contribution, which Bob happily invests in his retirement fund.
- Tom tells his parents that he needs a $3,000 computer to help with his studies at State U. The parents believe their son and buy the computer, which Tom promptly sells for $2,500 to another student, and Tom books a Caribbean cruise with his girlfriend with the proceeds.

In each of the preceding examples, the tort of fraud has been committed by Rose, Bob, and Tom, respectively, even though only the first example involves a contractual situation. In each case, the defrauded parties would be able to sue to recover their actual damages arising from the fraudulent misrepresentations (as well as punitive damages in most states).

Tortious Interference

Intentionally damaging a plaintiff's contract rights or business relationships results in the common law tort of tortious interference, which includes two separate torts: interference with contract rights and interference with business relationships.

Tortious interference with contract rights occurs when the defendant entices a party to breach an existing contract with the plaintiff or disrupts the ability of one party to perform her contractual obligations to another. In essence, the tort imposes a duty on outsiders not to interfere with the contract rights and obligations of others.

Tortious interference with business relationships occurs when a defendant intentionally acts to prevent the plaintiff from forming or maintaining business relationships.

Intentional Torts against Property

A second type of common tort involves interference with or damage to an individual's right to exclusively enjoy his personal and real property.

Trespass to Land

Trespass to land involves an intentional physical act that results in an unjustified intrusion onto another's land without the owner's consent. The tort is complete as soon as the trespass occurs; there is no requirement that any actual harm be done to the land. The tort seeks to compensate not damage to real estate, but rather the intrusion into another's land and the attendant interference with the owner's right to exclusively possess and enjoy the property. Remember from the preceding chapter that trespass is also a crime, and is also punishable as such in addition to the tort liability imposed on the trespasser.

Where no actual damage is caused to the land, the measure of damages awarded is usually slight, and may include only nominal damages (damages in name only, usually $1). Where the nature of the trespass is continuing or where damage is actually done to the land, substantial damage awards are likely. A property owner may also ask for an injunction from the judge—an order prohibiting the trespasser from continuing to trespass in the future. Injunctive relief is awarded by judges typically when trespass is of a continuing nature. Failing to observe an injunction can lead to stiff penalties (including jail time) for contempt of court.

As you will see in the chapter on real property in Unit V, ownership of land extends to the land itself, any permanent structures on it, and the space above and below the land. For purposes of the tort of trespass to land, any physical intrusion into another's real estate can give rise to the tort; walking on another's land, purposely throwing a ball on it, tunneling underneath it, or firing a gun or arrow over it all constitute the tort of trespass.

Where the trespass is innocent (e.g., the person did not realize she was entering another's land) or is the result of an emergency situation, such as fleeing a dangerous wild animal or entering land to assist someone in danger, the trespass is deemed excused. In this case, the trespasser must leave as soon as she learns she is trespassing or as soon as the emergency situation ends; otherwise, she will be subject to criminal and tort liability for the trespass.

Trespass to Personal Property

Just as the owner of real estate has the right to exclusively possess and enjoy her real property, the owner of personal property also has the exclusive right to enjoy and use his property free of outside interference. Any willful interference with that right results in the tort of trespass to personal property. As with trespass to real property, it is not necessary to prove that any damage was done to the property before a trespass action can be brought. The following example will illustrate:

- Fred, a good neighbor, wishes to surprise Victor, a mean malcontent whose sole existence seems to revolve around being miserable. Without Victor's permission or knowledge, Fred goes into Victor's garage and removes his old lawn mower, intending to tune it up and sharpen its blade before the mowing season starts. A week later, Fred returns the mower to its rightful place cleaned, blades sharpened, and with the oil and spark plug changed so that it is as good as new. When he informs Victor that he has revitalized his old mower, hoping to see the man smile for once in his life, the latter flies into a rage and decides to sue Fred for trespass to land and trespass to personal property. What is the likely result?

Fred will learn that no good deed goes unpunished when he defends himself against this lawsuit, for he is guilty of trespass to both land and personal property. Alas, his good intentions are irrelevant; the only issue is whether he willfully and without permission entered Victor's real estate and likewise without permission and willfully removed the old lawn mower from the garage, thereby depriving Victor temporarily of the exclusive right to its use and enjoyment. The damages likely to be awarded by a court in this case, however, are nominal damages only, such as $1 or less for the trespass to land and $1 or less for the trespass to personal property.

Conversion

The tort of conversion consists of permanently depriving the owner of personal property of its use and enjoyment through theft or destruction of the personal property. Where theft or willful destruction of the property is involved, the wrongdoer is also subject to criminal liability. If the destruction of the personal property is accomplished through mere carelessness, as opposed to willful conduct, tort damages are still available, although no criminal liability would attach to the act. The following examples will illustrate:

- José borrows Olga's textbook. While using the book, he accidentally drops a glass of grape juice over it, badly staining the pages. José is guilty of the tort of conversion, and liable to Olga for the cost of the book. He is not, however, guilty of any crime, since the conduct was unintentional.
- Cindy borrows Yetunde's camcorder and then sells it to Wendy (an innocent buyer), telling Yetunde that the camcorder was stolen. Cindy is guilty of the tort of conversion and of the crime of theft.
- Ben borrows Martha's personal watercraft and accidentally damages it beyond repair when he strikes a large boulder just under the surface of the water that causes the craft to sink. He is guilty of conversion of the watercraft and must pay its reasonable replacement value to Martha if it cannot be repaired. He is not, however, guilty of any crime because the damage was caused unintentionally.

Nuisance

The law recognizes the right of landowners, tenants, and the general public to live free from unreasonable interference from the land use activities of their neighbors that can diminish the quality of life or impair public safety. At common law, there are two separate torts involving public and private nuisance.

A public nuisance involves a property owner or renter who creates sounds, smells, pollution, or hazards that extend beyond his property boundaries into the property of others and unreasonably interfere with the rights of nearby owners and tenants to the quiet enjoyment of their property. Only one who owns or rents affected property has standing to sue for a private nuisance. Playing loud music in the wee hours of the morning, maintaining open piles of garbage on one's property that attract rodents to the property and to surrounding properties and emit foul odors, and maintaining a pig farm in a residential area could all appropriately result in successful nuisance suits. Today, the type of permissible land use is largely regulated by zoning statutes at the local level. Land use that is permitted by zoning and other land use statutes cannot generally be the basis of a private or public nuisance. Thus, if pig or chicken farms are allowed in a jurisdiction, the fact that property owners and the general public may find the odors emanating from these businesses to be unreasonably objectionable would not give rise to public or private nuisance suits. Where a zoning statute or noise ordinance does not cover the behavior, courts examine the reasonableness of the behavior and weigh the rights of property owners to engage in legal conduct with the quiet enjoyment rights of others in determining what a private nuisance is. Thus, the sound of an infant crying through the night, no matter how distressing, annoying, or disruptive to nearby neighbors, will not result in a successful private nuisance suit because it is unavoidable. But holding an all-night party with loud music would be, even if the city, town, or village does not have a specific noise ordinance.

A public nuisance involves activity in one's land that unduly interferes with the general public's rights in the areas of health, safety, or enjoyment of public land and public areas. While only an affected property owner or tenant may sue for a private nuisance, anyone who is affected by the conduct in question has standing to sue for a public nuisance. Thus, if a landowner dumps dangerous chemicals on his land that leech into the public water supply, anyone who has access to the water supply may sue for a public nuisance, and anyone who uses the sidewalk next to a manufacturing plant that releases noxious fumes into the air would have standing to sue for a public nuisance against the property owner.

Both equitable remedies such as injunctions and legal remedies such as compensatory damages are available to plaintiffs in public and private nuisance actions.

Questions

1. What is the basic difference between tort law and criminal law?
2. Can a failure to act lead to tort liability? Explain.
3. What is a basic prerequisite to tort liability?
4. List the four invasion of privacy torts.
5. What is the basic difference between false light and defamation?
6. What are the requirements of the tort of defamation?
7. When does malice need to be proven in a defamation action? How is malice defined?
8. What are the requirements for proving fraud?
9. Name four torts that involve interests in property.
10. What is disparagement?

Hypothetical Cases

1. Pamela Prankster, a practical joker who delights in subjecting her friends to sophomoric pranks, decides to dress up as a burglar and scare her friend Ariel as an April Fool's joke. She arrives at Ariel's door at midnight, dressed in typical cat-burglar garb, including a stocking over her face, and sporting a realistic-looking plastic toy gun. She breaks into Ariel's home by opening his ground-level bedroom window and climbing in. She then accosts the sleeping man, points the gun at his head, and yells "Wake up and die like a man!" at the top of her voice. He wakes up agitatedly and is immediately struck by a terror that leaves him unable to move or speak. After enjoying her friend's confusion and fear for a full minute, she removes the stocking from her face and yells out, good-naturedly, "Gotcha! April fool!" Ariel, who is not amused, decides to sue Pamela for civil damages. What torts can he sue for? What is the likely result of his case?

2. Assume the same facts as the last case. If Pamela, while she is pointing the fake gun at Ariel but before waking him, decides the joke is a bad idea and leaves the way she entered, is she guilty of any tort? Explain fully.
3. Vince borrows Dana's laptop computer over the weekend in order to complete a term paper for his Composition I class. While using the system, he runs a pirated game he had gotten from a friend on DVD that, unbeknownst to him, contained a computer virus. The virus causes the laptop's hard disk to be reformatted, and rewrites the computer's CMOS chip so that it no longer recognizes any peripherals and cannot be booted. Vince takes the computer to a local technician, who informs him that repairing the damage and reinstalling the software will cost more than the computer's $300 market price. Under what theory, if any, can Dana successfully sue Vince for the computer's market price? Is Vince guilty of any crime with regard to the incident?
4. Bob, a prominent state politician with aspirations to federal office, confides his marital infidelity to his friend Maurice, asking him to keep the matter secret, since its disclosure could harm his election chances. Five years later, when Bob is a candidate for national office, Maurice decides that fame and money are preferable to friendship and signs a lucrative book deal with Seedy Press to write a book about Bob's extramarital affair. Bob, furious at his friend's infidelity to him, sues Maurice for the tort of libel. What will he need to prove in order to prevail over Maurice? Will he prevail? What other tort could Bob sue Maurice under?

Ethics and the Law: Questions for Further Study

1. In this chapter, we have seen that some types of behavior can be both a crime and a tort, thus subjecting persons who engage in such behavior to both criminal and civil penalties. Do you think such double punishment is justifiable, or unduly harsh? Explain your answer fully.
2. Minors are generally held to be responsible for their own torts in most states, with some states exacting limited responsibility for minors' torts to their parents, often up to a set limit, such as $500–$2,000. What is your view on this issue? Should parents be held accountable for their minor children's torts? If so, should there be any limits set? If not, is it fair to the victims of minors' willful or negligent torts that they often have no immediate viable recourse against the penniless minors? Explain.

Negligence and Strict Liability

CHAPTER 8

Chapter Outline

Negligence
Defenses to Negligence
Strict Liability

As we saw in the preceding chapter, there can be no tort liability unless a duty of care owed by the defendant to the plaintiff has been breached, resulting in some injury to the plaintiff's rights. Chapter 7 introduced some of the more common intentional torts. In this chapter, we will explore two types of torts that can give rise to liability for unintentional harm: negligence and strict liability.

Negligence

Every member of society is charged with a duty to act with reasonable care at all times to avoid harming others through carelessness. The law imposes a duty on each of us to take the precautions that an imaginary reasonably prudent person would take to prevent inflicting foreseeable injury to others as we go about our daily routines. If a person falls short of this standard of care and causes foreseeable injury to others, liability for the tort of negligence will arise. A defendant to an action for negligence is not charged with willful conduct, but rather with failing to observe reasonable care under the circumstances. The reasonable person standard is an objective one; it requires each person in society to act in keeping with the standard of care that a reasonably prudent person would apply under the same circumstances. The reasonable person standard uses as its model a fictional member of society that represents a citizen of average intelligence, average common sense, and average skills.

To successfully bring a suit for negligence, the plaintiff must show that

1. the defendant breached a duty of care owed him;
2. the breach brought about foreseeable harm to the plaintiff; and
3. the breach was the proximate cause (direct, actual cause) of that harm.

The first requirement, a breach of a duty of care, is shown by convincing the trier of fact (usually a jury, or a judge where the parties waive the right to trial by jury) that the defendant failed to exercise the care that a reasonably prudent person would have exercised under the circumstances. In other words, one establishes negligence by proving legal carelessness—the failure to observe due care under the circumstances. The following instances all represent negligent action by the parties involved:

- Deidre, while driving on an icy road at 40 mph, fails to come to a complete stop at a red light and strikes another car crossing the intersection.
- Paula does not shovel her sidewalk after a snowstorm, and a neighbor walking on it slips and falls, fracturing a leg.

- John, while jogging, rounds the corner of a busy city street without stopping and crashes into Tom, who falls to the ground and chips a tooth.
- Peter, a New York City resident who likes to read *The New York Times* on his way to the subway station every morning, crashes against a legal street vendor's table on the sidewalk and causes extensive damage to the vendor's wares.

In each of the preceding examples, the persons involved breached the duty of care to the victims of their negligence in not exercising the care that a reasonably prudent person should have exercised under the circumstances.

The next question to be asked is whether the breach of that duty of care brought about a foreseeable harm. The answer for each of the preceding situations is yes. Deidre should have realized that driving too fast over slick roads could result in her striking or being struck by another vehicle when she failed to stop at a red light. Paula, likewise, should have known that failure to shovel and sand or salt an icy sidewalk could lead to someone slipping and falling on it. John should also have realized that running around a corner could result in slamming against an innocent pedestrian and that the person might then fall and injure himself. And Peter should have realized that reading the paper while walking could cause him to bump into one of the ubiquitous street vendors in his city.

The final test for negligence is whether the harm was proximately caused by the negligent act. To meet this test, the plaintiff must establish that the harm has been directly caused by the defendant's negligence and would not have occurred but for the negligence. Proximate cause requires a direct link between the cause of the harm and the negligent act. If any intervening circumstances contribute to the events leading to the injury, then negligence is not the cause of the injury in the eyes of the law. Intervening causes include any outside circumstance not caused by the defendant and not within the defendant's control. In addition, there must be a close link in space and time to the injury and the negligent act; if the person injured by the defendant's negligence was too distant in time or distance from the defendant's negligent act so as to be outside of the "zone of danger" provided by the defendant's negligence, the injury is not deemed to be proximately caused by the defendant's negligence. The following example should illustrate.

- Leona, a careless driver, runs a red light at an intersection. Marvin, an even worse driver, sees Leona run the red light three blocks away and panics; he swerves right, steps hard on the accelerator (mistaking it for the brake), and crashes through the display window of a storefront.

Despite the fact that Leona was clearly negligent in the preceding example in her failure to stop at a red light, she is not responsible for Mark's accident since her negligence was not its proximate cause. Leon was too far away (three blocks) to be in any danger when Leona crossed the intersection; his accident was the direct cause of his overreaction, not of Leona's negligence. Had he been only 50 feet away when Leona ran the light, he probably would have been within the zone of danger and his actions might possibly be attributed to Leona's negligence. But three city blocks away is simply too far, and the accident must be attributed to a separate intervening cause, namely, Leon's poor driving skills.

Defenses to Negligence

Even when negligence is established, it is still possible for a defendant to avoid tort liability by raising and proving one of three defenses: contributory negligence, comparative negligence, or assumption of the risk. The effect of these three defenses is to limit or completely avoid a defendant's tort liability.

Contributory Negligence

At common law, a person suing another for negligence could recover only if she were herself free of any negligence. If the plaintiff's negligence contributed even slightly to causing her injuries, the plaintiff's contributory negligence would bar her from recovering any damages from the defendant, even if the defendant's negligence far outweighed her own. When you consider that most accidents occur due to the negligence of both parties, the harshness of this rule becomes clear. Over time, a number of technical rules were developed to permit recovery by parties who were partially negligent under certain circumstances. Today most states have abandoned contributory negligence as a complete defense to negligence actions in favor of comparative negligence. But in states that still observe the traditional common law rule, contributory negligence still poses a complete bar to recovery.

Comparative Negligence

In the majority of states, a plaintiff whose own negligence contributed to his injuries may successfully sue a negligent defendant. A comparative negligence defense allows plaintiffs whose negligence contributed to their injuries to sue negligent defendants but limits their recovery to the percentage of their damages not caused by their own negligence. To put it another way, comparative negligence allows a reduction in a plaintiff's recovery proportional to his negligence. In the majority of jurisdictions that recognize comparative negligence, the jury is asked to assign a percentage of fault to each party in a negligence action—to decide, in essence, the relative fault of each person in causing the accident. After a jury assigns the proper percentage of culpability to each party, each party is entitled to recover from the other party damages equal to her actual damages minus a setoff for the percentage of her damages attributable to her own negligence. The following example will illustrate:

- Tom, Dick, and Harriet are involved in a three-way car accident in which they each share a part of the fault. A jury, after hearing all the evidence, assigns the following percentage of responsibility to each party for bringing about the accident: Tom, 60%; Dick, 30%; and Harriet, 10%. If each party suffered $10,000 in property damages, that party would each be entitled to recover the amount of damages set off by the percentage of fault shared in the accident. Tom, Dick, and Harriet, then, would each recover as follows:

    > Tom will receive $10,000 minus 60% of his damages.
    > ($10,000 – $6,000 = $4,000)
    > Dick will receive $10,000 minus 30% of his damages.
    > ($10,000 – $3,000 = $7,000)
    > Harriet will receive $10,000 minus 10% of her damages.
    > ($10,000 – $1,000 = $9,000)

Comparative negligence jurisdictions today are divided into two camps: those that recognize pure comparative negligence and those that recognize modified comparative negligence. Pure comparative negligence jurisdictions allow plaintiffs to recover no matter their percentage of negligence, whereas modified comparative negligence jurisdictions allow plaintiffs to recover only if they are less than 50% negligent themselves. In the minority of jurisdictions, like New York, that recognize pure comparative negligence, a plaintiff who is 99% responsible for causing an accident can still recover 1% of his damages from a defendant who was only 1% negligent in bringing about the accident. This can cause some interesting problems (and a legal dilemma) of its own, as the following example will illustrate:

- Dan Dunderhead, the proud owner of a brand new Ferrari, drives his automobile at 135 mph down the interstate. Sally Slowpoke, a good, cautious driver, merges into Dan's lane with her 2006 Toyota Corolla, not realizing Dan's excessive speed. Dan, unable to stop in time or to swerve out of the way, rear-ends Sally, causing a total loss to his car and Sally's. At trial, a jury finds Dan 90% negligent and Sally 10% negligent (for failing to better estimate Dan's excessive speed before merging into the highway). If Dan's car is worth $200,000 and Sally's is worth $1,000, Dan will have to pay Sally 90% of her loss ($1000 × 90% = $900), while Sally will have to pay Dan 10% of his loss ($200,000 × 10% = $20,000).

Comparative negligence (especially in its pure form) has generally resulted in increased litigation, higher jury awards, and higher liability insurance premiums for consumers in states that have adopted it.

Assumption of Risk

A third defense that is a total bar to a recovery in both negligence and intentional torts is assumption of risk. If a plaintiff suffers some injury from engaging in an activity he knows to be dangerous, he cannot sue for any injury he sustains as a result of engaging in such an activity. The key here is whether the plaintiff knew or should have known the inherent danger in engaging in the activity in question, and whether he voluntarily assumed that risk. One who voluntarily engages in a dangerous sport such as boxing, skydiving, skiing, or auto racing, for example, cannot successfully sue for any reasonably foreseeable injury received from engaging in the sport. The same holds true for a person who knowingly uses a defective product. In each of the following examples, the injured party would be barred from recovering for his damages based on a defense of assumption of risk:

- a baseball fan sitting along the first-base line who is hit by a line-drive foul;
- a person who borrows a car he knows to have badly worn brakes and who is later injured when the brakes fail;
- a driver who knowingly drives with a badly worn tire that blows out and causes him to lose control of the car;
- a person who plays with a dog known to bite and is bitten by it; and
- a skydiver injured by twisting a foot, landing atop a tree, or becoming entangled in a power line.

Keep in mind that the defenses of assumption of risk and its close cousin, product misuse, are available to defendants in any tort action, including the strict liability torts that we will discuss next.

Strict Liability

Under certain circumstances, a person who is neither negligent nor guilty of an intentional tort may still be required to pay damages for injuries that result from her activities. Strict liability (also called liability without fault) is imposed by law for injuries that result from certain kinds of activities that by their nature are highly dangerous. Strict liability torts arise out of three main activities: ultrahazardous activity, product liability, and damage done by wild animals. We will examine each of these areas in turn.

Ultrahazardous Activities

Some activities are by their very nature highly dangerous and cannot be made safe. Such activities are considered to be ultrahazardous, and anyone who is injured as a direct result of the activity is entitled to compensation as a matter of law, regardless of the level of care employed by the defendant to ensure safety. Ultrahazardous activities such as the manufacturing or handling of explosives, for example, can never be made completely safe because of the nature of the materials involved. Anyone who engages in such activity is strictly liable for foreseeable injuries to third parties that result directly from the activity. Persons who suffer an injury as a result of an ultrahazardous activity are entitled to compensation without needing to show the defendant's fault or negligence; once harm is linked to the ultrahazardous activity, liability is automatic, and the only issue becomes what compensation to award plaintiffs for their damages.

As with other torts, the defense of assumption of risk may be available to defendants in strict liability actions if it can be shown that a defendant knowingly and intentionally assumed the risk. Thus, while a defendant is normally strictly liable for harm caused by an ultrahazardous activity such as blasting or demolition work, a plaintiff who willfully walks into a building that is being demolished, ignoring obvious warnings to keep out, would be held to have assumed the risk of his injuries and barred from recovering damages for them.

Product Liability

Product liability places strict liability in tort on manufacturers, wholesalers, and retailers for defects in the design or manufacturing of products that render such products unreasonably dangerous to intended users. Examples of unreasonably dangerous products due to design or manufacturing defects would include spoiled food, automobile tires that experience blowouts due to a manufacturing defect during normal use, and a car that ignites when rear-ended because of a defective design.

For strict product liability to attach, the product must be unreasonably dangerous for its intended use due to a design or manufacturing defect, and the product must reach the consumer in unaltered form; products that are customized or otherwise changed after their manufacture and before they are sold to consumers are not subject to product liability claims (consumers injured by such altered products can still sue either the manufacturer or customizer under a negligence theory, however).

It should be noted that the mere fact that a product is dangerous will not subject its manufacturer to a product liability claim; the product must be unreasonably dangerous due to a design or manufacturing defect. Knives, guns, razor blades, and power tools all pose a danger even when properly used; before consumers can sue for product liability relating to these or any other product, they must show that the product was not merely dangerous, but unreasonably dangerous because of a design or manufacturing defect. Thus, a gun that explodes when fired, a drill that short-circuits and shocks the user when properly used, or a chain saw whose chain breaks and flies off during proper use would all qualify as strict product liability examples, provided they were properly used, arrived to the consumer from the manufacturer in unaltered form, and malfunctioned due to a manufacturing or design defect.

Wild Animals

The keeping of wild animals is deemed to be such a dangerous activity that anyone injured by them is entitled to recover from the animal's owner under a strict liability theory. For strict liability to attach, the animal in question must be a wild animal—defined as an animal that by its nature is not able to be domesticated. Wolves, tigers, elephants, lions, pythons, ferrets, and gorillas have been known to be kept as pets; any foreseeable personal injury or property damage caused by these animals, however, will subject the owner to strict liability in tort.

Note that the tort applies only to nondomestic animals. The law relating to domestic animals is somewhat different. Owners of domestic animals such as dogs, cats, horses, cattle, sheep, and other farm animals are generally responsible only for damage to persons or property that these animals cause when their owners fail to observe reasonable care under the circumstances (e.g., under a negligence theory). If a local ordinance requires dogs to be kept on a leash, for example, foreseeable harm done by a dog not restrained by a leash will be the responsibility of the owner, as failure to observe the leash law is negligence *per se*. On the other hand, if a dog bites a stranger and the dog had not bitten anyone before, the owner is liable only for the injuries caused by the dog in most states if he knew or should have known that the dog might bite. The owner of an aggressive dog (or a seemingly docile dog from an aggressive breed) must take special care to ensure his dogs do not injure others. As for the property damage these pets do, owners are strictly liable for it in most states if it is of a type that is reasonably foreseeable. Thus, if Fido attacks a neighbor, Fido's owner is liable for the attack only if the neighbor can show that Fido's owner was negligent in preventing the attack. If Fido bites the neighbor's cat or steals a roasted chicken from the neighbor's picnic table, on the other hand, Fido's owner will be strictly liable to the neighbor for the damage to the cat and the cost of the chicken, as biting felines and stealing savory food are activities well within the normal behavior of dogs.

Note that all three types of strict liability torts are closely related, and that the thread that binds them is the unreasonable danger posed to innocent third parties, be it from engaging in an ultrahazardous activity, creating an unreasonably dangerous product, or keeping a dangerous animal.

Questions

1. What is the essential breach of duty involved in the tort of negligence?
2. Is the reasonable person standard an objective or subjective standard for evaluating an individual's behavior?
3. What must a plaintiff prove in a negligence action to prevail over the defendant?
4. Define the concept of proximate cause.
5. Define contributory negligence.
6. At common law, what was the effect of a finding that the plaintiff was contributorily negligent?
7. What is the difference between contributory negligence and comparative negligence?
8. Distinguish pure from modified comparative negligence.
9. What are three defenses to tort liability?
10. What are the requirements for a products liability suit?

Hypothetical Cases

1. Pierce and Tai get into an automobile accident and sue each other for damages. At trial, it is determined that both parties were negligent. A jury finds that Pierce's responsibility for the accident was 60% and Tai's 40%. The jury also finds that Pierce suffered total damages in the amount of $10,000 and assesses Tai's damages at $5,000.
   A. Assuming a pure comparative negligence jurisdiction, what will each party's recovery in this case be, if any?
   B. Assuming a modified comparative negligence jurisdiction, what will each party recover in this case?
   C. Assuming a contributory negligence jurisdiction, what will be the result?
2. Donna asks Uri if she may borrow his bicycle to run a quick errand. Uri consents to Donna's request, but warns her that the brakes are weak and asks her to test the brakes thoroughly before driving off. Donna agrees and takes the bike, but fails to heed the warning and finds that she is unable to stop the bike from careening into a busy intersection at the bottom of a steep hill. She suffers serious injuries and sues Uri for negligence, claiming $5,000 in damages. Uri counterclaims in negligence for the cost of repairing or replacing his bike, $200. You are the judge hearing this case without a jury. How do you decide the case? Explain your answer fully.
3. Sandra and Althea are spectators in a mid-summer baseball game. During the game, Sandra is hit on the head by a foul ball, and Althea is knocked on the head by a beer bottle thrown by a rowdy drunken fan who purchased and drank a dozen beers from the concession stand during the game. In addition to the minor head injuries, both women suffer bad sunburns during the game. Because of their head injuries and bad sunburns, both women miss three days of work the following week and endure substantial pain and suffering. You are their attorney. (Congratulations! You've graduated from college, earned your Juris Doctor graduate degree, passed the bar exam, and have been admitted to practice—all in the span of this question.) Advise each woman of her possible claims against the ball club, the bottle thrower, and the player who hit the foul ball, respectively.
4. Martha's dog, Spot, has always been a loving, well-adjusted pet who has not so much as growled at a stranger in its life. Today, however, it ran up to the letter carrier and bit him on the leg after watching a dog perform a similar act on a network comedy show. The letter carrier sues Martha and the network that broadcast the show on a negligence theory. What is the likely result?
5. Would your answer to the previous question be the same if Spot were a wolf? Explain.

Ethics and the Law: Questions for Further Study

Although the law imposes no duty to act on members of society to help one another out of difficult situations, in most states Good Samaritans who take it upon themselves to render assistance to a person in need open themselves to liability for both intentional and negligent torts to persons they assist. Many jurisdictions have enacted legislation to protect medical personnel, such as doctors, nurses, and medical technicians, who administer emergency assistance at accident sites. Such personnel are only liable in many (but not all) jurisdictions for gross negligence or willfully tortious conduct. But in many jurisdictions, these "Good Samaritan" statutes do not apply to nonmedical personnel who render assistance to accident victims. Thus, it is possible for a person who saves an accident victim's life by rushing him to the hospital but causes some other injury in the process to be successfully sued for a tort by the ungrateful victim once he recovers. The safest conduct in most states is for passersby to not render assistance to accident victims. In your view, what is the reason for the law? Does the law encourage detachment and serve to discourage people of good conscience from rendering assistance in emergency situations for fear of being sued? Discuss the ethical and sociological ramifications with regard to this issue. Do you have any suggestions for a Model Good Samaritan Law that would protect the safety of accident victims while encouraging citizens to render assistance in emergency situations?

Unit I—Cases for Further Study

OBERGEFELL ET AL. *v.* HODGES, DIRECTOR, OHIO DEPARTMENT OF HEALTH, ET AL.
SUPREME COURT OF THE UNITED STATES
No. 14–556. Argued April 28, 2015—Decided June 26, 2015

576 U. S. ____ (2015)[1]

Michigan, Kentucky, Ohio, and Tennessee define marriage as a union between one man and one woman. The petitioners, 14 same-sex couples and two men whose same-sex partners are deceased, filed suits in Federal District Courts in their home States, claiming that respondent state officials violate the Fourteenth Amendment by denying them the right to marry or to have marriages lawfully performed in another State given full recognition. Each District Court ruled in petitioners' favor, but the Sixth Circuit consolidated the cases and reversed.

The Court Held (in a 5–4 decision) that the Fourteenth Amendment requires a State to license a marriage between two people of the same sex and to recognize a marriage between two people of the same sex when their marriage was lawfully licensed and performed out-of-State.

To the respondents, it would demean a timeless institution if marriage were extended to same-sex couples. But the petitioners, far from seeking to devalue marriage, seek it for themselves because of their respect—and need—for its privileges and responsibilities, as illustrated by the petitioners' own experiences. The history of marriage is one of both continuity and change. Changes, such as the decline of arranged marriages and the abandonment of the law of coverture, have worked deep transformations in the structure of marriage, affecting aspects of marriage once viewed as essential. These new insights have strengthened, not weakened, the institution. Changed understandings of marriage are characteristic of a Nation where new dimensions of freedom become apparent to new generations. This dynamic can be seen in the Nation's experience with gay and lesbian rights. Well into the 20th century, many States condemned same-sex intimacy as immoral, and homosexuality was treated as an illness. Later in the century, cultural and political developments allowed same-sex couples to lead more open and public lives. Extensive public and private dialogue followed, along with shifts in public attitudes. Questions about the legal treatment of gays and lesbians soon reached the courts, where they could be discussed in the formal discourse of the law. In 2003, this Court overruled its 1986 decision in *Bowers* v. *Hardwick*, 478 U. S. 186, which upheld a Georgia law that criminalized certain homosexual acts, concluding laws making same-sex intimacy a crime "demea[n] the lives of homosexual persons." *Lawrence* v. *Texas*, 539 U. S. 558, 575. In 2012, the federal Defense of Marriage Act was also struck down. *United States* v. *Windsor*, 570 U. S. ___. Numerous same-sex marriage cases reaching the federal courts and state supreme courts have added to the dialogue.

The Fourteenth Amendment requires a State to license a marriage between two people of the same sex. The fundamental liberties protected by the Fourteenth Amendment's Due Process Clause extend to certain personal choices central to individual dignity and autonomy, including intimate choices defining personal identity and beliefs. See, *e.g., Eisenstadt* v. *Baird*, 405 U. S. 438, 453; *Griswold* v. *Connecticut*, 381 U. S. 479, 484–486. Courts must exercise reasoned judgment in identifying interests of the person so fundamental that the State must accord them its respect. History and tradition guide and discipline the inquiry but do not set its outer boundaries. When new insight reveals discord between the Constitution's central protections and a received legal stricture, a claim to liberty must be addressed.

Applying these tenets, the Court has long held the right to marry is protected by the Constitution. For example, *Loving* v. *Virginia*, 388 U. S. 1, 12, invalidated bans on interracial unions, and *Turner* v. *Safley*, 482 U. S. 78, 95, held that prisoners could not be denied the right to marry. To be sure, these cases presumed a relationship involving opposite-sex partners, as did *Baker* v. *Nelson*, 409 U. S. 810, a one-line summary decision issued in 1972, holding that the exclusion of same-sex couples from marriage did not present a substantial federal question. But other, more instructive precedents have expressed broader principles.

---

[1] The page number is unavailable as of this writing. The full decision can be downloaded at http://www.supremecourt.gov/opinions/slipopinion/14 (last accessed December 22, 2015).

See, *e.g., Lawrence, supra,* at 574. In assessing whether the force and rationale of its cases apply to same-sex couples, the Court must respect the basic reasons why the right to marry has been long protected. See, *e.g., Eisenstadt, supra,* at 453–454. This analysis compels the conclusion that same-sex couples may exercise the right to marry.

Four principles and traditions demonstrate that the reasons marriage is fundamental under the Constitution apply with equal force to same-sex couples. The first premise of this Court's relevant precedents is that the right to personal choice regarding marriage is inherent in the concept of individual autonomy. This abiding connection between marriage and liberty is why *Loving* invalidated interracial marriage bans under the Due Process Clause. See 388 U. S., at 12. Decisions about marriage are among the most intimate that an individual can make. See *Lawrence, supra,* at 574. This is true for all persons, whatever their sexual orientation.

A second principle in this Court's jurisprudence is that the right to marry is fundamental because it supports a two-person union unlike any other in its importance to the committed individuals. The intimate association protected by this right was central to *Griswold* v. *Connecticut,* which held the Constitution protects the right of married couples to use contraception, 381 U. S., at 485, and was acknowledged in *Turner, supra,* at 95. Same-sex couples have the same right as opposite-sex couples to enjoy intimate association, a right extending beyond mere freedom from laws making same-sex intimacy a criminal offense. See *Lawrence, supra,* at 567.

A third basis for protecting the right to marry is that it safeguards children and families and thus draws meaning from related rights of childrearing, procreation, and education. See, *e.g., Pierce* v. *Society of Sisters,* 268 U. S. 510. Without the recognition, stability, and predictability marriage offers, children suffer the stigma of knowing their families are somehow lesser. They also suffer the significant material costs of being raised by unmarried parents, relegated to a more difficult and uncertain family life. The marriage laws at issue thus harm and humiliate the children of same-sex couples. See *Windsor, supra,* at ___. This does not mean that the right to marry is less meaningful for those who do not or cannot have children. Precedent protects the right of a married couple not to procreate, so the right to marry cannot be conditioned on the capacity or commitment to procreate.

Finally, this Court's cases and the Nation's traditions make clear that marriage is a keystone of the Nation's social order. See *Maynard* v. *Hill,* 125 U. S. 190, 211. States have contributed to the fundamental character of marriage by placing it at the center of many facets of the legal and social order. There is no difference between same- and opposite-sex couples with respect to this principle, yet same-sex couples are denied the constellation of benefits that the States have linked to marriage and are consigned to an instability many opposite-sex couples would find intolerable. It is demeaning to lock same-sex couples out of a central institution of the Nation's society, for they too may aspire to the transcendent purposes of marriage.

The limitation of marriage to opposite-sex couples may long have seemed natural and just, but its inconsistency with the central meaning of the fundamental right to marry is now manifest. The right of same-sex couples to marry is also derived from the Fourteenth Amendment's guarantee of equal protection. The Due Process Clause and the Equal Protection Clause are connected in a profound way. Rights implicit in liberty and rights secured by equal protection may rest on different precepts and are not always coextensive, yet each may be instructive as to the meaning and reach of the other. This dynamic is reflected in *Loving,* where the Court invoked both the Equal Protection Clause and the Due Process Clause; and in *Zablocki* v. *Redhail,* 434 U. S. 374, where the Court invalidated a law barring fathers delinquent on child-support payments from marrying. Indeed, recognizing that new insights and societal understandings can reveal unjustified inequality within fundamental institutions that once passed unnoticed and unchallenged, this Court has invoked equal protection principles to invalidate laws imposing sex-based inequality on marriage, see, *e.g., Kirchberg* v. *Feenstra,* 450 U. S. 455, 460–461, and confirmed the relation between liberty and equality, see, *e.g., M. L. B.* v. *S. L. J.,* 519 U. S. 102, 120–121.

The Court has acknowledged the interlocking nature of these constitutional safeguards in the context of the legal treatment of gays and lesbians. See *Lawrence,* 539 U. S., at 575. This dynamic also applies to same-sex marriage. The challenged laws burden the liberty of same-sex couples, and they abridge central precepts of equality. The marriage laws at issue are in essence unequal: Same-sex couples are denied benefits afforded opposite-sex couples and are barred from exercising a fundamental right. Especially against a long history of disapproval of their relationships, this denial works a grave and continuing harm, serving to disrespect and subordinate gays and lesbians. The right to marry is a fundamental right inherent in the liberty of the person, and under the Due Process and Equal Protection Clauses of the Fourteenth Amendment couples of the same-sex may not be deprived of that right and that liberty. Same-sex couples may exercise the fundamental right to marry. *Baker* v. *Nelson* is overruled. The State laws challenged by the petitioners in these cases are held invalid to the extent they exclude same-sex couples from civil marriage on the same terms and conditions as opposite-sex couples.

There may be an initial inclination to await further legislation, litigation, and debate, but referenda, legislative debates, and grassroots campaigns; studies and other writings; and extensive litigation in state and federal courts have led to an enhanced understanding of the issue. While the Constitution contemplates that democracy is the appropriate process for change, individuals who are harmed need not await legislative action before asserting a fundamental right. *Bowers,* in effect, upheld state action that denied gays and lesbians a fundamental right. Though it was eventually repudiated, men and women suffered pain and humiliation in the interim, and the effects of these injuries no doubt lingered long after *Bowers* was overruled. A ruling against same-sex couples would have the same effect and would be unjustified under the Fourteenth Amendment. The petitioners' stories show the urgency of the issue they present to the Court, which has a duty to address these claims and answer these questions. Respondents' argument that allowing same-sex couples to wed will harm marriage as an institution rests on a counter-intuitive view of opposite-sex couples' decisions about marriage and parenthood. Finally, the First Amendment ensures that religions, those who adhere to religious doctrines, and others have protection as they seek to teach the principles that are so fulfilling and so central to their lives and faiths.

The Fourteenth Amendment requires States to recognize same-sex marriages validly performed out of State. Since same-sex couples may now exercise the fundamental right to marry in all States, there is no lawful basis for a State to refuse to recognize a lawful same-sex marriage performed in another State on the ground of its same-sex character. 772 F. 3d 388, reversed.

KENNEDY, J., delivered the opinion of the Court, in which GINSBURG, BREYER, SOTOMAYOR, and KAGAN, JJ., joined. ROBERTS, C. J., filed a dissenting opinion, in which SCALIA and THOMAS, JJ., joined. SCALIA, J., filed a dissenting opinion, in which THOMAS, J., joined. THOMAS, J., filed a dissenting opinion, in which SCALIA, J., joined. ALITO, J., filed a dissenting opinion, in which SCALIA and THOMAS, JJ., joined.

Optional Assignments

1. Brief this abbreviated version of the case in a one-page, single-spaced brief (with double spaces between paragraphs) that contains the following four sections: (1) the basic facts of the case (Facts); (2) the legal issue the court is being asked to decide (Issue); (3) the holding of the court (how it decides the legal issue before it) (Holding); and (4) the rationale the court uses to support its decision (Rationale). If your instructor asks you to brief the case, she will give you additional instructions. Your instructor may also ask you to download and read the entire case before briefing it rather than the excerpt included here.
2. Do you agree or disagree with the majority decision in this case? Explain fully.
3. Assume that a state legislature passes a law that defines a marriage as "a union between two or more persons." Based on the reasoning of the five-justice majority in this case, how do you think the court should decide a case involving polygamists who, citing *Obergefell v. Hodges*, claim that the Fourteenth Amendment's equal protection clause requires every other state to recognize polygamist unions performed in the state that recognizes them? Would denying the right of polygamists to marry violate the U.S. Constitution in that case? Make an argument based on sound legal reasoning either for or against recognizing polygamy as a constitutional right.

WALKER, CHAIRMAN, TEXAS DEPARTMENT OF MOTOR VEHICLES BOARD, ET AL.

v.

TEXAS DIVISION, SONS OF CONFEDERATE VETERANS, INC., ET AL.

SUPREME COURT OF THE UNITED STATES

No. 14–144. Argued March 23, 2015—Decided June 18, 2015

576 U. S. ____ (2015)[2]

Texas offers automobile owners a choice between general-issue and specialty license plates. Those who want the State to issue a particular specialty plate may propose a plate design, comprising a slogan, a graphic, or both. If the Texas Department of Motor Vehicles Board approves the design, the State will make it available for display on vehicles registered in Texas. Here, the Texas Division of the Sons of Confederate Veterans and its officers (collectively SCV) filed suit against the Chairman and members of the Board (collectively Board), arguing that the Board's rejection of SCV's proposal for a specialty plate design featuring a Confederate battle flag violated the Free Speech

---

[2] The page number is unavailable as of this writing. The full decision can be downloaded at http://www.supremecourt.gov/opinions/slipopinion/14 (last accessed December 22, 2015).

Clause. The District Court entered judgment for the Board, but the Fifth Circuit reversed, holding that Texas's specialty license plate designs are private speech and that the Board engaged in constitutionally forbidden viewpoint discrimination when it refused to approve SCV's design.

The Court held that Texas's specialty license plate designs constitute government speech, and thus Texas was entitled to refuse to issue plates featuring SCV's proposed design.

When government speaks, it is not barred by the Free Speech Clause from determining the content of what it says. *Pleasant Grove City v. Summum*, 555 U. S. 460, 467–468. A government is generally entitled to promote a program, espouse a policy, or take a position. Were the Free Speech Clause interpreted otherwise, "it is not easy to imagine how government would function." Id., at 468. That is not to say that a government's ability to express itself is without restriction.

Constitutional and statutory provisions outside of the Free Speech Clause may limit government speech, and the Free Speech Clause itself may constrain the government's speech if, for example, the government seeks to compel private persons to convey the government's speech. This Court's precedents regarding government speech provide the appropriate framework through which to approach the case. The same analysis the Court used in *Summum*—to conclude that a city "accepting a privately donated monument and placing it on city property" was engaging in government speech, 555 U. S., at 464—leads to the conclusion that government speech is at issue here.

First, history shows that States, including Texas, have long used license plates to convey government speech, e.g., slogans urging action, promoting tourism, and touting local industries. Cf. id., at 470. Second, Texas license plate designs "are often closely identified in the public mind with the [State]." Id., at 472. Each plate is a government article serving the governmental purposes of vehicle registration and identification. The governmental nature of the plates is clear from their faces: the State places the name "TEXAS" in large letters across the top of every plate. Texas also requires Texas vehicle owners to display license plates, issues every Texas plate, and owns all of the designs on its plates. The plates are, essentially, government IDs, and ID issuers "typically do not permit" their IDs to contain "message[s] with which they do not wish to be associated," id., at 471. Third, like the city government in Summum, Texas "has effectively controlled the messages [conveyed] by exercising final approval authority over by exercising final approval authority over their selection." Id., at 473. These considerations, taken together, show that Texas's specialty plates are similar enough to the monuments in Summum to call for the same result.

Forum analysis, which applies to government restrictions on purely private speech occurring on government property, *Cornelius v. NAACP Legal Defense & Ed. Fund, Inc.*, 473 U. S. 788, 800, is not appropriate when the State is speaking on its own behalf. The parties agree that Texas's specialty license plates are not a traditional public forum.

Finally, the plates are not a nonpublic forum, where the "government is . . . a proprietor, managing its internal operations." *International Soc. for Krishna Consciousness, Inc. v. Lee*, 505 U. S. 672, 678–679. The fact that private parties take part in the design and propagation of a message does not extinguish the governmental nature of the message or transform the government's role into that of a mere forum provider. See *Summum*, supra, at 470–471. Nor does Texas's requirement that vehicle owners pay annual fees for specialty plates mean that the plates are a forum for private speech. And this case does not resemble other nonpublic forum cases. *Perry Ed. Assn.v. Perry Local Educators' Assn.*, 460 U. S. 37, 48–49; *Lehman v. Shaker Heights*, 418 U. S. 298; and *Cornelius*, supra, at 804–806, distinguished.

The determination that Texas's specialty license plate designs are government speech does not mean that the designs do not also implicate the free speech rights of private persons. The Court has acknowledged that drivers who display a State's selected license plate designs convey the messages communicated through those designs. See *Wooley v. Maynard*, 430 U. S. 705, 717, n. 15. The Court has also recognized that the First Amendment stringently limits a State's authority to compel a private party to express a view with which the private party disagrees. Just as Texas cannot require SCV to convey "the State's ideological message," id., at 715, SCV cannot force Texas to include a Confederate battle flag on its specialty license plates. 759 F. 3d 388, reversed.

[5–4 decision] BREYER, J., delivered the opinion of the Court, in which THOMAS, GINSBURG, SOTOMAYOR, and KAGAN, JJ., joined. ALITO, J., filed a dissenting opinion, in which ROBERTS, C. J., and SCALIA and KENNEDY, JJ., joined.

Optional Assignments

1. Brief this abbreviated version of the case in a one-page, single-spaced brief (with double spaces between paragraphs) that contains the following four sections: (1) the basic facts of the case (Facts); (2) the legal issue the court is being asked to decide (Issue); (3) the holding of the court (how it decides the legal issue before it) (Holding); and (4) the rationale the court uses to support its decision (Rationale). If your instructor asks you to brief the case, he will give you additional instructions. Your instructor may also ask you to download and read the entire case before briefing it rather than the excerpt included here.

2. Do you agree or disagree with the majority decision in this case? Explain fully.

UNIT 2

CONTRACTS

Lukas Gojda/Shutterstock

Introduction

A contract can be defined as an agreement between two or more parties that is enforceable in the courts. To rise to the level of an enforceable contract, an agreement must meet certain criteria: there must be a valid offer and acceptance, the agreement must be supported by consideration, the parties must have the legal capacity to enter into a contract, the agreement must be genuinely assented to by the parties involved, and it must be for a legal purpose. In some cases, the agreement must also be evidenced by a signed writing. If one of these necessary elements is missing from an agreement, a valid contract will not be formed.

In this unit, we examine the types of contracts (Chapter 9) and each element of a valid contract (Chapters 10 through 15). We also explore the rights of persons with regard to contracts that affect them directly but to which they are not parties (Chapter 16). We then examine the various means by which parties can discharge their contractual obligations and learn about the consequences that can result when a contract is breached (Chapter 17). Finally, we explore the remedies available to compensate parties who suffer a breach (Chapter 18).

CHAPTER 9
General Introduction to Contracts

CHAPTER 10
Offer and Acceptance

CHAPTER 11
Consideration

CHAPTER 12
Capacity

CHAPTER 13
Genuine Assent

CHAPTER 14
Legality

CHAPTER 15
Statute of Frauds

CHAPTER 16
Assignment of Contracts and Third-Party Beneficiaries

CHAPTER 17
Performance and Breach

CHAPTER 18
Remedies

General Introduction to Contracts

CHAPTER 9

Chapter Outline

Classification of Contracts

As previously noted, a contract is an enforceable agreement between two or more parties. All of us enter into numerous binding contracts on a daily basis without any conscious awareness that we do so. If you bought a cup of coffee before class; rode a bus, subway, or trolley car to get to campus earlier today as a commuting student; bought a ticket to an upcoming concert online; ate breakfast or lunch at a university restaurant or cafeteria; or bought a copy of your local newspaper, you have entered into a valid contract that gives rise to certain rights and responsibilities to you and to the other parties involved. We may not think of casual business transactions as contracts because such transactions are almost always completed to the mutual satisfaction of the parties involved, and there is seldom a reason to give them a second thought. You pay the agreed-upon fee for your choice of concert tickets and subsequently enjoy the performance, drink the coffee after paying for it, hop on the bus and eventually reach your destination (more or less on time), and live to enjoy the comforts of the food court another day. The significance of these contracts is important only in the rare case when parties do not perform as promised. The salad served at your favorite university eatery, for example, contains peanuts that cause a dangerous and potentially lethal allergic reaction in you, even though your server assured you that peanuts are not used in the salad. It is at these exceptional times that we need to be concerned about whether or not an underlying contract existed, and to examine the rights and responsibilities of the parties involved.

Although all contracts contain enforceable promises, not all promises rise to the level of a contract. While we may have a moral obligation to honor our promises, only promises that meet certain requisite criteria gain the special status of a contract. For a valid contract to be formed, each of the following criteria must be present:

1. There must be a valid offer and a valid acceptance to enter into a contract;
2. There must be valid consideration (something of legal value given and received by each party to the contract);
3. Each party to the contract has to have the mental capacity (or legal ability) to enter into a contract;
4. Each party has to freely give her consent to enter into the contract;
5. The contract must be for a legal purpose;
6. And, in certain cases, there must be written and signed evidence of the intent to enter into a contract for the contract to be enforceable.

In the chapters that follow, we examine each of these prerequisites to a valid contract in turn. For now, suffice it to say that if even one necessary criterion is missing, the underlying agreement will not rise to the level of a binding contract and will not be enforceable in the courts. A few brief examples will illustrate:

- John promises to give Ellen his stereo next week after he buys a new one. Ellen agrees to accept the gift. John then changes his mind and gives the stereo to Rachel. Ellen will not be able to successfully sue John for breach of contract because John's promise was not supported by consideration, and thus no contract was formed by Ellen's acceptance of his promise to give her a gift. (Ellen had not agreed to give anything of legal value in exchange for receiving the stereo.)
- Chuck agrees to turn over his Rolex watch to Tina in exchange for $100. Chuck makes the promise while Tina holds a gun to his head. No contract is formed (Chuck's assent to enter into the contract is not freely given; rather, it is the result of duress, and no valid contract is formed for lack of his genuine assent.)
- Ben, who has been judicially declared to be incompetent, orders 100 Napoleon Bonaparte costumes from a local supplier. The agreement is invalid, and no contract is formed, because Ben lacks the capacity to enter into a valid contract.

A popular misconception about contract law is that agreements between parties need to be expressed in writing in order to be enforceable. This has never been true. In fact, with limited exceptions to be covered in Chapter 15, verbal agreements are just as binding as written ones. In fact, it is possible to enter into a binding contract without either party uttering a single word. The intent to enter into a contract can be implied from the actions of the parties as well as from their oral or written words. What is crucial in contract law is the intention of the parties to enter into a binding agreement. Precisely how that intention is expressed is largely irrelevant to the validity of the underlying agreement.

Classification of Contracts

Contracts can be classified as express, implied, unilateral, bilateral, simple, and formal. Each of these classifications is examined next.

Express Contracts

Express contracts are formed when contracting parties specify the terms of their agreement orally or in writing. In an express contract, the *offeror* (the person who makes an offer to enter into a contract) articulates the terms of the offer to the *offeree* (the person to whom the offeror makes an offer to enter into a contract) either orally or in writing.

- Allison promises to install new windows in Bernie's home in exchange for Bernie's promise to pay her $8,000. The parties execute a signed agreement specifying when the work will be done and how payment is to be made. This is a typical express written contract.
- Frank verbally offers to mow Wendy's lawn for $10 an hour. Wendy verbally accepts Frank's offer. This is a typical express oral contract.

Implied in Fact Contracts

While most people usually specify contractual terms in some detail, it is possible to enter into a binding contract without uttering a single word if the action of the parties clearly indicates their intention to enter into a binding contract. In these situations, the resulting contract is said to be implied in fact, as the following example illustrates:

- Lenore walks into Barbara's bakery on a particularly busy day. She is in a hurry, so she grabs a loaf of Italian bread from the counter and waves it at Barbara, who nods in her direction and continues serving other customers.

In the preceding example, a binding implied in fact contract exists between Lenore and Barbara for the purchase of the bread on credit. Lenore will be obligated to pay Barbara the selling price of the bread within a reasonable time. If Lenore is a regular customer who purchases bread at the bakery every day, it will be presumed that she will pay for it tomorrow.

Bilateral Contracts

A bilateral contract is formed by the mutual exchange of promises between the contracting parties. In a bilateral contract, both parties make enforceable promises to each other as part of their contractual agreement. Consequently, a bilateral contract has two *promisors* (persons making contractual promises) and two *promisees* (persons to whom a contractual promise is made). To put it another way, bilateral contracts involve the mutual exchange of promises of present or future performance by the contracting parties, as the following examples illustrate:

- Jan agrees to purchase Rick's guitar for $75.
- Marie agrees to update the web pages for Jerry's law practice in exchange for Jerry drafting her will.
- Dawn agrees to create a client database for Glen's business for a $500 fee.

The preceding three examples all involve bilateral contracts since there is a mutual exchange of promises by both parties to each contract. Jan promises to pay $75 in exchange for Rick's promise to turn over his guitar to her; Marie promises to update Jerry's web pages in exchange for Jerry's promise to draft a will for her; Dawn agrees to create a database for Glen in exchange for Glen's promise to pay her $500. As with all bilateral contracts, these examples show that each contract contains two promisors and two promisees. Once the contract arises, there are two *obligors* (persons obligated to perform contractual promises) and two *obligees* (persons entitled to receive the benefit of the obligor's performance in a contract).

Unilateral Contracts

A unilateral contract is formed when one party exchanges a promise of future performance to induce another party to take some specific action. In other words, a unilateral contract is an exchange of a promise for an act. Unlike a bilateral contract, where there is a mutual exchange of promises making each party to the contract both a promisor/obligor and a promisee/obligee, a unilateral contract contains only one promisor/obligor. The promisor in a unilateral contract makes a conditional promise to the promisee to induce him to undertake some action. Note the following typical examples:

- Pamela Promisor tells Pepe Promisee that she will pay him $100 if he installs a security light in her backyard over the weekend.
- Pascuale Promisor tells Paula Promisee that he will pay her $250 if she will repair his deck over the next week.
- Peter Promisor tells Patricia Promisee that he will tune up her car if she cleans out his garage.

In the preceding three examples, unilateral promises are made by Pamela, Pascuale, and Peter, who are trying to induce some specific performance by Pepe, Paula, and Patricia.

The obligation of these promisors will come into existence only if the promisees undertake the desired action. Once the promisees complete the performance in question, the promisors will be obligated to perform as promised. But the promisees are not under any obligation to perform; it is completely up to them whether or not to accept the agreement offered by the promisors by beginning the requested performance.

Note that whether a contract is unilateral or bilateral depends on the terms offered by the promisor. If the promisor is seeking acceptance through the promisee's performance (a promise in exchange for an act), then the contract is unilateral; but if the promisor is seeking a present commitment for future performance by the promisee (a mutual exchange of promises), then the contract is bilateral.

Simple Contract

A simple contract is any agreement that need not follow a specific format to be enforceable. Simple contracts can be oral, written, express, or implied in fact. The vast majority of contracts entered into by businesses and individuals are simple contracts.

Formal Contract

At common law, the most common type of formal contract was one that needed to be in writing, signed, witnessed, and sealed by the parties. Today, most jurisdictions have abolished the significance of the seal for most contracts, and Article 2 of the Uniform Commercial Code (UCC) abolishes the significance of seal in all states for contracts involving the sale of goods, but the law still recognizes a number of formal contracts that are required to be in a specific form and contain certain specific language to be enforceable. They include negotiable instruments such as checks, drafts and notes, letters of credit (a promise to honor a demand instrument when it is presented for payment), and *recognizances* (formal acknowledgments of indebtedness made in court).

Questions

1. What is the basic definition of a contract?
2. What are the basic elements of a valid contract?
3. Is it true that oral contracts are unenforceable? Explain.
4. What is an implied in fact contract?
5. What is a bilateral contract?
6. What is a unilateral contract?
7. What is a formal contract?
8. Are most contracts simple or formal?

Hypothetical Cases

1. Dominic tells Rey, "I'm tired of eating mediocre food every day. If you prepare one of your gourmet dinners for me tomorrow, I'll gladly pay you $200." Rey does not respond.
   A. Is Dominic's offer to Rey for a unilateral or bilateral contract?
   B. Assuming that Rey wants to accept the offer under Dominic's terms, what must he do? Explain.
2. Chris tells John, "If you agree to provide me with all the firewood I need for next winter, I will agree to take care of all your gardening needs this spring and summer." John promptly accepts Chris's offer.
   A. Assume that a valid contract is formed. Is it express or implied in fact?
   B. Is this an offer for a unilateral or a bilateral contract? Explain.
3. Jane agrees to tutor Tom in accounting for three hours per week at $20 per hour throughout the semester. Both parties reduce their agreement to a writing that each signs in turn.
   A. Is this a simple or formal contract?
   B. Is it a bilateral or unilateral contract?
   C. Is this an express or an implied contract?
4. Joan, while browsing at a busy flea market, sees a vase she likes. The proprietor is busy several feet away, but she manages to get her attention by waiving a $5 bill and pointing to the vase. The proprietor nods in her direction, and she takes the vase, leaving $5 on the table, in clear view of the proprietor. The proprietor smiles at her and waves.
   A. Under the facts given, was a contract formed?
   B. Is this a simple or formal contract?
   C. Is this an express or an implied in fact contract?

Offer and Acceptance

CHAPTER 10

Chapter Outline

Requirements of a Valid Offer
Revocation of an Offer
Acceptance
Modes of Acceptance

As we have already seen, a contract is a legally enforceable agreement between two or more parties. As this definition implies, a contract depends on the consent of the parties to enter into a binding agreement. Assuming that the other requisite criteria are present (consideration, capacity, genuine assent, legality, and, where required, specific form), a binding contract is formed at the moment that a valid offer to enter into a contract is accepted. When a valid offer is accepted, the parties involved are obligated to render the agreed-upon performance and can be sued for breach of contract if they fail to do so.

Requirements of a Valid Offer

A valid offer must contain an unqualified, unambiguous promise to enter into a contract and must be communicated by the *offeror* (the person making the offer) to the *offeree* (the person to whom the offer is made). An offer that contains the requisite unqualified, unambiguous promise to enter into a contract and is communicated to the offeree can be accepted by the offeree to form a binding contract. In analyzing whether a valid offer exists, it's important to carefully examine the language and the circumstances surrounding the offer to determine whether the offer is unqualified and unambiguous, contains a valid promise, and has been communicated to the offeree. The following examples will illustrate some common problem areas:

- Rachel tells Ron, "I am considering selling my house for $100,000." Ron immediately replies, "I accept your offer."
- Stacy, angry that her motorcycle has broken down for the third time in two months, cries out, "I will sell this piece of junk motorcycle to the first person who gives me a nickel." Helen, who hears the statement, promptly tenders 5¢ to Stacy for the motorcycle.
- Arthur tells his friend Ranji, "I'll sell you my used 32-inch television set for $50." Before Ranji has a chance to reply, Sandy, who overheard the statement, cries out, "I accept your offer."

Although each of the preceding three examples seems to contain a valid offer, in fact none will form a valid contract when accepted under the facts given. In the first example, Rachel's statement does not contain a valid offer because it does not contain an unequivocal promise: Rachel says that she is considering selling her house, not that she promises to sell her house. Her statement is therefore not a clear offer, and no contract will be formed when Ron tries to accept it. In the second example, Stacy's statement certainly seems clear enough, yet under the circumstances it too is not an unequivocal offer, because the statement is made in anger or frustration and should not be interpreted as seriously intended by any offeree; in addition, the offer to sell a working motorcycle for a nickel also puts any potential offerees on notice that it is unlikely to be seriously intended. In the last example, Arthur's statement is a clear, unequivocal offer, but it cannot be accepted by Sandy because it was not communicated to her, but rather was made to Ranji. Only a person to whom an offer is communicated can accept it. (In that example, Ranji does have the power to accept Arthur's offer, since it is an unambiguous promise that was communicated to him.)

Revocation of an Offer

In general, a valid offer can be accepted at any time until it is either revoked or lapses. The offeror may revoke her offer at any time before it is accepted by communicating her intention to revoke to the offeree. Notice of revocation is effective when it is received by the offeree, whether or not he actually hears or reads it. The offer is also revoked if the offeree receives information from any source that clearly indicates the intention of the offeror to revoke the offer; an example of this is an offeree learning that a car that the offeror had offered to sell him has been sold to another party.

An offer may also be made to expire after a set period of time; if that is the case, the offeree must accept the offer during the stated time period that it is held open so as to form a contract. If Anne tells Bob, "I will sell you my old Xbox 360 for $75 if you accept my offer within 24 hours," then Bob must act within the stated time period; otherwise, the offer will expire. Even when a time period is specified, however, the offeror may still revoke the offer at any time before it automatically expires by communicating the desire to revoke the offer to the offeree. An exception to this rule is made if the offeree has given consideration for the offeror keeping the offer open. When such consideration is given, the offeree has a firm offer (also called an *option*) that is irrevocable by the offeror for its stated duration. Under Article 2 of the Uniform Commercial Code (UCC), a firm offer made by a merchant in a signed writing is also irrevocable, even if no additional consideration is given the merchant by the offeree for keeping the offer open.

When no time period is specified for acceptance by the offeree, an offer will terminate after the expiration of a reasonable period of time even if the offeror does not revoke it. What is a reasonable time period depends on the surrounding circumstances and hinges largely on the nature of the subject matter of the contract. If the subject matter of the contract is something with a fairly constant value, such as real estate in a stable housing market, a reasonable time might be three months or even longer. On the other hand, when the subject matter of the contract is subject to swift market fluctuations or has a limited useful life, the time period for acceptance of the offer can be very short. It can be measured in seconds when dealing with potentially volatile commodities such as pork belly, soybean, or crude oil futures, or be a day or so when highly perishable goods for immediate shipment, such as some fruits, vegetables, or flowers, are the subject of the offer.

Finally, an offer may automatically lapse by operation of law in a number of instances, such as the accidental destruction of the subject matter of the offer before it is accepted, or the death or incapacity of the offeror prior to acceptance of the offer by the offeree. Thus, if Sandy offers to sell her sailboat to Beatrice for $10,000 and the sailboat sinks in a storm before Beatrice accepts the offer, the offer automatically lapses; likewise, if Sanji offers to paint Beana's portrait for $500 and Sanji dies or becomes permanently incapacitated before Beana accepts the offer, Sanji's offer would lapse.

Acceptance

An offer is accepted by an offeree signaling his unqualified, unambiguous assent to the terms of the offeror's offer. To be valid, the offeree must communicate the acceptance to the offeror. In addition, the offeree's acceptance must be under the exact terms offered by the offeror; the terms in the acceptance must exactly mirror the terms in the offer for the acceptance to be valid. This requirement is referred to as the common law mirror image rule, which holds that any material deviation in the acceptance from the terms of the offer constitutes a rejection of the offer. The following example will illustrate:

- Steve offers to sell Barbara his English Racer for $350. Barbara can accept the offer only by agreeing to buy the bicycle under the offeror's terms. ("I accept," "I agree to your terms," "I'll take the bicycle," "Agreed," or any similar unequivocal, unambiguous response would constitute valid acceptance.)

In the preceding example, any of the following answers would violate the mirror image rule and automatically reject the offer, since each contains either additional or different terms from the original offer:

- "I'll take the bike for $300."
- "I'll take the bike provided you agree to coach me on racing for five hours at no additional cost."
- "I accept your offer provided you replace the worn front tire on the bike."

A counteroffer serves as an automatic rejection of the offer. Once a counteroffer is made, the original offeror now becomes the offeree of the counteroffer and can choose to either accept the counteroffer or reject it. The original offeree loses his ability to accept the original offer after making a counteroffer, as the next example illustrates:

- Celine offers to sell Biff her comic book collection for $1,500. Biff says he'll buy it for $1,250. Celine now has the right to accept Biff's counteroffer on his terms, reject it, or make another counteroffer of her own. If she rejects the counteroffer, Biff will no longer be able to accept the original offer to buy the comics for $1,500 to form a contract, since a counteroffer serves as a rejection of the original offer.

Like an offer, an acceptance must be unqualified and unambiguous. Although the word *accept* need not be used in a valid acceptance, the intent to accept must be unquestionably clear for a contract to be formed. Such responses as "I'm interested," "that sounds good," or "I could go for that" are all too ambiguous to form a valid acceptance.

Modes of Acceptance

An offer can be accepted through any reasonable means that communicates to the offeror the offeree's assent to the terms of the offer. As previously noted, acceptance of a valid offer immediately gives rise to a contract, provided that the other requirements for a valid contract are also present. This is not a problem in face-to-face negotiations, since the acceptance is immediately communicated to the offeror by the offeree and both parties are aware that a contract is formed. But what if an offeree decides to communicate his acceptance through the mail, by telegraph, or by use of email? In such cases, the acceptance is effective as of the moment that it is sent regardless of when or even whether it is received by the offeror. When acceptance is made by letter, it is effective as soon as a properly addressed envelope with sufficient postage is dropped in a mailbox or handed over to a postal employee for delivery. This is referred to as the *mailbox rule*. A similar rule applies in most states to letters carried by carrier services, telegraphs, and electronic or voice mail. The fact that an acceptance is valid when sent, rather than when received, can cause potential problems for offerors, as can be seen in the next example:

- Jim calls 10 friends offering to sell them his piano for $450—a bargain since its market value is $5,000. He tells them each to let him know within a week if they want to accept his offer. The next day, four of his friends write their acceptance in a letter that they deposit in a mailbox, properly addressed to Jim and containing the proper postage; three other friends leave him messages of acceptance on his answering machine at home; one sends him an electronic mail message of acceptance; one leaves an acceptance message with Jim's secretary; and one calls him at work and personally signals her acceptance. What is the likely result?

Jim in the preceding example had better hope that his friends are very understanding, for he has 10 valid contracts to sell his one piano. While only one of his friends will be able to successfully sue for the actual piano (the one who can prove he or she accepted first), the other nine friends are entitled to money damages (the difference between what they would have paid for the piano and its market value, in this case $4,550 each.)

This example illustrates the danger of making multiple general offers. How could Jim have protected himself in the preceding example? He could (and should) have done so by limiting acceptance to a specific means, such as "I will sell my piano to the first person who accepts my offer in person at my home." Note that even if the friend who called in her acceptance to Jim in person was the first to answer and therefore entitled to receive the piano, her acceptance would not revoke Jim's offer to the other nine offerees unless they independently learned of it prior to signaling their own acceptance of the offer.

Acceptance of a Unilateral Contract

As previously noted, a unilateral contract is an exchange of a promise for an act. What the offeror in a unilateral contract wants is not a promise by the offeree in return for her own promise, but rather for the offeree to accept the contract by performing the requested act. Acceptance of a unilateral contract, then, is made by the offeree only by beginning performance of the promisor's requested act. Once performance begins by the offeree, the offeror cannot withdraw the offer in most states and must allow the offeree to complete the task that is the subject matter of the contract. Acceptance by the offeree is complete when the task is finished, and the offeree is at that time entitled to receive the offeror's promised performance under the contract.

- Sherman offers to pay Sari $500 if she paints his garage within the next 72 hours. Sari says nothing but goes out to purchase the required supplies and begins performing the work the next morning.

Once Sari takes a substantial step toward rendering the requested performance, such as by purchasing the required supplies and preparing the garage for painting, Sherman may not withdraw the offer and must give Sari the opportunity to complete the work. If Sari does not complete the work on time, she will not be entitled to any payment, since she can accept the offer for a unilateral contract only by her full timely performance. On the other hand, if she completes the work on time, she will have accepted Sherman's offer and be entitled to payment of the $500.

Questions

1. What are the requirements of a valid offer?
2. What are four ways in which a valid offer can be revoked?
3. What effect does a counteroffer have on an offer?
4. What are the elements of a valid acceptance?
5. What means can be used by an offeree to communicate acceptance to the offeror?

Hypothetical Cases

1. Steve, while walking down the street, tells his friend Basili, "I would seriously consider selling you my antique gold Longines watch for $1,000." Basili does not answer. A month later, he writes Steve a letter stating that he accepts his offer to sell the Longines watch for $1,000. Is a contract formed? What is the effect of Basili's offer? Explain fully.
2. Assume the same facts as the last case. Would it make a difference if Basili had accepted the offer the next day? Do you think that a 30-day period is reasonable to accept an offer for the sale of an antique gold watch? Explain fully.
3. Olivia tells Bob, "If you agree to fix the leaky gutters in my house next week, I will agree to babysit your

daughter next weekend for up to 10 hours." Bob replies, "You've got a deal, provided that you give me $10 for the parts I'll need to do the work." Under these facts, is there a valid contract? Explain.

4. Osvaldo, an accountant, tells Luisa, "I'll gladly keep the books for your business for a yearly fee of $5,000." Ted, who overhears the offer, promptly answers, "I accept, Osvaldo."

A. Is there a valid contract between Osvaldo and Ted? Explain.
B. What is the proper legal term for Osvaldo's statement?
C. If Luisa writes Osvaldo a letter of acceptance and mails it the next day but forgets to put a stamp on the envelope, will a valid contract be formed? Explain.

# Consideration

CHAPTER 11

Chapter Outline

Illusory Promises
Past Consideration
Pre-existing Duty

Consideration can be defined as something of legal value given or received as an inducement to enter into a contract. For our purposes, you may think of consideration as the price of the contract. There are two elements to consideration: (1) a bargained-for-exchange and (2) something of legal value to the receiver or of legal detriment to the giver. To put it another way, consideration is whatever is given and received as the basis of the contract, and must represent something of legal value to the recipient or of legal detriment to the giver. Nearly anything that meets these two criteria and is not prohibited by law can be the basis of consideration for a contract.

In a bilateral contract, both parties must give consideration for the contract to be valid, as illustrated by the next example:

- Oksana offers to buy and install new brake pads on Eddy's car if he will allow her to use the car next weekend for a planned trip. If Eddy accepts the offer, a valid contract will be formed. The consideration each gets is clear: Eddy gets new brake pads and installation, and Oksana gets the use of an automobile for the weekend.

Note that consideration need not be money, although money is certainly valid consideration. There is also no requirement that the consideration exchanged be of equal value; all that courts generally look for is the existence of consideration that was freely agreed to. If one or both of the parties make a bad bargain, they will find no relief from the courts. If, in the preceding example, the value of new brake pads and installation for Eddy's car is $100 and the rental value of a car like Eddy's for the weekend is $300, the contract would be fully enforceable despite the disparate value of the consideration given by each party. As a general rule, courts will universally enforce contracts involving legal consideration without weighing the relative value of the consideration promised by each party. If the consideration agreed to by the parties is so disproportionate as to be unconscionable, however, a court can refuse to enforce the contract. To be unconscionable, the disparity in consideration would need to be so unreasonable and unfair as to shock the conscience of the court.

While consideration usually entails something of value to the receiver, it can also consist of something of detriment to the giver. If the giver of consideration agrees to do some legal act that he is not obligated to do, or give up the right to engage in activity that he has the lawful right to engage in, this constitutes consideration whether or not there is any tangible benefit to the receiver of the act or forbearance. The following example will illustrate:

- Florence offers Gary $1,000 if he will stop drinking coffee for six months. Gary accepts the offer in this unilateral contract and does not drink any coffee during the next six months. He is entitled to payment of the $1,000. He has a legal right to drink coffee and in giving up that right has given valid consideration.

> The preceding example involves forbearance (the giving up of one's right to engage in legal conduct as the basis of a contract), which is valid consideration. If the forbearance involves giving up illegal activity, it will not constitute consideration, and no contract will be formed. Thus, if Gary in the preceding example had been asked to give up snorting cocaine and had accepted, his forbearance would not constitute valid consideration because he has no legal right to use the illegal substance.

Illusory Promises

For there to be valid consideration in a contract, each party must give something of value to the other, or of detriment to themselves (e.g., forbearance). If the promised performance or forbearance is so vague as to be uncertain or if it is phrased in such a way as to make performance by one of the parties to a bilateral contract optional rather than mandatory, then the promised consideration is invalid. Promises that on their face appear to obligate one of the parties to render some performance but in fact do not obligate the party to perform are deemed illusory promises; such promises offer only the illusion of consideration. Each of the following offers contains an illusory promise:

- I promise to buy all the home heating oil I want from your company over the next heating season in exchange for your guarantee of a fixed price of $3.49 per gallon.
- I promise to let you do any plumbing work I might desire on my home over the next year if you promise to give me a 20% discount off your regular fee.
- I promise to take my auto to your shop for repair any time I wish for the next five years if you install a free set of tires in my car today.

The preceding three examples involve illusory promises because the promisor's statements are qualified by the words *wish*, *desire*, and *want*. Since there is no guarantee that the promisor will wish, desire, or want to do any business with the three promisees, the promisor is not actually obligated to do anything and, therefore, his promise contains no valid consideration. On the other hand, *requirements contracts* that obligate one party to purchase all the goods or services she will need over a specific period of time are valid. If, for example, Connie Consumer agrees to purchase all the home heating oil she needs to heat her home next winter from Independent Oil Co. at a fixed price of $3.49 per gallon, this is not an illusory promise but a valid contract. Even though there is no way to know exactly how much oil she will need over the next year, it is clear that she will need some oil if she has an oil-fired furnace and lives in an area of the country with cold winters. Her promise to buy all the oil she needs does represent valid consideration for Independent Oil Co.

The same holds true for *output contracts*, where a company agrees to sell all the goods it produces to a specific reseller for a stated price. Even though it may not be possible to know exactly what a company's production will be from one year to the next, it is enough to know that it will produce something, and whatever it produces, that is what it is obligated to sell at the agreed-upon price.

As you might suspect, requirements contracts and output contracts can easily be illusory contracts if one of the parties exercises bad faith. For instance, if home heating oil becomes too expensive in Connie's requirements contract with Independent Oil Co., she might opt to convert to gas heat or to install several wood-burning stoves in her home; likewise, if the price for the goods that manufacturer produces under an output contract falls precipitously, the manufacturer might be tempted to cut back production significantly to ameliorate its losses. What prevents both requirements contracts and output contracts from being illusory is that the Uniform Commercial Code (UCC) imposes a requirement of good faith and fair dealing on all contracts for the sale of goods. For contracts involving personal services, courts would generally hold the parties to an implied covenant of good faith as well when requirements or output contracts are involved in order to prevent these agreements from being illusory. This means that the parties cannot take unfair advantage of the requirement contract or output contract but must exercise good faith in dealing with such contracts. It would be a breach of contract, therefore, for Connie to convert to gas or wood as her home heating fuel. (She could, however, engage in reasonable conservation measures to lessen her need for fuel if its price rises, such as lowering the thermostat.) In determining reasonableness and good faith, courts would look at performance in previous years when requirements contracts or output contracts are involved, as well as to normal practices in the industry involved.

Past Consideration

As previously noted, consideration is defined as something of legal value given or received as an inducement to enter into a contract. As this definition implies, consideration must have a present value for the parties. A contract that cites consideration given in the past is unenforceable. To put it another way, past consideration is not valid consideration because nothing of present value is given as inducement to enter into a contract, as the next three examples illustrate:

- Adam tells Betty, "In consideration of your having been the best friend I've ever had over the past ten years, I hereby promise to buy you a brand new diamond bracelet for Christmas."
- Carla tells Donald at his retirement party, "In consideration of your 50 years of faithful service to Happy Co., we are pleased to award you a stipend of $500 per month above your normal pension benefit for the rest of your life."
- Edweena tells Frank, "In consideration of your having risked your life to save me from drowning, I hereby promise to place $50,000 in trust for your son's future education."

Even though the word *consideration* is used in these three examples, and even though there was certainly legal value in the services that Betty, Donald, and Frank provided, none of these promises is enforceable in court since the consideration cited is past consideration and not one of these individuals is obligated to do anything further under the terms of these agreements after the agreement is reached. If the promisees of these promises were obligated to render some new performance (even if minor), however, then there would be valid consideration and a contract would be formed. Therefore, if Carla's statement to Donald were to read "In consideration of your 50 years of faithful service to Happy Co. and your promise to remain on the job for another three months before retiring to assist with the transition of your replacement, we are pleased to award you a stipend of $500 per month above your normal pension benefit for the rest of your life," then the statement would contain valid consideration.

Pre-existing Duty

The pre-existing duty rule states that it is not valid consideration for parties to agree to do that which they are already obligated to do. While this may seem obvious, the rule has wide-ranging applications. The pre-existing duty rule makes modifications to existing contracts invalid unless they are accompanied by additional consideration or unless there is a good faith dispute as to the meaning of contract terms. Under Article 2 of the Uniform Commercial Code (UCC), contracts for the sale of goods can be modified in good faith without additional consideration by the mutual consent of the parties. Let's look at a few examples that illustrate the application of the rule:

- Alice borrows $5,000 from Beulah and agrees to repay it in two years with 7% interest. After six months, she wants to renegotiate the loan with Beulah to make it payable in three years at 5% interest. Even if Beulah agrees to the terms, Alice cannot enforce the changes to the contract since she is not giving any additional value in exchange for the modification to the contract. Beulah is free to accept less than she is entitled to under the contract. But if she changes her mind and demands that Alice honor the terms of the original agreement, Alice must do so.

If the parties wish to change the terms of the contract in the preceding example, Alice must give some additional consideration to Beulah for the changed contract to not run afoul of the pre-existing duty rule. She can do this by paying a higher interest rate, by changing the terms of payment to a monthly basis (so that Beulah gets payments earlier than she would otherwise be entitled to), by paying Beulah $20 for agreeing to the change, or by giving any other legal consideration to Beulah in exchange for the change in the terms of the original contract.

Note that regardless of problems with the pre-existing duty rule, past consideration, or illusory promises, parties are always free to honor agreements that they enter into, even if these are not legally enforceable; if they do so, they are in essence conveying a gift on the recipient of the contract's benefit. The point is that these agreements are not enforceable in the courts if promisors change their minds and refuse to honor them.

Questions

1. Define consideration.
2. Is consideration synonymous with money? Explain.
3. Explain how forbearance can be valid consideration.
4. What are illusory promises?
5. What is meant by a requirements contract?
6. What is meant by an output contract?
7. Are output and requirements contracts considered illusory and therefore void? Explain fully.
8. What is past consideration?
9. Why is past consideration invalid?
10. What is the basic thrust of the pre-existing duty rule?

Hypothetical Cases

1. Rob tells Sheniqua, "If you kiss me, I'll contribute $1,000 to your favorite charity." Sheniqua replies, "Are you serious, or are you pulling my leg?" whereupon Rob assures her that he is serious. She immediately kisses him and is informed by Rob that he was, after all, pulling her leg. Sheniqua is not amused and decides to sue Rob in small claims court to force him to make a $1,000 contribution to UNICEF. Rob defends on the grounds that there was no written contract and that even if there were it would be unenforceable, since he received no legal consideration from Sheniqua. You're the judge. Decide the case and give your legal analysis.

2. Ken, grateful that Letisha performed life-saving CPR on him after he had suffered a heart attack, executes a contract with the following language:
"In consideration of Letisha Washington having saved my life, I hereby promise to pay her $250 per week for life. Signed [Ken Smith]"
For the next three years, he faithfully makes the weekly payments, and then stops. Letisha, upset that Ken broke his word to her, sues him, seeking to reinstate his payments. Once again, you are the judge. Decide the case and state your legal reasoning for your decision.

3. Mark agrees to purchase from Nancy's farm stand "All the fruit I want, all the vegetables I desire, and all the apple cider I wish for the next two years in exchange for Nancy giving me a 20% discount off her normal retail price on the purchases." (Both he and Nancy sign the agreement.) He also enters into a separate agreement with Slippery Oil Corp. to purchase "All the home heating fuel I need for the next two years at a price of $3.75 per gallon." During the next two years, he buys no fruit, vegetables, or cider from Nancy and no home heating oil from Slippery Oil. Is he in breach of either contract? Explain.

4. Greg Greedy, a very popular but avaricious college lecturer, has a two-year contract with State U in which he agreed to teach nine credits per semester during that period in exchange for a yearly salary of $75,000. After his first year, he negotiates with the administration an additional $5,000 payment to be made to him at the end of the second year in exchange for his finishing out his two-year term. He also gets his students to agree to pay him $10 at the end of the semester in every class he teaches in exchange for his agreeing to remain as their instructor. In addition, he separately enters into an agreement with five of his students to tutor them individually after class in the evenings for a modest fee of $20 an hour each. If, at the end of his last semester, the college refuses to pay him the

$5,000 raise for having completed his contract, the students in his class refuse to pay him the $10 they each promised, and the students he had tutored also refuse to pay him for the agreed-upon tutorial sessions, what are Dr. Greedy's rights with respect to each of the three separate contracts?

Ethics and the Law: Questions for Further Study

It is sometimes easy to confuse what is legal with what is right. In a perfect world, the terms would be synonymous; alas, in the real world, too often they are not. Examine the following examples from both a legal and ethical perspective. What are the legal rights of the people involved? What are the ethical implications for each case? Do the law and ethics coincide? Would you suggest any changes to the law? Might changing the law create more problems than it solves?

- Albert Arsonist is trapped by his own blaze after setting fire to an occupied apartment building. Freida Firefighter is the first person on the scene. She rescues several victims from the burning building and then notices Albert on the roof, yelling for help—loudly admitting his crime and begging to be rescued. Freida, exhausted, yells back, telling him to wait for a helicopter that is on its way and will arrive in ample time to save him. Albert, who enjoys fire only when other people are being consumed by it, pleads with her to rescue him and offers to give her $25,000 in cash if she risks her life to extricate him from the flames. After much pleading on Albert's part, she re-enters the burning building and manages to rescue him from the flames. As thanks, Albert tells her he regrets that she did not burn to death on the way to rescue him, and that he has no intention of giving her the $25,000 he'd promised.
- Samantha, the owner of a restaurant, enters into a requirements contract with Pamela, a farmer, to supply all the fruits and vegetables that she needs in her business for a five-year period at a 20% discount over Pamela's normal retail price. Over the five-year period, Samantha always buys produce in quantity during seasonal periods when the price is low and stores it in huge freezers she purchased for that purpose. The result over the five-year period is a net loss of $25,000 to Pamela, whose farm loses money every year, and phenomenal success for Samantha, whose business prospers in great part due to the variety of excellent produce in her all-vegetarian menu. Pamela suspects that Samantha is abusing their contract, but will not bring legal action because she gave her word and believes that she is morally obligated to honor the agreement.

Capacity

CHAPTER 12

Chapter Outline

Definition of Capacity

Contracts involve a consensual relationship that requires parties to freely give their consent to enter into a contract. To put it another way, there must be a meeting of the minds between contracting parties before a binding agreement is formed. Two elements must be present for there to be valid consent given by contracting parties: (1) each party to the contract must have *contractual capacity* (the legal ability and power to enter into a contract); and (2) there must be *genuine assent* (consent that is freely given) by each party to enter into a contract. We will examine contractual capacity in this chapter and the closely related element of genuine assent in Chapter 13.

Definition of Capacity

Capacity is defined as the legal qualification, competence, or fitness to enter into a contract. To have the capacity to enter into a contract, a party must have both the mental competence to understand the nature of a contract and have reached the age of consent at the time that the contract is entered into. Problems with capacity, then, center around two basic areas: agreements entered into by persons lacking the mental capacity to enter into a contract and contracts entered into by minors. We'll examine each of these areas in turn.

Contracts by Incompetents

Contracts entered into by persons who have been judicially declared to be incompetent to handle their own affairs and have had a guardian appointed by a court are *void* (invalid and unenforceable). Persons who are judicially declared to be incompetent lose their capacity to enter into valid contracts, and contracts that they attempt to enter into are unenforceable. This is the case even when the other contracting party is unaware of the incompetence and acts in good faith in entering into the agreement.

Contracts entered into by persons who suffer from some mental illness or defect that prevents them from understanding the nature of a contract, but who have not been declared to be incompetent, are not void but voidable at the option of the incompetent person or his guardian. The distinction between void and voidable contracts is that a void contract can never be binding, whereas a voidable contract is binding unless the incompetent person sues to have the contract *rescinded* (declared invalid from its inception).

It should be noted that merely because a person suffers from some mental infirmity or defect does not necessarily mean that the person cannot enter into a fully binding contract. For a contract to be voidable for lack of capacity, it must be shown that the party seeking to void the contract did not understand the nature of a contract because of the mental infirmity. A person who suffers from depression or bipolar disorder, for example, would most likely be fully capable to enter into a contract as long as the disorder does not impair the ability to understand the nature of a contract. Whether or not a person's ability to understand the nature of a contract is impaired by a specific disorder is a question of fact to be determined by the trier of fact at trial (e.g., the jury, unless parties waive the right to a jury trial or the case is brought in small claims court, in which cases the judge would decide both questions of fact and of law).

Contracts by Intoxicated Persons

A person who enters into a contract while under the influence of alcohol or any other drug that can significantly impair mental ability is treated exactly the same as a person suffering from a mental disability who has not been judicially declared incompetent. In other words, contracts of intoxicated persons are generally voidable by such persons if they can show that their intoxication prevented them from understanding the nature of a contract at the time that they entered into the agreement. Most courts require some physical manifestation of inebriation at the time of entering into a contract before they will allow such contracts to be voided by reason of intoxication. The clearer the manifestation of intoxication at the time of the agreement, the likelier it is that a court will invalidate a contract.

Minors' Contracts

Every jurisdiction has a minimum age of consent for entering into binding agreements. While the age of majority can vary among the states, it is usually 18 years of age (19 in Alabama and Nebraska and 21 in Mississippi, though written and signed contracts for personal property by minors 18 or older are enforceable). When minors enter into a contract before attaining the age of majority, such contracts are generally voidable in every jurisdiction at the option of the minor. There is an exception for contracts involving necessaries—items or services essential to the maintenance of human life.

In most states, a minor has the option of voiding a contract entered into while a minor at any time during his minority. A minor who wishes to exercise the right to disaffirm a voidable contract must exercise that right before reaching the age of consent or a reasonable time thereafter; otherwise, the contract will be deemed automatically ratified.

Some states limit a minor's right to disaffirm a contract by statute to a specific period of time, such as one year from the date that the contract is entered into. In such states, the minor must disaffirm the contract within the specified time period, or it will be deemed to have been ratified.

In most states, the right of minors to disaffirm contracts is absolute. If the consideration they received under the contract has been damaged or worn from use, the minor is only obligated to return it in whatever condition it is in and, upon doing so, is entitled to a refund of whatever consideration he gave under the terms of the contract. Thus, if a minor buys a car at 16 in a state that recognizes 18 as the age of majority, he can return the car at any time until he reaches his 18th birthday, or a reasonable time thereafter (usually within a few weeks from his 18th birthday) and is entitled to a full refund of whatever consideration he paid for the car. It is irrelevant that a car after being used for two years is not worth the same as it was when purchased; it is not even relevant in most states if the car is damaged or even wholly destroyed; the child may still return the remains of the auto and be entitled to a full refund of its purchase price!

In some states, adults who deal with children are protected to some extent from situations such as the one just described by being able to sue in tort to recover whatever damage has been done to the underlying subject matter of the contract, as well as for the value of its use. But this is a minority view. In a majority of states, no such recovery is possible.

What if a minor lies about his age in order to induce an adult to enter into a contract? When that is the case, there is a split of opinion among the states. Some states allow the adult to recover damages from the minor for the tort of fraud, whereas others allow the minor to disaffirm even when the minor offered fraudulent proof of age to induce the adult to enter into the contract.

While the latter standard may seem harsh, keep in mind that it was developed at common law to protect children from being taken advantage of by unscrupulous adults. Whether or not the average child today in the waning days of infancy needs such protection is highly debatable; nevertheless, most states still retain a very paternalistic attitude toward protecting minors from themselves. How, then, can businesses protect themselves from the potential of minors' disaffirmance? Essentially in two ways: (1) require minors to obtain an adult cosigner for any contract they enter into, or (2) refuse to deal with minors altogether. The second option is seldom exercised because minors represent a very important market for most vendors. And, with the exception of large-ticket items, the first option is also often impractical. Why then do merchants deal with minors? Because the benefit of courting this profitable consumer segment far outweighs the potential cost of disaffirmance. As has been previously noted, minors may not disaffirm contracts for necessaries. Food, clothing, shelter, and medical care have been held to qualify as necessaries in most states. Educational expenses are also exempt from disaffirmance in many states, as are contracts involving credit.

In evaluating whether an item is a necessary or a luxury and therefore not exempt from disaffirmance, courts generally look at a child's needs in relation to her upbringing and the relative wealth of her parents. Thus, purchases involving articles of clothing that a child might normally wear are deemed necessaries, but not high-priced items of clothing not normally within the reach of the child's parents. For example, if the typical college professor's child purchases a $20,000 fur coat, it would likely be deemed a luxury, rather than a necessary, and the child could disaffirm the contract for its purchase as it is not an item of clothing that the child would normally be expected to wear. But if the child of wealthy parents purchases the same coat, it might well be deemed a necessary for the cost may not be an unreasonable extravagance for her. Keep in mind that while this double standard might seem unfair, all it means as applied here is that the relative wealth of a child's parents is a factor that can be considered in determining where to draw the line between a reasonable and an extravagant purchase. If an article of clothing is not deemed to be a luxury, then a contract for its purchase cannot be disaffirmed.

Contracts by Emancipated Minors

Contracts entered into by minors who are self-supporting and living apart from their parents are generally exempted from disaffirmance. Courts generally treat emancipated minors as adults for all purposes, including entering into fully binding contracts.

Minor's Business Contracts

As is the case with emancipated minors, the business contracts entered into by nonemancipated minors are also exempt from disaffirmance by the minors. The rationale here is clear: a minor who is mature enough to run her own business is also mature enough to be held responsible for contracts entered into on behalf of that business. If the child is not emancipated (e.g., is still a dependent of parents or guardians) but runs her own business, she is still free to disaffirm personal contracts she enters into that are unrelated to her business. Without this exception, minors could not participate in business ventures as a practical matter since their contracts would be unenforceable.

Questions

1. Define contractual capacity.
2. What is the effect of contracts entered into by persons who have been judicially declared to be incompetent?
3. What is the effect of contracts entered into by persons who have some mental defect or infirmity that does not permit them to understand the nature of a

contract but who have not been judicially declared to be incompetent?
4. What is the effect of contracts entered into by persons who suffer from some mental infirmity that does not prevent them from understanding the nature of a contract?
5. What are necessaries?
6. Give three examples of necessaries.
7. How are contracts with intoxicated persons treated?
8. What is the significance of minors' contracts?
9. May emancipated minors disaffirm contracts they enter into with adults?
10. What is the significance of minors' business contracts?

Hypothetical Cases

1. Leon believes himself to be Napoleon Bonaparte. Other than that one mental quirk, he is a happy, healthy, and quite successful businessperson. He has not been judicially declared to be incompetent and is currently undergoing therapy to address his delusion. At a business lunch, he enters into a million-dollar agreement with Lena, a supplier of raw materials for one of his business ventures. At the time of signing the agreement, Leon was dressed in his normal attire—that of a nineteenth-century French general—and was quite sober. The other party to the agreement had consumed three martinis and two glasses of wine during the two-hour lunch meeting, but was showing absolutely no sign of intoxication and seemed quite lucid and sober at the time that she signed the contract. Discuss fully whether either party (or both) would be able to rescind the agreement the next day based on a claim of incapacity.
2. Bernice is a 16-year-old high school student who runs a part-time document preparation service after school. She purchases a computer for her business and uses the same for almost two years quite successfully. On the day before her 18th birthday, she decides she'd like to upgrade her computer system and attempts to disaffirm the original contract. She contacts the original supplier from whom she'd purchased her computer system, informs them she was a minor at the time, and demands that they issue her a check for $2,000—the amount she had originally paid for the computer; she also tells them that she will, of course, return the computer to them, even though the hard drive and DVD burner no longer work. The supplier has a good laugh on the phone and then hangs up on her. She sues. What result? Explain fully.
3. Assume the same facts as in the last case, except that Bernice had purchased the computer system for her home use when she was 16 and only began using the computer for business use a month before she decides to disaffirm. What result? Explain fully.
4. Belinda is a 17-year-old college student. She enters into a written contract with Sal, an adult, for the purchase of Sal's 1964 Corvette for $2,000 in one week, when she reaches her 18th birthday. The day after signing the agreement, it dawns on Sal that he made a bad deal, since the car is worth many times his asking price. He calls Belinda and informs her that he wishes to disaffirm the contract. Belinda is furious and says she expects him to keep his word and turn over the car when promised.
   A. If Sal refuses to turn over the car as promised, may she successfully sue him for damages, or will Sal be able to successfully assert his disaffirmance of the contract?
   B. What if Belinda had lied to Sal about her age and even shown him false I.D. that stated she was 19 years old in a state that recognizes 18 as the age of majority? Would your answer be the same? Explain fully.

Ethics and the Law: Questions for Further Study

The special protection that the law affords to minors when it comes to disaffirming contracts stems from the common law notion that children need special protection—that they are innocent, gullible, and easy to be taken advantage of by adults. While this may be true of very young children, it is difficult to make that argument for the average 16- or 17-year-old in the twenty-first century. Should the law be changed? Is there still a need for offering special protection to minors? What about the adults who are victimized by unscrupulous "children" who take advantage of the system? At one time, women were afforded the same protection as children under the same paternalistic attitude that "the weaker sex needs protection from itself." Thankfully, those days are past. Is it not as condescending to knowledgeable young men and women to be treated as needing special protection when dealing with adults? What about gullible adults? Are they any less deserving of protection? What do you think? Make an argument for a just solution to this dilemma or for maintaining the status quo.

Genuine Assent

CHAPTER 13

Chapter Outline

Mutual Mistake
Duress
Fraud in the Inducement
Fraud in the Execution
Undue Influence

As noted in the preceding chapter, there must be a meeting of the minds of contracting parties before a valid contract can arise. This presupposes that the contracting parties have the capacity to enter into a binding contract, as discussed in Chapter 12, and that the parties give their genuine assent to enter into a binding agreement. *Genuine assent* is the requirement that the assent given to enter into a binding agreement be sincere and freely given by both contracting parties.

In this chapter, we will examine the circumstances that can undermine genuine assent and make a seemingly enforceable contract into either a void or voidable agreement. These circumstances include mutual mistake, duress, fraud in the execution, fraud in the inducement, and overreaching.

Mutual Mistake

If both parties to a contract are mistaken as to a material aspect of the contract, the contract is void. There can be no meeting of the minds, and therefore no binding contract, if both parties enter into an agreement based on a common mistake as to a material fact relating to the agreement. The following examples will help to illustrate this point:

- Sally offers to sell Bob "my iPhone for $50." Bob accepts the offer. Normally, a contract would result, but assume Sally owns two iPhones—an old, obsolete iPhone 3GS and a newer iPhone 5c of considerably greater value. Bob believes she is offering to sell the 5c, but Sally intended the offer to apply to the classic 3GS iPhone. No contract results because the parties were laboring under a mutual mistake of fact as to which phone was the subject matter of the contract.
- Sally offers to sell Bob "my tablet computer for $100." Bob accepts the offer after briefly inspecting the tablet and believing it to be an Apple Mini. In fact, the tablet is a generic 10-inch Android tablet that works perfectly well but is of considerably lesser value. Under these facts, a valid contract exists because only Bob is in error as to the brand of the tablet, and his unilateral mistake will not allow him to invalidate the contract.
- Sally offers to sell Bob "my Kindle Fire eBook reader for $100." Bob accepts the offer. Unbeknownst to Sally and Bob, the device was stolen from Sally's dorm room before she offered to sell it to Bob. Under these facts, no contract exists as both are mistaken as to a material fact relating to the contract—the fact that the Kindle Fire is no longer in Sally's possession. Theft or the destruction of the subject matter of a contract

outside of the control of the contracting parties will prevent the contract from being formed due to mutual mistake as to the subject matter's continued existence.

For a contract to be invalidated by reason of a mutual mistake as to a material fact, the mistake must relate to an assumption held in common by both parties to the contract. Again, if only one of the parties is mistaken, or if both parties are mistaken as to a nonmaterial fact, the contract is perfectly valid. Whether a fact is material or immaterial is determined by whether the parties relied on the fact in making their decision to enter into the contract or whether the fact would be material to a reasonable person under the circumstances. If both parties are mistaken as to a fact that was not a determining factor in the party's decision to enter into the contract, and if a reasonable person under similar circumstances would not be influenced by the fact in deciding to enter into the contract, the contract is fully binding. Thus, if two color-blind individuals enter into a contract for the sale of an automobile thinking it to be blue but it in fact is green, whether or not this is a material defect that would invalidate the contract depends on whether the color of the auto was a relevant consideration for the parties at the time of entering into the agreement. Assuming that a blue car is worth the same as a green one and that the parties are color blind, the color of the car is probably not a material factor in this contract.

Duress

Duress is perhaps the easiest factor to comprehend as invalidating a party's genuine assent. It is clear that if a person has a gun pointed at his head at the time that he agrees to enter into a contract, the assent given is not genuine, but is rather motivated by fear. Under such circumstances, it will come as no surprise that the contract is voidable by the person whose consent was obtained by duress.

While a gun to the head may be the simplest form of duress to grasp, duress can take many forms, each equally invalidating a contract. Physical coercion, such as the force or threat of force, constitutes duress, but so do threats of economic or social reprisals. What is important in determining whether a party acted under the threat of duress is whether the agreement to enter into the contract was motivated by the genuine desire to enter into a contract or by fear of some threat made by the other contracting party. Each of the following examples constitutes duress that would invalidate genuine assent:

- Samantha tells Benny, "If you don't sign this agreement, I'm going to punch your lights out." Benny believes the threat is real and signs the agreement.
- Steve tells Bertha, "Unless you sign this agreement, I will tell your husband that we're having an affair." Bertha, believing Steve to be serious, signs the agreement.
- Sandra tells Bernie "If you sign this partnership agreement, I won't tell everyone that you have AIDS." Bernie, who has AIDS and wants to keep the information private, signs the agreement.

Courts generally apply an objective test in determining whether a threat constitutes duress. Under an objective standard, a threat constitutes duress only if a reasonable person under the same circumstances would have deemed the threat believable and would have been motivated to action to avoid the consequences of the threat. Thus, if a 90-pound unarmed salesperson tells a 300-pound football player, "Unless you purchase this 50-inch television set right now, I'm going to beat you up," that would not constitute a believable threat to a reasonable person, and if the football player agrees to the contract, he will not be able to later invalidate it on grounds of duress.

Fraud in the Inducement

As we saw in our discussion of intentional torts in Chapter 7, fraud occurs whenever one person intentionally misleads another into undertaking some action that causes the defrauded party some harm. It stands to reason that of one of the parties to a contract consents to enter into the agreement because she is the victim of a fraud perpetrated by the other party, the assent given is not genuine and the contract can be invalidated.

The effect of fraud on a contract depends on whether fraud in the inducement or fraud in the execution is involved. Fraud in the inducement occurs whenever a party is misled into agreeing to enter into a contract by reasonably relying on the intentional misrepresentation relating to a material fact made by the other party. In other words, whenever one party purposely lies to another about important matters relating to the contract to induce that party to enter into the contract, fraud in the inducement is involved. The effect of fraud in the inducement is to make the resulting contract voidable at the option of the defrauded party. Whenever fraud in the inducement is involved, the party who has been intentionally misled into entering into the agreement has the option of having the agreement declared void in court. But the guilty party who perpetrated the fraud may not have the agreement declared void; if the defrauded party wishes to go through with the agreement when he learns of the fraud, he has the right to fully enforce the contract. For fraud in the inducement to be established as a defense to an otherwise valid contract, the following five elements must be present:

1. There must be a willful misrepresentation made by the offeror to the offeree;
2. The misrepresentation must relate to a material fact in connection to the proposed contract;
3. The representation must be made to induce the offeree to enter into the contract;
4. The offeree must reasonably rely on the misrepresentation; and
5. The offeree must suffer a loss as a result.

The following example should illustrate:

- Simon offers to sell Betty his used DVD recorder for $25. To induce her to buy the unit, he tells her that the DVD recorder has a digital tuner and can be used as a digital video recorder to record television shows with an antenna off the air without the need of a cable box. He also tells her that the DVD has surround sound capabilities. In fact, the DVD recorder can reproduce Dolby surround sound, but it does not have a video tuner and needs to be connected to a cable box or a separate tuner to be able to record television shows.

If Betty purchases the unit based on the misrepresentations, she may have the contract declared void at her option when she learns that the DVD recorder does not have an integrated tuner as claimed. On the other hand, if she is still willing to keep the unit despite the misrepresentations about it because of its low price, she is free to do so; Simon, however, will not be able to invalidate the contract based on his fraudulent statements.

Fraud in the Execution

When fraud in the execution is involved, the defrauded party has been intentionally induced to execute a legal instrument by a misrepresentation as to the nature of the instrument being signed. Unlike fraud in the inducement, in which one party is induced to enter into an otherwise valid agreement through the intentional misrepresentation of a material fact, when fraud in the execution is involved, the innocent party is induced to sign a written contract by having the nature of the instrument itself misrepresented as being something other than a contract. The following example will illustrate:

- Tawanda, a famous sports personality, is given a folded piece of paper by Frank, a fan, who asks her to sign her autograph. She complies. Unbeknownst to her, the piece of paper contains a contract wherein Tawanda agrees to hire Frank as her manager for a five-year term.

In the preceding example, Tawanda was misled not as to an aspect of the contract, but as to the very nature of the agreement itself. Her intent in signing her name to the paper was to give a fan an autograph, not to enter into a binding contract. She is a victim of fraud in the execution, since she was willfully misled into executing an agreement she never intended to effectuate. She was unaware that she was entering into an agreement at all when she signed her name to the paper; there was no meeting of the minds, and there is no valid contract.

Whenever fraud in the execution is involved, the victim does not intend to enter into an agreement at all; thus, the agreement that appears to result from the fraud is not merely voidable at the victim's option, but completely void and unenforceable by either party.

Undue Influence

Undue influence is involved when the contracting parties share a relationship based on trust and confidence and one party abuses that relationship to gain an unfair advantage over the other. Undue influence generally involves a fiduciary relationship (a relationship based on trust) such as the relationship between an attorney and her client or a doctor and her patient. Other common instances of overreaching involve parties with close personal or familial ties. The law recognizes that when such relationships are involved, parties are particularly vulnerable to manipulation because they are likely to let down their guard and allow the nature of the relationship to cloud their judgment.

A contract induced by undue influence is voidable at the option of the party who can show that she was induced to enter into a disadvantageous agreement because of the special relationship. A party seeking to avoid a contract based on undue influence needs to show that the assent given to enter into the contract was not genuine, but rather was clouded by the other party's taking unfair advantage of the fiduciary relationship in inducing her to enter into the contract. As with fraud in the inducement, contracts involving undue influence by one of the parties are voidable only by the party who is the victim of the undue influence.

Questions

1. Define genuine assent.
2. What is the effect of a mutual mistake of fact on a contract?
3. Will every mutual mistake of fact invalidate a contract?
4. What constitutes duress?
5. Is duress generally determined based on a subjective or objective test?
6. Define fraud in the inducement.
7. How is fraud in the execution different from fraud in the inducement?
8. What is the legal effect of fraud in the inducement and fraud in the execution on a contract?

Hypothetical Cases

1. Brandon enters into a contract with Sari whereby Sari agrees to ship 1,000 square yards of silk from India aboard the S.S. Freedom when the ship next sails. Unbeknownst to the parties at the time of entering into the contract, there are two S.S. Freedoms that sail from India to U.S. ports; the first sails in January and the second in March. Brandon meant for the goods to be shipped via the S.S. Freedom that sails in January, but Sari agreed to the contract based on the March sailing date of the S.S. Freedom she knew about. When the goods do not arrive at the end of January as expected, Brandon sues Sari for breach of contract. You are the judge. What result?
2. Rosa, while engaging in negotiations for the lease of Sam's commercial property for her new business, is upset by what she perceives to be Sam's unreasonable stubbornness in refusing to accept what she feels is an eminently fair offer for a five-year lease. After an hour of fruitless negotiation, she turns to Sam and says: "You know, you are the most pig-headed person I've ever had the unfortunate experience of dealing with. Unless you accept my offer, I'm going to beat you

senseless." Sam promptly accepts the offer and signs a commercial lease agreement with Rosa. A month later, unhappy with the arrangement, Sam wants to avoid the contract based on duress.

   A. Assume that Sam is a 300-pound ex-linebacker for the New York Giants and Rosa a slender, petite woman. Is Sam likely to succeed? Explain.

   B. Would your answer be different if Rosa had threatened to have Sam killed if he did not sign the agreement and Sam believed her to be serious?

3. Alisha, an attorney, enters into a contract with Clint, her client, whereby Clint agrees to sell her 10,000 shares of XYZ Company at $20 per share, the market value of the shares at the time of the contract. A month after the transfer of the shares, the price of the stock climbs to $40 per share due to conditions that were not foreseeable by Alisha or Clint at the time of their contract. Clint, upon learning of the doubling in value of the shares, decides that Alisha took advantage of their relationship and sues to have the contract voided. What result?

4. Assume the same facts as the last question, except that Alisha paid $17 for the stock when it had a market value of $20 per share. If Clint sues seeking to invalidate the contract, what result? What if after purchasing the stock for $17 it drops to $5 per share and Alisha sues to avoid the contract?

Legality

CHAPTER 14

It should come as no surprise that agreements that involve the commission of a crime or tort are void and unenforceable in the courts. In general, the courts will refuse to arbitrate disputes between parties to illegal contracts, leaving such parties without legal recourse. In this chapter, we will examine some common types of illegal contracts that courts will refuse to enforce and explore the consequences for parties to such contracts.

Chapter Outline

Contracts Involving the Commission of a Tort or a Crime
Restraint of Trade
Gambling Contracts
Usurious Contracts
Contracts Contrary to Public Policy

Contracts Involving the Commission of a Tort or a Crime

When the underlying subject matter of the contract involves the commission of a tort, a crime, or the violation of a state or federal statute, the agreement is void for illegality, and the parties are left with no legal recourse. The courts will generally not entertain petitions for the return of whatever consideration was given by the parties to such contracts, leaving the parties to the illegal contract in whatever position it finds them. Thus, if Albert pays Betty $10,000 to kill Charlie, and Betty performs her part of the agreement, Betty would not be able to sue Albert for breach of contract since the contract involves the commission of a crime. If Albert had paid the money to Betty, who then refused to carry out the murder of Charlie, Albert would also be prevented from suing Betty for breach of contract. In the latter example, Betty would be able to keep the $10,000 knowing that Albert had no legal recourse. In short, criminals who fail to honor their agreements are left to fend for themselves as the courts will refuse to hear suits from people "with unclean hands" (e.g., who are both guilty of entering into illegal contracts).

Restraint of Trade

A common type of illegal contract involves agreements in restraint of trade. The purpose of such contracts is to interfere with free competition in the marketplace. Contracts in restraint of trade include agreements involving price fixing, the establishment of monopolies, predatory trade practices, or other agreements whose purpose is to thwart competition and subvert the operation of the free market. Such agreements are made illegal by the federal Sherman and Clayton Acts when they unduly burden interstate commerce. As with most other illegal agreements, parties to contracts involving restraint of trade cannot sue for redress of grievances arising from such contracts. (The victims of such agreements can, of course, seek redress in the courts.) Thus, if Adam and Betty conspire to drive Carla out of business by a price-fixing scheme, neither Adam nor Betty would be able to sue one another if they breached their illegal agreement. But

Carla would be free to sue both parties for tort damages she suffered as a result of the illegal price fixing scheme, and recover reasonable attorneys' fees, court costs, and treble damages (punitive damages equal to three times her actual compensatory damages) under the civil provisions of the Clayton Act if the price fixing scheme involved interstate commerce.

Gambling Contracts

Perhaps the most common type of illegal contract involves gambling. At common law, gambling was perfectly legal in all forms. Today, in every jurisdiction, gambling is strictly controlled by statute. The extent to which gambling is allowed in each state varies widely. Some states actively welcome gambling as both a form of entertainment and an important source of state revenue; this includes not only the casino gambling of Nevada and New Jersey, but also the racetrack gambling and off-track betting allowed in many states, as well as the state-run lotteries prevalent in most states today. But even in states with liberal gambling policies, legal gambling is limited to that allowed by law and is strictly controlled. Whenever gambling that is not sanctioned by state law occurs, it is treated as any other illegal contract in most states, and the parties to illegal gambling agreements are not allowed to seek redress for breach of the gambling contracts in the courts. Thus, if Marty and Nate bet $500 on the outcome of the next Super Bowl game and the loser refuses to honor the illegal gambling agreement, the winner has no recourse in the courts.

Usurious Contracts

At common law, parties were free to enter into contracts for the borrowing and lending of money at any interest rate they freely agreed to pay. Today, the maximum rate of interest that can legally be charged for credit transactions is strictly regulated by law in most states. While the maximum rate allowed in states differs, most states impose a limit within the range of 10% and 21% per year on most in-state consumer credit transactions (rates that lenders can charge businesses are usually higher and often unregulated) as of this writing. If a credit agreement is entered into involving a rate of interest higher than the state law allows, the agreement is said to be usurious and void. A usurious contract is simply one that calls for the payment of a higher interest rate than the law allows.

Unlike most illegal contracts that the courts treat as void and completely unenforceable by the parties, agreements that involve usury are treated as enforceable in the majority of states, but the courts reform the contract by rewriting it to exclude the usurious rate of interest. In most states, courts reform usurious contracts by lowering the offending interest rate to fit within the legally allowed rate of interest in the state. Thus, if a state allows a maximum of 20% annual interest rate to be charged and a contract calls for a 30% rate of interest to be paid, the courts would enforce the contract by reforming it so that 20% interest is payable—the highest legal rate allowed in that state.

Usury law today is complicated because it is relatively easy for lenders to avoid state caps on interest by being chartered as a federal bank in a state that has no usury rate limit. Likewise, some lenders avoid state usury laws by affiliating themselves with native American tribes, which are not subject to state regulations (at least not for loans made in tribal lands; there is currently a split in the federal courts as to whether tribal-affiliated lenders who make loans outside of tribal lands are subject to state usury statutes).

Contracts Contrary to Public Policy

All courts have the right to hold contracts that are otherwise legal to be void and unenforceable if they violate the public policy of the state. Courts will refuse to enforce contracts that they deem harmful to the fabric of society or so unfair as to "shock the conscience of the court." The avoidance of contracts that a court finds offensive to public policy or unconscionable is within every court's equitable jurisdiction—the power of the court to award an extraordinary remedy when no just legal remedy exists.

There are no hard and fast rules as to what types of agreements the courts of any given state will find unconscionable or contrary to public policy. These determinations are made by judges on a case-by-case basis. As a general rule, however, courts are leery of exercising their equitable power to hold agreements to be unenforceable, as either unconscionable or void as against public policy, and exercise that power only in exceptional cases. That parties made a bad bargain or that some persons in society might deem an agreement objectionable are not grounds for declaring an otherwise valid agreement void. The types of agreements courts generally refuse to enforce as unconscionable involve shockingly unfair results for one of the parties or grossly unethical conduct as the subject matter of the agreement, as the following examples will illustrate.

- Jane, an expectant mother, agrees to turn over her baby at birth to the ABC Adoption Service in exchange for a fee of $50,000.
- Paul agrees to pay Paula $10,000 plus all medical expenses if she agrees to be artificially inseminated with his sperm and bear a child that she then will turn over to him for adoption.
- Tomás, a non-English-speaking resident alien, agrees to purchase a refrigerator from Enrique, who makes a sales presentation in Spanish and then asks Tomás to sign an agreement in English for the purchase of the refrigerator at $1,200 (including interest at the highest rate the law allows) for a refrigerator with a fair market value of $400.

The first two examples are typical of contracts void as against public policy, because they involve, essentially, thinly disguised baby selling agreements. The third example is typical of agreements that courts often find unconscionable. Note that the disparity in price and value in a contract of itself is not generally grounds for holding an agreement unconscionable; there must be additional factors that make the agreement shockingly unfair. In the last example, the fact that the sale was made in one language and the agreement signed in another, coupled with the disparity in the price paid for the appliance and its actual worth, is what would make it unconscionable in many courts.

Questions

1. What is the general effect of illegality on a contract?
2. What is the purpose of contracts in restraint of trade?
3. What is the legal effect of a contract in restraint of trade?
4. Were gambling contracts illegal at common law?
5. What determines the illegality or legality of a gambling contract today?
6. What is a usurious contract?
7. What is the effect of a usurious contract?
8. What are contracts contrary to public policy?

Hypothetical Cases

1. Carmen, Karen, and Xisco agree to pool their money to play their state's legal lottery every week. Each person agrees to pay $5 a week toward playing the same numbers that they each agree to for a whole year. Karen, who lives next to a lottery agent, agrees to play the numbers every week. After six months, one of the numbers picked by the group wins the lottery. Karen, who has been holding on to the tickets for the group, then refuses to share the proceeds with the ex-friends, who sue her for breach of contract. What result? Explain fully.
2. Frank asks Gina to place an illegal bet of $500 with her bookie on an upcoming baseball game, and promises to give her 10% of his winnings for her service if his team wins. Gina takes the money and makes the bet. Frank's team wins, but Gina's bookie, who has been arrested since she placed the bet with him, cannot be found to make payment on the bet. Frank, furious at the turn of events, sues Gina for $1,000 (the amount he would have recovered from her bookie); Gina, on the other hand, counterclaims for $100, the amount Frank had promised to pay her if he won. You are the judge. What result on both claims? Explain.
3. Wannabee Famous, a mediocre but aggressive figure skater, agrees to pay her bodyguard a salary of $100,000 per year in exchange for his services as

bodyguard, and his promise to assault all of her competitors a few days before major matches.

After a few matches, Wannabee decides that there's just too much competition and too little time, so she retires from skating and embarks on a new career as a lecturer on sports ethics and lands a book deal with a major publisher to write a book on *Making the Most of What Little Talent You Have*. Her bodyguard, furious at Wannabee's career change, sues for breach of contract. What result? Explain fully.

4. Desiree, a wealthy industrialist with failing eyesight and bad kidneys, enters into a contract with David wherein he agrees to sell one of his eyes and a kidney to her in exchange for a payment of $1,000,000 in cash plus all medical expenses. [The buying and selling of body parts is a crime under both federal and state law.] A week after the successful organ transplant, Desiree informs David that she's changed her mind about the agreed-upon payment because she could have gotten cheaper prices for the organs on the international organ black market and will only give him $25,000 and pay all medical expenses. David, furious, sues for breach of contract. You are the judge. What result? Explain fully.

Ethics and the Law: Questions for Further Study

As noted in this chapter, courts have the power under their equity jurisdiction to refuse enforcement of legal contracts that go against the public policy of the state. A problem when judges exercise this right is that they substitute their own sense of ethics (albeit acting for the common good) in place of the state legislature—the elected body entrusted with passing laws for the protection of the public safety and public morals—and the contracting parties themselves. It is legal to sell one's blood, whatever we may think of the practice. Why, then, should a person of sound mind not be able to sell a kidney that he does not need to live, or an eye for whatever price the market will bear? Why should a woman not be able to rent her womb for a price to incubate another woman's fertilized egg? Why not allow surrogate mothering agreements when all parties consent to the practice and no undue influence is exerted on the mother? In cases in which there is no direct effect to anyone outside of the contracting parties and the contracting parties freely agree to the terms of a contract, should such agreements be generally honored in the courts? Can you provide persuasive arguments against (or in support of) these "devil's advocate" statements?

Statute of Frauds

CHAPTER 15

Chapter Outline

Definition of a Signed Writing

Contracts That by Their Terms Cannot Be Performed within One Year

Contracts Transferring an Interest in Real Estate

Contracts for the Sale of Goods for $500 or More

Contracts Promising to Answer for the Debt of Another

Contracts of Executors and Administrators

Contracts in Consideration of Marriage

As we've previously seen, most contracts do not need to be expressed in a signed writing or follow any specific form to be enforceable. From early common law, an inherent problem with oral contracts has been their potential for fraud, as parties to oral contracts can easily lie in court about the specific terms of the agreement or about the existence of the agreement itself. Because of the potential for fraud inherent in oral contracts, the British Parliament enacted a statute in 1677 entitled an *Act for the Prevention of Frauds and Perjuries*. The statute required certain types of contracts to be evidenced by a signed writing to be enforceable, including transfers of interests in real estate, contracts of executors, leases of real estate for a term greater than three years, the creation of trusts, and contracts for the sale of goods with a value of £10 or greater, among others. An expanded modern version of this statute has been adopted by states in their own versions of the statute of frauds. Article 2 of the Uniform Commercial Code (UCC) also codifies a statute of frauds that applies to all contracts for the sale of goods with a value of $500 or more. Modern statutes of frauds require that certain types of contracts be evidenced by a signed writing by the party being charged with breach of contract before an action for breach of contract can be brought. Contracts that fall within a statute are unenforceable unless the party bringing the legal action can produce a writing that sets out the essential terms of the agreement. While the writing does not generally have to be very detailed, it must clearly show that a contract exists between the parties and the nature of the subject matter involved. Not every aspect of the contract needs to be covered by the writing. Under Article 2 of the Uniform Commercial Code, which covers sale of goods and has been adopted in all states except Louisiana,, for example, it is enough that a general description of the goods and their quantity are stated in the written and signed agreement. Once the contract is established, specific terms such as price or terms of delivery can be shown by oral testimony or through other written evidence. Statutes of frauds generally apply to executory contracts—contracts that have not yet been fully performed by the parties. Once parties fully perform as promised under an oral agreement, most contracts covered by the statute of frauds are deemed discharged by the performance, and the statute of frauds is inapplicable. Thus, if parties fully perform an oral contract that should have been evidenced by a signed writing, they can generally no longer raise the statute of frauds as a defense to the enforceability of the contract.

The statute of frauds in most jurisdictions today typically covers the following types of contracts:

- contracts that by their terms cannot be performed within one year;
- contracts for the transfer of an interest in real estate;
- contracts for the sale of goods worth $500 or more;
- contracts promising to answer for the debt of another;
- contracts of executors and administrators; and
- contracts in consideration of marriage.

Definition of a Signed Writing

For purposes of the statute of frauds, the requirements of both a writing and a signature are very broadly interpreted. As previously noted, the writing itself must merely evidence the existence of a contract in the broadest of terms. The writing can be made on paper or any other portable surface of any kind and with any type of equipment, including a typewriter, computer, pen, pencil, crayon, lipstick or, for that matter, by carving words on a piece of wood with a nail. Likewise, the requirement of a signature is broadly interpreted to mean any symbol or mark made by the contracting party intending it as her signature. Thus, a valid signature can be an X mark, the initials of the party, the party's typewritten name, and, of course, the party's name printed or signed by the party. In addition, a writing on a company's official letterhead, bill of sale, purchase order, or any other preprinted form is deemed to have been signed by that party if the writing is shown to be genuine and made by an employee of the company who is authorized to enter into a contract of the type involved on behalf of the company.

Keep in mind as you read the material in this chapter that it is possible for only one party to be bound by a signed writing. There is no requirement that the signatures of both parties appear in a writing in order for the contract to be enforceable—only that there be a signed writing by the party being sued. The importance of this distinction is illustrated in the next example:

- Zoreka and Betty discuss a large order for goods that Betty is considering buying from Zoreka's company. During the meeting, Betty borrows Zoreka's eyeliner and scribbles on a cocktail napkin "I agree to purchase 10,000 gizmos from Zoreka at $99.99 each for delivery June 8, 2017." She then initials the napkin and hands it over to Zoreka. If Betty fails to honor this agreement, her signed writing represented by the memorandum scribbled on the napkin will be enough to allow Zoreka to sue her. On the other hand, since Zoreka did not sign or initial the agreement, Betty will not be able to bind her to it if she refuses to perform as promised.

Contracts That by Their Terms Cannot Be Performed within One Year

If a contract by its terms cannot be performed within the space of one year, it must be evidenced by a signed writing to be enforceable. Common contracts that require more than one year to complete would include multiyear leases of real or personal property, employment contracts that run for more than one year, and construction contracts that by their terms cannot be completed in one year. If it is possible to fully perform a contract within a one-year term, no signed writing is required for it to be fully enforceable. Thus, a contract calling for the building of a bridge within the next 13 months need not be in writing, since it is possible for the builder to complete the project within a one-year term. Interestingly enough, the same holds true for a contract that is to run for a person's lifetime—since it is possible that the person may die within a year and thus fully discharge the contractual obligations. So a person's verbal agreement to work for an employer for his lifetime is perfectly valid, but an agreement to work for an employer for a two-year term must be evidenced by a signed writing to be enforceable, since by its terms it cannot be completed within 365 days.

Contracts Transferring an Interest in Real Estate

Contracts that transfer any interest in real property must be evidenced by a signed writing to be enforceable. As we will see in our coverage of real property law in Chapter 31, interests in real property include transfers of interests in real estate such as fee interests, life estates, and easements. Transfers of mere possessory or occupancy rights to real estate, such as leases and licenses, need not be evidenced by a signed writing, unless they run for a period longer than one year. The reason for this distinction is that leases and licenses do not give their holders a legal interest in real estate, but merely the right to occupy real estate.

Contracts for the Sale of Goods for $500 or More

As we will see in Chapter 19, goods can be defined as personal property that is tangible and movable. Nearly anything that can be owned other than real estate and intellectual property qualifies as goods. Books, electronic equipment, clothing, food, boats, cars, planes, pets, livestock, and other items with a physical existence that can be moved (or, to put it another way, that are not real estate or anything permanently attached to real estate) all constitute goods. Under UCC Section 2-201 (Statute of Frauds), whenever a contract for the sale of goods with a total price of $500 or more is entered into, it must be evidenced by a signed writing in order to be enforceable. For purposes of the statute, shipping costs or taxes paid in connection with the sale are not included in the price of the goods. On the other hand, the price of multiple goods purchased as part of a single transaction is added together to determine the price of the goods for purposes of the statute. Thus, an oral contract for a $300 television set and a $200 digital video recorder purchased at the same time is unenforceable because the total cost of the goods in the transaction is $500. But an oral contract for a $499.99 fax machine that costs $30 to ship and has $35 in sales taxes attached to it is perfectly binding, since neither sales taxes nor shipping costs are considered in the sale price.

Contracts Promising to Answer for the Debt of Another

A contract wherein the promisor agrees to answer for another's debt is unenforceable unless it is evidenced by a signed writing. This includes all surety, guarantee, and security interests given in consideration of a lender extending credit to any third party. It does not, however, include contracts entered into for another's benefit where the beneficiary of the contract is not the obligor. The following examples will illustrate:

- Gertrude agrees to guarantee payment on a loan by Dan to Carla. Gertrude cannot be bound to this guarantee unless Carla can produce a signed writing by Gertrude that shows the existence of the agreement.
- Bart purchases a computer printer for $400 from Sandra to give as a gift to Teresa. If this is an oral contract, it is fully enforceable against Bart by Sandra because it is not a contract to answer for the debt of another, but rather a gift purchased by Bart for Teresa's benefit. The obligor here is Bart, not Teresa, so no writing is required.

Contracts of Executors and Administrators

Executors of decedents' estates and administrators of incompetents' estates enter into contracts on behalf of the estates they serve on a regular basis. If they agree to be personally bound for contracts that benefit the estates, however, such an agreement must be evidenced by a signed writing before the promise is enforceable. Such contracts are, in effect, contracts promising to answer for the debt of another and are treated as such.

Contracts in Consideration of Marriage

The final type of contract required to be evidenced by a signed writing in order to be enforceable involves contracts wherein the consideration promised by one of the parties is marriage. This includes contracts made between prospective brides and grooms among themselves, as well as contracts between prospective brides and grooms and third parties. The most common type of agreement of this sort is a prenuptial agreement wherein the parties agree prior to their marriage how property will be distributed in the event that the marriage is subsequently dissolved. These agreements are generally legal, but they must be evidenced by a signed writing to be enforceable. These agreements are always subject to state law and may not apply to property acquired by the parties during the marriage in community property states, such as California, where such property generally belongs to both spouses subject to whatever exemptions are provided by the state (e.g., property inherited by the spouses during the marriage is typically exempt from joint ownership).

While contracts involving marriage as a consideration between prospective brides and grooms and third parties are not as common, these too are generally legal and enforceable provided they are evidenced by a signed writing. For example, prospective in-laws could offer to pay the bride and groom $1,000,000 if they marry and stay together for at least ten years; as long as the agreement is evidenced by a signed writing by the prospective in-laws, they would have to pay the agreed-upon consideration if the marriage lasts the agreed-upon term. On the other hand, an oral agreement to that effect would not generally be binding.

Questions

1. What types of contracts are covered under the statute of frauds?
2. Would a contract written and signed with a crayon on a brown paper bag satisfy the requirement of a writing?
3. What constitutes a signature for purposes of the statute?
4. Does a contract that is to run for a person's lifetime have to be evidenced by a signed writing? Explain.
5. Does a six-month lease need to be evidenced by a signed writing? Explain.
6. Does a contract for the purchase of a $450 digital camera and a $50 tripod have to be evidenced by a signed writing?
7. What types of contracts are considered contracts promising to answer for the debt of another?
8. Ben, a wealthy producer, and Brian, a poor, unemployed actor, enter into a written and signed prenuptial agreement that provides for Brian to receive only a $100,000 payment and no other support or distribution of property acquired during the marriage. Is this a valid contract? If Ben and Brian live in California, a community property state, and Ben earns $50,000,000 income and investments during the couple's marriage while Brian earns no income as a stay-at-home husband, will Brian be limited to the $100,000 provided for in the agreement? Explain.

Hypothetical Cases

1. Annette orally agrees to teach at State U for a two-year term. State U gives her a written memorandum of their agreement signed by the college president. The agreement states that Annette will be required to teach 12 credits per semester and be entitled to a salary of $70,000 per year. Annette is not asked to sign the agreement and does not do so. Six months into the contract, Annette receives a tenure-track offer from Private U at a higher salary and gives notice to State U that she will leave after completing the first year of her contract. Is Annette in breach of contract if she leaves after one year? If State U wished to fire Annette after one year because it found another better qualified instructor willing to teach the same courses for $50,000 per year, can it do so without being in breach of contract (assume that there is no collective bargaining agreement in place that would prevent the firing for purposes of this question)? Explain.
2. Henry orally promises to sell his house to Beanna for $225,000. On the day after the agreement is entered into, Bernard offers Henry $235,000 for the house, and Henry orally agrees to sell him the house. The next day, Tanya offers to rent the house from Henry for one year at $1,000 per month, and Henry orally agrees to the lease. If Beanna, Bernard, and Tanya sue Henry to enforce their respective agreements, what will a court decide? Contractual obligations aside, as among the three innocent parties, to whom does Henry owe the greater ethical duty to honor his agreement in your view? Why?
3. Miranda, the wealthy mother of Wendy, a spoiled brat, orally agrees to pay Harry Handsome, a movie star, $10,000,000 if he will marry her daughter. Harry agrees to the arrangement and marries Wendy. If Miranda then refuses to pay him the agreed-upon sum, can Harry sue for breach of contract? If Harry had scribbled on a note pad, "I hereby agree to marry Wendy in consideration of Miranda agreeing to pay me $10,000,000, Signed [Harry Handsome]," would your answer be the same? What if Miranda also initialed Harry's note? Explain.

4. Jerry, a young person with no previous credit history, asks his father to cosign a car loan. The father, who does not want to be bound by the agreement but wants the son to get the loan, illegibly scribbles his name on the loan application as guarantor, making sure that nobody will be able to read what the signature says. The loan is approved, and six months later, Jerry misses a few payments. The bank now wants to force Jerry's father to pay the loan on Jerry's behalf. He defends on grounds that his signature is illegible, does not look at all like his signature, and that he is therefore not liable as a guarantor. What result?

Assignment of Contracts and Third-Party Beneficiaries

CHAPTER 16

Chapter Outline

Assignment of Contract Rights

Novation

Rights of Third-Party Beneficiaries to Contracts

Although contracting parties usually perform their mutual obligations under contracts exactly as agreed upon, in some instances parties may wish to assign their rights under a contract to an outside party or may wish to have an outside party discharge their contractual obligations on their behalf. When all parties agree to such alterations in their original agreements, there is, of course, no problem. In this chapter, we will examine the rights of contracting parties to delegate their duties under contracts and to assign their contractual rights in the absence of consent between the parties. We will also explore the rights of individuals to enforce contracts that they have an interest in but to which they are not a party.

Assignment of Contract Rights

As we have seen previously, in every bilateral contract each party is obligated to render some type of performance in the form of whatever consideration is required under the contract, and is also entitled to receive whatever consideration the other party has promised as part of the contract. In other words, each party to a bilateral contract is an *obligor* (a person who is obligated to give the promised consideration) and an *obligee* (a person who is entitled to receive the consideration promised by the other contracting party). Consequently, each party to a bilateral contract has both certain rights as well as certain obligations that flow from the agreement.

Assignment of contract rights involves a party to a contract transferring whatever rights she has under a contract to one or more third parties. In general, contractual rights are freely assignable provided the following conditions are met:

- The rights to be assigned do not involve the performance of unique, nonstandardized personal services such as those rendered by physicians, attorneys, artists, and other professionals who exercise a high degree of personal judgment and discretion in rendering professional services for clients (standardized services, such as those performed by electricians, plumbers, or masons who must render performance in accordance with building codes are freely assignable);
- The assignment of contract rights does not place a significantly greater burden or risk on the obligor in rendering the promised performance;
- The contract itself does not prohibit assignment; and
- The assignment is not prohibited by law. (A common prohibition in many states, for example, prevents parties from assigning more than a set percentage of their wages, such as 25%, to third parties.)

When a permissible assignment of contract rights is involved, the consent of the obligor need not be obtained. Once the obligor is notified of the assignment of contract rights, he must perform whatever obligation he owed the *assignor* (the party who assigns contract rights) to the *assignee* (the party to whom the contract rights are assigned by the assignor).

Delegation of Contract Duties

Just as there are times when a party to a contract may wish to assign her contract rights, there are also times when parties may wish to delegate their contract duties. Delegation of duties involves an obligor obtaining a third party to perform his responsibilities under a contract in his stead. As is the case with assignment of contractual rights, delegation of contractual duties is generally allowed, provided that the following conditions are met:

- Unique, nonstandardized personal services such as those rendered by physicians, attorneys, artists, and other professionals who exercise a high degree of personal judgment and discretion in rendering professional services for clients cannot be delegated;
- The performance by the *delegatee* (the person to whom the obligor delegates his duties) is substantially the same as would have been given by the *delegator* (the party who delegates her duties to a delegatee);
- The contract does not prohibit delegation; and
- The delegation is not prohibited by law.

Rights and Responsibilities of Parties after Assignment or Delegation

After a valid assignment of contract rights by an assignor to an assignee, the assignee is entitled to performance by the obligor and can sue her directly if the obligation is not satisfactorily discharged. The assignee can also sue the assignor if the assignment was made to satisfy an obligation of the assignor to the assignee. The following example will illustrate:

- Alma owes Benedict $100. Benedict, in turn, owes Danielle $100. To extinguish his debt to Danielle, Benedict assigns his right to collect $100 from Alma to Danielle and notifies Alma of the assignment. Alma is now legally obligated to pay Danielle. In the event that Alma refuses to pay Danielle, Danielle has the right to sue either Alma or Benedict to collect the $100 owed her. If Alma only partially discharges her obligation by, say, paying Danielle only $90, Danielle can sue Alma for the remaining $10 or she can choose to sue Benedict for the remaining $10.

When a creditor agrees to pay back a loan over a long period of time, as is the case with a 30-year mortgage or federally guaranteed student loan that must be repaid over a period of 10 years, it is common for the debt to be assigned multiple times as the underlying note is discounted and sold from one creditor to another over the course of the payback period. When such a transfer occurs, the new assignee is entitled to receive payment for the remaining term of the loan after giving the debtor notice of the assignment. The terms of the loan, however, cannot change, so the debtor is entitled to continue to make payments under the same conditions of the original loan agreement. The payment amount, term of the loan, interest, and due date will remain the same. All that will change is the obligation of the debtor to send payment to the assignee.

When a valid delegation of duties is involved, the same rules apply: the *delegator* (the person who delegates contractual duties to a third party) remains obligated to the *obligee* (the person entitled to receive the benefit of the obligor's performance) until the *delegatee* (the person who performs the duties owed by the delegator) fully performs. If the delegatee does not perform at all, or renders an unacceptable performance of the delegator's contractual obligation, the obligee can sue either the delegator or the delegatee, at his option, as the following example illustrates:

- Ed, a general contractor, agrees to build a house for Frank for $200,000. Ed hires Gertrude as his painting contractor. If Gertrude does a poor job of painting the house, Frank can sue either Ed, the delegator of the duty to paint the house, or Gertrude, the delegatee of that duty. Ed's duty to Frank is discharged only after Gertrude completes the task of painting the house in an acceptable manner.

In the preceding example, if Gertrude does not paint the house or paints it in a way that is unacceptable under the contract (for example, if she paints the house the wrong color, paints the exterior of the house with an interior grade paint, or otherwise renders performance that falls short of acceptable performance under the contract), Frank can sue either Gertrude or Ed for damages, or he may sue them both. If he sues both, he can collect his entire damages from either party, or partial damages from each. If he sues and recovers damages from Ed, Ed would be able to recover from Gertrude any damages he had to pay due to her failure to perform—assuming, of course, that Gertrude is solvent.

Novation

When contracts cannot be assigned or delegated because of a contractual provision prohibiting assignment or delegation, or because the contract is of a type that is not assignable or delegable, the parties may still agree to substituted performance through what is called a *novation* (the substituting of one contract for another). When a novation is involved, both contracting parties agree that their original contract will be canceled and replaced by a new agreement that will substitute a new party for one of the original contracting parties. The following example will clarify the distinction between an assignment or delegation and a novation:

- Lina, a lawyer, agrees to represent Albert, an accused arsonist, in a criminal trial. This is a type of contract that is not delegable by Lina or assignable by Albert since it involves the unique, nonstandardized professional services of an attorney. Nevertheless, if Lina is unable to meet her obligation to defend Albert because of other commitments, she can, with Albert's consent, appoint her friend Luis to take over the case. If Lina and Albert both freely agree to the arrangement, then Lina's contract with Albert will be canceled and replaced with a new contract between Luis and Albert. The crucial distinction between assignment or delegation and novation is that novation can never be accomplished unless both contracting parties freely agree to it. If Albert demands that Lina defend him herself, the novation will not take place, and Lina will be liable for breach of contract to Albert if she fails to defend him due to other commitments. Lina could offer Albert some form of compensation as an inducement to agree to the novation. But additional consideration is not required for a novation to take place as the agreement by the parties to cancel and replace their original agreement contains legally sufficient consideration.

When a valid novation takes effect, the original contract between the parties is discharged and so are the duties of the original obligor, who is not liable for any breach of contract by the third party who takes over his obligations under the new contract.

Rights of Third-Party Beneficiaries to Contracts

It is not uncommon for persons who are not parties to a contract to have an interest in its performance. When a third party is intended to benefit from a contract to which she is not a party, the third party is termed an *intended beneficiary* of the contract. The typical example of an intended beneficiary is a beneficiary in a life insurance policy. When a third-party beneficiary is not intended by the parties to a contract to benefit from the contract, the third party is termed an *incidental beneficiary*. Examples of incidental beneficiaries are the employees of a contracting party; they may have a great personal stake in the contracts that the employer enters into, since their livelihood depends on them, but they are not directly intended to benefit from such contracts by the contracting parties.

The distinction between incidental and intended beneficiaries is of crucial importance because only intended beneficiaries can bring suit to enforce contracts to which they are not a party. The following example will illustrate:

- Ingrid takes out an insurance policy on her life with XYC Insurance Company and names her mother, Barb, as beneficiary. When Ingrid dies, XYZ refuses to pay the claim on grounds that Ingrid had not paid the last premium on time. Barb, as the intended beneficiary of this contract, can sue XYZ directly for breach of contract (assuming, of course, that the premiums had been paid and the policy was in force at the time of Ingrid's death).

- Caren, a primary building contractor, agrees to build a home for Harry for $250,000. After entering into the agreement, Harry changes his mind and decides to postpone the project for a year due to a downturn in the economy. Caren is willing to delay the project, but Eddy, an electrical contractor to whom Caren regularly subcontracts the electrical work on her building projects, is not as understanding as Caren and would like to sue Harry for breach of contract since he turned down some smaller projects in expectation of doing the electrical work on Harry's new home. Eddy has no standing to sue since he is not a party to the contract between Caren and Harry and is only an incidental beneficiary of that contract.

Questions

1. What is the difference between an assignment and a delegation?
2. What is an obligor?
3. What is an obligee?
4. How many obligors and obligees are there in every bilateral contract involving two parties?
5. What is an assignor?
6. What is an assignee?
7. Can contract rights be assigned by an assignor without the obligor's permission? If so, under what circumstances?
8. May contract duties be delegated under a contract without the obligee's permission? If so, under what circumstances?
9. Does an obligor who delegates her contractual duties to a third party remain liable to the obligee if the third party does not perform in accordance with the contract? Explain.
10. When may third-party beneficiaries sue to enforce a contract to which they are not a party but under which they stand to benefit?

Hypothetical Cases

1. Paul, a plumber, owes Olga $500 for a used laptop computer he purchased from her recently but has not yet paid for. Hanna owes Paul $500 for a new shower stall that Paul installed in her house. If Paul tells Hanna to send a check for $500 to Olga rather than to him to pay for the plumbing work, must Hanna honor the request? Explain.
2. Paul, a plumber, agrees to install a shower stall in Harry's home for a fee of $500. After entering into the contract, Paul subcontracts the work to Pauline, a licensed plumber who agrees to do the work for Paul for $400. When Harry learns of the delegation of contract duties by Paul, he is furious and wants to invalidate the contract. What result? If Harry accepts performance by Pauline but is unsatisfied by the work she performed, who can he sue for damages?
3. High Flying Industries, an airplane manufacturing company, enters into a contract with Western Airlines, a large carrier, for 40 new Super Duper Humongous Jets. After entering into the contract, but before accepting delivery of the planes, Western Airlines experiences financial difficulties and a protracted labor dispute that threaten to bankrupt the airline. In light of its financial difficulties, Western Air asks High

Flying Industries to postpone the plane deliveries until next year. Although unhappy about the arrangement, High Flying Industries agrees to the change because it wants Western Airlines to stay in business, and believes that it can turn its troubles around within a year if it is not forced to accept the delivery of the planes now. Several of High Flying Industries' subcontractors are not so understanding, however; if the contract is postponed, some may go out of business or at the very least have to lay off large numbers of employees, since their business is dependent on High Flying Industries' contracts for new planes. Several of these subcontractors band together and sue Western Airlines for breach of contract. What result?

4. Angela, an attorney, agrees to draft a will for Larry in exchange for a fee of $500. Before she has an opportunity to draft the will, she is retained by Killer Kong as a defense attorney in a multiple murder case that has gained national attention. Preparing Killer's defense will take all of Angela's resources and time over the next several months, so she would like to delegate all of her other business to Lenny, a friend and fellow legal practitioner in the same area. Can she delegate the preparation of Larry's will to Lenny without Larry's consent? Explain. Assuming that delegation is not possible, how can Angela still validly have Lenny prepare the will?

Ethics and the Law: Questions for Further Study

As we've seen in this chapter, in some instances delegation of duties can take place without the consent of the obligee. The law assumes that certain types of standardized services are identical, regardless of who performs them; the rationale is that plumbers, electricians, masons, roofers, carpenters, and other skilled workers who perform services according to some standard code or architectural plans all perform substantially identical work. Anyone who has hired any of these skilled professionals will quickly attest that there is a wide range of difference in acceptable performance among skilled professionals, and a wide range of pride in workmanship and professionalism among them as well. It is arguable that a fairly standard legal service such as the preparation of a will or the drafting of a power of attorney is in fact much more standardized than the wiring or framing of a house in terms of the uniformity of result that can be expected in these areas, given equally well-trained professionals. When you further consider that much of the routine work performed by lawyers is delegated to paraprofessionals such as paralegals, legal secretaries, and others who work under the direct supervision of the attorney, the distinction between standardized and nonstandardized professional services seems to blur even further. Do you believe this distinction, segregated largely between tasks performed by blue-collar and white-collar professionals, is justified? How can you protect yourself from an unwanted delegation or assignment of a contract to which you are a party?

Performance and Breach

CHAPTER 17

The vast majority of contracts end when all parties satisfactorily discharge their obligations. But in the performance of contracts, as in nearly all human endeavors, problems do crop up from time to time that result in a failure by one or both contracting parties to perform as promised. At times, such failure to perform is justified, and at others it is not. In this chapter, we will examine the various ways in which a contract can be discharged, as well as the consequences that result from the unexcused failure to render the performance promised in a valid contract.

Chapter Outline

Discharge through Performance
Discharge through Substantial Performance
Discharge through Impossibility of Performance
Discharge through Commercial Impracticability of Performance
Discharge through Frustration of Purpose
Discharge through Release
Discharge through Novation
Breach of Contract

Discharge through Performance

As previously noted, in the vast majority of cases contracting parties perform as promised. Once each party renders the agreed-upon consideration, the contract is deemed to be discharged through performance. A contract is discharged through performance when contracting parties have fully performed as promised. For a contract to be discharged through performance, there must be no substantial deviation from the performance promised to that which was actually rendered, and the performance must have been rendered on a timely basis. Nonconforming performance (performance that is materially different from what was promised under the contract) or conforming performance that is not rendered on a timely basis constitutes a breach of contract and will subject the breaching party to liability under the contract.

Discharge through Substantial Performance

If the obligor's performance fails to conform to the requirements of the contract in some minor way that does not impair the overall value of the contract for the obligee, the contract will be discharged, and the obligee will be required to pay the agreed-upon consideration minus the cost of curing the defect. For substantial performance to occur, the obligor's failure to perform must not be willful, and the deviation from the promised performance must be minor. The following example will illustrate:

- Bart Builder agrees to build Harriet Homeowner a new house to be completed one year from the date the contract is signed. On the date that the house must be completed under the terms of the agreement, Bart has not received a decorative custom-built stained glass window that is to be installed over the front door because the manufacturer went out of business a week before the delivery of the window was to be made. If Bart's performance otherwise conforms to the requirements of the contract, he will be entitled to payment from Harriet, but Harriet is entitled to offset the cost of installing the missing window from the contract price.

Discharge through Impossibility of Performance

At times parties who make a good-faith attempt at discharging their contractual obligations are unable to do so due to circumstances beyond their control. In such cases, the contract is deemed to be discharged by impossibility of performance, and the performance of all contracting parties is excused. For a contract to be discharged due to impossibility of performance, three criteria must be met: (1) the circumstances that make performance impossible must be beyond the control of the parties, (2) the circumstances must have been unforeseeable at the time that the parties entered into the contract, and (3) the parties must be objectively unable to perform. Common examples of circumstances that cause a contract to be discharged by impossibility of performance include the following:

- the destruction of the subject matter of the contract through circumstances outside the control of the parties;
- changes in the law that make performance illegal when such performance was legal at the time that the parties originally entered into the contract; and
- breaking out of hostilities between the countries of the contracting parties.

Parties whose contracts are discharged through impossibility of performance may not sue one another for breach of contract since the failure to perform is excused. If the external conditions that prevent the performance are of a temporary nature, then the duty to perform is merely suspended and the contract is not discharged. Likewise, if the external circumstances only partially impair the ability of one of the parties to perform, the parties will be obligated to offer whatever performance they can under the circumstances, and their duties under the contract will be discharged when they have done so. The following examples should help to clarify the applicable rules:

- Albert contracts with Betty to import 1,000 widgets a month for the next year. A month after entering into the agreement, Congress passes a law restricting imports from Betty's country to a maximum of 500 widgets per month for any U.S. importer. Albert's obligation under the contract will be discharged if he purchases the 500 widgets the law allows from Betty.
- Albert contracts with Betty to import 1,000 widgets a month for the next year. A month later Congress passes a law outlawing the importation of widgets. Albert's contract with Betty is fully discharged through impossibility of performance. (The subsequent illegality of the transaction makes it impossible to perform the terms of the contract.)
- Albert contracts with Betty to import 1,000 widgets a month for the next year. A month later, Congress passes a law placing a three-month moratorium on the importation of widgets. Albert is excused from performance for a three-month period due to impossibility of performance but must resume the monthly purchases once the moratorium is lifted for the remaining term of the contract.

Discharge through Commercial Impracticability of Performance

In some instances unforeseen changes in circumstances between the time that a contract is entered into and the time when performance is due make the contract possible to perform, but so difficult or costly as to be impracticable. At such times, performance may be excused. For a contract to be discharged through commercial impracticability, the party seeking to have the contract discharged needs to show that (1) the condition that arose after the contract was entered into was unforeseeable by the parties at the time of entering into the contract, and (2) the expense or problems incident to performance are so great as to make performance unreasonable. The mere fact that performance is more costly than anticipated by the parties will not cause a contract to be discharged if the increased cost was foreseeable at the time of entering into the contract. Whether or not performance in a given circumstance is commercially impracticable is a question of fact for the trier of fact to decide; it should be clear, however, that the costlier and the more difficult performance is, the more likely a jury is to find it commercially impracticable.

Commercial impracticability is recognized by Article 2 of the Uniform Commercial Code (UCC) with regard to transactions for the sale of goods. When contracts for other than the sale of goods are involved, only some states recognize commercial impracticability as a valid defense to a breach of contract action. Even in states that recognize impracticability of performance not involving the sale of goods, labor strikes and reasonable increases in the cost of goods or materials needed to perform the contract, while perhaps unexpected by the parties, are always deemed to be foreseeable. Thus, a party that is unable to perform because it suffers a labor strike by its employees is generally found to be in breach of contract.

Discharge through Frustration of Purpose

It is possible for conditions to change so drastically from the time that a contract is entered into until the time that performance is due that it becomes unreasonable to force the parties to go through with their agreement in light of the changed circumstances. When that happens, the contract is deemed discharged through frustration of purpose. For frustration of purpose to be relied on as the basis of discharging a contract, the party seeking to have the contract discharged needs to show that (1) a basic assumption made by the parties to the contract has been affected through no fault of the parties, and (2) there is no useful purpose to be served by allowing the contract to continue. A typical example of frustration of purpose would be a homeowner who contracts to have an attached garage built on his land, only to have the house struck by lightning and burned to the ground before the garage is built. While the contractor may be willing and able to perform, a court would be unlikely to allow the contractor to perform over the homeowner's objections since a basic assumption both parties made in entering into the contract—that there would be a house on which to attach the garage—is no longer true. If the court feels that allowing the contract to be performed under the circumstances is wasteful, it may declare the contract discharged and excuse all performance by the parties involved.

Discharge through Release

A release is a contract not to sue that parties can enter into so that they can discharge their contractual or tort obligations with one another. As with any contract, a release must generally be supported by new consideration. With regard to both tort and contract liability, the consideration given in exchange for the release can be anything of legal value, including a release by one party given in exchange for a release from the other. Thus, two persons who are involved in a minor automobile accident and do not wish to involve their insurance companies to avoid the premium rate increases that would ensue can exchange signed releases of liability with one another; both releases in that case are supported by consideration—a promise by each party not to bring a legal action against the other. The same is true for a release that relates to a contractual obligation. After a valid contract is entered into but before the parties have performed their obligations, either party can obtain from the other a signed release that excuses them from performance. If both parties want to get out of the contract, mutual releases can be executed, and they will be deemed to be supported by consideration, since both parties will give up their right to enforce the contract as consideration for the release from the other contracting party.

Discharge through Novation

As noted in the preceding chapter, novation is the substituting of one contract for another. When a novation is involved, both contracting parties agree that their original contract will be canceled and replaced by a new agreement that substitutes a third party for one of the original contracting parties. Once a valid novation of an existing contract is accomplished, the original contract is discharged, and the responsibilities of the parties under that agreement end.

Breach of Contract

The failure of any party to a binding contract to discharge their contractual obligations, either through rendering the promised performance or through the other means of obtaining a valid discharge of contract discussed in this chapter, constitutes a breach of contract. A party who suffers a breach of contract is entitled to sue for money damages or other remedies as will be discussed in the following chapter. A breach of contract can result from either a failure to perform the agreed-upon duties under a contract, or by the rendering of unacceptable, substandard performance in attempting to perform the duties under a contract. Thus, failing to perform at all or rendering significantly imperfect performance can constitute a breach of contract. The nature and extent of the breach, as we will see in the next chapter, will affect the damages the nonbreaching party is entitled to recover from the breaching party, as well as the specific remedies from which such a party may be able to choose.

Questions

1. How is a contract discharged though performance?
2. What is nonconforming performance?
3. What is discharge through impossibility of performance?
4. What are the requirements for impossibility of performance?
5. When can commercial impracticability be used to discharge a contract?
6. What will the party seeking to have a contract discharged by reason of commercial impracticability need to show?
7. What is a party required to show for a contract to be discharged for frustration of purpose?
8. What is a release?
9. How is a contract discharged through a novation?
10. What is a breach of contract?

Hypothetical Cases

1. Balthazar enters into a contract with Hunter wherein he agrees to build a garage within 60 days for $10,000. After entering into the contract, it dawns on Balthazar that he lacks the necessary skills to perform the agreed-upon task and institutes an action to have the contract invalidated for impossibility of performance, claiming it is impossible for him to perform as agreed. What result?
2. In the last example, assume that Balthazar performs as promised but takes 90 days to complete the job instead of the 60 agreed upon due to a labor strike by his workers. What result? What if Balthazar's lateness in completing the job were caused by an unforeseen flash flood that makes it impossible to work for 30 days?
3. Arsenio, an artist, agrees to paint a portrait of Jenny for $1,000. After entering into the contract but before either party has performed, Jenny is dismissed from her job and would like to cancel a contract that is now for her an unaffordable luxury.
   A. If Arsenio refuses to cancel the contract, can Jenny claim her impossibility to pay as circumstances that will discharge the contract?
   B. If Arsenio agrees to let Jenny off the hook, how should the parties go about discharging the contract?
   C. If both parties verbally agree not to sue one another, is there any real reason for executing a formal release?
4. In the last example, if Jenny still wants her portrait painted but Arsenio would like to get out of the contract without being in breach, what are his options for doing so?

Remedies

CHAPTER 18

When a contract is breached, the law provides the nonbreaching parties with a number of remedies to compensate them for any loss they suffer as a result of the breach. Available remedies can be classified into two distinct categories: legal remedies and equitable remedies. Legal remedies are available as a matter of right to parties who suffer a breach of contract as soon as they establish the breach. To be awarded a legal remedy, nonbreaching parties need only establish by a preponderance of the evidence that they suffered a breach and the extent of the damages they suffered as a direct consequence of the breach. Equitable remedies, on the other hand, are not available as a matter of right, but rather may be awarded at the sole discretion of a judge whenever the available legal remedies are insufficient to properly compensate nonbreaching parties for their loss. In this chapter, we will examine some common legal and equitable remedies available to parties who suffer a breach of contract.

Chapter Outline

Legal Remedies
Equitable Remedies
Election of Remedies
Mitigation of Damages

Legal Remedies

Parties who suffer a breach of contract may be entitled to legal remedies to compensate them for their loss. These include compensatory damages, nominal damages and, where appropriate and agreed to by the parties, liquidated damages.

Compensatory Damages

The basic purpose of compensatory damages is to place the nonbreaching party in the same position she would have been in had the breach not occurred. In other words, compensatory damages seek to offset the loss suffered by the nonbreaching party by a monetary award that will indemnify the party for her loss. Compensatory damages are available in four basic forms: loss of the bargain, cost of completion, incidental damages, and consequential damages.

Loss of the Bargain: Parties who suffer a breach of contract can recover their loss of the bargain damages. This remedy represents the difference between what the nonbreaching party was entitled to receive under the contract and what he actually received, minus any savings the innocent party realized because of the breach. To put it another way, loss of the bargain entails the difference between what the party was entitled to receive under the contract and what he actually got, less any cost saved by the innocent party in not having to perform its part of the contract. The following examples will illustrate:

- Samantha agrees to sell Carlos her 2003 Corvette with 100,000 miles for $8,000. After entering into the contract, Samantha is offered $12,000 for the car from a third party, Tom, and sells Tom the car. Samantha is in breach of the contract with Carlos, and Carlos is entitled to his loss of the bargain damages. In this case, assuming that the market price of the car in its current condition is $12,000, then Carlos's damages would be the difference between what he was entitled to receive (a car worth $12,000) minus what he would have paid for it ($8,000), or $4,000 in damages. ($12,000 − $8,000 = $4,000).

- Cathy, a computer retailer in California, agrees to ship 10 Dell desktop computers to Bob for his consulting business in Florida at $1,200 each delivered, for a total of $12,000. Before Cathy ships the computers, Bob informs her that he will not accept them because he has found a cheaper supplier. If Cathy pays $1,050 for each computer wholesale and if it would have cost $50 each to ship these from California to Florida, Cathy is entitled to compensatory damages representing her lost profits in the deal minus any cost savings in not having to perform the contract. In this case, she would have made $150 profit on each computer but would have spent $50 to ship each system. Consequently, she is entitled to damages of $150 × 10 (the profit she has lost) minus $50 × 10 (the shipping cost she has saved), or a total of $1,000 ($1,500 in lost profit offset by the $500 saved in shipping costs).

Cost of Curing the Defective Performance: Where the performance of one party is incomplete or nonconforming, the nonbreaching party may seek compensation for the reasonable cost of curing the defect in the tendered performance by having the performance completed by a third party. The following example will illustrate:

- Patrick agrees to paint Hugo's garage for $350. After Patrick paints 99% of the garage and only the trim around the garage doors and windows remains to be done, he falls ill and is unable to complete the job. Since the job was substantially completed, Hugo will have to pay the agreed-upon price but is entitled to compensation for the reasonable cost of curing the defective performance, which in this case would be the cost of having another house painter complete the trim work on his garage. If Hugo furnishes the court with estimates of $100 from local painters to finish the trim work, Patrick would be entitled to payment of $250 for his work (the contract price minus the reasonable cost of completing his performance).

Incidental Damages: Foreseeable damages that flow directly from a breach of contract are termed incidental damages and are recoverable by the nonbreaching party. The following example will illustrate:

- Frank orders 50 bushels of apples from Maria to sell on his fruit stand. Maria mistakenly ships 50 bushels of pears. Since the fruit sent is not the same as that ordered, Maria is in breach of contract for failure to ship conforming goods. Frank is entitled to the loss of bargain damages. He can also recover any incidental expenses that flow directly from the breach, such as the cost of shipping the goods back to Maria and the cost of storing the goods while awaiting instructions from Maria as to how to ship them back.

Consequential Damages: Damages that are not caused directly by a breach but result as a direct, foreseeable consequence of the breach are termed consequential damages. Typical consequential damages include lost profits and personal injury or property damage flowing as a direct consequence of the breach. The following example will illustrate:

- Tai orders 200 pounds of soybean burgers to sell in his Veggie Burger establishment from XYZ Foods. XYZ mistakenly ships 200 pounds of all-beef hamburger patties. As a result of the mix-up, Tai has to close his restaurant for a day until he can procure the needed ingredients for his veggie burgers from another source. In addition to his loss of the bargain damages and the incidental damages of storing and shipping back the nonconforming goods, Tai can sue XYZ Foods for the foreseeable consequential damages of his lost profits for the day he had to close his business, a consequence that flowed directly from the breach.

Foreseeability of the damages at the time that the parties entered into the contract is a prerequisite to consequential damages being awardable. In addition to showing that the consequential damages were foreseeable by the breaching party at the time of entering into the contract, the party asking for consequential damages must be able to prove those damages with a high degree of certainty; courts will normally refuse to award damages that are speculative in nature. In the preceding example, Tai could prove his lost profits by showing the profits made by the business over the past several weeks on the same day of the week that it had to be closed as a result of the breach. Thus, assuming that the business had to be closed on Monday, Tai could prove his lost profits by relying on the average lost profits he'd made on the Monday preceding and the Monday following the day of the business closure or in some similar objective manner (such as the average profits for his business on Mondays over the last quarter).

Nominal Damages

Whenever a contract is breached that does not cause any real loss to the nonbreaching party, a court can award nominal damages. As the name implies, nominal damages are damages in name only, usually $1.00 or $0.05. It is a way for courts to acknowledge that a legal wrong has been done to one of the parties, but that the party has suffered no real injury. Parties do not ask for nominal damages; they are awarded by a court when a breach of contract is proven but the plaintiff cannot prove any actual damages as a result of the breach.

Liquidated Damages

In cases in which it is expected that actual damages will be difficult to assess as the result of a breach, parties often agree ahead of time to a liquidated damages provision in the contract that states what damages will be payable by each party in the event of a breach. Generally speaking, parties to a contract may agree to liquidated damages as long as they are reasonable. If the liquidated damages are set at a high value so as to discourage parties from breaching a contract, courts will determine the damages to be intended as a penalty and universally refuse to enforce them. For liquidated damages to be enforceable, they must be reasonable and related to the actual loss anticipated by one or both parties in the event that the contract is breached.

Equitable Remedies

On some occasions none of the available legal remedies will properly compensate a party for the loss occasioned by a breach of contract. In those rare instances, courts have the power to grant extraordinary remedies based on a court's inherent power to award equitable relief when the available legal remedies will not serve the ends of justice. Among a court's equity powers is the ability to award the remedies of specific performance, injunction, and quasi contract. We'll examine each of these in turn.

Specific Performance

Specific performance is an order by a court requiring that the breaching party perform the contract as agreed. Although courts do not generally force parties to honor their contractual obligations, they will do so when the subject matter of the agreement is unique and money damages would not properly compensate aggrieved parties for their loss. The types of contracts for which courts often award specific performance include the sale of real estate, antiques, art, and similar unique subject matter.

It is solely within the discretion of a court whether to allow specific performance; in general, judges are wary of awarding this remedy, preferring to award monetary damages whenever that is a viable remedy. Specific performance is not available as a remedy in cases involving ordinary goods or in personal service contracts.

Injunction

A second equitable remedy within the discretion of the courts is the power to grant injunctive relief. An injunction is a court order that prohibits specific action. In breach of contract cases, injunctive relief can be granted to prevent the sale or removal from the state of unique goods or the transfer of real estate pending the resolution of the breach of contract action. Thus, if a party is seeking specific performance of a sales contract for, say, a rare painting, a court would be asked to issue an injunction preventing the defendant in that action from moving, selling, or otherwise disposing of the painting pending the outcome of the case.

Quasi Contract

Quasi contract is essentially a legal fiction that courts engage in so as to hold parties liable for nonexistent contracts to prevent the unjust enrichment by one party at the expense of the other. Typical examples where quasi contract could be invoked involve gross unfairness or a miscarriage of justice, as the following examples illustrate:

- Belinda, while shopping at Marty's Market, gives Marty a $100 bill in payment for a pack of gum, thinking it a $1 bill. Marty gives her two quarters and, while he is reaching for the remaining $99 change in bills, Belinda turns around and walks away. Even though there is clearly no contractual duty here from Marty to return the excess $99 to Belinda, who has walked away without waiting for the rest of her change, courts would generally impose such a duty on him under a quasi contract theory to avoid his unjust enrichment at Belinda's expense due to her mistake.

- Anne, Stephanie's aunt, promises Stephanie that she will pay for Stephanie to attend any university in the world when she graduates high school in six months. Stephanie, who has always enjoyed a good relationship with her wealthy aunt, promptly applies to several universities and turns down employment offers she had been contemplating. She enrolls at a pricey Ivy League university and agrees to attend in the fall. When Stephanie receives her bill for tuition, housing, and related fees and forwards it to her aunt, Anne informs her that she has changed her mind and is no longer willing to pay for Stephanie's tuition. Under the circumstances, a great injustice would be done to Stephanie if Anne is allowed to renege on her promise, and most courts would hold Anne to her promise under quasi contract despite the fact that it is unsupported by consideration and, therefore, not a valid contract.

Before courts will impose quasi contract to bind a promisor to a promise that is not supported by consideration, the promisee will need to show that he (1) justifiably relied on the promise, (2) changed his condition in reliance on the promise, (3) suffered some loss as a result, and (4) that an injustice would result if the promisor is not made to honor the promise. In the preceding example, Stephanie meets each of the requirements for quasi contract since she justifiably relied on her aunt's promise in thinking that a wealthy aunt with whom she had a good relationship would be willing to pay for her education, changed her condition (turned down the employment offers and enrolled in an expensive university in reliance on her aunt's promise), suffered a loss (has to pay tuition, fees, and housing expenses), and it would be unjust to leave her no recourse under the circumstances. It should be noted, though, that courts will not necessarily enforce the entire promise—only enough of it to prevent an injustice from being done. Thus, in this example, a court may not order the aunt to pay for room, board, and tuition for all four years of college. However, it would likely order the aunt to bear the cost of at least one full year of tuition, room, and board and related expenses—long enough to allow the niece to transfer to another school or to look for another job back home if she is unable or unwilling to remain at the school at her own expense.

Election of Remedies

Since the basic purpose of awarding remedies for breach of contract is to place the parties in the same position they would have been in had the breach not occurred (or, to put it another way, to compensate parties for their loss), parties are not allowed to have duplicate recoveries, and punitive damages (awards intended to punish defendants for their actions) are not awardable in actions for breach of contract. In a suit involving breach of contract, plaintiffs must elect the remedies they believe themselves to be entitled to and prove their damages to the court (with the exception of nominal damages, which a court will award on its own when appropriate). If a plaintiff wants specific performance but asks only for compensatory damages, he'll be out of luck. Likewise, if a plaintiff is entitled to loss of the bargain damages as well as incidental and consequential damages, she must specifically ask for each remedy; otherwise, it will not generally be awarded.

Some of the available remedies are mutually exclusive: a person who wishes to sue for money damages for loss of the bargain cannot also receive specific performance, for obvious reasons. Likewise, a person who sues to recover liquidated damages under a valid liquidated damages provision in a contract cannot also recover other compensatory damages. What damages to ask for is usually an important question of strategy for attorneys, who must decide which of the available remedies are available to their clients and then select the most advantageous from the ones available. They usually can ask for mutually exclusive remedies in the alternative; this is especially useful when the most beneficial remedy is an equitable one that a court may or may not award at its discretion. Thus, a person who wishes specific performance of a contract can ask for that as the primary remedy and for compensatory damages in the alternative (e.g., in case the court refuses to honor the request for the equitable remedy of choice).

Mitigation of Damages

In most instances, parties who sue for breach of contract are held to have an affirmative duty to mitigate their damages; this means that contracting parties must take any steps reasonably necessary to lessen the breaching party's damages when a contract breach occurs. The Uniform Commercial Code (UCC) specifically imposes the duty to mitigate damages in cases dealing with the sale of goods. If parties do not attempt in good faith to lessen their damages when a breach occurs, most courts will refuse to compensate nonbreaching parties for the extent of the damages they suffered but could have avoided through a reasonable effort at mitigating or lessening the damages. For instance, a tenant who breaches an apartment lease by leaving six months before it expires is liable to the landlord for the remaining six months' rent. But courts in most states impose on landlords the duty to mitigate the tenant's damages by making a good-faith effort to rerent the apartment to new tenants. If the landlord makes no such effort and a court finds that the apartment would have been rented in 30 days if a good-faith effort were expended by the landlord, then the landlord will be able to collect rent only for the 30-day period that the apartment was likely to remain empty had he attempted to mitigate the tenant's damages. In addition, he will be barred from collecting rent for the months when the apartment would have been rented had he exerted a good-faith effort to find new tenants by advertising and showing the rental apartment to prospective tenants or by hiring a realtor. Note too that if the landlord advertises the apartment or hires a realtor at her expense to show the apartment, these reasonable expenses are chargeable to the tenant who breached the lease. These expenses are in addition to the rent for time that the apartment remains unoccupied despite the landlord's reasonable efforts to rerent it.

Questions

1. What are four basic legal remedies available to parties who suffer a breach of contract?
2. What are three basic equitable remedies available to parties who suffer a breach of contract?
3. How are loss of the bargain damages computed?
4. What is meant by the cost of curing the defective performance?
5. What are incidental damages?
6. What are consequential damages?
7. What are nominal damages?

8. What are liquidated damages, and when may they be used?
9. What is specific performance, and when is specific performance awardable as a remedy?
10. What is an injunction, and when is it likely to be awarded in a contract action as a remedy?
11. What is quasi contract?

Hypothetical Cases

1. Silvia agrees to sell her 2012 Ford Taurus to Earl for $7,500 in a signed writing. At the time that the parties enter into the contract, the market value of the car is $8,500. When Earl presents a check to Silvia for the agreed-upon price, she informs him that she has changed her mind and will be selling the car to Tina for $8,500. Earl is furious at Silvia's breach and sues her for breach of contract. In his suit, he asks for injunctive relief preventing Silvia from transferring the car to Tina while the suit is pending, as well as specific performance of the contract and, in the alternative, compensatory damages of $1,000. You are the judge. Decide the case and rule on what damages are awardable.

2. Sanford agrees to sell his mint-condition 1954 Ford Thunderbird to Gina for $20,000. After entering into a valid written agreement for the sale of the car, Sanford has a change of heart and refuses to part with the automobile. Gina sues. What remedies can she reasonably ask for?

3. In preparation for the grand opening of his new business, Dan's Diet Delights, Dan orders 1,000 pounds of assorted dietetic sweets. Two days before his scheduled grand opening, his supplier ships 1,000 pounds of rich, high-calorie sweets by mistake. As a result, Dan has to postpone his grand opening for a week (until the right goods arrive) and, in addition, has to spend $500 for new advertising and posters with the new grand opening day. He also has to pay one week's salary to two sales employees, who have nothing to do in that time since the goods for the store have not arrived, for a total of $800. In addition, he spends $100 to ship the goods back to the supplier at the nonconforming supplier's suggestion. After the right goods finally arrive, he sues the supplier. What damages can he ask for, and what damages is he likely to receive?

4. Manny agreed to work as the manager of Patricia's Pet Store for three years in exchange for compensation of $40,000 per year and a percentage of the profits. After the first year of the three-year contract, Manny informed Patricia that he would not complete the remaining two-year term because he had found a more lucrative job elsewhere. Patricia immediately began interviewing for Manny's replacement and spent approximately $1,000 in search-related expenses before she found a suitable manager for her store willing to take the job for the same compensation as Manny. If she decides to sue Manny for breach of the employment contract, what, if any, damages will she recover? Would your answer be the same if she found someone to take Manny's job for $35,000 per year and the same percentage of the profits as Manny had received? What if no qualified person can be found to do the same job for under $42,000 with the same profit sharing arrangement as Manny had in his contract? Explain fully.

Ethics and the Law: Questions for Further Study

It is an unfortunate fact of life that many legal wrongs go unremedied. Most textbooks on law, including this one, focus on the legal rights and duties of citizens in their dealings with one another without paying much attention to real-world realities. As a practical matter, however unpleasant and unsung, a sizable percentage of judgments that parties obtain from courts after prevailing in contract or tort actions never get collected. The fact that a court awards damages does not guarantee that defendants will ultimately pay them. And while judgment holders have a number of recourses available to them for collecting outstanding judgments, including attaching the real and personal property of judgment debtors and garnishing wages, for example, collecting through these and other legal means can take time and money, such as the fees charged by attorneys, collection agencies, private investigators, and forensic accountants to trace debtor's assets and their attempts to hide or fraudulently transfer assets to avoid paying outstanding judgments. As is often the case, many who habitually violate the law are quite adept at avoiding its consequences. At common law in England, debtors' prison was available as a last resort to punish those who would not pay their debts, including the discharging of outstanding judgments. Even today, in many countries around the world, debtors can be jailed for failing to pay their bills or for ignoring civil judgments. While indiscriminately jailing debtors would have unacceptable social consequences and certainly have a disproportionate impact on the poor, it is equally true that there is no incentive now for persons who are judgment-proof (e.g., the indigent, persons on public assistance, and those who derive their income from the underground economy without traceable income or assets) to act in a responsible manner, since there are no real consequences for their refusal to honor financial obligations or judgments. How do you feel about this issue? What recommendations would you make to achieve a fair balance between protecting the truly needy from creditors' predatory practices and preventing abuses of the system by those with significant resources who refuse with impunity to honor their obligations?

Unit II—Cases for Further Study

DOUGLASS V. PFLUEGER HAWAII, INC
Supreme Court of Hawaii
110 Haw. 520 (Haw. 2006)

This appeal concerns the sole question whether plaintiff-appellant Adrian D. Douglass, a minor at the time he was hired by defendant-appellee Pflueger Hawai`i, Inc. dba Pflueger Acura (Pflueger), is contractually bound by an arbitration provision set forth in Pflueger's Employee Handbook. Douglass appeals the December 30, 2003 order of the Circuit Court of the First Circuit, the Honorable Victoria S. Marks presiding, granting Pflueger's motion to stay action and to compel arbitration of the claims asserted by Douglass in his complaint.

I. Background

On or about November 29, 2001, Douglass was injured on the job when a coworker sprayed him on the buttocks area with an air hose. Subsequently, on May 2, 2002, Douglass filed a complaint with the Hawai`i Civil Rights Commission (HCRC). In response to his request to withdraw his HCRC complaint and pursue the matter in court, the HCRC, on September 25, 2002, issued a right-to-sue letter to Douglass, pursuant to HRS § 368-12 (1993). Thereafter, on December 17, 2002, Douglass filed an action against Pflueger in the circuit court. The complaint essentially asserted that: (1) Douglass was sexually assaulted in an attack in which his supervisor at Pflueger's car lot "took an air hose, held it against and/or in close proximity to his buttocks, and unleashed a blast of compressed air"; (2) Douglass' anus, rectum and colon were instantaneously penetrated, inflated, and dilated by the force of the blast; (3) Douglass was treated at the Emergency Department of the Kapiolani Medical Center for Women and Children; and (4) he was admitted to the hospital overnight for further observation and treatment. In his complaint, Douglass alleged five employment law claims: (1) Hostile, Intimidating and/or Offensive Working Environment; (2) Unsafe Working Environment; (3) Sexual Assault and Sexual Discrimination; (4) Negligent Training (of its Supervisor); and (5) Negligent Supervision.

III. Discussion

A. The Infancy Doctrine

Hawai`i has long recognized the common law rule—referred to as "the infancy doctrine" or "the infancy law doctrine"—that contracts entered into by minors are voidable. *See, e.g., Jellings v. Pioneer Mill Co.,* 30 Haw. 184 (1927); *Zen v. Koon Chan,* 27 Haw. 369 (1923); *McCandless v. Lansing,* 19 Haw. 474 (1909). Under this doctrine, a minor may, upon reaching the age of majority, choose either to ratify or avoid contractual obligations entered into during his or her minority. *See* 4 Richard A. Lord, *Williston on Contracts* § 8:14 (4th ed. 1992); *see also* Restatement (Second) of Contracts, §§ 7, 12, and 14 (1979); 7 Joseph M. Perillo, *Corbin on Contracts* § 27.4 (2002 ed.). Traditionally, the reasoning behind the infancy doctrine was based on the well-established common law principles that the law should protect children from the detrimental consequences of their youthful and improvident acts. As the California Court of Appeals explained in *Michaelis v. Schori,* 20 Cal.App.4th 133, 24 Cal.Rptr.2d 380 (1993):

> The rule has traditionally been that the law shields minors from their lack of judgment and experience and under certain conditions vests in them the right to disaffirm their contracts. Although in many instances such disaffirmance may be a hardship upon those who deal with an infant, the right to avoid his contracts is conferred by law upon a minor for his protection against his own improvidence and the designs of others. *It is the policy of the law to protect a minor against himself and his indiscretions and immaturity as well as against the machinations of other people and to discourage adults from contracting with an infant. Any loss occasioned by the disaffirmance of a minor's contract might have been avoided by declining to enter into the contract.*
>
> *Id.* at 381; *see also Dodson v. Shrader,* 824 S.W.2d 545,547 (Tenn. 1992) ("[T]he underlying purpose of the infancy doctrine . . . is to protect minors from their

lack of judgment and from squandering their wealth through improvident contracts with crafty adults who would take advantage of them in the marketplace." [citation omitted]).

The rule that a minor's contracts are voidable, however, is not absolute. An exception to the rule is that a minor may not avoid a contract for goods or services necessary for his health and sustenance. *See* 5 Richard A. Lord, *Williston on Contracts* § 9:18 (4th ed. 1993); *see also Creech v. Melnik,* 147 N.C.App. 471, 556 S.E.2d 587, 590-91 (2001); *Garay v. Overholtzer,* 332 Md. 339, 631 A.2d 429, 443-45 (1993). Such contracts are binding, even if entered into during minority, and a minor, upon reaching majority, may not, as a matter of law, disaffirm them. *See Muller v. CES Credit Union,* 161 Ohio App.3d 771, 832 N.E.2d 80, 85 n. 4 (2005) (stating that contracts for the purchase of necessities, which "are food, medicine, clothes, shelter or personal services usually considered reasonably essential for the preservation and enjoyment of life[,]" are valid exceptions to the general rule) (citation and internal quotation marks omitted); *see also Yale Diagnostic Radiology v. Estate of Harun Found.,* 267 Conn. 351, 838 A.2d 179, 182 (2004). As the Maryland Court of Appeals summarized in *Schmidt v. Prince George's Hospital,* 366 Md. 535, 784 A.2d 1112 (Ct.App. 2001):

> *By the common law, persons, under the age of twenty-one years, are not bound by their contracts, except for necessaries, nor can they do any act, to the injury of their property, which they may not avoid, when arrived at full age. ...*
>
> *They are allowed to contract for their benefit with power in most cases, to recede from their contract when it may prove prejudicial to them, but in their contract for necessaries, such as board, apparel, medical aid, teaching and instruction, and other necessaries, they are absolutely bound, and may be sued and charged in execution; but it must appear that the things were absolutely necessary, and suitable to their circumstances, and whoever trusts them does so at his peril, or as it is said, deals with them at arms' length.*
>
> *Their power, thus[,] to contract for necessaries, is for their benefit, because the procurement of these things is essential to their existence, and if they were not permitted so to bind themselves they might suffer.* [citation omitted].

It is apparent that the Hawai'i Legislature has, through the enactment of several statutory provisions codified the principle that contracts relating to medical care, hospital care, and drug or alcohol abuse treatment are contracts for "necessaries" (*i.e.,* medical aid). These statutes explicitly provide that minors who enter into contracts for the medical services described therein cannot later disaffirm them by reason of their minority status.

Inasmuch as none of the parties to this appeal contend that Douglass' employment was "a necessary," it would appear that under the well-recognized infancy doctrine, Douglass would be entitled to disaffirm his employment contract, including the purported arbitration agreement. However, a review of Hawaii's child labor law—specifically HRS § 390-2 (1993 Supp. 2005)—evinces the legislature's intent to incorporate the rationale underlying the common law infancy doctrine—that is, to protect children from the detrimental consequences of their youthful and improvident acts—into the statutory scheme and impose upon the Department of Labor and Industrial Relations (DLIR) the responsibility of promulgating rules and regulations to effectuate such intent.

Prior to 1969, *all* minors seeking employment were required to obtain a certificate of employment, which, as previously noted, requires the signature of a parent or guardian of the minor, as well as information from the employer as to, *inter alia,* the hours of work and the nature of the employment. [But] ... since 1969, sixteen- and seventeen-year-olds are no longer required to secure parental consent, and the DLIR does not require any information from the employer; sixteen- and seventeen-year-olds are merely required to present his or her certificate of age to a prospective employer, which the minor obtains from the DLIR after producing an acceptable proof of age document.

With respect to contracts of employment, it is apparent that, by relaxing the requirements for sixteen- and seventeen-year-olds to obtain employment, the legislature clearly viewed minors in this particular age group—being only one to two years from adulthood—as capable and competent to contract for gainful employment and, therefore, should be bound by the terms of such contracts. Similarly, inasmuch as the parent or guardian of a minor under sixteen is required to sign the application for a certificate of employment, which contains specific information regarding the nature and conditions of that employment, before entering into an employment contract, any such contract is equally binding on said minor. However, consistent with the policy of protecting minors until they attain the age of majority, the legislature provided an additional safeguard by authorizing the DLIR to "suspend, revoke or invalidate" any certificate of employment or age previously issued if the minor's employment is later found to be detrimental to the minor. *See* HRS § 390-4 [citation omitted]. Thus, based on the foregoing reasoning, we conclude that, inasmuch as the protections of the infancy doctrine have been incorporated into the statutory scheme of Hawaii's child labor law, the general rule that contracts entered into by minors are voidable is not applicable in the employment context.

In applying the foregoing discussion to the circumstances of the instant case, we recognize that the record does not indicate whether Douglass had, in fact, obtained an age certificate prior to his employment with Pflueger. However, even if he did not, Douglass should, nevertheless, be bound by the terms of his employment contract with Pflueger. First, there is nothing in the statutory scheme of the child labor law that renders Douglass' employment invalid or illegal based on his failure to obtain an age certificate. Second, it is undisputed that Douglass was, at the time he was hired, a seventeen-year-old high school graduate, who was only four months away from majority. And, third, there is nothing in the record to suggest that "the nature or condition of [Douglass'] employment [as a lot technician was] such as to injuriously affect [his] health, safety or well-being . . . or contribute towards [his] delinquency" so as to trigger the suspension, revocation, or invalidation authority bestowed upon the DLIR director pursuant to HRS § 390-4. In other words, whether Douglass did or did not obtain an age certificate is irrelevant; it does not change the fact that Hawaii's child labor law provides for the protections of the infancy doctrine and renders inapplicable the general rule that contracts entered into by minors are voidable in the employment context. To conclude otherwise would be inconsistent with the clear legislative policy that sixteen- and seventeen-year-old minors do not, in accordance with the common law infancy doctrine, have an absolute right to disaffirm their employment contracts.

Accordingly, we hold that the circuit court properly rejected Douglass' argument that he is entitled to disaffirm his employment contract, including the arbitration provision, by reason of his minority status. *Mossman v. Hawaiian Trust Co., Ltd.*, 45 Haw. 1, 15-16, 361 P.2d 374, 382 (1961) (agreeing with determination of the trial court, but for different reason); *see also Ko`olau Agric. Co., Ltd. v. Comm'n on Water Res. Mgmt.*, 83 Hawai`i 484, 493, 927 P.2d 1367, 1376 (1996) (same).

Optional Assignments

1. Brief the preceding abbreviated version of the case in a one-page, single-spaced brief (with double spaces between paragraphs) that contains the following four sections: (1) The basic facts of the case [Facts]; (2) The legal issue the court is being asked to decide [Issue]; (3) The holding of the court (how it decides the legal issue before it) [Holding]; and (4) The rationale the court uses to support its decision [Rationale]. If your instructor asks you to brief the case, she will give you additional instructions.

2. In the omitted portion of the case, the court examines the validity of the arbitration clause in the employment contract and concludes that the clause is valid. Because it treats the employment contract containing the clause as a "necessary" that precludes the minor from disaffirming the contract, the court goes on to order that the case must be decided by arbitration and dismisses the appellant minor's appeal. Do you think this is a just decision? Explain.

IN THE COURT OF APPEALS OF OHIO
SECOND APPELLATE DISTRICT CLARK COUNTY
Ayres v. Burnett
2014 Ohio 4404
[2014]

FAIN, J.,

Plaintiffs-appellants Diana and Richard Ayres appeal from a judgment of the Clark County Court of Common Pleas rendered upon their complaint against defendants-appellees Diana and David Burnett. They contend that the trial court erred by considering parol evidence of modification of the lease agreement between the parties. Alternatively, they contend that there was no consideration for any modification.

We conclude that the trial court erred to the extent that it considered evidence of conversations extrinsic to the lease before February 2004, because that evidence is barred by the parol evidence rule. We further conclude that the evidence of conversations concerning the modification made in February 2004 is not barred by the parol evidence rule. We conclude that the trial court erred in finding that there was evidence of consideration for modification as of that date. Finally, we conclude that there is competent, credible evidence upon which the trial court could rely in finding that in August 2006, the parties orally agreed to modify the monthly rent under the lease agreement as of August 2006, and that the modification of the rent amount was supported by sufficient consideration.

Accordingly, the judgment of the trial court is Reversed, and this cause is Remanded for further proceedings.

V. The Lease

The Ayreses are the owners of a commercial building at 89 East Clark Street, North Hampton, Ohio. On October 2, 2002, they executed an "Offer to Lease" with the Burnetts, which provided for monthly rent in the amount of $1,950. The Burnetts opened a day-care business in the property in July 2003. A lease was executed between the parties on October 13, 2003. The lease had an effective period from July 2003 through June 30, 2006. The lease contained the provision for monthly rent as the Offer to Lease—$1,950. No rent payments were made until February 2004, when the Burnetts began paying $1,500 per month. On September 1, 2006, the Burnetts began paying $1,650 per month for rent, until April 2007, when they vacated the premises.

The Ayreses brought this action against the Burnetts for unpaid rent, as well as damages to the building. At trial, Mr. Burnett testified that Mr. Ayres agreed to accept the sum of $1,500 as full rent. He further testified that the parties agreed to the sum of $1,650 beginning September 2006. Mr. Burnett testified that Ayres gave them receipts for the monthly payments and never indicated that there was an underpayment.

Mrs. Burnett testified that Mr. Ayres approached her about using his building for a daycare business. She testified that Mr. Ayres prepared a business plan for her, but did not include an amount for rent. According to Mrs. Burnett, Mr. Ayres told her that the rent would "probably [be] between $800 or $900." Tr. p. 316-317. The business opened in July 2003. She testified that Mr. Ayres told her that she and her husband should get the business going and they would discuss the rent payments later. Ayres did not contact her again until October 2003, when he brought the written lease agreement to them for signature. Mrs. Burnett testified that she told Mr. Ayres that the rent payment set forth in the lease agreement was not the amount agreed upon; he told her not to worry about it, that he had already had his attorney prepare the lease and they would "take care of it in a few months and see what the rent would be."

Mrs. Burnett testified that she next discussed the matter with Ayres in early February 2004, when he came to the daycare to discuss the rent. She testified that he asked her how much she could pay, and she told him that she could afford to pay $1,500 per month. Mrs. Burnett testified that Mr. Ayres agreed to that amount. She also testified that he agreed to accept their business tax refund as payment for past rent. She testified that she personally gave him a check for $8,500, which he accepted for the past rent. Mrs. Burnett testified that in August 2006, when the lease term expired, Mr. Ayres told her that he wanted the sum of $2,200 as rent. She testified that they agreed to the sum of $1,650, which she and her husband paid through March 2007. They vacated the premises in April 2007.

Mr. Ayres, who is an accountant, testified that the building had previously been used for a daycare business and that he marketed it to the Burnetts for that use. He testified that he never agreed to a reduction in rent. He testified that he accepted the $1,500, and later the $1,650 in rental payments from the Burnetts, but that the "balance was never forgiven. It was deferred." He testified that the receipts he gave the Burnetts did not indicate any balance due in the section used for showing deficiencies, and that he did not present them with an invoice for the balance. He further testified that he did not take any steps to evict or to sue the Burnetts during the time they occupied the premises. He filed suit in August 2008.

II. The Course of Proceedings

Following trial, the magistrate found that the parties had modified the terms of the lease. The magistrate's decision stated, in pertinent part, as follows:

> *The [Ayreses] and the [Burnetts] entered into an Offer to Lease dated June 26, 2002 and a lease agreement for the lease of 89 East Clark Street, North Hampton, Ohio on or about October 13, 2003. The lease, by its terms, was to have commenced on July 1, 2003 and was to end on June 30, 2006. The [Burnetts] possessed the option to renew the lease for an additional three years providing certain conditions were met. The option to renew the lease for an additional three years was to have been memorialized by a writing and, in the absence thereof, the tenant was to be considered as holding over and a tenant at will. The Court finds that the [Burnetts] continued to occupy the leased premises into April, 2007 with the agreement of the [Ayreses] but that they were tenants at will.*
>
> *The Court finds that, based on their course of dealing as evidenced by the testimony and exhibits, the [parties] agreed that the rent for the premises, after June 30, 2006 was to be $1,650.00 per month which the [Burnetts] paid through March, 2007. Prior to that date, the parties, by their course of dealing, as evidenced by the testimony and exhibits, had agreed this rent would be reduced to $1,500 per month. The consideration for such amendments was the continued occupancy of [the Burnetts] on [the Ayreses] premises. The [Burnetts] vacated the premises in April, 2007 but agreed to pay*

the [Ayreses] April rent but failed to do so. The Court, therefore, finds that the [Ayreses are] due that rent as well as the ten percent (10%) penalty provided for under the lease for a total of $1,715.00.

The Court further finds that, as to [the Ayreses'] claim for rent due from the inception of the lease until the termination of the initial three-year term, that the parties subsequently modified the lease terms to provide for a lesser amount of monthly rent than that originally provided for and the parties' course of conduct over the three years of the original term was probative of their modification. Accordingly, the Court finds in favor of the [Burnetts] upon the claim of the [Ayreses] for unpaid rent during the [Burnett's] occupancy of the premises during the initial three-year term [citation omitted].

The Ayreses filed objections to the magistrate's decision, which the trial court overruled. From the judgment rendered by the trial court, the Ayreses appeal.

III. [Held:] The Trial Court Erred by Considering Parol Evidence of a Modification of the Lease Agreement Before August, 2006

Agreements Unsupported by Consideration

The Ayreses contend that evidence of any modification of the rental amount set forth in the lease is barred by the parol evidence rule. Alternatively, they contend that any finding of modification is improper, because no consideration was given for a reduction in the amount of rent.

"As a rule of substantive law, the parol evidence rule provides that extrinsic evidence is not admissible to contradict or vary the terms of an unambiguous contract." Mangano v. Dawson, 7th Dist. Columbiana No. 93-C-72, (June 13, 1995). "The rule results from the presumption that the intent of the parties to a contract resides in the language they choose to employ in the agreement." Id. "The rule 'operates to prevent a party from introducing extrinsic evidence of negotiations that occurred before or while the agreement was being reduced to its final written form [.]' " Bellman v. Am. Internatl. Group, 113 Ohio St.3d 323. "The parol evidence rule does not apply to evidence of subsequent modifications of a written agreement or to waiver of an agreement's terms by language or conduct." Star Leasing Co. v. G & S Metal Consultants, Inc., 10th Dist. Franklin No. 08AP-713 [citation omitted].

In this case, the lease did not contain a clause prohibiting oral modification of the lease. There is evidence that the parties engaged in general discussions, prior to, and contemporaneous with, the signing of the lease, to the effect that the monthly rent would be less than $1,000. This evidence is barred by the parol evidence rule. However, we conclude that there was competent, credible evidence upon which the magistrate could rely in finding that the parties engaged in conversations in February 2004, after the execution of the lease, that could serve to modify the amount of rent subsequent to the execution of the lease. The parol evidence rule is inapplicable to those discussions.

We must determine whether there was any consideration to support an oral modification of rent as a result of the discussions in February 2004. "Leases are contracts and are subject to traditional rules of contract interpretation." EAC Properties, LLC v. Brightwell, 10th Dist. Franklin No. 10AP-853. "A tenancy is possession or occupancy of land by right or title, especially under a lease, which is a contract by which an owner or rightful possessor of real property conveys the right to use and occupy the property in exchange for consideration, usually rent." Kanistros v. Holeman, 2d Dist. Montgomery No. 20528 [citation omitted].

"Oral modification of a written contract must be supported by new and distinct consideration." Coldwell Banker Residential Real Estate Services v. Sophista Homes, Inc., 2d Dist. Montgomery No. 13191 (Oct. 26, 1992). "It is elementary that neither the promise to do a thing, nor the actual doing of it will constitute a sufficient consideration to support a contract if it is merely a thing which the party is already bound to do, either by law or a subsisting contract with the other party." Id. quoting Rhoades v. Rhoades, 40 Ohio App. 2d 559 (1st Dist. 1974). "The pre-existing duty rule prohibits one from being forced to modify a contract whereby one is already bound to perform without adding some additional consideration." O'Brien v. Production Engineering Sales Co., 2d Dist. Montgomery No. 10417 [citation omitted] (Jan. 8, 1988). "The burden of proving consideration is on the party who seeks to prove modification." Coldwell Banker, supra. The existence of consideration is a question of fact. Id. In a civil case, "[j]udgments supported by some competent, credible evidence going to all the essential elements of the case will not be reversed by a reviewing court as being against the manifest weight of the evidence." C.E. Morris Co. v. Foley Constr. Co., 54 Ohio St.2d 279 (1978).

In this case, the Burnetts were already bound by the lease to rent the premises for a term of three years at the rate of $1,950 per month. The mere fact that the Burnetts promised to pay, and did pay, a lesser sum than they were required to pay does not constitute consideration sufficient to create a new contract. Lawhorn v. Lawhorn, 2d Dist. Montgomery No. 11914 [citation omitted] (Sept. 7 1990). "[A] mere agreement by the lessor to accept less rental than that provided in the lease, is without consideration and, therefore, not binding." Adams Recreation Palace, Inc. v. Griffith, 58 Ohio App. 216 (2d Dist. 1937). However, as of August 2006, the initial three-year lease term had expired, and the Burnetts became tenants at will, holding over under the lease. As stated above, there is evidence that the parties orally agreed, in August, that the rental amount would be $1,650. The trial court was free to credit the Burnetts' testimony over that of Mr. Ayres regarding the modification. We do not find the Burnetts' testimony unworthy of belief. This modification was supported by sufficient consideration, in that the Burnetts continued in possession of the premises, enabling the Ayreses to continue to earn income, after the expiration of the original lease term. Thus, we conclude, based upon the facts found by the trial court, that from August 2006 until the parties vacated the premises, the agreed-upon monthly rent was $1,650, which the Burnetts paid.

We conclude that the trial court erred to the extent that it permitted the use of parol evidence to support a finding of modification prior to the February 2004 conversations between Mr. Ayres and the Burnetts. Thus, the finding of modification prior to that date was improper. Furthermore, there was no consideration for a modification before the expiration of the lease term in 2006. We conclude that there was evidence of conversations suggesting a modification as of February 2004; however, again the record does not demonstrate consideration sufficient to support an agreement to modify. We conclude that the trial court's finding of modification was, therefore, error with regard to the period from February 2004 until August 2006. The trial court did not err in finding consideration sufficient to support the claimed modification for the period from August 2006, during the holdover period until the premises were vacated.

The trial court's decision with regard to modification prior to August 2006 is not supported by the record. The decision finding both modification with sufficient consideration following August 2006 is supported by the evidence. Thus, the sole assignment of error is sustained in part and overruled in part.

I. Conclusion

The sole assignment of error being sustained in part and overruled in part, the judgment of the trial court is Reversed, and this cause is Remanded for further proceedings consistent with this opinion.

Optional Assignments

1. Brief the preceding abbreviated version of the case in a one-page, single-spaced brief (with double spaces between paragraphs) that contains the following four sections: (1) The basic facts of the case [Facts]; 2. The legal issue the court is being asked to decide [Issue]; (3) The holding of the court (how it decides the legal issue before it) [Holding]; and (4) The rationale the court uses to support its decision [Rationale]. If your instructor asks you to brief the case, he will give you additional instructions.
2. It is a well-established principle of law that modifications to a contract made without additional consideration to support them are invalid because they run afoul of the pre-existing duty rule. One cannot renegotiate a contract that has one of the parties give more or less consideration than they originally promised unless some additional consideration is given to that party to justify the change. Nevertheless, the Article 2 of the Uniform Commercial Code (UCC) changed the common law rule that still generally applies to other contracts and permits good faith modifications to sales contracts agreed to by the parties to be effective even without additional consideration being given. Which do you think is the better rule? Why?

SALES, LEASES, COMMERCIAL PAPER, AND SECURED TRANSACTIONS UNDER THE UNIFORM COMMERCIAL CODE

UNIT 3

Lukas Gojda/Shutterstock

Introduction to the Uniform Commercial Code

The Uniform Commercial Code (UCC) was drafted in 1949 by the National Conference of Commissioners on Uniform State Laws (NCCUSL), an organization composed of preeminent legal experts from throughout the country, in an effort to unify laws affecting business throughout the U.S. By 1967, the UCC was adopted with only minor changes by the legislatures of all the states, with the exception of Louisiana, which has not adopted Articles 2 or 2A. (Louisiana's law is still heavily influenced by the French civil law, and as such, Louisiana law tends to differ in significant ways from that of the other 49 states.) Since 1949, the NCCUSL has offered amendments from time to time, most recently in 1993 when the NCCUSL amended the UCC to reflect the realities of electronic commerce, but it will be some time before a majority of the states adopts the new amendments. More recent amendments to Article 2 proposed in 2001 and 2003 failed to gain support in any state and were withdrawn. No proposed amendments are available as of this writing.

Because the UCC effectively unifies the law in key areas in all states, it is a statute of paramount importance to business. Thus, the UCC affords to companies that conduct business in more than one state the uniformity and predictability that is essential to commerce.

In this unit, we will examine salient provisions of key articles of the UCC: Article 2 (Sales), Article 2A (Leases), Article 3 (Commercial Paper), and Article 9 (Secured Transactions).

CHAPTER 19
Introduction to UCC Article 2 (Sales) and Article 2A (Leases)

CHAPTER 20
Rights and Duties of Parties in the Performance and Breach of Sales and Lease Contracts

CHAPTER 21
Warranties

CHAPTER 22
Remedies for Breach of Sales and Lease Contracts

CHAPTER 23
Introduction to UCC Article 3 (Commercial Paper)

CHAPTER 24
Transfer and Negotiation of Commercial Paper and Rights of Holders

CHAPTER 25
Liability of Parties to Commercial Paper and Warranties of Transfer and of Presentment

CHAPTER 26
Introduction to UCC Article 9 (Secured Transactions)

Introduction to UCC Article 2 (Sales) and Article 2A (Leases)

CHAPTER 19

Chapter Outline

Applicability of Article 2

Applicability of Article 2A

Formal Requirements and Rules of Construction

Statute of Frauds [§ 2-201(1), § 2A-201(1)]

Parol Evidence Rule [§ 2-202, § 2A-202]

Inapplicability of Seals [§ 2-203, § 2A-203]

Contract Formation

Contracts for International Sale of Goods

Article 2 of the UCC concerns itself with contracts for the sale of goods, and Article 2A covers contracts for leases involving goods. In general, the UCC codifies the common law of contracts and makes some significant changes whenever contracts involve the sale or lease of goods.

It is crucial to emphasize from the outset that Article 2 and 2A apply only to contracts involving the sale or lease of goods. As we will see in this chapter, goods can be defined as tangible, movable personal property. Contracts for other than goods (e.g., service contracts, contracts involving interests in real estate, and contracts involving intangible personal property, such as stocks, bonds, patents, and copyrights) are not covered by the changes to the common law of contracts provided by Article 2. Likewise, Article 2A does not apply to consumer or commercial leases of real estate.

In this chapter, we will examine the most significant changes to the law of contracts made by UCC Articles 2 and 2A. As you read the material that follows, keep in mind that what you learned about contract law in Chapters 9–18 is still applicable when sales contracts are involved unless the law has been modified by Articles 2 or 2A. For the most part, this chapter will focus on highlighting the most significant changes to the common law of contracts made by UCC with regard to contracts for the sale or lease of goods. As you read the material in this chapter, it will help to understand the changes if you keep in mind two basic principles applicable to the UCC: (1) a major purpose of the UCC is to simplify the law and make it easier for parties to enter into binding contracts; and (2) the UCC will often hold merchants to a higher standard than nonmerchants. Section 2-104 (1) of the UCC defines a merchant as follows:

> "Merchant" means a person who deals in goods of the kind or otherwise by his occupation holds himself out as having knowledge or skill peculiar to the practices or goods involved in the transaction or to whom such knowledge or skill may be attributed by his employment of an agent or broker or other intermediary who by his occupation holds himself out as having such knowledge or skill.

Thus, a merchant is one who either (1) deals in goods of the type involved in the contract in question, or (2) has specific expertise in the types of goods involved either through specialized personal knowledge or through the hiring of persons to act on her behalf that have such knowledge.

Applicability of Article 2

Under Section 2-105 (1), goods are defined as including "all things (including specially manufactured goods) which are movable at the time of identification to the contract for sale . . . [and] the unborn young of animals and growing crops. . . ." Furthermore, under Section 2-107 (1), goods also includes contracts for the sale of minerals, oil, and gas if these are severed (removed) from the realty by the seller; when these items are to be severed from the land by the buyer, the contract is not considered one for the sale of goods and is therefore not covered by Article 2.

Applicability of Article 2A

Article 2A covers contracts for the lease of goods [§ 2A-102] as well as contracts for subleasing goods [§ 2A-103 (1) (k)].

Formal Requirements and Rules of Construction

The UCC makes some changes to the common law of contracts with regards to the enforceability of oral contracts and specifies to what extent written agreements may be contradicted by extraneous evidence.

Statute of Frauds [§ 2-201(1), § 2A-201(1)]

A contract involving the sale of goods with a price of $500 or more or a lease involving payment of $1,000 or more must be evidenced by a signed writing by the party being charged with a breach if it is to be enforceable. Despite the general rule that a signed writing is required to enforce contracts for the sale of goods with a price of $500 or more, the UCC relaxes the statute of frauds by three important exceptions to its application as follows:

- Section 2-201 (2) states that when both parties are merchants, a signed writing in confirmation of the contract by one of the parties will bind both parties unless it is objected to in writing within ten days of receipt by the receiving merchant;
- Section 2-201 (3) and Section 2A-201 (4) (a) further state that if goods are to be specially manufactured for the buyer by the seller or lessor and are not resalable by the seller or suitable for lease or sale by the lessor in the regular course of business, the seller or lessor can bind the buyer or lessee of the specially manufactured goods even without a signed writing by the buyer or lessee once the seller or lessor has made "either a substantial beginning of their manufacture or commitments for their procurement";
- Section 2-201 (4) (a) and Section 2A-201 (4) (b) additionally state that oral contracts involving the sale of goods with a value of $500 or more and contracts for the lease of goods requiring payment of $1,000 or more are enforceable against a buyer, seller, lessee, or lessor who admits that an oral contract existed during testimony in open court or in pleadings. Under this exception, however, the contract is enforceable only for the quantity of goods actually admitted to in the pleadings or in the party's testimony; and
- Section 2-201 (4) (b) states that the statute of frauds cannot be used as a defense to the enforcement of an oral contract to the extent that goods under the contract have been accepted and paid for. In other words, Section 2-201 can be used only to prevent the enforcement of executory oral contracts, but not contracts that have been fully executed and discharged through performance.

Parol Evidence Rule [§ 2-202, § 2A-202]

The UCC states that when parties have executed a signed writing relating to a contract for the sale or lease of goods that is intended to embody the final agreement of the parties, such written agreements cannot be contradicted by *parol evidence* (oral or extraneous evidence). Terms in such contracts can, however, be explained by course of dealing, usage of trade, course of performance, and by additional consistent terms (unless a court finds the written agreement was intended to embody the complete and exclusive agreement between the parties). For purposes of the UCC, course of dealing, course of performance, and usage of trade are defined as follows:

- **Course of Dealing** [§ 1-205 (1)]: Course of dealing is previous conduct by the parties that establishes a common basis of understanding for interpreting specific contract provisions and the conduct of the parties. The assumption is that when parties do business with one another, an understanding may arise as to the interpretation of common contract provisions from their past experience. Thus, if a buyer and seller have been doing business with each other for three years on a net 30 credit basis and no specific credit terms are noted on their latest contract, it could be inferred from their course of dealing that a net 30 credit term was assumed to apply.

- **Usage of Trade** [§ 1-205 (2)]: The UCC defines usage of trade as "any practice or method of dealing having such regularity of observance in a place, vocation or trade as to justify an expectation that it will be observed with respect to the transaction in question." The UCC recognizes that common language might have special meaning in a given trade or industry, and will allow parol evidence as to such meaning to be introduced in sales contracts. In the lumber industry, for example, an order for 2" by 4" by 8' lumber will in fact not result in lumber being shipped that is actually 2" high by 4" wide by 8' in length; the dimensions will be somewhat smaller since it is understood that the 2" by 4" by 8' measurements apply to green wood, which can be expected to shrink as it dries. Thus, in a contract calling for the delivery of lumber, the stated dimensions would be subject to interpretation by what is acceptable in the trade.

- **Course of Performance** (Practical Construction) [§ 2-208]: In a contract for the sale of goods that requires repeated performance over a period of time, the actual performance tendered and accepted is relevant to explaining the terms of a contract. Thus, in a contract that calls for 12 monthly shipments of goods, if the buyer accepts without complaint the first 11 shipments but refuses the twelfth, his acceptance without objection of the first 11 shipments would be relevant in determining the conformity (acceptability) of the goods to the contract.

Inapplicability of Seals [§ 2-203, § 2A-203]

As noted in Chapter 9, at common law a seal had special significance and is still required today in some formal contracts. But the UCC specifically states that seals are inoperative in contracts involving the sale or lease of goods; thus, the presence or absence of a seal on a sales contract has no effect on the contract.

Contract Formation

The UCC makes some significant changes to the common law of contracts in the areas of contract formation, particularly with regard to the requirements of offer and acceptance.

Contract Formation in General [§ 2-204, § 2A-204]

At common law, a contract was formed at the precise moment that a valid offer was accepted; thus, a clear, unequivocal offer and a clear, unequivocal acceptance were prerequisites to the formation of a valid contract. Furthermore, no valid agreement would be found to exist unless it was very clear just what the parties were agreeing to. The UCC, however, greatly relaxes these traditional requirements of contract formation by stating that a valid sales contract can exist even if it is impossible to clearly determine the moment of its making. In addition, the UCC makes contracts involving the sale or lease of goods valid even if one or more material terms are omitted or purposely left open as long as "the parties have intended to make a contract and there is a reasonably certain basis for giving an appropriate remedy" [§ 2-204 (3), § 2A-204 (3)].

Offer and Acceptance in Formation of Sales [§ 2-206] and Lease of Goods Contracts [§ 2A-206]

Unless the offer unambiguously states otherwise, the UCC allows acceptance through any reasonable means, and states that an offer for the shipment of goods can be accepted either by a promise to ship or by actual shipment of either conforming or nonconforming goods. If nonconforming goods are shipped, this is at once acceptance and a breach of the sales contract, unless the seller specifically notifies the buyer that the nonconforming goods are being shipped as an accommodation. Thus, if a buyer orders a television set and says he prefers acceptance by letter, the seller can accept either by forwarding the requested acceptance letter, by promising to ship the set via a telegram, by shipping the set, or even by shipping a stereo (nonconforming goods), in which case the seller would both accept the contract for the sale of the television set on the buyer's terms and breach it at the same time. Note that Section 2-206 and Section 2A-206 liberalize the common law rules of contract acceptance in favor of making it easier for the parties to enter into binding contracts. These sections also provide that when acceptance may reasonably be made by beginning performance (e.g., unilateral contracts), the offeror may treat the offer as lapsed if he has not received notification that the offeree has begun performance within a reasonable time of the offer being made [§ 2-206 (2) and § 2A-206 (2)].

Additional Terms in Acceptance or Confirmation [§ 2-207]

Another major change to the common law of contracts is effected by Section 2-207, which essentially curtails the mirror image rule. You may remember from Chapter 9 that an offer needs to exactly mirror an acceptance if a contract is to be formed; any material changes in the acceptance render the acceptance a counteroffer and automatically reject the original offer. The UCC changes this rule with regard to sales contracts by stating that an acceptance that contains additional terms is valid unless it is conditioned on the offeror accepting the offeree's additional terms. In other words, the effect of the additional terms varies depending on whether or not the parties are both merchants. If none or only one of the parties is a merchant, the additional terms are ignored. If both parties are merchants, the additional terms become part of the contract unless (1) they are objected to within a reasonable time of receipt of the acceptance, (2) the additional terms materially alter the contract, or (3) the offer specifically limits acceptance to the stated terms. The following examples will illustrate how Section 2-207 works:

- Seller offers to sell buyer 100 widgets for $1,000. Buyer accepts through a letter that states: "please ship the 100 widgets for $1,000. I assume you will ship via Federal Express Ground." If one or none of the parties is a merchant, the additional terms relating to the delivery are simply ignored, and seller may ship the goods via any commercially reasonable means. If buyer and seller are merchants, the additional terms become a part of the contract providing seller does not object to them within a reasonable time and further providing that the cost of Federal Express shipping is not substantially higher than the other available means of shipment. (If it is substantially higher, then the term would not apply even between merchants since it would be a material alteration to the terms of the contract.)
- Seller offers to sell buyer a boat for $5,000. Buyer accepts the offer as follows: "I agree to purchase your boat provided that you also throw in four life preservers and water skis." Whether or not the parties are merchants, the acceptance is invalid because it is conditioned on acceptance of the additional terms, making the attempted acceptance into a counteroffer. Words that signal a conditional acceptance include *if, provided that, as long as,* and *on condition of.*

Unconscionable Contract or Clause [§ 2-302]

The UCC gives courts wide latitude in dealing with contracts that they deem unconscionable as a matter of law. If a court finds a contract or a contract clause unconscionable, it may refuse to enforce the contract, or enforce the contract without the unconscionable clause, or rewrite the contract to avoid the unconscionable result. For purposes of the UCC as for other contracts, an unconscionable contract can be defined as "one which no man in his senses would make, on the one hand, and which no fair and honest man would accept, on the other" (*Hume v. U.S.*, 132 U.S. 406, 10 S.Ct. 134 (1889)). Generally speaking, courts will not invalidate contracts based merely on one party having made a bad bargain or on the bargain being unfair to one party. Gross unfairness of a type that shocks the conscience of the court is typically required for a contract to be held voidable on the grounds of unconscionability.

Auction Sales [§ 2-328]

Under the UCC, auction sales are deemed to be complete when the auctioneer signals her assent to the bidder's offer by the fall of the hammer, or in any other customary manner. If a bid is made while the hammer is falling, the auctioneer has the option to deem the goods sold under the bid for which the hammer was falling, or she may reopen bidding at her discretion.

Auctions can be either with reserve or without reserve. In auctions with reserve, the auctioneer reserves the right to withdraw any item from bidding if, in his sole discretion, the bids offered are unacceptably low. Auctions without reserve, on the other hand, obligate the auctioneer to sell the item outright for the highest bid. Whether an auction is with or without reserve is in the discretion of the auctioneer; if terms are not stated, the auction is deemed to be with reserve.

Finally, in all bids except forced sales, such as foreclosures and sheriff's sales, an auctioneer may not knowingly receive a bid on the seller's behalf unless it is made known prior to the bidding that the seller has reserved the right to bid on the auctioned item(s). If a bid is made in violation of this rule, the bidder may either at his option avoid the sale or take the goods at the highest good-faith bid (the highest bid before a bid was made on the seller's behalf). The reason for this rule is obvious: to avoid sellers artificially inflating bids at an auction by bidding against other bidders for their own goods unless the other bidders are given notice that the seller may be bidding on her own goods.

Statute of Limitations in Contracts for Sale [§ 2-725]

The statute of limitations for contracts involving the sale of goods is four years from the date that the cause of action *accrues* (a cause of action accrues when the breach occurs). Parties may not extend the period of limitation, but they can shorten it to a period of not less than one year by their mutual agreement.

Contracts for International Sale of Goods

As we have seen, contracts for the sale of goods in the United States are governed by Article 2 of UCC in every state except Louisiana. When contracts for the sale of goods involve individuals or businesses in the United States and other countries, however, the UCC is inapplicable, and contracting parties must contend with what are often marked differences in the laws of their respective countries. Fortunately, there are numerous international conventions and treaties whose purpose it is to facilitate international commerce between countries willing to adopt them. One such agreement is the United Nations Convention on Contracts for the International Sale of Goods (CISG). The CISG went into effect January 1, 1988, with the United States as a signatory country and by 2006 had been adopted by 72 countries from Argentina to Zambia. It includes many of our key trading partners in Europe; North, South, and Central America; the Middle East and Asia; including Canada, Mexico, China, South Korea, and most of our European trading partners (but not the United Kingdom as of this writing).

Like the UCC, the CISG attempts to simplify and facilitate contract formation. Unlike the UCC, which applies to all sales of goods transactions, however, the CISG applies only to the sale of goods transactions where both parties are merchants and therefore excludes consumer sales transactions. Another major difference between the UCC and CISG is that the CISG contains no statute of frauds and therefore makes all oral contracts valid, regardless of the value of the goods sold. Like the UCC, the CISG recognizes the irrevocability of merchants' firm offers, but unlike the UCC it does not require a firm offer to be made in writing for it to be effective.

As is the case with UCC Article 2, the CISG allows contracting parties the flexibility to set the specific terms of their agreement. It also serves largely to fill the gap when the contracting parties do not specify important contractual terms in their agreement. The CISG even allows contracting merchants to make its provisions wholly inapplicable simply by including a clause in their sales contract that the CISG will not apply to the transaction. The parties are also free to set by their mutual agreement that their contract will be ruled by any country's laws and to adopt another code such as UCC Article 2 as applicable instead of the CISG.

Questions

1. What types of transactions do Articles 2 and 2A of the UCC apply to?
2. Define goods.
3. Do Articles 2 and 2A of the UCC essentially do away with the common law of contracts?
4. Under what circumstances will a written and signed confirmation of a contract bind both parties to a contract?
5. Under the statute of frauds sections of the UCC [§ 2-201 and § 2A-201], what is the limit on the enforceability of oral contracts for the sale or lease of goods?
6. What is parol evidence?
7. What type of parol evidence can be used to explain written agreements?
8. What is the significance of a seal under the Articles 2 and 2A of the UCC?
9. What is the effect of shipping nonconforming goods in response to a sales order?
10. In general, what is the effect of nonmaterial additional terms in an acceptance with regard to contracts for the sale or lease of goods?
11. What is an unconscionable contract?
12. What is the difference between an auction with reserve and one without reserve?
13. Does the CISG apply to all international contracts between signatory countries? Explain.
14. When the CISG is applicable to their agreement, to what extent are parties able to modify provisions of the CISG by their mutual agreement?

Hypothetical Cases

1. Ben Buyer calls Sally Seller by phone and orders a color laser printer for $300.00, a replacement black toner cartridge for $100.00, and a 17-inch LCD monitor for $99.00. The total price of the order is $499.99 plus $35.00 in sales taxes and $25.00 for shipping for a grand total of $559.99. A day after placing the order, Ben has a change of heart and calls Sally to cancel. Sally informs him that she has already shipped the goods and that it is, therefore, too late for him to cancel the order. When the goods arrive five days later, Ben refuses delivery, whereupon Sally sues him in small claims court to recover her loss of the bargain damages plus the incidental expenses of paying for shipping the goods to Ben and back to her after his rejection of their delivery. You are the judge. Decide this case and give the legal justification for your decision.

2. Bernice Buyer sends a purchase order to Sam Seller that reads as follows: "Ship 20 notebook computers with the following minimum configuration at $2,500 each: Intel i7 processor, 750 GB hard disks, 6 GB RAM, dual layer DVD-R/RW drive." When the purchase order arrives, Sam promptly ships 20 current Apple Macintosh notebook computers of comparable value. When the computers arrive, Bernice rejects their delivery claiming that the term *PCs* clearly implied IBM-compatible machines, rather than Apple computers. The term *PC* is not in Bernice's order. Sam, on the other hand, claims that since no actual type of computer was specified, he was free to ship any commercially reasonable system that met the buyer's specifications. The parol evidence rule notwithstanding, what type of extraneous evidence, if any, can both parties provide in court to bolster their arguments?

3. Bart Buyer, the owner of Bart's Bargain Basement, sends a purchase order to Salena Seller for 1,000 My Little Autopsy toy sets—the season's hottest selling toy that, to the dismay of parents everywhere, allows children to simulate the thrills and chills of performing a real autopsy on an anatomically correct doll whose body parts can be removed with realistic blood and gore effects. Salena, who does not have the popular toy in stock, ships 1,000 My Undead Mummy dolls to Bart with a note that states: "These are shipped as an accommodation to your order at a 10% reduction off our regular wholesale price." When the dolls arrive, Bart rejects them (they are not gory enough, in his view, to suit the tastes of discriminating five-year-olds) and sues Salena for breach of contract. What result?

4. Benigno Buyer writes Francene Farmer a letter that states he is willing to purchase 1,000 pounds of apples at a price of $.50 per pound.
   A. How can Francene accept this contract?
   B. If Francene writes back stating, "Your terms are agreeable, provided you purchase a minimum of 1,200 pounds of apples." What is the effect of Francene's statement? Will it matter whether or not Benigno is also a merchant?
   C. Assume that the wholesale price of apples is $1 per pound at the time that the offer is made. If Francene accepts it, will she be likely to successfully assert a defense of unconscionability if she later refuses to honor the contract's terms?

Rights and Duties of Parties in the Performance and Breach of Sales and Lease Contracts

CHAPTER 20

Chapter Outline

Delivery of Goods [§ 2-308]

Time Frame for Delivery of Goods and Notice of Termination [§ 2-309]

Contract Options and Duty of Cooperation [§ 2-311]

Shipment by Common Carrier [§ 2-311]

F.O.B. and F.A.S. Shipment Terms and Risk of Loss [§ 2-319]

C. I. F. and C. & F. Terms [§ 2-320]

Sale on Approval, Sale or Return, and Consignment Sales [§ 2-326]

Risk of Loss with Regard to Sale on Approval and Sale or Return [§ 2-327]

Passing of Title to Goods [§ 2-401]

Insurable Interest on Goods [§ 2-501]

Seller's Tender of Delivery [§ 2-503]

Shipment by Seller [§ 2-504]

Effect of Seller's Tender of Delivery [§ 2-507]

Risk of Loss [§ 2-509]

Buyer's Right to Inspect Goods [§ 2-507]

Buyer's Rights on Improper Delivery [§ 2-601]

Merchant Buyer's Duties as to Rightfully Rejected Goods [§ 2-603]

Anticipatory Repudiation [§ 2-610]

Casualty to Identified Goods [§ 2-613]

Substituted Performance [§ 2-614]

In this chapter, we will cover the basic rules set out by the UCC affecting the rights and responsibilities of parties to sales contracts both during their performance and after their breach. As is usually the case with the UCC, these rules generally apply in the absence of parties' agreement to the contrary. With few exceptions, parties are free to modify nearly all of the provisions that follow through specific language in the sales contract; but if they do not do so, the UCC spells out some key rights and responsibilities of parties in an attempt to reflect their probable intent. As previously noted, one of the main purposes of the UCC is to facilitate commerce, to make it easier for people to enter into binding agreements. Because sales contracts are often not very detailed (although they certainly can be), the UCC provides a basic framework of key rights and duties of the parties that are incorporated into every sales agreement unless the parties agree otherwise.

Delivery of Goods [§ 2-308]

Unless the parties agree otherwise, the place for delivery of goods by the seller to the buyer is the buyer's place of business or, if he has no place of business, the buyer's residence. If, at the time of entering into a contract, both parties know that the goods are in another place, then delivery is to be made at the place where the goods are.

Time Frame for Delivery of Goods and Notice of Termination [§ 2-309]

If no specific time for delivery is set, delivery must be within a reasonable time. With regard to contracts that have an indefinite duration, they are valid for a reasonable time but are subject to termination by either party at any time. To terminate such agreements, parties must receive notification of termination before the contract is terminated; parties cannot contract away the need for notification of termination.

Contract Options and Duty of Cooperation [§ 2-311]

A sales contract that allows one of the parties to specify the particulars of performance is valid if it otherwise meets the requirements for a valid sales contract. In such cases, the party with the right to specify the particulars relating to performance has to exercise good faith and be bound by the limits of commercial reasonableness. In addition, the party with the right to specify the performance must exercise the option in a timely basis. Failure to do so constitutes a breach of the sales contract.

Shipment by Common Carrier [§ 2-311]

Sales contracts very often require goods to be shipped by the seller to the buyer through a common carrier (a company that offers transportation services to the general public, such as UPS; Federal Express; air, train, and bus transportation companies and the U.S. Postal Service). The type of method chosen for delivery of goods can have an effect on such factors as the risk of loss of goods in transit, the time when the buyer obtains an insurable interest, and the buyer's right to inspect and reject the goods, as well as who bears the cost of delivery, as we will see from the analysis of the following code sections.

F.O.B. and F.A.S. Shipment Terms and Risk of Loss [§ 2-319]

F.O.B. and *F.A.S.* are shipping terms that mean *free on board* and *free alongside a vessel*, respectively. When F.O.B. and F.A.S. are involved, the seller bears the responsibility (and cost, if any) of getting the goods in the possession of the carrier. If the contract calls for F.O.B. or F.A.S. at a specific destination (e.g., F.O.B. buyer's plant or F.A.S. buyer's port), then the seller bears the cost and risk of loss of getting the goods to the named destination.

With F.O.B. and F.A.S. contracts, the seller's risk of loss for the goods ends as soon as she discharges her responsibility of delivering the goods over to the carrier. At that point, if the goods are lost, stolen, or damaged in transit, the loss is borne by the buyer (who may then sue the carrier for the loss of goods in transit if the carrier's liability has not been waived).

When F.O.B. or F.A.S. to a specific location other than the seller's plant or seller's home port is involved, the seller retains the risk of loss for goods that are lost, stolen, or damaged in transit until the delivery of the goods is tendered to the buyer. Once delivery is tendered, it is the buyer's responsibility (and his expense) to get the goods loaded off the common carrier.

C. I. F. and C. & F. Terms [§ 2-320]

The acronyms *C. I. F.* and *C. & F.* in sales contracts relate to shipping terms and stand for *cost, insurance, and freight* and *cost and freight*, respectively. In a C.I.F. contract, the costs of shipping and insurance are included in the sale price, whereas in a C. & F. contract, the cost of shipping (freight) is included in the sales price, but not the cost of insurance, which the buyer must pay for and procure on her own, if she desires.

Sale on Approval, Sale or Return, and Consignment Sales [§ 2-326]

A sale on approval occurs whenever a buyer is given by the seller the right to return goods after delivery is made, even if conforming goods are involved. Purchases made by a consumer for goods that carry a free home trial period for a specified period of time, for example, are considered a sale on approval. A sale or return involves goods sold to a merchant buyer for resale with the understanding that if they are not resold by the buyer they can be returned to the seller for credit. The distinction between a sale on approval and a sale or return is of importance when the buyer is insolvent. Goods purchased by a buyer for his personal use on a sale on approval basis are not subject to attachment by the buyer's general creditors while the goods are in his possession until the buyer clearly evidences the intent to keep the goods. When a sale or return is involved, however, the goods that are the subject matter of the sale are considered the buyer's property and can be reached by the buyer's general creditors if the buyer becomes insolvent after purchasing the goods.

For purposes of the UCC, consignment sales are deemed to be sale or return sales unless the goods are clearly labeled as being consigned goods. (In a consignment sale, the owner of goods places them in the hands of a merchant who normally deals in the sale of the type of goods involved, and the merchant then sells the goods for a fee.)

Risk of Loss with Regard to Sale on Approval and Sale or Return [§ 2-327]

Unless the parties agree otherwise, in a sale on approval, the risk of loss does not pass to the purchaser until she has accepted the goods, and the seller bears the cost of the buyer shipping the goods back to the seller if acceptance is refused. Failure to notify the seller of acceptance after the trial period expires constitutes acceptance. Return of goods in a sale or return contract is at the buyer's risk and expense. Thus, if a seller ships goods to a buyer for a 15-day free trial and the buyer keeps them for 15 days without shipping them back, the buyer has accepted the goods and the risk of their loss shifts to him. But if goods are stolen, lost, or destroyed while in a buyer's possession during the trial period in a sale on approval, the risk of loss is the seller's, and the buyer need not pay for the lost, stolen, or destroyed goods. (If the buyer purposely or negligently destroys the goods, however, such destruction will constitute acceptance of the goods, and he must pay for them.) On the other hand, if a seller ships goods to a merchant buyer for sale or return and the goods are lost, stolen, or accidentally destroyed in transit or while in the buyer's possession, the buyer must pay for them, since the risk of loss for goods in a sale or return is with the buyer.

Passing of Title to Goods [§ 2-401]

In general, title to goods passes to the buyer at the time and place where the seller completes his performance with reference to the physical delivery of the goods, but parties may modify when and where title passes by their mutual agreement. This means that, in part, when title passes depends on the delivery terms specified in the contract. In carrier cases involving F.O.B. seller's plant, for example, title passes to the buyer as soon as the goods are placed in the hands of the carrier. In F.O.B. buyer's plant, however, title will not pass to the buyer until the goods arrive at the buyer's plant. And in cases in which the seller is required to actually deliver the goods to the buyer as part of the sales contract (rather than an F.O.B. or F.A.S. contract in which the buyer has the burden of unloading the goods from the carrier), such as the usual in-home delivery customarily available for consumer sales transactions, the title to the goods passes on tender of delivery of the goods at their final destination.

Insurable Interest on Goods [§ 2-501]

A buyer obtains an insurable interest on goods that are in existence at the time of entering into the contract. When future goods are involved (goods that are not in existence at the time of entering into the contract, such as goods that the seller is to manufacture or order for the buyer), the buyer obtains an insurable interest as soon as the goods are "shipped, marked or otherwise designated by the seller as goods to which the contract refers" [§ 2-501 (1) (b)]. If the future goods are crops or the unborn young of animals, the buyer obtains an insurable interest as soon as the crops are planted or the animals conceived. Sellers, on the other hand, retain an insurable interest in goods for as long as they have title in the goods or for as long as they retain a security interest in them.

Seller's Tender of Delivery [§ 2-503]

A seller must tender conforming goods to the buyer and give the buyer reasonable notice that the goods are available for delivery. Unless the parties agree otherwise, *tender of delivery* (the notification to buyer by seller or his agent that goods are available for delivery or pickup) must be at a reasonable hour, and the buyer must be given sufficient time to pick up or request delivery of the goods once tender of delivery is made. When goods are in the possession of a *bailee* (a person who temporarily holds goods belonging to another) and will be delivered to the buyer without actually being moved (such as when they are in the possession of a warehouse from which the buyer will pick them up), the seller must tender delivery by tendering a negotiable instrument of title. For example, the seller must tender a warehouse receipt or bill of lading, or otherwise notify the bailee of the buyer's right to take delivery of the goods. The following examples will illustrate:

- Buyer orders a washing machine from Home Appliance Company for in-store delivery. When the appliance arrives at the selected store location, Home Appliance Company must tender delivery by notifying the customer that the washing machine is available for pickup and then give the customer a reasonable amount of time to pick it up. Notification by a postcard would be sufficient, as would a phone call. But if a customer is notified by phone, a single call at 1:00 PM on Sunday would not be reasonable tender of delivery if the customer is not at home. Likewise, contacting the customer and telling her that she must pick up the washing machine within the next two hours would also not be reasonable tender of delivery.
- Buyer orders an automobile in Florida and agrees to take delivery of the car from the manufacturer's plant in Michigan. If the automobile is available in one of the seller's warehouses in Detroit, the seller must either tender a negotiable instrument of title to the buyer or notify its warehouse of the buyer's right to pick up the car within a reasonable time and then give the buyer a reasonable opportunity to travel to Detroit to pick up the car.
- Buyer purchases a 60-inch LCD television set from Hi-Tech Video Sales. Under the terms of the contract, Hi-Tech will have its delivery department deliver the set to buyer's home and set it up for her within two weeks. If, a week after entering into the contract, the set is ready for delivery, Hi-Tech must make a reasonable effort to notify the buyer that delivery is available and can be made at a reasonable time. If Hi-Tech phones buyer at 1:00 PM on Monday, at 1:02 PM on Monday, and at 1:05 PM on Monday and is unable to reach the buyer, a proper tender of delivery has not been made. (Calling three times to attempt delivery may be reasonable, but not within a five-minute period on the same day!)

Shipment by Seller [§ 2-504]

When the seller will not personally deliver the goods to the buyer under the terms of the sales contract but rather will ship them via carrier, the seller must place the goods in the hands of the carrier and make arrangements for their delivery in accordance with the terms of the sales contract. If applicable, the seller must also promptly send any required documents of title that buyer may need to claim the goods from the carrier and promptly notify the buyer of the goods' shipment.

Effect of Seller's Tender of Delivery [§ 2-507]

Once the seller properly tenders delivery of the goods to the buyer, the buyer is obligated to accept and pay for the goods. Failure of the buyer to accept or pay for conforming goods once they are tendered constitutes a breach of contract.

Risk of Loss [§ 2-509]

In the absence of agreement to the contrary, the exact moment at which the risk of loss for goods being shipped by carrier passes to the buyer from the seller depends on the terms of the contract. When F.O.B. buyer's plant or F.A.S. buyer's port shipping terms are involved, the risk of loss passes to the buyer as soon as the seller turns over the goods to the carrier for shipment or as soon as the goods are placed alongside a vessel for loading. If the shipping terms call for shipping to a specific destination by carrier, such as F.O.B. buyer's plant or F.A.S. buyer's port, then the risk of loss for the goods shifts from the seller to the buyer as soon as the goods are tendered at their final destination. Remember that tender does not mean the same as delivered; goods are tendered as soon as the buyer is notified that the goods are ready to be picked up or ready to be delivered at their final destination. Thus, if F.O.B. buyer's plant is involved in a contract, the seller will bear responsibility for any loss occurring during transit from loss, theft, or any damage to the goods. The risk for such loss, however, will shift to the buyer as soon as the goods arrive at their destination and the buyer is notified of their arrival and given a reasonable opportunity to pick them up. On the other hand, if goods are purchased F.O.B. seller's plant, the risk of loss will pass to the buyer as soon as the seller turns the goods over to the carrier (usually in the seller's loading dock).

In cases in which goods are in the possession of a third-party bailee and no movement of the goods is intended by the parties, the risk of loss passes to the buyer as soon as the buyer receives a negotiable document of title (such as a negotiable warehouse receipt) or when the buyer is notified by the bailee of his right to pick up the goods.

Finally, in cases in which goods are not shipped by carrier, but rather delivered directly to the buyer by the seller or picked up directly by the buyer from the seller, the risk of loss passes to the buyer when he picks up the goods if the seller is a merchant or when the goods are tendered to him if the seller is not a merchant. As is often the case, this means that merchant sellers are held to a higher duty of care than nonmerchants and must bear the loss of any goods they sell until they are actually delivered or picked up by their customers, but nonmerchant sellers bear the risk of loss for such goods only until tender of delivery is made. The following example will illustrate:

- Stephanie sells a used bicycle to Irving for $50. Irving pays for the bike but asks Stephanie if she will hold it for him until the next day. That evening, the bicycle is stolen from Stephanie's garage. If Stephanie is in the business of selling bicycles, the risk of loss would pass to Irving only upon actual physical delivery of the bike, so that Stephanie would bear the risk of loss and have to return the money to Irving if she cannot deliver the goods as promised. But if Stephanie is not a merchant, the risk of loss would pass to Irving as soon as the goods are tendered for delivery; in this case, the bike was tendered when it was bought, since he could have taken it at that time, so Irving would bear the loss of its subsequent theft.

Keep in mind that the parties are always free to reallocate the risk of loss any way they wish by mutual agreement. Furthermore, these rules are only effective assuming that conforming goods are tendered. If there is a breach of contract involved and the goods tendered are nonconforming because they do not meet the requirements of the contract (e.g., wrong goods, defective goods), then the risk of loss remains with the seller until they are either accepted by the buyer despite the nonconformity or the defect is cured by the seller [§ 2-510].

Buyer's Right to Inspect Goods [§ 2-507]

In general, a buyer has the right to inspect goods before paying for them to ensure that they conform to the requirements of the contract. Any expense for inspecting the goods must be borne by the buyer, but the expense is recoverable from the seller if the goods turn out to be nonconforming and the buyer rejects them. In cases in which goods are shipped C.O.D. (cash on delivery), however, a buyer must pay for the goods without first inspecting them. (If there is a defect in goods ordered C.O.D., the buyer can, of course, demand that the seller rectify the defect and sue the seller for breach of contract if she refuses to do so.)

Buyer's Rights on Improper Delivery [§ 2-601]

Whenever any delivery contains nonconforming goods in whole or in part, the buyer has the right to either reject the whole delivery, accept the whole delivery, or accept any commercial unit or units and reject the rest. Thus, if a liquor store owner orders ten cases of a particular California vintner's cabernet sauvignon wine and the distributor mistakenly ships one case of cabernet sauvignon and nine cases of merlot wine from the appropriate vineyard, the buyer may accept only the one case of conforming goods and reject the nine cases of nonconforming goods, or he can reject the whole shipment or accept the whole shipment despite the nonconformity.

If the nonconforming shipment is a part of an installment contract, where a number of individual deliveries are made over a period of time as part of a larger contract, the UCC makes it harder to reject the shipment. In such cases, the buyer may reject an installment only for nonconformity "if the non-conformity substantially impairs the value of that installment and cannot be cured or if the non-conformity is a defect in the required documents [of title]" [§ 2-612 (2)]. If the nonconformity of any single shipment in an installment contract can be cured by the seller, the buyer must accept the shipment and then allow the seller to cure the defect.

Merchant Buyer's Duties as to Rightfully Rejected Goods [§ 2-603]

As is often the case with the UCC, merchant buyers are held to a higher duty of care with respect to goods that they rightfully reject as nonconforming than are nonmerchants. A merchant buyer who rightfully refuses to accept nonconforming goods in his possession must follow the reasonable instructions of the seller with regard to the goods and, if no instruction is given by the seller, must make a reasonable effort to sell them on behalf of the seller if the goods are perishable or otherwise are likely to decrease rapidly in value. The reasonable incidental costs incurred by the buyer in caring for and disposing of the nonconforming goods on behalf of the seller are reimbursable to her by the seller. In addition, where the buyer is under a duty to sell the goods for the seller to prevent their spoilage or loss of value, the buyer is entitled to a reasonable commission for her services.

Anticipatory Repudiation [§ 2-610]

At common law, a breach of contract was not deemed to occur until a party obligated to render performance under a contract refused to do so. For that reason, when one party gave notice to the other that he would not or could not discharge performance of his obligations under the contract, the other party could not obtain any legal remedy until the actual deadline for the performance had passed. Thus, if a buyer contracted with a seller January 1 for shipment of 1,000 widgets on July 1 and the seller informed the buyer on January 2 that it could not or would not honor the contract, the buyer could not sue the seller or pursue any other remedy until after July 1—the day when the performance was due. The UCC changes this rule by giving aggrieved parties various options when sellers inform them of an *anticipatory repudiation* (notice by one party to the other that the promised performance in a contract will not be given when due). When anticipatory repudiation occurs, the aggrieved party (either the buyer or seller) can await performance by the repudiating party for a reasonable time, or opt to immediately resort to any available remedy for breach and simultaneously suspend his own performance.

Casualty to Identified Goods [§ 2-613]

When goods identified for shipment or delivery under a sales contract are damaged or destroyed without the fault of either contracting party, the contract is avoided if the loss to the goods is total. If the loss is only partial, or if the goods have deteriorated so that they no longer conform to the contract, the buyer has a choice of either treating the contract as avoided or accepting the goods with an adjustment in price for the deterioration or partial loss. If acceptance with price adjustment is elected, the buyer may not assert any other remedy against the seller. For example, if 25% of goods are damaged due to a fire and the buyer elects to take delivery of the remaining 75% of nondamaged goods with a reduction of 25% in the contract price, she cannot then ask the seller to ship another 25% of goods at the contract price.

Substituted Performance [§ 2-614]

Whenever an agreed-upon common carrier for shipment or the facilities for loading or unloading goods become unavailable due to circumstances beyond the control of the contracting parties, a commercially reasonable substitute may be selected and must be accepted. If, for example, the agreed-upon carrier is unavailable because of a labor dispute, the seller can select a commercially reasonable alternative, and the buyer must accept that substitution. This section also provides for substitute methods of payment in cases in which foreign or domestic governmental regulations make the agreed-upon method of payment unavailable. If this happens before goods are delivered, the seller may stop delivery until the buyer provides a commercially acceptable substitute method of payment. If delivery has already been made, then the seller must accept payment in the method provided for in the governmental regulation.

Questions

1. Unless the parties agree otherwise, where must the seller deliver goods to the buyer?
2. What is a common carrier?
3. What do the acronyms *F.O.B.* and *F.A.S.* stand for?
4. In an F.O.B. seller's plant or F.A.S. seller's port shipping contract, who bears the risk of loss for the goods while they are in transit to the buyer and in the hands of the carrier?
5. What do the acronyms *C. I. F.* and *C. & F.* stand for?
6. Define the terms *sale on approval, sale or return,* and *consignment sale*.
7. Who bears the risk of loss for goods that are in a buyer's possession under a sale on approval contract during the trial period before the buyer accepts the goods?
8. In general, when does title to goods pass from the seller to the buyer in a sales contract?
9. When does a buyer obtain an insurable interest to goods in a sales contract?
10. Define tender of delivery.

Hypothetical Cases

1. Beatrice Buyer orders 2,000 square yards of material from Sonya Seller. The contract calls for shipment F.O.B. buyer's plant. Based on these facts, answer the following questions:
   A. Who bears the risk of loss for the goods when they are placed in the hands of the carrier?
   B. Who pays for the shipment of the goods in this contract?
   C. Assuming that these goods are in existence in the seller's warehouse when the contract is made, when does the buyer obtain an insurable interest in the goods?
2. Bubba Buyer orders 1,000 cartons of "grade A jumbo" eggs from Sam Seller. Sam ships 100 cartons of "grade A jumbo" eggs and 900 cartons of "grade A medium" eggs. Answer the following questions based on these facts:
   A. If Bubba spends $50 to have the eggs inspected and then discovers that 900 cartons do not conform to the requirements of the contract, who is ultimately responsible for the cost of the inspection? Explain.
   B. What are Bubba's options with regard to the goods?
   C. If the shipment were a part of an installment contract calling for a delivery of 1,000 cartons of eggs every month for a year, will Bubba be able to reject the whole shipment? Explain.
3. Bertha Buyer orders five bushels of oranges from Sal Seller. Sal sends his truck out to deliver five bushels of tangerines. Since Bertha is not home at the time that the delivery is attempted, the driver unloads the tangerines onto Bertha's front porch and leaves them there, along with the bill. A day later, Bertha arrives home to find the tangerines rapidly spoiling in the sun. If she is not a fruit merchant, what are her responsibilities with regard to the fruit? Would your answer be the same if she were a fruit merchant? Explain.

4. Fred Farmer agrees to sell three tons of wheat stored in one of his silos to Betty Buyer. Under the terms of the contract, the wheat is to be delivered in three months, but Betty agrees to pay 50% of the sales price at the current market rate in 30 days, with the remaining 50% price payable upon delivery at the then-prevalent market rate. A week after entering into the contract, a fire erupts in the grain silo containing the wheat, and 20% of the wheat is completely destroyed before the fire is put out. In addition, another 30% of the wheat is damaged by the fire (but is still marketable at a reduced price), and 50% of the wheat is unaffected. When Fred informs Betty of the loss, what are her rights with regard to the contract?

Warranties

CHAPTER 21

In every contract for the sale or lease of goods under UCC Articles 2 and 2A, warranties can arise either by the express words or actions of the seller or lessor concerning the goods being sold (express warranties) or by operation of law (implied warranties). In this chapter, we will briefly examine the general provisions of the UCC relating to the creation, application, and waiver of warranties in contracts involving the sale or lease of goods.

Chapter Outline

Express Warranties [§ 2-313, § 2A-210)]

Implied Warranties

Third-Party Beneficiaries of Warranties Express or Implied [§ 2-318, § 2A-216]

Express Warranties [§ 2-313, § 2A-210)]

Sections 2-313 and 2A-210 of the UCC state that express warranties can be created by sellers in any of the following ways.

Express Statement or Promise about Goods

Any express affirmation of fact or promise made by the seller or lessee to the buyer about the goods being sold creates an express warranty that the goods will conform to the statement or promise. For a warranty to arise, the statement or promise has to be made during the bargaining process; statements made after goods are purchased do not qualify as warranties. Likewise, the statement or promise has to be specific. General statements about the quality of goods (even if exaggerated) do not qualify as warranties. So if a salesperson says to a buyer, "This blender represents a great value," "This car gets great mileage," or "This is the best toaster on the market," these statements are too general to constitute warranties and are considered as mere sales puffery of the products. But statements such as "This car gets 25 miles to the gallon in city driving" or "This toaster will toast bread in 30 seconds" or "We will repair or replace the blender within two years if it breaks down" are all clear and specific enough to constitute warranties.

Description of the Goods

Any description of the goods made as part of the basis of the bargain creates an express warranty that the goods will conform to the description. For a description of the goods to rise to the level of a warranty, it must be concrete and made by the seller to the buyer during the bargaining process for the goods. There is no requirement that the words *guarantee* or *warranty* be used for an express warranty to arise. As with express statements and promises, general statements about the quality or value for the goods that merely express the seller's opinion or constitute sales puffery are excluded. The following examples will illustrate:

- This is a marvelous car and a great value. It gets wonderful gas mileage, provides exceptional acceleration, and goes quite fast on the open road. In addition, it is a sturdy car in solid condition. And it looks great. (No express warranties are made in this description. It is merely subjective, over-broad sales puffery that, in typical fashion, says absolutely nothing concrete about the car.)
- This car is a 2014 Ford Explorer with 50,000 miles, automatic transmission, air conditioning, navigation system, and antilock brakes. (Every one of the descriptive statements in this sentence creates a warrantee as to the used car being sold as to the car's make, model, mileage, transmission, air conditioning, navigation system, and brakes.)

Use of Sample or Model during Sale

Whenever a salesperson uses a model or sample in trying to close a sale or lease deal, an express warranty arises that the goods delivered will conform to the model or sample shown the buyer or lessee. For this warranty to arise, the buyer or lessee must actually have inspected the sample or model of the goods before agreeing to the purchase. If the buyer or lessee is clearly told or knows that there are differences between the goods being purchased and the model she is shown, however, the warranty will not arise. Thus, agreeing to lease or purchase a car after inspecting the showroom model, which includes a ten-disk CD changer and on-board navigational computer, does not mean that a warranty is made that the model delivered will also have this optional equipment if the buyer is told, or should realize, that the equipment is optional. But if a salesperson tells a prospective buyer, "You can have a car equipped just like that one for $20,000" and points to a car loaded with options, the salesperson has made a warranty to the person who inspects it prior to agreeing to the sale that the car ordered will be equipped exactly as the sample.

Implied Warranties

In addition to express warranties that can arise from the noted circumstances, a number of implied warranties also attach automatically to every sale and lease contract, whereas others arise only when merchant sellers or lessors are involved. We'll examine these in turn.

Warranty of Title and Against Infringement [§ 2-312]

Every seller (merchant or nonmerchant) makes a warranty of title that guarantees he has good title to the goods and that the transfer is rightful. The warranty also guarantees that the goods are transferred free from any security interest, lien, or other encumbrance that the buyer is not aware of as of the time of entering into the contract.

In addition to the warranty of title, a merchant seller also guarantees that the goods are free of any claim of copyright or patent infringement or similar claim by third parties. An exception is granted to the warranty against infringement to merchant sellers who manufacture goods to specifications furnished by the buyer; such specially manufactured goods are not warranted against claims of infringement by third parties, since it is the buyer's responsibility to furnish specifications that do not infringe on others' patents, copyrights, or similar intellectual property rights. The following example will illustrate:

- ABC Company buys 100 television sets from Sam Seller. Unknown to either ABC or Sam at the time of the sale, the manufacturer of the sets has misappropriated trade secrets and infringed on numerous patents from XYZ Company in the manufacture of the set. If XYZ sues ABC seeking an injunction against the resale of the sets or for any other damages, ABC can recover any incidental or consequential damages from Sam for breach of the implied warranty against infringement that Sam as a merchant seller made to ABC as part of the sale. (Sam could then sue the manufacturer of the set for his damages caused by its infringement.)

Lessees are offered similar implied warranty protection by Section 2A-211, which provides that lessors warrant to lessees that during the lease term no person holds a claim or interest to the goods that can interfere with the lessee's enjoyment of the leasehold interest and also offers protection against claims of infringement by third parties.

The warranty of title and against infringement can be waived only by specific language or by circumstances which give the buyer notice that the seller does not claim title to the goods being sold. Purchasing the goods from a sheriff's sale, for example, would give notice to the buyer that the goods are sold subject to possible liens or other claims by others.

Warranty of Fitness for a Particular Purpose [§ 2-315, § 2A-213]

In any sale or lease where the seller knows that the buyer is relying on the seller's or lessor's skill or judgment in selecting goods suitable to the buyer's specific needs, a warranty arises that the goods sold will be suitable to the buyer's or lessee's special needs. This warranty is made by both merchant and nonmerchant sellers and lessors. For the warranty to arise, it is imperative that the buyer or lessee rely on the seller's or lessor's superior skill in selecting goods suitable to his specific needs and that the seller or lessor be aware that the buyer or lessee is relying on her superior knowledge or skill with regard to the goods being sold, as the following example illustrates:

- Lenny, who has never skied before, notices a pair of cross-country skis in Rhonda's garage sale. He asks Rhonda if the skis are suitable for downhill skiing, a sport he has been considering taking up. Rhonda, who wants to sell the skis, assures him that they will be perfectly suitable for that purpose. Rhonda has breached the warranty of fitness for a particular purpose in making a recommendation to Lenny knowing that he was relying on her superior knowledge of skiing. (Notice that she is also guilty of fraud in the inducement.) As a consequence, she will have to refund Lenny's money on demand and could be held liable for any damage that he suffers as a consequence of her breach of warranty.

Warranty of Merchantability [§ 2-314]

In every sale or lease by a merchant, an implied warranty is made that the goods will be merchantable, which is to say that they will pass without objection in the trade under the contract description, be fit for the ordinary purposes for which such goods are used, are adequately packaged and labeled (if appropriate) and, if labeled, conform to the description or promises made in the label. If the goods are *fungible* (of a type where one part is substantially identical to other parts, such as grain, gasoline, and vegetable oil), then they must be of at least fair, average quality within their description.

Exclusion or Modification of Warranties [§ 2-316, § 2A-214]

Generally speaking, warranties may be modified or completely excluded either orally or in writing. All that the UCC requires is that the exclusion or limitation be clear. With regard to the warranty of merchantability, it can be excluded only by language that specifically mentions merchantability and, if in writing, must be conspicuous. In addition, an exclusion of the warranty of fitness for a particular purpose must be in writing and conspicuous.

All implied warranties may be excluded by such language as "There are no warranties which extend beyond the face hereof," [§ 2-316 (2)] and by expressions such as *as is, with all faults* "or other language which in common understanding calls the buyer's attention to the exclusion of warranties and makes plain that there is no implied warranty" [§ 2-316 (3) (a), § 2A-214 (3) (a)]. A buyer who is given the opportunity to examine a sample prior to entering into a contract and examines the goods or refuses to do so cannot claim a breach of an implied warranty with regard to "defects which an examination ought in the circumstances to have revealed" [§ 2-316 (3) (b), § 2A-214 (3) (b)]. In addition, "an implied warranty can also be excluded or modified by course of dealing or course of performance or usage of trade" [§ 2-316 (3) (c), § 2A-214 (3) (c)].

Third-Party Beneficiaries of Warranties Express or Implied [§ 2-318, § 2A-216]

Sections 2-318 and 2A-216 of the UCC expressly extend warranty coverage to persons injured by defective goods but who had not purchased or leased the goods themselves. These sections address the common law privity of contract problems that prevent a person from suing to recover for injuries suffered from defective products unless they had actually purchased the product themselves. (Only persons who are parties to a contract are in *privity of contract* with one another.) The UCC provides three alternatives for states to adopt that extend coverage to any natural person injured by a defective product as follows:

- Alternative A extends warranty coverage to any member or guest of the buyer's or lessee's household who could reasonably be expected to use, consume, or be affected by the defective goods and who is personally injured by a breach of the product's warranty.
- Alternative B extends warranty protection to any natural person who may reasonably be expected to use, consume, or be affected by the goods and is personally injured by a breach of the warranty.
- Alternative C extends warranty protection to any person who may reasonably be expected to use, consume, or be affected by the goods and who is injured by a breach of the warranty.

For purposes of these sections, a "natural person" is a human being as distinguished from business entities such as corporations or limited liability companies. Only alternative C is not specifically limited to "natural persons," and only Alternative C would allow nonpersonal injury claims by injured persons (e.g., personal property damage claims). These sections cover all express and implied warranties, and their effectiveness cannot be waived by contract.

Questions

1. What are three ways in which express warranties can come into existence?
2. Name four implied warranties.
3. Generally speaking, how do implied warranties come into existence?
4. Which implied warranties are made only by merchant sellers?
5. Can implied warranties be modified or waived? If so, how? If not, why not?
6. Which warranty protection can never be waived?
7. Who makes a warranty of title, and what does it guarantee?
8. What is the warranty against infringement, and how does it arise?
9. Would a person who is given a gift that causes him injury due to a design defect be able to sue the seller of the defective product in a state that has adopted Alternative A of UCC Sections 2-318 and 2A-216? Explain.
10. Would a person who is given a gift that causes him injury due to a design defect be able to sue the seller of the defective product in a state that has adopted either Alternatives B or C of UCC Sections 2-318 and 2A-216? Explain.

Hypothetical Cases

1. Benito Buyer purchases a screwdriver at a garage sale for 50¢ from Sandra Seller who is not a hardware merchant. What warranties, if any, are made as part of this transaction?
2. Benito Buyer purchases a screwdriver for $2 from Sally's Hardware Store. He lends the screwdriver to his neighbor, Dan Dimwit, who uses the screwdriver as a chisel to break up a piece of crumbling cement in his backyard in order to rebuild it. While Dan is hammering at the screwdriver with a sledge hammer, it breaks and a piece of the handle flies into his eye, causing him a minor eye injury. Explain which warranties attach to this sale and then analyze Dan's chances of suing Sally's Hardware Store for breach of warranty

if his state has adopted UCC Section 2-318 Alternative A. Would your answer be the same if the state has adopted Section 2-318 Alternative C? Explain fully.

3. Botswain Buyer asks the proprietor of his local home center for advice on thawing a water pipe in his Montana home that froze during a particularly nasty winter cold spell. The seller recommends an oxygen-acetylene torch to do the job—a tool that is not well suited to the job or for use by a homeowner. Botswain, relying on the advice, purchases a $500 welding kit and proceeds to melt part of the water main into his house in an attempt at defrosting it, turning his basement into an unwanted indoor swimming pool. He wants to sue the seller to recover his damages under a theory of breach of contract, breach of the implied warranty of merchantability, and breach of the implied warranty of suitability for a particular purpose. What result? Explain fully.

4. Bruce Buyer purchased a used electric drill at a hardware store. The drill was in a basket with other assorted hardware items and tools. Over the basket, a large sign clearly read: "All of the items in this box are sold as is." Bruce read the sign before purchasing the drill. After taking the drill home, he plugged it in and received a tremendous shock which nearly killed him and required his brief hospitalization. He now wants to sue the seller for breach of warranty. Will he succeed? If so, which warranty in particular was breached by the seller? If not, why not?

Remedies for Breach of Sales and Lease Contracts

CHAPTER 22

As with other areas of contract law, the Uniform Commercial Code has made some important modifications to the common law remedies available to contracting parties who suffer a breach of contract. While the basic common law remedies for breach of contract discussed in Chapter 18 are still available when a breach of a sales contract occurs, they have been both expanded and limited in varying degrees by the UCC, as we will see in this chapter. Here we will examine the specific remedies available to sellers, buyers, lessors, and lessees under the UCC.

Chapter Outline

Seller's and Lessor's Remedies
Seller's Remedies
Buyer's Remedies
Lessee's Remedies
General Rules Affecting Buyers, Sellers, Lessees, and Lessors
Liquidation of Damages [§ 2-718, § 2A-504)]
Contractual Modification or Limitation of Remedies [§ 2-719, § 2A-503]
Statute of Limitations [§ 2-725, § 2A-506]

Seller's and Lessor's Remedies

The UCC specifies in substantial detail the specific remedies available to sellers in Sections 2-703 through 2-710 and to lessors in Sections 2A-523 through 2A-531. We'll examine the most significant of these UCC sections next in our discussion.

Seller's Remedies

Seller's Remedies in General [§ 2-703]

After a buyer's wrongful rejection, revocation of acceptance of goods, failure to pay for goods when due, or wrongful repudiation, a seller may withhold delivery of goods, stop delivery of the goods in the hands of a third party (shipping or warehouse delivery contracts), cancel the contract, or pursue any of the other remedies provided under the UCC.

Seller's Right to Salvage Unfinished Goods [§ 2-704]

When a buyer breaches a contract calling for specially manufactured goods after the seller has begun the manufacturing process but before the manufacture of the goods has been completed, the seller may either sell the partially manufactured goods for their salvage or scrap value or may elect to complete the manufacture of the goods and resell them to another buyer. Any amount recovered by the seller from such a sale would help offset his damages against the buyer if another remedy is pursued against it.

Seller's Right to Stop Delivery [§ 2-705]

A seller may stop delivery of goods in the hands of a carrier or other bailee (such as a warehouse) upon learning of the buyer's insolvency, or if the seller refuses to pay for the goods prior to delivery if payment is then due.

Seller's Right to Resell Goods [§ 2-706]

After a breach by buyer, the seller may resell the goods to another buyer and recover the difference between the resale price and the contract price, along with any incidental and consequential damages.

Seller's Damages for Non-Acceptance or Repudiation [§ 2-708]

The measure of damages for the buyer's wrongful nonacceptance or repudiation of goods is the difference between the market price at the time and place that delivery is tendered and the contract price, along with incidental and consequential damages less any expenses the seller saves due to the buyer's breach. Thus, if a buyer on October 1 agrees to take delivery of goods on January 1 in New York from a seller in California and then breaches the contract on October 2, the seller's damages will be the market price of the goods in New York on January 1 minus the contract price (the amount payable for the goods under the contract) minus any expenses saved by the seller as a consequence of the breach (such as the cost of shipping to New York if it was an F.O.B. buyer's plant contract). If the seller suffers any additional incidental and consequential damages as a result of the breach, these too are recoverable from the buyer.

In cases in which the market price minus contract price differential does not adequately compensate the seller for the breach, the seller can opt to recover her lost profits from the sale along with any incidental and consequential damages.

Action for the Price [§ 2-709]

The seller may recover the contract price from a buyer for goods that the buyer has accepted or goods that have been lost, damaged, or destroyed in transit after the risk for their loss had shifted to the buyer. A seller may also recover the contract price for goods that he cannot resell after a reasonable effort, such as when there is no ready market for the goods.

Seller's Incidental Damages [§ 2-710]

A seller's incidental damages recoverable from a buyer after a breach include any "commercially reasonable charges, expenses or commissions incurred in stopping delivery, in the transportation, care and custody of goods after the buyer's breach, in connection with return or resale of the goods or otherwise resulting from the breach."

Lessor's Remedies in General [§ 2A-523]

If the lessee wrongfully rejects or revokes acceptance, or fails to make a payment when due, the lessee is in default and the lessor may avail herself of remedies similar to those available to a seller after a buyer's breach of contract. These include the right to cancel the lease contract [§2A-505 (1)], proceed with respect to goods not identified to the contract [§2A-524], withhold delivery of the goods and take possession of previously delivered goods [§2A-525], stop delivery of the goods in the possession of a bailee [§2A-526], dispose of the goods and recover damages [§2A-527], retain the goods and recover damages [§2A-528], or in a proper case recover rent for the goods under the lease [§2A-529]. The lessor may also recover incidental damages from the lessee [§2A-530], such as the reasonable expenses or commissions incurred in stopping delivery of goods or in the transportation, care, and custody of goods after the lessee's default.

Buyer's Remedies

As with seller's remedies, the UCC details the specific remedies available to buyers in Sections 2-711 through 2-717. We'll examine the most significant of these UCC sections next.

Buyer's Remedies in General; Buyer's Security Interest in Rejected Goods [§ 2-711]

Upon a seller's breach, a buyer may elect to cancel the contract and recover any money paid to the seller as well as exercise any other remedy allowed by the UCC. In addition, the buyer has a security interest for goods in her possession after a rightful rejection or revocation to the extent of any money paid to the seller for their sale.

Cover; Buyer's Procurement of Substitute Goods [§ 2-712]

After a breach, a buyer may cover his damages by procuring in good faith and without unreasonable delay the purchase of substitute goods from another seller. Cover can be defined as the right of a buyer after a breach of contract to purchase goods from a third party in substitution for the goods he was entitled to receive from the seller. If this remedy is selected, the buyer may recover from the seller the difference between the contract price and the cover price plus incidental and consequential damages minus any expense saved as a result of the breach.

Cover is an optional remedy, and the failure of a buyer to elect to cover his damages within a reasonable period of time will not bar him from pursuing other available remedies.

Buyer's Damages for Non-Delivery or Repudiation [§ 2-713]

The measure of damages for nondelivery or repudiation by the seller is the difference between the market price and the contract price at the time that the buyer learned of the breach. The market price is to be based on the place where tender of delivery was due under the contract. As usual, incidental and consequential damages are also recoverable, and any expenses saved by the buyer as a result of the breach are deducted from his damages.

Buyer's Damages for Breach in Regard to Accepted Goods [§ 2-714]

After accepting nonconforming goods, buyers may recover damages for any reasonable loss resulting from the nonconformity. The measure of damages is the difference in value at the time and place of acceptance between the accepted nonconforming goods and the value of conforming goods. Incidental and consequential damages are also recoverable, if appropriate.

Buyer's Incidental and Consequential Damages [§ 2-715]

The buyer's incidental and consequential damages resulting from the seller's breach include reasonable costs incurred in inspecting, receiving, transporting, and caring for rightfully rejected goods, as well as commercially reasonable charges incurred in connection with affecting cover for nonconforming goods. Consequential damages include any loss resulting from the general or particular circumstances of the buyer that the seller, at the time of entering into the contract, had reason to know and that could not be reasonably prevented through cover or otherwise. Such damages also include personal injury or property damage directly caused by and resulting from the breach of any sales warranty.

Buyer's Right to Specific Performance or Replevin [§ 2-716]

A court may award specific performance where the goods are unique or in other proper circumstances. A buyer may also sue for *replevin* (an action at law requiring the person who has goods in his possession to turn them over to their rightful owner) when he is unable to effect cover for goods identified to the contract.

Deduction of Damages from the Price [§ 2-717]

A buyer may, after duly notifying the seller of his intent to do so, deduct part or all of her damages from any payment still due from her to the seller for the same contract. A buyer cannot, however, deduct her damages for one sales contract from money due the seller for other contracts not involved in the breach.

Liquidation or Limitation of Damages [§ 2-718]

Parties may agree to liquidated damage provisions in sales contracts as long as these are reasonable and anticipate the actual harm that may be caused by a breach. Liquidated damage provisions that are unreasonably high are void as penalties.

Lessee's Remedies

Lessee's remedies under Article 2A of the UCC are similar in scope and purpose to the remedies provided to buyers under Article 2 of the UCC. We'll briefly examine these next.

Lessee's Remedies Generally [§ 2A-508]

Upon breach by the lessor of the lease agreement, the lessee may avail himself of any of the following remedies:

- cancel the lease contract [§ 2A-505 (1)];
- recover a just portion of the rent or security given under the lease agreement;
- cover and recover damages as to goods affected [§§ 2A-518, 2A-520] (e.g., obtain the goods elsewhere and seek compensation for costs above those that would have been incurred in the lease) or recover damages for nondelivery [§§ 2A-519, 2A-520];
- pursue any other rights or remedies provided for in the lease agreement (such as liquidated damages, if applicable);
- recover identified goods upon the lessor's failure to deliver the goods in conformity to the lease contract or repudiation of the lease contract [§ 2A-522];
- obtain specific performance or replevin in an appropriate case (e.g., when unique goods are involved) [§ 2A-521];
- recover damages for breach of any implied or express warranty;
- in case of a rightful rejection or justifiable revocation of acceptance, a lessee retains a security interest in the goods in her possession to cover the reasonable cost of inspecting, caring for, storing, or shipping goods back to the lessor. Section 2A-508 (5) allows a lessee under such circumstances to hold and dispose of the goods in good faith and in a commercially reasonable manner;
- deduct damages in whole or in part from any rent due under the lease in the event of a default by the lessor as long as the lessee informs the lessor of his intention to do so.

General Rules Affecting Buyers, Sellers, Lessees, and Lessors

In addition to the sections affecting remedies we've just examined, the UCC provides a number of rules relating to remedies that apply equally to buyers, sellers, lessees, and lessors. We'll touch on these next.

Liquidation of Damages [§ 2-718, § 2A-504)]

Parties may provide for liquidated damages for both buyers and sellers in sales contracts as long as they are reasonably calculated to compensate the parties for their actual anticipated losses in the event of a breach. Unreasonably large liquidated damage provisions are void as penalties.

Contractual Modification or Limitation of Remedies [§ 2-719, § 2A-503]

Parties are free to limit or provide remedies in addition to those in the UCC by their mutual agreement. But if parties do limit the available remedies and the exclusive remedy selected fails in its essential purpose or is found to be unconscionable, the parties may resort to any remedy provided by the UCC. In other words, if the remedy selected by the parties through their mutual agreement turns out to be unreasonable under the circumstances, a court will ignore the limitation of remedies provision in the contract and award any remedy provided by the UCC. In addition, the parties may limit or exclude incidental or consequential damages through their mutual agreement, but this provision will also be ignored by the courts if it is found to be unconscionable.

Statute of Limitations [§ 2-725, § 2A-506]

An action involving the breach of a contract for the sale or lease of goods must be initiated within four years from the date it accrues. Parties to both sales and lease contracts may reduce that time period by mutual consent, but not to less than one year.

Questions

1. What is the seller's right to salvage unfinished goods?
2. What is the measure of a seller's damages after the buyer's nonacceptance or repudiation of goods?
3. What are the incidental damages that a seller may recover after a breach by the buyer?
4. What is cover?
5. What are the buyer's or lessee's incidental and consequential damages?
6. When may a court award specific performance?
7. Are liquidated damage provisions valid in contracts for the sale or lease or goods?
8. Are agreements to limit remedies in sales or lease contracts enforceable?
9. What is the statute of limitations for cases involving the sale or lease of goods?
10. Under what conditions are liquidated damages clauses in sales or lease of goods contracts enforceable?

Hypothetical Cases

1. Buyer orders 1,000 widgets from seller to be manufactured to the buyer's specifications. After the seller orders the necessary raw materials to manufacture the widgets but before the manufacture of the goods is completed, the buyer informs the seller that he will not accept delivery of the goods because he has found a cheaper supplier. Seller wishes to sue for breach of contract. Discuss what remedies are available to the seller under such circumstances.
2. Seller, a Nevada corporation, agrees to sell to buyer, a Colorado company, 1,000 widgets for $100 each by contract signed January 1. Under the terms of the agreement, the goods are to be delivered to seller on February 1. On January 15, seller informs buyer that it will be

unable to ship the widgets. The market price for widgets in Colorado and Nevada is given in the following table. What are buyer's exact cover damages given these facts?

Date	State	Market Price Of Widgets
January 1	Nevada	$95
January 1	Colorado	$97
January 15	Nevada	$105
January 15	Colorado	$110
February 1	Nevada	$135
February 1	Colorado	$150

3. Buyer agrees to purchase a Picasso painting from seller for $5,000,000. At the time of the contract, the market price of the painting is $4,800,000. After entering into the contract but before delivering the painting, seller has a change of heart and informs the buyer that he will not honor the agreement. At the time that the seller informs the buyer of his intention to breach the contract, the market price of the painting is unchanged. What remedy may the buyer successfully demand in court?

4. Lessee, a Georgia corporation, enters into a lease agreement for a fleet of 1,000 flexible fuel delivery trucks for its local delivery business from Lessor, a Kentucky company that specializes in retrofitting regular gasoline and diesel cars and trucks to run on a variety of flexible fuels including diesel/biofuel, gas and electric, gas and ethanol hybrids, as well as all electric and hydrogen fuel-cell-powered vehicles. Leasing these vehicles adds 25% to the overall cost over leasing traditional gas- or diesel-powered vehicles, but the lessee estimates that it will save a modest $250 per year over the life of its five-year lease per vehicle above and beyond the higher lease price in lower fuel costs. But, more importantly, the vehicles represent a statement about the company's commitment to the environment, and the company has invested $250,000 in a new marketing campaign highlighting its investment in an environment-friendly fleet of delivery vehicles and in promoting its new slogan: "Why ship with Brown if you can save money by going Green?" A month before the new vehicles were to be delivered, the lessor informs the lessee that it will be unable to make delivery when promised and tenders to the lessee a check for $1,000—the liquidated damages agreed to by the parties in the lease contract in the event that either the lessor or lessee failed to perform as promised. Under these facts, discuss fully what specific damages, if any, the lessee is entitled to recover from the lessor.

Introduction to UCC Article 3 (Commercial Paper)

CHAPTER 23

Chapter Outline

Parties to Commercial Paper

Form of Negotiable Instruments [§ 3-104]

Type of Negotiable Instruments

Requirements for Negotiability

General Rules Applicable to Commercial Paper

Although it is technically possible to carry out business strictly on a cash basis, the realities of commerce necessitate the use of readily acceptable substitutes for cash as well as financial instruments that make it easy to lend and borrow money. It's simply not practical—or safe—to carry what can often be very large sums of paper money needed for business transactions. It should come as no surprise, then, that the majority of business transactions are carried out by check.

Article 3 of the Uniform Commercial Code concerns itself with commercial paper in its four basic forms: checks, drafts, notes, and certificates of deposit. They serve both as substitutes for cash (checks and drafts) and as a means of facilitating the extension of credit (notes and certificates of deposit). While these instruments have been around for many centuries, the UCC has consolidated the common law into a single comprehensive code, updating and modernizing the law as needed. The 1990 revision of Article 3 has been adopted in every state except New York as well as in Washington D.C., Puerto Rico, and the Virgin Islands. New York has legislation pending for its adoption that has not been voted on as of this writing. A newer revised version of Article 3 (as well as Article 4 dealing with bank collections) was released in 2002 by the National Conference of Commissioners on Uniform State Laws (NCCUSL) for adoption by the states. The 2002 revisions approved by the NCCUSL and the American Law Institute amend Articles 3 and 4 relating to e-commerce. As of this writing, the 2002 amendments have been adopted by only 11 states and Washington D.C., and legislation is pending for its approval in Massachusetts.

For commercial paper to be readily accepted as a substitute for money or as a means of extending credit, persons accepting such instruments must have some clear assurance that they will be honored when they are presented for payment. As an incentive to make commercial paper attractive to persons who accept it in the normal course of business, the law provides certain guarantees to those who accept such instruments in good faith and pay value for them. We will explore the specifics of the protection afforded to holders in the next chapter, but it is essential to understand the fundamental distinction of commercial paper from other financial or contractual instruments from the outset; otherwise, the significance of these instruments will not be apparent.

The distinguishing characteristic of a negotiable instrument is that it can give special protection to persons to whom it is legally negotiated in the course of business. Provided certain conditions are met for due negotiation, persons who take negotiable instruments in good faith and give some value for them take such instruments free of most defenses against their payment.

Parties to Commercial Paper

Before we continue our discussion of commercial paper, it will be helpful to introduce the major parties who play a role in the creation, negotiation, and payment of negotiable instruments. We will encounter these parties throughout the rest of this unit, and it will be helpful if we become familiar with the basic role of each party now.

- **Drawer:** The party who makes or executes a draft.
- **Drawee:** The party who is directed to pay a draft or a note. (If the draft is a check, the drawee is always a bank or other financial institution.)
- **Maker:** The party who makes or executes a note.
- **Payee:** The party to whom a note or draft is made payable.
- **Bearer:** The party in possession of a note or draft made out to him as payee or made out to bearer.
- **Accommodation Party:** A party who signs a note or draft of a maker or drawer as a maker, drawer, acceptor, or indorser to guarantee payment if the note or draft is dishonored when presented for payment.
- **Acceptor:** A drawee of a draft who binds herself to pay the payee the face value of the draft when it is presented for payment by signing as acceptor on the face of the draft.
- **Guarantor:** A party who signs a note or draft on its face guaranteeing payment in case the note or draft is dishonored when it is presented for payment.
- **Indorser:** The party who signs her name on the back of a note or draft naming her as payee to obtain payment on it or negotiate it to a third party.
- **Indorsee:** The party to whom a negotiable instrument is indorsed as the new payee.

Form of Negotiable Instruments [§ 3-104]

As previously noted, there are four basic forms of negotiable instruments: drafts, checks, notes, and certificates of deposit. Regardless of their form, all negotiable instruments must meet the following criteria:

- The instrument must be in writing;
- It must be signed by the maker or drawer (the person who creates the instrument);
- It must contain an unconditional promise or order to pay a *sum certain* (a specifically identifiable amount) in money;
- It must contain no other promise or obligation;
- It must be payable on demand or at a definite time; and
- It must be payable to order or bearer.

An instrument that meets all of the noted criteria qualifies as a negotiable instrument; an instrument that fails to meet one or more of the noted criteria may still be a valid instrument, but it will not qualify for the special status of a negotiable instrument.

Type of Negotiable Instruments

A negotiable instrument will take one of four forms: it can be a draft, check, note, or certificate of deposit. Note carefully the basic characteristics of each of these instruments.

```
Navarre Beach, Florida
                                        February 1, 2016

PAY TO THE ORDER OF  PAUL PAYEE

Five thousand and no/100----------DOLLARS  $5,000.00



To  Dan Drawee                          Denise Drawer
    Toledo, Ohio
```

FIGURE 23.1 Sample Draft in Which Denise Is the Drawer, Who Orders Dan (the Drawee) to Pay Paul (the Payee) a Sum Certain in Money ($5,000.00)

Draft

A draft is an order by a *drawer* (the person who draws, or executes, the draft) to a *drawee* (the person ordered by the drawer to pay the draft) to pay a sum certain in money on demand or at a specified date to the order of a specified *payee* (the person the drawer orders the drawee to pay) or to *bearer* (anyone in possession of the draft). A draft is used as a substitute for money. For an example of a draft, see Figure 23.1.

Check

A check is nothing more than a draft that is drawn on a bank. In other words, the drawer of a check is a depositor who orders the drawee (his bank) to pay the payee a specific amount of money. As with a draft, a check is also a substitute for money. For an example of a check, see Figure 23.2.

Note

Unlike drafts and checks that serve as substitutes for money, a note serves as evidence of debt. The drafter of the note is called the maker, and the person for whose benefit the note is drafted is called the payee. Invariably, the maker of a note drafts it in exchange for having received something of present value (a loan, the purchase of a home, or the

```
Dom and Denise Drawer                                              1027
   101 Lovely Lane
   Americus, GA 31710

                                            February 1, 2016

PAY TO THE ORDER OF  PAULETTE PAYEE--------------
Five thousand and no/100-----------------DOLLARS   $5,000.00


First Drawee Bank of Georgia
   111 Washington Street
   Albany, GA 31721


Memo:                                       Denise Drawer
           0011957:0597087:87159-095
```

FIGURE 23.2 Sample Check

> **PROMISSORY NOTE**
>
> $ 25,000.00   December 31, 2016
>
> Three years after date (without grace) I promise to pay to the order of Pedro Payee the sum of twenty five thousand and no/100 dollars for the value received with interest of 5.49 percent per annum compounded daily from the above date until paid. Both principal and interest are payable only in lawful money of the United States.
>
> **Payable at:** 107 Pleasant Avenue, Richmond, VA 23249 **Due:** December 31, 2019
>
> *Darlene Drawer*
> Signature

FIGURE 23.3 Sample Promissory Note

purchase of a car, for example) for which he agrees to pay the payee in the future under terms specified by the note. For an example of a note, see Figure 23.3.

Certificate of Deposit

Like a note, a certificate of deposit is also an instrument that evidences debt (see Figure 23.4). The only difference between a note and a CD is that a CD is only issued by a bank or other financial institution as evidence of its debt to a named creditor/depositor. Whenever you invest in a bank CD, you might think of the transaction as a deposit of money; in reality, however, you are lending the bank money under the terms specified by the CD, for which the bank issues you its promise to repay you at a stated time in the future your principal plus interest at a specified rate.

Requirements for Negotiability

As we've already seen, an instrument must meet certain specific requirements to qualify for the special status of a negotiable instrument. The qualifying criteria bear a closer look, since each criterion is essential for an instrument to gain the status of a negotiable instrument.

The Requirement of a Signed Writing

The UCC does not define what constitutes a writing for purposes of creating a negotiable instrument, but the requirement has been liberally construed by the courts to include words written on nearly any portable surface that affords some permanence. No specific words need to be used in creating a negotiable instrument as long as the writing meets all the requirements for negotiability. Thus, even though most checks are routinely written on preprinted forms supplied by the financial institution in which the drawer maintains

> **CERTIFICATE OF DEPOSIT**
>
> DATE: October 1, 2016
>
> For value received, the LAST BANK OF EREHWON promises to pay to Dennis and Denise Depositors the principal sum of Ten Thousand Dollars ($10,000.00) with interest eighteen months (18 months) from the date hereof at the rate of One and One Quarter Percent (1.25%) per annum compounded daily. The said principal and interest shall be payable in lawful money of the United States of America at 123 Main Street, in the State of California, or at any branch of the LAST BANK OF EREHWON in the state.
>
> LAST BANK OF EREHWON   *Orlando Officer*
> 123 Main Street   Senior Vice President
> Mojave, CA 93501

FIGURE 23.4 Sample Certificate of Deposit

a checking account, a check can technically be written on nearly any surface capable of accepting writing. A valid check, note, draft, or even a CD can be written on a legal pad, loose-leaf paper, a shirt, or even a coconut shell (though it might take some convincing to get someone to accept such an instrument!). Likewise, the writing can be created with a typewriter, computer printer, pen, crayon, pencil, or even lipstick. Using any medium that is easy to erase, however, can lead to problems if the instrument is later altered. And, as with a negotiable coconut, using an exotic writing surface or implement may well make the instrument unacceptable to most payees.

As is the case with the type of paper or writing implement used to create a negotiable instrument, the requirement of a signature is rather liberally construed by the courts. The UCC specifically states: "A signature may be made (i) manually or by means of a device or machine, and (ii) by the use of any name, including any trade or assumed name, or by a word, mark, or symbol executed or adopted by a person with present intention to authenticate a writing" [§ 3-401(b)]. So an X on paper, a scanned signature, or a signature reproduced on a rubber stamp are all perfectly valid, as is the signed or printed name or initials of any signer, as long as these are used intentionally as a signature. Instruments may also be electronically signed. Adding /s/ immediately before typing one's name on an email or online form is sufficient as a signature, for example, as is true of other online authentication protocols such as clicking on a link to electronically insert an "electronic signature" on a document.

The Requirement of an Unconditional Promise

To be negotiable, an instrument must on its face make an unconditional promise to pay a specific amount of money by a drawer or maker to a named payee or to bearer. With some limited exceptions noted in Section 3-106 of the UCC, a conditional promise destroys the negotiable nature of an instrument. Hence, a check that reads "Pay to the order of Paul Payee $200 if the U.S. wins the 2019 Women's Soccer World Cup Championship" is not a negotiable instrument, since the promise to pay is conditioned on the happening of a future event.

The Requirement of a Sum Certain in Money

A negotiable instrument must be payable in cash, and the amount payable on the instrument must be ascertainable from the instrument itself. The requirement that the instrument be payable in money is met if it is payable in the legal tender of any country; thus, a draft payable in yen, euros, pounds sterling, and pesos is perfectly negotiable if it meets all the other requirements of a negotiable instrument. An instrument payable in a foreign currency, unless otherwise noted on the instrument itself, can be paid in the stated currency or in the U.S. equivalent of the currency at the time and place of its presentment for payment [§ 3-107]. In addition, the fact that an instrument is payable with fixed or variable interest will not affect negotiability, even if the interest payable must be ascertained by reference to information not provided in the instrument. If the interest cannot be ascertained from the instrument itself or by reference to outside information, then interest is payable at the judgment rate at the place of payment at the time and in the place that the interest first accrues [§ 3-112 (b)].

The Requirement of No Other Promise or Obligation

Negotiable instruments must contain only an unconditional promise to pay a sum certain in currency. If there are other obligations or promises cited in the instrument along with the promise to pay money, the instrument will not be negotiable. For example, an instrument that promises to pay payee "one hundred dollars and two ounces of gold" is nonnegotiable, as is a promise by a carpenter to "pay $50 and build a deck." The additional promises of payment of gold and the building of a deck make the respective instrument nonnegotiable.

The Requirement That the Instrument Be Payable on Demand or at a Specific Time

Negotiable instruments must be payable either on demand or at a specifically ascertainable date. Instruments such as checks that are not usually payable at a specific time are demand instruments and are payable at any time on demand as soon as they are issued. For instruments that are payable on or after a specific date, all that is required is that it be clear from the instrument itself when it is payable. Thus, an instrument that is payable "30 days from today" or "on July 1, 2020" is a time instrument and satisfies the requirement of specificity as to the date when it is payable. The mere fact that an instrument is subject to acceleration upon the happening of an event (such as the maker's late payment of an instrument payable on a monthly basis) will not destroy negotiability, nor will the fact that the instrument is subject to an extension upon the request of one or more of the parties [§ 3-108 (b)]. But if the instrument is payable only upon an event that is not certain to occur (such as "when the New York Yankees next win the World Series"), then it is not negotiable.

The Requirement That the Instrument Be Payable to Order or to Bearer

An instrument must either be payable to the order of a specific person (or persons) or company or to bearer. An instrument is payable to order if it states that it is payable to a specifically ascertainable person, company, or group of people. An instrument is payable to bearer if it is payable to no specifically identifiable person [§ 3-109 (a) (3)], but rather can be paid to anyone who lawfully has it in his possession. An instrument is made payable to bearer by such terms as pay to bearer, pay to the order of bearer, pay to cash, pay to the order of cash, or any language that makes the instrument payable to no specifically ascertainable person or company. (See Sections 3-109 (a) (1), (2), and (3)). A check made payable to "life, the universe, and everything," for example, is a bearer instrument, since it names no specifically ascertainable person; its effect is the same as drawing a check to the order of cash as a payee. On the other hand, a check made payable to the order of "First National Bank of Ohio savings account # A123456" would be payable to the registered owner or owners of the account and would be a negotiable instrument, since there is sufficient information on the face of the instrument with which to identify the specific payee or payees. (See Section 3-110 (c) (1)).

General Rules Applicable to Commercial Paper

Antedating and Postdating the Date on Negotiable Instruments [§ 3-113]

The negotiability of an instrument is unaffected by postdating or antedating. If, for example, a check issued on August 1 is postdated for September 1, it is still a negotiable instrument.

Incomplete Instruments [§ 3-115]

A negotiable instrument that has not been completely filled out by the maker or drawer cannot be enforced until it is complete. But it is permissible for the holder of an incomplete instrument to complete it by filling in missing information as long as the completion is authorized. If a completion is unauthorized, the rules relating to material alteration apply, and the instrument is generally void. The burden of proving an unauthorized material alteration is on the party making the assertion that the instrument has been materially altered without authorization.

The significance of this section is that good-faith additions to negotiable instruments by persons who have the instrument in their possession are generally lawful unless they are unauthorized. A person receiving a check in which the date has been omitted, for example, could safely insert the date that the check was negotiated to him. In addition, a blank check (a check that is signed by the maker but is otherwise incomplete) can also be lawfully filled out by the person to whom it is given as long as the drawer intended to authorize the person to do so.

Instruments Payable to Two or More Persons [§ 3-110 (d)]

An instrument payable to two or more parties in the alternative can be negotiated by any of the named parties alone. If an instrument is negotiated to two or more parties jointly, however, the signatures of both parties are necessary to effect lawful negotiation. If, for example, a check is made payable to Jane or John Doe (payable in the alternative), either John or Jane may cash the entire check. If the check is made out to John and Jane Doe (payable jointly), however, both John's and Jane's signatures would be required to negotiate the check.

Contradictory Terms of Instrument [§ 3-114]

When an instrument contains contradictory terms, "typewritten terms prevail over pre-printed terms, handwritten terms prevail over both and words prevail over numbers."

Statute of Limitations [§118]

In general, the statute of limitations for enforcing commercial paper is as follows:

- An action to collect on note payable at a definite time must be instituted within six years of the due date.
- An action to enforce a demand note must be instituted within six years of the demand for payment. Actions to enforce payment of a demand note are barred after ten years if neither interest nor principal is paid for a continuous period of ten years.
- An action to enforce an unaccepted draft must be begun within three years after dishonor of the draft, or after ten years of the date of the draft if the draft is not presented for payment and dishonored, whichever occurs first.
- An action to enforce the obligation of an acceptor of a certified check or the issuer of a cashier's check, teller's check, or traveler's check must be begun within three years after demand for payment is made of the acceptor or issuer.
- An action to collect on a dishonored certificate of deposit must be commenced within six years of the CD's due date.
- An action to enforce an accepted draft (other than a check) must be commenced within six years after the due date or dates stated in the draft, or within six years of the acceptance if the obligation of the acceptor is payable on demand.

Questions

1. What are the four basic types of negotiable instruments?
2. What is the fundamental difference between a note and a certificate of deposit? What function do these two instruments serve?
3. What is the fundamental difference between a draft and a check? What purpose do both instruments serve?
4. What are the basic requirements that every instrument must meet to be a negotiable instrument?
5. What is the effect of antedating or postdating a check?
6. How must an instrument that is made payable to Tom, Dick, and Harriet Jones be negotiated?
7. What type of instrument is a check made payable to "A billion grains of sand"? Is such an instrument valid?
8. A check made payable to Jane Doe has $100 written in figures in the box provided for the amount, but states "One thousand dollars" in writing on the space provided to state the amount of the check in writing.

Is the check valid? If so, for what amount? If not, why not?
9. Peter Payee receives a check as a birthday gift from his grandmother. The check is made out for $50 to him as payee, but the drawer neglected to write in a date on the space provided and also forgot to write in the amount in words in the space provided on the check. Peter, eager to buy two new games for his new game console on sale that week for $25 each, fills out the missing date and the words "Fifty and NO/100 dollars" on the check and negotiates it to his local games dealer. Is the check valid? Has Peter committed an unlawful act in completing the check?
10. Mark Maker issues a note to Percival Payee for $500. The note is made payable one year from the date of issue with interest, but no interest rate is specified. Is the instrument valid and, if so, what interest rate is payable?

Hypothetical Cases

1. Bob borrows $500 from his friend Lina. In exchange for the money, he gives her a piece of paper like the one that follows. Is this a negotiable instrument? Explain.

> Date: May 1, 2017
>
> I, Bob Borrower, hereby acknowledge that I owe Leona Lender the sum of $500.
>
> *Bob Borrower*

2. Albert and Betty find themselves shipwrecked on a deserted island in the South Pacific after their small boat capsizes. Fearing that they will not be rescued and wishing to alleviate his guilty conscience, Albert decides to pay off a long-standing debt to Betty of $10,000. Feeling generous in his belief that the two may well have to spend the rest of their lives alone in the island, he tells Betty that he would like to give her $20,000 as payment of the debt and the interest that has accrued over the past ten years. Since the parties have neither paper nor writing implements handy, Albert tears off a piece of board from the remains of their boat and uses a rusty nail to scratch out the following message on its surface:

> Date: July 4, 2017
> To: Third Bank of Nevada (A/C 123-45678)
> Pay to the order of Betty Lender $20,000 (twenty thousand and no/100 dollars)
> Albert Debtor

The next day, much to Albert's surprise, they are rescued by a passing cruise ship. Is the instrument that Albert executed valid? If so, what type of an instrument is it?

3. On June 1, 2016, Darlene issues a check to Daniel that is dated July 1, 2016. The instrument is made payable to Daniel's order "If the Florida Marlins win the World Series." Is the instrument negotiable? Explain.

4. Answer the questions that follow based on this instrument:

> Date: 1/1/2017
> TO: Sam Shoemaker, President
>   ABC Industries
> One year from today, pay to the order of Sandy Jones $1,000.00 (two thousand dollars and xx/100) plus simple interest at 7% per annum.
>   *Benjamin Brewster*
> Payment Guaranteed: *Rhoda Roberts*

A. What type of instrument is this?
B. What is Benjamin Brewster's function in relation to the instrument?
C. What is Sam Shoemaker's (of ABC Industries) function in relation to the instrument?
D. What is Sandy Jones's function in relation to the instrument?
E. What is Rhoda Roberts's function in relation to the instrument?
F. Is the instrument valid as written and, if so, exactly how much will be payable under the instrument when it is presented for payment on January 1, 2018?

Transfer and Negotiation of Commercial Paper and Rights of Holders

CHAPTER 24

Chapter Outline

Transfer of Negotiable Instruments and the Transferee's Right to an Indorsement

Negotiation [§ 3-201]

Indorsement [§ 3-204]

Rights of a Holder

Rights of a Holder in Due Course

Unlike the transfer of an ownership interest in most tangible personal property, which can be accomplished without any specific formalities, the transfer of negotiable instruments requires following a set procedure for the *transferee* (the person to whom the instrument is transferred) to gain the special status of a holder of the instrument. In this chapter, we will explore the statutory requirements for transferring commercial paper.

Transfer of Negotiable Instruments and the Transferee's Right to an Indorsement

Generally speaking, the legal transfer of an interest in a negotiable instrument from one person to another is accomplished by an *indorsement* (a signature placed by the holder of the instrument on the back of the instrument) and the delivery of the instrument to the person intended to be the instrument's new holder. The accomplishment of such a transfer is termed a negotiation of the instrument and generally transfers to the new holder whatever rights the *transferor* had in the instrument. If the transferor of a negotiable instrument neglects to indorse the instrument, Section 3-203 (c) gives the *transferee* (the person to whom the instrument is transferred) the unqualified right to obtain specific performance of the transferor's indorsement if the instrument was transferred for value. Negotiation of the instrument, however, does not occur until the indorsement is made.

Negotiation [§ 3-201]

Negotiation is defined as "a transfer of possession, whether voluntary or involuntary, of an instrument by a person other than the issuer to a person that thereby becomes its holder" [§ 3-201 (a)]. An instrument payable to the order of a specific person or company is negotiated by the physical transfer of the instrument containing the indorsement of the holder, and a *bearer instrument* (one that is payable to cash, to bearer, or payable to the order of no specifically identifiable party) is negotiated merely through possession alone, without the requirement that it be indorsed by the transferor [§ 3-201 (b)].

Indorsement [§ 3-204]

An indorsement is defined as a "signature, other than that of a signer as maker, drawer or acceptor, that alone or accompanied by other words is made on an instrument for the purpose of (i) negotiating the instrument, (ii) restricting payment of the instrument, or (iii) incurring indorser's liability on the instrument" [§ 3-204 (a)].

175

We have already seen that the order of a drawer of a draft to the drawee to pay the payee, as well as the promise of the maker to pay the payee must be unconditional. But the indorser of a negotiable instrument can make the indorsement conditional without destroying its negotiability. Thus, an indorsement that reads "Pay to Jane Doe if the Yankees win the World Series" is a valid indorsement. (We'll take a look at special and restrictive indorsements in the following two sections in this chapter.)

The UCC provides that an indorsement must be written by the indorser or on his behalf on the instrument, or on a separate piece of paper that is permanently attached to the instrument [§ 3-204 (a)]. Stapling, gluing, or otherwise permanently affixing a separate sheet of paper to a negotiable instrument for indorsements when the space in the back of the instrument is used up is perfectly valid. When an additional sheet of paper is required to be attached to a negotiable instrument for additional indorsements, it is called an *allonge*.

In the event that an instrument is made payable to a person with her name misspelled or even with a mistaken name, it is lawful for the payee to indorse the instrument either under her correctly spelled or true name, as well as under the misspelled or incorrect name. A person accepting transfer of the instrument, however, can demand that the indorsee in such circumstances sign both with the correct and misspelled or incorrect names [§ 3-204 (d)].

Special, Blank, and Anomalous Indorsements [§ 3-205]

A special indorsement specifies the person or persons to whom the instrument is made payable. When an instrument is specially indorsed to a specifically identifiable person or company, the instrument cannot be further negotiated without that person's indorsement [§ 3-205 (a)]. For example, if Albert makes out a check to Betty and Betty indorses it as follows: "Pay Carmen" or "Pay to the order of Carmen," the check is specially indorsed, and Carmen will need to indorse it next before it can be further negotiated to any other person.

A blank indorsement, on the other hand, does not specify any specific person but merely consists of a signature or a signature preceded by words such as "Pay to cash," "Pay bearer," or "Pay anybody." A check that is indorsed in blank is a bearer instrument and can be further negotiated merely by transferring it to a third party [§ 3-205 (b)].

If a person who is not a holder of an instrument attempts to indorse it, such an indorsement is termed an anomalous indorsement, and is invalid and does not affect the manner in which the instrument may be negotiated.

The nature of a negotiable instrument is determined by examining the instrument's last indorsement. An instrument indorsed in blank is bearer paper, whereas a specially indorsed instrument is order paper.

Restrictive Indorsements [§ 3-206]

A restrictive indorsement is one that fits one of the following criteria:

- A conditional indorsement (such as "pay to Jane Doe if a Democrat wins the next presidential election") or an indorsement that purports to prohibit further transfer of the instrument (such as "pay Jane Doe only"). Such indorsements do not affect the negotiability of the instrument under Section 3-206 (b), and the named indorsee is free to further negotiate the instrument regardless of whether or not the restrictive condition is met.

- Indorsements that signal a purpose of deposit or collection by part of the indorsee in negotiating the instrument (e.g., "for deposit," "pay any bank," or "for collection"). Such indorsements are generally valid, and any person, bank, or entity that takes the instrument for value inconsistent with the indorsement converts the instrument.

- Indorsements made to agents, trustees, or other fiduciaries (such as Pay Lina Lawyer as attorney for Clint Client). Persons who purchase instruments from indorsees in good faith under such circumstances may pay the indorsees the instrument's value without regard to whether the indorsee violates a fiduciary duty to the principal. Thus, a bank may safely pay a check indorsed to "Larry Lawyer, attorney for Clara Client" unless it knows that Larry is cashing the check intending to defraud his client by keeping the proceeds for himself.

Rights of a Holder

The UCC defines a holder as "the person in possession [of a negotiable instrument] if the instrument is payable to bearer or, in the cases of an instrument payable to an identified person, if the identified person is in possession" [§ 1-201 (20)]. Thus, the original payee of a note or draft is a holder when the instrument is delivered to him, as are all persons to whom instruments are transferred with special indorsements in their benefit or with blank indorsements.

A person who obtains the status of a holder of a negotiable instrument gains the right to further transfer or negotiate it, and to enforce its payment whether or not she is the instrument's true owner [§ 3-301]. Anyone may transfer a negotiable instrument once the status of holder is achieved. This can present problems, especially when bearer instruments are involved, since anyone (even a thief) can negotiate them. Even though persons who wrongfully cash or otherwise negotiate instruments breach the presentment and transfer warranties or title (as we'll see later), it can still be a problem when such persons cannot be found or are found to be insolvent after a wrongful transfer. The reason is that the rightful issuer or owner of the instrument may not then be able to successfully sue for the loss resulting from the wrongful negotiation.

When a holder transfers an instrument, however, he does so subject to any claims that can be asserted to payment of the instrument by third parties, as well as all normal claims and defenses based on breach of contract [§ 3-306]. Thus, even though a holder might have the legal right (or power, if you prefer) to transfer an instrument, she will generally be subject to liability if the transfer is wrongful. For example, if a thief finds a check indorsed in blank, he can negotiate it to an innocent third party or cash it at his bank. However, he will be subject to civil liability (as well as criminal penalties) for the wrongful transfer and conversion of the instrument if he is sued by the drawer of the check or any person to whom he wrongfully transferred it. Likewise, a person who receives a check as his consideration under a contract will be able to cash the check but will be subject to liability to the drawer for the value of the check if he does not properly perform his end of the bargain.

Rights of a Holder in Due Course

A person is a holder in due course under the definition of Section 3-302 if he takes a negotiable instrument

- for value; and
- in good faith; and
- without notice that it is overdue or has been dishonored or that there is an uncured default with respect to payment on another instrument issued as part of the same series; and
- without notice that the instrument contains an unauthorized signature or has been altered; and
- without notice of any claim of a property interest or possessory right in the instrument or its proceeds by another; and
- without notice that any party has a defense or claim in recoupment if the claim arose from the transaction that gave rise to the instrument (for example, if there was a breach of contract giving the drawer or maker of the instrument a valid claim against the payee to whom the instrument was issued as consideration of the breached contract).

The significance of holder in due course status is that a holder in due course (HDC) takes an instrument free from most defenses to its payment. A payee or indorsee who qualifies for HDC status is in an excellent position when demanding payment of a negotiable instrument because only real defenses that relate to the validity of the instrument itself can be asserted against an HDC. Thus, an HDC takes an instrument free of all defenses other than the real defenses enumerated in Section 3-305 (a) (1), which include

- infancy, to the extent that it is a defense to a simple contract;
- duress, lack of legal capacity, or illegality of the transaction, which nullifies the obligation of the obligor;
- misrepresentation that induces a party to sign a negotiable instrument without understanding its character or its terms (fraud in the execution);
- discharge in insolvency proceedings.

The following example will illustrate the significance of the holder in due course status:

- Buyer gives seller a check for $1,000 in exchange for seller's promise to ship a 60-inch high-definition LCD television set. As soon as he receives the check, the seller indorses it to XYZ Oil Company to pay for a delivery of fuel oil in that amount. XYZ in turn indorses the check and deposits it in its account at Second National Bank. If the television set that eventually arrives at buyer's home is a 37-inch rather than a 60-inch set, can the buyer demand that either XYZ or Second National Bank refund the amount they were paid upon negotiation of the check?

The answer here depends on whether or not XYZ Oil Company and Second National Bank are holders in due course. Since they each accepted the negotiable instrument for value, in good faith and without notice that there were any claims against it, they qualify as holders in due course and are not subject to the defense of breach of contract that buyer has against seller—the original payee and subsequent transferor of the instrument. Does the original payee also qualify for holder in due course status, or can the buyer force it to refund the amount it received from negotiating the check? Clearly, the seller is not a holder in due course, since he obviously knew that that there would be a claim against payment of the check for breach of contract when he shipped the nonconforming goods to the buyer.

Questions

1. What are the two steps required to transfer a negotiable instrument?
2. What is a negotiation?
3. Is a conditional indorsement valid?
4. If a drawer misspells a payee's name, how can the payee negotiate the instrument?
5. What are special and blank indorsements?
6. What are restrictive indorsements?
7. What is the UCC definition of the term *holder*?
8. How does a person become a holder in due course?
9. What is the significance of holder in due course status?
10. What defenses are valid even against a holder in due course?

Hypothetical Cases

1. Danielle Drawer writes a check payable to Pablo Payee for $50. Pablo, who owes Inga Indorsee $50, signs his name on the reverse of the check and hands it to her. Answer the following questions based on these facts:

    A. What type of indorsement did Pablo make?
    B. After Pablo's indorsement, is the instrument order paper or bearer paper?
    C. If a thief were to steal the check after Pablo's indorsement, would the thief be able to cash the check?

2. Don Drawer gives a check to his friend Pamela Payee as a birthday gift. Pamela indorses the check "Pay any bank, [signed] Pam Payee." Answer the following questions based on these facts:
   A. Is Pamela a holder of the instrument when Don gives her the check?
   B. Is Pamela a holder in due course of the instrument? Explain.
   C. Is Pamela's bank a holder in due course after it accepts the check and credits her account? Explain.
3. Assume the same facts as the previous question:
   A. What type of indorsement is involved?
   B. Is the negotiation from Pamela to her bank valid given that she signed her name as Pam Payee rather than Pamela Payee?
4. Matthew Maker drafted a note payable to Sam Slimy for $1,000 payable on demand. At the time that Matthew drafted the note, Sam held a gun to his head. A day later, Sam indorses the note to Irene Innocent in exchange for $1,000 in cash. When Irene tries to cash the note with Matthew, will Matthew have to pay it? Would your answer be the same if Irene had taken the note in exchange for $200 in cash? Explain fully.

Liability of Parties to Commercial Paper and Warranties of Transfer and of Presentment

CHAPTER 25

Chapter Outline

Liability of Parties to Commercial Paper

Warranties on Presentment and Transfer

Presentment and Notice of Dishonor

As we've already seen, the primary purpose of negotiable instruments is to facilitate commercial transactions by acting as a substitute for cash or as evidence of debt and a guarantee of its repayment. We've also seen that there is an element of risk to persons who issue negotiable instruments since they must generally pay holders in due course under the terms of the instrument and are barred from asserting most defenses to its payment. If we ended our discussion of commercial paper here, it might well seem that the risk inherent in the negotiation of these instruments is an unacceptable one. Fortunately, the makers and drawers of negotiable instruments do have a measure of protection against most adverse circumstances that can arise out of the transfer of these instruments through the contractual and signature liability that arises from the transfer of a negotiable instrument and from the warranties that automatically attach when such instruments are negotiated or presented for payment to the drawees or makers. In this chapter, we will explore the liability of parties to commercial paper as well as the warranties of transfer and presentment that arise from their negotiation.

Liability of Parties to Commercial Paper

Parties to commercial paper can have essentially two types of liability: signature liability and contractual liability. Signature liability arises from the act of signing a negotiable instrument to create or transfer it, while contractual liability attaches based on the relationship that parties have to one another with regard to the instrument being created or negotiated. We'll examine both types of liability in turn.

Signature Liability

Before a person can be found to have any liability on a negotiable instrument, the person's signature must appear on the instrument, or the instrument must be signed by an authorized agent on the person's behalf [§ 3-401 (1)]. As we've previously seen, the UCC is rather liberal in determining what constitutes a signature, essentially holding any mark made by a party with the intention of having it serve as a signature to be a valid signature [§ 3-401 (2)]. Since no person is liable on an instrument unless her signature appears on it, the drawee of a draft or check is not liable on the instrument at the time that the drawer draws the instrument. However, the drawee becomes liable to pay it upon signaling his intention to do so by signing on the face of an instrument as an acceptor. If the drawee is a bank, rather than a person, it also has no liability on a draft [§ 3-408]. A bank is, of course, liable on a bank check where it is both the drawer and drawee of the instrument and signs as drawer on the face of the instrument.

The mere fact that a person's signature appears on commercial paper can subject the signer to liability for the instrument. It is not necessary that the signer receive any consideration for signing or have any relationship to the instrument; all that is required is that the signature be genuine and that the signer intentionally placed it on the instrument. If, for example, Albert asks Betty to carry a check over to Charlie, who is ten feet away, and Betty signs on the reverse of the check before giving it to Charlie, she has signature liability as an indorser of the check—even though she was not asked to sign, had no need to sign, and certainly received no consideration for signing her name on the check.

Unauthorized Signatures

In general, individuals are not liable to pay on negotiable instruments unless they sign the instruments. If an unauthorized signature is placed on a negotiable instrument (a forged signature, for example), the signature is ineffective. Similarly, if a person claiming to act as an agent on behalf of a principal signs a negotiable instrument on the principal's behalf but does so without the principal's authority, the unauthorized signature is ineffective as to the principal but will constitute the valid signature of the unauthorized signer unless the principal subsequently ratifies the agent's unauthorized signature [§ 3-403 (a)]. On the other hand, if a person's negligence contributes to the forgery [§3-406 (a)], such as the leaving of a signature stamp in plain sight where a forger avails himself of it to affix an unauthorized, genuine signature to a check, then the defense of unauthorized signature may not be asserted against a holder in due course.

Contractual Liability

Parties who sign commercial paper incur contractual liability for payment of an instrument that can be either primary or secondary, depending on the relation of the parties to the instrument. The maker of a note, cashier's check, or other draft drawn on the drawee has primary liability for payment of the instrument [§ 3-412], as does the acceptor of a draft or bank that certifies a check drawn on it by a depositor [§ 3 413]. Once a draft has been accepted by a bank, the drawer's liability is discharged [§ 3-414 (c)]. If a draft is accepted by a drawee that is not a bank, and the acceptor subsequently dishonors the draft when it is presented for payment, the drawer retains secondary liability on the draft [§ 3-414 (d)] to the payee and to any indorsers. The drawer of a draft or check that has not been accepted by the drawee, on the other hand, has secondary liability for its payment that does not arise unless the drawee dishonors the draft or check when it is presented to it for payment [§ 3-414 (b)]. In addition, Section 3-414 (e) allows the drawer to limit even his contractual liability for payment of an instrument by drawing the instrument "without recourse," which limits the right of the payee to seek payment on the instrument only from the drawee.

Indorsers of negotiable instruments are all secondarily liable for payment of the instrument if the primarily liable parties fail to discharge the instrument when it is presented for payment. If an instrument is dishonored, an indorser must pay any person who has indorsed the instrument after him [§ 3-415 (a)] after being given proper notice of dishonor [§ 3-503 (a)] by such subsequent indorsers.

In addition to drawers and indorsers, accommodation parties who sign an instrument in order to bolster its acceptance by a payee or indorser can also be either primarily or secondarily liable on the instrument, depending on whether they sign it on its face or as indorsers, and on the nature of their signature. An accommodation party may sign as maker, drawer, acceptor, or indorser and is obligated to pay the instrument in accordance with the capacity in which he signs [§ 3-419 (b)]. Accommodation parties who sign as guarantors (e.g., attaching such terms as "payment guaranteed" or "guarantor" along with their signatures) bear secondary liability and must pay on the instrument if it is dishonored once an execution of judgment against the accommodated party has been returned unsatisfied, or if the accommodated party is insolvent, undergoing insolvency proceedings, cannot be served with process, or when it is otherwise apparent that payment cannot be obtained [§ 3-419 (d)].

The contractual liability of parties to an instrument can be summarized as follows:

- Drawer: Secondarily liable on a check or draft it has drawn (pays if the instrument is dishonored when presented for payment to the drawee).
- Drawee: Primarily liable on a check or draft it has accepted.
- Maker: Primarily liable on a note or CD it has executed.
- Accommodation Party: Secondarily liable for payment of a note or draft it has indorsed in order to guarantee its payment. Primarily liable on a note or draft it has signed as a primary party (such as comaker).
- Guarantor: Secondarily liable for payment of a note or draft for which it has guaranteed payment by signing as guarantor on its face. (The guarantor must use language that unequivocally identifies it as a guarantor rather than as a comaker.)
- Indorser: Secondarily liable to all parties to whom a note or draft is negotiated after it negotiates the instrument. Must refund whatever consideration it received for negotiating the draft if it is dishonored by the primarily liable parties.

Warranties on Presentment and Transfer

In addition to the contractual liability of parties to commercial paper, there are implied warranties that attach to the transfer of a negotiable instrument and to its presentment for payment.

Presentment Warranties

Section 3-417 (a) of the UCC specifies that any person who receives payment or acceptance of a draft and all other previous transferors of the draft make the following three implied warranties to the drawee or acceptor of the draft:

1. that at the time of transfer the warrantor had the right to enforce the draft or obtain payment or acceptance of the draft on behalf of a person entitled to enforce it;
2. that the draft has not been dishonored; and
3. that the warrantor has no knowledge that the signature of the drawer of the draft is unauthorized.

Transfer Warranties

Section 3-416 of the UCC provides that any person who transfers a negotiable instrument for consideration makes the following five warranties to the transferee (the person to whom the instrument is transferred):

1. the warrantor is entitled to enforce the instrument;
2. all signatures are authentic and authorized;
3. the instrument has not been altered;
4. the instrument is not subject to a defense or claim in recoupment of any party which can be asserted against the warrantor; and
5. the warrantor has no knowledge of any insolvency proceeding commenced with respect to the maker or acceptor or, in the case of an unaccepted draft, the drawee.

Presentment and Notice of Dishonor

Presentment of an instrument is a demand made by a person entitled to enforce the instrument that it be paid or *accepted* (an acknowledgment by a maker or drawee that the instrument is valid and will be paid when due) [see § 3-501 (a)]. In general, presentment of an instrument to the primarily liable party for acceptance is a prerequisite to invoking secondary liability on an instrument. Presentment may be made at the place of payment of the instrument (and must be made at the place of payment if the instrument is payable at a bank in the United States), may be made by any commercially reasonable means, and is effective when the demand for payment or acceptance is received [§ 3-501 (b) (1)].

The party to whom presentment is made may treat presentment as occurring on the next business day after the day of presentment if it has established a cutoff hour not earlier than 2:00 PM for the review and processing of instruments presented for payment or acceptance and the presentment is made after the cutoff hour [§ 3-501 (4)].

Notice of Dishonor

Notice of dishonor may be given by any commercially reasonable means including written, oral, and electronic communications [§ 3-405 (b)]. If the notice of dishonor is given by a bank that has taken the instrument for collection, it must give such notice by midnight of the next banking day following the banking day in which the bank itself receives notice of dishonor of the instrument [§ 3-503 (c)]. Notice of dishonor given by any other person taking an instrument for collection must be given within 30 days following the day the person receives the notice of dishonor [§ 3-503 (c)]. With respect to any other instrument (e.g., instruments not taken for collection), notice of dishonor must be given within 30 days following the day on which dishonor occurs [§ 3-5-3 (c)]. But an indorser can disclaim his contractual liability by indorsing the instrument "without recourse" [§ 3-415 (b)]. For example, if a lawyer accepts a check made out to her that is intended for her client, the lawyer can indorse the check "without recourse" and negotiate it to the client. If the check is later dishonored, the lawyer would have no contractual liability. The client would accept the check under these circumstances with the "without recourse" indorsement because the client is aware that the lawyer is merely acting as an agent when indorsing the check and bears no personal liability for the validity of the check.

Questions

1. What are the two types of liability that parties to commercial paper have?
2. What parties to commercial paper have primary liability for its payment?
3. What parties have secondary contractual liability for payment of commercial paper?
4. What two basic types of warranties are involved in commercial paper transactions?
5. What are the warranties of presentment and when are they available?
6. What are the warranties of transfer and to whom do they apply?
7. When must presentment be made when the instrument does not specify a time for presentment?
8. What is the time frame within which an instrument presented for acceptance must be accepted?
9. What is the time frame within which an instrument presented for payment must be accepted?
10. What is the time frame within which notice of dishonor needs to be given by a bank and a party who is not a bank?

Hypothetical Cases

1. Examine the sample negotiable instrument that follows and answer the questions that relate to it:

> January 10, 2017
> Two years from date, I promise to pay Ed Biosca $2,000.00 (two thousand dollars and xx/100) with interest at the rate of 5.50% per annum, compounded daily.
>
> *Beulah Borrower*
>
> Payment Guaranteed: *Nat Toobright*

   A. What type of instrument is this?
   B. Who is/are the primarily liable party or parties to this instrument?
   C. Is there a secondarily liable party to this instrument? If so, who is it?

2. Assume the same facts as in the previous question. Assume further that on January 10, 2019, Ed Biosca presents this note to Beulah Borrower. When must Beulah pay the instrument?

3. Sam Slick, a crook, finds a check made out to Pamela Payee in the amount of $10 on Pamela's desk at work. He steals the check, changes the amount to $100, forges Pam's signature, and specially indorses the check to himself as indorsee. The next day, Sam negotiates the instrument to Ignacio Innocent, a coworker, who does not know of the theft or alteration of the check and who pays Sam $100 for the instrument.

   A. What transfer warranties has Sam breached in negotiating the check to Ignacio?
   B. What transfer warranty or warranties has Sam not breached in negotiating the instrument?

4. Examine the sample instrument that follows and then answer the questions that relate to it:

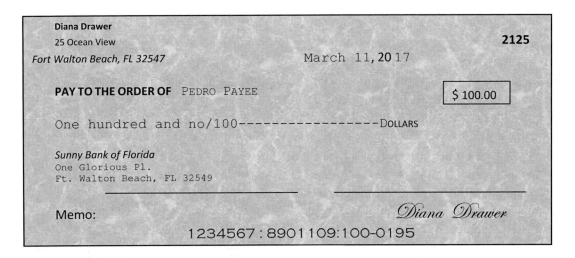

   A. What type of instrument is this?
   B. If Pedro deposits the check in his account and it turns out that Diane did not have sufficient funds to cover the instrument, how long does Pedro's bank have to notify him of the dishonor when it learns of it?
   C. How may the bank notify Pedro of the dishonor?

Introduction to UCC Article 9 (Secured Transactions)

CHAPTER 26

A large portion of business transactions at the wholesale and retail levels involving personal property are done on a credit basis. Some of them involve unsecured debt, such as transactions paid by credit cards or unsecured personal bank loans (also called signature loans). When large loans are involved, or when dealing with consumers or businesses whose credit histories make them bad credit risks, sellers often protect themselves by retaining a security interest in the goods sold or in other personal property belonging to the debtor as security in the event that the debtor defaults on the debt.

Chapter Outline

Applicability
Basic Terminology
Creating a Security Interest
Perfecting a Security Interest
Duration of a Perfected Security Interest
Priorities among Conflicting Security Interests in the Same Collateral
Default

Applicability

Article 9 of the UCC generally applies to secured transactions relating to personal property or fixtures, agricultural liens, a sale of accounts, *chattel paper* (a writing that evidences a monetary obligation and security interest in goods or a lease of goods), intangible personal property (including patents and copyrights), and *consignments* (transactions wherein goods are delivered to merchants for sale) [§ 9-109 (a)]. UCC Article 9 does not apply, however, when preempted by other federal or state laws or the applicable laws of another country with respect to the creation or enforcement of security interests [§ 9-109 (c)]. Article 9 also does not apply to the following [§ 9-109 (d)]:

- nonagricultural landlord's liens, a sale of accounts chattel paper, paper intangibles, or promissory notes as part of the sale of a business out of which they arose;
- assignments of accounts, chattel paper, payment intangibles or promissory notes for the purposes of collection (e.g., the assignment of delinquent accounts to collection agencies for collection);
- the creation or transfer of interests in or liens on real property (mortgages on real property, for example, are not covered by this article).

The National Conference of Commissioners on Uniform State Laws (NCCUSL) promulgated a revised version of Article 9 in 2010 that has been adopted by all 50 states, Washington D.C., and Puerto Rico. (The U.S. Virgin Islands as of this writing has not adopted the 2010 revision; it has adopted the 1998 version of the act.)

187

Basic Terminology

Before we continue our discussion of secured transactions, it will be useful to define some basic terms (Section 9-102 (a) contains 80 key definitions):

- **Collateral:** Property subject to a security interest or agricultural lien [§ 9-102 (a) 12)];
- **Consignee:** A person to whom goods are delivered in a consignment [§ 9-102 (a) (19)];
- **Consignment:** A transaction, regardless or its form, in which a person delivers goods to a merchant for the purpose of sale and the merchant deals in goods of the kind under a name other than that of the consignor; the merchant is not an auctioneer and is not generally known to his creditors to be involved in the business of selling the goods of others [§ 9-102 (a) (20)];
- **Consignor:** A person who delivers goods to a consignee in a consignment [§ 9-102 (a) (21)];
- **Debtor:** A person having an interest, other than a security interest or other lien, in the collateral (e.g., a person who has an ownership interest or the right to possess and use the property purchased on credit or under a lease agreement) [§ 9-102 (a) (28)];
- **Financing statement:** A record or records composed of an initial financing statement and any filed record relating to the initial financing statement [§ 9-102 (a) (39)];
- **Fixtures:** Goods that have become so related to particular real property that an interest in them arises under real property law (e.g., they become part of the real estate by being permanently affixed to it) [§ 9-102 (a) (41)];
- **Secured party:** Any creditor who has a security interest in the debtor's collateral, including a person who holds an agricultural lien; a consignor; or the purchaser of chattel paper, payment intangibles, or promissory notes [§ 9-102 (a) (72)];
- **Security agreement:** An agreement that creates or provides for a security interest [§ 9-102 (a) (73)].

Creating a Security Interest

For a creditor to obtain a security interest in the property of a debtor, three conditions must exist:

1. value has been given to the debtor in exchange for the security interest [§ 9-203 (b) (1)];
2. the debtor has rights in the collateral [§ 9-203 (b) (2)]; and
3. the collateral is in the possession of the secured party or the debtor has authenticated a security agreement that provides a description of the collateral [§ 9-203 (b) (3)].

The value that a debtor receives in exchange for the security interest is usually the extension of credit or the sale of goods to which the security interest attaches. However, the value need not relate to the transaction involving the personal property that is the subject of the security interest. For example, a debtor who is in default of an unsecured loan for having missed several monthly payments could offer a security interest in tangible or intangible personal property that she owns to a creditor in exchange for the creditor providing her different terms on the loan or an extension of time to pay it. In this case she would receive "value" for the security interest that she gives the creditor (the avoidance of a default judgment).

The requirement that a debtor have "rights in the collateral" means that debtors may give a security interest only in property that they own or otherwise have the right to possess and then only to the extent of their ownership or possessory interest in the property.

Finally, creditors may obtain a security interest only to property that is in their possession (e.g., that a debtor has turned over to their custody) or to which the debtor has provided a description, if it is not in the creditor's possession. This means that a debtor may enter into a valid oral security agreement only if he turns the property over to the creditor. If the debtor retains the property or otherwise leaves it out of the creditor's control, then the security interest will not arise unless the debtor has authenticated the agreement by providing either a description of the personal property in a signed writing or in an electronic form that has been authenticated by a unique symbol, encryption, or similar process used to identify the person in an email or other form of electronic communication [§ 9-102 (a) (7)].

Perfecting a Security Interest

Perfection is the legal process by which creditors with a security interest in personal property protect themselves against claims from other creditors who may also have a security interest in the same property. If a creditor follows the prescribed process and perfects her security interest, her right to use the property covered by the security interest to satisfy the debtor's debt in the event of a default will be superior to that of other creditors with a similar security interest in the property. The process of perfecting a security interest is intended to give third parties notice of the secured party's security interest. To that end, it usually requires the filing of either a *financing statement* (a document that gives notice of the security interest) or a copy of the security agreement with the appropriate state office (typically the secretary of state).

The filing of a financing statement requires communication of a record to a filing office with the appropriate filing fee or acceptance of the record by the filing office [§ 9-516 (a)]. The record must include the initial financing statement that contains a name for the debtor, a name and address for the secured party, an indication of whether the debtor is an individual or an organization and, if an organization, the type or organization and jurisdiction of its organization. (For example, "the debtor is a corporation organized under the laws of the state of Delaware and having its principal offices in North Carolina.") [See § 9-516 (b).] The financing statement must also contain a statement describing the collateral it covers. If the secured interest relates to *fixtures* (goods permanently attached to realty), the financing statement must be filed in the state office where mortgages on real estate are filed [§ 9-501 (a) (1) (B)] and must include a description of the real estate to which they are attached.

For some types of personal property, the security interest is perfected automatically without requiring the secured party to file a financing statement. Some of these are enumerated in § 9-309 and include

- purchase money security interests in consumer goods (transactions involving consumer credit where the seller extends credit to the consumer for goods sold and retains a security interest in the goods);
- assignments of accounts or payment intangibles that do not constitute a significant part of the assignor's outstanding accounts or payment intangibles;
- the sale of a promissory note;
- a security interest in investment property created by a broker or securities intermediary.

Other instances of security interests that do not require the filing of a financing statement to be perfected include instances when negotiable documents, goods, money, or tangible chattel paper are in the possession of the secured party [§ 9-313 (a)], where perfection of the interest happens automatically upon the goods being placed under the control of the secured party. When goods covered by a certificate of title are involved, perfection of the security interest for the goods is covered by the law of the jurisdiction in which the goods are titled [§ 9-303]. For example, if automobiles and boats of a certain size are required to be titled in the state, state law will control the process for creating and perfecting a security interest in such goods by having the security interest noted on the title.

Duration of a Perfected Security Interest

A financing statement is generally effective for five years after the date of filing [§ 9-515 (a)]. But a continuation statement may be filed before the filed financing statement lapses. For a continuation statement to be effective, it must be filed within six months of the financing statement's lapse (e.g., within the last six months of its effective period) and will extend the effectiveness of the security interest for another five years from the date when it would otherwise lapse. Continuations may be filed in succession, effectively extending the coverage of the perfected security interest every five years *ad infinitum* [see § 9-515 (c) (d) (e)].

Priorities among Conflicting Security Interests in the Same Collateral

Generally speaking, first in time is first in right when it comes to conflicting perfected security interests that are enforced according to their time of filing or perfection [§ 9-322 (a) (1)]. And perfected security interests take priority over unperfected security interests [§ 9-322 (a) (2)]. But there are exceptions to the general rule. One of these covers perfected purchase money security interests of noninventory purchases of goods; it provides a preference for these over other security interests perfected before it if the purchase money security interest is perfected within 20 days of the debtor taking possession of the collateral [§ 9-324 (a)]. Therefore, if Betty Businesswoman gives a general security interest in all present and future business property to Candice Creditor in exchange for a loan and then purchases new fixtures for her business from Frank's Fixtures, giving Frank a purchase money security interest in the fixtures, Frank's security interest will take priority over Candice's, even though hers was perfected first. When a perfected purchase money security interest in goods that qualify as inventory are involved, such a security interest has priority over other security interests in the same inventory [§ 9-324 (b)]. Thus, if Barb Businesswoman has given to Ben Banker a security interest in her inventory to secure a line of credit and she places an order for goods for resale in her store from Sandra Seller secured by a purchase money security interest, Sandra's interest in the goods will take priority over Ben's.

Default

Article 9 does not define what constitutes a default, but it allows the parties to define for themselves what constitutes default by their mutual agreement in any manner that is reasonable [§ 9-601 (a), § 9-603 (a)]. When a default occurs, the secured party may reduce the claim to judgment (e.g., sue for default of the underlying note or draft), foreclose, or otherwise enforce the claim, security interest, or agricultural lien by any available judicial procedure [§ 9-601 (a) (1)]. If the collateral is documents, the secured party may proceed either as to the documents or as to the goods they cover [§ 9-601 (a) (2)]. For example, if the collateral is a warehouse receipt for goods in the hands of a third party and the debtor defaults on the debt, the secured party could either transfer the negotiable instrument and use the proceeds to settle the debt or use the warehouse receipt to take possession of the goods it covers and then sell the goods itself to satisfy the debt. If the personal property that is the subject of the security interest is insufficient to cover the full debt, the secured party can obtain a deficiency judgment against the debtor for the difference. If the security interest involves property worth more than the debtor's debt, the debtor is generally entitled to a return of any excess proceeds from the sale or other disposition of the property offset by the reasonable costs related to caring for or disposing of the property [see § 9-615 (a) (1) (2)].

Questions

1. What types of property are covered by Article 9 of the UCC?
2. What are fixtures? Are fixtures covered by UCC Article 9?
3. For a creditor to obtain a security interest in the property of a debtor, what three conditions must exist?
4. What is "perfection" of a security interest?
5. What is the purpose of perfecting a security interest, and how is it generally accomplished?
6. If the financing statement relates to fixtures, where must it be filed?
7. How long does a perfected security interest last?

8. How many times may a perfected security interest be extended?
9. What is the general rule concerning conflicting security interests in the same collateral?
10. What are the basic rights of a secured party when a default occurs?

Hypothetical Cases

1. Harry Homeowner needs to buy a new boiler for his home to upgrade his heating system for a total cost of $7,500, which includes $5,000 for the cost of a new high-efficiency furnace and $2,500 for labor, transportation, and taxes. He wants to purchase the unit on credit from Penelope, a licensed HVAC contractor, who is willing to finance the purchase and installation in exchange for a security interest in the boiler for $7,500.
    A. A month after the boiler is installed, Harry loses his job and is unable to make the second monthly payment to Penelope. If he offers to give a security interest to Penelope in his entire art collection worth $100,000 in exchange for Penelope giving him a three-month grace period on making further payments on the boiler and Penelope accepts, may she perfect a security interest in the artwork as well as in the boiler?
    B. Assuming that the security interest in the artwork may be given by Harry to Penelope, what must Penelope do to perfect her interest in the artwork?
    C. If Harry fails to make payments after the grace period ends because he has been unable to find another job, what are Penelope's legal options?
2. Assume the same facts as in the previous question:
    A. If Harry defaults and Penelope has taken possession of his $100,000 art collection, what are her rights with regard to the artwork?
    B. If Harry's art collection is made up of ten paintings, each with a value of $10,000, what are Penelope's rights with regard to her security interest in the collection?
    C. If Penelope wants to keep one of the paintings in satisfaction of the debt, may she do so? Explain fully.
3. Bernard wants to buy a 60-inch high-definition television from his local appliance store, Rip M Off, Inc. The store, which caters to low-income clientele and offers electronics and other household goods at highly inflated prices and at the highest interest rate that the law allows in his state, agrees to sell the set to him at a price of $5,000 financed over a six-year period at a 25% rate of interest. The financing agreement makes it clear that the store retains a purchase money security interest in the television set. As part of the deal, Bernard also executes a second security agreement covering his $5,000 synthesizer (he is a professional musician) and a $2,000 diamond ring that he inherited from his dad. He turns the ring over to the appliance store as security in a verbal agreement, but it is agreed that he will be allowed to keep the synthesizer as long as he makes timely payments, and he provides a written, signed copy of an agreement to this effect to Rip M Off. Rip M Off promptly perfects its interest in the synthesizer by forwarding a financing statement to his state's secretary of state with the appropriate fee and in the form required by local law, but it does not send financing statements covering the television set or ring to the secretary of state.
    Two years later, Bernard stops making payments on the television set because he realizes that he made a bad bargain when agreeing to buy the set.
    A. Has Rip M Off perfected its security interest with regard to the ring under the facts given?
    B. May Rip M Off enforce the security agreement against the synthesizer if the outstanding loan amount at the time of Bernard's default is $4,000 and the actual value of the television set at the time is $500?
    C. If the value of the synthesizer at the time of the debtor's default is $3,000 and the market value of the television set is $500, what are the creditor's rights with regard to the secured property? Discuss fully.
4. Assume the same facts as in the previous question:
    A. If you were to represent Bernard, what argument would you make (if any) in his defense if Rip M Off chooses to sue him personally for the outstanding loan balance?
    B. While Bernard might argue that Rip M Off engages in predatory practices in enticing consumers residing in the poorest neighborhoods to enter into purchases that they can ill afford, Rip M Off would counter that selling expensive equipment to individuals with no credit or poor credit histories and limited means is a high-risk business and that its high prices and high interest rates are merely the only means to cover its business risk and the extremely high default rates of customers who are often judgment-proof. Analyze this issue and argue either for or against the validity of Rip M Off's business practices from the perspective of law, business, and ethics.

Unit III—Cases for Further Study

**MAEDER BROTHERS QUALITY WOOD PELLETS, INC., v.
HAMMOND DRIVES & EQUIPMENT, INC.**

No. 320362

COURT OF APPEALS OF MICHIGAN

April 14, 2015, Decided

[Unpublished Slip Decision[1]]

Before: OWENS, P.J., and JANSEN and MURRAY, JJ. PER CURIAM.

Plaintiff appeals as of right the trial court's order granting defendant's motion for summary disposition under MCR 2.116(C)(8) (failure to state a claim on which relief can be granted) and MCR 2.116(C)(10) (no genuine issue of material fact) in this breach of contract and warranties case. We affirm.

I. Factual Background

Plaintiff purchased a Bliss Pellet Mill in 2006 and second mill in 2008. The machine is used to transform sawdust and wood chips into pellets that are marketed for heating and power purposes. The mechanics of both machines required the use of bearings. The written information that the mill manufacturer provided to plaintiff directed it to use "Timken" bearings. Neither plaintiff's president, Richard Maeder, nor its secretary and general manager, Christi Densmore, could recall if the manufacturer's instructions stated to only use Timken bearings. Because the bearings would wear out approximately every 90 days, plaintiff constantly needed to purchase replacements. The parties stipulated that the cost to plaintiff of purchasing replacement Timken bearings was approximately $40,000 a year.

Looking to cut costs, plaintiff, through Densmore, inquired of defendant if it could find a cheaper bearing that could also do the job consistent with the Timken bearing. Densmore acknowledged that when she made this request she merely provided defendant with the part number and gave defendant no further technical specifications. Densmore stated that when ordering bearings and other parts from defendant in the past, she also had merely provided the part number. The replacement bearing that defendant provided to plaintiff was manufactured by a company other than Timken. Densmore acknowledged that the substitute bearing operated consistently with the Timken bearings at first. However, plaintiff soon began to experience problems that resulted in substantial damage to both pellet mills. A subsequent investigation revealed that the substitute bearings were the cause of this damage because they were made of softer steel than the Timken bearings.

Neither Densmore nor Maeder recalled any written contract regarding the purchase of substitute bearings or any other express statement or writing from defendant on how they would perform. Maeder further acknowledged that he did not know if defendant's representative who handled the purchase had any specialized background or expertise in bearings. He acknowledged that defendant was not a manufacturer, but simply a distributor.

Plaintiff filed a four count complaint alleging breach of contract, negligence, breach of implied warranty, and breach of express warranty. While the complaint did not specifically state that the claims were based on Michigan's version of the Uniform Commercial Code (UCC), the complaint clearly shows that the substance of the allegations concerned a dispute over the commercial sale of bearings, which are considered a "good" under the UCC.

Defendant moved for summary disposition, arguing... that the deposition testimony of Maeder and Densmore showed no express warranty existed. [and that] the implied

---

[1] This is an excerpt of an unpublished slip decision; the published decision is not yet available as of this writing. A PDF version of the full complete slip decision is available at http://www.michbar.org/file/opinions/appeals/2015/041415/59691.pdf (last accessed January 9, 2016).

warranty claim was barred by portions of Michigan's product liability law. In plaintiff's response it alleged that its express and implied warranty counts were governed by the UCC. At the hearing on defendant's motion, defendant claimed that plaintiff could not argue that the UCC applied because plaintiff did not specifically mention the UCC in its complaint.

The trial court granted defendant's motion for summary disposition on all counts of plaintiff's complaint. . . . On plaintiff's express warranty claim, the trial court granted the motion because it determined that both Maeder's and Densmore's deposition testimony showed that no express warranty was ever made. Finally, the trial court granted summary disposition on plaintiff's implied warranty claim because it determined that plaintiff failed to plead a UCC claim or, in the alternative, because plaintiff failed to establish the elements of either of the two types of UCC implied warranties.

II. Standard of Review

This Court reviews de novo the trial court's grant of summary disposition pursuant to MCR 2.116(C)(8) and (C)(10). *Maiden v Rozwood*, 461 Mich 109, 118; 597 NW2d 817 (1999).

III. Analysis

"A motion under MCR 2.116(C)(8) tests the legal sufficiency of the complaint." *Id.* at 119. The plaintiff's factual allegations are accepted as true and the motion may only be granted where "no factual development could possibly justify recovery." *Id.* "[C]onclusory statements that are unsupported by allegations of fact on which they may be based will not suffice." *State v CVS Caremark Corp*, 496 Mich 45, 63; 852 NW2d 103 (2014). The court must also accept all reasonable inferences that can be drawn from the factual allegations as true. *Id.* "MCR 2.116(I)(5) requires that if summary disposition is appropriate under MCR 2.116(C)(8) . . . plaintiffs shall be given the opportunity to amend their pleadings, unless the amendment would be futile." *Granam v Does*, 303 Mich App 522, 543; 845 NW2d 128 (2014).

"A motion under MCR 2.116(C)(10) tests the factual sufficiency of the complaint." *Maiden*, 461 Mich at 120. The court considers affidavits, pleadings, depositions, admissions, and other evidence in a light most favorable to the non-moving party. *Id.* "In presenting a motion for summary disposition, the moving party has the initial burden of supporting its position by affidavits, depositions, admissions, or other documentary evidence." *Quinto v Cross & Peters Co*, 451 Mich 358, 362; 547 NW2d 314 (1996). Then the burden shifts to the party opposing the motion "to establish that a genuine issue of disputed fact exists." *Id.* "A litigant's mere pledge to establish an issue of fact at trial cannot survive summary disposition under MCR 2.116(C) (10)." *Maiden*, 461 Mich at 121. It is necessary to "set forth specific facts at the time of the motion showing a genuine issue for trial." *Id.*

"Michigan is a notice-pleading state." *Johnson v QFD, Inc.*, 292 Mich App 359, 368; 807 NW2d 719 (2011). A complaint must contain "[a] statement of the facts, without repetition, on which the pleader relies in stating the cause of action, with the specific allegations necessary reasonably to inform the adverse party of the nature of the claims the adverse party is called on to defend." MCR 2.111(B)(1). "[I]t is well settled that [courts] will look beyond mere procedural labels and read the complaint as a whole when ascertaining the exact nature of a plaintiff's claims." *Johnson*, 292 Mich App at 368.

Michigan's adopted version of Article 2 of the UCC, MCL 440.2102 *et seq.*, governs the transactions of sale of goods. "[W]here a plaintiff seeks to recover for economic loss caused by a defective product purchased for commercial purposes, the exclusive remedy is provided by the UCC. . . ." *Neibarger v Universal Coops*, 439 Mich 512, 527-528; 486 NW2d 612 (1992). There is no dispute that the present controversy involves the sale of goods.

In the present case, the court placed great emphasis on the fact that plaintiff did not specifically mention the UCC in its complaint, and defendant again argues this point on appeal. Although true, plaintiff's complaint does state that the dispute is over bearings it purchased from defendant. Thus, defendant was on notice that it was being sued by an entity to which it sold goods and that the subject matter of the suit involved the sale of those goods. This provided sufficient notice for defendant to know that the case would be governed by Article 2 of the UCC.

* * *

C. Plaintiff's Breach of Express Warranty Claim

An express warranty is created by "[a]n affirmation of fact or promise made by the seller," by "[a] description of the goods," or by "[a] sample or model which is made part of the basis of the bargain." MCL 440.2313(1). Both Maeder and Densmore testified that neither defendant nor any representative of defendant ever made any express statement to them about how long the substitute bearings would last or what type of steel the bearings were made of. Plaintiff presented no admissible evidence to contradict this. While plaintiff argued that an express warranty existed, it merely attached four pages from Maeder's deposition to its response to defendant's motion, on which we do not find any admissible evidence that any affirmation of fact or promise was made to him by defendant. Therefore, the trial court did not err in granting defendant's motion for summary disposition under MCR 2.116(C)(10) with respect to plaintiff's breach of express warranty claims.

D. Plaintiff's Breach of Implied Warranty Claim

The UCC describes two types of implied warranties. The first is the implied warranty of merchantability. MCL 440.2314. The second is the implied warranty of fitness for a particular purpose. MCL 440.2315. Plaintiff's complaint does not specify which implied warranty forms the basis of its claim, but it referred to both types in its response to defendant's motion for summary disposition.

1. Implied Warrant of Merchantability

"[A] warranty that goods shall be merchantable is implied in a contract for their sale if the seller is a merchant with respect to goods of that kind." MCL 440.2314(1). "'In general the question whether a party may be a merchant as that term is used in the UCC is a question of law for the courts to decide by applying the UCC definition of merchant to the facts in the case.'" *Bev Smith, Inc v Atwell*, 301 Mich App 670, 681; 836 NW2d 872 (2013) (citation omitted). A merchant is defined as "a person that deals in goods of the kind or otherwise by the person's occupation holds itself out as having knowledge or skill peculiar to the practices or goods involved in the transaction." MCL 440.2104. The official comments provide further guidance on the definition of a merchant for purposes of the implied warranty of merchantability:

> [I]n Section 2-314 on the warranty of merchantability, such warranty is implied only "if the seller is a merchant with respect to goods of that kind." Obviously this qualification restricts the implied warranty to a much smaller group than everyone who is engaged in business and requires a professional status as to particular kinds of goods.... [MCL 440.2104, UCC comment 2.]

Plaintiff alleged that defendant "is engaged and has continuously engaged at all times relevant to this lawsuit in the business of buying, selling, distributing and handling parts of all kinds for power transmissions, hydraulic and pneumatic systems and materials for all types of drives and equipment." Accepting this allegation as true and all reasonable inferences that can be drawn from it, plaintiff has alleged that defendant does "deal[] in goods of the kind or otherwise by the person's occupation holds itself out as having knowledge or skill peculiar to the practices or goods involved in the transaction." MCL 440.2104. Although the term "bearings" is not used, the allegation was that defendant is the seller of "parts of all kinds" for machines like plaintiff's Bliss Pellet Mill, which would include the bearings in issue. Therefore, to the extent the trial court granted defendant's motion for summary disposition on plaintiff's implied warranty of merchantability claim under MCR 2.116(C)(8) it committed error.

However, a motion for summary disposition under MCR 2.116(C)(10) requires more than just an allegation in the complaint. It is a factual test of the allegation and requires the plaintiff to produce admissible evidence that would support the allegations. *Maiden*, 461 Mich at 120. Again, nothing in the pages of Maeder's deposition submitted by plaintiff to the court provides any type of evidence or even any assertion that defendant is a merchant, i.e., a person that deals in bearing or holds itself out to have knowledge or skill in bearings. Indeed, Maeder testified that he did not know if defendant's representative was an expert or what his background in bearings was. Therefore, the trial court properly determined that defendant was entitled to summary disposition under MCR 2.116(C)(10) to the extent that plaintiff's claim addressed the implied warranty of merchantability.

2. Implied Warranty of Fitness for a Particular Purpose MCL 440.2315 provides as follows:

> Where the seller at the time of contracting has reason to know any particular purpose for which the goods are required and that the buyer is relying on the seller's skill or judgment to select or furnish suitable goods, there is unless excluded or modified under the next section an implied warranty that the goods shall be fit for such purpose.

Regarding defendant's motion for summary disposition under MCR 2.116(C)(8), the question is whether plaintiff pleaded facts in its complaint that if proven true would establish both that defendant had reason to know of the particular purpose plaintiff was to use the bearing for and that defendant had reason to know that plaintiff was relying on defendant's skill or judgment to select a suitable bearing. Plaintiff does allege that it purchased bearings from defendant in the past and that it asked defendant to select a cheaper bearing that could do the job. If proven true, this would establish that defendant had knowledge of the purpose for which plaintiff would use the bearings.

However, in order for the warranty of fitness for a particular purpose to apply, plaintiff was also required to plead facts that, if true, would establish that defendant had knowledge that plaintiff was relying on defendant's skill and judgment. Plaintiff does allege that the substitute bearings were provided "with the affirmative statement and promise by [defendant] to [plaintiff] that these bearings would perform the same function in the same manner as Timken roller bearings, but at less cost." However, all this alleges is that defendant made an express warranty to plaintiff. It does not allege that defendant had reason to know that plaintiff was relying on defendant's expertise. Nowhere in plaintiff's complaint does it allege that defendant had reason to know plaintiff was relying on its skill and expertise in bearings Additionally, it is questionable whether the implied warranty of fitness for a particular purpose would even apply to a situation like the present case, where the buyer was using the goods for the ordinary purpose for which they were intended. The comments to the UCC's implied warranty of fitness for a particular purpose state:

> A "particular purpose" differs from the ordinary purpose for which the goods are used in that it envisages a specific use by the buyer which is peculiar to the nature of his business whereas the ordinary purposes for which goods are used are those envisaged in the concept of merchantability and go to uses which are customarily made of the goods in question. . . . [MCL 440.2315, UCC comment 2.]

There is nothing in plaintiff's complaint or in the depositions that would suggest that plaintiff intended to use the bearings for something other than the ordinary purpose for which such bearings were used. Thus, to the extent plaintiff's implied warranty count is based on the implied warranty of fitness for a particular purpose, the trial court correctly granted summary disposition under MCR 2.116(C)(8).

Affirmed. Defendant, having prevailed on appeal, may tax its costs pursuant to MCR

/s/ Donald S. Owens
/s/ Kathleen Jansen
/s/ Christopher M. Murray

Optional Assignments

1. Brief the preceding abbreviated version of the case in a one- to two-page, single-spaced brief (with double spaces between paragraphs) that contains the following four sections: (1) The basic facts of the case [Facts]; (2) The legal issue the court is being asked to decide [Issue]; (3) The holding of the court (how it decides the legal issue before it) [Holding]; and (4) The rationale the court uses to support its decision [Rationale]. If your instructor asks you to brief the case, she will give you additional instructions.
2. On the issue of the implied warranty of fitness for a particular purpose, if the plaintiff had shown evidence that it told the defendant what the bearings would be used for and asked the defendant to recommend a suitable less expensive replacement for the bearings it had been using, would the result have been the same? Explain.
3. If the plaintiff had provided evidence that the defendant in fact knew the type of business it was engaged in and what the bearings would be used for, do you think the outcome would have been the same if all other facts remained the same? Explain.

[The text of this Vermont trial court opinion is unofficial. It has been reformatted from the original. The accuracy of the text and the accompanying data included in the Vermont trial court opinion database is not guaranteed.]

PETER DERNIER & NICOLE DERNIER v. U.S. BANK NATIONAL ASS'N.
STATE OF VERMONT
SUPERIOR COURT CIVIL DIVISION Windsor Unit
Docket No. 144-3-11 Wrcv (January 26, 2015)

Opinion and Order RE: Motion for Summary Judgment (#12)

The Defendant, U.S. Bank National Association, has moved for summary judgment. The Plaintiffs, Peter and Nicole Dernier, oppose the motion. Upon review of submitted briefs and supporting statements of facts, the Defendant's motion is denied.

Procedural History

This is a declaratory judgment action between the Plaintiff homeowners and the Defendant bank, filed by the Plaintiffs on March 23, 2011 and seeking a declaration of the Defendant's rights to enforce the Plaintiffs' mortgage and promissory note. On October 20, 2011, the Plaintiffs moved for leave to file a second amended complaint. On

June 12, 2012, the court denied the Plaintiffs' motion and granted the Defendant's motion to dismiss. The Plaintiffs appealed the dismissal to the Vermont Supreme Court as *Dernier v. Mortgage Network, Inc.*, 2013 VT 96, 195 Vt. 113. On appeal, the Court affirmed the court's dismissal as to some issues in the Plaintiffs' second amended complaint and reversed and remanded as to others. It is now before this court on remand.

On December 1, 2014, the Defendant moved for summary judgment on the remaining issues. On January 5, 2015, the Plaintiffs responded. This decision follows.

The Defendant is represented by Andre D. Bouffard, Esq. The Plaintiff is represented by Russell D. Barr, Esq.

Summary Judgment Standard

Under Vermont Rule of Civil Procedure 56, summary judgment is appropriate "if the movant shows that there is no genuine dispute as to any material fact and the movant is entitled to judgment as a matter of law." V.R.C.P. 56(a). When ruling on a motion for summary judgment, the court must take the evidence in a light most favorable to the party opposed to summary judgment. Summary judgment must not be utilized as a substitute for a determination on the merits of the claims if there is any evidence presented by the party opposed to summary judgment that creates an issue of material fact. The trial court must not consider the relative weight of the evidence. *Fritzeen v. Trudell Consulting Engineers, Inc.*, 170 Vt. 632 (2000). It is not the function of the trial court to make findings of fact in connection with a motion for summary judgment even where the record appears to lean strongly in one direction. *Booska v. Hubbard Insurance Agency, Inc.*, 160 Vt. 305, 309 (1993). The court must resolve all doubts in favor of the non-moving party. *Dillon v. Champion Jog Bra, Inc.*, 175 Vt. 1 (2002). The court must allow the non-moving party the benefit of all reasonable doubts and inferences. *Foster & Gridley v. Winner*, 169 Vt. 621 (1999).

In ruling on a motion for summary judgment, the court must regard all properly supported allegations of fact presented by the party opposed to summary judgment as true. *Mellin v. Flood Brook Union School Dist.*, 173 Vt. 202 (2001). The party opposed to summary judgment may not rest on the allegations in the pleadings to rebut credible documentary evidence or affidavits. *Gore v. Green Mountain Lakes, Inc.* 140 Vt. 262 (1981). Where a witness gives contradictory or internally inconsistent testimony the court will construe the testimony in a light most favorable to the party opposed to summary judgment.

The factual basis for this order is derived from the Plaintiffs' and the Defendant's statements of facts. Many of the facts alleged by both parties are not material to the dispute or are material only to issues already disposed of by the Supreme Court. Accordingly, this is a redacted recitation of facts.

1. On October 7, 2005, Plaintiff Peter Dernier executed a promissory note for $245,250.00, naming Kittridge Mortgage Corporation as lender.
2. There is a version of the promissory note that bears one indorsement, from Kittridge Mortgage Corporation to Mortgage Network, Inc. (Plaintiffs' Exhibit A).
3. There is a version of the promissory note that purportedly bears two indorsements, one from Kittridge Mortgage Corporation to Mortgage Network, Inc., and one from Mortgage Network, Inc. in blank. (Plaintiffs' Exhibit 5).
4. The alleged indorsement from Mortgage Network, Inc. in blank is an affixed stamp which reads:
Pay to the order of ** Without
Recourse Mortgage Network, Inc.
By: Chad M. Goodwin
Pipeline Manager
5. A signature is superimposed over the stamp.
6. The authenticity of this signature is disputed. The Plaintiffs have supplied an affidavit of a Chad M. Goodwin, stating that he was an employee of Mortgage Network, Inc.
7. There is, according to the Defendant, a version of the promissory note which bears a specific indorsement from Mortgage Network, Inc. to the Defendant rather than an indorsement in blank. This version of the promissory note was not attached to the motion and for that reason is disregarded by the court.[1]
8. On October 7, 2005, the Plaintiffs also executed a mortgage deed to Kittridge Mortgage Corporation.
9. The mortgage was assigned from Kittridge Mortgage Corporation to Mortgage Electronic Registration Systems, Inc., as nominee for Mortgage Network, Inc., and from Mortgage Electronic Registration Systems, Inc. to the Defendant, by August 5, 2013 at the latest.
10. The Defendant, directly or through its agents, has possession of the note and mortgage.
11. Mortgage Network, Inc. has disclaimed its interest, if any, in the Plaintiffs' mortgage loan.

---

[1] The discussion below would be no different even if this alleged version of the note were considered.

Discussion

As noted, this case was previously appealed to the Vermont Supreme Court as *Dernier v. Mortgage Network, Inc.* On remand, the sole question before this court is whether the Defendant presently lacks the right to enforce the Plaintiffs' promissory note because the note was stolen.

Promissory notes are governed by the Uniform Commercial Code as adopted in Vermont, codified as Title 9A of the Vermont Statutes. Generally, a person is entitled to enforce a negotiable instrument if they have possession of the instrument and the instrument is payable to them. 9A V.S.A. § 3-301. In the case of a bearer instrument, transfer of possession of the instrument, whether voluntary or involuntary, is sufficient by itself to constitute a negotiation making the transferee a holder entitled to enforce the instrument. § 3-201.

For the purposes of this motion, the Plaintiffs do not challenge the Defendant's actual possession of the note, though of course, the Defendant would have to prove possession of the note in order to enforce it at any further proceeding. Rather, the Plaintiffs allege that the instrument was not properly negotiated to the Defendant because the indorsement in blank affixed to the note is a forgery. Essentially, the Plaintiffs rely on § 3-305(c), which states that "an obligor is not obliged to pay the instrument if the person seeking enforcement of the instrument whether the Plaintiffs have offered sufficient evidence to prove that the instrument is a lost or stolen instrument.[2]

Although Vermont's § 3-305(c) adopts the language of the Uniform Commercial Code without alteration, there is surprisingly little guidance on this particular clause from any jurisdiction. In *Mbaku v. Bank of America*, the District of Colorado cited this section only to place the burden of proof on the party resisting enforcement to prove that a note is lost or stolen. *Mbaku v. Bank of America*, Docket No. 12-cv-00190-PAB-KLM, 2014 WL 4099313, at *7 (D. Colo. Aug. 20, 20140). In *Sepehry-Fard v. MB Financial Services*, the Northern District of California cited this clause only to reject its application on standing grounds. *Sepehry-Fard v. MB Financial Services*, Docket No. C 13-02784 JSW, 2014 WL 122436, at *4 (N.D. Cal. Jan. 13, 2014). The remaining cases either refer to § 3-305(c) in passing or deal with the more complicated issue of whether an obligor is a holder in due course. Accordingly, the court's application of § 3-305(c) to this context is a matter of first impression in the truest sense.

As an initial matter, the court notes that the official comment's only reference to this clause of § 3-305(c) illustrates a completely different situation. Namely, the official comment states that "[t]he last sentence of subsection (c) allows the issuer of an instrument such as a cashier's check to refuse payment in the rare case in which the issuer can prove that the instrument is a lost or stolen instrument and the person seeking enforcement does not have rights of a holder in due course." § 3-305(c), official comment at 4. Nevertheless, because the language of the statute itself is broad, the court concludes for the clause can apply to this case.

The question, then, is whether the Plaintiffs can sufficiently show that the note was lost or stolen so as to survive summary judgment. The court concludes that the Plaintiffs have made such a showing.

Although the Plaintiffs have offered no direct evidence that the note was stolen, they have offered the affidavit of a Chad M. Goodwin, swearing that he is a former employee of Mortgage Network, Inc. and that the signature on the indorsement is not his own. Taken in the light most favorable to the Plaintiffs, a finder of fact could conclude that the indorsement was forged, and that, therefore, the note is not a bearer instrument. Further, a finder of fact could infer that because the indorsment was forged, the Defendant's possession of the note is wrongful. In such an eventuality, Mortgage Network, Inc. would have the right to enforce the note, not the Defendants.

In opposition, the Defendant has offered a reasonable argument for enforcement notwithstanding the allegedly irregular indorsement. It is true that, under § 3-403, an unauthorized or forged signature is nevertheless good "as the signature of the unauthorized indorsement in blank would still be valid. § 3-403(a). It is also true that a forged signature "can be ratified for all purposes of [Article 3]." § 3-403(a). However, the standard for summary judgment is clear that "summary judgment is improper where the evidence is subject to conflicting interpretations, regardless of a judge's perceptions of the comparative plausibility of facts offered by either party or the likelihood that a party might prevail at trial." *Provost v. Fletcher Allen Health Care, Inc.*, 2005 VT 115, ¶ 15, 179 Vt. 545. Accordingly, the Defendant's motion for summary judgment must be denied in favor of a trial on the merits.

---

[2] The Defendant could also ultimately prevail by showing that they are a holder in due course. However, the Plaintiffs allege that the Defendant has refused to disclose through the discovery process any evidence regarding their negotiation for the Plaintiffs' note. Accordingly, the court assumes for the purposes of this motion that the Defendant is not a holder in due course.

Order

The Defendant's motion for summary judgment is DENIED.
Dated at Woodstock, Vermont, this _____ day of January, 2015.

Judge Theresa S. DiMauro
Superior Court Judge

Optional Assignments

1. Brief the preceding abbreviated version of the case in a one- to two-page, single-spaced brief (with double spaces between paragraphs) that contains the following four sections: (1) The basic facts of the case [Facts]; (2) The legal issue the court is being asked to decide [Issue]; (3) The holding of the court (how it decides the legal issue before it) [Holding]; and (4) The rationale the court uses to support its decision [Rationale]. If your instructor asks you to brief the case, he will give you additional instructions.

2. Do you agree or disagree with the opinion? Why?

UNIT 4

BANKRUPTCY

Lukas Gojda/Shutterstock

CHAPTER 27
Liquidation, Reorganization, and Adjustment of Debts

Liquidation, Reorganization, and Adjustment of Debts

CHAPTER 27

Chapter Outline

Introduction

Chapter 7: Liquidation

Chapter 11: Reorganization

Chapter 13: Adjustment of Debts of an Individual with Regular Income

Introduction

Under early common law in Great Britain, individuals who were unable to pay their debts when they became due were subject to incarceration in debtor's prisons until they (or their family and friends) paid their debts. While this practice punished irresponsible individuals who borrowed beyond their means and provided to creditors significant leverage in collecting unpaid debts, it also caused much hardship to the innocent families of delinquent debtors who would often be left with no means of support when the primary breadwinner was jailed and denied the ability to make a living. The unintended but unavoidable effect of punishing innocent children and dependent spouses for the inability of husbands or wives to pay their debts eventually resulted in the abandonment of the practice of jailing debtors unable to pay their debts.

In the United States, Article I, Section 8 of the U.S. Constitution gives Congress the power to create uniform laws regulating bankruptcy. Today, bankruptcy law in the United States is codified in the United States Bankruptcy Code (Title 11 of the United States Code) and was most recently amended by the Bankruptcy Abuse Prevention and Consumer Protection Act of 2005 (BAPCPA) [Pub. L. 109-8]. The provisions of greatest interest to most individuals and businesses are contained in Chapters 7, 11, and 13 of the code. Chapter 7 deals with straight bankruptcy or *liquidation*, which involves the discharge of a debtor's debts after the collection and sale at auction of all of the debtor's nonexempt property for the benefit of creditors. Chapter 11 concerns itself not with the liquidation or forgiveness of debt, but rather its *reorganization* or restructuring to allow the debtor to continue in business, and Chapter 13 involves the *adjustment of debt* similar to Chapter 11 reorganization but available only to individual debtors with regular income. In this chapter, we will survey the essential provisions of Chapters 7, 11, and 13 of the Bankruptcy Code. We will also see how the code attempts to provide a fresh start to debtors who are unable to pay their debts when they become due while offering creditors the opportunity to satisfy a portion of their claims out of the insolvent debtor's remaining assets.

Chapter 7: Liquidation

A Chapter 7 liquidation proceeding allows individuals and businesses who are unable to meet their financial obligations to have their debts discharged by turning over substantially all of their property to a trustee with the oversight of the bankruptcy court in order that it may be sold for the benefit of the debtor's creditors. In essence, Chapter 7 allows a debtor to make a fresh start by removing the burden of debts that are beyond the debtor's ability to repay. A measure of protection is also afforded to the debtor's creditors who may force liquidation proceedings under certain circumstances when a debtor is unable or unwilling to repay his debts.

Who May Bring Chapter 7 Proceedings

Chapter 7 applies to all debtors *other than* railroads, domestic insurance companies, banks, savings and loan associations, homestead associations, new market venture capital companies, small business investment companies licensed by the Small Business Administration, and credit unions, which are specifically excluded. Individuals, corporations, and partnerships can avail themselves of bankruptcy protection. Municipalities may also generally avail themselves of Chapter 7 protection.

Liquidation proceedings under Chapter 7 may be brought by the debtor (voluntary liquidation) or by the debtor's creditors (involuntary liquidation). For creditors to force liquidation on a debtor, the debtor must have a minimum combined unsecured debt of $15,325. If the total number of creditors is 12 or more, three creditors must join in the petition for involuntary liquidation to which the debtor owes an undisputed combined unsecured claim of at least $15,325. If there are fewer than 12 creditors (excluding employees and insiders of the debtor) with an aggregate debt of at least $15,325 in unsecured debt, then any one or more creditors may file a petition for involuntary liquidation as long as the combined unsecured debt of the petitioning creditors is at least $15,325. The following example will illustrate:

- Adam owes Betty $6,000, Carla $10,000 and Don $16,000. He has no other debts. If the debt to the three creditors is unsecured (e.g., not backed by a security interest such as a mortgage on real property or a lien on personal property) and Adam is unable to pay his debts when they become due to all three creditors, Betty and Carla can force Adam into Chapter 7 bankruptcy (or Chapter 11 reorganization), since their combined debts are at least $15,325. Don could also force Adam into Chapter 7 or Chapter 11 involuntary bankruptcy or reorganization since Adam's debt to him meets the minimum amount for an involuntary petition. Of course, Betty, Carla, and Don could all join together and force an involuntary Chapter 7 or Chapter 11 petition.

Appointment of Interim Trustee

After a voluntary or involuntary petition for relief is filed, a court will issue an order for relief that will relieve the debtor from the obligation to continue to pay his debts pending a final adjudication by the court of the bankruptcy petition. The bankruptcy court then appoints an interim trustee whose responsibility it is to collect the property of the debtor not specifically exempted from attachment. The trustee then manages the property until a final determination is made by the court in the bankruptcy proceedings. Creditors are given the opportunity to replace the interim trustee with a trustee of their own choosing through a formal selection process under the supervision of the court. The trustee then manages the debtor's property and sees to its liquidation by sale at auction with the proceeds to be used to pay off the creditor's claims on a prorated basis.

Bankruptcy Decree

Finally, a trial is held. If it is found that the debtor is insolvent and if he has fulfilled his obligations under the code, such as disclosing and turning over to the trustee all nonexempt property, the court enters a bankruptcy decree that will permanently discharge all of the debtor's outstanding debts. The decree also allows creditors to recover a prorated share of the creditor's debt from the proceeds of the property turned over to the trustee in the following priority order:

1. secured creditors are paid first to the extent of their security interest;
2. allowed unsecured claims for domestic support obligations are paid for spousal or child support and trustee's allowed administrative expenses;
3. administrative expenses of the estate (court costs, attorneys' fees, and related expenses);

4. *gap creditors'* claims (a gap creditor is one who became a creditor in the normal course of business after the filing of the bankruptcy petition but before the appointment of a trustee);
5. up to $12,475 in unpaid wages, salaries, or commissions earned by employee creditors within 180 days prior to the filing for bankruptcy or 180 days from the date of the cessation of the debtor's business, whichever occurs first;
6. allowed claims for contributions to employee benefit plans (health, life, and pension benefits) within 180 days of the filing for bankruptcy or 180 days from the cessation of business, whichever occurs first (up to a maximum of $12,475 *in combination with* wages, salaries, or commissions);
7. claims of up to $6,150 by farmers against a grain storage facility debtor or by fishermen against debtors who operate a fish storage facility;
8. up to $2,775 for claims of individuals for the deposit of money for the purchase, lease, or rental of property or the purchase of services for personal, family, or household use (e.g., consumer transactions) if such money was deposited before the bankruptcy petition was filed and the goods or service were never provided;
9. claims by a municipality for unpaid taxes for the year prior to the filing of the petition;
10. allowed unsecured claims by a federal depositary institution to maintain the capital of an insured depository institution;
11. allowed claims for personal injury arising out of the intoxicated use of a motor vehicle or boat;
12. all other unsecured claims of creditors.

The dollar amounts noted above along with dollar amounts in other key sections of the code noted in this chapter are current as of this writing; they are adjusted by April 1 every three years by the Judicial Conference of the United States based on the Consumer Price Index. The new rates, rounded to the nearest $25, have been published in the *Federal Register* by March 1 every three years since 1998.

In the event that there are insufficient funds to pay all of the members of a class their full debt, the debt is prorated for the members of the class. For example, if an estate has only $1,000 left when it comes time to pay the holders of the second-lowest priority claim (tax liens) and the debtor owed $1,000 to the state in unpaid income taxes and $500 to the local government in unpaid real property taxes (assume for the moment that both have an equal priority), the state would get two-thirds of the remaining sum and the local government one-third ($666.67 to the state and $333.33 to the local government). In the event that the money runs out prior to claims in all priority classes being discharged (as is usually the case), all debts are nevertheless generally discharged and the debtor will not need to repay them. On the down side, a judgment of bankruptcy goes on the debtor's credit report for seven years and makes it difficult for the debtor to rebuild his credit rating.

Debtor's Property Exempt from Attachment

The basic principle behind Chapter 7 is that a debtor turns in to the court whatever real and personal property he owns to be sold for the benefit of his creditors and in return has his debts forgiven to the extent that his assets are insufficient to cover his debt. Forcing a debtor to turn in all of his worldly possessions to be granted the protection of Chapter 7 might cause a severe hardship for debtors who would be left penniless and possibly without the means of earning a living. The Bankruptcy Act, therefore, allows debtors to keep some of their property after a voluntary or an involuntary Chapter 7 proceeding by statutorily exempting certain types of property from attachment. Figure 27.1 lists property that is statutorily exempt from attachment under the Bankruptcy Act. The act does not preempt state action and permits states, if they choose to do so, to provide different exemptions to debtors that can be more or less generous than the federal exemptions. For example, the homestead exemption in New York currently ranges from $75,000 to $150,000 for an individual depending on the county of residence ($150,000 to $300,000 for a husband and

d. The following property may be exempted under subsection (b)(2) of this section:
   1. The debtor's aggregate interest, not to exceed $22,975 in value, in real property or personal property that the debtor or a dependent of the debtor uses as a residence, in a cooperative that owns property that the debtor or a dependent of the debtor uses as a residence, or in a burial plot for the debtor or a dependent of the debtor.
   2. The debtor's interest, not to exceed $3,675 in value, in one motor vehicle.
   3. The debtor's interest, not to exceed $575 in value in any particular item or $12,250 in aggregate value, in household furnishings, household goods, wearing apparel, appliances, books, animals, crops, or musical instruments, that are held primarily for the personal, family, or household use of the debtor or a dependent of the debtor.
   4. The debtor's aggregate interest, not to exceed $1,550 in value, in jewelry held primarily for the personal, family, or household use of the debtor or a dependent of the debtor.
   5. The debtor's aggregate interest in any property, not to exceed in value $1,225 plus up to $11,500 of any unused amount of the exemption provided under paragraph (1) of this subsection.
   6. The debtor's aggregate interest, not to exceed $2,300 in value, in any implements, professional books, or tools, of the trade of the debtor or the trade of a dependent of the debtor.
   7. Any unmatured life insurance contract owned by the debtor, other than a credit life insurance contract.
   8. The debtor's aggregate interest, not to exceed in value $12,250 less any amount of property of the estate transferred in the manner specified in section 542(d) of this title, in any accrued dividend or interest under, or loan value of, any unmatured life insurance contract owned by the debtor under which the insured is the debtor or an individual of whom the debtor is a dependent.
   9. Professionally prescribed health aids for the debtor or a dependent of the debtor.
   10. The debtor's right to receive—
       A. a social security benefit, unemployment compensation, or a local public assistance benefit;
       B. a veterans' benefit;
       C. a disability, illness, or unemployment benefit;
       D. alimony, support, or separate maintenance, to the extent reasonably necessary for the support of the debtor and any dependent of the debtor;
       E. a payment under a stock bonus, pension, profit sharing, annuity, or similar plan or contract on account of illness, disability, death, age, or length of service, to the extent reasonably necessary for the support of the debtor and any dependent of the debtor, unless—
           i. such plan or contract was established by or under the auspices of an insider that employed the debtor at the time the debtor's rights under such plan or contract arose;
           ii. such payment is on account of age or length of service; and
           iii. such plan or contract does not qualify under section 401(a), 403(a), 403(b), or 408 of the Internal Revenue Code of 1986.
   11. The debtor's right to receive, or property that is traceable to—
       A. an award under a crime victim's reparation law;
       B. a payment on account of the wrongful death of an individual of whom the debtor was a dependent, to the extent reasonably necessary for the support of the debtor and any dependent of the debtor;
       C. a payment under a life insurance contract that insured the life of an individual of whom the debtor was a dependent on the date of such individual's death, to the extent reasonably necessary for the support of the debtor and any dependent of the debtor;
       D. a payment, not to exceed $22,975, on account of personal bodily injury, not including pain and suffering or compensation for actual pecuniary loss, of the debtor or an individual of whom the debtor is a dependent; or
       E. a payment in compensation of loss of future earnings of the debtor or an individual of whom the debtor is or was a dependent, to the extent reasonably necessary for the support of the debtor and any dependent of the debtor.
   12. Retirement funds to the extent that those funds are in a fund or account that is exempt from taxation under section 401, 403, 408, 408A, 414, 457, or 501(a) of the Internal Revenue Code of 1986.

FIGURE 27.1 Property Exempt from Attachment in Chapter 7 Liquidation [11 U.S.C. § 522(d)(1-12)]

wife who file jointly for protection under the Bankruptcy Act) in the value of a primary residence. Florida allows an unlimited homestead exemption for an individual filer if the home was purchased 730 days prior to filing the bankruptcy petition. In California, on the other hand, the homestead exemption for individual filers is up to $75,000 of the equity in their home; $100,000 if the filer lives with a family member; $175,000 if the filer is 65 or older, or physically or mentally disabled; and $175,000 if 55 or older, single, and earns a gross annual income under $25,000. As of this writing, 19 states and Washington D.C. allow filers to choose between the state exemption or the federal exemption, while 31 states have passed legislation restricting filers to the state exemptions only.

Chapter 11: Reorganization

Under Chapter 11, individuals and businesses that have gotten into financial difficulties are given the opportunity to restructure their debts and formulate a plan for their repayment. Unlike Chapter 7 liquidation, which allows for the forgiveness of debt beyond an individual's or business's ability to repay it, Chapter 11 permits for the repayment of debt to be made under different terms than those under which the debt was originally incurred. The reorganization of debt often involves changing the way debt is repaid, such as by extending the debt's term, in an attempt to provide businesses with financial difficulties some needed breathing room to keep them afloat and prevent Chapter 7 liquidation.

Who May Bring Chapter 11 Proceeding

Any person who qualifies for Chapter 7 protection may also file under Chapter 11, except for stockbrokers and commodity brokers, who are specifically excluded. In addition, railroads may also file for Chapter 11 protection, even though they are excluded from filing for Chapter 7 protection.

Appointment of Committee of Creditors

After the court enters an order of relief, the United States Trustee appoints a committee of creditors holding unsecured claims against the debtor. The trustee may also appoint other committees of creditors if she deems it appropriate (such as when there are many creditors with different classes of claims), and the court can order the trustee to appoint additional committees at the request of any party in interest. This committee "shall ordinarily consist of the persons, willing to serve, that hold the seven largest claims against the debtor of the kinds represented on such [a] committee . . ." [11 U.S.C. § 1102 (b) (1)]. This committee (or committees, where more than one are appointed) serves as the primary negotiating body in formulating the reorganization plan. The committee is specifically empowered to

1. consult with the trustee or debtor in possession concerning the administration of the case;
2. investigate the acts, conduct, assets, liabilities, and financial condition of the debtor, the operation of the debtor's business and the desirability of the continuance of such business, and any other matter relevant to the case or to the formulation of a plan;
3. participate in the formulation of a plan, advise those represented by such committee of such committee's determinations as to any plan formulated, and collect and file with the court acceptances or rejections of a plan;
4. request the appointment of a trustee or examiner under section 1104 of this title; and
5. perform such other services as are in the interest of those represented [11 U.S.C. § 1103(c)].

As you can see, the committee of creditors have broad powers to investigate the debtor and to study the feasibility of a reorganization plan. If such a plan is deemed feasible by the debtors, the committee is then primarily responsible for coming up with and submitting a specific plan of reorganization for the debtor.

Appointment of Trustee or Examiner

After the case is started but before the court approves a final reorganization plan, a trustee or examiner is appointed. The court can appoint a trustee for cause if it believes that there has been fraud, dishonesty, incompetence, or gross mismanagement of the affairs of the debtor by current management, either before or after the commencement of the case, or simply if the court believes such an appointment to be in the best interests of the creditors. If a trustee is not appointed and the debtor is allowed to continue managing the business, then any interested party may request the appointment of an examiner. The examiner will investigate any allegations of fraud, dishonesty, incompetence, misconduct, mismanagement, or irregularity in the management of the affairs of the debtor of or by current or former management of the debtor if the court believes the appointment of an examiner will be in the interest of any interested party, or if the debtor's unsecured debts exceed $5,000,000.

Duties of Trustee

If a trustee is appointed, she is given the following duties:

1. accountability for all property received;
2. examine proofs of claims of creditors and object to any deemed improper;
3. furnish information about the estate and estate administration at the request of any party in interest;
4. furnish information to the court, to the United States Trustee and to any interested government agencies entitled to collect taxes, periodic reports, and summaries about the operation of the debtor's business, including information about business receipts and disbursements;
5. make a final report and a final account of the administration of the estate to the court and to the U.S. Trustee;
6. provide notice to any party entitled to receive domestic support from the debtor about the discharge and notice that it does not extinguish the domestic support obligations of the debtor;
7. continue to perform the obligations of a debtor who served as an administrator of an employee benefit plan at the time of the filing of the Chapter 11 petition;
8. use all reasonable best efforts to transfer patients from a health care business that is in the process of being closed to an appropriate health care business that provides similar services with a reasonable quality of care in the vicinity of the closing health care facility;
9. file a list of the debtor's creditors, a schedule of the debtor's current assets, liabilities, income, expenses, and a financial statement (if the debtor has not already done so);
10. investigate the acts, conduct, assets, liabilities, and financial condition of the debtor, the operation of the debtor's business, and the desirability of the continuance of the business, and any other matter relevant to the case or to the formulation of a plan;
11. report the results of her investigation to the court and to creditors' committees, equity security holders' committees, indenture trustees, and any other entity the court designates;
12. file a plan or report why a plan cannot be formulated, recommend conversion to liquidation (Chapter 7) or to an individual repayment plan case (Chapter 13), or recommend dismissal. (If the trustee formulates a plan of reorganization, she will do so in consultation with the debtors.) [11 U.S.C. § 1106 (a) (1-8)]

Duties of Examiner

If an examiner is appointed instead of a trustee, the examiner has the following duties:

1. investigating the acts, conduct, assets, liabilities, and financial condition of the debtor, the operation of the debtor's business, and the desirability of the continuance of the business, and any other matter relevant to the case or to the formulation of a plan; and

2. reporting the results of his investigation to the court and to creditors' committees, equity security holders' committees, indenture trustees, and any other entity the court designates. [11 U.S.C. § 1106(b)]

Filing of Reorganization Plan

As is true of liquidation, reorganization may be voluntary or involuntary. A Chapter 11 case may be begun voluntarily by a debtor filing a plan of reorganization at any time (even after an involuntary case is begun). The debtor is given an exclusive right to file a plan within the first 120 days from the court's order of relief granted upon the proper filing of a case under this chapter. Other interested parties may also propose a plan if a trustee has been appointed, if the debtor does not meet the 120-day deadline, or if the debtor meets the 120-day deadline but fails to obtain approval of the plan by the creditors within 180 days of the court's order for relief, but the court may extend or reduce these time periods for cause. A court may extend the 120-day deadline to a maximum of 18 months and the 180-day deadline for up to 20 months from the date that it grants the order of relief.

Acceptance of Reorganization Plan

Before it becomes effective, a reorganization plan must be accepted by the members of each class of debtors that the plan will affect. For a class of creditors to accept the plan, not less than half of the members of a class who together hold a minimum of two-thirds of the total amount of debt for the entire class must vote to accept the plan.

Confirmation of Reorganization Plan

After acceptance of a reorganization plan, it must be confirmed by the court. A plan will be confirmed by the court only if it is found to meet minimum criteria, including:

1. the plan complies with the applicable provisions of Chapter 11;
2. the proponent of the plan complies with all applicable provisions of Chapter 11;
3. the plan has been proposed in good faith;
4. all costs and expenses under the plan are approved by the court as reasonable;
5. the identities and affiliations of any individuals who will serve as a director, officer, or voting trustee of the debtor serve as successors to the debtor under the plan or participate in any joint plan with the debtor;
6. the identities and compensation of any insiders that will be retained under the reorganization plan by the debtor are disclosed;
7. debtors in each class have either accepted the plan or will be guaranteed a minimum claim under the reorganization as they would have received under Chapter 7 liquidation;
8. confirmation of the plan is not likely to be followed by liquidation or further financial reorganization in the future.

Effect of Reorganization Plan's Confirmation

Once a plan is confirmed, the debtor and all creditors are bound by its terms. Debts of the debtor that arose before the filing for Chapter 11 reorganization are excused after all required payments under the plan are made, except as specifically provided for in the reorganization plan or under the provisions of the Bankruptcy Act (e.g., some tax liability is nondischargeable for corporate debtors under Chapter 11). Unlike in Chapter 7 proceedings, the debtor in Chapter 11 proceedings retains ownership of his property and may continue in business under the specific guidelines of the reorganization plan.

Chapter 13: Adjustment of Debts of an Individual with Regular Income

Chapter 13 allows an individual with regular income to file a plan with the court for the adjustment of debt. If the plan is approved, the individual's debts will be forgiven if he honors the repayment plan approved by the court.

Who May Bring Chapter 13 Proceedings

Chapter 13 proceedings may be brought by any individuals (other than stock brokers or commodity brokers) who have a stable income from wages or other reliable sources that would allow them to meet their obligations under a repayment plan. For purposes of this chapter, persons on fixed income, including pensions, Social Security, disability, or public assistance all qualify as persons having a regular income. Such income can be derived from self-employment in a business (provided such income is steady and reliable), but the business entity itself cannot be the subject of the reorganization. (As we've just seen, business reorganization would, of course, be covered by Chapter 11 of the Bankruptcy Code.)

In addition to the requirement of a regular income, the total unsecured debt for an individual (or an individual and a spouse filing jointly) must be less than $383,175, and the total secured debt must be less than $1,149,525.

Instituting Chapter 13 Proceedings

Unlike Chapter 7 and Chapter 11 proceedings, which may be instituted voluntarily at the request of the debtor or involuntarily at the request of the creditors, Chapter 13 proceedings may only be brought voluntarily by the debtor. The rationale for not permitting involuntary Chapter 13 cases is perhaps best expressed in the Senate's own report on Section 303 of the Bankruptcy Act governing the commencement of involuntary cases:

> Involuntary Chapter 13 cases are not permitted. . . . To do so would constitute bad policy, because Chapter 13 only works when there is a willing debtor that wants to repay his creditors. Short of involuntary servitude, it is difficult to keep a debtor working for his creditors when he does not want to pay them back. [Senate Report No. 95-989]

Lest it seem unfair to deny creditors the ability to bring an involuntary case under Chapter 13, keep in mind that they *can* bring either an involuntary Chapter 7 or Chapter 11 action. The purpose of Chapter 13 is to make it simpler for debtors who meet the eligibility criteria for Chapter 13 to come up with a voluntary plan to reorganize their debts without having to jump through all the hoops required by the standard Chapter 11 reorganization.

Filing and Contents of Plan

The debtor must file a plan for the adjustment of her debts under Chapter 13. The debtor's plan must contain the following provisions:

1. the debtor must provide for the submission of all future income (or as much of it as necessary to effectuate the plan) to the trustee;
2. it must provide for the deferred payment of all claims entitled to a priority under section 507 of the Bankruptcy Code (see Figure 27.2) unless the holders of such claims agree to different treatment;
3. if the plan classifies claims, it must provide identical treatment for all claims of a particular class;
4. the plan may provide for less than full payment to a priority claim for support under § 507(a)(1)(B) if the plan provides that all of the projected disposable income of the debtor will be applied to make payments under the plan for five years;
5. the plan may not provide a payment period longer than three years (although the court may extend the period to not more than five years if the debtor can show cause).

Confirmation of the Plan

A court will confirm the debtor's plan for the repayment of her debts if it meets the following criteria:

1. it complies with the provisions of Chapter 13 and other applicable provisions of the Bankruptcy Code;
2. all required fees that must be paid before confirmation have been paid;
3. the plan has been proposed in good faith by the debtor;

11 U.S.C. § 507 – Priorities

a. The following expenses and claims have priority in the following order:
   1. First:
      A. Allowed unsecured claims for domestic support obligations that, as of the date of the filing of the petition in a case under this title, are owed to or recoverable by a spouse, former spouse, or child of the debtor, or such child's parent, legal guardian, or responsible relative, without regard to whether the claim is filed by such person or is filed by a governmental unit on behalf of such person, on the condition that funds received under this paragraph by a governmental unit under this title after the date of the filing of the petition shall be applied and distributed in accordance with applicable nonbankruptcy law.
      B. Subject to claims under subparagraph (A), allowed unsecured claims for domestic support obligations that, as of the date of the filing of the petition, are assigned by a spouse, former spouse, child of the debtor, or such child's parent, legal guardian, or responsible relative to a governmental unit (unless such obligation is assigned voluntarily by the spouse, former spouse, child, parent, legal guardian, or responsible relative of the child for the purpose of collecting the debt) or are owed directly to or recoverable by a governmental unit under applicable nonbankruptcy law, on the condition that funds received under this paragraph by a governmental unit under this title after the date of the filing of the petition be applied and distributed in accordance with applicable nonbankruptcy law.
      C. If a trustee is appointed or elected under section 701, 702, 703, 1104, 1202, or 1302, the administrative expenses of the trustee allowed under paragraphs (1)(A), (2), and (6) of section 503(b) shall be paid before payment of claims under subparagraphs (A) and (B), to the extent that the trustee administers assets that are otherwise available for the payment of such claims.
   2. Second, administrative expenses allowed under section 503(b) of this title, unsecured claims of any Federal reserve bank related to loans made through programs or facilities authorized under section 13(3) of the Federal Reserve Act (12 U.S.C. 343), and any fees and charges assessed against the estate under chapter 123 of title 28.
   3. Third, unsecured claims allowed under section 502(f) of this title.
   4. Fourth, allowed unsecured claims, but only to the extent of $12,475 for each individual or corporation, as the case may be, earned within 180 days before the date of the filing of the petition or the date of the cessation of the debtor's business, whichever occurs first, for—
      A. wages, salaries, or commissions, including vacation, severance, and sick leave pay earned by an individual; or
      B. sales commissions earned by an individual or by a corporation with only 1 employee, acting as an independent contractor in the sale of goods or services for the debtor in the ordinary course of the debtor's business if, and only if, during the 12 months preceding that date, at least 75 percent of the amount that the individual or corporation earned by acting as an independent contractor in the sale of goods or services was earned from the debtor.
   5. Fifth, allowed unsecured claims for contributions to an employee benefit plan—
      A. arising from services rendered within 180 days before the date of the filing of the petition or the date of the cessation of the debtor's business, whichever occurs first; but only
      B. for each such plan, to the extent of—
         i. the number of employees covered by each such plan multiplied by $12,475; less
         ii. the aggregate amount paid to such employees under paragraph (4) of this subsection, plus the aggregate amount paid by the estate on behalf of such employees to any other employee benefit plan.
   6. Sixth, allowed unsecured claims of persons—
      A. engaged in the production or raising of grain, as defined in section 557(b) of this title, against a debtor who owns or operates a grain storage facility, as defined in section 557(b) of this title, for grain or the proceeds of grain, or
      B. engaged as a United States fisherman against a debtor who has acquired fish or fish produce from a fisherman through a sale or conversion, and who is engaged in operating a fish produce storage or processing facility—but only to the extent of $6,150 for each such individual.
   7. Seventh, allowed unsecured claims of individuals, to the extent of $2,775 for each such individual, arising from the deposit, before the commencement of the case, of money in connection with the purchase, lease, or rental of property, or the purchase of services, for the personal, family, or household use of such individuals, that were not delivered or provided.

FIGURE 27.2 Priority Order for Creditors' Claims under Chapters 7, 11, and 13 [11 U.S.C. § 507]

11 U.S.C. § 507 – Priorities (continued)

8. Eighth, allowed unsecured claims of governmental units, only to the extent that such claims are for—
    A. a tax on or measured by income or gross receipts for a taxable year ending on or before the date of the filing of the petition—
        i. for which a return, if required, is last due, including extensions, after three years before the date of the filing of the petition;
        ii. assessed within 240 days before the date of the filing of the petition, exclusive of—
            I. any time during which an offer in compromise with respect to that tax was pending or in effect during that 240-day period, plus 30 days; and
            II. any time during which a stay of proceedings against collections was in effect in a prior case under this title during that 240-day period, plus 90 days; or
        iii. other than a tax of a kind specified in section 523(a)(1)(B) or 523(a)(1)(C) of this title, not assessed before, but assessable, under applicable law or by agreement, after, the commencement of the case;
    B. a property tax incurred before the commencement of the case and last payable without penalty after one year before the date of the filing of the petition;
    C. a tax required to be collected or withheld and for which the debtor is liable in whatever capacity;
    D. an employment tax on a wage, salary, or commission of a kind specified in paragraph (4) of this subsection earned from the debtor before the date of the filing of the petition, whether or not actually paid before such date, for which a return is last due, under applicable law or under any extension, after three years before the date of the filing of the petition;
    E. an excise tax on—
        i. a transaction occurring before the date of the filing of the petition for which a return, if required, is last due, under applicable law or under any extension, after three years before the date of the filing of the petition; or
        ii. if a return is not required, a transaction occurring during the three years immediately preceding the date of the filing of the petition;
    F. a customs duty arising out of the importation of merchandise—
        i. entered for consumption within one year before the date of the filing of the petition;
        ii. covered by an entry liquidated or reliquidated within one year before the date of the filing of the petition; or
        iii. entered for consumption within four years before the date of the filing of the petition but unliquidated on such date, if the Secretary of the Treasury certifies that failure to liquidate such entry was due to an investigation pending on such date into assessment of antidumping or countervailing duties or fraud, or if information needed for the proper appraisement or classification of such merchandise was not available to the appropriate customs officer before such date; or
    G. a penalty related to a claim of a kind specified in this paragraph and in compensation for actual pecuniary loss.
    An otherwise applicable time period specified in this paragraph shall be suspended for any period during which a governmental unit is prohibited under applicable nonbankruptcy law from collecting a tax as a result of a request by the debtor for a hearing and an appeal of any collection action taken or proposed against the debtor, plus 90 days; plus any time during which the stay of proceedings was in effect in a prior case under this title or during which collection was precluded by the existence of 1 or more confirmed plans under this title, plus 90 days.
9. Ninth, allowed unsecured claims based upon any commitment by the debtor to a Federal depository institutions regulatory agency (or predecessor to such agency) to maintain the capital of an insured depository institution.
10. Tenth, allowed claims for death or personal injury resulting from the operation of a motor vehicle or vessel if such operation was unlawful because the debtor was intoxicated from using alcohol, a drug, or another substance.

FIGURE 27.2 (Continued)

> b. If the trustee, under section 362, 363, or 364 of this title, provides adequate protection of the interest of a holder of a claim secured by a lien on property of the debtor and if, notwithstanding such protection, such creditor has a claim allowable under subsection (a)(2) of this section arising from the stay of action against such property under section 362 of this title, from the use, sale, or lease of such property under section 363 of this title, or from the granting of a lien under section 364(d) of this title, then such creditor's claim under such subsection shall have priority over every other claim allowable under such subsection.
> c. For the purpose of subsection (a) of this section, a claim of a governmental unit arising from an erroneous refund or credit of a tax has the same priority as a claim for the tax to which such refund or credit relates.
> d. An entity that is subrogated to the rights of a holder of a claim of a kind specified in subsection (a)(1), (a)(4), (a)(5), (a)(6), (a)(7), (a)(8), or (a)(9) of this section is not subrogated to the right of the holder of such claim to priority under such subsection.

FIGURE 27.2 (Continued)

4. the amount payable to each unsecured claim is not less than the amount that would have been paid if the estate of the debtor were liquidated under Chapter 7;
5. the holders of secured claims provided for in the plan have accepted the plan;
6. the debtor will be able to make all payments under the plan and comply with the plan;
7. the debtor's action in filing the petition was in good faith;
8. the debtor has paid all amounts required to be paid under domestic support obligations; and
9. the debtor has filed all required federal, state, and local tax returns.

Payments by Debtor

Unless a court orders otherwise, a debtor is required to commence making payments within 30 days of filing the proposed plan or the order for relief, whichever is earlier. Payments are made to the trustee in the amount proposed by the plan, Payments due for leases of personal property are paid directly to the lessor, with evidence of payment sent to the trustee. Payments made to the trustee are held by the trustee until the plan is confirmed by the court, at which time the trustee is charged with distributing those payments as soon as practicable.

If the plan is confirmed, the trustee will continue to receive payments as provided for under the plan and distribute these to the debtors in accordance with the provisions of the plan. If the plan is not approved by the court, the trustee must return all monies received from the debtor (minus the trustee's allowable fee).

Effect of Confirmation

After confirmation, the debtor must make payments to the trustee as provided for in the plan. The property in the debtor's estate, however, will vest in her free of debtors' claims as long as the debtor adheres to the accepted repayment plan.

Discharge

After the debtor makes the final payment under the terms of the plan, the court will issue an order discharging the debtor from all debt covered by the plan. A court may also grant a discharge even before the debtor completes the agreed-upon payments under the plan if the court finds that the debtor's failure to keep making payments is brought about by circumstances for which the debtor should not be held accountable, as long as each creditor has been paid an amount equal to what they would have received under a Chapter 7 liquidation or Chapter 11 reorganization of the debtor's estate.

Limitation on Refiling for Protection under the Bankruptcy Code

Debtors whose debts are discharged by a Chapter 7 bankruptcy and subsequently get into additional economic difficulties can file for Chapter 7 bankruptcy protection again after eight years from the bankruptcy decree and can also file for Chapter 11 or Chapter 13 reorganization after only six years from a discharge in bankruptcy.

Bankruptcy Abuse Prevention and Consumer Protection Act of 2005

The Bankruptcy Abuse Prevention and Consumer Protection Act of 2005 (Pub. L. 109-8) went into effect October 17, 2005. The intent of Congress in passing the act was to address the increase in consumer bankruptcy filings that in 1998 had reached the 1 million mark for the first time, with bankruptcy filings doubling in the decade preceding passage of the act and reaching 1.6 million filings in fiscal year 2004, according to the U.S. House of Representatives Judiciary Committee Report 109-031. The act was an attempt by Congress to make bankruptcy filing a matter of last resort to stem the losses for creditors that result from abusive use of bankruptcy filings that are then passed on to all consumers in the form of higher interest rates, higher prices, and higher downpayments required for consumer goods and services.

The act makes it harder and more expensive to file for bankruptcy in a number of ways. For example, the act now requires individuals to complete credit counseling with an agency approved by the United States Trustee's Office prior to filing for Chapter 7 or Chapter 13 protection. A second counseling session on personal financial management is required at the conclusion of the bankruptcy case before a discharge order is entered. The new rules also require a means test before individuals can file for Chapter 7 protection. Individuals who do not pass the means test (whose monthly income over allowed expenses is higher than the act allows) are precluded from filing for Chapter 7 protection and are limited to a Chapter 13 or Chapter 11 filing. The valuation of personal property not subject to attachment also changes under the act to reflect the property's retail market value (what it would cost to purchase the property in its used condition at retail, rather than the old measure of value as what a consumer could sell the property for at an auction). This raises the valuation of exempt property over the old system, making filers able to keep less personal property under the allowed exemptions. Because state exemptions vary widely, especially with regard to the homestead exemption (the equity value on a primary residence that the filer is allowed to keep), the act sets up limits on the ability of filers to shop for a friendlier filing venue. The time period required for a resident to live in a state prior to being able to claim the state exemptions was increased from three months under the prior law to two years. And residence for 40 months is required prior to being able to claim a state's homestead exemption. Filers who do not meet these new time limits may use only the exemptions from the state in which they lived during the statutory period prior to the filing. The new rules also give priority to spouses and children of debtors with regard to alimony and child support payments, giving these a preference over all unsecured creditors.

The new rules also require that lawyers who represent bankruptcy filers personally attest to the accuracy of the information provided in the bankruptcy filing. This new requirement subjects the lawyer to potential liability for false or fraudulent information contained in the filing, and effectively forces the attorney to verify the accuracy of critical information provided by the client. This has significantly increased the workload required for filings, and therefore the cost to clients seeking the protection of the Bankruptcy Act. In addition to significantly higher costs for consumers seeking bankruptcy protection, the increased personal and professional liability risk to attorneys may also result in fewer attorneys willing to practice in the bankruptcy area in the future as well as significantly higher costs to consumers seeking the relief of the bankruptcy courts.

Questions

1. Which chapter of Title 11 of the United States Code deals with liquidation?
2. Which chapter of Title 11 of the United States Code deals with reorganization?
3. What types of debtors may *not* file for Chapter 7 protection?
4. What are the requirements for bringing involuntary liquidation proceedings against a debtor under Chapter 7?
5. What chapter of the Bankruptcy Act does not allow for involuntary proceedings to be instituted against creditors?
6. Under the federal exemptions listed under the Bankruptcy Act, how much of the equity in a homeowner's primary residence is exempt in a Chapter 7 filing?
7. What is the basic difference between Chapter 7 and Chapter 11?
8. What types of debtors may bring a Chapter 11 reorganization proceeding?
9. Name four of the duties of a trustee under Chapter 11 reorganization proceedings?
10. Who may bring a Chapter 13 proceeding?
11. What provisions must be contained in a debtor's plan under Chapter 13?

Hypothetical Cases

1. Beautiful Homes, Inc., a closely held company in the business of providing home decorating services that is wholly owned by Jenny Chang, finds itself in financial difficulties. Its assets, including the good will of the business, its long-term commercial lease, and its account receivables total $150,000, and the total debts of the business are $250,000. Although the business is generally healthy, Jenny's problems stem primarily from her having financed a recent expansion through short-term, variable interest loans just before interest rates began to rise. The result is that she can no longer meet the monthly payments on her loan.
   A. Under the facts given, would Jenny be wise to file for Chapter 7 protection of her business? Explain fully.
   B. Should Jenny file for Chapter 11 protection of her business? Explain fully.
   C. Could Jenny file for Chapter 13 protection of her business enterprise? Explain.
2. Debby Debtor has just been informed that her $100,000 per year middle management position is being eliminated as part of her company's downsizing. Debby's basic assets include a car worth $20,000, $30,000 equity in her home, $10,000 in bank CDs, and $2,000 in savings. Her monthly payments on her home, car, credit cards, utilities, and property taxes total $2,500. Her total unsecured debt is $20,000, and her secured debt (primarily her home and auto financing) is $300,000. Afraid that she will need many months to find another job and that selling her home in the present real estate market in her area would not be feasible, she is considering filing for protection under the Bankruptcy Act.
   A. May Debby file under Chapter 7? Should she?
   B. May she file under Chapter 11? Should she?
   C. May she file under Chapter 13? Explain fully.
3. Don Broke has managed to obtain $200,000 in unsecured loans (mostly from unsolicited credit cards with high credit lines and even higher interest rates). He also owes $30,000 in a homeowner's loan secured by a mortgage on his home. Don's only source of income is his job at a fast-food restaurant in which he makes $10 per hour for a gross monthly income of $1,400. He owns a house he inherited from his parents, and it is worth $160,000. He also owns a classic car with a value of $15,000 that he inherited from his grandmother. Finally, he owns approximately $5,000 worth of personal property and household goods, including a $3,000 70-inch 3D television set. After being unable to pay his monthly bills for several months, Don decides he must avail himself of the protection offered by the Bankruptcy Act.
   A. Does Don qualify for Chapter 7, 11, or 13 protection?
   B. Should Don file for liquidation or reorganization? Explain.
   C. Assume that Don files for liquidation under Chapter 7. How much of his personal or real property will he be able to keep assuming that his state does not provide greater exemptions than the Bankruptcy Act affords? (To put it another way, how much of his property will be exempt from attachment under Chapter 7?)
4. Peter Penniless files for bankruptcy under Chapter 7. At the time of filing, his assets subject to attachment totaled $3,000. His debts included the following: $2,500 in allowed administrative expenses in bringing the case; $5,000 to Visa, $4,000 to MasterCard, and $1,000 to American Express in unsecured debt.
   A. How much of the administrative expense claim will be paid? Explain fully.
   B. How much of the unsecured debt will be paid to the credit card creditors? Explain fully.

Unit IV—Cases for Further Study

SUPREME COURT OF THE UNITED STATES
No. 12–5196
STEPHEN LAW, PETITIONER v. ALFRED H. SIEGEL, CHAPTER 7 TRUSTEE
ON WRIT OF CERTIORARI TO THE UNITED STATES
COURT OF APPEALS FOR THE NINTH CIRCUIT
[March 4, 2014]

JUSTICE SCALIA delivered the opinion of the Court. The Bankruptcy Code provides that a debtor may exempt certain assets from the bankruptcy estate. It further provides that exempt assets generally are not liable for any expenses associated with administering the estate. In this case, we consider whether a bankruptcy court nonetheless may order that a debtor's exempt assets be used to pay administrative expenses incurred as a result of the debtor's misconduct.

I. Background

A

Chapter 7 of the Bankruptcy Code gives an insolvent debtor the opportunity to discharge his debts by liquidating his assets to pay his creditors. 11 U. S. C. §§ 704(a)(1), 726, 727. The filing of a bankruptcy petition under Chapter 7 creates a bankruptcy "estate" generally comprising all of the debtor's property. § 541(a)(1). The estate is placed under the control of a trustee, who is responsible for managing liquidation of the estate's assets and distribution of the proceeds. § 704(a)(1). The Code authorizes the debtor to "exempt," however, certain kinds of property from the estate, enabling him to retain those assets post bankruptcy. § 522(b)(1). Except in particular situations specified in the Code, exempt property "is not liable" for the payment of "any [prepetition] debt" or "any administrative expense." § 522(c), (k). Section 522(d) of the Code provides a number of exemptions unless they are specifically prohibited by state law. § 522(b)(2), (d). One, commonly known as the "homestead exemption," protects up to $22,975 in equity in the debtor's residence. § 522(d)(1) and note following § 522; see Owen v. Owen, 500 U. S. 305, 310 (1991). The debtor may elect, however, to forgo the § 522(d) exemptions and instead claim whatever exemptions are available under applicable state or local law. § 522(b)(3)(A). Some States provide homestead exemptions that are more generous than the federal exemption; some provide less generous versions; but nearly every State provides some type of homestead exemption. See López, State Homestead Exemptions and Bankruptcy Law: Is It Time for Congress To Close the Loophole? 7 Rutgers Bus. L. J. 143, 149–165 (2010) (listing state exemptions).

B

Petitioner, Stephen Law, filed for Chapter 7 bankruptcy in 2004, and respondent, Alfred H. Siegel, was appointed to serve as trustee. The estate's only significant asset was Law's house in Hacienda Heights, California. On a schedule filed with the Bankruptcy Court, Law valued the house at $363,348 and claimed that $75,000 of its value was covered by California's homestead exemption. See Cal. Civ. Proc. Code Ann. § 704.730(a)(1) (West Supp. 2014). He also reported that the house was subject to two voluntary liens: a note and deed of trust for $147,156.52 in favor of Washington Mutual Bank, and a second note and deed of trust for $156,929.04 in favor of "Lin's Mortgage & Associates." Law thus represented that there was no equity in the house that could be recovered for his other creditors, because the sum of the two liens exceeded the house's nonexempt value. If Law's representations had been accurate, he presumably would have been able to retain the house, since Siegel would have had no reason to pursue its sale. Instead, a few months after Law's petition was filed, Siegel initiated an adversary proceeding alleging that the lien in favor of "Lin's Mortgage & Associates" was fraudulent. The deed of trust supporting that lien had been recorded by Law in 1999 and reflected a debt to someone named "Lili Lin." Not one but two individuals claiming to be

Lili Lin ultimately responded to Siegel's complaint. One, Lili Lin of Artesia, California, was a former acquaintance of Law's who denied ever having loaned him money and described his repeated efforts to involve her in various sham transactions relating to the disputed deed of trust. That Lili Lin promptly entered into a stipulated judgment disclaiming any interest in the house. But that was not the end of the matter, because the second "Lili Lin" claimed to be the true beneficiary of the disputed deed of trust. Over the next five years, this "Lili Lin" managed—despite supposedly living in China and speaking no English—to engage in extensive and costly litigation, including several appeals, contesting the avoidance of the deed of trust and Siegel's subsequent sale of the house.

Finally, in 2009, the Bankruptcy Court entered an order concluding that "no person named Lili Lin ever made a loan to [Law] in exchange for the disputed deed of trust." In re Law, 401 B. R. 447, 453 (Bkrtcy. Ct. CD Cal.). The court found that "the loan was a fiction, meant to preserve [Law's] equity in his residence beyond what he was entitled to exempt" by perpetrating "a fraud on his creditors and the court." Ibid. With regard to the second "Lili Lin," the court declared itself "unpersuaded that Lili Lin of China signed or approved any declaration or pleading purporting to come from her." Ibid. Rather, it said, the "most plausible conclusion" was that Law himself had "authored, signed, and filed some or all of these papers." Ibid. It also found that Law had submitted false evidence "in an effort to persuade the court that Lili Lin of China—rather than Lili Lin of Artesia—was the true holder of the lien on his residence." Id., at 452. The court determined that Siegel had incurred more than $500,000 in attorney's fees overcoming Law's fraudulent misrepresentations. It therefore granted Siegel's motion to "surcharge" the entirety of Law's $75,000 homestead exemption, making those funds available to defray Siegel's attorney's fees. The Ninth Circuit Bankruptcy Appellate Panel affirmed. BAP No. CC–09–1077–PaMkH, 2009 WL 7751415 (Oct. 22, 2009) (per curiam). It held that the Bankruptcy Court's factual findings regarding Law's fraud were not clearly erroneous and that the court had not abused its discretion by surcharging Law's exempt assets. It explained that in Latman v. Burdette, 366 F. 3d 774 (2004), the Ninth Circuit had recognized a bankruptcy court's power to "equitably surcharge a debtor's statutory exemptions" in exceptional circumstances, such as "when a debtor engages in inequitable or fraudulent conduct." 2009 WL 7751415, *5, *7. The Bankruptcy Appellate Panel acknowledged that the Tenth Circuit had disagreed with Latman, see In re Scrivner, 535 F. 3d 1258, 1263–1265 (2008), but the panel affirmed that Latman was correct. 2009 WL 7751415, *7, n. 10. Judge Markell filed a concurring opinion agreeing with the panel's application of Latman but questioning "whether Latman remains good policy." 2009 WL 7751415, *10.

The Ninth Circuit affirmed. In re Law, 435 Fed. Appx. 697 (2011) (per curiam). It held that the surcharge was proper because it was "calculated to compensate the estate for the actual monetary costs imposed by the debtor's misconduct, and was warranted to protect the integrity of the bankruptcy process." Id., at 698. We granted certiorari. 570 U. S. ___ (2013).

II. Analysis

A

A bankruptcy court has statutory authority to "issue any order, process, or judgment that is necessary or appropriate to carry out the provisions of" the Bankruptcy Code. 11 U. S. C. § 105(a). And it may also possess "inherent power . . . to sanction 'abusive litigation practices.'" Marrama v. Citizens Bank of Mass., 549 U. S. 365, 375–376 (2007). But in exercising those statutory and inherent powers, a bankruptcy court may not contravene specific statutory provisions.

It is hornbook law that § 105(a) "does not allow the bankruptcy court to override explicit mandates of other sections of the Bankruptcy Code." 2 Collier on Bankruptcy ¶105.01[2], p. 105–6 (16th ed. 2013). Section 105(a) confers authority to "carry out" the provisions of the Code, but it is quite impossible to do that by taking action that the Code prohibits. That is simply an application of the axiom that a statute's general permission to take actions of a certain type must yield to a specific prohibition found elsewhere. See Morton v. Mancari, 417 U. S. 535, 550–551 (1974); D. Ginsberg & Sons, Inc. v. Popkin, 285 U. S. 204, 206–208 (1932) [Footnote omitted]. Courts' inherent sanctioning powers are likewise subordinate to valid statutory directives and prohibitions. Degen v. United States, 517 U. S. 820, 823 (1996); Chambers v. NASCO, Inc., 501 U. S. 32, 47 (1991). We have long held that "whatever equitable powers remain in the bankruptcy courts must and can only be exercised within the confines of " the Bankruptcy Code. Norwest Bank Worthington v. Ahlers, 485 U. S. 197, 206 (1988); see, e.g., Raleigh v. Illinois Dept. of Revenue, 530 U. S. 15, 24–25 (2000); United States v. Noland, 517 U. S. 535, 543 (1996); SEC v. United States Realty & Improvement Co., 310 U. S. 434, 455 (1940).

Thus, the Bankruptcy Court's "surcharge" was unauthorized if it contravened a specific provision of the Code. We conclude that it did. Section 522 (by reference to California law) entitled Law to exempt $75,000 of equity in his home from the bankruptcy estate. § 522(b)(3)(A). And it made that $75,000 "not liable for payment of any administrative expense." § 522(k) [Footnote omitted]. The reasonable attorney's fees Siegel incurred defeating the "Lili Lin" lien were indubitably an administrative expense, as a short march through a few statutory cross-references makes plain: Section 503(b)(2) provides that administrative expenses include "compensation . . . awarded under" § 330(a); § 330(a)(1) authorizes "reasonable compensation for actual, necessary services rendered" by a "professional person employed under" § 327; and § 327(a) authorizes the trustee to "employ one or more attorneys . . . to represent or assist the trustee in carrying out the trustee's duties under this title." Siegel argues that even though attorney's fees incurred responding to a debtor's fraud qualify as "administrative expenses" for purposes of determining the trustee's right to reimbursement under § 503(b), they do not so qualify for purposes of § 522(k); but he gives us no reason to depart from the "'normal rule of statutory construction'" that words repeated in different parts of the same statute generally have the same meaning. See Department of Revenue of Ore. v. ACF Industries, Inc., 510 U. S. 332, 342 (1994) (quoting Sorenson v. Secretary of Treasury, 475 U. S. 851, 860 (1986)).

The Bankruptcy Court thus violated § 522's express terms when it ordered that the $75,000 protected by Law's homestead exemption be made available to pay Siegel's attorney's fees, an administrative expense. In doing so, the court exceeded the limits of its authority under § 105(a) and its inherent powers.

B

Siegel does not dispute the premise that a bankruptcy court's § 105(a) and inherent powers may not be exercised in contravention of the Code. Instead, his main argument is that the Bankruptcy Court's surcharge did not contravene § 522. That statute, Siegel contends, "establish[es] the procedure by which a debtor may seek to claim exemptions" but "contains no directive requiring [courts] to allow [an exemption] regardless of the circumstances." Brief for Respondent 35. Thus, he says, recognition of an equitable power in the Bankruptcy Court to deny an exemption by "surcharging" the exempt property in response to the debtor's misconduct can coexist comfortably with § 522. The United States, appearing in support of Siegel, agrees, arguing that § 522 "neither gives debtors an absolute right to retain exempt property nor limits a court's authority to impose an equitable surcharge on such property." Brief for United States as Amicus Curiae 23.

Insofar as Siegel and the United States equate the Bankruptcy Court's surcharge with an outright denial of Law's homestead exemption, their arguments founder upon this case's procedural history. The Bankruptcy Appellate Panel stated that because no one "timely oppose[d] [Law]'s homestead exemption claim," the exemption "became final" before the Bankruptcy Court imposed the surcharge. 2009 WL 7751415, at *2. We have held that a trustee's failure to make a timely objection prevents him from challenging an exemption. Taylor v. Freeland & Kronz, 503 U. S. 638, 643–644 (1992).

But even assuming the Bankruptcy Court could have revisited Law's entitlement to the exemption, § 522 does not give courts discretion to grant or withhold exemptions based on whatever considerations they deem appropriate. Rather, the statute exhaustively specifies the criteria that will render property exempt. See § 522(b), (d). Siegel insists that because § 522(b) says that the debtor "may exempt" certain property, rather than that he "shall be entitled" to do so, the court retains discretion to grant or deny exemptions even when the statutory criteria are met. But the subject of "may exempt" in § 522(b) is the debtor, not the court, so it is the debtor in whom the statute vests discretion. A debtor need not invoke an exemption to which the statute entitles him; but if he does, the court may not refuse to honor the exemption absent a valid statutory basis for doing so.

Moreover, § 522 sets forth a number of carefully calibrated exceptions and limitations, some of which relate to the debtor's misconduct. For example, § 522(c) makes exempt property liable for certain kinds of prepetition debts, including debts arising from tax fraud, fraud in connection with student loans, and other specified types of wrongdoing. Section 522(o) prevents a debtor from claiming a homestead exemption to the extent he acquired the homestead with nonexempt property in the previous 10 years "with the intent to hinder, delay, or defraud a creditor." And § 522(q) caps a debtor's homestead exemption at approximately $150,000 (but does not eliminate it entirely) where the debtor has been convicted of a felony that shows "that the filing of the case was an abuse of the provisions of" the Code, or where the debtor owes a debt arising from specified wrongful acts—such as securities fraud, civil violations of the Racketeer Influenced and Corrupt Organizations Act, or "any criminal act, intentional tort, or willful or reckless misconduct that caused serious physical injury or death to another individual in the preceding 5 years." § 522(q) and note following § 522. The Code's meticulous—not to say mind-numbingly detailed—enumeration of exemptions and exceptions to those exemptions confirms that courts are not authorized to create additional exceptions. See Hillman v. Maretta, 569 U. S. ___, ___ (2013) (slip op., at 12); TRW Inc. v. Andrews, 534 U. S. 19, 28–29 (2001).

Siegel points out that a handful of courts have claimed authority to disallow an exemption (or to bar a debtor from amending his schedules to claim an exemption, which is much the same thing) based on the debtor's fraudulent concealment of the asset alleged to be exempt. See, e.g., In re Yonikus, 996 F. 2d 866, 872–873 (CA7 1993); In re Doan, 672 F. 2d 831, 833 (CA11 1982) (per curiam); Stewart v. Ganey, 116 F. 2d 1010, 1011 (CA5 1940). He suggests that those decisions reflect a general, equitable power in bankruptcy courts to deny exemptions based on a debtor's bad-faith conduct. For the reasons we have given, the Bankruptcy Code admits no such power. It is of course true that when a debtor claims a state-created exemption, the exemption's scope is determined by state law, which may provide that certain types of debtor misconduct warrant denial of the exemption. E.g., In re Sholdan, 217 F. 3d 1006, 1008 (CA8 2000); see 4 Collier on Bankruptcy ¶522.08[1]–[2], at 522–45 to 522–47. Some of the early decisions on which Siegel relies, and which the Fifth Circuit cited in Stewart, are instances in which federal courts applied state law to disallow state-created exemptions. See In re Denson, 195 F. 857, 858 (ND Ala. 1912); Cowan v. Burchfield, 180 F. 614, 619 (ND Ala. 1910); In re Ansley Bros., 153 F. 983, 984 (EDNC 1907). But federal law provides no authority for bankruptcy courts to deny an exemption on a ground not specified in the Code.

C

Our decision in Marrama v. Citizens Bank, on which Siegel and the United States heavily rely, does not point toward a different result. The question there was whether a debtor's bad-faith conduct was a valid basis for a bankruptcy court to refuse to convert the debtor's bankruptcy from a liquidation under Chapter 7 to a reorganization under Chapter 13. Although § 706(a) of the Code gave the debtor a right to convert the case, § 706(d) "expressly conditioned" that right on the debtor's "ability to qualify as a 'debtor' under Chapter 13." 549 U. S., at 372. And § 1307(c) provided that a proceeding under Chapter 13 could be dismissed or converted to a Chapter 7 proceeding "for cause," which the Court interpreted to authorize dismissal or conversion for bad-faith conduct. In light of § 1307(c), the Court held that the debtor's bad faith could stop him from qualifying as a debtor under Chapter 13, thus preventing him from satisfying § 706(d)'s express condition on conversion. Id., at 372–373. That holding has no relevance here, since no one suggests that Law failed to satisfy any express statutory condition on his claiming of the homestead exemption.

True, the Court in Marrama also opined that the Bankruptcy Court's refusal to convert the case was authorized under § 105(a) and might have been authorized under the court's inherent powers. Id., at 375–376. But even that dictum does not support Siegel's position. In Marrama, the Court reasoned that if the case had been converted to Chapter 13, § 1307(c) would have required it to be either dismissed or reconverted to Chapter 7 in light of the debtor's bad faith. Therefore, the Court suggested, even if the Bankruptcy Court's refusal to convert the case had not been expressly authorized by § 706(d), that action could have been justified as a way of providing a "prompt, rather than a delayed, ruling on [the debtor's] unmeritorious attempt to qualify" under § 1307(c). Id., at 376. At most, Marrama's dictum suggests that in some circumstances a bankruptcy court may be authorized to dispense with futile procedural niceties in order to reach more expeditiously an end result required by the Code. Marrama most certainly did not endorse, even in dictum, the view that equitable considerations permit a bankruptcy court to contravene express provisions of the Code.

D

We acknowledge that our ruling forces Siegel to shoulder a heavy financial burden resulting from Law's egregious misconduct, and that it may produce inequitable results for trustees and creditors in other cases. We have recognized, however, that in crafting the provisions of § 522, "Congress balanced the difficult choices that exemption limits impose on debtors with the economic harm that exemptions visit on creditors." Schwab v. Reilly, 560 U. S. 770, 791 (2010). The same can be said of the limits imposed on recovery of administrative expenses by trustees. For the reasons we have explained, it is not for courts to alter the balance struck by the statute. Cf. Guidry v. Sheet Metal Workers Nat. Pension Fund, 493 U. S. 365, 376–377 (1990).

* * *

Our decision today does not denude bankruptcy courts of the essential "authority to respond to debtor misconduct with meaningful sanctions." Brief for United States as Amicus Curiae 17. There is ample authority to deny the dishonest debtor a discharge. See § 727(a)(2)–(6). (That sanction lacks bite here, since by reason of a postpetition settlement between Siegel and Law's major creditor, Law has no debts left to discharge; but that will not often be the case.) In addition, Federal Rule of Bankruptcy Procedure 9011—bankruptcy's analogue to Civil Rule 11—authorizes the court to impose sanctions for bad-faith litigation conduct, which may include "an order directing payment. . . of some or all of the reasonable attorneys' fees and other expenses incurred as a direct result of the violation." Fed. Rule Bkrtcy. Proc. 9011(c)(2). The court may also possess further sanctioning authority under either § 105(a) or its inherent powers. Cf. Chambers, 501 U. S., at 45–49. And because it arises postpetition, a bankruptcy court's monetary sanction survives the bankruptcy case and is thereafter enforceable through the normal procedures for collecting money judgments. See § 727(b). Fraudulent conduct in a bankruptcy case may also subject a debtor to criminal prosecution under 18 U. S. C. § 152, which carries a maximum penalty of five years' imprisonment.

But whatever other sanctions a bankruptcy court may impose on a dishonest debtor, it may not contravene express provisions of the Bankruptcy Code by ordering that the debtor's exempt property be used to pay debts and expenses for which that property is not liable under the Code.

The judgment of the Court of Appeals is reversed, and the case is remanded for further proceedings consistent with this opinion.

It is so ordered.

Optional Assignments

1. Brief the preceding abbreviated version of the case in a one- to two-page, single-spaced brief (with double spaces between paragraphs) that contains the following four sections: (1) The basic facts of the case [Facts]; (2) The legal issue the court is being asked to decide [Issue]; (3) The holding of the court (how it decides the legal issue before it) [Holding]; and (4) The rationale the court uses to support its decision [Rationale]. If your instructor asks you to brief the case, she will give you additional instructions.

2. Do you agree or disagree with the opinion? Why?

UNIT 5

PROPERTY AND INSURANCE

Lukas Gojda/Shutterstock

CHAPTER 28
Personal Property

CHAPTER 29
Intellectual Property

CHAPTER 30
Bailments

CHAPTER 31
Real Property

CHAPTER 32
Creation and Transfer of Interests in Real Property

CHAPTER 33
Landlords' and Tenants' Rights and Responsibilities

CHAPTER 34
Insurance

CHAPTER 35
Wills

CHAPTER 36
Trusts

Introduction to Property

The term *property* is used to describe anything that is capable of ownership. An ownership right in property, regardless of its nature, gives the owner a whole bundle of rights that the government sanctions and protects. For instance, the owner of real estate or personal property has the right to use it, sell it, give it away, rent it, possess it, prevent others from possessing or interfering with it, and with some exceptions even to destroy it. Ownership of property carries with it the exclusive right to use, possess, and dispose of the thing over which one has an ownership interest. Government sanctions property rights by recognizing the rights of individuals to private property ownership. It also protects those rights through criminal statutes that make interfering with the property rights of others a punishable offense (e.g., theft, arson, criminal mischief), and allows individuals to use the courts to defend their property rights and to seek civil damages against those who interfere with them (e.g., actions in tort and contract).

Property can be divided into two basic types: real and personal. Real property essentially consists of land and anything permanently attached to it, whereas personal property consists of anything else that is capable of ownership. Personal property can be further divided into both tangible and intangible types. We have already been exposed to tangible personal property (also called *goods* and *chattels*) in our discussion of Article 2 of the Uniform Commercial Code (UCC) covering the sale of goods. Intangible personal property, on the other hand, covers ownership rights over things that do not have physical existence such as intellectual property (copyrights, patents, trademarks, and the like), stocks, bonds, contract rights, and commercial paper.

In this unit, we will explore personal and real property rights, as well as the rights and responsibilities of parties incidental to owning, renting, borrowing, and giving away real and personal property during the owner's life and after death. We will also examine the role of insurance as a means of protecting property and managing risk.

Personal Property

CHAPTER 28

Chapter Outline

Acquiring Title to Personal Property through Possession

Acquiring Title to Property through Purchase

Acquiring Title to Personal Property through Manufacturing

Acquiring Title to Personal Property through Accession

Acquiring Title to Personal Property through a Gift

As you are doubtless aware, nearly everything on earth is capable of ownership. Even at early common law, where all real property and wild animals in England were deemed to belong to the crown (which in turn could gift parts of it to favored nobles as it saw fit), serfs were allowed limited rights to own personal property. Then, as now, there were five basic ways in which rights to personal property could be acquired: by possession, by purchase, by manufacture, by *accession* (the adding of value to the property by one's labor), and by gift. In this chapter, we will examine the creation and transfer of rights to both tangible and intangible personal property.

Acquiring Title to Personal Property through Possession

While the oft-repeated phrase "possession is nine-tenths of the law" is generally untrue, it contains a grain of truth, for possession alone can convey a property interest in at least two instances: the lawful killing or capture of wild animals and the finding of abandoned property.

Wild Animals

Under modern personal property law, wild animals belong to no one while they are free. A wild animal can, however, become personal property if it is lawfully killed and retrieved by a hunter or lawfully trapped or captured alive. Thus, a hunter who kills a deer using an approved means and possessing a valid hunting license owns the deer as soon as he takes possession of it. Likewise, fish swimming in a pond, river, or ocean are subject to personal ownership if they are caught in season by a fisherman with a valid fishing license (where one is required). If fish or game are illegally killed or caught, however, ownership does not pass to the hunter or fisherman; rather, the ownership vests in the state. Thus, a deer killed out of season, by a hunter without a license, or by a hunter using an unapproved weapon (e.g., a rifle in a jurisdiction that allows only the taking of deer by the use of a shotgun or a bow and arrow) or a fish that does not meet the required size or weight standards belongs to the state.

A wild animal that is lawfully captured alive and then escapes is considered personal property only as long as it was in captivity; as soon as it regains its freedom, the property interest of its captor ends and the animal can become the property of anyone who ultimately kills and takes possession of it or recaptures it alive (assuming that the killing or capture of the animal is legal under applicable state or federal law). Note too that the mere lawful killing of a wild animal does not convey a property interest; the animal becomes personal property only when the hunter takes possession of it. The traditional common law rule holds that the person taking possession of a dead wild animal owns it, regardless of who killed it (as long as the killing was lawful). Keep in mind, however, that states are free to modify the traditional common law through judicial decisions or legislative enactments.

Abandoned Property

The finder of abandoned property obtains a property right to it by possession of the property. Property is deemed abandoned if its true owner voluntarily relinquishes interest to such property through a clearly manifested intention to divest herself of the property. A homeowner who puts an old television set by the curb next to his garbage for collection on the day that trash is normally picked up, for example, has clearly abandoned the property, and it may be claimed by any passerby who takes it.

In determining whether property is abandoned, the intent of the owner is of paramount importance; that property appears to be abandoned does not mean that it necessarily is. A wallet that falls into a wastepaper basket, for example, is not abandoned property but rather qualifies as lost property, even though it might appear to be abandoned property to a person who later picks it out of the garbage pail. The same would be true of property placed by the curb for pickup as refuse or in a garbage pail by someone who does not own it; only the true owner can relinquish her property rights to personal property. Whether or not property was actually abandoned by its owner is a question of fact that must be resolved by the trier of fact if the issue is litigated at trial.

It is important to distinguish between abandoned property and lost or mislaid property for purposes of ownership by possession because the finder of lost or mislaid property does *not* gain ownership of it. *Mislaid property* is property that the true owner purposely placed somewhere and then forgot to retrieve. Leaving a briefcase in a cab, forgetting a pocketbook at a restaurant table, and leaving a wallet at a checkout counter at a supermarket after paying for groceries are all examples of mislaid property. *Lost property*, on the other hand, is property that the owner involuntarily lost custody of by accident or negligence and does not know where to find. A wallet dropped by accident in the middle of the street and a camera that drops inadvertently from the neck of its owner when the strap breaks are both examples of lost property. As we'll see in our discussion of bailments in Chapter 30, the finder of lost or mislaid property does not become its owner but rather an involuntary bailee of it who has a responsibility to make a reasonable attempt to find its true owner. (See Figure 28.1 for an example of a statute that defines the rights and responsibilities of finders of lost property.)

Acquiring Title to Property through Purchase

The most common means of acquiring both tangible and intangible personal property is through its purchase. As we've already seen from our discussion of the sale or goods, title to tangible personal property generally passes upon delivery of the property from the seller to the buyer pursuant to a sales contract. When you go to a bakery and pay $3 for a large loaf of Italian bread, you gain ownership over the bread as soon as the bakery attendant hands it to you and you pay for it. The same is true for any other tangible or intangible property: once property is delivered and paid for pursuant to a binding agreement for its sale, the item's ownership passes from the seller to the buyer, and the buyer acquires whatever ownership interest the seller had to give. This is true whether a cash, credit, or barter transaction is involved. If an electrician agrees to purchase a painter's painting in exchange for wiring the painter's home, title to the painting will pass as soon as it is turned over to the electrician, subject to her keeping her end of the bargain and properly wiring the painter's home. The same would be true if the electrician paid $1,000 in cash for the painting, gave a check for $1,000 for it or charged the painting on her Visa or MasterCard.

When title is acquired through purchase, the purchaser obtains exactly whatever title the seller had to give; thus, if the seller is a thief, the purchaser will generally acquire no title to the goods (one exception is goods sold by a merchant to whom the goods were

Finders Keepers?

While conventional wisdom may hold that the finder of lost property may keep it for her own use, the law has never supported that point of view. Ownership rights to personal property can only be transferred through one of the traditional means discussed in this chapter and are not lost through the negligence of the owner who leaves behind or loses personal property. From early common law, the finder of lost or mislaid property had a legal duty imposed on him to make some effort to find the true owner of the property, and was held to be holding the property as a bailee or caretaker for the true owner until the owner could be found. The finder of lost property could use the property after conducting a reasonable search for its true owner, but had to return it to her should she show up in the future and claim the property. At common law and generally today, one who finds lost or mislaid property and immediately appropriates it for his use without a reasonable effort to find the true owner is guilty of a crime (theft) and a tort (conversion).

Many states have codified the responsibility of the finder of lost property into a statute. In New York, for example, such a statute can be found in Article 7-B of the Personal Property Law. [NY Pers Prop L § 252 (2014)] paragraphs 1 and 3 of the statute, quoted below in part, require finders of property with a value of $20 or more to turn in lost property to police. Failing to do so can result in a misdemeanor conviction. On the plus side, complying with the statute allows the found property to vest in the finder after a period of time that ranges from three months to three years depending on the property's value (see paragraph 7 below). In order to obtain title to the property after the statutory period noted below, however, the finder will need to pay for the cost of storage or care of the property while in police custody (if any).

1. [A]ny person who finds **lost property** of the value of twenty dollars or more . . . shall, within ten days after the finding or acquisition of possession thereof, either return it to the owner or report such finding or acquisition of possession and deposit such property in a police station or police headquarters of the city where the finding occurred or possession was acquired. . . .
2. [A]ny person who finds an instrument or comes into possession of an instrument with knowledge that it has been found shall, within ten days after the finding or acquisition of possession thereof, either return it to a person entitled thereto or report the finding or acquisition of possession and deposit the instrument in a police station or police headquarters, as provided in subdivision one of this section, as if such instrument were lost property having a value of ten dollars or more.
3. [A]ny person who shall refuse or willfully neglect to comply with the provisions of subdivision one or subdivision two of this section shall be guilty of a misdemeanor and upon conviction thereof shall be punished by a fine of not more than one hundred dollars or imprisonment not exceeding six months or both.
   - NY Pers Prop L § 253 (7) (2014) further provides that the lost property [or its value if the property is sold at auction by police] is to be given to the finder if the true owner does not claim it as follows:
     1. after three months and the property has a value of less than $100, or
     2. after six months if it has a value of at least $100 but less than $500, or
     3. after one year if the property has a value of at least $500 but less than $5,000, or
   - After three years if the property has a value of at least $5,000.

FIGURE 28.1 Some States Provide a Statutory Framework Defining the Duties of Finders of Lost Property. The Applicable New York Statute Excerpted Here [Ny Pers Prop L §§ 252-253] Requires Finders of Lost Property with a Value of $20 or More to Turn it Over to Police. Failing to Do so Can Result in a Misdemeanor Conviction

entrusted by the true owner, as we'll see in Chapter 30 in our discussion of bailments). The general rule is that a seller passes exactly the title he has to the goods being sold; since a thief has no title to the goods sold, he passes no title to them.

Acquiring Title to Personal Property through Manufacturing

The act of creation conveys a property interest in the creator in the fruits of his labor. Thus, a person who combines paint and paper to manufacture a painting owns the painting; likewise, a person who writes a poem or the lyrics or music to a song acquires an ownership interest to these intangible intellectual properties. If goods are manufactured with material not owned by the manufacturer, however, then ownership will not vest with the creator but rather will remain with the owner of the material used by the person who created the new substance. If, for example, a thief steals lumber and other building supplies from a construction site and uses them to construct a house on his land, the thief will *not* obtain title to the finished home despite the fact that he manufactured it; rather, the title to the house, if it can be moved from the land, or to its value if it cannot, will remain with the true owner of the building supplies.

Acquiring Title to Personal Property through Accession

Accession can be defined as an increase to the value of property one owns through either one's own input or through some external force. For example, if you purchase an old, unseaworthy boat for $50 and restore it into a splendid vessel worth $25,000, the boat will have added $24,950 to its value, and your property will have benefited from an accession brought about by your work. Likewise, if you own a cow that becomes pregnant, you will own the milk it produces and the calf it eventually bears. This may all be obvious, but the issue of who owns property that benefits from an accession can become clouded when the property of one person is improved—either willfully or through a mistake—by the work of another.

Whenever accession is made by one person to the property of another, the question of who is entitled to benefit from the accession depends on the surrounding circumstances. When the accession is made by one person in bad faith, with the knowledge that the property belongs to another, for example, the property in its improved form belongs to the true owner and there is no need to compensate the person who added to its value. Thus, a thief who paints a stolen car and puts a new engine into it will not be entitled to compensation by the car's true owner for the value added to the vehicle. When the accession is innocently made, which is to say under circumstances when the person adding value to another's property did so in good faith, under a mistaken assumption as to the ownership of the property or the owner's intention to abandon it, the person making the accession is entitled to compensation by the true owner of the property. In most instances, the true owner is entitled to keep the property but must either return the improvement made to the property, where it is possible to do so, or its reasonable value. In cases in which the property is transformed from its original form into something of superior value because of the accession, the person who innocently transformed the property is generally entitled to keep it but must pay its true owner the reasonable value of the property in its original form.

The following examples will illustrate:

- Elizabeth, an artist, finds a very bad oil painting in front of Elijah's house and, believing that he intends to throw it out, takes it home with her. She then sets to work on it and imbues the painting with new life—and a new aesthetic and material value. When Elijah learns of Elizabeth's mistake, he demands that she return the painting and claims that the accession she has caused to his property rightfully belongs to him. Elizabeth counters that the painting belongs to her, since she acted in good faith and reasonably believed the painting had been abandoned.

- Elizabeth, an artist, sees a painting hanging in Elijah's living room of the type created in assembly-line fashion that are sometimes sold in shopping malls and in some department stores. She finds the painting to be so bad as to be offensive and an insult to art lovers the world over. She rips it down from the wall in disgust and (without Elijah's knowledge or consent) takes it home and paints over it with fresh oils, transforming a $100 eyesore into a $5,000 true work of art. When Elijah learns of Elizabeth's actions, he demands that she turn over his painting, claiming that the accession it to rightfully belongs to him. Elizabeth refuses to turn over her artwork but offers to pay him the $100 his original oil painting was worth.

In the first example, Elizabeth innocently transforms the painting into something of great value. Because the accession was done in good faith and under the reasonable belief that the painting had been abandoned, Elizabeth may keep the painting but must pay Elijah whatever the original painting was worth. In the second example, however, Elizabeth acts with the knowledge that the painting belongs to Elijah and is, therefore, not entitled to *any* compensation for its accession.

Acquiring Title to Personal Property through a Gift

The final means by which title can be obtained to personal property is by being the recipient of a gift. For title to personal property to pass by gift, the following criteria must be met:

- the giver of the gift (the donor) must intend to part with the property for the benefit of the receiver (the donee) out of detached, disinterested generosity;
- there must be a delivery of the property from the donor of the gift to the donee; and
- there must be an acceptance of the gift by the donee.

To make a valid gift, the donor must have the legal capacity to dispose of property that is the same as that required for entering into a valid contract. With regard to the competence of the donor, the same rules apply as to contracts; gifts by judicially declared incompetents are void, while gifts by minors or persons with diminished capacity who have not been adjudged incompetent are voidable. If the donor expects to receive some consideration in return for making the "gift," then there is no valid gift but rather a contract, and standard contract law applies to the transaction.

The requirement of delivery normally entails the physical transfer of the property from the donor to the donee either directly or through an agent (such as a delivery by messenger or common carrier). In cases in which physical delivery is impossible or impractical, a valid constructive delivery can be made by the donor taking some affirmative step to deliver either the property itself or the means of obtaining the property to the donee. For example, if a donor wishes to make a gift to the donee of a gold watch that is in the donor's safety deposit box in a bank, giving the donee the key to the safety deposit box along with written authorization to the bank to allow the donee to access the safety deposit box would construe a valid constructive delivery of the watch itself. Likewise, giving the keys and signed registration and title to a car by a donor to the donee constitutes constructive delivery of the automobile, regardless of where the automobile itself is located at the time that the keys, title, and registration are transferred.

Acceptance of a gift by the donee requires words or actions that clearly and unequivocally evidence the intent to accept the gift.

Inter Vivos Gifts

When the subject matter of the gift is transferred during the lifetime of the donor to the donee, the transfer is termed an *inter vivos* gift (a gift between the living). *Inter vivos* gifts are generally irrevocable. Thus, when a donor with the intention of making a gift delivers it to the donee and the donee accepts it, the gift is complete and the title to the property passes from the donor to the donee. Once the transfer is effectuated, the donor cannot change his mind and recall the property, for it no longer belongs to him. The donor can, however, change his mind at any time before all three conditions to a valid gift are met. In addition, a gift such as an engagement ring that is given in consideration of a marriage that fails to take place when the parties break off the engagement may be recoverable by the giver as Figure 28.2 illustrates.

Since a valid *inter vivos* gift requires an intention to make a valid gift by the giver, gifts that are the product of undue influence, fraud, or made by a person without the capacity to enter into a contract are voidable at the option of the giver.

> ### Engagement Rings
>
> Engagement rings are classified as gifts made with an implied condition that a marriage between the donor and donee will occur. If the engagement is subsequently broken by either party and the marriage does not take place, the donor is usually entitled to return of the ring. Under the traditional common law rule, if the marriage is broken by the donor of the gift without just cause, the donee may keep the ring. Likewise, if the donee of the ring breaks the engagement without just cause, the donor is entitled to the return of the ring. The courts of some states, such as Pennsylvania, have abandoned the common law rule in favor of a modern trend that applies a no-fault approach that requires the donee to return the ring regardless of whether the engagement was broken by the donee or donor with or without cause.

FIGURE 28.2 After a Wedding Engagement Is Broken, Who Owns the Engagement Ring?

Gifts *Causa Mortis*

A gift *causa mortis* is one made during the donor's lifetime in contemplation of death. When a gift *causa mortis* is involved, the donor intends to make a gift only because he fears that he is about to die. Such gifts are valid, but unlike normal *inter vivos* gifts, are revocable by the donor if he does not die of the cause he contemplates dying from at the time of making the gift. A typical gift *causa mortis* would include a person who is about to undergo surgery giving a ring to a loved one and saying, "I want you to have this ring now, since I fear I'll die during the operation." If the person dies, the gift is effective. If the person survives the operation, however, he can reclaim the gift from the donee within a reasonable time of his recovery.

Testamentary Gifts

A testamentary gift is one that the donor intends not to take effect until after her death. Unlike gifts *inter vivos*, which require no specific formalities as long as they meet the three criteria for a valid gift, testamentary gifts are typically made through a will and must conform to the formalities for such instruments. (We'll discuss wills in detail in Chapter 35.) Testamentary gifts are revocable during the lifetime of the testator or testatrix (the man or woman, respectively, who drafts a will to make testamentary gifts to take effect upon his or her death).

Questions

1. How does one obtain title to wild animals?
2. To whom does a deer killed out of season by a poacher belong?
3. How does one obtain title to abandoned property?
4. Does the finder of lost or mislaid property automatically become its owner?
5. What is accession?
6. What are the three requirements that must be met for a valid *inter vivos* gift?
7. What is an *inter vivos* gift?
8. What is a gift *causa mortis*?
9. Are either gifts *causa mortis* or *inter vivos* revocable? If so, under what circumstances?
10. What are testamentary gifts?

Hypothetical Cases

1. Andrea, Bart, and Cathy notice a bunny while walking in the woods. Andrea immediately yells out, "I'm gonna get that rabbit and make a couple of lucky rabbit's feet out of it." Bart cries out: "Over my dead body; I saw him first and I'm gonna grab it and make rabbit stew!" Cathy exclaims: "I'll brain the first idiot who touches that adorable bunny! I want him for a pet!" The three then run toward the poor bunny, who tries its best to elude them. Andrea catches it first, loudly proclaiming her victory; but the bunny bites her thumb and she drops it, unharmed. Bart grabs at the poor creature next and tries to stuff it in his pocket but drops him when Cathy tackles him from behind. Cathy then grabs at the bunny and manages to capture and hold it, taking

it home with great care. Andrea and Bart, nursing their bruises and egos, solemnly vow revenge.
   A. Assume that rabbits are considered pests in the state where all this occurred and that there are no laws relating to the killing or live taking of rabbits. Further assume that Andrea and Bart both sue Cathy for the return of the bunny that they claim rightfully belongs to them. Whose bunny is it, anyway? Explain fully.
2. Michael buys a motorboat in poor condition from Terry for $500. Unknown to Michael, the boat was stolen by a thief who had sold it to Terry six months earlier. Michael fixes the engine and restores the boat to excellent seaworthy condition by spending $50 in parts and materials and 100 hours of his time. By the time he finishes the restoration, the boat is worth $5,000. On the first day that he puts the boat in the water, its true owner appears and claims it. Michael claims that the boat rightfully belongs to him, since he was a good-faith purchaser of it and paid its fair market price. The case ends up in small claims court and you are the judge. Decide this case and justify your decision with sound legal reasoning.
3. Assume the same facts as above except that Michael rebuilds the dead outboard engine for $250 and does no other work to the boat before the owner surfaces and claims the vehicle. What result?
4. Fred purchases a 50-inch LCD television set as a gift to his friend Gina and has it shipped to her home as a surprise gift. On the day that the set was to be delivered, Fred has a falling out with Gina and tells her: "I had bought a large screen television as a birthday gift for you that was supposed to be delivered today, but I've changed my mind and I'm going to have the delivery canceled." Gina immediately retorts, "Too late, I accept your gift."
   A. Can George cancel the delivery, or is he too late to rescind the gift? Explain.
   B. If the television set had already been delivered and accepted by Gina before the falling out and Fred stopped payment on the check he'd used to pay for the set, would the gift be revoked?

Ethics and the Law: Questions for Further Study

The law generally requires the finder of lost or mislaid property to make a reasonable search for its true owner or risk prosecution for theft, regardless of the value of the item that is lost, in the absence of a state statute to the contrary. In addition, there is no requirement that the finder be compensated by the true owner when the item is claimed, other than for any reasonable expenses incurred in relation to the care of the item or advertisements relating to its loss. This imposes an arguably unfair burden on finders of lost property and might encourage persons who find the property to refuse to pick it up so as not to have to fulfill the legal obligation of searching for the property's true owner. Should the law force the true owner of lost or mislaid property to compensate the finder for the reasonable value of his services in attempting to locate the owner? Might this encourage persons who find lost or mislaid goods to turn them into police or attempt to search for the property's true owners? Aren't we in fact encouraging persons who find such property to break the law and keep it by giving them no incentive to "do the right thing"? What do you think?

Intellectual Property

CHAPTER 29

Chapter Outline

Patents

Copyrights

Trademarks

Service Marks, Collective Marks, and Certification Marks

Remedies for Infringement of a Registered Mark

Trade Secrets

Intellectual Property in the International Arena

As we saw in the preceding chapter, the very act of creation can convey a property interest to the creator in the object of her creation. This is equally true for tangible personal property, such as manufactured goods, as well as intangible personal property, such as a writer's work or an actor's performance. In the eyes of the law, a wordsmith's work is as much worthy of protection as a silversmith's creations. But intellectual property is harder to protect against theft and infringement than is tangible personal property. It is easier to prove interference with tangible property rights than intangible ones. For instance, if a carpenter's creation, say a chair, is stolen, damaged, or used by another without the carpenter's consent, the carpenter will have relatively little trouble proving the infringement. But a singer whose song or music is stolen, or inappropriately "borrowed" by another in whole or in part, will often have a harder time making his case. Interference with intangible property rights is often easily accomplished and often difficult to trace. Indeed, most people infringe on others' intangible property rights on a regular basis, often unaware that they are doing so. Copying commercial software or a DVD from a friend; illegally downloading copyrighted music or video from the Internet or via peer-to-peer file transfers; ripping mp3, wav, or mp4 files from legally purchased downloads, CDs, or DVDs and uploading these to a friend's media player; and incorporating the ideas of others in term papers or other writing without giving credit—all constitute unlawful interference with intangible property rights. In this chapter, we will examine the basic laws that protect intellectual property rights in the U.S. in the form of patents, copyrights, service marks, and trademarks.

The U.S. Constitution gives to Congress in Article I, Section 8 the power to "promote the progress of science and useful arts, by securing for limited times to authors and inventors the exclusive right to their respective writings and discoveries." Congress has secured these rights through appropriate legislation and the creation of the U.S. Patent and Trademark Office and the U.S. Copyright Office to regulate the issuance of patents, copyrights, and trademarks in accordance with Congressional guidelines.

Patents

A patent is an exclusive right granted to an inventor by the federal government to profit from the use of her invention for a period of 14 years for design patents and 20 years for utility and plant patents from the date of filing the patent application. During the 14- or 20-year period that the inventor alone is given the exclusive right to exploit the invention covered by the patent, the patent itself is deemed intangible personal property; as such, it can be sold, given away, or leased to anyone the inventor chooses for whatever consideration is mutually agreed upon. After the patent expires, the invention becomes public domain and may be used by anyone without the need to compensate the inventor.

To be patentable, the subject matter for which a patent is sought must be new and must not infringe on any other existing patent. While most patents involve some type of device, it is also possible to patent new chemical substances, such as a new drug or a better lubricant. New compositions of matter, such as genetically engineered microorganisms or plants with special properties, are also patentable. Novel manufacturing techniques or processes may also be patented, provided they are both new and useful. For example, if a process were discovered to better extract sap from maple trees to make maple syrup, the process could be patented, as could a new method of extracting oil from shale rock.

Application for a patent is made to the U.S. Patent and Trademark Office (USPTO). In the application, the inventor must show both how the invention works, including detailed technical drawings and other supporting evidence of how the device can be manufactured, as well as a narrative detailing the novelty and usefulness of the object that make it worthy of patenting. Upon the grant of a patent, the inventor is protected from any infringement during the patent's useful life. Any unauthorized use of the patented idea by a third party will result in a valid civil suit for damages by the inventor against the infringing party, regardless of the infringer's good faith or lack of actual knowledge of the existence of the patent. If the infringement is malicious, a court is empowered to award both actual damages (such as lost royalties) as well as punitive damages equal to three times the actual damages caused by the infringement, as well as court costs and attorneys' fees if the judge deems it appropriate. Where patent infringement is not malicious, but rather caused by negligence or ignorance of the infringer, the typical damages awarded are a reasonable royalty for use of the inventor's patent.

Copyrights

The Federal Copyright Act provides protection to authors of literary, dramatic, musical, choreographic, and artistic works, including motion pictures and other audio-visual works. The act is very broad in scope and is intended to cover any original work of authorship, regardless of the medium. The act includes computer software (both electronic programs and written program listings).

Any qualifying work can be copyrighted by registering with the U.S. Copyright Office in Washington D.C., but registration is not necessary to invoke copyright protection. A work is deemed copyrighted as soon as it is expressed in some tangible form, such as by writing it down or typing it into a computer and saving it as a file. Nevertheless, it is a good idea to formally register copyrighted work because registration is a prerequisite to being able to bring an infringement action and recover damages.

For works created after January 1, 1978, copyright protection lasts throughout the author's life and for an additional 70 years after the author's death. Copyrights owned by publishers, such as works produced by authors on a work-for-hire basis, last for 95 years from the date of publication or 120 years from the date of creation, whichever comes first. During the copyright period, the author (and the author's estate for 70 years after the author's death) has the exclusive right to reproduce the work or to make any derivative works based on it. Authors are also entitled to royalty payments upon public use of copyrighted works, such as the broadcasting of a song or music video over the airwaves or the public performance of a play.

Limited *fair use* of copyrighted work can be made without it constituting copyright infringement for educational purposes, as well as for news reporting and literary criticism. To qualify as fair use, the portion of the copyrighted work must be relatively small and not unduly infringe on the work as a whole. For example, quoting from one page of a novel for purposes of literary criticism or copying one article from a newspaper for classroom distribution is likely to be covered under fair use. But if the amount of material used is excessive, a copyright infringement occurs. In determining whether a specific instance of alleged copyright infringement is covered by the *fair use doctrine*, and is thus exempt from liability, the courts perform a balancing test between the author's right to profit from his work and the educational or literary value of the infringement. Courts in recent years have shown decreasing tolerance for allowing a fair use exception to copyright infringement actions, even in not-for-profit educational settings. Penalties for copyright infringement can include civil damages for infringement, as well as punitive damages and criminal penalties for willful infringement.

In addition, the Digital Millennium Copyright Act of 1998 and the No Electronic Theft Act of 1997 passed by Congress significantly enhanced the protection offered by the Copyright Act of 1976 for copyrighted material in digital form and provide stiff penalties for copyright infringement of up to $250,000, even for private, noncommercial infringement.

Trademarks

A trademark is any symbol, picture, design, or words adopted by a manufacturer to distinguish its products from other similar products in the market. To be capable of being registered with the U.S. Patent and Trademark Office, a trademark must be unique and cannot be a generic name. Product names, such as *Coca-Cola*® and *Coke*®, can be registered trademarks, as well as slogans adopted to identify a product (*The real thing* relating to Coke®, for example). But the generic words *cola* and *soda* by themselves cannot be trademarks, since they are not unique but rather descriptive of a type of product. Company logos and graphic designs are also capable of being registered trademarks. Thus, *7-Up*® and *The Uncola*® are registered trademarks for the well-known soft drink, and so is the red dot used by the soft drink maker in its advertising and as part of its product's name. Likewise, the distinctive design in product labels can be covered by a trademark.

When a trademark is registered, it may be contested by any company that claims an infringement of its own trademark for a period of five years. If a new trademark is not contested within that time period, it becomes incontestable.

Once issued, a new registered trademark can be renewed after five years and is renewable every ten years thereafter upon a showing that it is still in use and has not been abandoned. Trademarks registered before 1990 are renewable every 20 years. Application to renew a trademark must be made within three months of its expiration. Like all personal property, a trademark may be sold or assigned by its owner.

Service Marks, Collective Marks, and Certification Marks

Service marks, collective marks, and certification marks are closely related to trademarks and treated in exactly the same way for purposes of federal registration and renewal. A service mark is any distinctive mark used by a service industry for purposes of advertising or sales. The radio and television network designations of ABC, NBC, CBS, and FOX, for example, are all service marks, as are the CBS eye symbol, and the NBC peacock. Likewise the symbols used by book publishers along with their names on book spines.

Collective marks are a type of trademark or service mark owned by a collective and used by its members to denote membership in the organization and to distinguish their products or services from those offered by nonmembers. CPA is an example of a collective mark to denote membership in the Society of Certified Public Accountants. Another example is the letters ILGWU found on garments created by members of the International Ladies' Garment Workers' Union.

Certification marks, on the other hand, are specific words or symbols adopted by a group of companies or government agencies to denote the quality, origin, or some other attribute relating to the goods. Typical certification marks include USDA Choice, UL [Underwriter's Laboratories] Approved, and the Union Label attached to goods manufactured in the U.S. by textile and other unionized workers.

Remedies for Infringement of a Registered Mark

It is an infringement of a registered mark to reproduce such a mark or an imitation of such a mark without the consent of the registrant by any means for a commercial purpose whenever doing so would tend to confuse or deceive the public as to the genuineness of the goods involved. This means that third parties cannot misappropriate the registered mark of another (trademark, service mark, or certification mark), and even a misleading approximation of such a mark cannot be used for commercial purposes if the public may be misled as to the identity of the goods. Consequently, a new soft drink maker cannot use the name Pepsi Cola or any registered mark associated with the nationally known soft drink, and it can't even use a name or adopt a logo that is close enough to confuse the general public. Peppy Cola, for example, *might* be an allowable trade name for such a drink, but if the manufacturers adopt a lettering style or can design that approximates the *Pepsi Cola*® trademarks for these, it would constitute trademark infringement. The question of whether a particular trade name or trademark is sufficiently similar to the existing registered marks of a product is usually one of fact for the trier of fact to determine.

The damages allowable for infringement of a registered mark vary depending on the nature of the infringement. Where an infringement is innocently made by a printer who manufactures literature, packaging, or any other material to be used in the sale or marketing of the product, the only remedy available against the printer is an injunction to prevent it from continuing to create such infringing material. Injunctive relief is likewise the only remedy available against a television station, newspaper, or other medium that innocently runs commercials containing infringing material. Where the infringement is intentional, however, and made for the purpose of confusing or deceiving the public, the party who suffers an infringement of a registered mark not only may be awarded injunctive relief, but also may recover any profits made by the infringer from the infringement, as well as any damages sustained by the holder of the infringed registered mark as a result of the infringement. *Treble damages* (three times the actual damages of the infringer's actual profits made from the infringement) may also be awarded, as well as court costs and attorneys' fees.

Trade Secrets

Trade secrets include business plans, mechanisms, manufacturing techniques, and compiled data that give a business an advantage over its competitors. Although some trade secrets, such as formulas for the manufacture of products, could be patented, they often are not in order to extend the useful life of the formula and to keep it secret. If, for example, the formula for making Coca-Cola® had been patented, its ingredients would be a part of the public record and would only have given the company a 20-year monopoly on its manufacture. By maintaining a formula as a trade secret, the company can maintain its monopoly over the manufacture of a given product indefinitely, or until its competitors can duplicate or reverse-engineer the formula themselves, whichever comes first. Likewise, customer lists and other information vital to the running of a business are considered trade secrets.

The significance of trade secrets is that they are protected in two ways. First, employees who have access to such information are under an obligation not to divulge it and can be enjoined from doing so; indeed, they can be sued for damages if they misappropriate or divulge trade secrets to which they had access as employees. Second, because trade secrets are considered the personal property of a company, any illegal access to or theft of such secret information is both a crime and a tort that can subject violators to criminal and civil liability. If the information contained in a trade secret is discovered through lawful means, however, the discoverer is free to use it. So if a new company stumbles on another's secret manufacturing techniques or formulas by chance or by its independent research into the product, it is free to use that formula or manufacturing technique itself unless these are covered by a patent.

Intellectual Property in the International Arena

Intellectual property protection does not extend beyond the borders of a sovereign nation because countries cannot impose their laws on other sovereign nations. Therefore, the fact that the U.S. Patent Office grants a patent to Jane Doe does not mean that Jane's patent provides her with any protection outside the U.S. As is true of international law generally, countries cannot force one another to recognize their laws other than by negotiated treaties or, in extreme cases, by going to war.

In the intellectual property arena, the protection of intellectual property rights is governed by various international treaties and protocols applicable to signatory nations. Nations that do not sign on to international agreements are not bound to give any protection to the intellectual property of foreign nationals and many do not. Even when nations agree to bind themselves to treaties, there is no guarantee that they will strictly enforce them; there is no shortage of examples of trading partners that turn a blind eye to copyright and patent infringement within their borders. Enforcement then becomes an issue that aggrieved nations pursue through diplomatic channels, weighing options such as exerting international pressure through the United Nations, threatening to impose trade sanctions or reduce foreign aid, and so on.

International Copyright Protection

Copyright protection in the international arena is provided by two principal international conventions: the Berne Convention for the Protection of Literary and Artistic Works (Berne Convention) and the Universal Copyright Convention (UCC). Both conventions offer protections to authors who live in countries that are signatories of the conventions from infringement of their work in other signatory countries. The protection is automatic and arises when a work is copyrighted in any signatory country. As of this writing, 168 nations are signatories of the Berne Convention, and 100 countries have signed the UCC. Any specific formal requirements for copyright protection under the UCC can be fulfilled by authors attaching a copyright notice that includes the letter *C* in a circle © along with the year that the work was copyrighted and the author's name (e.g., © 2017 Amanda Author). Under the international conventions, countries essentially agree to provide copyright owners of other signatory countries the same legal rights that they extend to their own citizens. Thus, if the U.S. provides an individual copyright owner protection throughout his life and 70 years after his death, and Angola (a Berne Convention signatory as is the U.S.) provides protection for the author's life and for 50 years after his death, and only 25 years after death for photographic works and applied arts, then the copyright of a U.S. photographer for his photographs would last only for his life and for 25 years after his death in Angola—the same as would apply to Angola nationals. (For additional detailed information about the Berne Convention, you can visit the World Intellectual Property Organization (WIPO) site at http://www.wipo.int/treaties/en/ip/berne/.)

International Patent Protection

Unfortunately for inventors, patent protection does not generally apply outside their country of nationality. International conventions such as the Madrid Protocol, which, like the copyright conventions, are sponsored under the auspices of the United Nations, do not provide reciprocal rights for signatory members—only a simplified, centralized way to apply for patent protection in countries that are signatories to the agreement. In other words, a patent holder in the U.S. has no protection of any kind anywhere else in the world. To protect her idea, an inventor needs to apply for a patent in every country in which she wants to protect her idea through a patent, and there is no guarantee that a patent will be issued. Even when applying to multiple countries for patents under an international agreement like the Madrid Protocol, which allows for applications to be made to a single office, the applicant has to pay for fees and translations into languages other than English. These fees, unlike the modest copyright registration fee, can quickly rise to thousands of dollars per application. Moreover, there is no real protection offered to inventors whose patents are infringed by foreign nationals in countries where the inventor has not secured a patent other than to prevent goods manufactured under the infringed patent from being imported into the U.S. Finally, it should be noted that even when inventors are willing to bear the cost of seeking patent protection in other countries, there is no guarantee that a patent will be issued, and business process patents are usually not recognized outside the United States.

International Trademark Protection

The treatment of trademarks in the international arena is similar to that of patents as described previously and is also subject to the Madrid Protocol. Registration of a trademark for signatory countries is handled by application to a single office with payments for registration applications for each selected country. If granted, trademark protection needs to be periodically renewed, and the trademark must remain in continuous use for the renewal to be granted. (For sample forms and additional information about applications through the Madrid Protocol, you can visit the World Intellectual Property Organization (WIPO) site at http://www.wipo.int/madrid/en/forms/.)

Questions

1. What is a patent?
2. What government office is in charge of granting patents?
3. Can a state grant patents?
4. Are sculptures, paintings, photographs, and choreographed dances protected by copyright? Explain.
5. How does a work become copyrighted?
6. How long does copyright protection last?
7. What is a trademark?
8. What is a service mark?
9. What are certification marks?
10. How long do registered trademarks last?

Hypothetical Cases

1. Imalia Inventor invents the proverbial better mousetrap. She promptly begins its manufacture in her garage and starts selling the mousetraps to local businesses and private individuals through a direct marketing campaign. Sales are brisk, and she soon turns her invention into a profitable business that catches the attention of other mousetrap manufacturers throughout the world. Within six months, mousetraps identical to hers flood the market at a much lower price and drive her out of business. Furious at this injustice, she wants to sue for patent infringement and for interference with trade secrets. What result?

2. Wanda Writer compiled a book of her poetry as well as a rough draft of a novel using her computer. She never printed the material since she considered it a work in progress, preferring to do all revisions on her computer. Every week, she burned a backup of the material into a DVD. When the work was completed, she took the DVD to work, intending to use her color laser printer there to print the material out to send to selected publishers for their consideration. On her way to work, however, she had her purse stolen by a thief in the subway. The thief took her valuables but threw the DVD disk away, having no use for literature. The DVD was later found by chance by an English professor who, impressed with the work and unable to determine its rightful owner, published the novel in his own name and copied two of the 100 poems for distribution in his class. Wanda eventually learned of the professor's actions and decided to sue him for copyright infringement, both for the publication of the novel in his own name and for the unauthorized use of her poetry in the classroom. What result on both claims? Explain fully.

3. The makers of a new toothpaste called *West* launch their new product on the market with a heavy ad campaign in newspapers, magazines, and television stations across the nation. The ads feature a western theme that revolves around cowboys, gunfighters, and similar characters endorsing the product. While the commercials are unique, the packaging and lettering of the toothpaste are very similar to another leading dentifrice, *Crest*®.

    Based on these facts, answer the following questions:
    A. Does there seem to be a trademark infringement here? What will the makers of *Crest*® need to show in order to succeed in a trademark infringement action?

- B. Assuming that the lettering and designs are found to infringe on Crest's registered trademark, what damages should be assessed against the manufacturer of West toothpaste?
- C. What damages can the makers of Crest seek against the media for running the infringing commercials?
4. A food services company invents an artificial sweetener that tastes exactly like sugar, has no calories, and is cheaper than sugar to manufacture. It seeks a patent for its new invention and begins production of the new product. Answer the following questions based on these facts.
   - A. If the company wants to register the product under the name Sugar, will it succeed?
   - B. Assume that the company obtains a registered trademark for the product under the name *Natural Sweet*. Six years later, when the product has captured a 90% share of the artificial sweetener market, a competitor sues for trademark infringement, claiming that the product is too closely linked to its own trademark, both in the name and in the appearance of the lettering in the registered trademark's logo. Assume that both of these allegations are true. What result?
   - C. Twenty-one years after the introduction of the product into the market, a competitor clones the product and markets it under its own trademark. The inventor of the product sues to protect its product, claiming both an infringement of its patent and a violation of its valuable trade secrets by the appropriation of its formula. What result?

Bailments

CHAPTER 30

In the previous two chapters, we discussed ownership interests to personal property. In this chapter, we will explore the rights and responsibilities of parties to personal property that is transferred by an owner to a third party for temporary custody.

Chapter Outline

Introduction to Bailments

Introduction to Bailments

A *bailment* occurs when possession of personal property is transferred by its true owner to a third party for temporary custody with the understanding that the property must be returned to its true owner at some time in the future. The owner of the property who gives over custody of it to a third party is called the *bailor*, and the person to whom custody of goods is temporarily entrusted is called the *bailee*.

For a valid bailment to occur, personal property (either tangible or intangible) must be involved, and the following must occur:

- there must be a transfer of property from the bailor to the bailee;
- the transfer must be of a temporary nature with the understanding that the bailed property will be returned to the bailor in the future;
- there must be a willful acceptance of the bailed property by the bailee.

When these conditions are met, a bailment arises that conveys certain rights and obligations to the parties involved that depend in part on the type of bailment involved. The three basic types of bailments that parties can enter into are (1) bailments for the sole benefit of the bailor; (2) bailments for the sole benefit of the bailee; and (3) mutual benefit bailments.

Bailments for the Sole Benefit of the Bailor

A bailment for the sole benefit of the bailor, as the name implies, is one that benefits only the bailor (owner) of the bailed property. This type of bailment is gratuitous (the bailee is not paid for his services and derives no benefit from the bailment) and places on the bailee only a slight duty of care with regard to the bailed goods. When this type of bailment is involved, the bailee is not responsible for any damage or loss of the bailor's property unless he was grossly negligent in caring for it or unless he damages the property himself.

A bailment for the sole benefit of the bailor typically occurs in situations in which the bailor asks the bailee as a favor to temporarily look after his property. Each of the following situations entails a bailment for the sole benefit of the bailor:

- Sam asks Samantha to keep an eye on his books in the student cafeteria while he goes to the men's room;
- Pam asks Peter to hold her camera and snap her picture;
- Bernard asks Beatrice to keep an eye on several bags of groceries while he goes to get his car from the parking lot.

Each of the preceding situations involves the bailee doing a favor for the bailor. Since the bailee is not deriving any benefit from the bailment, her duty of care with regard to the bailed goods is slight. In the preceding examples, for instance, the bailees would not be responsible for any theft or damage to the bailed goods unless they themselves stole or damaged the goods or were grossly negligent with regard to their care. As long as the three bailees stayed within a reasonable distance from the goods and made some effort to watch them, they would not be responsible for their loss or theft should the goods be stolen or damaged by a third party. Note, too, that the bailment in these three examples will not arise unless the bailees *agree to look after the goods*. Thus, if Cindy asks Chuck to look after her pocketbook while she goes to the lady's room and leaves before he agrees to do so by his word or deed, no bailment occurs and Chuck has absolutely no responsibility with regard to the pocketbook.

Bailments for the Sole Benefit of the Bailee

A bailment for the sole benefit of the bailee is a gratuitous bailment from which only the bailee derives a benefit. Unlike bailments for the sole benefit of the bailor, where the bailee's duty of care is slight, the bailee's duty of care with regard to the bailed goods in a bailment for the sole benefit of the bailee is great. In such a bailment, the bailee has an absolute duty to ensure the safety and integrity of the bailed goods and will generally be liable to the bailor for any damage, however slight, to the bailor's property that the bailee could have prevented while it was in his care. Common examples of such bailments include the following:

- Henry borrows Hannah's automobile to drive a friend to the hospital;
- Martha borrows Muhammad's digital SLR camera to take pictures of her Hawaiian vacation;
- Ranji borrows Rhoda's boat to go on a fishing trip.

If a stone lifted by a truck on the highway cracks Hanna's windshield on the way to the hospital, an unexpected wave splashes water on Muhammad's camera on Maui, or an unseen rock scrapes the bottom of Rhoda's boat, Henry, Martha, and Ranji will need to pay for the repair or replacement of the bailed property regardless of how carefully they cared for it while borrowing it.

Mutual Benefit Bailments

A mutual benefit bailment is one in which both the bailor and bailee derive some legal benefit from the bailment of the goods involved. Typical mutual benefit bailments include (but are not limited to) rental agreements involving personal property. When such bailments are involved, one person typically pays money to another in exchange for the temporary use of the other's personal property. But money need not be the consideration given by the bailee; anything of legal value given by the bailee as consideration for being allowed to use the bailed property will suffice to make the bailment one of mutual benefit. Thus, the routine car rental and DVD movie rental agreements clearly involve mutual benefit bailments, but so do the following situations:

- Liv borrows Lenny's power saw to work on a home construction project with the understanding that she will buy Lenny three new blades for the saw when she returns it;

- Pamela, who lives close to the local airport, agrees to allow Pascuale to leave his car in her garage while he goes on a two-month vacation abroad in exchange for being allowed to use the car during that time period;
- Teresa allows Tai to borrow her snow blower during a winter season in exchange for Tai's agreement to clear her driveway and sidewalk after every snowstorm.

The duty of care involved in a mutual benefit bailment is *reasonable care* under the circumstances. To put it another way, the duty of care for such bailments is greater than that of bailments for the sole benefit of the bailor, but not as great as that of bailments for the sole benefit of the bailee. In practical terms, this means that ordinary wear and tear with regard to the bailed goods is permissible in such bailments, but the bailee has a duty to take reasonable care of the bailed property and is responsible for any damage above reasonable wear and tear caused by his negligence. As always, what is reasonable care under the circumstances is a question of fact to be determined by the trier of fact.

Bailor's Rights and Duties in a Bailment

Bailors in all bailments have certain rights and responsibilities arising from the bailment. The principal rights of bailors include the right to have the property returned to them by the bailee in the same condition it was in when the bailee received it and the right to receive the agreed-upon consideration from the bailee for the bailment (unless, of course, a gratuitous bailment is involved). The responsibilities of the bailor, on the other hand, include turning over the bailed property to the bailee as agreed and warning the bailee of any known defects in the property that might cause injury or other loss to the bailee. The duty to warn bailee depends in part on the nature of the bailment. Where bailments for the sole benefit of the bailee are involved, the duty of the bailor to warn extends only to known hidden defects in the goods of which he is aware and which would not be obvious to the bailee. When mutual benefit bailments are involved, the bailor is responsible not only to warn the bailee of any known defects, but also of any defect which the bailor *could* have discovered through a reasonable inspection. The same is true in a bailment for the sole benefit of the bailor.

Bailee's Rights and Duties in a Bailment

The bailee has the right to possess the bailed property and, if the bailment agreement so provides, to use it during the term of the bailment. He also has the right to be indemnified for any reasonably necessary cost incurred with respect to caring for or emergency repairs to the property not caused by the bailee's negligence. The bailee is also entitled to compensation for any injury sustained by him as a result of the bailor's failure to warn him of defects in the bailed property. His duties with regard to the bailed property include caring for it in accordance with the nature of the bailment and returning the bailed property to the bailor at the end of the bailment.

Limitations of Rights and Duties of Parties to Bailments

Parties to bailments are generally free to limit or alter their respective rights and duties through their contractual agreement. The express agreement between the parties will control with regard to their rights and responsibilities. Contractual provisions that limit or increase the responsibility of one or both parties are generally enforceable as long as they are not unconscionable and as long as they are freely agreed to by both parties. Waiver of liability clauses by bailees, for example, are generally binding, as are clauses imposing strict liability on bailees for damage to the bailed goods. Thus, a bailment agreement concerning an automobile that is entrusted to a parking attendant at a garage can limit the liability of the garage for loss or injury to the vehicle or its contents not caused by garage employees. For such a waiver to be valid, however, the bailor must be made aware of it at the time of the bailment. If notice of the waiver is given only on the back of the parking stub in small, hard-to-read print, the waiver would most likely not be enforced by a court (a court could find the attempted waiver void as unconscionable or ineffective because it is not reasonably communicated to the bailor). But if legible signs to the effect of the garage's waiver of liability are clearly visible to the bailor at the time that she entrusts the car to the garage and a legible waiver of liability is included in the ticket stub, the waiver would be valid.

Special Bailments

Certain types of bailments are treated differently with regard to the bailee's liability to goods entrusted to her care, making the bailee strictly liable for damage or loss of such goods. The most common types of special bailments involve common carriers and innkeepers. A *common carrier* is any company in the business of transporting people or cargo that offers its services to the general public, while *innkeepers* include all companies in the hospitality industry providing lodging services. Whenever a special bailment is involved, the bailee is strictly liable for theft, loss, or damage to bailed goods regardless of the level of care extended in caring for the goods or the lack of fault in their loss with the exception of acts of God or of the public enemy. At common law, innkeepers were strictly liable for damage to the personal property of their guests in their premises, and common carriers for the property of passengers and goods in transit. Today, the liability has been limited by federal and state legislation to a set dollar amount in most cases. In addition, hotels may limit their liability for guests' property in most states by providing a safe in which guests may place their valuables and advising their guests of the availability of the safe. Common carriers are also able to limit or waive their liability contractually for goods entrusted for shipment.

Constructive Bailments

Although bailments require that the owner of personal property willfully give up his control of the property and place it in the hands of the bailee for her temporary control, and likewise require the acceptance of the bailed property by the bailee, there are times when the courts will treat property in the hands of a person who does not own it as a constructive bailment. A *constructive bailment* is nothing more than a legal fiction used by the courts to hold persons who have property lawfully belonging to others in their possession to make such persons responsible for the reasonable care of such property. Finders of lost or mislaid property, for example, are constructive bailees of the property until the true owner can be found or ownership to the property lawfully passes to them by operation of law. Likewise, thieves and embezzlers are also held to be constructive bailees of the property wrongfully in their possession. In much the same vein, a person who mistakenly takes the property of another thinking it her own is also a constructive bailee of that property until she returns it to its true owner.

Questions

1. What is a bailment?
2. What are the necessary criteria for a bailment to arise?
3. What is a bailment for the sole benefit of the bailor?
4. What is a bailment for the sole benefit of the bailee?
5. What is the duty of care for a bailee in a mutual benefit bailment, a bailment for the sole benefit of the bailor, and a bailment for the sole benefit of the bailee?
6. What are the principal rights of bailors with regard to bailed property?
7. What are the principal rights of the bailee with regard to bailed property?
8. What are the two most common types of special bailments?
9. What is the significance of a special bailment?
10. What are innkeepers? What is the innkeeper's liability for bailed goods?

Hypothetical Cases

1. Sari asks Steve to look after her dog as a favor while she goes on vacation for two weeks, and Steve agrees to care for the dog during that time. During the two-week period, Steve spends $50 on dog food and $50 on a visit to the vet when the dog became violently ill for undetermined reasons. In addition, Steve spends $200 in lumber to build the dog a custom-made doghouse. After Sari returns home, Steve presents her with a bill for each of the noted expenses, including $250 for his time in building the doghouse and $100 for his services as a "doggie sitter" during the period in question. Sari refuses to pay any of the charges, claiming that Steve was supposed to have looked after the dog as a favor and that any money spent by him on the dog was merely a gift. You are the judge. What result? Explain your decision fully.
2. Karl lends his DVD recorder to Karun so that she may dub an old video tape of her wedding using her VCR. In exchange for borrowing the DVD recorder over the weekend, Karun promises to give Karl a pack of 25 blank DVDs as consideration for borrowing the recorder. While the DVD recorder was in her care, it received a small, accidental scratch on its plastic case. What type of bailment was involved here? Is Karun responsible for the damage to the DVD recorder? Explain fully.
3. Priscilla parks in a private parking lot in the downtown area of her city, which charges $19.99 plus tax for all-day parking. She pulls into the lot and is directed by the parking attendant to park in parking space #125. She does so and then goes to the attendant to pay the parking fee. The attendant does not ask for, nor does Priscilla offer, her car keys. At the attendant's booth, a large sign in bold, red letters reads: *ATTENTION: Customers park here at their own risk. Lock your car and take all valuables from it. Management assumes no responsibility for losses of any kind to customers' cars or their contents while in this lot.* She reads the sign, and gives the attendant the required fee, taking from him a parking stub that contains the same language. When she returns to her car later that evening, she finds that it has been broken into; the upholstery has been ripped in various places; two windows have been smashed; and her GPS navigation system, cellular phone, and pocketbook (which she'd left in the car's glove compartment) have been stolen. Furious, she sues the parking lot owners, alleging failure to observe the reasonable care required to avoid the damage to her vehicle as required under a mutual benefit bailment. What result? Explain fully.
4. Frank and Fiona go into a restaurant inside a hotel at which they are not staying as guests. On their way in, Frank hangs up his coat and hat in a coat rack by the entrance to the restaurant. After they are seated, a busboy offers to check Fiona's fur coat for her, and she assents. A short time later, the busboy returns with a coat check ticket, which he gives to Fiona. After a wonderful meal, Frank discovers that his hat and coat are missing from the coat rack, as is the fur that was checked by the busboy into the hotel's coat checkroom. They sue the restaurant for breach of the bailment agreement with regard to both articles of clothing and for strict liability, claiming a special bailment existed. Will either theory of liability be successful? Explain fully.

Real Property

CHAPTER 31

Chapter Outline

Estates in Land
Freehold Estates
Nonfreehold Estates
Future Interests
Nonpossessory Interests in Land
Easements
Profits à Prendre
Licenses

Real property can be defined as land and anything that is permanently attached to land, including buildings, trees, and growing crops. What distinguishes real from personal property is that real property is fixed and unmovable, whereas personal property (both tangible and intangible) is movable. Whenever personal property is permanently affixed to real property, such as in the installation of a ceiling fan or dishwasher, it becomes a fixture and its nature changes from personal to real property.

The owner of real estate owns not only the land itself and anything permanently attached to it, but also everything below the land, including minerals and precious metals, as well as the space above the land up to a height set by local ordinances (typically up to several hundred feet above the highest structure in the land). With few exceptions, such as easements discussed in the following sections, the owner of real estate has the right to exclusively use the property and to prevent others from using it without permission. As we've seen in our discussion of criminal law and torts, the willful entry into the real estate of another without the owner's assent can constitute trespass, which is both a crime and a tort.

Real property by its nature is eternal; land has existed since the earth's birth and will endure until its demise. This contrasts sharply with personal property, which by its nature has an ephemeral, finite existence. Tangible personal property generally wears out or is used up over time, and property interests in intangible personal property such as patents and copyrights can expire after a specific number of years. In part because real property lasts forever, the law has come to recognize a number of varying *degrees* of interests in real estate that range from absolute present and future ownership of real estate forever (fee simple absolute) to a number of lesser interests that will be examined in this chapter. In addition, we will explore the means of obtaining and transferring interests to real property that, as we will see, require far greater formalities than does the acquisition and transfer of title to personal property.

Estates in Land

Interests in real property are classified in accordance with the rights they convey to the real estate involved. These can range from absolute ownership of property to the mere right to occupy property for a preset period of time or to gain access to property for a limited purpose. Ownership interests in land that last forever or for an undetermined period of time (including a person's lifetime) are called *freehold estates*, while interests that are limited to a specific period of time are called *leasehold estates*. A *freehold* estate is a right of title to land, as distinguished from a *leasehold* estate, which is a mere possessory interest in land without title.

Freehold Estates

Fee Simple Absolute

Fee simple absolute is the most complete ownership interest in land that can be possessed. It conveys to the owner of the land the absolute, unqualified right to own, possess, and dispose of land forever.

Determinable Fee

A determinable fee (also referred to as a *base fee* or *qualified fee*) is a fee estate with some qualification or limitation attached to it. Typically, such estates are conferred only upon the happening of a future event, or are subject to termination upon some future circumstance. For instance, if land is transferred by a father to his daughter subject to her not marrying before his death, a determinable fee estate is created. Whether or not the property will pass to the daughter depends on whether or not the condition attached to its grant is met; if the daughter marries during the grantor's lifetime, her interest in the property is terminated; but if the grantor dies before the daughter has married, then a fee simple absolute interest in the land would vest in the daughter.

Life Estate

A life estate is a fee interest that lasts during the life of a specific individual. The holder of a life estate interest in land has a proprietary interest in the land during the life of a specific individual. Usually, the estate runs for the lifetime of the *grantee* (the person to whom the life estate is granted), but a life estate can also be based on the life of a third person other than the grantee. For example, a mother can grant a life estate to her son that lasts for the son's lifetime, or the mother's lifetime, or the lifetime of any other person. Because the life estate has a limited duration, the owner of a life estate does not enjoy the same rights to the land as does the owner of a fee simple absolute estate. The owner of a life estate is entitled to the exclusive possession of the realty during the life of the person on whose life the estate is based. During that lifetime, the owner of the life estate may exclusively possess the realty, may put it to any lawful use, and may lease or sell outright his interest in the realty to any third person. But owners of life estates are prohibited from unreasonably interfering with or limiting the value of the real estate to the future holders of a fee interest in the estate.

An owner of a life estate who abuses her rights respecting the realty by destroying its future value to the prejudice of a future heir to the property is guilty of *waste* and can be sued for damages by any person or persons whose future interest in the land are damaged. The holder of a life estate may benefit from all that the land has to offer, including mining the land for its mineral or precious metal content, farming the land and using timber on the land during the duration of the life estate, as long as such use does not unreasonably hamper the rights of subsequent owners of the land. If, for example, land covered by the life estate has a gold mine in it that produced 100 ounces of gold every month before the grant of the life estate, the grantee of the life estate may continue to mine the land and retrieve from it 100 ounces of gold per month during the duration of her estate, but may not significantly increase the mining operations. Likewise, the owner of a life estate containing timber may make reasonable use of the timber for his own needs, but may not sell all the timber in the land to a logging company.

Dower

Dower is a special type of life estate reserved for widows to property owned by the husband during his life. At common law, widows had a one-third interest for their lifetimes in any land that their deceased husbands owned in fee to provide for their sustenance and that of any children of the marriage. Upon the wife's death, the land would typically pass in fee to her children by the deceased husband, if any survived her, or otherwise as provided in the husband's will. Dower has been modified or abolished in most jurisdictions today, but an analogous provision guaranteeing a share of a decedent spouse's estate is available in states where dower has been abolished.

Curtesy

Curtesy is an analogous provision to dower for widowers, giving them either a fee interest or a life estate in their wives' land provided that the marriage produced at least one child. Like dower, curtesy has been either modified or abolished in most states and replaced by a guaranteed right of husbands and wives to inherit a minimum portion of a deceased spouse's estate.

Nonfreehold Estates

Estate for Years

An estate for years is a possessory interest in land that grants its holder the right to occupy land for a set period of time. As is the case with all leasehold estates, an estate for years conveys only a possessory interest to the grantee and does not convey a fee or ownership interest. A one-year apartment lease and a 99-year commercial lease are estates for years, as is a nine-month student housing lease, even though it lasts for less than one year.

Periodic Tenancy

A periodic tenancy, like an estate for years, is a nonfee, possessory interest in real estate that lasts for a specified period of time, such as week to week or month to month, and is automatically renewed at the end of each rental period. Absent local regulations to the contrary, the landlord and the tenant may unilaterally end a periodic tenancy by giving notice of at least one rental period of their intention to end the tenancy. Thus, a tenant in a month-to-month tenancy must give her landlord one month's notice of her intention not to renew, and the landlord must give similar notice to the tenant if he wishes not to renew the tenancy. If rent is payable on a weekly basis, then one week's notice would need to be given by either party, and so on.

Tenancy at Will

A tenancy at will is a tenancy that has no fixed term of duration and can be ended at any time by either the landlord or the tenant. Tenancy at will typically involves a tenant who is not required to pay rent by the landlord, since payment of rent on a regular basis automatically results in a periodic tenancy. For example, if Lana allows Ted, a friend, to live rent free in an apartment that she owns as a favor, a tenancy at will is involved and Ted can leave at any time or be asked to leave at any time without the need of prior notice. The same would be true if Lana allows Ted to pay "whatever he can whenever he can," and Ted gives Lana some money from time to time in varying amounts and at irregular intervals.

Future Interests

Future interests in real property are possessory or ownership interests that do not exist at present but rather will or might arise in the future. When a life estate is granted, for example, a future fee interest is retained in the property after the death of the holder of the life estate. With regard to fee interests in real property, we need to be aware of two main future interests, reversions and remainders, that can be either absolute or contingent upon the happening of an event, as we will see next.

Reversionary Interests

A reversionary interest is a future interest in real estate that is retained by the grantor of real property by transferring to a grantee something less than a fee simple absolute interest in the real estate involved. When a reversionary interest is retained, real property transferred by the grantor will vest once again in the grantor or in her estate at some time in the future. If a grantor grants a fee simple absolute interest in real estate, she retains no interest in the property, since by definition such a grant involves an absolute transfer of whatever ownership interest the grantor has in the property to the grantee forever. If less than a fee simple absolute interest in land is transferred, such as by a life estate or an estate for years, then the grantor retains an interest in the land that will *revert* to her upon the natural termination of the grantee's interest in the land. If, for example, Ted transfers a life estate to Lenore in Blackacre, Ted retains a reversionary interest in Blackacre, since he will regain a fee simple absolute interest in the land as soon as Lenore dies.

It is also possible to retain a contingent reversionary interest in land (also called *the possibility of a reverter*) through the transfer of a determinable fee interest. If, for example, Ted transfers to Lenore his interest in Blackacre subject to her successfully completing college before her 22nd birthday, Ted retains the possibility of a reverter to Blackacre since it will revert to him in the event that Lenore fails to graduate college by the required age.

Remainder Interests

A remainder interest is a future interest to real estate that is given to a third party by a grantor through an express grant to a grantee of less than a fee simple interest in property with a provision that the property will or may vest in a third party upon the passage of time or the happening of an event in the future. As is the case with a reversionary interest, a remainder interest may be either absolute or contingent. If, for example, a grantor grants Blackacre "to my daughter, Darlene, for life then to my son, Sam," a present life estate is given to Darlene with Sam receiving an absolute remainder interest (Darlene is certain to die at some point in the future, and Sam or his heirs will then inherit Blackacre in fee simple absolute). A contingent remainder interest could be conveyed to Sam by a grant such as the following: "To my daughter, Darlene, for life, then to my son, Sam, if he is then alive." In the preceding example, Sam receives only a grant of a contingent remainder interest, since he will receive the property in question in fee simple only if he outlives his sister. Assuming that Sam dies before Darlene in the last example, what will happen to Blackacre? It will revert to the grantor's estate. (The grantor has retained a contingent reversionary interest in the property under the last example in the event that the son dies before the daughter.)

Nonpossessory Interests in Land

The fee and leasehold interests we've discussed thus far are all possessory interests in real property, since the holder of any of the preceding interests has either a present or a future contingent or absolute right to occupy or *possess* real property. In addition to these possessory interests in real property, the law recognizes a number of nonpossessory interests giving the holder the right not to occupy land, but rather to make some limited use of it. Such nonpossessory interests include easements, *profits à prendre*, and licenses.

Easements

An easement is a right to use the property of another for a limited purpose. The most common kinds of easement involve the right to travel over the property of another to gain access to one's land, as well as those granting public utilities the right to transport power, water, gas, or phone lines over or under land to provide needed services. When an easement is granted over one piece of land for the benefit of another, the benefited land is called the dominant estate, and the land that is burdened by the easement is called the servient estate. Generally speaking, easements can have perpetual existence or be created to last for a specified period of time.

Affirmative Easements

An affirmative easement is one that grants to its holder the right to pass over the land of another or otherwise gain access into it for the permitted purpose named in the easement.

If the owner of Whiteacre has an easement over Greenacre to gain access to his property from a main road, for example, such an easement would be considered an affirmative easement, with Whiteacre as the dominant tenement and Greenacre the servient tenement.

Negative Easements

A negative easement is an easement that prohibits certain kinds of otherwise lawful activity from being carried out in the servient tenement to benefit the owner of the dominant tenement. If, for example, the owner of Redacre is concerned that the owner of Blueacre next door might decide to plant tall trees or build a tall structure on his land and thereby obstruct his view, he can try to obtain a negative easement from the owner of Blueacre, preventing him from planting trees or erecting any structure higher than one story on his land. Negative easements can be procured for any agreed-upon consideration and are often included in land that is sold by developers as part of a planned community for the benefit of the community as a whole. For example, lots sold by a developer might contain a negative easement prohibiting the purchaser from putting a trailer on the land where trailers are otherwise allowed by the local zoning laws.

Easement Appurtenant

Easements appurtenant are easements attached to one piece of land for the benefit of another. An appurtenant easement runs with the land forever, unless it is canceled by the owner of the dominant tenement, and is transferred to any subsequent owners of both the servient and dominant tenements.

Easement in Gross

Unlike easements appurtenant, which attach to the land and are transferred with its sale, an easement in gross is personal in nature and gives its holder the right to make a limited use of another's land for her personal benefit. Easements in gross benefit an individual rather than a dominant tenement.

Creation of an Easement

Easements are considered nonpossessory interests in real property and are subject to the same formalities of creation as any other transfer of an interest in real property. We will examine the transfer of interests in real property in the next chapter, but for now, it should be noted that easements can arise in a number of ways. An easement can arise from an *express grant* by the grantor executing a valid deed containing the terms of the easement and transferring it to the grantee. An easement can also arise by *reservation* when the transferor of real property reserves to himself in the deed the right to use the property for a particular purpose, or by transferring the property by a deed containing a negative easement. Easements can also arise by implication through the transfer of property under circumstances where the clear intention of the parties was to reserve an easement but they neglected to expressly do so in transferring the property. Finally, an easement can arise out of necessity in instances where, for example, there is no means of gaining access to a person's land other than through the land of another.

Profits à Prendre

A *profit à prendre* is another nonpossessory right in real estate that gives its holder the right to go onto the land of another and to remove something from it or to make some use of the soil of another. Common *profits à prendre* involve mining rights, logging rights, and water rights in another's land. The distinguishing characteristic between a *profit à prendre* and an easement is that the former involve the right to remove something from the land, whereas the latter merely involve the right to go onto or pass through the land of another for a specific purpose. Because *profits à prendre* confer an interest in real property, they must be created subject to the same formalities as any other real property interest.

Licenses

A license is a revocable, temporary privilege to go on another's land for a specific purpose. Unlike easements and *profits à prendre*, licenses are *not* considered interests in land. Like easements and *profits à prendre*, licenses can be conferred free of charge or for a fee. Because they are not interests in real estate, licenses can be created and revoked orally or in writing without any special requirements or formalities.

Because a license is revocable at any time by the owner or person in lawful possession of the real property, a person who is on another's land as a licensee must leave as soon as the license expires or is revoked; otherwise, he becomes trespasser. This is true even when a fee was paid for the license. Thus, guests in your home must leave as soon as you tell them to, or *revoke their license* to be in your home, and patrons of a movie theater must leave whenever management asks them to do so—with or without just cause. If a licensee who has given consideration for his license, such as the patron of a movie theater, is asked to leave the premises without cause, he is entitled to a refund of whatever consideration he paid for the license under a theory of breach of contract. If a license for which a fee has been paid is revoked for cause, such as for theater patrons who talk loudly during a movie, throw popcorn, talk on a cell phone during a performance, allow their kids to run around the theater, or engage in other disruptive conduct that interferes with the enjoyment of the movie by other patrons, then no refund need be made by the grantor of the license since no breach of contract is involved.

Questions

1. What are freehold estates?
2. What is the most complete ownership interest in land that can be possessed?
3. What is a determinable fee?
4. What is a reversionary interest?
5. What is a remainder interest?
6. What is the main distinction between easements and profits à prendre?
7. What is a license?
8. What is an easement appurtenant?
9. What is an easement in gross, and how is it different from an easement appurtenant?
10. What is the distinction between affirmative and negative easements?

Hypothetical Cases

1. Leroy Landowner transfers title to real estate he owns by a deed that contains the following transfer language:
    To my son, Steve, for life, then to Steve's children. If Steve should die childless, then to my daughter, Donna.
    A. What type of interest does Steve have to the land?
    B. What interest do Steve's unborn children have with regard to this transfer of land?
    C. What is Donna's interest in the land?
    D. What interest, if any, has Leroy reserved for himself or his estate? Explain fully.
2. Tasha, a college student at State U, agrees to rent a studio apartment from Luisa and to pay her $100 per week. The parties make no other provision in their agreement, and the agreement is not reduced to a writing.
    A. What kind of interest in real estate does Tasha have as a result of this agreement? Be specific.
    B. Does Tasha gain a fee interest as a result of this agreement? Explain.
    C. How long will this arrangement last? What if either Tasha or Luisa is unhappy with the arrangement after a few months go by?
3. Ben, the owner of Blackacre, would like to obtain permission to fish in Gwendolyn's pond in Greenacre, a property that adjoins his own. He would also like the right to cross over Greenacre with his car to avoid a lengthy traffic light on the main road in which his property is situated. In addition, he would like to obtain assurances from Gwendolyn that she will never build any structure within 300 feet of his property line or within 1,000 feet of her pond. He negotiates a deal with Gwendolyn giving him precisely what he wants in exchange for an undisclosed dollar amount.

Gwendolyn executes a deed granting Ben the right to fish on her pond throughout his life, and the right for Ben or any person who purchases Blackacre from him in the future to cross over Greenacre in order to get access to a secondary road. The deed also grants to Ben and any future owners of Blackacre the assurance that no structure will ever be built on Greenacre within 300 feet of Blackacre, and that no structure will be built within 1,000 feet of Greenacre's pond during Ben's life. State in precise terms the nature of the interest in Greenacre that Ben has procured with regard to the above. Be specific.

4. A group of college students go on a club-sponsored trip to a theme park in their state. Each of the students pays the $100 access fee to the park and enters after being given a set of rules that apply to patrons' conduct while in the park. The rules prohibit alcoholic beverages from being taken into or consumed by patrons in the park and require patrons to wear shoes at all times in the park. No other rules are posted. Before the day is over, one of the students is kicked out of the park for drinking a beer that she'd brought into the park (she was 21 and of legal drinking age in the state involved), a second student is ejected for wandering about the park in his underwear (but wearing sneakers), and a third student is expelled for using obscene and abusive language to one of the park's employees and repeatedly pulling the ears in the victim's rabbit costume. The park refuses to refund the money of any of the three students, and they decide to sue in small claims court for a refund of their $100 fees and for other incidental and consequential damages flowing from an alleged breach of contract.

   A. With regard to real property law, what was the status of the three students while they were visiting the park?
   B. Did the park have the legal authority to eject the students from its premises? Explain.
   C. Will any of the students succeed in their claims against the park? Explain.

Creation and Transfer of Interests in Real Property

CHAPTER 32

Interests in real property can be created and transferred in two ways. The first and more common is through the execution and transfer of a deed, and the second is by *adverse possession* (obtaining possession to the property of another and holding onto it to the exclusion of all others, while claiming it as one's own for a period of time ranging from 3 to 30 years).

Chapter Outline

Transfer by Deed
Title through *Inter Vivos* and Testamentary Gifts
Title through Eminent Domain
Recording Statutes
Title through Adverse Possession
Concurrent Ownership
Public and Private Restrictions on Land Use

Transfer by Deed

The creation and transfer of an interest in land is almost always accomplished by the execution and delivery of a valid deed to the property from the *grantor* (the seller and transferor of the property) to the *grantee* (the buyer and transferee of the property). When a valid deed is delivered to the grantee, title to the underlying real estate passes; delivery of the deed is the legal equivalent of delivering the land itself.

To be valid, a deed must meet certain requirements. It must (1) be in writing; (2) list the name or names of the grantor(s) and the grantee(s); (3) contain words that unequivocally show an intent to transfer land; (4) offer a clear description of the land being transferred; and (5) contain the signature(s) of the grantor(s). As long as these five requirements are met, a deed will be valid. Even though most deeds are executed by filling in the blanks of ready-made forms, there is no requirement that a specific form be used in most jurisdictions, and a handwritten deed would be perfectly valid, as long as it contained the five noted requirements.

A deed can be used to transfer any present or future interest in realty, including fee interests such as fee simple and life estate transfers as well as nonfee interests, such as easements and profit à prendre.

Warranty Deed

A warranty deed is a deed in which the grantor gives assurances to the grantee that she has valid title to the land being transferred and obligates herself to make reparations to the grantee or anyone to whom the grantee may subsequently transfer the land if her title was somehow defective.

Quitclaim Deed

A quitclaim deed is a deed in which the grantor transfers whatever title he has to a given piece of land to the grantee. Unlike a warranty deed, a quitclaim deed contains no assurance that the grantor has good title and no promise to make any future reparations if title is defective. Such deeds are typically granted when a defect in title of the transferor is suspected or when the transferor purchased the land as an agent for a third party and subsequently needs to transfer title to the third party. As you might suspect, there is an element of risk in purchasing property with a quitclaim deed, which usually affects its selling price. In addition, title insurance is generally unavailable for property purchased with a quitclaim deed, and most banks will not issue a standard mortgage for such property.

Contract of Sale

Although a contract of sale is not necessary to the transfer of real estate, contracts of sale are invariably found in transactions involving the purchase and sale of real estate. Such contracts are ruled by the applicable contract law in the jurisdiction where the contract is entered into or the real estate is situated. Because such contracts involve an interest in real estate, they must be evidenced by a writing signed by the buyer(s) and seller(s) to be enforceable by both parties under the statute of frauds. If a verbal contract for the sale of real estate is involved, the parties may still honor their agreement and validly transfer the property upon the execution and delivery of a valid deed, but such a contract would not be enforceable in the courts if either party refused to go through with the verbal agreement. On the other hand, because real estate is unique, written, signed contracts by parties are enforceable in the courts to secure damages for breach if either party reneges on the agreement, and the equitable remedy of specific performance is also available to buyers who wish to force sellers to transfer a deed pursuant to a valid contract of sale.

Title through *Inter Vivos* and Testamentary Gifts

As previously noted, a contract is unnecessary as a means of conveying real estate. While the purchase of real estate is the most common means of obtaining title to it, title can also be obtained by means of a gift. An *inter vivos* transfer of an interest in realty can occur by gift from the transfer of a deed for which no money or a nominal fee of $1 is paid. As with all transfers of real estate, the delivery of a valid deed by the transferor to the transferee accomplishes the transfer. If a grantor makes a testamentary disposition of real estate by a provision in a will, it is the executor or executrix as the legal representative of the deceased testator who executes and delivers a valid deed to the person for whose benefit the testamentary gift was made.

Title through Eminent Domain

Another means of effectuating a transfer of real estate without need for a contract of sale is a transfer to the state or federal government under its powers of eminent domain. *Eminent domain* is the power of the federal, state, or local government to condemn private property for public use upon paying its owner the property's market price. In the U.S., the federal government is given the power of eminent domain by the Fifth Amendment to the U.S. Constitution. Such a power is also found in the constitutions of the individual states. If the government wishes to use private land for public use, its owners with few exceptions have no choice but to deed over to the government all or whatever part of the land it requires. Typical exercises of the government's eminent domain powers extend to the building of roads, expansion of parks, and the construction of similar public projects. But it is also possible for the government to seize private land for private development if it does so for a valid public purpose, such as creating jobs, stimulating economic development, increasing tax revenues, attracting tourism, or otherwise improving the quality of life for its citizens pursuant to a development plan. Not only individuals but entire towns may be called upon to transfer their land to the government (usually quite unhappily) for such projects as new construction or expansion of reservoirs, dams, and similar public works projects.

Eminent domain is also relied on in granting necessary easements for power and telephone lines that must pass over private lands. The same is true for government takings of only partial real estate rights, such as the subsurface rights to private land to build a subway system. When such a partial taking of private land for private use is involved, the landowner is compensated for the partial taking at market value and is otherwise free to use or sell whatever portion of the land was not seized for public use.

Recording Statutes

Every jurisdiction provides for the means of recording deeds to give notice to subsequent purchasers of the property of previous transfers of the property. While it is not generally required that deeds be recorded to effectively pass title to land, recording a deed offers protection to the purchaser of real property from previous or subsequent fraudulent transfers of title or attachment of liens to the same land by a previous owner or by his creditors. A typical problem in this area arises when a grantor executes multiple deeds to the same property, with the intention of defrauding the grantees. Since there can be only one true owner of real estate in such circumstances, the question becomes who has the greater interest. At common law, the answer was simple: first in time, first in right, so the first grantee of the land would be entitled to it. Today, states have addressed the problem through the adoption of recording statutes that provide a simple means of giving notice to third parties of owners of record to real estate, and provide for a means of resolving multiple claims by innocent grantees to the same land.

Three basic types of recording statutes are in use today: notice acts, race acts, and race-notice acts.

Notice Acts

Jurisdictions that use notice acts as their recording statutes prevent persons with actual notice of a previous transfer of the property from having a greater interest in the property than the previous transferee of the property who has not recorded its deed. In other words, in such jurisdictions a transferee takes property subject to any previous ownership interests that he has constructive knowledge of because the deeds detailing these interests have been officially recorded and subject to any previous transfer of the property that he has actual knowledge of, regardless of whether or not such transfer has been recorded.

Race Acts

Under race acts, the first person to record a deed has the greater right to the underlying property, regardless of any actual knowledge of previous unrecorded transfers of the property. Race acts get their name from the fact that new transferees of property must race to the recording office to have their interest in the property protected from previous or subsequent transfers; where more than one transfer has been made to the same property, the person who wins the race to the recording office gets the superior interest to the land, regardless of whether or not she was aware that other transfers had been made prior to her own.

Race-Notice Acts

As the name implies, race-notice recording acts combine the provisions of both the race and notice acts by providing that the first person to record a deed without notice of any prior recorded or unrecorded transfers of property obtains the greater interest to the underlying property. In other words, race-notice acts require that a transferee of property take it without any actual or constructive knowledge of any previous transfers of the property by the same grantor that would conflict with the grantee's interest.

Title through Adverse Possession

Adverse possession is a means of acquiring property by maintaining possession of it during a statutorily defined period and meeting certain additional criteria. Unlike more common means of obtaining property that require the transfer of a deed, with adverse possession, title is obtained by meeting the statutorily defined criteria, which include the following:

- the possession must be actual and exclusive;
- the possession must be continuous for the entire statutory period (commonly 10 years, but it can be as short as 3 and as long as 30 years);
- the possession must be open and notorious;
- the possession must be hostile and adverse.

To put it another way, for title to property to pass by adverse possession, the possession must be actual, open, notorious, and exclusive during the statutory period, and the possessor of the property must show that he held it without the owner's permission.

The requirement that possession be open, actual, and exclusive means that the adverse possessor must exclusively occupy the land during the statutory period without the owner having access to it or joint use of it. The requirement that possession be continuous means that the adverse possessor cannot stop using the land for the entire statutory period; there can be no breaks in the period of usage by the adverse possessor for the entire statutory period. If, for example, the period of adverse possession in a state is ten years and an adverse possessor uses land belonging to another for five years and then stops using it for a year (or allows the owner to make use of it again for a period of time after five years) and then resumes the adverse possession, the statute begins to run again and he must continue to use the land exclusively for another uninterrupted period of ten years before owning it under adverse possession. The requirement that the possession be open and notorious means that the adverse possession must be out in the open for the whole world to see. Finally, the requirement that the possession be hostile and adverse means that the adverse possessor must use the land, holding it out to be his own without the permission of the true owner throughout the statutory period. If the owner gives permission to use of the land, there can be no adverse possession.

Adverse possession presents a particularly serious problem for absentee landowners, especially in states with relatively brief statutory periods, such as five or ten years. The law requires property owners to take some affirmative steps to protect their property from others' infringement by taking timely action against trespassers before they can perfect their interest in the land under the adverse possession statute. To put it another way, adverse possession is really a statute of limitations that requires landowners to protect their property rights against infringement by others within a certain period of time or risk losing them. Keep in mind that not all adverse possession claims are nefarious in nature, and many arise out of honest mistakes, such as a landowner building a structure that is in whole or in part on a neighbor's land due to a mistake as to the land boundaries. In any case, whether the adverse possession is innocent or willful, the claim of the adverse possessor extends only to the land actually occupied and used by her during the period of adverse possession. Thus, if Henrietta builds a homestead on one acre of Harry's ten-acre land, she will eventually own only the one acre she has exclusively used throughout the statutory period, and not the entire ten-acre tract.

Concurrent Ownership

Like personal property, real property can be owned individually or jointly by two or more persons or companies. You should be aware of three distinct types of joint ownership options: joint tenancy, tenancy in common, and tenancy by the entirety.

Joint Tenancy

Joint tenancy is a means of two or more persons owning real estate together. The most significant feature of joint tenancy is that the property owned by the joint tenants passes automatically to the survivor upon the death of the cotenant. If two people own real estate as joint tenants, then the survivor automatically owns the whole upon one joint tenant's death. If more than two persons own real estate as joint tenants, the share of any joint tenant who dies is distributed equally among the survivors. For example, if four friends own a home equally as joint tenants and one dies, the share of each survivor in the property increases from a 25% interest to a 33.33% interest.

Each joint tenant does not need to have an equal share in the property. It is possible to have two joint tenants with vastly different ownership interests in the underlying real estate; nevertheless, if any one of them dies, that person's share passes to the survivors in equal shares. Thus, if two friends own property as joint tenants in which one holds a 95% interest and the other a 5% interest, the survivor would automatically obtain title to the whole property, regardless of her investment in it.

Joint tenants share in the responsibility for upkeep of a home, payment of taxes, and other expenses that naturally result from the ownership of real property in proportion to their ownership interest of the property. Thus, a 10% joint owner of property pays 10% of the property's expenses and receives 10% of any rent or other income that the property produces. But the right of joint tenants to occupy or use real estate is not related to their ownership interest of it; a 10% owner has the right to occupy 100% of the house at all times. This potential problem is resolved by a separate contractual agreement between the joint owners detailing their rights of occupancy.

The interest of a joint tenant to real property is freely transferable during the joint tenant's life. It can be sold, leased, or given away at will. This presents another potential problem for joint tenants, since any one of them has the power to freely dispose of her property interest to any person or persons she wishes. For this reason, joint tenants often have a separate contract detailing restrictions on the transfer of the property and/or a right of first refusal of the cotenants to purchase the interest of a joint tenant who wishes to sell her interest in the property before an offering is made to the general public. If a joint tenant's interest is transferred, the new tenant becomes a tenant in common rather than a joint tenant, so his interest passes to his heirs upon his death rather than to his cotenants.

A joint tenancy is generally severable at any time by any one joint tenant who can petition a court to partition the property or to force its sale.

Tenancy in Common

Tenancy in common is similar in all respects to joint tenancy with one important exception: the interest of a tenant in common who dies passes to her estate, rather than to the surviving tenants in common. In other words, tenants in common enjoy the same rights and responsibilities as joint tenants except that there is no survivorship provision in the tenancy.

Tenancy by the Entirety

Tenancy by the entirety is a form of joint tenancy reserved for married couples. The main difference between joint tenancy and tenancy by the entirety is that, unlike tenants in common or joint tenants, a tenant by the entirety cannot transfer his interest in the underlying property without the signature of the cotenant. The creditors and holders of unsatisfied judgments against each spouse may, however, attach a lien on the spouse's interest in a tenancy by the entirety.

Public and Private Restrictions on Land Use

Generally speaking, the owner of real estate has the right to use his land in any way he sees fit, provided that the use is one permitted by law. But there are limits to these rights that can be imposed by the government and through private agreements among landowners.

Zoning

Government exerts control over the private use of land through its zoning regulations. States have the power to control the private use of land under their general police powers, through which states regulate private conduct to promote the general welfare of citizens in such areas as health, safety, and ethics regulations. Public land use regulation is carried out primarily at the local level, with the state empowering local city or town zoning boards to regulate local land use through zoning regulations. Zoning regulations relate to architectural and structural building designs, as well as the limitation of allowed land uses, such as dividing communities into areas that permit farming, heavy and light industry, and residential use of real estate, or any combination of these.

When an existing land use classification is changed by a zoning board, persons who had previously used their property in a way that now becomes illegal are typically allowed to continue their *nonconforming use* of their land at least for a period of time—usually as long as the existing owner retains title to the land and continues to use it in the nonconforming way. In addition, zoning authorities have the power to grant a *variance* to any person or business that petitions the authority for an exemption to the zoning regulations—usually by claiming hardship or special circumstances. Variances permitting deviation from the zoning ordinance are typically not granted unless the petitioner can convince the authority that the zoning ordinance represent an undue hardship.

Private Restrictions of Land Use

In addition to the zoning ordinances in a given area, individuals also have the ability to restrict otherwise permissible uses of land through private agreements. We have already seen one way of accomplishing such voluntary restrictions on land use by means of negative easements. For instance, if members of a given community want to make sure that some permissible land uses they find disagreeable are not carried out by any of its members, they can execute a negative easement preventing such use of their land. As has been previously noted, this is often done in new subdivisions and in planned communities. Such restrictive covenants can be included in the original deeds to land as easements appurtenant that run with the land, so all subsequent owners of the property are bound by them.

Questions

1. What is a warranty deed?
2. What is a quitclaim deed?
3. May property be transferred without a contract of sale?
4. What are the requirements for a valid deed?
5. What purpose do recording statutes serve, and what are the three types of recording acts in use today?
6. What is adverse possession? What are the criteria for establishing title through adverse possession?
7. Define joint tenancy, tenancy in common, and tenancy by the entirety.
8. What is a variance?
9. What is generally required for a variance to be granted?
10. What is a private means of effectuating a restriction of land use?

Hypothetical Cases

1. Greg Grantor wishes to make a gift of a one-acre tract of land he owns to his friend Gina. He orally tells her in front of ten reliable witnesses that the land is hers forever and that she may dispose of it at will. Gina promptly accepts the gift and takes possession of the land. A month later, Greg dies and his executor serves notice on Gina that she must vacate the land. Gina refuses to do so, claiming the land is rightfully hers. What result?

2. Assume the same facts as in the last question except that after making the oral statement of his intention to give Gina the land, Greg writes on a piece of paper with a pen the following:

   I, Greg Grantor, hereby give to Gina Grantee all my rights and interest in a one-acre tract of land I own called Blackacre with the intent that she be the owner of the land forever.

   [signed] Greg Grantee

   Greg then gives the paper to Gina and dies a month later.
   A. Based on these facts, if Greg's executor demands that Gina quit the premises, what result?
   B. What interest, if any, does Gina have after the transfer of the paper to her?
   C. Will she be able to record the instrument as a deed? If so, what type of deed is it?

3. Francene Fink, a not very nice person with a long history of defrauding others, executes ten valid quitclaim

deeds to a piece of property she owns at ten separate closings during a two-day period. She then leaves for a warmer climate in a country with no extradition treaty. If her state has a recording statute based on a race-notice act, answer the following questions based on these facts.
   A. Who will ultimately have the best title to the property?
   B. Does the fact that a quitclaim deed was given by Francene preclude any of the ten grantees from acquiring a valid title to the land?
   C. Assuming that Francene is apprehended before she could flee the country, would any of the grantees be able to successfully sue her for damages? If so, under what theory? If not, why not?
4. Sam Slick moves into a 100-acre tract of land belonging to Irma Innocent, an absentee landowner. He builds a log home on the land and builds a barbed wire fence around a one-acre tract of land surrounding his home. He tells everyone he meets that he owns the entire 100 acres of land, even though he only actually takes possession of the one-acre tract. Whenever anyone attempts to approach his home, he drives them away. After nine years of living in Irma's land, he decides to move to another state and leaves his homestead for a six-month period, telling everyone that he will return in six months and posting no trespassing signs around the perimeter of the one-acre land surrounding his home.
   A. If the state with Sam's homestead requires a five-year period of adverse possession, who owns Sam's homestead after Sam returns to the state? Assuming that Sam would be the owner under adverse possession, how much land would he own?
   B. If the state involved has a ten-year requirement for adverse possession, how long must Sam wait before he actually owns the homestead after he returns from his six-month trip?
   C. If Sam had moved into the land with Irma's consent but, once in it, he began telling everyone (except Irma) that he owned it and met the other requirements for adverse possession, would he own the land after the required time period expired? Explain.

Ethics and the Law: Questions for Further Study

It can be argued that adverse possession rewards criminal conduct by allowing a trespasser who illegally seizes the land of another to eventually become its true owner. Can adverse possession be justified on moral grounds as the valid public policy of a state? Or is this an outmoded wrinkle in the fabric of real property law that states should iron out? Take a stand on the issue that is ethically defensible.

Landlords' and Tenants' Rights and Responsibilities

CHAPTER 33

> Agreements involving the rental of real property carry with them certain rights and obligations for the landlord and tenant that are imposed by law. Generally speaking, however, the parties are free to modify these implied rights and duties, as well as to create different ones by their express agreement. In this chapter, we will primarily focus on these implied rights and obligations which operate in the absence of a contrary agreement by the parties.

Chapter Outline

Creation of the Landlord-Tenant Relationship

Termination of the Landlord-Tenant Relationship

Unlawful Termination of the Landlord-Tenant Relationship

Tenant's Rights and Responsibilities

Landlord's Remedies Upon Breach of the Rental Agreement

Tenant's Remedies Upon Breach of a Rental Agreement

Creation of the Landlord-Tenant Relationship

As we saw in Chapter 31, three basic leasehold estates can be created and convey to the tenant the right to possess real property without a freehold interest in such property. Whether the tenancy involved is a tenancy for years, a periodic tenancy, or a tenancy at will, the same rules apply to its formation. Such tenancies can be created either orally or by a written agreement between the parties that can be as detailed or as brief as the parties wish. Where the agreement is detailed, as is the case with rental agreements involving standard leases (see Figures 33.1 and 33.2), the rights and responsibilities of the parties are primarily determined by the agreement itself; where it is brief or nonexistent, the common law of real property steps in and defines the rights and duties of the parties.

Termination of the Landlord-Tenant Relationship

A landlord-tenant relationship can be terminated in one of three ways: by the expiration of the specified period involved in a tenancy for years, by either the landlord or tenant serving notice on one another that she wishes to terminate a periodic tenancy or a tenancy at will, or by a breach of the tenancy agreement by either the landlord or the tenant.

A tenancy at will can be terminated at any time by either party serving notice upon the other of his intention to terminate the tenancy. A periodic tenancy, however, requires a one-period notice to be provided prior to termination by the landlord or the tenant; if, for example, the tenancy is from month to month, then one month's notice is required prior to termination, while one week's notice would be required for a tenancy from week to week.

Unlawful Termination of the Landlord-Tenant Relationship

A tenancy unlawfully terminates upon a breach by either the landlord or tenant of a material duty they owe one another. Upon the unlawful termination of a lease by a tenant, the tenant remains liable for payment of rent throughout the

RESIDENTIAL LEASE

LEASE AGREEMENT, made between _____ (Landlord) and _____ (Tenant). For good consideration it is agreed between the parties as follows:

1. Landlord hereby leases and rents to Tenant the premises described as follows: _____

2. This Lease shall be in effect for a term of _____ years, commencing on _____, 20__ and terminating on _____, 20__.

3. Tenant shall pay Landlord the annual rent of $_____ during said term, in monthly payments of $_____ each, payable monthly in advance.

4. Tenant shall at its own expense provide the following utilities: _____

5. Tenant further agrees that:
   a) Upon the expiration of the lease it will return possession of the leased premises in its present condition, reasonable wear and tear, and fire casualty excepted. Tenant shall commit no waste to the leased premises.
   b) It shall not assign or sub-let or allow any other person to occupy the leased premises without Landlord's prior written consent.
   c) It shall not make any material or structural alterations to the leased premises without Landlord's prior written consent.
   d) It shall comply with all building, zoning and health codes and other applicable laws for said leased premises.
   e) It shall not conduct a business deemed extra hazardous, a nuisance or requiring an increase in fire insurance premiums.
   f) In the event of any breach of the payment of rent or any other allowed charge, or other breach of this Lease, Landlord shall have full rights to terminate this Lease in accordance with state law and re-enter and claim possession of the leased premises, in addition to such other remedies available at law or equity to Landlord arising from said breach.

6. This Lease shall be binding upon and inure to the benefit of the parties, their successors, assigns and personal representatives.

7. Additional Lease terms: _____

Signed and sealed this _____ day of _____, 20__.

_____ (Seal) Tenant
_____ (Seal) Landlord

FIGURE 33.1 Sample Residential Lease (Short Form)

remaining lease period. But the landlord must make a reasonable effort to mitigate or lessen the tenant's liability in most states by attempting to rent the premises as quickly as possible to another tenant. As soon as the premises are rented to another tenant, the rent paid by the new tenant is used to set off the previous tenant's obligation, and the breaching tenant is required to pay any shortfall between the due rent and the rent paid by the new tenant. In addition, the landlord is entitled to recover from the breaching tenant any

COMMERCIAL LEASE

This Lease (*Lease*) is made this ___ day of _____, 20__ by and between _____ (hereinafter *Landlord*) and _____ (hereinafter *Tenant*).

In consideration for the mutual promises and covenants contained herein, and for other good and valuable consideration, the parties hereby agree as follows:

1. The Landlord leases to the Tenant, and the Tenant rents from the Landlord the following described premises:
   _____
   _____

2. The term of the Lease shall be for _____ commencing _____, 20__ and ending _____, 20__.

3. The Tenant shall pay to Landlord as rent $_____ per year in equal monthly installments of $_____ payable in advance at _____.

4. This Lease is subject to all present or future mortgages affecting the premises.

5. Tenant shall use and occupy the premises only as a _____ subject at all times to the approval of the Landlord.

6. The Tenant shall not make any alterations in, additions to or improvements to the premises without the prior written consent of the Landlord.

7. The Landlord, at his own expense, shall furnish the following utilities or amenities for the benefit of the Tenant:
   _____
   _____

8. The Tenant, at his own expense, shall furnish the following:
   _____
   _____

9. The Tenant shall purchase at his own expense public liability insurance in the amount of $_____ as well as fire and hazard insurance in the amount of $_____ for the premises and shall provide satisfactory evidence thereof to the Landlord and shall continue same in force and effect throughout the Lease term hereof.

10. The Tenant shall not permit or commit waste to the premises.

11. The Tenant shall comply with all rules, regulations, ordinances codes and laws of all governmental authorities having jurisdiction over the premises.

12. The Tenant shall not permit or engage in any activity which will effect an increase in the rate of insurance for the Building in which the premises is contained nor shall the Tenant permit or commit any nuisance thereon.

13. The Tenant shall not sub-let or assign the premises nor allow any other person or business to use or occupy the premises without the prior written consent of the Landlord, which consent may not be unreasonably withheld.

14. At the end of the term of this Lease, the Tenant shall surrender and deliver up the premises in the same condition (subject to any additions, alterations or improvements, if any) as presently exists, reasonable wear and tear excluded.

15. Upon default in any term or condition of this Lease, the Landlord shall have the right to undertake any or all other remedies permitted by Law.

16. This Lease shall be binding upon, and inure to the benefit of, the parties, their heirs, successors, and assigns.

Signed this _____ day of _____, 20__.

_____   _____
        Tenant   Landlord

FIGURE 33.2 Sample Commercial Lease (Short Form)

incidental and consequential expenses caused by the breach, such as the cost of advertising for new tenants or the charges paid to a realtor for listing the apartment.

Tenant's Rights and Responsibilities

The tenant's primary responsibility is to pay the agreed-upon rent on the due date. In addition, the tenant has the responsibility to not unreasonably disturb other tenants. The tenant is also responsible for making minor repairs to the rental property, and to warn the landlord of the need for any major repairs should he become aware of such a need. Minor repairs would include unstopping a clogged sink or fixing a leaking faucet, while major repairs include structural repairs to the building, such as fixing a roof or repairing a sagging floor. In addition, the tenant must refrain from unduly harming the rental property; any damage done to rental property beyond normal and reasonable wear and tear is the responsibility of the tenant. The tenant is also responsible for quitting the rental premises upon the termination of the rental period. Although these are the main responsibilities of tenants, other responsibilities can, and usually are, spelled out in the rental agreement.

The tenant's rights, on the other hand, include the right to exclusively possess and use the premises under the terms of the lease. In addition, the tenant is entitled to quiet enjoyment of the rental premises, and the landlord must take affirmative steps to remove any impediment to such quiet enjoyment that is reasonably within his power to remove. For example, unreasonably noisy tenants or tenants who are engaged in illicit activities that can affect the health and safety of other tenants in the same building, such as the manufacturing or distribution of illegal drugs, must be evicted by the landlord upon a tenant's request and proof of such activity. Tenants are also entitled to premises that are reasonably safe and habitable; a landlord who provides rental premises that contain unreasonable safety hazards or who fails to provide necessary services such as heat (when required) and hot water is in breach of the rental agreement, and such a breach constitutes a wrongful constructive eviction of the tenants. Unless the rental agreement states otherwise, the tenant also has the right to sublet or assign the right to occupy the rental premises to third parties during the lease period. If premises are sublet, the tenant and the sublessee are jointly responsible for the payment of rent and for any damage done to the rental premises. Other rights may be provided by state laws and the rental agreement.

The landlord's primary responsibility is to provide habitable premises to the tenant throughout the lease period, and to protect the right of the tenant to quietly and exclusively possess the premises during the rental period. In addition, the landlord is obligated to make necessary repairs to common areas and to rental premises on a timely manner when needed, and to provide necessary essential services, such as heat and hot water (unless, of course, the tenant is responsible for such services under the rental agreement).

The landlord is entitled to payment of the rent when it is due and to have the tenant maintain reasonable care of the premises during the tenancy. The landlord is also entitled to have the tenant quit the rental premises at the end of the tenancy, as well as to any other rights she has expressly reserved to herself in the rental agreement.

Landlord's Remedies Upon Breach of the Rental Agreement

Landlords have wide latitude in the remedies that they may reserve to themselves upon a tenant's breach by expressly providing for remedies in the lease. Unless a lease provision relating to remedies is deemed to be unconscionable or violates local laws, it will generally be enforced. This is particularly the case in commercial leases, where courts are much less likely to hold a remedy reserved by the landlord to be unconscionable if it is freely agreed to by the tenant. Even provisions that would be void as penalties in residential leases are often upheld in commercial leases in many states, such as rent acceleration clauses that require a tenant to immediately pay the rent due for the entire long-term lease upon any breach of the lease, including a late rent payment. Leases may also contain valid forfeiture clauses in most states that annul the tenant's rights to occupy the property upon any breach of the lease, including the nonpayment of rent or the failure to maintain the premises in a reasonable state of repair. In addition, a landlord can include a clause in a lease to the effect that the lease automatically terminates upon any breach by the tenant. When such clauses are contained in a lease, a landlord can bring an action for a summary judgment against the tenant and an order of eviction merely by proving that a breach has occurred. Some jurisdictions also allow landlords to forcibly re-enter their premises after a breach by a tenant who refuses to quit the premises; such a remedy, termed *self-help*, is not universally available, however. In jurisdictions that provide an expedited method for landlords to reclaim property from tenants who wrongfully retain it after breaching a lease, self-help is generally not available.

In addition to extraordinary remedies that a landlord might reserve to herself in a lease, every landlord has the power to treat a lease as terminated after a breach by the tenant and to sue the tenant for damages (including incidental and consequential damages) caused by the breach. A landlord may also opt to continue a lease in force after a tenant's breach and recover from him any damages that are caused by the breach. Regardless of which remedy a landlord pursues after a tenant's breach, a growing number of states impose a duty on the landlord to mitigate the tenant's damages. If, for example, a tenant with a two-year lease leaves after one year without the landlord's permission, the landlord can treat the lease as still in force and sue the tenant for damages, but in many jurisdictions the landlord must make a reasonable effort to rerent the premises within a reasonable time after the breach.

Tenant's Remedies Upon Breach of a Rental Agreement

Tenant's remedies for a landlord's breach of a material duty owed under a lease include the right to terminate the lease and recover damages or to continue the lease and recover damages. A tenant wishing to terminate for a landlord's failure to live up to a material obligation must first give the landlord notice and provide her with the opportunity to remedy the situation within a reasonable time. If a landlord fails to remedy the breach within a reasonable time of having been notified of it, the tenant may treat the lease as terminated and sue the landlord for any actual damages suffered as a result of the breach (including incidental and consequential damages). If a tenant does not wish to treat the lease as terminated upon a landlord's failure to live up to her contractual obligations, the tenant may continue the lease and sue for damages. A tenant may recover money damages to compensate him for the breach (typically the difference between the value of the premises as promised and the value of the premises after the landlord's breach).

Statutes in some jurisdictions also allow a tenant to withhold rent if a landlord is in breach, such as by not providing heat or hot water in winter or otherwise breaching the warranty of habitability; under such statutes, a tenant must generally deposit the rent in an escrow account until the situation is remedied. Some states also provide tenants either by statute or through judicial decisions with the right to make required repairs to rental premises if the landlord refuses to do so and to deduct the reasonable cost of these repairs from the rent. Finally, a tenant may treat a landlord's failure to make necessary repairs or to provide required services as constructive eviction or a breach of warranty of habitability and treat the lease as terminated. Court intervention is usually required before a tenant can resort to any self-help provisions such as using rent money to perform the landlord's obligations.

Questions

1. Must lease agreements be in any specific form?
2. What are the three lawful means by which a landlord-tenant relationship can be terminated?
3. What are the basic responsibilities of a tenant?
4. What are the tenant's basic rights with regard to the rental property?
5. What are the landlord's basic duties?
6. What are the landlord's essential rights?
7. Are lease provisions that provide specific remedies to landlords generally enforced in the courts?
8. What remedies are available to a landlord who does not specifically provide for extraordinary remedies in a lease?
9. In states that require it, what must a landlord do to mitigate damages if a tenant leaves the premises after six months in a two-year lease?
10. What remedies are available to a tenant who wishes to remain in the rental property after a material breach of the lease by the landlord?

Hypothetical Cases

1. Ted is a tenant of Leopold. He has never entered into a formal lease agreement of the premises but has been living in Leopold's house for ten years. He pays his rent on the first of every month and has done so (with several rent increases) on a timely basis throughout his tenancy.
   A. What type of tenancy do Ted and Leopold have?
   B. If Ted wants to leave his apartment because he intends to purchase a home, what must he do?
   C. What if Leopold wants to oust Ted to give the apartment to someone else?
   D. What if Leopold wants to allow Ted to remain as a tenant but wants to also increase his rent by $100 per month?
2. Timmy is a tenant in Liana's apartment building and has a two-year lease. Timmy would like to sublet part of his apartment to Tawana to help with the rent payments. When the landlord finds out about the arrangement, she is furious and wants to evict Timmy and Tawana on grounds that Timmy breached the lease. If the lease made no provisions as to subletting, what result? What if Timmy had subleased the entire apartment to Tawana without Liana's permission and the lease was likewise silent on the issue of subleasing?
3. In the last question, if Timmy subleases the apartment to Tawana after one month of the two-year lease, who will be responsible for the rent payments when they are due? What will be the effect of Tawana breaking the lease?
4. Tasha, a tenant in Leo's two-family home, has a two-year lease that specifies she must pay for the utilities she uses in her apartment, but that the landlord is responsible for providing heat and hot water. In January, during a particularly cold period, the boiler breaks, leaving Tasha without heat for two days. Leo, who is also without heat during that period, has the furnace looked at immediately but is told the repair will take two days due to the need to have a replacement part shipped from an out-of-town supplier. Leo offers to lend Tasha two space heaters to tide her over until the boiler is fixed, but Tasha, who hates the cold, immediately moves to another apartment and sues Leo for breach of the lease, seeking compensatory damages of $300 (for the unused month's rent) and incidental and consequential damages of $1,800 ($1,200 moving expenses and a $600 fee she paid a realtor to help find her a new apartment). Leo, on the other hand, counterclaims for damages for breach of the lease, claiming Tasha had no right to quit the premises under the circumstances. You are the judge. Resolve this dispute based on your knowledge of the applicable law.

Ethics and the Law: Questions for Further Study

Generally speaking, courts are likelier to enforce extraordinary remedies written into commercial leases than the same remedies written into residential leases. Why do you think this is so? Is it fair to give greater protection to all residential tenants over all commercial tenants even though a given residential tenant might be a real estate attorney intimately familiar with the relevant law and a commercial tenant might be a high school dropout attempting to get an entrepreneurial venture off the ground? Attack or defend the practice from a perspective of ethics rather than law.

Insurance

CHAPTER 34

Chapter Outline

The Insurance Contract

Types of Insurance Contracts

Risk is an unavoidable part of life. The difference between success and failure in both our business enterprises and in our personal lives often depends on managing risk through appropriate planning and the development of strategies for minimizing its potentially destructive effects. Insurance plays a key role in helping to manage known risks for businesses and individuals by allowing the insured to shift the risk to an insurance company for a price. The premium that the insurer charges includes the anticipated cost of all claims from its policy holders in addition to the insurer's overhead and profits. When the cost of covering insured claims rises for an insurer, such as the cost of reimbursing homeowners for property damage after a particularly active hurricane season, the costs are typically passed along to policy holders as higher premiums.

The Insurance Contract

At its core, insurance involves a contractual relationship between an insured party (the insured) and an insurance company (the insurer) whereby the insurer agrees to indemnify the insured for certain covered losses as stated in the insurance contract (the policy) in exchange for the insured paying the insurer an agreed-upon price (the premium). In addition to the contracting parties, an insurance contract may be for the benefit of a third party (the beneficiary) who will receive the benefit of the contract upon the happening of an insured event. This is the case, for example, with a life insurance contract in which a beneficiary receives the face amount of the policy upon the death of the insured.

Insurance contracts must meet the traditional requirements of a valid offer and acceptance, consideration, capacity, genuine assent, and legality. The would-be insured makes the offer to enter into an insurance contract by filling out an application for insurance through an insurance agent or independent broker. The contract does not become effective until the insured accepts the offer by issuing a policy to the insured. Although an insured will often not know for a period of weeks or longer whether the insurance application is accepted, agents and brokers will often issue a binder to an insurance applicant that provides immediate coverage pending the insurer's formal acceptance of the insurance application. Binders are common in contracts involving property and liability insurance such as automobile insurance and homeowner's insurance policies and offer temporary protection that lasts until a policy is issued or until the insurance application is rejected, whichever comes first.

Material misrepresentations on insurance applications can result in a voidable insurance contract at the option of the insurer or in reduced coverage, depending on the nature of the misrepresentation. If the insurer would not have issued the policy had the truth been disclosed by the insurance applicant, then the policy is voidable at the option of the insurer. On the other hand, if the insurer would have issued a policy had the truth been disclosed but at a higher premium, then the face value of the policy will be reformed to reflect modified coverage based on the premium paid. For example, if a business misrepresents the existence of a sprinkler system in an application for insurance and the insurer would not have issued the policy without a valid sprinkler system in place, then the insurer can void the policy when it learns about the material misrepresentation and will not need to pay fire or smoke-related claims should these accrue. (It will, however, have to return premiums paid to the insured.) Likewise, if an insured lies about having been diagnosed with cancer in a life insurance policy, the policy will be voidable at the option of the insurer if it would not normally issue life insurance to someone diagnosed with the disease. But lying about one's age or about having smoked cigarettes on a life insurance policy will not render it void in most instances; rather, the face value of the policy will be changed to reflect the amount of coverage the premiums would buy for someone who is the actual age of the insured or the amount of insurance the same premium would have purchased for a smoker.

Insurable Interest

To obtain insurance, one must have an insurable interest in the property or life one seeks to protect. For public policy reasons, individuals may insure only against risks that they have a sufficient economic interest or personal stake in protecting. An insurance contract issued to an individual with no insurable interest is at best a gambling contract (e.g., the individual is betting that harm will come to another's property or person) and at worst would provide an incentive for unscrupulous individuals to do harm to the persons or property of others to collect insurance proceeds. For these reasons, obtaining insurance without an insurable interest is illegal and renders the policy void.

A valid insurable interest exists in business or personal property that one owns or has the right to use or occupy, but only to the extent of one's interest in the property. Thus, we can obtain liability insurance coverage for an automobile we own or lease, and for real property that we own or lease to insure against harm to ourselves or others through our negligent use or maintenance of the property. But we can insure such property only from the harm of theft or destruction from fire, wind, or water to the extent of our ownership interest in it or financial responsibility for it. Therefore, we can insure a car we own against theft for its full value, but not a car we lease unless we are legally responsible for the full price of the vehicle in the event of theft under the lease agreement. Likewise, we can purchase protection against the theft of personal property in real estate we own or lease but can insure only ourselves against the destruction of the real estate itself (e.g., buildings and fixtures in a personal residence) if we own the property or if we have legal responsibility for its loss. In a similar vein, we have an insurable interest in our own lives, in the lives of close family members such as spouses and children, and in the lives of key business associates, such as our partners in a partnership. A person who has an insurable interest in her own life may purchase life insurance and make anyone she wishes its beneficiary; however, only someone with an insurable interest in her, such as a husband, a parent, or a business partner, may purchase a life insurance policy on her life without her consent.

Form and Interpretation of Insurance Contracts

The statutes of frauds in some states require insurance contracts to be evidenced by a signed writing. In a majority of states, however, oral insurance contracts are fully binding.

Normal rules of construction apply to insurance contracts so that courts will interpret contractual language according to its plain meaning and will resolve any ambiguous or contradictory language in favor of the party who did not draft the agreement (e.g., the insured).

Cancellation and Lapse of Insurance Contracts

Insurance contracts automatically lapse at the end of the period of coverage unless they are renewed by the mutual consent of the parties. A contract lapses if the insured does not pay the required premium to keep the policy in force when it is due, but states often require the insurer to provide a grace period (typically 30 days) for an insured to reinstate a lapsed policy and maintain continuous coverage. A policy may also be canceled by either the insured or the insurer based on the terms of their agreement or as provided by law. The insured may typically cancel a policy by notifying the insurer of her intention to discontinue the coverage, and the insurer by notifying the insured of its decision not to continue coverage, typically after the expiration of the policy's current period of coverage. For example, an insurer may cancel coverage for an individual insured based on his claims history and may cancel all policies in a geographic area based on its claims experience. Insurers may also cancel policies at any time for fraud.

Types of Insurance Contracts

Insurance is classified in accordance with the type of protection it provides. Next, we will briefly examine the major classifications of property, life, liability insurance, and health insurance contracts.

Property Insurance Contracts

Property insurance contracts involve an agreement by an insurer to indemnify an insured for covered losses to real or personal property in which he has an insurable interest. Typically, these contracts cover losses from fire, lightning, wind, or hail as well as smoke and water damage from a fire. These policies also contain a list of excluded events for which there is no coverage. These typically include acts of the public enemy (e.g., war or terrorist attacks), flood damage, damage from nuclear fallout, and the willful acts of the property owner.

Life Insurance Contracts

Life insurance contracts provide a payment upon the death of the insured and are available in three basic types: term, universal life, and whole life. Term contracts are the least expensive type of coverage available with premiums increasing over time to reflect the statistically greater chance of death as one ages. These can be renewable yearly or after a set number of years (5-, 10-, or 20-year level term plans are common); level term plans maintain the same premium rate for their entire duration, while yearly renewable term plans experience gradual rate increases every year as they are renewed. The entire amount of the premium reflects the actuarial risk or loss and the profit for the company; thus, these types of insurance contracts do not accumulate a cash value over time.

Another popular type of life insurance contract is a universal life policy. These are essentially term policies, with substantially higher premiums than straight term policies, that develop an accumulation fund on which interest at competitive rates is paid by the insurer. The accumulation fund and the tax-deferred interest it earns help to lower the overall cost of the term coverage over time and can accumulate significant cash surrender value, especially for individuals who take out such policies early in life. Part of each premium goes to pay the cost of term insurance coverage, and part is retained in interest earning accounts that typically pay interest rates that are often higher than bank certificates of deposit or money market funds.

The third type of life insurance policy is the traditional whole life policy that carries a relatively high premium cost but builds up cash at a guaranteed rate over time and may also earn dividends for the insured if purchased from a mutual company (a company that is owned by its policyholders). Like universal life policies, these policies build up cash reserves over time that the insured can borrow against or take as cash by surrendering the policy for its cash value later in life.

Liability Insurance Contracts

As the name implies, liability insurance contracts protect the insured against liability for negligent acts within the limits of the policy. Such coverage is available for real and personal property owned or rented by the insured (e.g., homeowner's, apartment dweller's, auto, and boat insurance) and covers injuries suffered by third parties as a result of the negligence of the insured in the maintenance or use of the covered property. The willful acts of the insured are generally excluded from coverage. Business liability insurance covers the liability of business owners for their own and their employees' negligence, as well as some willful acts (such as defamation or false arrest).

Malpractice insurance is a type of liability insurance that covers negligence in professional practices such as medicine and law. Worker's compensation insurance is also a specialized form of liability insurance that covers the employer's statutory responsibility for employees' work-related injuries under a state's worker's compensation statute.

Health Insurance Contracts

Health insurance policies protect individuals and families from many of the costs associated with healthcare. Typically, these come in two types: hospitalization and major medical. Hospitalization policies typically cover the costs associated with in-hospital care and surgical procedures as well as diagnostic tests associated with such procedures and surgeons' and anesthesiologists' fees. Major medical policies cover routine and specialty medical care and diagnostic exams and procedures that do not require hospitalization. The cost and coverage in these policies vary widely, as does the ability of the insured to choose primary care and specialty physicians and hospitals. In general, the wider the choice of physicians, facilities, and services provided, the larger the cost for premiums and co-insurance payment required of the insured.

Changes Required by the Affordable Healthcare Act (ACA)

In 2010 Congress passed and President Obama signed the Patient Protection and Affordable Care Act commonly referred to as Obamacare. The act imposes a number of major changes that impact businesses and individuals. First, ACA requires all individuals who are not covered for health insurance through work or through qualifying private insurance and who do not qualify for Medicare or Medicaid to purchase qualifying insurance through either state or federal exchanges or pay a tax penalty equal to 1% of their income. The act removes pre-existing condition exclusions from insurance contracts and allows parents to have adult children covered through their health insurance plans up to the age of 26. The act provides tax credits for small businesses with up to 25 employees for 50% of the healthcare premium cost for their employees if they offer healthcare coverage. The act also requires employers with 100 or more employees to provide health insurance to their employees or face a tax penalty of $2,000 per employee. (As of this writing, it is unclear whether the deadline will be extended beyond 2015.) Employers with 50–99 employees have until 2016 to provide coverage or face a similar tax. Companies with fewer than 50 employees are not required to provide health insurance and will have no tax penalties imposed if they fail to do so.

The Constitutionality of the ACA was challenged in the courts, but the U.S. Supreme Court held in a 5–4 decision that the act was constitutional [*National Federation of Independent Business v. Sebelius*, 648 F. 3d 1235 (2012)]. The court ruled that Congress could not require individuals to purchase health insurance under the Commerce Clause (as Congress intended), but Congress under its very broad power to tax could impose a tax on businesses that do not provide coverage for their employees and to individuals whose employers do not provide health insurance and who refuse to purchase their own through the federal or state exchanges. A subsequent second challenge to the ACA in the U.S. Supreme Court seeking to invalidate the ability of the federal government to provide health insurance through a federal exchange in states that refused to implement their own exchanges also failed in a 6–3 decision [*King v. Burwell*, 576 U. S. ____ (2015)].

Questions

1. How would you categorize the relationship between an insurer and the insured?
2. What role does insurance play in the management of personal and business risks?
3. What is the function of a binder?
4. What is the effect of a material misrepresentation on an insurance application by a person seeking insurance?
5. What is the effect of obtaining insurance without an insurable interest?
6. What are property insurance contracts?
7. Why do term life contracts carry lower premiums than universal life or whole life contracts?
8. What is malpractice insurance?
9. What are the two major types of health insurance policies available?
10. What is the typical grace period allowed by some states for an insured person to reinstate a policy that has lapsed due to nonpayment of premiums?

Hypothetical Cases

1. Ingrid fills out an application for life insurance from an agent of XYZ Insurance Company who makes a sales call at her home and sells her on buying a $100,000 whole life policy at a cost of $100 per month. In the insurance application, she misstates her age as 35 (she is actually 50) and falsely claims that she has not smoked cigarettes or used any tobacco product for the past two years. (In fact, she smokes two packs of cigarettes a day and chews tobacco when at her desk at work where she is unable to smoke.) The sales agent, who wants to make the sale (he will earn 55% of the first year's premium as his commission and 10% of her yearly premiums thereafter), ignores the fact that there is an open pack of cigarettes on the dining room table where he has made his sales presentation to her, as well as a spittoon in plain sight, a tin of chewing tobacco, an ashtray containing about 15 cigarette butts, and a pungent aroma of tobacco in the air. The amount of whole life insurance that Ingrid would be able to buy for $100 a month at her age as a smoker with this particular company would be $20,000. Based on these facts, answer the following questions:
   A. If the insurance company learns that Ingrid lied about her age and use of tobacco products, what will it be able to do with regard to this policy?
   B. If Ingrid dies after the company issued the policy and the company later discovers Ingrid's misrepresentations, what will Ingrid's beneficiary receive as a death benefit?
   C. What legal liability and what ethical responsibility does the salesperson bear under the facts given?

2. John and Karen are living together in a committed relationship but are not married. Karen earns twice as much as John and pays the bulk of the household expenses for a home that they purchased some years ago as joint tenants. They have a six-year-old son together, Lenny. Under these facts, please answer the following questions:
   A. May John purchase a $250,000 policy on Karen's life with himself as beneficiary in order to guard against her loss of income should she die unexpectedly?
   B. May Karen purchase a $100,000 life insurance policy on John's life and list their son, Lenny, as the beneficiary?
   C. If both John and Karen would like to have $250,000 coverage on each other's lives in case of death, what would you advise them to do?

3. Ken has lease on a new BMW automobile with a market value of approximately $50,000. Under the terms of the lease, he is responsible for $10,000 in the event that the car is stolen or destroyed by fire or a road hazard. In the event of accidental damage to the car resulting from a collision with another vehicle or property, he is responsible for up to the market value of the automobile. What is the maximum amount of comprehensive insurance that he may carry with regard to the automobile in case of fire or theft? Is there a limit to the personal liability insurance that he can purchase with regard to damage he or others with his permission may do to other people while driving the car?

4. Dan, Eddy, and Francine decide to go into business together providing computer consulting services. They have decided to organize the business as a partnership and are concerned about their exposure to potential lawsuits from individuals who might injure themselves while on the business premises. They would also like to obtain some health insurance coverage to protect them in case of hospitalization. Finally, they are concerned about the impact of any of them dying on their fledgling business and would like to take out the least expensive life insurance coverage they can find for $500,000 for each partner with the other partners as beneficiaries. Given these facts, please answer the questions that follow:
   A. Assuming that they rent a small storefront and have no significant partnership property in the leased property, what type of insurance would you suggest that they take to protect them from the risk of lawsuits?
   B. Given their concerns and tight budget, and also given that they expect that the business will experience steady growth in coming years, what type of life insurance contract would you recommend?

Wills

CHAPTER 35

Chapter Outline

An Introduction to Wills

Requirements of a Valid Will

Holographic and Nuncupative Wills

Revocation of a Will

Disinheritance of Spouses and Children

Intestacy

In our discussion of property thus far, we have seen that it is possible to transfer both real and personal property in a variety of ways, including by gift. Up until now, we have only discussed *inter vivos* and *causa mortis* gifts, which constitute a present transfer of both title to property as well as the property itself. It is also possible to make future transfers of gifts of real or personal property through the use of a will. In this chapter, we will examine the basic laws relating to wills and learn how this instrument can be used to convey interests to real and personal property. We will also examine how the property of a person who dies without leaving a valid will is distributed.

An Introduction to Wills

A will is an instrument that allows a person to make a distribution of her property that will become effective upon her death. Wills are by their nature revocable at any time by the person who creates them until the person's death.

A valid will can serve five main functions: (1) making positive dispositions of real and personal property; (2) directing how property is *not* to be distributed (e.g., disinheriting individuals in whole or in part who would otherwise be entitled to a distribution of property under intestacy); (3) making arrangements for the disposing of one's body after death; (4) providing for the guardianship of minor children; and (5) naming a person to act as executor or executrix of the estate. (See Figure 35.1 for a sample will.)

Definitions

Before we explore the substantive law of wills, it is important to become familiar with some relevant terminology.

- Decedent: a person who has died (with or without a valid will).
- Testator: a man who executes a valid will.
- Testatrix: a woman who executes a valid will.
- Executor: a man appointed by a testator or testatrix to serve as a personal representative to carry out the wishes and provisions expressed in a will, to pay debts of the estate, and to dispose of property in accordance with the testamentary provisions after the death of the testator or testatrix.
- Executrix: a woman appointed by a testator or testatrix to serve as a personal representative to carry out the wishes and provisions expressed in a will, to pay debts of the estate, and to dispose of property in accordance with the testamentary provisions after the death of the testator or testatrix.

WILL

LAST WILL AND TESTAMENT OF: _____

I, _____, a resident of _____ County, in the state of _____ declare that this is my will.

FIRST:

I revoke all Wills and Codicils that I have previously made.

SECOND:

I am not currently married. I have no children now living, nor have I any deceased children who died and left issue.

THIRD:

I give all my jewelry, clothing, household furniture and furnishings, personal automobiles and other tangible articles of a personal nature, or my interest in any such property not otherwise disposed of by this will or in any other manner together with any insurance on the property, to _____ who presently resides at _____, if he or she survives me by thirty (30) days, and if he or she does not so survive me, then I give said property to _____, who presently resides at _____, and if she or he does not survive me by thirty (30) days, then to _____ who presently resides at _____, otherwise to pass with the residency of my estate.

FOURTH:

I give the residue of my estate as follows:

1. To _____ who presently resides at _____ should he or she survive me by thirty (30) days.
2. If _____ who presently resides at _____, does not survive me by thirty (30) days, I give his or her interest to _____ who presently resides at _____, and if she does not survive me by thirty (30) days, then to _____ who presently resides at _____ should he or she survive me by thirty (30) days, and if he or she should not so survive me, then I give the rest and residue of my estate to those persons who would have taken said property under the interstate laws of the state of _____.

FIFTH:

I nominate _____ as Executor of this Will, to serve without bond. If he shall for any reason fail to qualify as Executor, I nominate _____ as Executrix to serve without bond. The term "my Executor" as used in this Will shall include any personal representative of my estate.

I authorize my Executor to sell, with or without notice, at either public or private sale, and to lease any property belonging to my estate, subject only to such confirmation of court as may be required by law.

I authorize my Executor to invest and reinvest any surplus money in the Executor's hands in every kind of property, real, personal, or mixed and every kind of investment, specifically including but not limited to interest bearing accounts, corporate obligations of every kind, preferred or common stocks, shares of investment trusts, investment companies, mutual funds, or common trust funds, including funds administered by the Executor, and mortgage participations, that men of prudence, discretion, and intelligence acquire for their own account.

SIXTH:

I direct that all inheritance, estate, or other death taxes (excluding any additional tax imposed under Internal Revenue Code or any state tax that may be reason of my death, be attributable to my probate estate or any portion of it, or to any property or transfers of property outside my probate estate, shall be paid by my Executor out of the residue of my estate disposed of by this Will, without adjustment among the residuary beneficiaries,

FIGURE 35.1 Sample Will

and shall not be charged against or collected from any beneficiary of my probate estate, or from any transferee or beneficiary of any property outside my probate estate.

SEVENTH:

If any beneficiary under this Will in any manner, directly or indirectly, contests or attacks this Will or any of its provisions, any share or interest in my estate given to the contesting beneficiary under this Will is revoked and shall be disposed of in the same manner provided herein as if that contesting beneficiary had predeceased me without issue.

I subscribe my name to this Will on _____, 20__, at _____.

_____

On the date written below, _____ declared to us, the undersigned, that this instrument, consisting of these few pages including the page signed by us as witnesses, was his or her Will and requested us to act as witnesses to it. He or she thereupon signed this Will in our presence, all of us being present at the same time. We now, at his or her request, in his or her presence and in the presence of each other, subscribe our names as witnesses.

Each states that the testator is not a minor and appears to be of sound mind and that we have no knowledge or any facts indicating that the foregoing instrument, or any part of it, was procured by duress, menace, fraud or undue influence.

We, each of himself or herself, declare that each of us is over the age of majority, and that each of us is, and the others appear to be of sound mind.

We, each for himself or herself, declare under penalty of perjury that the foregoing is true and correct and that this attestation and this declaration are executed on the _____ day of _____, 20__ at __ _____.

_____ residing at _____
_____ residing at _____
_____ residing at _____

FIGURE 35.1 (Continued)

- Intestacy: the state of dying without having executed a valid will.
- Intestate: without a valid will. A person dies *intestate* when he or she has not left a will, or has left a will that is void for failure to meet the technical requirements for a valid will.
- Intestate Succession: the laws in a state that determine how a decedent's property is to be distributed when the decedent died without having left a valid will.
- Intestacy Statute: a state's statute that determines how a decedent's property is to be distributed when the decedent has died without a valid will.
- Distributee: a person entitled to take or to share in a decedent's property under the laws governing intestacy.
- Issue: descendants in any degree from a common ancestor (includes adopted children).
- Per Capita: a distribution made to named individuals or to a class of individuals in which each takes an equal share (the term literally means a distribution *by the heads* in a "share and share alike" basis).
- Per Stirpes: a distribution made by *the roots*, or by lineage, where interested individuals take a proportionate share of a distribution that a deceased ancestor would have been entitled to had he or she survived the testator or testatrix. (When a distribution is made *per stirpes*, as is often the case in intestacy statutes, descendants of a common ancestor by blood or through adoption share in any distribution intended for the deceased ancestor.)

An example will help to illustrate. Assume Tammy testatrix dies leaving all of her property to her two children, Charles and Donna. Charles has a son of his own, Carl, and Donna has three children, Dom, Danielle, and Darnell. If Donna predeceases Tammy and Tammy had left her property to Charles and Donna *per stirpes*, then Charles gets one-half of Tammy's estate, and Donna's children share Donna's share of the estate equally, each taking a third of whatever property she would have inherited if alive (for a one-sixth share each). If the property had been left to Charles and Donna *per capita*, on the other hand, then all surviving heirs would take an equal share of the estate, so that Charles would get not a one-half share, but a one-quarter share with his nephews and niece as survivors of Donna taking each a one-quarter share and sharing equally in the estate. Thus, if Tammy's estate after all final expenses, taxes, and outstanding debt are paid is $1,200,000 and Donna predeceases Tammy, the *per stirpes* share for the survivors would be $600,000 for Charles and $200,000 each for Donna's children. A *per capita* distribution, on the other hand, would have all survivors share in the estate equally, giving Charles and his niece and nephews a $300,000 share each.

- Bequest: a gift of personal property by will (also called a *legacy*).
- Devise: a gift of real property by will.
- Codicil: a supplement to a will that alters, revokes, or affirms any provision in the will. (A codicil must be executed in exactly the same way as a will in order to be valid.)

Requirements of a Valid Will

Although laws relating to the creation of a valid will vary somewhat among the 50 states, the essential requirements for the creation of a valid will tend to be relatively uniform. With the exception of holographic and nuncupative wills that we will discuss shortly, all wills must meet the following criteria to be valid:

- the testator or testatrix must be of legal age;
- the testator or testatrix must have the legal capacity to dispose of property;
- the will must be written (unless it is a nuncupative will) and generally signed by the testator or testatrix at its end; (A signature appearing before the end of the will invalidates any provisions in the will that appear after the signature. Holographic wills need not be signed or witnessed in some states.)
- the will must be signed before witnesses or acknowledged before witnesses by the testator or testatrix who must then sign as witnesses to the will (two or three witnesses are required, depending on the jurisdiction);
- in some jurisdictions, the will needs to be published.

Requirement of Legal Age

A testator or testatrix must be of legal age (generally 18 years of age) to execute a valid will. A will executed by a minor is void and s *not* deemed ratified when the minor reaches legal age.

Requirement of Legal Capacity

For a will to be valid, the testator or testatrix must have the legal capacity to dispose of property at the time of executing the will. Wills drafted by incompetents, like those drafted by minors, are void. Competence is measured as of the time that the will is drafted. That a legally competent person becomes incompetent subsequent to drafting the will does not invalidate the instrument.

Fraud, duress, and undue influence can invalidate a testator's or testatrix's capacity in much the same way as they serve to invalidate genuine assent to a contract. Thus, a will that is shown to have been drafted as a result of fraud, duress, or undue influence is void.

Requirement of a Signed Writing

There is no special form that needs to be used in drafting a valid will, and writing of any sort on any type of paper with any type of writing instrument is generally acceptable if the writing conforms to the requirements for a valid will. The signature of the testator must appear at the end of the will, following all its provisions. If, by some mistake, it appears otherwise than at the end of the will, any provisions following the signature are ignored, but the will is still valid minus such provisions in most jurisdictions.

The requirement of a signature is liberally construed, as is generally the case in other legal instruments. Any mark made by the testator or testatrix on the will intended as a signature will satisfy the requirement of a signature.

Requirement of Witnessing the Will

Most jurisdictions require that wills be witnessed by at least two or three witnesses who sign either after seeing the testator sign before them or after having the testator acknowledge his signature on the will to them. If the testator does not sign immediately before the witnesses, the witnessing of the will must usually take place within a set time of the testator's signing of the will. (In New York, for example, a will must be witnessed within 30 days of its execution by the testator or testatrix.)

Witnesses are not required to know what is in the will and, in fact, ought not be allowed to read it unless the testator expresses the wish that they do so, since witnesses are not acknowledging the contents of the will, but rather that the testator signed with the intention of creating the will.

If more than the required number of witnesses sign the will, any excess witnesses are referred to as *supernumeraries*. The presence of supernumeraries does not affect the validity of the will; in fact, supernumeraries can be useful when witnesses are required to testify as to their witnessing the will or to the testator's or testatrix's state of mind (especially in cases involving contests of the will) since witnesses can die, move from a jurisdiction, or have lapses of memory.

A problem can arise with witnesses who are also entitled to receive a bequest or devise under the will. Generally speaking, such witnesses do not invalidate the will, but are generally barred from taking under the terms of the will (unless they are also entitled to take under the laws of intestacy, in which case they cannot receive a benefit that is greater than their intestate share). If that is the case, then an interested witness may take the *lesser* of her intestate share or the bequest or device provided for in the will. If there is a conflict involving an interested witness but the will can be validated without the interested witness's signature because of the existence of a supernumerary, then the interested witness may take his full share under the terms of the will.

Attorneys who prepare wills generally have witnesses execute a self-proving affidavit immediately after witnessing the will that states that the testator or testatrix published and acknowledged the instrument as his last will and testament, signed the instrument in their presence, and asked them in turn to sign as witness to the will. The name and addresses of each witness is noted next to their signature, and the affidavit is then notarized and attached to the end of the will. This generally avoids the requirement of having to find the witnesses in the future to acknowledge their having witnessed the will when the will is probated.

Requirement of Publication of the Will

Some jurisdictions require that a will be not only witnessed but also published by the testator or testatrix. The publication requirement is fulfilled, however, merely by the communication of the testator or testatrix to the witnesses that the instrument they are asked to sign is the last will and testament of the testator or testatrix. For example, a will is published by the testator asking each of his witnesses to sign as follows: "This is my last will and testament. Please acknowledge my signature and sign as a witness in the space provided." Any similar words that clearly convey to the witnesses that the instrument is the last will and testament of the testator or testatrix will generally suffice as fulfilling the requirement of publication, where one exists.

Holographic and Nuncupative Wills

As previously noted, two types of wills that are recognized in many states represent a departure from the traditional will format and do not require the same formalities as traditional wills.

Holographic Wills

A holographic will is one that is completely written out in the testator's handwriting. In states that recognize such wills as having a special status, the requirement of a signature, of witnessing, and of publication are typically dispensed with. The rationale for treating holographic wills differently than traditional wills is that it is far less likely for a holographic will to be forged than is the case for a traditional form will. In states that do not recognize holographic wills as such, a will that is entirely written in the hand of the testator or testatrix is still perfectly valid but must also be signed, witnessed, and published the same as any other will.

Nuncupative Wills

A nuncupative will is an oral will that is dictated by the testator or testatrix to two or more witnesses. Many states recognize such wills but place strict limitations on their validity, usually recognizing them as valid only if they are dictated by a soldier during active duty in an armed conflict or a mariner at sea. For this reason, such wills are also commonly referred to as "soldiers and sailors wills."

States that recognize nuncupative wills also generally place a time limit on their effectiveness. Typically, a nuncupative will dictated by a soldier is valid for up to one year after the cessation of the hostilities in which the soldier was taking part at the time of dictating the will. In cases of mariners at sea, a nuncupative will is also limited in duration to a set period after the sailor reaches land.

The purpose for these wills is to allow soldiers and sailors to make informal wills at a time when they might be otherwise unable to execute a traditional will due to their special circumstances. If these oral wills are not re-executed as valid traditional wills within the time specified in the state's statute, then they expire and the testator's estate will be distributed under the intestacy statute when he dies.

Since these wills are not reduced to a writing by the testator, they are proven by the testimony of the witnesses as to the wishes of the testator. Interested witnesses to a nuncupative will are treated exactly the same as interested witnesses to a traditional will and can generally not benefit from the will.

Revocation of a Will

A will is revocable at any time prior to the death of the testator or testatrix, and may be revoked by any unequivocal act that clearly shows an intent to revoke the will. Thus, a testator who writes "void" across all pages of a will and initials each page will effectively cancel the will, as does one who tears up the entire will with the intent to destroy it. But an attempt to cancel or change a part of a will is ineffectual; so crossing out a provision in a will and initialing it will have no effect on that provision or on the validity of the will. Crossing out a beneficiary's name and replacing it with that of another is likewise ineffectual. Such changes can be accomplished only through a codicil.

Although the destruction of a will does not necessarily imply its revocation, if a will that was last known to be in the hands of the decedent is not found upon his death, a revocation of the will is presumed.

Writing a new will revokes an existing will only if the new will contains a revocation clause. If a revocation clause is not contained in a new will, it will revoke an existing will only to the extent that it contains provisions that are inconsistent with the existing will.

Consistent provisions in both wills are read together. For this reason, the revocation of all prior wills is typically the first clause in every will.

Partial revocation of wills also occurs in most states by operation of law upon the marriage or divorce of the testator, or the birth or adoption of a child that occurs after a testator's last will. If a testator marries subsequent to making a will, the spouse will be entitled to an intestate share of the testator's estate in most states (the share she or he would receive if the testator died without a will) and an existing will drafted before the marriage will be modified as needed to accommodate the spouse's rights to inherit. A divorce decree in most states will have a similar impact on an existing will. The will itself will remain valid, but any provision made for the benefit of the divorced spouse will be nullified and the assets redistributed under the terms of the will or the laws of intestacy if the entire estate had previously been left to the former spouse. The birth or adoption of a child by a testator or testatrix after making a will also alters the will to accommodate the child in most states under the presumption that the decedent would not have intended to disinherit the child. Absent actual evidence of such intent, the child will take an intestate share in the estate if he or she is entitled to a share of the estate under the state's intestacy statute.

Disinheritance of Spouses and Children

As previously noted, two of the five main functions that a valid will can serve include making positive dispositions of real and personal property and directing how property is *not* to be distributed. While a testator or testatrix is free to dispose of her property in any way she sees fit, there are limits on a testator's right to disinherit spouses and children. In every state, it is impossible to wholly disinherit a spouse to whom one is legally married at death. If an attempt to disinherit a spouse is made, the spouse will be able to assert his rights to a statutory minimum portion of the decedent's estate under the state's applicable intestacy statute or under the common law right of dower and curtesy.

Under English common law, a spouse was absolutely entitled to a portion of a decedent spouse's estate. If the surviving spouse was a widow, she was entitled to *dower*, a life estate in one-third of all the husband's real property upon his death in order to assure her sustenance and that of her children. A surviving widower was likewise entitled to assert his right of *curtesy,* which entitled a husband to a life estate in all of a deceased wife's real property if the marriage had produced a legitimate child who was born alive and might inherit the estate. While dower and curtesy have been largely abolished or modified in the vast majority of states, an analogous right for both husbands and wives is retained today in the form of an intestacy share. In every state, a surviving spouse is entitled to either a life estate in the property owned by the deceased spouse or to a percentage of such spouse's real and personal property at the time of death.

Children are not given protection from disinheritance in most states. While some states require that a nominal sum be awarded to a surviving child (such as $1) or that the child be specifically named in order to be disinherited, in most states a parent can disinherit children simply by failing to make any provisions for them in a will.

Intestacy

Whenever a decedent dies without leaving a valid will, he is said to have died intestate, and the state determines how the decedent's property will be distributed to the decedent's family. State intestacy statutes detail how a decedent's estate is to be distributed after death. While such statutes generally reflect an attempt to distribute a decedent's assets in accordance with what a state's legislature believes would be the wishes of most residents of the state, the provisions in any given state's intestacy statute may not accurately reflect the assumptions that many individuals make as to who will be the beneficiaries of their estates if they die without a will and the actual share of the estate that these beneficiaries will inherit. For this reason, it is important that all individuals become familiar with their state's intestacy statute and to execute a valid will if their wishes are not appropriately reflected in it. (Figure 35.2 illustrates New York's intestacy statute.)

> **[New York State Intestacy Statute]**
> **Estates, Powers and Trusts Laws Article 4**
>
> § 4-1.1:
>
> (a) If a decedent is survived by:
>   1. A spouse and issue, fifty thousand dollars and one-half of the residue to the spouse, and the balance thereof to the issue by representation.
>   2. A spouse and no issue, the whole to the spouse.
>   3. Issue and no spouse, the whole to the issue, by representation.
>   4. One or both parents, and no spouse and no issue, the whole to the surviving parent or parents.
>   5. Issue of parents, and no spouse, issue or parent, the whole to the issue of the parents, by representation.
>   6. One or more grandparents or the issue of grandparents (as hereinafter defined), and no spouse, issue, parent or issue of parents, one-half to the surviving paternal grandparent or grandparents, or if neither of them survives the decedent, to their issue, by representation, and the other one-half to the surviving maternal grandparent or grandparents, or if neither of them survives the decedent, to their issue, by representation; provided that if the decedent was not survived by a grandparent or grandparents on one side or by the issue of such grandparents, the whole to the surviving grandparent or grandparents on the other side, or if neither of them survives the decedent, to their issue, by representation, in the same manner as the one-half. For the purposes of this subparagraph, issue of grandparents shall not include issue more remote than grandchildren of such grandparents.
>   7. Great-grandchildren of grandparents, and no spouse, issue, parent, issue of parents, grandparent, children of grandparents or grandchildren of grandparents, one-half to the great-grandchildren of the paternal grandparents, per capita, and the other one-half to the great-grandchildren of the maternal grandparents, per capita; provided that if the decedent was not survived by great-grandchildren of grandparents on one side, the whole to the great-grandchildren of grandparents on the other side, in the same manner as the one-half.
> (b) For all purposes of this section, decedent's relatives of the half blood shall be treated as if they were relatives of the whole blood.
> (c) Distributees of the decedent, conceived before his or her death but born alive thereafter, take as if they were born in his or her lifetime.
> (d) The right of an adopted child to take a distributive share and the right of succession to the estate of an adopted child continue as provided in the domestic relations law.
> (e) A distributive share passing to a surviving spouse under this section is in lieu of any right of dower to which such spouse may be entitled.

FIGURE 35.2 Sample Intestacy Statute (New York State)

Questions

1. What is a will? What basic functions do wills serve?
2. What is the effect of a will drafted by a child under the age of consent?
3. How many witnesses are typically required for a valid will?
4. What is a supernumerary?
5. Do witnesses generally need to know what is in the will? Is there an exception to this rule?
6. In jurisdictions that require the publication of a will, does the will have to be published in a newspaper of general circulation? Explain.
7. What are holographic and nuncupative wills?
8. How can a valid will be revoked?
9. Can children and spouses be disinherited? Explain.
10. What is intestacy, and what is the net result of dying intestate?

Hypothetical Cases

1. Sandy Soldier, while at her barracks in her home state in time of peace, decides it would be a good idea to make a will. She asks three friends to be witnesses to her will and tells them that it is her intent to leave all of her personal and real property to her parents share and share alike, except that she wants her valuable stamp collection to go to her brother, Benny. While she spoke, one of the three witnesses, William, took notes. When Sandy noticed that William had taken notes, she read them and, finding them an accurate reflection of

her wishes, she initialed them at the end. Six months later, Sandy dies of an automobile accident.
   A. Did she effectively create a will by dictating it under the circumstances? Explain fully.
   B. Did Sandy create a valid will by initialing William's notes. Explain.
   C. How will Sandy's property be distributed?
2. Tiffany Testatrix, a young woman of 16, wants to create a will after learning of a friend's tragic death. She does a little bit of background reading on the subject, and then writes out the following document completely in her own hand:

I, Tiffany Testatrix, being of sound and disposing mind hereby make my last Will and Testament.
I leave my porcelain doll collection and my music CDs to Jane Jones, my best friend. I also leave all of my personal papers and photographs to Jane.
I leave the money in my savings and checking accounts to my parents per stirpes.
I name my brother, Michael, to act as my executor. If Michael is unable or unwilling to act in that capacity, then I name my father as executor of my estate.
I wish my eyes, kidneys, liver, and heart to be donated to a local hospital for use in transplants that might give others a second chance at life. I wish the remainder of my remains to be cremated and scattered at sea.
The rest, residue, and remainder of my estate is to go to the American Red Cross.

[Initialed] T.T.

Answer the following questions based on the facts given:
   A. What type of will is involved here?
   B. Is the will valid?
   C. Do the initials suffice as a signature in this will?
   D. If Tiffany dies upon reaching her 90th birthday without having drafted another will, how will her property be distributed?

3. Assume the same facts as in the previous question, except that Tiffany is 18 and of legal age at the time that she executed the instrument.
   A. Is this a valid will? Explain fully.
   B. Assuming that Tiffany's state recognizes the type of will involved here, does the fact that it has not been witnessed invalidate it?
   C. Assume for the sake of this question that the instrument is valid and that upon her death Tiffany has amassed a billion-dollar real estate empire, that her collection of porcelain dolls is worth $1,000,000 and that she has $250,000 in savings and checking accounts. Further assume that her parents have died before Tiffany, but that her childhood friend, Jane, and her brother, Michael, are still alive. How will her assets be distributed?
   D. Assume that brother Michael is unhappy with the will and wishes to contest its validity. In the event that he is successful in showing that Tiffany did not have the capacity to draft a valid will when she was 18 due to some mental illness, how is the property likely to be distributed?

4. Thomas Testator drafted a valid will when he was 30 years old and single in which he left all of his estate to his parents, and, if they predeceased him, to various charities. At 35, Thomas married Tawana and remained married to her until his death at the ripe old age of 100, with Tawana surviving him. He never changed his will, and at his death both parents had predeceased him.
   A. Who gets his estate? Be specific.
   B. Assume that soon after marrying, Thomas took out his will and crossed out the provision giving his property to his parents and replaced Tawana's name where it had previously read to the parents if they survived him, else to the named charities. What is the effect of this change?
   C. What if Thomas has written VOID across each page of the will and initialed each page after doing so?

Ethics and the Law: Questions for Further Study

Most states permit children to be disinherited, but not spouses. The prohibition against disinheriting a spouse is absolute, regardless of the underlying relationship between the parties, the length of the marriage, or the support (or lack thereof) that the spouses provided to one another during their married lives. Would you characterize this as a just and ethical law? How about the ability to disinherit children, regardless of the underlying relationship or support that children might have given to the parent throughout their lives? Should a bad marriage convey greater interests in the estate of a deceased spouse than a good, nurturing, supportive, and loving child obtains as a birthright and by affinity of blood? What arguments based on sound ethical principles can you make for the maintenance of the current law or for its change? Should the law recognize similar rights for unmarried domestic partners in long-term, committed relationships?

Trusts

CHAPTER 36

Chapter Outline

Creation of Express Trusts
Requirements, Rights, and Responsibilities of Trustees
Irrevocable and Revocable Trusts
Totten Trusts
Creation of Testamentary Trusts
Creation of a Resulting Trust
Creation of a Constructive Trust
Termination of Trusts

Up until now, our discussion has focused on transfers of property that involve ownership interests. But it is also possible to transfer less than a full ownership right in property by giving or selling to someone the right to benefit from property owned by another. We have already been exposed to this concept in our study of real property, where we've seen that it is possible to give or sell to someone less than a full fee simple interest in property, such as by the transfer of a life estate or an estate for years, where the recipient of the property interest obtains the right to benefit from it for life or for a set period of time, but not full ownership of the property. The same concept applies to a trust, where the actual property is held by a third party (the trustee) who is its legal owner but must manage the property for the benefit of the trust beneficiary.

A *trust* is an arrangement whereby property is transferred by its owner to some third party or parties who are entrusted with its management for the benefit of a named beneficiary. A trust involves a *fiduciary relationship* (a confidential relationship based on trust) in which the trustee (the person entrusted with the property) must exercise the highest duty of care and honesty in exercising her duties and place the interests of the beneficiary of the trust above her own.

Before we continue with our discussion, it will be useful to define some terms:

- Trust: an arrangement whereby real or personal property is held by one person entrusted with its management and care for the benefit of another.
- Trustee: a person entrusted with the care of property held in trust for the benefit of another.
- Beneficiary: a person who receives the income or other benefits derived from property under the care of a trustee.
- Trust Corpus: the underlying property that forms the basis of the trust (literally the *body of the trust*).
- Trust Settlor: the creator of a trust who gives the trust corpus over to the trustee for the benefit of the beneficiary. (The settlor is also commonly referred to as the trustor.)
- Express Trust: a trust created by the express wishes of the settlor.
- Resulting Trust: a trust that arises by implication of law or the requirements of equity from the implied intent of the settlor in creating a trust. (The most common resulting trust is a trust in favor of the settlor when an express trust fails upon the death of an express beneficiary when the settlor had not made express provisions for a secondary beneficiary.)

- Constructive Trust: a fictional trust imposed by courts as an equitable remedy to avoid unjust enrichment in cases in which property is obtained through unlawful means such as by fraud or duress.
- Private Trust: an express trust for the benefit of specific beneficiaries.
- Charitable Trust: a trust for religious, educational, or other philanthropic purpose that does not benefit specific individual beneficiaries, but rather charitable organizations or the public at large.
- *Inter Vivos* Trust: a trust created by the settlor during her lifetime.
- Testamentary Trust: a trust created by a provision in a will that is not to take effect until the settlor's death.

Creation of Express Trusts

The creation of an express trust requires that the trust settlor deliver to the trustee (or trustees) the trust corpus with the intention of creating a trust for the benefit of the trust beneficiary. When an *inter vivos* trust is involved, the settlor personally delivers the trust corpus to the trustees; in a testamentary trust, it is the executor of the estate who is charged with delivering the trust corpus to the trustees.

For a valid trust to be created, the trust must be for a lawful purpose. As long as the noted requirements are met, a trust can be created orally or through a signed writing. But if an interest in real estate is involved as the trust corpus, a signed writing is required to satisfy the statute of frauds.

Requirements, Rights, and Responsibilities of Trustees

Individuals who wish to serve as trustees must be of legal age and cannot be incompetent. States often impose other requirements on trustees, such as that they not be convicted felons or unable to execute their duties due to alcohol or drug addiction. A residency requirement may also be imposed by states on trustees.

During the period that the trust is in force, the trustees are the legal owners of the trust corpus. If more than one trustee is named in a trust, then the trustees own property as joint tenants. Trustees must use reasonable care in the management of trust property and can be sued for any loss resulting from mismanagement of the trust that arises out of negligence or incompetence. Because trustees perform a valuable service to the trust beneficiary, they are entitled to reasonable compensation for their services unless they specifically agree to serve gratuitously.

Upon the termination of a trust that is either revocable by its nature or set to automatically expire upon the happening of an event or the passage of time, the trust corpus revests in the settlor or otherwise as provided in the trust instrument, and the trustees' interest in the trust corpus ends.

Irrevocable and Revocable Trusts

A trust is irrevocable unless the settlor specifically reserves the power to revoke the trust (see Figures 36.1 and 36.2). In a typical revocable trust, the settlor retains the right to revoke the trust or to alter its beneficiaries, trustees, or the trust's income provisions during the settlor's lifetime (see Figure 36.3). A settlor can also reserve the right to appoint the remainder interest in the trust by will. In addition, a trust can be set up to automatically terminate at a future date or upon the happening of an event. If the power to revoke is retained by the settlor, then she or he also retains a reversionary interest in the trust corpus,

IRREVOCABLE TRUST

TRUST AGREEMENT made this ____ day of _____, 20___, between _____ (the "Grantor"), and _____ and _____ (the "Trustees").

1. TRUST PROPERTY. The Grantor, desiring to create trusts for the benefit of his adult children and for other good and valuable consideration, irrevocably assigned to the Trustees of the property described in attached Schedule A (the "Trust Property"), in trust, for the purposes and on the conditions hereinafter stated.

2. DISPOSITIVE PROVISIONS. The Trustees shall hold the property for the primary benefit of _____ and _____ (the "Beneficiaries"), and the Trustees shall hold, manage, and invest the trust property, and shall collect and receive the income, and after deducting all necessary expenses incident to the administration of the trusts, shall dispose of the corpus and income of the trusts as follows:

    (a) The Trustees shall pay the entire net income of the trust, quarter annually, to the beneficiaries of the trust, provided that there shall be paid over absolutely to the beneficiaries at age _____ the corpus of the trust.

    (b) If any of the beneficiaries shall die before attaining the age of _____ years, the trust for his or her benefit shall cease, and the corpus, together with any undistributed income, shall be paid over absolutely to the issue of the beneficiary then living per stirpes; but if there be no issue, then to the other beneficiaries if living, either outright, or, if the other beneficiary shall not have then attained the age of _____ years, in trust, to be added to, held, administered, and distributed as part of the trust for the other beneficiary; but if the other beneficiary is not then living, then absolutely to the then living issue of the other beneficiary per stirpes; and if there is no issue, then to the estate of the beneficiary for whom the trust was being held originally.

    (c) Notwithstanding anything contained to the contrary, if at any time while the trusts are in force any financial emergency arises in the affairs of either of the primary beneficiaries of the trusts, or if the independent income of either of the beneficiaries (exclusive of the income from any trust created for his or her benefit by the Grantor) and all other means of support are insufficient for the support of the beneficiary, in the judgment of the Trustees, the Trustees shall pay over to the beneficiary, solely out of the corpus of the trust for his or her benefit, at any time and from time to time, the sum or sums as the Trustees shall deem necessary or appropriate in their discretion.

3. TRUSTEES' POWERS. In the administration of the trusts, the Trustees shall have the following powers, all of which shall be exercised in the fiduciary capacity, primarily in the interest of the beneficiaries:

    (a) To hold and continue to hold as an investment the property, of any additional property which may be received by them, so long as they deem proper, and to invest and reinvest in any securities or property, whether or not income-producing, deemed by them to be for the best interest of the trusts and the beneficiaries.

    (b) To rent or lease any property of the trusts for the time and upon the terms and for the price or prices as in their discretion and judgment may seem just and proper and for the best interest of the trusts and the beneficiaries.

    (c) To sell and convey any of the property of the trusts or any interest, or to exchange it for other property, for the price or prices and upon the terms as in their discretion and judgment may be deemed for the best interest of the trusts and the beneficiaries.

    (d) To make all repairs and improvements at any time deemed necessary and proper to and upon real property constituting a part of the trusts.

    (e) To deduct, retain, expend, and pay out of any money belonging to the trusts any and all necessary and proper expenses in connection with the operation and conduct of the trusts.

    (f) To vote upon all securities belonging to the trusts, and to become a party to any stockholders' agreements deemed advisable by them in connection with the securities.

    (g) To consent to the reorganization, consolidation, merger, liquidation, readjustment of, or other change in any corporation, company, or association.

    (h) To compromise, settle, arbitrate, or defend any claim or demand in favor of or against the trusts.

    (i) To incur and pay the ordinary and necessary expenses of administration, including (but not by way of limitation) reasonable attorneys' fees, accountants' fees, investment counsel fees, and the like.

FIGURE 36.1 Sample Irrevocable Trust

> (j) To act through an agent or attorney-in-fact, by and under power of attorney duly executed by the Trustees, in carrying out any of the authorized powers and duties.
> (k) To borrow money for any purposes of the trusts, or incidental to their administration, upon their bond or promissory note as trustees, and to secure their repayment by mortgaging, creating a security interest in, or pledging or otherwise encumbering any part or all of the property of the trusts.
> (l) To lend money to any person or persons upon the terms and in the ways and with the security as they may deem advisable for the best interest of the trusts and the beneficiaries.
> (m) To engage in business with the property of the trusts as sole proprietor, or as a general or limited partner, with all the powers customarily exercised by an individual so engaged in business, and to hold an undivided interest in any property as tenant in common or as tenant in partnership.
> (n) To determine the manner in which the expenses incidental to or in connection with the administration of the trusts shall be apportioned as between corpus and income.
> (o) The Trustees may freely act under all or any of the powers by this Agreement given to them in all matters concerning the trusts, after forming their judgment based upon all the circumstances of any particular situation as to the wisest and best course to pursue in the interest of the trusts and the beneficiaries, without the necessity of obtaining the consent or permission of any interested person, or the consent or approval of any court.
>
> The powers granted to the Trustees may be exercised in whole or in part, from time to time, and shall be deemed to be supplementary to and not exclusive of the general powers of trustees pursuant to law, and shall include all powers necessary to carry them into effect.

FIGURE 36.1 (Continued)

and a resulting trust by reversion vests the trust corpus on the settlor if the power of revocation is exercised in the future, or if the corpus is set to revest in the settlor upon the happening of an event or the expiration of a set period of time. For example, a settlor who creates a trust for the benefit of a child that is to run for the child's lifetime reserves for himself a resulting trust by reversion upon the child's death.

Totten Trusts

A Totten trust gets its name from the case that led to its recognition in New York [*Matter of Totten*, 179 N.Y. 112 (1904)], but such trusts are also recognized in many other states. In a Totten trust, the settlor opens a bank account in her own name *in trust for* a named beneficiary. During the settlor's life, the trust is freely revocable by the settlor in whole or in part by either closing the account or removing money from it. If the settlor has not revoked the account at her death, however, the funds in the account vest in the beneficiary.

In addition to being subject to revocation by the settlor during her life, a Totten trust can also be revoked by a will (in New York, at least) in which the testator or testatrix leaves the money in the Totten trust account to someone other than the beneficiary named on the account. To revoke a Totten trust by will, the testator or testatrix must specifically name the bank account, give its account number, and state the bank at which the account is held and the name of the beneficiary named in the account.

In addition to being revocable during the settlor's lifetime, Totten trusts are subject to attachment by creditors of the settlor after death, and are subject to the surviving spouse's elective share (the unalienable one-third intestate share that a spouse is entitled to in most states) if the surviving spouse has not been provided with at least the minimum required share by the decedent's will.

Finally, if a beneficiary of a Totten trust predeceases the settlor of the trust, the trust is automatically revoked and the corpus revests in the settlor.

4. LIMITATION ON POWERS. Notwithstanding anything contained to the contrary, no powers enumerated or accorded to trustees generally pursuant to law shall be construed to enable the Grantor, or the Trustees or either of them, or any other person, to sell, purchase, exchange, or otherwise deal with or dispose of all or any parts of the corpus or income of the trusts for less than an adequate consideration in money or monies worth, or to enable the Grantor to borrow all or any part of the corpus or income of the trusts, directly or indirectly, without adequate interest or security.
5. CORPUS AND INCOME. The Trustees shall have the power to determine the allocation of receipts between corpus and income and to apportion extraordinary and share dividends between corpus and income.
6. TRUSTEES' AUTHORITY AND THIRD PARTIES. No person purchasing, renting, or leasing any of the property of the trusts, or in any manner dealing with the trusts or with the Trustees, shall be required to inquire into the authority of the Trustees to enter into any transaction, or to account for the application of any money paid to the Trustees on any account.
7. ADDITIONAL PROPERTY. The Grantor reserves the right to himself or to any other person at any time, by deed or will, to add to the corpus of either or both of the trusts, and any property added shall be held, administered, and distributed as part of the trust or trusts. The additional property shall be allocated between the trusts in accordance with any directions given in the instrument of transfer.
8. ACCOUNTING BY TRUSTEES. The Trustees may render an accounting at any time to the beneficiaries of the trust, and the written approval of a beneficiary shall be final, binding, and conclusive upon all persons then or thereafter interested in the trust for that beneficiary. The Trustees may at any time render a judicial account of their proceedings for either or both of the trusts.
9. COMPENSATION OF TRUSTEES. The Trustees waive the payment of any compensation for their services, but this waiver shall not apply to any successor trustee who qualifies and acts under this Agreement except that no person who adds to the corpus of either or both of the trusts shall ever be entitled to any compensation.
10. SUCCESSOR TRUSTEES. Either of Trustees shall have the power to appoint his or her successor Trustee. If either of the named Trustees shall die, resign, become incapacitated, or refuse to act further as Trustee, without having appointed a successor Trustee, the other named Trustee may, but shall not be required to, appoint a successor Trustee. The appointment of a successor Trustee shall be made by a duly acknowledged instrument delivered to the primary beneficiaries and to the person, if any, then acting as Trustee.
11. BOND AND LIABILITY OF TRUSTEES. Neither of the two (2) named Trustees shall be required to give any bond or other security. The Trustees shall not be liable for any mistake or error of judgment in the administration of the trusts, except for willful misconduct, so long as they continue to exercise their duties and powers in a fiduciary capacity primarily in the interests of the beneficiaries.
12. IRREVOCABILITY. The trusts shall be irrevocable, and the Grantor expressly waives all rights and powers, whether alone or in conjunction with others, and regardless of when or from what source he may have acquired such rights or powers, to alter, amend, revoke, or terminate the trusts, or any of the terms of this Agreement, in whole or in part. By this instrument the Grantor relinquishes absolutely and forever all his possession or enjoyment of, or right to the income from, the trust property, and all his right and power, whether alone or in conjunction with others, to designate the persons who shall possess or enjoy the trust property, or the income.
13. SITUS. This trust has been executed and delivered in the State of _____ and shall be construed and administered according to the laws of that state.

In witness whereof the Grantor and the Trustees have executed this Agreement in the City of _____, County of _____

_____
Grantor

_____
Trustee

FIGURE 36.2 Sample Irrevocable Trust (Continued)

> **REVOCABLE TRUST**
>
> _____, SETTLOR, of _____ in the County of _____, have this day conveyed and transferred to _____, a _____ located at and off _____, State of _____, TRUSTEE, the property as listed and set forth in Schedule A attached hereto and made a part hereof, and the said Trustee hereby makes and executes this Declaration of Trust and hereby agrees for itself and its successors in effect, to hold said property and any property from time to time added hereto IN TRUST NEVERTHELESS upon the following uses and benefits, that is to say:
>
> FIRST: The property shall be held, managed, invested and re-invested by the Trustee, and its successor or successors, with all the powers to the Trustee as herein provided.
>
> SECOND: The Trustee shall divide the Trust Property into equal shares for each of the beneficiaries, namely: _____, and shall pay to, or apply for the benefit of, said named beneficiaries such amount, or amounts, of the net income and/or principal from each of said shares as the Trustee in its uncontrolled discretion may determine, any net income in any year which is not paid to, or applied for the benefit of, the beneficiary of each said share shall be added to the principal of said share at the end of the year.
>
> THIRD: The Trustee shall pay to each of said beneficiaries the principal of the share held for his or her benefit, free and discharged from any Trust in or within one (1) year from the date of the death of the last surviving settlor unless this trust is sooner revoked.
>
> FOURTH: In extension and not in limitation of the powers given them by law or other provisions of this instrument the Trustee and any successor or successors shall have the full power with respect to any property in any Trust established hereunder, to deal with the same as if he/she were the owner thereof without order or license of any Court.
>
> FIFTH: The interest of each beneficiary in the income and principal of a trust under this instrument shall be free from the control or interference of any creditor of the beneficiary or any spouse of a married beneficiary and shall not be subject to attachment or susceptible of anticipation or alienation.
>
> SIXTH: This Declaration of Trust is revocable and the Settlor retains the power to alter, amend or revoke this instrument either in whole or in part at any time. Revocation shall be accomplished by a certificate of the Settlor delivered to the Trustee personally or by certified mail.
>
> IN WITNESS WHEREOF _____ and _____, Settlors, and _____, Trustee, have hereunto set their hands and seals this ___ day of _____, 20_____.
>
> In presence of: _____   _____
>   Notary Public   Settlor
>
> _____   _____
>   Notary's Seal   Settlor

FIGURE 36.3 Sample Revocable Trust

Creation of Testamentary Trusts

As previously noted, testamentary trusts are created by a provision in a will and do not take effect until the testator's death. It is the responsibility of executors or executrixes to turn over the trust corpus to the trustees after the death of the testator/settlor after the will has been probated.

Creation of a Resulting Trust

A resulting trust is a trust implied from the intentions of the settlor when an express trust fails. Thus, a resulting trust arises by operation of law and is not expressly created by the settlor. As previously noted, the most common type of a resulting trust is one that results in favor of the settlor when an express trust fails and no other provisions are made by the settlor for the disposition of the trust corpus. For instance, if A creates a trust in favor of B but makes no provisions for what is to happen to the trust corpus upon B's death, a resulting trust will be created by implication when B dies in favor of A or A's estate, the assumption being that the settlor intends to retain a future interest in the property once an express trust ends or fails unless express provisions are made to the contrary.

Creation of a Constructive Trust

Like a resulting trust, a constructive trust arises automatically by operation of law. A constructive trust, in fact, is not a trust at all but rather a legal fiction that the courts engage in so as to prevent unjust enrichment (much like the equitable *quasi contract* theory we have seen in contract law). Whenever persons illegally obtain property that belongs to another, such as by theft, fraud, duress, or by undue influence, a constructive trust comes into effect and holds the person in possession of the property to be a trustee (albeit an unwilling one) for the benefit of the true owner of the property, who is both the constructive settlor and the constructive beneficiary of the trust. A constructive trust is, in effect, a legal remedy available to anyone who is illegally or fraudulently parted from his property to obtain both the return of the property and any gains made to it by the wrongdoer/"trustee" while the property was in his possession.

Termination of Trusts

When a trust terminates depends on such factors as its terms and whether it is a revocable or irrevocable trust. Both revocable and irrevocable trusts automatically terminate upon the accomplishment of their stated purpose, as, for example, the expiration of a set time period or the end of the beneficiary's life (if the trust was set to last for the beneficiary's lifetime). In addition, both revocable and irrevocable trusts end upon the depletion of the trust corpus. Finally, revocable trusts can be terminated at any time by the settlor.

Questions

1. What is a trust?
2. How is a trust created?
3. Does the creation of a trust require a writing?
4. Are trusts generally revocable or irrevocable?
5. How is a Totten trust created?
6. Are Totten trusts revocable? If so, how?
7. How are testamentary trusts created?
8. What is a resulting trust?
9. What is a constructive trust? How does such a trust come into existence?
10. How does a revocable trust terminate?

Hypothetical Cases

1. Alissa verbally tells Barry that she would like him to manage her stock portfolio for Charlie's benefit while Charlie attends college. She signs over all of her stocks to Barry, who agrees to make periodic distributions to Charlie out of the dividend earnings from those stocks and to reconvey these stocks to Alissa when Charlie graduates.
    A. Is a trust created by the above agreement? Assuming for the moment that a trust is created, what type of trust is it?

B. How would you characterize Alissa, Barry, and Charlie with respect to the agreement (assuming for the moment that a valid trust is created)?
C. Assuming a trust is created, what would happen if Charlie dies prior to completing college?
D. Assume for the moment that no trust is created here because a writing is required. If Alissa transfers the stock certificates to Barry under an oral agreement, how would you characterize the arrangement and Barry's obligation thereunder?

2. Michelle opens a savings account with $500 in her own name *in trust for* Michael. In the year that follows, she gets into a bit of a financial bind and withdraws $495 from the account. But when her financial situation improves, she deposits various amounts into the account, with the result that at her death the account contains $150,000. Michelle's only other significant assets at her death are a checking account with $500 in it and an automobile with a market value of $500.
   A. If Michelle dies leaving no living relatives entitled to an intestate distribution, what will Michael be entitled to receive from the account?
   B. If Michelle dies leaving only a daughter and no other living relatives, what would Michael receive? What about the daughter?
   C. What if Michelle has a husband and no other living relatives upon her death?

3. Simeone Settlor called her attorney and told him that she wished to create a trust in favor of her nephew, Simon, for $200,000. She instructed the lawyer (who was also to be the trustee) that she wanted Simon to benefit from the income of the trust during his life, with the corpus to be divided among Simon's children at his death, or, if he dies childless, to the American Heart Association. She further authorized the lawyer, who has a valid power of attorney to act on her behalf, to withdraw the funds from one of her accounts at State Bank. If she dies an hour after the communication with the lawyer, is a valid trust created? Explain fully.

4. Vinnie Victim is swindled out of $10,000 by a con man who invests the money in a speculative venture that results in a ten-fold increase of his investment. Vinnie wants to sue the swindler. What are his rights?

Unit V—Cases for Further Study

SUPREME COURT OF THE UNITED STATES

No. 04–108

SUSETTE KELO, ET AL., PETITIONERS v. CITY OF NEW LONDON, CONNECTICUT, ET AL.

ON WRIT OF CERTIORARI TO THE SUPREME COURT OF CONNECTICUT

545 U. S. 469 (2005)

Opinion of the Court*

I

The city of New London (hereinafter City) sits at the junction of the Thames River and the Long Island Sound in southeastern Connecticut. Decades of economic decline led a state agency in 1990 to designate the City a "distressed municipality." In 1996, the Federal Government closed the Naval Undersea Warfare Center, which had been located in the Fort Trumbull area of the City and had employed over 1,500 people. In 1998, the City's unemployment rate was nearly double that of the State, and its population of just under 24,000 residents was at its lowest since 1920.

These conditions prompted state and local officials to target New London, and particularly its Fort Trumbull area, for economic revitalization. To this end, respondent New London Development Corporation (NLDC), a private nonprofit entity established some years earlier to assist the City in planning economic development, was reactivated. In January 1998, the State authorized a $5.35 million bond issue to support the NLDC's planning activities and a $10 million bond issue toward the creation of a Fort Trumbull State Park. In February, the pharmaceutical company Pfizer Inc. announced that it would build a $300 million research facility on a site immediately adjacent to Fort Trumbull; local planners hoped that Pfizer would draw new business to the area, thereby serving as a catalyst to the area's rejuvenation. After receiving initial approval from the city council, the NLDC continued its planning activities and held a series of neighborhood meetings to educate the public about the process. In May, the city council authorized the NLDC to formally submit its plans to the relevant state agencies for review. Upon obtaining state-level approval, the NLDC finalized an integrated development plan focused on 90 acres of the Fort Trumbull area.

The Fort Trumbull area is situated on a peninsula that juts into the Thames River. The area comprises approximately 115 privately owned properties, as well as the 32 acres of land formerly occupied by the naval facility (Trumbull State Park now occupies 18 of those 32 acres). The development plan encompasses seven parcels. Parcel 1 is designated for a waterfront conference hotel at the center of a "small urban village" that will include restaurants and shopping. This parcel will also have marinas for both recreational and commercial uses. A pedestrian "riverwalk" will originate here and continue down the coast, connecting the waterfront areas of the development. Parcel 2 will be the site of approximately 80 new residences organized into an urban neighborhood and linked by public walkway to the remainder of the development, including the state park. This parcel also includes space reserved for a new U.S. Coast Guard Museum. Parcel 3, which is located immediately north of the Pfizer facility, will contain at least 90,000 square feet of research and development office space. Parcel 4A is a 2.4-acre site that will be used either to support the adjacent state park, by providing parking or retail services for visitors, or to support the nearby marina. Parcel 4B will include a renovated marina, as well as the final stretch of the riverwalk. Parcels 5, 6, and 7 will

---

*Footnotes have been omitted. Some material has been excerpted for the sake of brevity.

provide land for office and retail space, parking, and water-dependent commercial uses. 1 App. 109–113.

The NLDC intended the development plan to capitalize on the arrival of the Pfizer facility and the new commerce it was expected to attract. In addition to creating jobs, generating tax revenue, and helping to "build momentum for the revitalization of downtown New London," id., at 92, the plan was also designed to make the City more attractive and to create leisure and recreational opportunities on the waterfront and in the park.

The city council approved the plan in January 2000, and designated the NLDC as its development agent in charge of implementation. See Conn. Gen. Stat. § 8–188 (2005). The city council also authorized the NLDC to purchase property or to acquire property by exercising eminent domain in the City's name. § 8–193. The NLDC successfully negotiated the purchase of most of the real estate in the 90-acre area, but its negotiations with petitioners failed. As a consequence, in November 2000, the NLDC initiated the condemnation proceedings that gave rise to this case.

II

Petitioner Susette Kelo has lived in the Fort Trumbull area since 1997. She has made extensive improvements to her house, which she prizes for its water view. Petitioner Wilhelmina Dery was born in her Fort Trumbull house in 1918 and has lived there her entire life. Her husband Charles (also a petitioner) has lived in the house since they married some 60 years ago. In all, the nine petitioners own 15 properties in Fort Trumbull—4 in parcel 3 of the development plan and 11 in parcel 4A. Ten of the parcels are occupied by the owner or a family member; the other five are held as investment properties. There is no allegation that any of these properties is blighted or otherwise in poor condition; rather, they were condemned only because they happen to be located in the development area.

In December 2000, petitioners brought this action in the New London Superior Court. They claimed, among other things, that the taking of their properties would violate the "public use" restriction in the Fifth Amendment. After a 7-day bench trial, the Superior Court granted a permanent restraining order prohibiting the taking of the properties located in parcel 4A (park or marina support). It, however, denied petitioners relief as to the properties located in parcel 3 (office space). 2 App. to Pet. for Cert. 343–350.

After the Superior Court ruled, both sides took appeals to the Supreme Court of Connecticut. That court held, over a dissent, that all of the City's proposed takings were valid. It began by upholding the lower court's determination that the takings were authorized by chapter 132, the State's municipal development statute. See Conn. Gen. Stat. § 8–186 et seq. (2005). That statute expresses a legislative determination that the taking of land, even developed land, as part of an economic development project is a "public use" and in the "public interest." 268 Conn., at 18–28, 843 A. 2d, at 515–521. Next, relying on cases such as *Hawaii Housing Authority* v. *Midkiff*, 467 U.S. 229 (1984), and *Berman* v. *Parker*, 348 U.S. 26 (1954), the court held that such economic development qualified as a valid public use under both the Federal and State Constitutions. 268 Conn., at 40, 843 A. 2d, at 527.

Finally, adhering to its precedents, the court went on to determine, first, whether the takings of the particular properties at issue were "reasonably necessary" to achieving the City's intended public use, id., at 82, 843 A. 2d, at 552–553, and, second, whether the takings were for "reasonably foreseeable needs," id., at 93, 843 A. 2d, at 558–559. The court upheld the trial court's factual findings as to parcel 3, but reversed the trial court as to parcel 4A, agreeing with the City that the intended use of this land was sufficiently definite and had been given "reasonable attention" during the planning process. Id., at 120–121, 843 A. 2d, at 574.

The three dissenting justices would have imposed a "heightened" standard of judicial review for takings justified by economic development. Although they agreed that the plan was intended to serve a valid public use, they would have found all the takings unconstitutional because the City had failed to adduce "clear and convincing evidence" that the economic benefits of the plan would in fact come to pass. Id., at 144, 146, 843 A. 2d, at 587, 588 (Zarella, J., joined by Sullivan, C. J., and Katz, J., concurring in part and dissenting in part).

We granted certiorari to determine whether a city's decision to take property for the purpose of economic development satisfies the "public use" requirement of the Fifth Amendment. 542 U.S. ___ (2004).

III

Two polar propositions are perfectly clear. On the one hand, it has long been accepted that the sovereign may not take the property of *A* for the sole purpose of transferring it to another private party *B*, even though *A* is paid just compensation. On the other hand, it is equally clear that a State may transfer property from one private party to another if future "use by the public" is the purpose of the taking; the condemnation of land for a railroad with common-carrier duties is a familiar example. Neither of these propositions, however, determines the disposition of this case.

As for the first proposition, the City would no doubt be forbidden from taking petitioners' land for the purpose of conferring a private benefit on a particular private party. See *Midkiff*, 467 U.S., at 245 ("A purely private taking could not withstand the scrutiny of the public use requirement; it would serve no legitimate purpose of government and would thus be void"); *Missouri Pacific R. Co.* v. *Nebraska,* 164 U.S. 403 (1896). Nor would the City be allowed to take property under the mere pretext of a public purpose, when its actual purpose was to bestow a private benefit. The takings before us, however, would be executed pursuant to a "carefully considered" development plan. 268 Conn., at 54, 843 A. 2d, at 536. The trial judge and all the members of the Supreme Court of Connecticut agreed that there was no evidence of an illegitimate purpose in this case. Therefore, as was true of the statute challenged in *Midkiff*, 467 U.S., at 245, the City's development plan was not adopted "to benefit a particular class of identifiable individuals."

On the other hand, this is not a case in which the City is planning to open the condemned land—at least not in its entirety—to use by the general public. Nor will the private lessees of the land in any sense be required to operate like common carriers, making their services available to all comers. But although such a projected use would be sufficient to satisfy the public use requirement, this "Court long ago rejected any literal requirement that condemned property be put into use for the general public." *Id.*, at 244. Indeed, while many state courts in the mid-19th century endorsed "use by the public" as the proper definition of public use, that narrow view steadily eroded over time. Not only was the "use by the public" test difficult to administer (*e.g.*, what proportion of the public need have access to the property? at what price?), but it proved to be impractical given the diverse and always evolving needs of society. Accordingly, when this Court began applying the Fifth Amendment to the States at the close of the 19th century, it embraced the broader and more natural interpretation of public use as "public purpose." See, *e.g.*, *Fallbrook Irrigation Dist.* v. *Bradley*, 164 U.S. 112, 158–164 (1896). Thus, in a case upholding a mining company's use of an aerial bucket line to transport ore over property it did not own, Justice Holmes' opinion for the Court stressed "the inadequacy of use by the general public as a universal test." *Strickley* v. *Highland Boy Gold Mining Co.*, 200 U.S. 527, 531 (1906). We have repeatedly and consistently rejected that narrow test ever since.

The disposition of this case therefore turns on the question whether the City's development plan serves a "public purpose." Without exception, our cases have defined that concept broadly, reflecting our longstanding policy of deference to legislative judgments in this field.

In *Berman* v. *Parker*, 348 U.S. 26 (1954), this Court upheld a redevelopment plan targeting a blighted area of Washington, D.C., in which most of the housing for the area's 5,000 inhabitants was beyond repair. Under the plan, the area would be condemned and part of it utilized for the construction of streets, schools, and other public facilities. The remainder of the land would be leased or sold to private parties for the purpose of redevelopment, including the construction of low-cost housing.

The owner of a department store located in the area challenged the condemnation, pointing out that his store was not itself blighted and arguing that the creation of a "better balanced, more attractive community" was not a valid public use. *Id.*, at 31. Writing for a unanimous Court, Justice Douglas refused to evaluate this claim in isolation, deferring instead to the legislative and agency judgment that the area "must be planned as a whole" for the plan to be successful. *Id.*, at 34. The Court explained that "community redevelopment programs need not, by force of the Constitution, be on a piecemeal basis—lot by lot, building by building." *Id.*, at 35. The public use underlying the taking was unequivocally affirmed:

"We do not sit to determine whether a particular housing project is or is not desirable. The concept of the public welfare is broad and inclusive. . . . The values it represents are spiritual as well as physical, aesthetic as well as monetary. It is within the power of the legislature to determine that the community should be beautiful as well as healthy, spacious as well as clean, well-balanced as well as carefully patrolled. In the present case, the Congress and its authorized agencies have made determinations that take into account a wide variety of values. It is not for us to reappraise them. If those who govern the District of Columbia decide that the Nation's Capital should be beautiful as well as sanitary, there is nothing in the Fifth Amendment that stands in the way." *Id.*, at 33.

In *Hawaii Housing Authority* v. *Midkiff*, 467 U.S. 229 (1984), the Court considered a Hawaii statute whereby fee title was taken from lessors and transferred to lessees (for just compensation) in order to reduce the concentration of land ownership. We unanimously upheld the statute and rejected the Ninth Circuit's view that it was "a naked attempt on the part of the state of Hawaii to take the property of A and transfer it to B solely for B's private use and benefit." *Id.*, at 235 (internal quotation marks omitted). Reaffirming *Berman*'s deferential approach to legislative judgments in this field, we concluded that the State's purpose of eliminating the "social and economic evils of a land oligopoly" qualified as a valid public use. 467 U.S., at 241–242. Our opinion also rejected the contention that the mere fact that the State immediately transferred the properties to private individuals upon condemnation somehow diminished the public character of the taking. "[I]t is only the taking's purpose, and not its mechanics," we explained, that matters in determining public use. *Id.*, at 244.

In that same Term we decided another public use case that arose in a purely economic context. In *Ruckelshaus* v. *Monsanto, Co.*, 467 U.S. 986 (1984), the Court dealt with provisions of the Federal Insecticide, Fungicide, and Rodenticide Act under which the Environmental Protection Agency could consider the data (including trade secrets) submitted by a prior pesticide applicant in evaluating a subsequent application, so long as the second applicant paid just compensation for the data. We acknowledged that the "most direct beneficiaries" of these provisions were the subsequent applicants, *id.*, at 1014, but we nevertheless upheld the statute under *Berman* and *Midkiff*. We found sufficient Congress' belief that sparing applicants the cost of time-consuming research eliminated a significant barrier to entry in the pesticide market and thereby enhanced competition. 467 U.S., at 1015.

Viewed as a whole, our jurisprudence has recognized that the needs of society have varied between different parts of the Nation, just as they have evolved over time in response to changed circumstances. Our earliest cases in particular embodied a strong theme of federalism, emphasizing the "great respect" that we owe to state legislatures and state courts in discerning local public needs. See *Hairston* v. *Danville & Western R. Co.*, 208 U.S. 598, 606–607 (1908) (noting that these needs were likely to vary depending on a State's "resources, the capacity of the soil, the relative importance of industries to the general public welfare, and the long-established methods and habits of the people"). For more than a century, our public use jurisprudence has wisely eschewed rigid formulas and intrusive scrutiny in favor of affording legislatures broad latitude in determining what public needs justify the use of the takings power.

IV

Those who govern the City were not confronted with the need to remove blight in the Fort Trumbull area, but their determination that the area was sufficiently distressed to justify a program of economic rejuvenation is entitled to our deference. The City has carefully formulated an economic development plan that it believes will provide appreciable benefits to the community, including—but by no means limited to—new jobs and increased tax revenue. As with other exercises in urban planning and development, the City is endeavoring to coordinate a variety of commercial, residential, and recreational uses of land, with the hope that they will form a whole greater than the sum of its parts. To effectuate this plan, the City has invoked a state statute that specifically authorizes the use of eminent domain to promote economic development. Given the comprehensive character of the plan, the thorough deliberation that preceded its adoption, and the limited scope of our review, it is appropriate for us, as it was in *Berman*, to resolve the challenges of the individual owners, not on a piecemeal basis, but rather in light of the entire plan. Because that plan unquestionably serves a public purpose, the takings challenged here satisfy the public use requirement of the Fifth Amendment.

To avoid this result, petitioners urge us to adopt a new bright-line rule that economic development does not qualify as a public use. Putting aside the unpersuasive suggestion that the City's plan will provide only purely economic benefits, neither precedent nor logic supports petitioners' proposal. Promoting economic development is a traditional and long accepted function of government. There is, moreover, no principled way of distinguishing economic development from the other public purposes that we have recognized. In our cases upholding takings that facilitated agriculture and mining, for example, we emphasized the importance of those industries to the welfare of the States in question, see, *e.g., Strickley*, 200 U.S. 527; in *Berman*, we endorsed the purpose of transforming a blighted area into a "well-balanced" community through redevelopment, 348 U.S., at 33; in *Midkiff*, we upheld the interest in breaking up a land oligopoly that "created artificial deterrents to the normal functioning of the State's residential land market," 467 U.S., at 242; and in *Monsanto*, we accepted Congress' purpose of eliminating a "significant barrier to entry in the pesticide market," 467 U.S., at 1014–1015. It would be incongruous to hold that the City's interest in the economic benefits to be derived from the development of the Fort Trumbull area has less of a public character than any of those other interests. Clearly, there is no basis for exempting economic development from our traditionally broad understanding of public purpose.

Petitioners contend that using eminent domain for economic development impermissibly blurs the boundary between public and private takings. Again, our cases foreclose this objection. Quite simply, the government's pursuit of a public purpose will often benefit individual private parties. For example, in *Midkiff*, the forced transfer of property conferred a direct and significant benefit on those lessees who were previously unable to purchase their homes. In *Monsanto*, we recognized that the "most direct beneficiaries" of the data-sharing provisions were the subsequent pesticide applicants, but benefiting them in this way was necessary to promoting competition in the pesticide market. 467 U.S., at 1014. The owner of the department store in *Berman* objected to "taking from one businessman for the benefit of another businessman," 348 U.S., at 33, referring to the fact that under the redevelopment plan land would be leased or sold to private developers for redevelopment. Our rejection of that contention has particular relevance to the instant case: "The public end may be as well or better served through an agency of private enterprise than through a department of government—or so the Congress might conclude. We cannot say that public ownership is the sole method of promoting the public purposes of community redevelopment projects." *Id.*, at 34.

It is further argued that without a bright-line rule nothing would stop a city from transferring citizen *A*'s property to citizen *B* for the sole reason that citizen *B* will put the property to a more productive use and thus pay more taxes. Such a one-to-one transfer of property, executed outside the confines of an integrated development plan, is not presented in this case. While such an unusual exercise of government power would certainly raise a suspicion that a private purpose was afoot, the hypothetical cases posited by petitioners can be confronted if and when they arise. They do not warrant the crafting of an artificial restriction on the concept of public use.

Alternatively, petitioners maintain that for takings of this kind we should require a "reasonable certainty" that the expected public benefits will actually accrue. Such a rule, however, would represent an even greater departure from our precedent. "When the legislature's purpose is legitimate and its means are not irrational, our cases make clear that empirical debates over the wisdom of takings—no less than debates over the wisdom of other kinds of socioeconomic legislation—are not to be carried out in the federal courts." *Midkiff,* 467 U.S., at 242. Indeed, earlier this Term we explained why similar practical concerns (among others) undermined the use of the "substantially advances" formula in our regulatory takings doctrine. See *Lingle* v. *Chevron U.S. A. Inc.*, 544 U.S. ___, ___ (2005) (slip op., at 14–15) (noting that this formula "would empower—and might often require—courts to substitute their predictive judgments for those of elected legislatures and expert agencies"). The disadvantages of a heightened form of review are especially pronounced in this type of case. Orderly implementation of a comprehensive redevelopment plan obviously requires that the legal rights of all interested parties be established before new construction can be commenced. A constitutional rule that required postponement of the judicial approval of every condemnation until the likelihood of success of the plan had been assured would unquestionably impose a significant impediment to the successful consummation of many such plans.

Just as we decline to second-guess the City's considered judgments about the efficacy of its development plan, we also decline to second-guess the City's determinations as to what lands it needs to acquire in order to effectuate the project. "It is not for the courts to oversee the choice of the boundary line nor to sit in review on the size of a particular project area. Once the question of the public purpose has been decided, the amount and character of land to be taken for the project and the need for a particular tract to complete the integrated plan rests in the discretion of the legislative branch." *Berman,* 348 U.S., at 35–36.

In affirming the City's authority to take petitioners' properties, we do not minimize the hardship that condemnations may entail, notwithstanding the payment of just compensation. We emphasize that nothing in our opinion precludes any State from placing further restrictions on its exercise of the takings power. Indeed, many States already impose "public use" requirements that are stricter than the federal baseline. Some of these requirements have been established as a matter of state constitutional law, while others are expressed in state eminent domain statutes that carefully limit the grounds upon which takings may be exercised. As the submissions of the parties and their *amici* make clear, the necessity and wisdom of using eminent domain to promote economic development are certainly matters of legitimate public debate. This Court's authority, however, extends only to determining whether the City's proposed condemnations are for a "public use" within the meaning of the Fifth Amendment to the Federal Constitution. Because over a century of our case law interpreting that provision dictates an affirmative answer to that question, we may not grant petitioners the relief that they seek.

The judgment of the Supreme Court of Connecticut is affirmed.

It is so ordered.

Optional Assignments

1. Brief the preceding abbreviated version of the case in a one- to two-page, single-spaced brief (with double spaces between paragraphs) that contains the following four sections: (1) The basic facts of the case [Facts]; (2) The legal issue the court is being asked to decide [Issue]; (3) The holding of the court (how it decides the legal issue before it) [Holding]; and (4) The rationale the court uses to support its decision [Rationale]. If your instructor asks you to brief the case, she will give you additional instructions.

2. Do you agree or disagree with the opinion? Why?

SCHOENHOLZ v. HINZMAN
Supreme Court of Kansas.
295 Kan. 786 (2012)
[Case excerpt]

The opinion of the court was delivered by ROSEN, J.:

This is an unfortunate story of a business and familial relationship gone bad. Rodney Schoenholz entered into an oral agreement with his sister, Janine Hinzman, for the bailment of farm animals and farm equipment on her land. Four years after their cooperative effort to breed horses broke down, Hinzman sold her farm and the horses. Schoenholz subsequently retrieved most of his equipment from the farm and sued Hinzman for conversion and breach of the bailment contract. Hinzman counterclaimed for the expenses of maintaining the equipment and caring for the horses.

The district court awarded no damages. The Court of Appeals affirmed the rulings against Schoenholz but found the district court had erred in denying Hinzman compensation for caring for some of the horses and had abused its discretion in denying sanctions against Schoenholz. We disagree with the principal parts of the Court of Appeals' decision and remand the case to the district court for further proceedings.

The dates and substance of the parties' actions are significant to our analysis. In 1999, Schoenholz and Hinzman orally agreed to operate a joint horse-breeding enterprise. Schoenholz was to provide breeding horses, and Hinzman was to take care of the horses on her farm and would promote breeding with her own horses. Schoenholz would store equipment, including a tractor, and materials on her farm to aid in the enterprise, and the two would evenly split the proceeds from the sale of the horses.

In August 2002, after an argument about payments, Schoenholz and Hinzman ended the joint enterprise, and Schoenholz agreed to remove his animals from the farm by April 2003. As of April 2003, he had removed neither his horses nor his equipment. He did not remove any of his equipment other than his tractor until 2007. He explained that he refused to retrieve his property because he had no place to store it.

Hinzman stopped using the tractor in 2003, and it sat idle on her farm for more than 3 years until Schoenholz retrieved it at the end of 2006. Hinzman provided all the care for the horses, including not only the original horses that Schoenholz had provided but also the unsold offspring of those horses, from April 2003 until she sold them.

One of Schoenholz' horses, World Ruler, developed health problems and had to be quarantined. Hinzman initially boarded World Ruler at her daughter's farm, and then moved the horse to her own farm for a period of 1,260 days after April 2003.

The parties had multiple conversations during which Hinzman complained about Schoenholz storing his equipment on her farm. During the course of one of these discussions, when Hinzman asked him to remove the horses and equipment, Schoenholz struck Hinzman, and he was charged with battery.

On September 22, 2006, Schoenholz entered into a diversion agreement for the battery, one condition of which was that he would "remove all of his personal property, of whatever kind, from the victim's residence . . . within sixty (60) days of the signing of the diversion." A provision was made that he would "be accompanied by law enforcement if deemed appropriate by the victim." On August 6, 2007, the State filed a motion to dismiss the charges with prejudice based on Schoenholz' alleged satisfaction of the terms of the diversion agreement. The district court granted the motion, even though Schoenholz had not removed his property from his sister's farm.

Finally, in 2006, Hinzman sold her farm and the horses. In 2007, after Hinzman had turned the farm over to a new owner, Schoenholz removed his property from the farm.

On May 3, 2007, Schoenholz filed a petition in district court seeking damages for horses that were not returned, depreciation of the tractor, and loss of fencing materials, a bale fork and link, and other farm-related materials. Hinzman filed an answer and counterclaim for the costs associated with storing Schoenholz' equipment and caring for his horses. Following unsuccessful motions for summary judgment and sanctions, a trial was held on January 24–25, 2008. The district court essentially ruled against both parties on all claims and counterclaims, as well as on requests for sanctions.

The Court of Appeals, in an unpublished opinion, affirmed the district court in denying Schoenholz' claims but reversed the district court's finding that Hinzman was not entitled to damages for the care of the horses and in finding that Hinzman was not entitled to costs for violations of a discovery order. *Schoenholz v. Hinzman,* No. 101,063, 2010 WL 445693 (Kan.App.2010) (unpublished opinion).

Schoenholz filed a petition for review, which this court granted. Hinzman did not file a petition for review of the issues on her cross-appeal.

Preliminary Discussion of the Law of Farm Bailments and Gratuitous Bailments

Although the parties did not base their claims on or address the statutory scheme, the Kansas Legislature has enacted several statutes that govern bailments of livestock and unpaid costs for feeding and caring for that livestock. K.S.A. 58-207 *et seq.* has been in effect, with only minor modifications, since 1868.

As a general principle, a statutory remedy will supersede a common-law remedy so long as the statute provides an adequate substitute remedy. [Citation omitted.] For this reason, we must examine the parties' claims and counterclaims in light of the statutory requirements, notwithstanding the parties' arguments that are grounded in the common law.

K.S.A. 58-207 establishes a lien on boarded livestock and allows a bailee of horses to sell the horses if the bailor fails to pay for their feed and care for 60 days after a demand is made:

> "The keepers of livery stables, *and all others engaged in feeding horses,* cattle, hogs, or other livestock, *shall have a lien upon such property for the feed and care* bestowed by them upon the same, *and if reasonable or stipulated charges for such feed and care be not paid within sixty (60) days after the same becomes due, the property, or so much thereof as may be necessary to pay such charges and the expenses of publication and sale, may be sold as provided in this act: Provided, however,* That any lien created by this act may be assigned." (Emphasis added.)

K.S.A. 58-208 allows a bailee to sell goods left in the possession of the bailee for more than 6 months, if there is a lien on the goods and if the bailee properly advertises the sale:

> "*Any* forwarding merchant, warehouse keeper, stage, express or railway company, hotelkeeper, carrier, or other *bailee* not hereinbefore named, *having a lien upon goods which may have remained in store or in the possession of such bailee for six months or more, may proceed to sell such goods,* or so much thereof as may be necessary to pay the amount of the lien and expenses, according to the provisions of this act: *Provided, That such sale may be advertised* and made by any carrier in any city of the first, second or third class through which its line runs, where, in the judgment of such carrier, the best price can be obtained for the property to be sold." (Emphasis added.)

K.S.A. 58-209 allows a bailee of livestock and perishable property to dispose of the property in order to pay for the expenses of maintaining the livestock or other perishable property 30 days after charges for the upkeep become due:

> "*If the property bailed or kept be horses,* cattle, hogs, or other livestock, or is of a perishable nature and will be greatly injured by delay, or be insufficient to pay such charges for any further keeping, *the person to whom such charges may be due may, after the expiration of thirty days from the time when such charges shall have become due, proceed to dispose of so much of such property as may be necessary to pay such charges and expenses* as herein provided." (Emphasis added.)

K.S.A. 58-211 requires the bailee to provide *written notice* to the bailor before disposing of property if the name and residence of the owner is known:

> "*Before any such property shall be sold, if the name and residence of the owner thereof is known, notice of such sale shall be given the owner in writing,* either personally or by mail, or by leaving a notice in writing at such person's residence or place of doing business. If the name and residence is not known, the person having the possession of such property shall cause a notice of the time and place of sale, and containing a description of the property, to be published at least once a week for three consecutive weeks in a newspaper, if there is one published in the county where such sale is advertised to take place, and if there is no newspaper published in such county, then the notice shall be published in some newspaper of general circulation in such county. If the value of the property does not exceed $100, such notice may be given by written or printed handbills posted in at least five public places in the township or city where the bailee resides or the sale is to take place, one of which shall be in a conspicuous part of the bailee's place of business. *Notices given under this section shall state that if the amount due with storage keeping and sale costs is not paid within 15 days from the date of mailing, personally giving or posting of the notice (as the case may be), the property will be sold at public auction.*" (Emphasis added.)

Hinzman fell within the provisions of these statutes. She had the option of selling Schoenholz' horses, or shares of horses, but only after she had made a demand for the reasonable costs of upkeep and only after providing printed notice of the sale. She did not follow the statutory mandates for disposing of the horses, and, as a consequence, she incurred certain ongoing responsibilities for taking care of them.

* * *

Damages for the Tractor

Schoenholz sought damages for the alleged deterioration of the tractor that he left sitting out in the open on Hinzman's farm. The district court found that the parties created an implied bailment of the tractor in 1999 when Hinzman accepted the use of the tractor on her farm and allowed Schoenholz to leave the tractor on her premises. The court then noted a legal presumption that the bailee is at fault if bailment property is damaged while in the exclusive possession and control of the bailee. The court found that the tractor suffered damage between 1999 and 2006 and that the tractor was not used after the spring of 2003 by either party. The district court concluded, however, that there was no evidence of when the damage occurred to the tractor and the statute of limitations barred any recovery for the deterioration. The Court of Appeals agreed that the statute of limitations had run for any negligence claim with respect to the tractor.

As with the horses, Hinzman allowed Schoenholz to keep his tractor on her farm. Although the tractor was not the subject of a lien statute as the horses were, she did not forfeit her status as a bailee simply because Schoenholz did not retrieve or maintain his tractor. Her bailee status did not, however, oblige her to take positive steps to keep the tractor in the same condition in which Schoenholz left it.

A gratuitous bailee is not liable for any injury arising from "nonfeasance," that is, from inaction. [Citation omitted.] Hinzman was not under a special duty to service the tractor and move it to some sheltered place different from where her brother had left it. She was therefore not liable for any loss in value that the tractor may have suffered. While the district court erred in finding that the statute of limitations barred recovery, we affirm the conclusion that Schoenholz was not entitled to damages to the tractor as having been right for the wrong reason. [Citation omitted.]

* * *

The judgment of the Court of Appeals is affirmed in part and reversed in part. The judgment of the district court is affirmed in part, reversed in part, and remanded with directions.

Optional Assignments

1. Brief the preceding abbreviated version of the case in a one- to two-page, single-spaced brief (with double spaces between paragraphs) that contains the following four sections: (1) The basic facts of the case [Facts]; (2) The legal issue the court is being asked to decide [Issue]; (3) The holding of the court (how it decides the legal issue before it) [Holding]; and (4) The rationale the court uses to support its decision [Rationale]. If your instructor asks you to brief the case, he will give you additional instructions.

2. Leaving the question of law aside for the moment, does the case obtain a just result? Explain.

IN THE MATTER OF THE ESTATE OF RAY MERLE BURTON. VICTOR WHITE, APPELLANT, V. RICHARD DIDRICKSEN, RESPONDENT.

No. 46441-1-II

COURT OF APPEALS OF WASHINGTON, DIVISION TWO

June 30, 2015, Oral Argument
August 18, 2015, Filed

[Case excerpt]

PRIOR HISTORY: Appeal from Pierce County Superior Court. Docket No: 14-4-00545-1. Judge signing: Honorable Ronald E Culpepper. Judgment or order under review. Date filed: 05/30/2014.

SUMMARY:

WASHINGTON OFFICIAL REPORTS SUMMARY
Nature of Action: A decedent's former assistant and caretaker claimed that he was willed the decedent's estate under testamentary documents that were drafted and signed by the decedent at different times and that were witnessed and signed by separate individuals. The decedent's cousin and legal heir moved for an order declaring that the decedent died intestate.

Superior Court: The Superior Court for Pierce County, No. 14-4-00545-1, Ronald E. Culpepper, J., on May 30, 2014, entered an order declaring that the decedent died intestate.

Court of Appeals: Holding that the decedent's testamentary documents did not constitute a valid will because they did not satisfy statutory attestation requirements, the court affirms the trial court's order.

JUDGES: Authored by Bradley A. Maxa. Concurring: Linda Cj Lee, Lisa Sutton.

OPINION BY: Bradley A. Maxa

OPINION

1 Maxa, J. — Victor White appeals the trial court's order declaring that Ray Burton died intestate. RCW 11.12.020(1) states that wills must be signed by the testator and attested by two witnesses to be valid. White submitted evidence that Burton drafted and signed a document leaving his entire estate to White. The document was signed by one witness, but subsequently was lost. Burton later drafted a second, purportedly similar, document leaving his entire estate to White. That document was signed by a different witness. Richard Didricksen, Burton's legal heir, challenges the validity of the document under RCW 11.12.020(1). White argues that because two witnesses attested to Burton's testamentary intent to leave his estate to White, the documents together constituted a validly executed will under both strict compliance and substantial compliance theories.

¶2 We hold that Burton's testamentary documents do not constitute a valid will because Burton did not strictly comply with the requirement in RCW 11.12.020(1) that two witnesses attest to a will. We also hold that even assuming the substantial compliance doctrine applies to RCW 11.12.020(1), Burton did not substantially comply with the attestation requirement. Accordingly, we affirm the trial court's order declaring that Burton died intestate. [Footnote omitted.]

FACTS

¶3 Burton was a successful businessman with substantial assets, including two gold mines and a number of collectible cars. He allegedly was estranged from his living relatives and considered himself without family. Beginning in 2011, White helped the elderly Burton with a variety of tasks around his home. At some point, Burton allegedly began to prepare White to take over his business dealings after he died. Burton was hospitalized for pneumonia in 2013, and after his release White became his caretaker. Burton also received home nurse visits, and later hospice care. Throughout this time, Burton apparently had no will.

¶4 Shortly before he died, Burton handwrote and signed a document in red ink that was witnessed and signed by Lisa Erickson, a nurse. Erickson stated in a declaration that the document was for the purpose of Burton leaving his property to White. However, Erickson provided no testimony regarding the actual language used in that document, and she does not know what happened to the document.

¶5 The day before he died, Burton handwrote another testamentary statement, again in red ink, on a blank portion of a preprinted healthcare directive form. He apparently needed some assistance from another nurse, Shirley Outson, to complete the writing. The final statement, which is difficult to read, appears to state:

Thank [Footnote omitted] Victor White remain my caretaker til I go to sleep/die. The transfer of Gold Mines Montecarlo and Black Hawk One, all my collector cars and real estate located at 36619 Mountain Hwy E, Eatonville, WA 98320. I wish all my worldly possessions to go to Victor White.

Clerk's Papers at 13. Burton signed the form below the statement, as did Outson. But no other witness signed the document.

¶6 Burton died on January 25, 2014. White petitioned the trial court to recognize Burton's statement on the healthcare directive form as his will and to name White as personal representative of Burton's estate. Didricksen, Burton's cousin and legal heir, moved for an order declaring that Burton died intestate. The trial court granted Didricksen's motion, finding that Burton had not executed a valid will and therefore had died intestate. White moved for reconsideration, which the trial court denied. In denying White's motion for reconsideration, the trial court noted that White was free to pursue other legal remedies.

¶7 White appeals the trial court's order declaring that Burton died intestate and its denial of his motion to reconsider that order.

ANALYSIS

A. Strict Compliance with Two Witness Requirement

¶8 White argues that the trial court erred by concluding that Burton died intestate because Burton complied with the requirements of RCW 11.12.020(1) and executed a valid will by creating two equivalent documents, each witnessed by a different person. We disagree. [Footnote omitted.]

1. Standard of Review

¶9 White challenges the trial court's legal conclusion that Burton's testamentary documents did not comply with RCW 11.12.020(1). We review a trial court's conclusions of law de novo. In re Estate of Jones, 152 Wn.2d 1, 8-9, 93 P.3d 147 (2004). We also review questions of statutory interpretation de novo. Id.

¶10 If the plain meaning of a statute is unambiguous, we apply that plain meaning as an expression of legislative intent without considering extrinsic sources. Jametsky v. Olsen, 179 Wn.2d 756, 762, 317 P.3d 1003 (2014). We give words their usual and ordinary meaning and interpret them in the context of the statute in which they appear. Lake v. Woodcreek Homeowners Ass'n, 169 Wn.2d 516, 526, 243 P.3d 1283 (2010).

2. No Strict Compliance

¶11 RCW 11.12.020(1) requires that a will meet three basic formalities:

Every will shall be [1] in writing [2] signed by the testator or by some other person under the testator's direction in the testator's presence, and shall be [3] attested by two or more competent witnesses, by subscribing their names to the will, or by signing an affidavit that complies with RCW 11.20.020(2), while in the presence of the testator and at the testator's direction or request.

Attestation by two witnesses always is required, and Washington does not recognize "holographic" wills.[*] In re Brown's Estate, 101 Wash. 314, 317, 172 P. 247 (1918).

¶12 White argues that the healthcare directive document is a valid will that complies with the two witness requirement. But that document was signed by only one witness. Therefore, on its face the document does not comply with RCW 11.12.020(1).

¶13 However, White argues that two witnesses did attest to Burton's will. White claims that they attested to the will in counterparts, separately signing two counterpart documents describing the same testamentary gift. White notes that nothing in RCW 11.12.020(1) prohibits executing a will in counterparts and that no Washington cases address this situation.

¶14 Even if we assume that witnesses can attest to a will in counterparts, the facts here show that Burton's witnesses did not sign counterpart documents. A "counterpart" is "one of two corresponding copies of a legal instrument"; a synonym is "duplicate." Webster's Third New

---

[*] Only nuncupative wills—restricted to members of the armed forces or merchant marine and testamentary gifts of personal property amounting to $1,000 or less—are exempt from some of these formality requirements. RCW 11.12.025.5 HN8A holographic will is a will handwritten, dated, and signed by the testator that may be validated on the basis of the testator's handwriting rather than any witness attestations. See In re Bauer's Estate, 5 Wn.2d 165, 171, 105 P.2d 11 (1940). In his petition to the trial court, White characterized the healthcare directive document as a holographic will. However, he does not argue on appeal that the document was valid as a holographic will and appears to recognize that Washington courts will not give effect to such wills.

Int'l Dictionary, 520 (2002). Here, there is no evidence that Burton prepared duplicative copies of any testamentary document. The witnesses stated that the two handwritten testamentary documents both left Burton's entire estate to White, but neither witness stated that the documents were identical. Having one witness sign one testamentary document and having another witness sign a different testamentary document does not constitute signing one document in counterparts.

¶15 White also argues that the two documents must be viewed as a single integrated document that was signed by two witnesses. However, even if we assume that these documents somehow formed a single will, there were no witnesses that signed that will. Erickson and Outson each signed a portion of the will, but neither witnessed the "integrated" document.

¶16 Without evidence that two witnesses signed the same document, or at least identical duplicates of that document, White cannot show that Burton complied with RCW 11.12.020(1). Because only one witness signed the healthcare directive document—the only testamentary writing signed by Burton in the record—we hold that Burton did not strictly comply with the two witness requirement in RCW 11.12.020(1).

B. Substantial Compliance

¶17 White argues that even if Burton did not strictly comply with the two witness requirement in RCW 11.12.020(1), we should conclude that he executed a valid will because he substantially complied with that requirement. We disagree.

1. Legal Principles

¶18 Under the substantial compliance doctrine a party complies with statutory requirements by "satisfaction of the substance essential to the purpose of the statute." Crosby v. Spokane County, 137 Wn.2d 296, 302, 971 P.2d 32 (1999); accord In re Santore, 28 Wn. App. 319, 327, 623 P.2d 702 (1981). Courts may invoke the doctrine where a party has "substantially complied with the requirements crucial to the underlying design intended by the legislature." Murphy v. Campbell Inv. Co., 79 Wn.2d 417, 422, 486 P.2d 1080 (1971). However, some statutes are not susceptible to substantial compliance. See, e.g., Medina v. Pub. Utility Dist. No. 1 of Benton County, 147 Wn.2d 303, 317-18, 53 P.3d 993 (2002) (failure to comply with a statutory time limitation cannot be considered substantial compliance with the statute).

2. Substantial Compliance and RCW 11.12.020(1)

¶19 Washington courts have not applied the substantial compliance doctrine to the requirements of RCW 11.12.020(1). The only Washington case that even mentions substantial compliance with regard to RCW 11.12.020(1) is In Re Estate of Ricketts, 54 Wn. App. 221, 773 P.2d 93 (1989). In that case, the two witnesses to a will codicil did not subscribe their names to the codicil, but instead signed an affidavit that was stapled to it. Id. at 221. It was undisputed that this procedure did not strictly conform with the requirements of the version of RCW 11.12.020(1) then in effect.[Footnote omitted.] Id. at 222. But the proponent of the will cited to a number of cases approving probate of wills despite irregularities in the placement of witnesses' signatures. Id. at 223.

¶20 The court in Ricketts discussed an Oklahoma case in which a will was admitted to probate when the testator signed at the end of the will near the bottom of the page and the subscribing witnesses signed on the following page. Id. The court stated that the record in that case "show[ed] much more substantial compliance with the requirements for execution than here present." Id. at 224.

¶21 Ricketts could be interpreted as accepting the notion that a testator can comply with RCW 11.12.020(1) through substantial compliance. However, the court did not specifically address that issue and in fact did not find substantial compliance. Instead, the court applied the requirements of RCW 11.12.020(1) and reversed the trial court's decision to admit the codicil to probate. Id. at 225.

¶22 Regardless of the significance of Ricketts, in order to assess the merits of the present case we assume without deciding that the substantial compliance doctrine applies to RCW 11.12.020(1).

3. Substantial Compliance with Will Validity Provisions

¶23 Even assuming that substantial compliance is sufficient to satisfy the two witness requirement of RCW 11.12.020(1), Didricksen argues that there was no substantial compliance here. We agree.

¶24 The deficiency with Burton's testamentary documents was more than merely technical or procedural. The fundamental problem is that only Erickson saw and witnessed the first document and only Outson saw and witnessed the second, different document. If Erickson and Outson had seen an identical document but both signatures for some reason were not on that document, White's substantial compliance argument might be more compelling. But the fact that Erickson and Outson signed different documents precludes any finding of substantial compliance of the requirement in RCW 11.12.020(1) that two witnesses attest to the will.

¶25 Applying substantial compliance here also would work against the purposes of RCW 11.12.020. The statutory purposes underlying the formality requirements of the statute are "to ensure that the testator has a definite and complete intention to dispose of his or her property and to prevent, as far as possible, fraud, perjury, mistake and the chance of one instrument being substituted for another." In re Estate of Malloy, 134 Wn.2d 316, 322-23, 949 P.2d 804 (1998). Here, the risk of mistake—if not fraud—would be high if we allowed probate of a testamentary document signed by only one witness when the second "witness" never saw that document.

¶26 We hold that under the facts of this case, Burton's healthcare directive document did not substantially comply with RCW 11.12.020(1).

C. Attorney Fees

¶27 Didricksen requests an award of reasonable attorney fees under the Trust and Estate Dispute Resolution Act (TEDRA), chapter 11.96A RCW. We decline to award Didricksen attorney fees.

¶28 Under RCW 11.96A.150, we have discretion to award reasonable attorney fees in cases involving a decedent's estate. See Kitsap Bank v. Denley, 177 Wn. App. 559, 580-81, 582, 312 P.3d 711 (2013). Although this is not a TEDRA case, the TEDRA attorney fee provision applies to "'[a]ll matters concerning the estates and assets of . . . deceased persons.'" Id. (quoting RCW 11.96A.020(1)(a)). In exercising our discretion, we "may consider any and all factors that [we] deem to be relevant and appropriate." RCW 11.96A.150(1).

¶29 Here, the evidence suggests that White is acting to enforce Burton's testamentary intent. And this is not a frivolous appeal—it raises a novel issue of law. Such appeals should not be discouraged by awarding attorney fees to an opponent if the court decides the issue in that opponent's favor. Cf. Bale v. Allison, 173 Wn. App. 435, 461, 294 P.3d 789 (2013) (declining to award attorney fees on appeal because the case involved a unique issue). Under the circumstances, we do not award Didricksen attorney fees on appeal.

¶30 We affirm the trial court's order declaring that Burton died intestate.

Lee and Sutton, JJ., concur.

Optional Assignments

1. Brief the preceding abbreviated version of the case in a one- to two-page, single-spaced brief (with double spaces between paragraphs) that contains the following four sections: (1) The basic facts of the case [Facts]; (2) The legal issue the court is being asked to decide [Issue]; (3) The holding of the court (how it decides the legal issue before it) [Holding]; and (4) The rationale the court uses to support its decision [Rationale]. If your instructor asks you to brief the case, she will give you additional instructions.

2. Judges in Washington State have the discretion to award attorneys' fees under the Trust and Estate Dispute Resolution Act (TEDRA), chapter 11.96A RCW in cases involving disputes that arise from a decedent's estate. In this case the court refuses to grant reasonable attorneys' fees as discussed in paragraphs 27–29 above. Unlike in most of the rest of the world where losing parties to litigation (both trial and appellate) must pay the prevailing party's reasonable attorneys' fees in whole or in part, the United States departed from the world standard "loser pays" rule (often referred to as the "English Rule" in the colonial era in favor of the "American Rule" that every person pays his own attorney's fees, win or lose, except in the rare case when a federal or state statute specifically allows judges to award attorneys' fees to the prevailing party. It can be argued that the American Rule encourages litigation even by persons with weak cases since the losing party does not have to worry about paying the winning party's lawyer's fees and directly contributes to giving the United States the dubious distinction of being the most litigious nation on earth and contributes to the backlog in civil courts that can require three to five years for a trial to be held from the date that it is first filed in the civil courts of large U.S. cities.[1] On the other hand, defenders of the "American Rule" argue that adopting the "loser pays" standard would restrict access to the courts, especially for individuals with limited means who may refrain from pursuing remedies in the courts out of fear that they may have to pay the defendant's legal fees if they lose the case. Access to justice is an important issue from both a legal and an ethical perspective. What are your thoughts on the issue?

---

[1] For a full discussion of the issue, see e.g., Victor D. López and Eugene T. Maccarrone, "Leading the World in the Wrong Direction: Is It Time for the U.S. to Adopt the World Standard 'Loser Pays' Rule in Civil Litigation?" NEJLS Vol. 32 pp. 1–20 (Fall 2014). An online version of the article is available at http://nealsb.info/j2014.html. (Last accessed September 26, 2015.)

UNIT 6

AGENCY

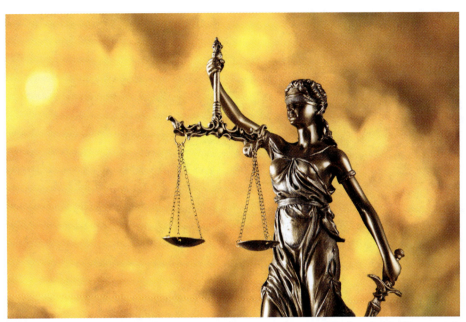
Lukas Gojda/Shutterstock

CHAPTER 37
Agency

Agency

CHAPTER 37

Introduction

In business as well as in our personal lives, we often need to have others act on our behalf to carry out routine tasks that we may not have the time or expertise to perform ourselves. An entrepreneur might go into business for herself and initially perform all of the required tasks personally while the enterprise is in its early stages. But if the business is successful and the owner wants to expand her operations, it will be impossible for her to do so without hiring additional help to take on some of the responsibilities of the expanding venture. As new employees are hired, they become agents of the owner and are empowered by her to carry out certain tasks in her place. To put it another way, the owner of a business delegates some of her responsibilities to agents whom we normally call employees and empowers these agents to act on her behalf in accordance with the terms of employment. Thus, a used car salesman hired by the owner of a used car lot is empowered to sell cars on the owner's behalf, and can bind the owner to sales contracts he enters into with third parties (used car buyers). Similarly, an individual can authorize another to act as his agent for the purpose of carrying out any legal task by executing a valid power of attorney. In both of these instances, if the agent acts on behalf of the principal (the person on whose behalf the agent acts) with the principal's authority, the acts of the agent bind the principal exactly as if the principal had acted herself. This simple principle forms the basis of agency law, and is of critical importance to the formation of the business organizations we will discuss in the next unit (partnerships, limited partnerships, corporations, and limited liability companies).

In this unit, we will explore the basic principles of the law of agency and discuss its application in employment relationships.

Agency is a consensual relationship that comes into existence when one person authorizes another to act on his behalf to conduct some lawful business. An agent acts as a stand-in for the person she represents (called the principal) and is empowered to conduct most any legal business on the principal's behalf. When a duly authorized agent acts on behalf of a principal, it is as if the principal had acted herself.

Chapter Outline

Introduction
Creation of an Agency
Agent's Authority
Agent's Apparent Authority
Agency by Estoppel
Termination of an Agency
Principal's Duties in an Agency Agreement
Agent's Duties in an Agency Agreement
Liability of Principal for Agent's Torts
Liability of Agents for Contracts Entered Into on the Principal's Behalf
Agent's Unauthorized Contracts
Agent's Authorized Contracts on Behalf of a Fully Disclosed Principal
Agent's Authorized Contracts on Behalf of a Partially Disclosed Principal
Agent's Authorized Contracts on Behalf of an Undisclosed Principal

Creation of an Agency

Agency is a consensual relationship. As such, it requires the principal to have the mental capacity to enter into a contract with the agent. Incompetents and minors, therefore, can generally disaffirm agency agreements, and judicially declared incompetents cannot enter into agency agreements at all (the same rules apply as to contractual capacity). Interestingly, there is no requirement that the agent be competent. In most states, any person may be an agent, including incompetents and children. Principals are free to choose whomever they wish to act on their behalf, and this includes persons lacking full mental capacity.

Generally speaking, no formalities are necessary for the creation of a valid agency. Oral instructions as well as written ones can lead to the creation of an agency. The only exception is when the agent is empowered to take some action on the principal's behalf that will require a written, signed contract to be executed by the agent under the requirements of the statute of frauds. In such instances, the agency agreement must also be represented by a signed writing if it is to be enforceable. This requirement is referred to as the *equal dignities rule*. Simply stated, the equal dignities rule requires that an agency agreement conform to the same formalities as any agreement that the agent will subsequently enter into on the principal's behalf. Thus, if a principal hires an agent to purchase real estate, the agency agreement must be evidenced by a signed writing, since a contract for the purchase of realty requires a signed writing.

Perhaps the most common means of creating an agency relationship is by the execution of a power of attorney, whereby the principal authorizes the holder of the power of attorney (called the attorney-in-fact) to act as his agent with respect to matters specified in the power of attorney.

Agent's Authority

Agents may act on behalf of their principals in accordance with their actual or apparent authority. Agents who act under the aegis of actual or apparent authority will bind their principals to contracts entered into on their behalf.

An agent acts with actual authority if he acts pursuant to the express or implied instructions of his principal. Actual express authority can be found in any oral or written instructions given the agent by his principal, while implied actual authority includes any reasonable steps that an agent takes to carry out the express authority granted by the principal. For example, if Peter Principal instructs Angela Agent to purchase a used Japanese-built automobile with less than 70,000 miles for a price not to exceed $5,000, Angela would have the express authority to purchase any vehicle in her discretion that meets the conditions expressed by the principal. In addition, Angela would have the implied authority to take any steps reasonably necessary to carry out her instructions. Under this example, Angela could purchase a 2010 Toyota Corolla with 50,000 miles for $5,000, since doing so would clearly come within her actual express authority. She could also pay the required taxes and registration fee for such a vehicle and arrange its transportation at a commercially reasonable cost; her authority to perform these tasks would be implied from her express authority, since it is commercially reasonable (necessary, in fact) to pay sales taxes and registration fees and to transport an automobile after its purchase.

In determining an agent's implied authority, one must look to the actual express authority granted by the principal. Any steps that are reasonably required for the agent to carry out the actual express authority granted by the principal will generally be deemed to have been implicitly authorized by the principal. For example, the express authority by the principal who hires an agent to act as general manager of her business enterprise would include the implied authority to hire, train, supervise, and fire employees, as well as to contract for necessary services—all of which are implicitly necessary for the agent to carry out the expressly granted authority to manage the business.

Agent's Apparent Authority

Like implied authority, an agent has apparent authority that flows directly from an express grant of actual authority by the principal. Apparent authority can be defined as the authority that an agent seems (or appears) to have to a reasonable person under the circumstances based on the nature of the agency. Such authority generally flows from the customs and practices of an industry or the general assumptions about a person's position that a reasonably prudent person might make. For example, since it is generally true that the director of human resources has the power to hire new employees, an interviewee who is offered a job by a company's director of human resources can accept such an offer and bind the principal to honor it even if the specific HR director was not authorized by management to make employment offers.

The same is true of contracts entered into by employees who have been fired on behalf of their previous employers unbeknownst to innocent third parties with whom they deal. If, for instance, the purchasing manager for XYZ Company enters into a million-dollar equipment purchase contract the day after he is fired by XYZ, the company would be bound by the contract unless the supplier with whom the ex-purchasing manager contracted was aware of the employee's lack of actual authority. After an agency terminates, ex-agents have apparent authority to bind their principals until the principal lets third parties who have dealt with the agent in the normal course of business know that the agency has terminated. With regard to third parties who have dealt with the agent in the past, the principal must provide actual notification of the agency's termination, and such notification is generally effective when it is received by the third party.

Therefore, if Peter Principal fires Angela Agent, Angela's implied authority continues until every person with whom she has dealt as Peter's agent is given actual notice that the agency has terminated or learns of that fact by independent means, such as by actually reading a legal notice in the newspaper that states Angela is no longer Peter's agent. Persons who may have been aware of the agency but who did not deal with Angela directly can be given constructive notice of the termination of the agency by publication of a legal notice in a newspaper of general circulation in the geographic area or areas in which Angela acted as Peter's agent. Constructive notice will effectively destroy an agent's implied authority to bind her principal with respect to third parties who have never dealt with the agent, but not with regard to third parties with whom the agent has dealt as an agent for her principal.

The termination of an agency by operation of law (covered below) automatically terminates all authority by the agent, including apparent authority.

Agency by Estoppel

In some instances, a principal who has not actually empowered an agent to act on his behalf can be bound by acts of the agent under an estoppel theory. If the principal misleads a third party into believing that a person who is not an agent is in fact the principal's agent, then the principal will be unable to disavow acts of the purported agent. For instance, if a sole proprietor leads an innocent third party to believe that a specific person is his agent when no actual agency exists, any contracts that the third party enters into with the purported agent in reliance on the principal's misrepresentations will bind that principal as if the purported agent were in fact a duly authorized agent. Note, though, that a purported agent's misrepresentations will not bind the principal unless they are made in the presence of the principal who does not disavow them. The following examples will illustrate:

- Arnold misrepresents himself to be Paula's new purchasing agent to Tom, an innocent third party, in the presence of Paula who does not correct Arnold's misstatement. Arnold subsequently sends Tom, a wholesaler, a written order for $100,000 worth of electronics equipment for resale in Paula's business. If Paula rejects the shipment when it arrives, Tom is entitled to sue her for damages, including his lost profits and shipping and insurance costs, as Tom had apparent authority to order the goods as Paula's purported agent.
- Archibald, an unemployed charlatan, tells Tina that he is a new partner in the accounting firm of Adam, Bloom, and Chang, P.C., a prestigious small firm in Tina's city. Tina, believing his assertions, pays him a sizable retainer for his purported firm to handle her company's payroll and maintain her books. If Archibald cashes the check and skips town, Tina has no recourse against Adam, Bloom, and Chang, P.C., as the firm did not mislead her. She did not verify Archibald's statements with the firm, and the firm is not responsible for allowing her to be misled by the false statement.

Termination of an Agency

An agency can be terminated in one of three ways: by the consent of the parties, by the completion of the agency purpose or expiration of the agency period, or by operation of law.

Termination by Consent of the Parties

Generally speaking, an agency can be terminated at any time by the mutual consent of the principal and agent, or by the unilateral wish of either party. This is generally true even in cases in which a contract exists between the parties that prevents an agency from being dissolved or states that the agency will run for a specified period of time. If an agency is wrongfully terminated by one of the parties unilaterally, damages may be available to the aggrieved party for breach of contract. Thus, say an agent agrees to serve as agent for a principal for a period of five years and quits at the end of the first year. In this case, the principal may be able to recover compensatory damages that would include the difference between what he would have paid the agent under their agreement and what he must pay a replacement agent for the remaining period in the breached agency agreement. He may also recover incidental and consequential damages, such as the cost of conducting an employment search to replace the agent. But the agency itself will be effectively terminated upon the wish of either the principal or the agent.

Termination by Completion of Agency Purpose or Expiration of Agency Period

An agency automatically terminates on the completion of its stated purpose when the agency is entered into in order to complete a single purpose. For example, an agency that is created for the purpose of the agent purchasing a specific piece of real estate for the principal automatically expires when the agent completes his assigned task. Likewise, an agency that is set up to expire after a set period of time or upon the happening of a given event automatically terminates when the specified time period expires or the specified event happens.

Termination by Operation of Law

An agency automatically terminates by operation of law upon the death, incompetence, or bankruptcy of the principal, or upon the death of the agent. (Note that the incompetence or bankruptcy of the agent does not necessarily terminate an agency.) Subsequent illegality and impossibility of performance also cause an agency to be terminated by operation of law, since the purpose of the agency cannot be fulfilled. If the impossibility of performance or illegality is only temporary, then the agency resumes as soon as the impediment to the completion of the agency purpose is removed. For example, if XYZ Corp. hires Adam Agent to purchase electronics goods from a specific country for resale in the U.S. during the next five years at a set salary and Congress places an embargo on that country for alleged civil rights abuses a year after the contract was entered into, the agency terminates by operation of law. But if Congress removes the sanctions a year later because of an improvement in that country's civil rights record, then the agency would resume for the remaining three-year period called for in the original agreement. Likewise, if Congress imposes a one-year moratorium on imports and exports to that country, the agency is suspended only for the one-year period in which it is legally impossible for the agent to carry out her duties.

Principal's Duties in an Agency Agreement

A principal owes certain duties to the agent in every agency. These include the duty to compensate the agent for her services (unless compensation is waived by the agent), the duty to indemnify the agent for any reasonable costs incurred or losses suffered as a result of the agency, and the duty to cooperate with the agent in carrying out the purposes of the agency. In addition to these duties that arise by operation of law in every agency, the principal can have other duties specified in the agency agreement. A principal who breaches any duty owed his agent will be liable to the agent for damages.

Duty to Compensate Agent

Unless it is clear that a gratuitous agency was intended, the agent is entitled to be compensated for her service to the principal. If compensation is not discussed, the agent is entitled to compensation for the reasonable value of the services rendered.

Duty of Reimbursement and Indemnification

An agent will often need to spend money on behalf of the principal to carry out the duties of the agency. If these expenditures are reasonable and necessary to further the interests of the principal, the agent is entitled to reimbursement from the principal for these expenses upon giving an accounting of them. In addition, agents can sometimes suffer personal losses while engaged in the business of the agency. As long as these losses were reasonably foreseeable by the principal at the time of entering into the agency and were not caused by the willful acts of the agent, the agent is entitled to indemnification for such losses. For example, if an agent is injured through the fault of a third party or though his own negligence while conducting agency business, the principal must indemnify the agent for all medical expenses and reasonably foreseeable related losses flowing from the injury. Likewise, an agent whose personal property is damaged or destroyed while carrying out agency business is generally entitled to indemnification by the principal for such losses.

Duty of Cooperation

A principal must render any reasonable assistance necessary to allow the agent to carry out the responsibilities of the agency. This duty extends to providing the agent with any necessary information or resources reasonably needed to perform the assigned agency duties, and also includes a duty of the principal not to interfere with the agent while the agent attempts to carry out the duties of the agency.

Agent's Duties in an Agency Agreement

Like the principal, the agent has certain obligations that flow from the agency agreement by operation of law and by the express terms of the agency agreement. The agent's duties arising by operation of law include the duty of loyalty, the duty of obedience, the duty to inform the principal of relevant facts relating to the agency learned by the agent, the duty to exercise due care in carrying out the responsibilities of the agency, and the duty to render an accurate accounting of expenses or income received by the agent in conducting agency business.

Duty of Loyalty

The duty of loyalty requires that the agent place the interests of the principal above his own, and requires the agent to deal honestly and in good faith in carrying out his duties as assigned by the principal. Agency is a *fiduciary relationship* (a relationship based on trust in which the agent must exercise absolute good faith in his dealings on behalf of the principal).

An agent can breach the duty of loyalty in a number of ways, including through the obvious means of stealing or misappropriating funds from the principal, and the much more subtle means of competing with the principal or using information learned by means of the agency relationship to further his own interests rather than those of the principal. An agent cannot even keep gifts (or illicit bribes, for that matter) he receives in the normal course of conducting agency business on the principal's behalf; such gains are considered the rightful property of the principal and must be turned over to the principal by the agent who receives them.

Duty of Obedience

The agent's duty of obedience to her principal requires her to follow the reasonable instructions of the principal relating to the agency. Failure to do so will subject the agent to liability for any resulting loss suffered by the principal.

Duty to Communicate to the Principal Relevant Information Learned about the Agency

A principal is deemed to have constructive knowledge of any relevant information that the agent learns during the course of performing her duties as an agent. Because as a matter of law the principal is presumed to know relevant information that the agent learned, agents must communicate any relevant information they learn relating to the agency to their principals immediately. If they fail to do so, they can be held personally responsible for any losses suffered by the principal as a result of their failure to disclose the relevant information.

Duty to Exercise Due Care in Conducting Agency Business

Agents must exercise the duties of their agency with reasonable care. Failure to do so can result in tort liability for negligence. Agents who have special skills, such as attorneys, physicians, architects, or accountants must exercise a level of professionalism and expertise that is acceptable in their profession; failure to do so can result in liability for malpractice.

Duty to Render an Accounting

Agents must keep accurate records of expenses incurred on behalf of their principals for which they are entitled to reimbursement or indemnification, as well as of any income or other benefit derived from the agency to which the principal is entitled. Agents must render a formal accounting to their principals from time to time, whenever the principal reasonably requests an accounting or as otherwise provided by the agency agreement.

Liability of Principal for Agent's Torts

Principals are liable for harm caused by the agent's negligent acts to third parties during the scope of their agency, but not generally for the willful torts or crimes committed by the agent without her knowledge or consent. The agent, of course, is also liable for his own negligence with regard to third parties whom the agent injures due to his negligence while engaged in agency business, as well as for damage caused by his willful torts or crimes. For the principal to be held liable for the agent's negligence, two tests must be met: (1) there must be a master-servant relationship, wherein the agent is under the direct control of the principal (e.g., the agent must be an employee of the principal); and (2) the tort must have been committed by the agent while engaged in conducting agency business. If, for example, the driver of a delivery truck who fails to stop at a red light while making a delivery injures an innocent person, the injured person can hold the driver's employer liable for the injuries suffered. But not so if the driver injures someone while driving his own car on the way to work, since he would not at that time have engaged in conducting agency business.

Independent contractors are not deemed agents of their employers, but rather are deemed to be self-employed and solely responsible for their own torts. In determining whether a given person is an employee or an independent contractor, courts weigh a number of factors, including the level of control exerted by the principal over the details of the work performed by the person, the number of hours worked by the person on the principal's behalf every week, whether the person has other clients, and whether the person exerts independent judgment in carrying out her duties. Thus, a gardener who works for the Jones family 2 hours per week and has 20 other clients in the area is not an employee, but rather an independent contractor, but a gardener who works exclusively for the Jones family for 20 hours per week and has no other clients probably is an employee; the difference can be crucial if the gardener negligently injures himself or someone else during the course of his employment, for the Jones family would not be responsible for such injuries in the former case but would be liable for them in the latter.

Liability of Agents for Contracts Entered Into on the Principal's Behalf

Agents are not generally personally liable for contracts they enter into on behalf of their principals within the scope of their authority. When an authorized agent enters into a contract on behalf of a principal, it is as if the principal had entered into the contract personally. The agent is merely a facilitator who stands in the place of the principal when entering into an authorized contract and is not a party to the contract. A problem arises, however, when agents enter into unauthorized contracts and when agents act on behalf of principals who wish to keep their identities secret from the other contracting parties. In such instances, the agent may be solely liable under the resulting contract, or may be jointly liable with the principal, depending on the circumstances.

Agent's Unauthorized Contracts

If an agent enters into a contract with a third party on behalf of a principal without having either actual, implied, or apparent authority to do so, the principal is not bound under the resulting agreement, and the agent is personally liable under the contract. For example, if Alec Agent is authorized by Pancho Principal to bid up to $100,000 at auction for a piece of unimproved real estate and Alec bids $120,000 on the property, Pancho is not bound by the resulting agreement, since Alec acted without express or implied authority, but Alec is bound by it and is liable to the third party with whom he contracted (e.g., the auctioneer) for breach of contract if he does not purchase the land at the agreed-upon price.

Principals are free to honor unauthorized contracts entered into by their agents if they choose, but are under no obligation to do so. If a principal elects to honor an unauthorized contract entered into on his behalf by an agent, he ratifies the agreement and is afterward bound by it. Ratification involves the principal's affirmance of a previously unauthorized act by the agent. Once the principal ratifies an unauthorized contract, the agent is no longer liable under it, since the liability for performing the contract is assumed by the principal upon its ratification.

Agent's Authorized Contracts on Behalf of a Fully Disclosed Principal

An agent has no liability for authorized contracts entered into on behalf of a fully disclosed principal. A principal is fully disclosed when the party with whom the agent deals on the principal's behalf is aware that the agent is acting as an agent for a particular principal and is aware of the principal's identity. As previously noted, the agent in such instances is merely a facilitator—a conduit, if you will—for the principal entering into a contract through his authorized agent, and does not become a party to the contract. If either the principal or the third party subsequently breaches the contract, they can only sue each other (and not the agent) for the breach.

Agent's Authorized Contracts on Behalf of a Partially Disclosed Principal

When a partially disclosed principal is involved, the agent discloses to the third party with whom she is contracting that she is acting on behalf of a principal but refuses to disclose the identity of the principal. Such contracts are common in instances in which the principal fears that the third party might be unwilling to deal with him, or the identity of the principal might drive up the price of the contract if it were known. In such contracts, both the principal and the agent have joint liability, and both can be sued if the contract is breached if the third party independently learns of the principal's identity or if a court compels the agent to disclose the principal's identity at the request of the third party.

Agent's Authorized Contracts on Behalf of an Undisclosed Principal

In contracts involving an undisclosed principal, the third party with whom the agent contracts is unaware that the agent is acting on behalf of a principal. As far as the third party is concerned, the agent acts solely on his own behalf and is thus personally liable for the performance of the contract if the undisclosed principal fails to perform. If the third party later learns of the undisclosed principal's identity, the third party may hold both the agent and the undisclosed principal liable under the contract.

Questions

1. What is agency?
2. What formalities are necessary to enter into an agency agreement?
3. How does the equal dignities rule apply?
4. What are the three basic means by which an agency can be terminated?
5. What effect does the death of the agent have on an agency? The death of the principal?
6. What effect does the bankruptcy of the agent have on an agency? What about the bankruptcy of the principal?
7. What are the basic duties owed by a principal to an agent in every agency relationship?
8. What are the basic duties that all agents owe their principals?
9. What is the contractual liability of agents who enter into unauthorized contracts on behalf of their principals?
10. What is the agent's contractual liability in contracts entered into with third parties on behalf of disclosed principals? Partially disclosed principals? Undisclosed principals?

Hypothetical Cases

1. Marsha asks Muhammad, a fellow student at State U who is a computer whiz, to purchase a computer for her that in his best judgment would best meet her needs. She tells him that he can spend up to $1,500 on a complete system, including an inexpensive printer. Muhammad, after many hours of research to put together the most cost-effective system at the lowest possible price for Marsha, places an order with Computer World on Marsha's behalf and asks that the complete system be shipped to Marsha.
   A. Is Muhammad Marsha's agent under the facts given? If so, does he need written authorization before he can purchase the system on Marsha's behalf?
   B. If Muhammad orders a system for $1,500 from Computer World after identifying himself as Marsha's agent, is Muhammad liable on the contract if Marsha refuses the computer system when it is delivered? Explain.
   C. If Muhammad finds a $4,000 computer system on clearance for $2,000 and orders it for Marsha, who is liable on the contract if Marsha refuses to accept it when the system is delivered, assuming that there is no issue with the statute of frauds? Explain.
2. Assume the same facts as in the last question:
   A. If payment for Muhammad's services was not discussed when Marsha asked him to purchase the computer system, will Muhammad nevertheless be entitled to be paid for his services? Explain.
   B. If Muhammad purchases a system that is inappropriate for Marsha's needs, what recourse will she have?
3. Barbara hires Enrique as a consultant to set up and maintain her computer network. Enrique works at Barbara's business site approximately five to ten hours per week and bills Barbara at a rate of $125 per hour for his work. He does not have an office in Barbara's place of business and is not on the payroll. He works

unsupervised and sets his own schedule and hours on an as-needed basis. In addition to working for Barbara, Enrique does consulting work for several other clients on an ongoing basis.
   A. Is Enrique an employee or an independent contractor?
   B. What practical difference does it make whether Enrique is an independent contractor or an employee?
   C. Would Enrique be considered an employee under the previous facts if he worked 20 hours per week for the past three years for Barbara and had no other clients?
4. Jasmine hires Jemal to run her business as general manager under a three-year contract. After six months, the parties have a falling out and Jemal gives Jasmine notice of his intention to resign from his position and expresses the willingness to stay on for up to 60 days to allow Jasmine to recruit a suitable successor.
   A. If Jasmine is unwilling to release Jemal from his contractual obligation, can she force him to stay on as her agent for the contractual three-year term?
   B. If Jasmine cannot convince Jemal to stay on as her general manager, what recourse does she have against him? Explain.
   C. Assuming that Jasmine can find several suitable replacements for Jemal for a lesser salary than she had agreed to pay him, what recourse will she have against Jemal?

Unit VI—Cases for Further Study

DISTRICT COURT OF APPEAL OF FLORIDA
THIRD DISTRICT.
REGIONS BANK, ETC., ET AL., APPELLANTS, V.
MAROONE CHEVROLET, L.L.C., APPELLEE.
No. 3D10–1656.
Decided: July 17, 2013

Before SHEPHERD, C.J., and SUAREZ and FERNANDEZ, JJ.[*] Garbett, Stiphany, Allen & Roza, Philip A. Allen, III, and David S. Garbett, for appellants. Colson Hicks Eidson, Roberto Martinez, and Barbara A. Silverman, for appellee.

Regions Bank, formerly known as Union Planters Bank, N.A., First Source Bank, Peninsula Bank, and Ocean Banks (collectively "the banks") appeal from a final judgment entered in favor of Maroone Chevrolet, L.L.C. We reverse in part and affirm in part.

This case arose from a business relationship between InterAmerican Car Rental, Inc. and Maroone Chevrolet for the purchase of InterAmerican's fleet of rental vehicles. The relationship existed from August 1999 until September 2002, when InterAmerican ceased operations. The parties' practice followed the norm in the industry. Maroone would receive an order for a group of vehicles from InterAmerican, and would place an order for the vehicles with the manufacturer. The manufacturer would ship the vehicles directly to InterAmerican but invoice Maroone. Maroone would in turn invoice InterAmerican for the amount due on the vehicles delivered. Additionally, Maroone would prepare applications for certificates of title on the vehicles, including any financing lien holders designated by InterAmerican. Upon InterAmerican's receipt of the vehicles, it would submit a draw request to a financing bank, which would issue a check for the purchase money loan on the subject vehicles payable solely to Maroone or payable jointly to Maroone and InterAmerican. The checks now at issue were then delivered to InterAmerican.

InterAmerican ultimately went out of business and was unable to repay money owed to Maroone. Consequently, Maroone sued InterAmerican's depository bank and financing banks for statutory and common law conversion and negligence, alleging mishandling of the financing checks.[1] Specifically, Maroone claimed Regions Bank accepted for deposit into InterAmerican's operating account, and the financing banks issued payment on, nine financing checks made payable: 1) to Maroone; or, 2) to both InterAmerican and Maroone, but were not properly endorsed by Maroone. Five checks, issued by Peninsula Bank to both payees, were included in the latter category: Check No. 7005252 for $655,130.85, Check No. 7006426 for $446,297.87, Check No. 7006452 for $439,346.21, Check No. 7006454 for $387.767.66, and Check No. 7003036078 for $406,070.85. Four checks, issued solely to Maroone, were included in the first category. The first, Check No. 620761, issued by Ocean Bank for $72,361.65, and three other checks issued by First Source Bank: Check No. 67154 for $120,802.43, Check No. 70340 for $516,064.00, and Check No. 71337 for $25,803.20.

On its negligence claim, Maroone sought $4.8 million in consequential damages for InterAmerican's outstanding receivables based on its claim that Maroone would have stopped doing business with InterAmerican sooner if the banks had timely alerted Maroone to InterAmerican's practice of forging Maroone's endorsement.

After a bench trial, the lower court entered the final judgment appealed from which denied the consequential damages claim as speculative, but found that the banks breached their duty of ordinary care in their handling of the checks which included Maroone as a payee. It also found that InterAmerican had directly paid Maroone for

---

[*]SUAREZ, J.

[1]InterAmerican maintained its operating account at Regions Bank. Peninsula, Ocean, and First Source Banks provided InterAmerican with financing for their vehicle purchases.

some of the financed vehicles, and accordingly deducted that amount from the damages awarded. The final judgment awarded Maroone: $406,070.85, representing the face amount of Peninsula Bank Check No. 3036078; $25,803.20 for the face amount of First Source Bank Check No. 71337; and $72,361.65 for the face amount of Ocean Bank Check No. 620761. Additionally, the trial court awarded Maroone prejudgment interest on each of these awards at the rate of nine percent beginning in 2002.

The banks now appeal that judgment. They contend the trial court erred in entering judgment in favor of Maroone on the single-payee checks because Maroone never proved InterAmerican was its agent for purposes of delivery. As to the remaining checks, appellants raise several errors, all of which we conclude are meritless. Lastly, appellants claim the trial court erred in the prejudgment interest award. We address the claims regarding the single-payee checks and prejudgment interest in this opinion.

The appellants do not challenge the lower court's findings of fact. Thus, because appellants' arguments rest on questions of law, our review is de novo. See Miami–Dade County v. Wilson, 44 So.3d 1266, 1270 (Fla. 3d DCA 2010).

We turn first to the argument that Maroone's statutory conversion claim fails for lack of delivery. This claim is based on section 673.4201(1)(b), Florida Statutes (1997), which provides in relevant part: "An action for conversion of an instrument may not be brought by . . . [a] payee or indorsee who did not receive delivery of the instrument either directly or through delivery to an agent or a copayee." The banks contend Maroone did not meet the requirements for statutory conversion because it did not prove the subject checks were delivered to either Maroone or its agent. The parties' briefs concentrate on whether actual or merely constructive delivery is required to satisfy the statute.[2] We conclude instead that application of the statutory exclusion turns on the existence of an agency relationship between Maroone and InterAmerican. The question is whether, in receiving the single-payee checks, InterAmerican was acting as Maroone's representative.

It is well settled that an agency relationship may be express or implied from apparent authority, and the burden of proving the agency belongs to the party asserting it. See, e.g., City Nat'l Bank of Detroit v. Basic Food Indus., Inc., 520 F.2d 336, 337 (5th Cir.1975) ("[A]n agent's authority need not be conferred in express terms, but may be implied under justifying circumstances."); Roessler v. Novak, 858 So.2d 1158, 1162 (Fla. 2d DCA 2003) ("Although some agencies are based upon an express agreement, a principal may be liable to a third party for acts of its agent which are within the agent's apparent authority."); Robbins v. Hess, 659 So.2d 424, 427 (Fla. 1st DCA 1995) ("The party alleging the agency relationship bears the burden to prove it."). Moreover, because "apparent authority is a form of estoppel [which arises] from 'the authority a principal knowingly tolerates or allows an agent to assume, or which the principal by his actions or words holds the agent out as possessing,'" apparent agency exists only where the principal creates the appearance of authority. Jackson Hewitt, Inc. v. Kaman, 100 So.3d 19, 31 (Fla. 2d DCA 2011) (quoting Owen Indus., Inc. v. Taylor, 354 So.2d 1259, 1261 (Fla. 2d DCA 1978)). Therefore, the focus is on the conduct or words of the principal, not those of the purported agent or the understanding of the person dealing with the purported agent. However, "the third party's reliance on the purported agent's apparent authority must be reasonable." Izquierdo v. Hialeah Hosp., Inc., 709 So.2d 187, 188 (Fla. 3d DCA 1998); see also Jackson Hewitt, 100 So.3d at 32; Roessler, 858 So.2d at 1161–62 n. 3.

Here, the allegations in Maroone's complaint and the testimony at trial incorrectly focused on the understanding of the purported agent, InterAmerican, and the entity dealing with the purported agent, the financing banks, rather than the conduct of the principal, Maroone. The complaint alleges the financing banks delivered checks payable to Maroone to InterAmerican for the benefit and use of Maroone. Representatives of the financing banks and InterAmerican generally confirmed this fact. However, Maroone asserted below that it was unaware InterAmerican was accepting financing checks on its behalf. Maroone could not have authorized InterAmerican to do something of which it was unaware. Thus, not surprisingly, the appellants presented no evidence that Maroone did anything to create an agency by placing apparent authority with InterAmerican. On the contrary, other than to avoid the statutory delivery exclusion, Maroone cannot claim InterAmerican as its agent because to do so would legitimize InterAmerican's actions, including the forging of Maroone's endorsements. This would be unreasonable.

Accordingly, we conclude Maroone's claims on the single-payee checks fail for lack of delivery. We, therefore, reverse that part of the final judgment awarding Maroone $25,803.20 for the face amount of First Source Bank Check No. 71337 and $72,361.65 for the face amount of Ocean Bank Check No. 620761.

Maroone presented the following evidence at trial regarding the two-payee checks:

A. Peninsula Bank.

Check No. 7005252 for $655,130.85—In August 1999, InterAmerican ordered sixty-two Hyundai cars, naming

---

[2] It seems clear that constructive delivery to a payee's agent or copayee is sufficient. See Attorney's Title Ins. Fund, Inc. v. Regions Bank, 491 F.Supp.2d 1087 (S.D.Fla.2007) (discussing why "delivery" encompasses both physical and constructive delivery); see also Racso Diagnostic, Inc. v. Cmty. Bank of Homestead, 735 So.2d 519, 520 (Fla. 3d DCA 1999).

Peninsula Bank as the lien holder. In September 1999, Peninsula Bank delivered to InterAmerican a check payable to InterAmerican and Maroone for sixty-one of the sixty-two cars. InterAmerican typed Maroone's name on the back of the check and deposited it into InterAmerican's operating account with Regions Bank. In December 1999, Peninsula Bank delivered to InterAmerican another check payable to InterAmerican and Maroone in payment of the final car. This time, InterAmerican endorsed the check and delivered it to Maroone along with InterAmerican's check payable to Maroone for twenty-one of the sixty-two cars in the order. Between December 30, 1999, and April 1, 2000, InterAmerican sent three checks to Maroone in payment for the remaining cars. This order, therefore, was paid in full.

Check No. 7006426 for $446,297.87—In March 2002, InterAmerican ordered twenty-three Chevrolet cars, naming Peninsula Bank as the lien holder. Later that month, Peninsula sent a check payable to InterAmerican and Maroone in the amount of $446,297.87 for the order. InterAmerican again typed Maroone's name on the back of the check and deposited it into its account. In June 2002, InterAmerican sent a check to Maroone for eighteen cars from this order. Later that same month, it appears InterAmerican paid the manufacturer directly for two other cars. At trial, the banks' expert testified that Maroone's ledgers showed a credit for the balance owed on the remaining cars. Thus, the evidence demonstrated the order tied to this check was also paid in full.

Check No. 7006452 for $439,346.21—In April 2002, InterAmerican placed an order for an additional twenty-three Chevrolets with Peninsula Bank as the lien holder. Peninsula sent a check for that order to InterAmerican in the amount of $439,346.21 payable to InterAmerican and Maroone. InterAmerican negotiated the check by typing Maroone's name on the back and depositing it. In June 2002, InterAmerican sent a check to Maroone that included payment for one of the cars in this order. InterAmerican later sent a second check to Maroone which included payment for another seventeen cars in this order. Additionally, two cars from this order were repaid by InterAmerican's June check sent in payment for eighteen cars from the March order. The banks' expert again testified that Maroone's ledgers showed InterAmerican paid for the remaining three cars in this order. Thus, no outstanding balance remained in connection with this check.

Check No. 7006454 for $387.767.66—InterAmerican made a second order in April that consisted of twenty Chevrolet cars, naming Peninsula Bank as the lien holder. The same month, Peninsula gave a check to InterAmerican in the amount of $387,767.66, payable to InterAmerican and Maroone for the order. InterAmerican typed Maroone's name on the back and deposited the check. InterAmerican then paid Maroone for two of these cars through the June check, which included payment for the initial April order. InterAmerican sent another check in June to Maroone for another seven cars from this order. Maroone's ledger showed full payment on the remaining balance of this order.

Check No. 7003036078 for $406,070.85—In June 2002, InterAmerican ordered nineteen Ford vehicles, naming Peninsula as the lien holder. Peninsula sent a check for this order to InterAmerican in the amount of $406,070.85, which was payable to InterAmerican and Maroone. InterAmerican again negotiated the check by typing Maroone's name on the back and deposited it into its account. There is no evidence in the record indicating Maroone received payment for any of these cars. Therefore, the full amount of $406,070.85 remained owing from this order.

It is axiomatic that a plaintiff must prove damages resulting from the defendant's wrongdoing to be entitled to recover. See, e.g., Bank of Miami Beach v. Newman, 163 So.2d 333, 333 (Fla. 3d DCA 1964) ("It is fundamental that a person is not entitled to recover damages if he has suffered no injury."). To prove a prima facie case of conversion, the plaintiff must show evidence of damage, not just liability. See, e.g., Saewitz v. Saewitz, 79 So.3d 831, 833 (Fla. 3d DCA 2012); accord Star Fruit Co. v. Eagle Lake Growers, 33 So.2d 858, 861 (Fla.1948) (reversing because "[t]here was no evidence introduced concerning value" of the specific items allegedly converted). Moreover, the plaintiff must present evidence regarding a "reasonable certainty" as to its amount of damages, and a plaintiff's claim cannot be based upon "speculation or guesswork." Saewitz, 79 So.3d at 833–34. The plaintiff seeking damages must "adduce evidence . . . from which [the trier of facts] could properly determine" the extent of the plaintiff's alleged economic damages. See, e.g., U.S.B. Acquisition Co. v. Stamm, 660 So.2d. 1075, 1079 (Fla. 4th DCA 1995).

Because the record here is devoid of evidence supporting damages attributable to the banks' mishandling of the subject financing checks, with the exception of Peninsula Bank Check No. 7003036078, we affirm the award of damages only to the extent of the amount of this check, $406,070.85, plus any prejudgment interest on this amount. The remaining amount is reversed because there was no evidence to support it. We conclude the trial court properly rejected the claim for consequential damages as speculative.

Lastly, the trial court did not err in calculating prejudgment interest. The amount of prejudgment interest is an element of the plaintiff's damages, and thus is incorporated into the amount of the judgment in cases in which prejudgment interest is due. See Argonaut Ins. Co. v. May Plumbing Co., 474 So.2d 212, 215 (Fla.1985). The interest compensates the plaintiff for the loss of use of the amount awarded, and thus interest accrues from the date the money was due until the date of the judgment. Id. ("[T]he loss itself is a wrongful deprivation by the defendant of the plaintiff's property.").

Under Florida law, the rate of both prejudgment and postjudgment interest is set by statute. § 687.01, Fla. Stat. (1994); § 55.03, Fla. Stat. (2003). Section 687.01 refers to section 55.03, Florida Statutes (2003), for the rate to be used for prejudgment interest where no contractual interest rate applies. The governing version of section 55.03 provides that Florida's Chief Financial Officer shall set the interest rate on January 1 of each year and that "[t]he interest rate established at the time a judgment is obtained shall remain the same until the judgment is paid." § 55.03(1), (3), Fla. Stat. (2003). The same should apply to prejudgment interest. Once the rate is obtained based on the date of loss, it should remain the same. See Genser v. Reef Condo. Ass'n, 100 So.3d 760, 762–63 (Fla. 4th DCA 2012) (applying a fixed rate to prejudgment interest calculations under section 55.03, Florida Statutes (2003)). Thus, the trial court properly determined prejudgment interest.

Accordingly, we reverse the final judgment award of $25,803.20 (for First Source Bank Check No. 71337) and $72,361.65 (for Ocean Bank Check No. 620761). We affirm the award of $406,070.85 (for Peninsula Bank Check No. 7003036078) and affirm the award of prejudgment interest, but remand for calculation of prejudgment interest consistent with this opinion.

Affirmed in part, reversed in part, and remanded.

Optional Assignments

1. Brief the preceding case in a one- to two-page, single-spaced brief (with double spaces between paragraphs) that contains the following four sections: (1) The basic facts of the case [Facts]; (2) The legal issue the court is being asked to decide [Issue]; (3) The holding of the court (how it decides the legal issue before it) [Holding]; and (4) The rationale the court uses to support its decision [Rationale]. If your instructor asks you to brief the case, she will give you additional instructions.

2. Discuss whether you agree with the court's decision and whether the decision obtains a just result in your view.

UNIT 7

GOVERNMENT REGULATION OF BUSINESS

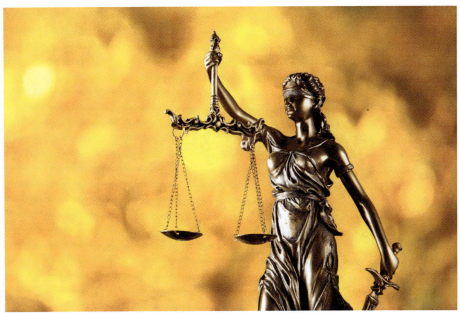
Lukas Gojda/Shutterstock

CHAPTER 38
Employment Relations

CHAPTER 39
Federal Securities Acts

CHAPTER 40
Federal Antitrust Law

Introduction

The first half of the twentieth century saw a remarkable change in American law fueled by a variety of economic, social, and political factors. It is this time period that largely gives birth to labor law in the United States as a distinct discipline, thanks to various federal acts that, among other things, recognize the rights of workers to join unions and engage in collective bargaining through representatives of their own choosing and impose controls on abusive practices first by employers and then by unions. With the assistance of U.S. Supreme Court decisions that broadly interpreted the Commerce Clause to provide Congress with the ability to exert wide control over almost any activity that could have an impact on interstate or international commerce, federal regulation of business has become the established norm in a wide range of areas that include labor management relations, employee protection from illegal discrimination and an unsafe workplace, securities and antitrust regulation, and the establishment of some protection for employee pensions in companies that provide pensions to their workers, among many others. In this unit, we will examine some of the salient regulations in these areas. Keep in mind as you read on that we are only scratching the surface of what is very extensive federal regulation of business, and that states often provide additional regulations that can go well beyond the federal minimum standards examined here.

Employment Relations

CHAPTER 38

Chapter Outline

Rights and Responsibilities of Employers and Employees Based on Agency

Rights and Responsibilities of Employers and Employees Based on Contract Law

Governmental Regulation of Labor-Management Relations

Additional Federal Regulation Affecting Employment

At early common law, labor law did not exist as a separate field of law. The relationship between employers (masters) and employees (servants) was governed by the law of agency and contracts. Because employees are considered agents of their employers when they are actively engaged in performing their assigned duties, they can avail themselves of the rights of agents under the law of agency as discussed in the preceding chapter. Employees who asserted their rights as agents under the law of agency (e.g., seeking indemnification for work-related injuries) could be summarily fired, however. As to the rights of employees under contract law, it will come as no surprise that the law generally favored the employer rather than the employee in most matters relating to the employment relationship. Employees' rights under employment contracts were generally limited to the terms of the employment agreement. Since the terms of employment are generally dictated by the employer, employment contracts with rare exception contained little legal protection for the employee beyond the guarantee of receiving the bargained-for wages. More often than not, the sole practical remedy available to employees who felt unjustly treated by an employer was to resign their positions and seek employment elsewhere.

Today, agency and contract law are still at the heart of labor law, but a significant amount of federal and state legislation has been enacted that helps to define the rights and responsibilities of employers and employees in a number of key areas, including collective bargaining; occupational safety; and protection from discrimination based on sex, race, color, religion, national origin, age, and physical disability.

Rights and Responsibilities of Employers and Employees Based on Agency

Employees are considered agents of the employers for whom they work and, as such, have the rights and responsibilities of agents as discussed in Chapter 37. Thus, an employer owes the employee the duties of compensation, reimbursement, and indemnification as well as the duty of cooperation; whereas the employee owes the employer the duties of loyalty and obedience, the duty to make an accounting, and the duty to exercise due care in the performance of employment responsibilities.

The rights and responsibilities dictated by the law of agency for employers and employees do not extend to the relationship between employers and independent contractors. Unlike employees, who are deemed to be agents of their employers, independent contractors are considered to be self-employed and are owed no duty by persons who hire them, beyond those covered in the contract through which their services are obtained.

The distinction between employees and independent contractors can be crucial when third parties are injured through the negligence of the independent contractor, or when the independent contractor suffers injury or other loss while working for the employer. Since an agency relationship does not exist between independent contractors and those who obtain their services, independent contractors are solely responsible for their own torts (including their negligence), and they are not given the protection available to employees when they suffer injury or other loss while performing their contractual responsibilities.

At times, a thorny issue develops as to whether a given person is an independent contractor or an employee. In deciding such questions, courts weigh a number of factors in an attempt to determine the nature of the relationship. Relevant factors include the extent of control exercised by the employer over the individual's performance of contractual duties (the greater the control, the likelier it is that the worker is an employee rather than an independent contractor); the duration of the employment contract and the exclusiveness of the relationship (the longer the relationship, the likelier an employee is involved; the more clients a worker works for, the less likely it is that she is an employee of any of them); and whether the worker works out of the employer's premises and uses her own tools rather than tools provided by the employer also plays a factor in determining whether an individual is an employee or an independent contractor. (Having an office or other workspace in the employer's premises tends to indicate an employment relationship, as does having tools required for the job provided by the employer, while bringing one's own tools or equipment to the job site is an indication of independent contractor status.)

Rights and Responsibilities of Employers and Employees Based on Contract Law

As previously noted, at common law the precise rights and responsibilities of the employer and employee were almost exclusively dictated by general agency law and the employment contract. While other factors come into play today, the employment contract is still of critical importance in determining the rights and responsibilities of the parties. Parties are free to define the nature of the employment relationship through oral or written contracts as long as these do not conflict with federal or state law. The length of employment, precise duties of the employee, compensation, and benefits package are all typically defined in the employment contract. In most cases, the employer as offeror of the employment contract defines these terms, and the employee as offeree either accepts or rejects the offer on the employer's terms. Employees can, of course, bargain for better terms than those offered by the employer, but most employees in reality have little bargaining power, especially in tight job markets or in positions requiring few specialized skills.

To a large extent, the efforts of both the federal and state governments to regulate labor law through legislation can be seen as an effort to level the playing field between employers and employees by setting limits on the terms that employers (and, to a lesser extent, unions) may impose on employees through the employment contract. Throughout the remainder of this chapter, we'll spotlight a cross section of salient legislative efforts in the area of business law to gain an overview of the limits that have been placed on employers in dictating the terms of employment for their employees. Keep in mind from this point on that employment is still (at least technically) at will, which is to say that employers and employees are free to negotiate the terms of employment within the boundaries of the law and that the employer or employee may generally unilaterally terminate any employment contract that does not have a fixed duration at any time with or without just cause, as long as no federal or state law is violated by the termination.

Governmental Regulation of Labor-Management Relations

The history of labor-management relations in the U.S. through the first three decades of the last century was not an auspicious one from the workers' perspective. There was no formal protection for workers' rights to form unions or bargain collectively with management. While these rights had been long recognized in Europe, where a greater emphasis on workers' rights had been (and remains) a focal point of that continent's industrialized democracies, in the U.S. most organized labor activities were deemed to violate either criminal or civil laws. The mere act of joining a union could (and often did) result in termination of an employee. Likewise, employees who banded together and instituted boycotts or strikes against an employer could be prosecuted for criminal antitrust violations under the 1914 Clayton Act, which made illegal all conspiracies to restrain trade or interfere with commerce. Organizers of boycotts or strikes could also be sued in many states for civil damages under a tort theory such as willful interference with contract rights. Most state courts readily granted injunctions at management's request, preventing employees from engaging in illegal boycotts, as did the federal courts prior to the Norris La Guardia Act of 1932. In addition, since a worker had no protected right to join a union or to engage in collective bargaining, employers were free to insist on including a clause in employment contracts that prevented employees from ever joining a union as a condition of being hired. These contractual provisions, which came to be known as yellow dog contracts by union sympathizers, were usually enforced by the courts and served to effectively deny workers the ability to unionize or bargain collectively with employers. By 1932, the political climate had begun to change, and what had been very effective roadblocks to the labor movement were slowly removed through a series of acts passed by Congress granting some measure of protection to workers and curtailing the most egregious abuses of power by management.

Norris La Guardia Act of 1932

The Norris La Guardia Act accomplished two important goals: declaring agreements prohibiting workers from joining unions as a condition of being hired (yellow dog contracts) illegal as against public policy and unenforceable, and restricting the power of federal judges to issue injunctions against union boycotts.

While the act did not prevent employers from seeking injunctive relief against employee boycotts in state courts, many states eventually also prevented their courts from issuing such injunctions.

National Labor Relations Act of 1935

The National Labor Relations Act of 1935 (also known as the Wagner Act) granted to employees for the first time the right to organize, to bargain collectively through representatives of their own choosing, and to engage in activities for the purpose of collective bargaining or other mutual aid or protection. The act also prohibited five unfair labor practices by employers:

1. interference with attempts of employees to unionize or join unions;
2. domination or interference with the formation or administration of any labor union or contributing financial or other support to it;
3. discrimination in hiring, tenure of employment, or any term or condition of employment to encourage or discourage membership in any labor organization;
4. discharge or discrimination against an employee for filing charges or giving testimony under the act; and
5. refusing to bargain collectively with the chosen representatives of the employees.

The act also made unlawful closed shop agreements that require employers to hire only union workers. Union shop agreements, in which employees need not be union members when hired but must join the union after being hired, were not made illegal by the act, however. In addition, the act established the National Labor Relations Board (NLRB) to hear and adjudicate complaints from employees about employers' unfair labor practices. NLRB decisions on such matters are automatically reviewed by District Courts of Appeals, which issue orders of enforcement if they concur with the findings of the NLRB.

Fair Labor Standards Act (1938)

The Fair Labor Standards Act of 1938 fixed for the first time minimum wage and maximum hours provisions. The act set the maximum workweek at 44 hours for the first year after its adoption, 42 hours after one year, and 40 hours per week thereafter, requiring employers to pay all hourly employees time and a half for any work required beyond the stated maximum. (Executive, administrative, and professional employees are exempt.) The act also set minimum wage provisions on a sliding scale that were set to increase from $0.25 an hour for the first year, $0.30 per hour for the next six years, and $0.40 per hour thereafter. The minimum wage requirements have been raised periodically thereafter, starting with an increase to $0.75 per hour in 1949. As of this writing, the federal hourly minimum wage is $7.25. States and cities are free to impose a higher minimum wage and many do. The act does not generally cover business enterprises with less than $500,000 in annual volume. The act also does not cover hospitals; nursing homes; higher education institutions; and federal, state, and local government agencies.

Under the federal law, a lower minimum wage can legally to be paid to certain workers. Full-time students employed in retail or service stores, agriculture, or colleges and universities can be paid not less than 85% of the current minimum wage provided the employer obtains a certificate from the Department of Labor and the student works a maximum of 8 hours per day and not more than 20 hours per week during the school year, and not more than 40 hours per week when classes are not in session. In addition, workers under the age of 20 can be paid any wage above $4.25 per hour for the first 90 calendar days after they are employed. Workers who work in jobs where they earn tips and make at least $30 in tips per month can also be paid less than the prevailing federal minimum wage, but not less than $2.12 per hour as of this writing, as long as the employee earns at least the federal minimum wage when the tips are added to the sub-minimum wage hourly rate. Therefore, an employee who works at a restaurant and earns $15 per hour in tips need only be paid $2.12 per hour in wages by the employer, but an employee who works at a car wash 40 hours per week and earns $40 per week in tips must be paid a minimum of $6.25 in hourly wages (the hourly wage plus the tips must at least equal the minimum wage).

The Fair Labor Standards Act also requires covered workers to be paid time and a half for overtime work after 40 hours per week. There is no maximum number of hours that an employer can ask an employee to work each week as long as time and a half is paid after 40 hours. Overtime pay need not be provided for workers who work weekends or holidays. And employees may be asked to work more than 8 hours per day without overtime as long as the weekly total is not more than 40 hours. An employee who is required to work for 12 hours on Mondays, Wednesdays, and Thursdays and 4 hours on Sundays is not entitled to overtime pay under the federal law.

Most states have enacted minimum wage laws that give their workers greater benefits than provided under federal law. The Department of Labor publishes current information on the federal minimum wage as well as current minimum wage information for all states and territories on its web site at http://www.dol.gov.

Labor Management Relations Act (1947)

The Labor Management Relations Act of 1947 (also known as the Taft–Hartley Act) essentially modified the 1935 National Labor Relations Act (the Wagner Act) in a number of significant ways. Chief among these modifications is the extension of unfair labor practices to unions as well as employers. The act makes it an unfair labor practice for unions to engage in the following three prohibited activities:

1. coercing or restraining employees in their choice of a union to represent them, or coercing or restraining employers in the choice of their own bargaining representatives;
2. compelling an employer to fire an employee in a union shop for other than non payment of dues; and
3. refusing to bargain in good faith.

The act has also given the president the right to seek an injunction to force striking workers back to work for a period of up to 60 days in strikes that in his view imperil national health or safety. If the dispute is not settled during the 60-day cooling-off period, the president can ask for a 20-day extension of the injunction if the strike threatens a national emergency.

Labor Management Reporting and Disclosure Act (1959)

The Labor Management Reporting and Disclosure Act of 1959 (also known as the Landrum–Griffin Act), like the Labor Management Relations Act (the Taft–Hartley Act) before it, further modified the National Labor Relations Act of 1935 (the Wagner Act), primarily tightening up control of unions' internal affairs.

The act imposed fiduciary duties on union leadership and provided for criminal punishment of union officials who violated the trust of their office. Federal monitoring of unions' financial status was imposed, and unions were required for the first time to report both to the federal government and to their members how union funds are used. The act also regulates union elections, including instituting the requirement that union elections be run through secret ballots. Furthermore, protection is extended to members who state their opposition to union leadership or policies making it illegal for the union to punish such dissenting members. Finally, unions are required under the act to provide members with copies of collective bargaining agreements and to make their members aware of their rights under the act.

Additional Federal Regulation Affecting Employment

In addition to the labor-specific federal acts just noted, other federal (and, to a lesser extent, state) legislation has had a crucial role in redefining the employer-employee relationship.

From the early 1930s through the late 1950s, Congress set into place the foundation of American labor law through the landmark acts we've just briefly reviewed. In so doing, Congress set itself up as the primary source of law relating to employment, preempting state legislation and regulation of labor in areas it elects to regulate. Since the 1960s, Congress has maintained its leadership role in legislation affecting employment through its passage of a number of important acts that further define the rights and responsibilities of employers and employees in a number of key areas that we will examine next.

Employment Discrimination

Title VII of the 1964 Civil Rights Act is the single most important legislation protecting workers from illegal discrimination on the job. The act makes it an unlawful employment practice for an employer

1. to fail or refuse to hire or to discharge any individual, or otherwise to discriminate against any individual with respect to compensation, terms, conditions, or privileges of employment, because of such individual's race, color, religion, sex, or national origin; or
2. to limit, segregate, or classify employees or applicants for employment in any way that would deprive or tend to deprive any individual of employment opportunities or otherwise adversely affect his/her status as an employee, because of such individual's race, color, religion, sex, or national origin.

The 1964 Civil Rights Act created the Equal Employment Opportunity Commission (E.E.O.C.) and empowered it to enforce the act. The E.E.O.C., an independent commission made up of five members appointed by the president and confirmed by Congress, investigates charges of discrimination and enforces the law against covered employers, labor unions, or employment agencies it believes to be guilty of unlawful discrimination.

For employers, unions, and employment agencies to be covered by the act, they must be engaged in activities that have an impact on interstate commerce (as we have previously seen, nearly any activity can be seen as having an impact in interstate commerce) and employ at least an average of 15 persons for a minimum of 20 weeks during the year. Employers that do not meet this criterion do not come within the act because their activities are deemed too insignificant to have an impact on interstate commerce and thus fall outside of the congressional regulatory power.

Not all forms of discrimination are prohibited by the act. Discrimination is permissible if it is pursuant to a bona fide occupational qualification reasonably necessary for the operation of the business enterprise. Thus, the Catholic Church may choose to ordain only male Catholics for the priesthood, since being both male and Catholic are deemed necessary qualifications for being a Catholic priest. Likewise, a motion picture producer who wishes to make a film about the life of Dr. Martin Luther King may recruit only black males who speak American-accented English for the role. On the other hand, an airline may not hire only female flight attendants merely because it can show its business customers prefer female attendants.

The act's prohibition against discrimination based on sex has been interpreted by the courts to date only as preventing unjustified discrimination based on a person's biological sex. Discrimination based on sexual orientation or preference, however, is not covered as such.

Sexual Harassment

Sexual harassment on the job can constitute employment discrimination within the 1964 Civil Rights Act under certain circumstances. This is an area of the law that is still evolving. The E.E.O.C. has issued guidelines for defining sexual harassment as follows [E.E.O.C. Guidelines 1604.11(f)]:

> Unwelcome sexual advances, requests for sexual favors, and other verbal or physical conduct of a sexual nature constitute sexual harassment when:
>
> 1. Submission to such conduct is made either explicitly or implicitly a term or condition of an individual's employment, [or]
> 2. Submission or rejection of such conduct has the purpose or effect of unreasonably interfering with an individual's work performance or creating an intimidating, hostile or offensive working environment.

While the E.E.O.C. guidelines do not have the force of law, they have persuasive power for judges who must ultimately define the types of conduct that comprise sexual harassment as they decide cases in which such harassment is alleged to have occurred. The bulk of decided cases up to the present have concerned the first definition of sexual harassment under the E.E.O.C. guidelines. Primarily, these involve instances of a supervisor abusing her position of authority in attempting to exact sexual favors from a subordinate employee. Such conduct is universally held to be an unfair labor practice and a violation of Title VII of the 1964 Civil Rights Act. A much harder question involves the secondary definition of sexual harassment under the E.E.O.C. guidelines, since it is not as clear what types of conduct constitute "unreasonably interfering with an individual's work performance" or what constitutes "creating an intimidating, hostile or offensive working environment." For example, is it sexual harassment for a supervisor to keep a calendar in his office that features women in bathing suits if an employee finds it offensive? What about a print of a nude painting, such as Goya's *La Maja Desnuda*? Arguably, tolerating any sexually explicit language in the workplace—even by other employees—constitutes sexual harassment if any employee finds that such language creates an "intimidating, hostile or offensive working environment." These issues continue to be litigated regularly, and the courts are forced to grapple with the free speech and free expression implications as they define the limits of acceptable behavior in the workplace.

Age Discrimination

The Age Discrimination in Employment Act of 1986 (A.D.E.A.) protects men and women over the age of 40 against discrimination because of their age in hiring or promotion. Like Title VII of the 1964 Civil Rights Act, the A.D.E.A. applies to employers, unions, and employment agencies engaged in interstate commerce. The act also effectively outlaws mandatory retirement solely because of age with few exceptions.

Unemployment Benefits

The Social Security Act of 1935 provides the framework for unemployment compensation that is funded through mandatory contributions by employers and employees. The unemployment insurance provisions of the act are administered by state agencies under federal coordination. Requirements for eligibility of benefits, duration of benefits, and the amount of benefits payable are controlled by local laws, though states tend to adopt similar regulations in these areas. Railroad workers, farm workers, domestic workers, and federal workers are not covered under the act, although railroad and federal employees have coverage under separate federal legislation.

In general, employees must work a minimum number of weeks per calendar year to be eligible for coverage, and only employees who are dismissed from their jobs without just cause are entitled to receive benefits; employees who quit a job out of choice are not eligible for unemployment insurance, nor are employees who are fired for wrongful conduct, such as embezzlement or illegal drug use on the job.

Health and Safety

The Occupational Safety and Health Act of 1970 was passed by Congress to ensure employee health and safety on the job. Under the act, the Secretary of Labor is given the responsibility of promulgating standards for ensuring worker's health and safety on the job as well as the power to enforce these standards in the courts.

The act imposes on employers a duty to furnish a workplace to all employees free from recognized hazards that are likely to cause death or serious injury. Employers are also required to keep records of all occupational injuries or illnesses that result in death, loss of consciousness, loss of one or more workdays, or medical treatment other than first aid.

The act created a dedicated agency within the Department of Labor, the Occupational Safety and Health Administration (O.S.H.A.), to handle matters relating to administration and enforcement of the act. The agency is charged with conducting safety inspections of workplaces with a poor safety record and with forcing compliance with the act through the courts when employers do not voluntarily resolve safety or health problems identified by the agency. O.S.H.A. also investigates allegations of safety or health violations at the request of employees, who are protected against reprisals for making such allegations or otherwise asserting their rights under the act.

Workers' Compensation

Every state has adopted a workers' compensation statute that provides compensation for employees for job-related injuries. Coverage varies from state to state, with some states limiting coverage to employees engaged in manual labor, whereas others cover nearly all employees regardless of the nature of the employment. Covered employees who suffer injuries arising out of the course of their employment are guaranteed compensation for their loss as well as payment of medical bills, but give up the right to sue the employer under a tort or contract theory for damages resulting from the injury. States generally limit damages recoverable by injured employees to statutorily provided amounts that are modest when compared to jury awards for similar tort injuries. States' workers' compensation statutes, thus, provide some measure of protection to employees who suffer injuries on the job by guaranteeing them prompt medical care of no cost to them (even if the injury is caused by their own negligence), but also serve to effectively limit the common law rights of employees to later sue the employer for the damages for the same injury.

Pension Plans

Employers are not generally required to provide retirement plans or health plans to employees. If they choose to do so, however, these private retirement and health plans are covered by the Employment Retirement Income Security Act of 1974 (ERISA) which sets standards for most retirement and health plans that are voluntarily provided in the private sector. The act requires employers to provide basic information about health and retirement plans to employees, including a summary of benefits under these plans and information on how they operate as well as a yearly annual report summary covering the plan's assets. The same information along with a full annual report detailing plan assets must also be filed with the Department of Labor. The act also imposes fiduciary responsibilities on plan administrators.

The Consolidated Omnibus Budget Reconciliation Act of 1985 (COBRA) amended ERISA to provide workers and their families who lose their health benefits due to a qualifying event the right to choose to continue group health benefits provided by their group health plan for a limited period of time. A qualifying event for an individual includes a voluntary or involuntary termination of employment other than for gross misconduct or the loss of eligibility for health coverage due to a reduction in work hours that makes the employee ineligible for coverage (e.g., going from full-time to part-time employment status if only full-time employees are offered health coverage by the employer). A qualifying event for a dependent of a covered employee includes such circumstances as the divorce of a spouse, the death of the covered employee, and the loss of coverage by a dependent child who loses dependent status under the plan. Qualified individuals who avail themselves of a temporary COBRA extension of coverage may be required to pay 102% of the entire premium for healthcare. Thus, if the employee paid $200 per month and the employer paid $800 per month for health coverage for the employee and his family, the employee could be asked to pay $1,020 per month for COBRA coverage (102% of the employer and employee contribution). COBRA temporary coverage is generally available if the employer sponsored a health plan for 20 or more employees in the prior year. COBRA applies to private sector employers and to state and local governments that provide health insurance to their employees. COBRA continuation coverage may generally be maintained for up to 18 months.

The Health Insurance Portability and Accountability Act of 1996 (HIPAA) provided another significant amendment to ERISA. The act protects individuals and families covered by group health plans from the exclusion of coverage for pre-existing medical conditions when employees change health plans. HIPAA generally limits the maximum period for excluding pre-existing conditions from coverage to 12 months from an individual's enrollment date (18 months for late enrollees). And HIPAA requires a new employer's plan to give individuals credit for the length of time they had prior continuous health coverage, without a break in coverage of 63 days or more, to reduce or eliminate the exclusion period. Therefore, an employee who had health insurance coverage for the 12 months immediately preceding the start of a new job with no break in coverage greater than 63 days will have 12 months of credit toward the exclusionary period and will qualify for pre-existing condition coverage on the date of enrollment in the new plan.

Family and Medical Leave Act of 1993

The Family and Medical Leave Act of 1993 allows public and private sector employees who have worked for the same employer for one year for a minimum of 1,250 hours to take up to 12 weeks of unpaid leave in any 12-month period for any of the following reasons:

1. the birth or adoption of a child;
2. the placement of a foster child;
3. the serious illness of a spouse, child, or parent; or
4. the serious illness of the employee.

The act covers employers who hire 50 or more employees full or part time during the year who live within 75 miles of the worksite. Employees must work for a covered employer for at least one year and have worked a minimum of 1,250 hours for the employer in the past year to be eligible for coverage. Employers may require and employees may elect to include paid leave (such as vacation or sick time) as a part of the 12-week period.

Employees are under the obligation to provide 30 days' notice prior to taking leave in cases in which the need for leave is foreseeable. In addition, the employer is entitled to demand proof of the underlying reason for the leave (such as medical certification of illness or legal proof of adoption, birth, or new foster parent status). In cases in which both a husband and wife work for the same employer, the combined period of leave taken by the couple may not exceed 12 weeks per calendar year.

Covered employees who take medical or family leave under the act are entitled to return to their job at the end of the leave period. If the employer cannot reasonably find a temporary replacement for the employee on leave, it can hire a permanent replacement and offer a comparable job to the employee upon his return from leave.

Employees whose earnings are in the top 10% in the company have more limited rights under the act. They can take medical or family leave, but the employer need not keep their jobs open or rehire them in any capacity at the end of the leave period. The employer must, however, keep health insurance in force for these employees during the leave period if health insurance is offered to employees.

Americans with Disabilities Act

The Americans with Disabilities Act of 1990 (ADA) contains two principal parts. Title I of the ADA forbids discrimination against qualified individuals with physical or mental disabilities in hiring, firing, or promotion, and requires employers to make reasonable accommodations for disabled employees. Title III of the ADA mandates accessibility for the disabled to new and existing public and private facilities that are open to the general public.

This landmark legislation expands the 1973 Rehabilitation Act that prohibited discrimination in hiring on the basis of handicap in federal employment and by federal contractors and companies receiving federal assistance. The ADA is enforced by the Equal Employment Opportunity Commission (E.E.O.C.) and, as of July 25, 1994, has applied to all employers engaged in interstate commerce who employ at least 15 employees per day for at least 20 weeks per year. The U.S. and corporations wholly owned by the U.S. are excluded from the act, as are Indian tribes and social clubs that are not open to the general public. The salient provisions of Title I of the ADA include the following:

- prohibits discrimination against qualified disabled individuals based on their disability in hiring, retention, or promotion;
- mandates that reasonable accommodation be made for qualified disabled individuals by employers unless such accommodations would impose an undue hardship on the business operation;
- allows private individuals to bring lawsuits to enforce the act through injunction (but not for money damages);
- allows the U.S. Attorney General to bring legal action that includes injunctions, fines, and/or damages against employers who violate the act (including reasonable attorneys' fees, court costs, reinstatement, and treble damages, where appropriate).

In its regulations relating to the ADA, the Equal Employment Opportunity Commission defines an individual as qualified for a specific job if she "satisfies the requisite skill, experience, and education requirements of the employment position" [29 CFR 1630.2(m)]. The ADA does not require lesser-qualified disabled individuals to be hired; it only forbids discrimination against otherwise qualified individuals merely because of their disability.

Under the ADA, an individual is considered to be disabled if he suffers from a physical or mental impairment that substantially limits one or more major life functions [29 CFR 1630.2(j)]. A major life function is any essential function such as walking, thinking, seeing, hearing, or reproducing. In addition, the impairment must be permanent in nature and be substantial. For instance, a person who sprains an ankle while jogging would not be considered to be disabled for purposes of the act even if he is unable to walk as a result of the sprain, since it is a temporary condition. Likewise, someone suffering from mild arthritis who can get around well but is somewhat slowed down by the disease is probably not disabled. (A person suffering from severe arthritis whose mobility is substantially impaired would be disabled, however.)

Title III of the ADA requires greater accessibility by all to places open to the public. The act mandates in great detail changes to existing and new construction to make it accessible to the physically challenged. The detailed regulations mandate greater accessibility through a number of means, including detailed building code changes controlling the height of water fountains, the number of restrooms in buildings, and the installation of elevators in all-new construction taller than two stories or with more than 3,000 square feet per floor. The regulations go as far as to detail the number of parking spaces that must be set aside for handicapped drivers, the number of theater seats that must be made handicapped-accessible, and the height of dining tables in restaurants. In addition, telephone companies are mandated to provide telecommunications devices for the deaf. All new construction must comply with the ADA guidelines, and existing structures must be made handicapped-accessible unless doing so would prove an undue hardship. Social clubs, religious institutions, residential facilities covered by fair housing laws, and owner-occupied inns with fewer than six rooms to rent are all exempt from the act.

The ADA also covers accessibility to public transportation by the disabled.

Affordable Healthcare Act (ACA) of 2010

As we saw in Chapter 34, the Patient Protection and Affordable Care Act of 2010 provides a tax incentive to small businesses that employ no more than 25 employees to provide healthcare to their employees by providing a tax credit of 50% of the healthcare premium cost for their employees if they offer healthcare coverage. You may remember that the act also requires employers with 100 or more employees to provide health insurance to their employees or face a tax penalty of $2,000 per employee. (As of this writing, it is unclear whether the deadline will be extended beyond 2015.) Employers with 50–99 employees have until 2016 to provide coverage or face a similar tax. Companies with fewer than 50 employees are not required to provide health insurance and will have no tax penalties imposed if they fail to do so. The ACA does not require employers to provide health insurance to employees; rather it provides a carrot and stick approach to encourage businesses to do so. Because the tax penalty of $2,000 per employee for employers with 100 or more employees is far less costly than providing medical coverage to employees and their families, it remains to be seen how many businesses will opt to pay the penalty and leave their employees with the unpleasant choice of purchasing their own insurance through the federal or state exchanges or paying the tax penalty of 1% of their income if they fail to do so.

Questions

1. What two branches of law does labor law primarily stem from?
2. What are the two most significant provisions of the Norris–La Guardia Act of 1932?
3. What are the basic provisions of the National Labor Relations Act of 1935 (the Wagner Act)?
4. What are the basic provisions of the Fair Labor Standards Act of 1938?
5. What are the basic provisions of the Labor Management Relations Act of 1947 (the Taft–Hartley Act)?
6. What are the basic provisions of the Labor Management Reporting and Disclosure Act of 1959 (Landrum–Griffin)?
7. The 1964 Civil Rights Act makes what type of discrimination in employment illegal?
8. How does the Equal Employment Opportunity Commission define sexual harassment in its guidelines?
9. What federal act was passed by Congress in 1970 to oversee employees' health and safety on the job? What federal agency is charged with enforcement of the act?
10. What are the two main areas covered by the 1993 Americans with Disabilities Act?

Hypothetical Cases

1. Devon hires Rex to do odd jobs around his house on a fairly regular basis. Over the past year, Rex worked an average of six hours per week for Devon performing a variety of tasks, which included gardening, house painting, snow removal, and minor household repairs. Rex also works for a number of other homeowners in the community performing similar tasks for them on a regular basis. He is paid a flat hourly fee by Devon and uses both his own tools and tools provided by Devon in the performance of his job.
   A. During a late October afternoon while performing leaf pickup for Devon, Rex decides to gather leaves in a large steel drum and burn them without Devon's knowledge or consent. A gust of wind carries a burning leaf to Angela's house next door, starting a fire that causes extensive property damage. Is Devon responsible for the damage? What is the main issue on which this answer depends? Explain.
   B. Would it make a difference in the last question if Rex worked 20 hours per week exclusively for Devon? Explain.

2. Benny Bigot owns a small business that employs ten part-time and three full-time workers throughout the year. He places an ad in a local paper for a full-time receptionist. He subsequently interviews a number of applicants and refuses to hire several qualified applicants for the following reasons: Barbara because she is Jewish; David because he is male; Linda because she is black; Harry because he is gay.
   A. All are outraged when Benny tells them the reason he will not hire them and all file a complaint with the Equal Employment Opportunity Commission. What result under federal law?
   B. If Benny expands his business and hires 20 part-time and full-time workers year round, what result? Explain fully.
   C. What would be the result under the above facts if Benny ran a seasonal business employing 100 persons for three months every year?

3. Samantha, the general manager of ABC Corporation, asks Sam, her secretary, out for drinks after work. Sam believes this to be a sexual advance on Samantha's part and is deeply offended by it. He immediately calls the E.E.O.C. to file a sexual harassment complaint. What result?

4. Emma is fired from her middle management job at ABC Company after ten years of employment due to corporate restructuring and decides to go into business for herself as a management consultant. Her severance package provides her with one year's salary and a continuation of all health benefits for one year after her separation from the company. (The company will continue to pay $1,000 per month for her medical plan and will continue to deduct her $100 per month plan contribution from her monthly severance paychecks.)
   A. After the one-year period, will Emma be able to continue her medical coverage through COBRA? If so, for how long and at what maximum cost?
   B. Assume Emma decides to look for employment after her ABC healthcare coverage ends and waives her right to a COBRA extension of her coverage because she cannot afford the cost. If she finds employment with XYZ Company and enrolls in its health plan 60 days after her health coverage through ABC expires, and XYZ has a 12-month exclusionary period for pre-existing conditions in its healthcare plan, how long must she wait before being covered for pre-existing conditions by her new plan?
   C. If Emma finds employment three months after her health coverage at ABC expires and is diagnosed with a medical condition requiring emergency surgery a month after being in her new job, will her new health insurance pay for the medical costs related to the surgery if the new coverage has a six-month waiting period before pre-existing conditions are covered?

5. Martha, an automobile mechanic, is injured when an article of loose clothing becomes entangled in the alternator pulley of an engine she is diagnosing. She suffers severe injuries requiring her to be hospitalized for a week and to undergo several surgical procedures. After the operations, she is unable to return to work for two months.
   A. If she is found to have been negligent in wearing loose clothing while working on a running engine in violation of the shop's safety guidelines, who will bear the cost of her medical injuries and her time lost from work?
   B. If she is unhappy with the award given her by the Worker's Compensation Board in her state in compensation for her injuries, can Martha sue her employer under a contract or tort theory?

6. Frank, a legally blind attorney who has just been admitted to practice in his state, applies for a position as an associate at a law firm, answering an advertisement that lists as one of the requirements of the job a minimum of five years of relevant experience. In his letter of application, he notes that he is legally blind but claims to be capable of performing the necessary duties with only minor accommodations by the

employer. He is not granted an interview and decides to sue, claiming that he was discriminated against in violation of the Americans with Disabilities Act.
A. What result?
B. If instead of having just been admitted to practice Frank had been employed as an attorney by another firm for ten years, would your answer to the last question change? Explain.
C. Assume that Frank is one of the finest attorneys in his state who has recently begun to lose his vision due to irreversible glaucoma. Further assume that his current employer dismisses him, claiming he can no longer perform his regular job duties. If Frank can show that he would be able to continue performing his job if the employer purchased a larger computer monitor for him to use, as well as furnished him with better lighting in his office, would he likely succeed in his case if the total cost of the new equipment would be $5,000 for the employer and the employer were a large law firm? What if a small firm with just two partners were involved?

Ethics and the Law

The Family and Medical Leave Act allows married couples who are covered employees under the act and who work for the same employer to take a maximum of 12 *combined* weeks of medical leave, effectively forcing them to share their medical leave privileges when no such requirement is made of unmarried domestic partners who are each free to take up to 12 weeks of medical or family leave each year. Arguably, this unfairly penalizes married couples and rewards individuals who choose not to marry. Nor is this the only example of federal legislation that provides less preferable treatment to married couples and their nuclear families. The federal tax code has long provided and has only fairly recently made an effort to address the "marriage penalty" for married couples who have for many years been subjected to higher taxes than nonmarried couples living together. Many federal and state entitlement programs also arguably discourage marriage by lessening benefits for married couples for whom benefits are based on the combined income of the husband and wife, while not generally counting the income available to domestic partners who are not declared to live in the same household, thereby arguably encouraging single-parent households and denying many children the well-documented benefits of living in a two-parent household. While societies routinely and appropriately use the law to engage in social engineering for the benefit of their citizens, is providing disincentives to marriage, even if minor or unintended, ethically justifiable in our society? What do you think?

Federal Securities Acts

CHAPTER 39

In the aftermath of the stock market crash of 1929, Congress passed the Securities Act of 1933 and the Securities Exchange Act of 1934. These landmark acts regulate the original issue of securities and the subsequent trading of securities in the secondary markets, respectively. These acts as amended require companies to provide investors with accurate information about their finances, and they punish fraudulent and deceptive activities in the issuance and sale of securities.

Chapter Outline

Securities Act of 1933
Sanctions under the Securities Act of 1933
Securities Exchange Act of 1934
Sarbanes–Oxley Act of 2002
Securities Regulation by the States

Securities Act of 1933

The Securities Act of 1933 requires that securities be registered prior to being offered for sale for the first time in interstate commerce, with few exceptions. The act defines securities broadly to include a range of instruments such as stocks, bonds, debentures, evidence of indebtedness, voting trust certificates, investment contracts, and fractional undivided interests in oil, gas, or mineral rights. In *SEC v. W. J. Howey Co.* (328 U.S. 293), the U.S. Supreme Court held that an investment contract constitutes a security under the act. An investment contract under the *Howey* test is defined as any transaction in which a person

- invests
- in a common enterprise
- reasonably expecting profits that are
- derived primarily or substantially from the managerial or entrepreneurial efforts of others.

Registration

Before any new security can be offered to the public through the mails or through any interstate commerce facility such as a stock exchange or the use of the Internet, the issuer must file a registration statement with the Securities and Exchange Commission (SEC). The registration statement must be written in plain language and include all of the following:

- a description of the significant provisions of the security offered for sale that includes the relationship between the security and other capital securities of the company;
- a description of the company's properties and business;
- a description of the company's management that includes information on the management's security holdings, compensation, and benefits;

331

- a financial statement certified by an independent public accounting firm; and
- a description of pending lawsuits involving the company.

Prior to the filing for registration with the SEC (the *prefiling period*), a company must avoid publicity about the new security and may not sell or offer to sell the security to anyone. Once the company files the registration statement with the SEC and its approval is pending (the *waiting period*), the company may still not sell the security but may begin to offer the security for sale through limited advertisements in ads that tell prospective investors where they may request a prospectus for the new security while stating that the ad is not an offer to sell securities (*tombstone ads*). At this point, a company may make available a preliminary prospectus to investors that does not include the price of the security. Once the SEC declares the registration effective and prospective buyers are given a final prospectus (the *post-effective period*), the company may finally offer and sell the new security.

Securities Exempt from Registration

As noted previously, there are some limited exemptions to the requirement that new securities be registered with the SEC prior to their being offered to the public. The Securities Act of 1933 exempts the following securities from registration:

- all bank securities sold prior to July 27, 1933;
- commercial paper (such as checks, drafts, notes, and certificates of deposit) with a maturity date of not more than nine months;
- government-issued securities;
- securities issued by nonprofit religious, charitable, educational, benevolent, or fraternal organizations;
- securities issued by a bank or savings and loan;
- securities issued by common carriers regulated by the Interstate Commerce Commission;
- an insurance policy or an annuity contract.

Under Rule 147, securities offered for sale solely in one state by a company that does at least 80% of its business in the state are also exempt from filing. State securities regulations, however, may require the company to file with the SEC. Resale of these securities is also restricted to residents of the state for nine months following the initial sale. In addition to the intrastate sale exemption and security exemptions noted here, the act allows several additional exemptions involving small securities offerings. These include the following:

- ***Rule 506 of Regulation D:*** This rule exempts private offerings to *accredited investors* (expert investors such as banks, executive officers, directors, and partners of the business issuing the security and wealthy investors) and limited offerings to not more than 35 nonaccredited investors (e.g., regular, nonexpert investors).
- ***Rule 504 of Regulation D***: Nonpublic issuers may sell up to $1 million of securities in a 12-month period to any purchaser. General advertising of the issue is permitted, as long as the dollar limit of the issue is not exceeded.
- ***Rule 505 of Regulation D***: Any issuer may sell up to $5 million of securities in a 12-month period to fewer than 35 unaccredited investors and to an unlimited number of accredited investors. General advertising of the issue is not permitted, however.
- ***Regulation A***: Any nonpublic issuer may sell up to $5 million of securities in a one-year period with no limit on the number of purchasers and no purchaser sophistication requirement. The offering circular is considered the disclosure document for such a filing and must be filed with the SEC, but registration of the offering itself is not required.

Securities purchased under Rules 504, 505, and 506 must generally be held for one year prior to resale; otherwise, the seller may be subject to penalties as an underwriter of an unregistered security.

Sanctions under the Securities Act of 1933

Section 12 (a) (2) prohibits misstatements or omissions of material fact in any written or oral communication in connection with the general distribution of any security by an issuer, and section 17 (a) prohibits the use of any device or artifice to defraud, or the use of any untrue or misleading statement, in connection with the offer or sale of any security.

The act provides for civil and criminal sanctions for willful and negligent violations. The SEC is given the power to investigate and bring civil enforcement proceedings under the act and allows the SEC to seek injunctive relief against violators of the act. Section 11 of the act provides civil liability for damages when a registration statement misstates or omits a material fact on its effective date. A purchaser may file suit for damages caused by misstatement or omission without having to prove reliance on the misstatement or omission in purchasing the securities or prove that defendant negligently or intentionally misstated or omitted a material fact. However, a defendant can escape liability by proving the purchaser knew of the misstatement or omission when the security was purchased. In addition, defendants can successfully assert the defense of *due diligence* and escape liability if they can establish that after a *reasonable investigation* they had reasonable grounds to believe and did believe that the registration statement was true and contained no omission of material fact.

Section 24 of the 1933 act provides for criminal liability for any person who willfully violates the act or its rules and regulations with violators subject to fines of up to $10,000 and/or imprisonment for up to five years for each criminal violation of the act. Criminal violations of the act are prosecuted by the Department of Justice.

Securities Exchange Act of 1934

Unlike the disclosure requirements of the Securities Act of 1933, which applies only to the initial public offering of a security, the Securities Exchange Act of 1934 regulates the trading of securities after their original public offering. The act also regulates securities brokers, dealers, securities exchanges, and national securities associations. In addition, the act created the Securities and Exchange Commission (SEC) and empowered it to enforce the securities laws under the 1933 and 1934 acts.

Under the Securities Exchange Act of 1934, companies whose securities are traded on any public securities exchange and companies with assets in excess of $10 million whose stock is owned by 500 or more shareholders are required to file information on an annual and quarterly basis with the SEC. Companies are also required to provide the SEC with notification of material changes when they occur by means of a monthly report. The reported information is then made available to prospective investors and to the general public through the EDGAR (Electronic Data Gathering Analysis and Retrieval) database maintained by the SEC. EDGAR is available online at http://www.sec.gov/edgar.shtml.

The act also requires company insiders, defined as corporate officers, directors, and anyone who controls 10% or more of any company's class of equity securities, to disclose their holdings and transactions in company securities. Proxy solicitations are also regulated under the act.

Violations of the Securities Exchange Act of 1934

Both civil and criminal sanctions are available under the act. These include the following:

> Section 18 of the act imposes liability on any person responsible for a false or misleading statement of a material fact in any filing under the act. Anyone who relies on the false or misleading statement may sue for damages without the need to prove that

the defendant was negligent in providing the false or misleading information to the SEC. However, a defendant may avoid liability by proving that the false or misleading information was provided in good faith.

Section 10(b) prohibits the use of manipulative or deceptive devices through misstatement or omission of a material fact in the sale of securities. A material fact can be defined as any information where there is substantial likelihood that a reasonable investor would consider it important in making the decision to purchase the security. A seller is not liable under section 10 (b) unless she acts with *scienter* (with the mental state embracing the intent to deceive, manipulate, or defraud). The prohibition is made applicable to all transactions in securities under Rule 10 (b) (5), whether or not the securities need to be registered with the SEC under the 1933 or 1934 acts.

Section 32 provides criminal liability for violations of the act of up to $5 million in fines and imprisonment up to 20 years for willful violations of the act. Businesses may be fined up to $25 million for violations of the act.

Sarbanes–Oxley Act of 2002

(Public Company Accounting Reform and Investor Protection Act of 2002)

The highly publicized management and accounting scandals involving Enron, Tyco International, WorldCom, and other companies in the recent past led Congress to adopt the Sarbanes–Oxley Act (SOX) in 2002 with near unanimity in both the House of Representatives and the Senate. The legislation established new or enhanced standards for the boards of all U.S. publicly traded companies, their management, and all public accounting firms. Criminal penalties are imposed for certain violations of the act, and the SEC is charged with implementing rules for compliance with the provisions of the act. SOX creates a new agency, the Public Company Accounting Oversight Board (PCAOB), which is charged with the oversight, inspection, regulation, and disciplining of accounting firms in their roles as auditors of public companies.

Following are some of the key provisions of the act:

- Section 906 requires chief executive officers and chief financial officers of most publicly traded companies to certify the accuracy of financial statements filed with the SEC.
- Section 302 requires both quarterly and annual statements to be certified by the CEO and CFO of reporting companies as having been reviewed by a signing officer of the company and to contain no factual errors to the best knowledge of the signing officer. The signing officer must also certify the existence of an internal control system to identify all material information that must be reported by the company.
- Section 806 provides protection for employees who report securities violations (whistleblower protection), preventing employers from firing or taking other retaliatory action against such employees.
- Enhanced penalties are provided under the act, including fines of up to $5 million and/or up to 20 years in jail for criminal violations of the Section 906 certification requirements.

Securities Regulation by the States

Federal securities regulation does not preempt the states from also regulating the sale of securities within their borders. In cases in which the issuance or sale of securities is not covered by the federal acts, such as in the case of intrastate offerings, states impose their own regulatory requirements on issuers under what are often referred to as *blue sky laws*. Every state has its own regulatory scheme covering the issuance and sale of securities. In most states, securities regulation is patterned after the federal acts.

Questions

1. When must securities be registered with the SEC under the Securities Act of 1933?
2. What types of securities are covered under the 1933 act?
3. What is the definition of an investment contract under the Howey test?
4. What type of information must be included in a registration statement under the 1933 act?
5. What kinds of securities are exempt from registration under the 1933 act?
6. What are the maximum penalties for violating the Securities Act of 1933?
7. What is the threshold for registering securities under the 1934 act and having to file periodic reports about these securities?
8. What is the maximum criminal penalty available under the 1934 act?
9. What is the function of the Public Company Accounting Oversight Board created by Sarbanes–Oxley?
10. What is the maximum criminal penalty for violating the certification requirements of Sarbanes–Oxley?

Hypothetical Cases

1. Private University, a private not-for-profit educational institution located in California, decides to issue "Shares in Learning" certificates in a one-time offering to the public. These shares will be sold for $500 each and entitle the bearer to redeem each certificate for two undergraduate or one graduate college credit in any of its schools at any time in the future. The shares may also be resold without restriction by the initial purchaser. The offering will be made via the Internet.
   A. Assuming that the "Shares in Learning" are securities for purposes of the Securities Act of 1933, will the issue need to be registered with the SEC under the act? Explain.
   B. Assume for purposes of this question that the "Shares in Learning" are issued by Private College, a proprietary for-profit institution licensed to do business in California. Will the securities need to be registered with the SEC if the college does business only in California, the securities are advertised and sold only to California residents via telephone solicitation, and 5 of the 500 institution's current students are from out of state? Explain fully.
   C. If State University is a proprietary, for-profit institution that does business in all 50 states and around the world by offering its degrees online, will the security offering come under the 1933 act?
2. ABC Corporation decides to issue a new corporate bond in order to raise $500 million to finance the expansion of its manufacturing facilities and a new building to house its corporate headquarters. The issue is to be marketed only to wealthy investors and institutional investors. Will this new bond issue need to be registered with the SEC? Explain.
3. XYZ Company is an entrepreneurial venture with assets of $11 million that is wholly owned by Jemal and Julia, who are husband and wife. The couple would like to raise $5 million in new capital either through equity or debt financing and want to remain free of the requirement to register the new securities under the Securities Act of 1933 and also want to remain free of the reporting requirements of the Securities Exchange Act of 1934. What are their options? Explain fully.
4. In the last example, assume that both Jemal and Julia innocently materially overstate the company's net worth to prospective investors due to errors in their financial statements provided by their accounting firm. As a result, they are sued by an investor who claims that he would not have purchased bonds for the offered rate of interest were it not for the misrepresentations about the company's finances.
   A. Do Jemal and Julia have a valid defense against a civil suit from the investor?
   B. May Jemal and Julia be successfully prosecuted under the 1934 act for the misstatement?
   C. Had the material misrepresentation been knowingly made in order to induce investors to buy the new securities, what would be the maximum penalty that Jemal and Julia could be subject to?

Federal Antitrust Law

CHAPTER 40

Chapter Outline
The Sherman Antitrust Act of 1890
The Clayton Act of 1914

The strength and integrity of our economic system depend on free competition, with companies gaining competitive advantages based on such factors as the quality, uniqueness, and price of the products and services they provide and the effectiveness of their marketing efforts in differentiating their products from those of their competitors in the minds of consumers. But the system can be undermined if companies are allowed to engage in anticompetitive practices that artificially manipulate prices by limiting competition, restricting the availability of products, or fixing prices by agreements that undermine basic market forces. While the states and the federal government both regulate and punish anticompetitive practices, it is the federal government that regulates anticompetitive practices that can impact interstate commerce, primarily through the Sherman Antitrust Act and Clayton Act as amended. In this chapter, we will focus on these two acts and examine the basic tenets of federal antitrust law.

The Sherman Antitrust Act of 1890

Section 1 of the Sherman Antitrust Act [15 U.S.C. § 1] as amended declares illegal every "contract, combination in the form of trust or otherwise, or conspiracy, in restraint of trade or commerce among the several States, or with foreign nations. . . ." Violation of the act is punishable as a felony and carries a maximum penalty of up to $10 million if the violator is a corporation and a maximum fine of $350,000 and/or imprisonment of up to three years if the violator is an individual. Because contracts and conspiracies require the participation of two or more persons, Section 1 of the act applies only to concerted efforts by two or more persons or entities to restrain trade or commerce. (Section 3 of the act extends the same prohibition and penalties for conduct in restraint of trade affecting Washington D.C. and U.S. territories.)

Section 2 of the act [15 U.S.C. § 2] makes it a felony to "monopolize . . . or conspire with any other person or persons, to monopolize any part of the trade or commerce among the several States, or with foreign nations. . . ." The maximum violation for persons or corporations found guilty of violating Section 2 of the act is the same as for violations of Section 1, namely a maximum fine of $10 million for corporations and $350,000 and/or imprisonment for up to three years for individuals. Under this section, individual and concerted action to artificially create a monopoly is criminalized. Note that monopolies as such are not prohibited; rather, it is the effort to artificially create a monopoly by practices in restraint of trade that is criminalized. An individual or corporation may in theory create and maintain a monopoly as long as it is done without engaging in illegal anticompetitive activity. Thus, if an inventor were to invent an engine that runs on tap water, she could patent the invention and be guaranteed a manufacturing monopoly for a period of 20 years from the date that she files her patent application once the patent is issued. Likewise, if a corporation discovers a new process for genetically engineering a bacterium that ingests waste products and excretes crude oil, it could either patent the new organism or protect its manufacturing as a trade secret and thereby guarantee for itself a monopoly on the production of what would be a highly lucrative commodity without violating the Sherman Antitrust Act. In other words, domination of a market by producing a superior product or service at a lower price than the competition is not a violation of the act.

Section 2 of the act also prohibits attempts to monopolize a market. To successfully prosecute a person or company for an attempt to monopolize interstate or foreign commerce, the prosecutor must prove that the defendant willfully engaged in conduct intended to destroy competition and create a monopoly. Individuals and companies can also be prosecuted for taking part in a conspiracy to create a monopoly. To successfully prosecute individuals or companies for a conspiracy to monopolize, the prosecutor must establish that the defendants planned a course of action with the intent to destroy competition to create a monopoly and that they engaged in some overt act to carry out that plan.

In addition to the criminal penalties discussed here, Section 4 of the act [15 U.S.C. § 4] gives U.S. attorneys under the direction of the U.S. Attorney General the power to obtain injunctive relief (such as cease and desist orders) in federal district courts against violators of the act.

The Sherman Act also provides civil penalties to individuals or companies harmed by those who violate the act that include *treble damages* (triple the amount of actual damages suffered by a plaintiff due to a defendant's violation of the act).

Violations of the Act

The courts apply a "rule of reason" test first announced by the U.S. Supreme Court in *Standard Oil Co. v. U.S.* [221 U.S. 1 (1911)] to determine whether specific actions that may arguably result in restraint of trade under the act are illegal. Under the rule of reason test, conspiracies in restraint of trade are held to be illegal only if they constitute undue or unreasonable restraints of trade and unreasonable attempts to monopolize under the Sherman Act. Therefore, only contracts or actions that are unduly restrictive of trade are deemed to violate the act. Some types of agreements are so harmful to free competition, however, that they are held to be *per se* violations of the act and punishable in themselves without having to examine their reasonableness or potential restraint on commerce. Common examples of *per se* violations of the act include agreements among competitors to fix prices or limit the availability of commodities, group boycotts in which groups of sellers refuse to deal with a specific company or person, and agreements by competitors to carve out geographic areas in which they will not compete with one another. The following examples will illustrate:

- Three gasoline retailers in a suburban town agree to charge $3.50 per gallon of regular gas at a time when the average price for gasoline in their region of the state is $3.00 per gallon. This is a price-fixing agreement and a *per se* violation of Section 1 of the act.
- Slick's Lube Works and Do-Em-Fast Oil Changes, two national competing chains specializing in oil changes and related automotive services, agree to divide areas of each state in which they do business so that only one of the companies does business in any given city or town in each state. This agreement, intended to lessen competition and increase the profitability of each franchise for both companies, is a *per se* violation of the act.
- Three major food retailers, ABC Corp., DEF Corp., and GHI Corp., agree not to purchase produce from JKL Corp., a produce wholesaler, until JKL makes major price concessions to each company. This is an illegal boycott and a *per se* violation of the act.

The Clayton Act of 1914

The Clayton Act modifies and strengthens the antitrust provisions of the Sherman Act in a number of significant ways. We'll explore some of these next.

Prohibition on Price Discrimination

Section 2 of the Clayton Act [15 U.S.C. § 13] prohibits sellers from charging different competitive buyers different prices for "commodities of like grade and quality." Temporary price reductions are permitted if made in a good faith effort to meet a competitor's price reductions. Different prices may also be charged to reflect higher shipping costs when delivering commodities to buyers in different geographic areas. Quantity discounts are also allowable, provided they are available to all buyers who purchase similar quantities of goods. Giving and soliciting discriminatory pricing are punished equally under the act. Schools, colleges, universities, public libraries, churches, hospitals, and not-for-profit charitable institutions are not subject to the provisions of this section of the act. Violation of this section of the act is punishable by fines of not more than $5,000 and/or imprisonment for not more than one year.

Prohibition on Sale and Lease Contracts That Prevent the Buyer from Purchasing Commodities from the Seller's Competitors

Section 3 of the act [15 U.S.C. § 14] makes it illegal for sellers of commodities involved in commerce to enter into sale or lease contracts that restrict the ability of buyers to purchase the goods or services of the seller's competitors when the effect is to lessen competition or tend to create a monopoly in any line of commerce. The effect of this section is to prohibit exclusive dealing contracts and tie-in sales arrangements in which a buyer must agree to purchase one or more product lines as a precondition to being able to purchase what is typically a highly desirable product line with limited availability.

Antitrust Laws Inapplicable to Labor Organizations

Section 6 of the act [15 U.S.C. § 17] exempts labor organizations from coverage under antitrust laws, stating that "[t]he labor of a human being is not a commodity or article of commerce" and that the lawful activities of unions cannot be "held or construed to be illegal combinations or conspiracies in restraint of trade, under the antitrust laws."

Acquisition by One Corporation of the Stock of Another

Section 7 of the act [15 U.S.C. § 18] generally prohibits the acquisition of one company's stock by another company when "the effect of such acquisition may be substantially to lessen competition, or to tend to create a monopoly." Corporations may, however, expand their operations through subsidiaries and purchase the stock of subsidiary companies when the effect is not to substantially lessen competition.

Premerger Notification

Section 7A of the act [15 U.S.C. § 18a] requires notification of the Federal Trade Commission (FTC) and the Assistant Attorney General in Charge of the Antitrust Division of the Department of Justice prior to the acquisition of voting securities when the acquisition would leave the acquirer with voting securities and aggregate assets in the company whose securities are being acquired of $200 million or more. In certain circumstances, the threshold amount is set at $50 million. The amounts are adjusted annually as of September 30, 2004, and were raised to $305.1 million and $76.3 million, respectively, as of January 2015 (the latest data available as of this writing). A waiting period of 30 days (15 days for cash tender offers) is imposed prior to the consummation of acquisitions requiring notification of the FTC and Department of Justice, with the waiting period starting on the day that the notification is received by the FTC.

Prohibition on Officers and Directors Serving Competing Companies

Section 8 of the act [15 U.S.C. § 19] prohibits interlocking directorates and officers serving competing companies if both companies have aggregate capital, surplus and undivided profits of $10 million or more each. (The FTC adjusts the amount annually; it was $15.3 million as of January 2015.) Directors and officers serving two companies that meet the minimum capital amount may still lawfully serve both companies as long as one of the following conditions is met:

1. the competitive sales of either company are less than $1,000,000 ($1,525,300 as adjusted for 2015);
2. the competitive sales of either corporation are less than 2% of that corporation's total sales; or
3. the competitive sales of each corporation are less than 4% of that corporation's total sales.

Directors and officers of banks, banking associations, and trust companies are exempt from the provisions of this section.

Violations of the Act

The Department of Justice through the Assistant Attorney General in Charge of the Antitrust Division, state attorneys general, and the FTC all have jurisdiction over violations of the act. The federal and state attorneys general may seek injunctive relief such as cease and desist orders in federal district courts. The act also provides treble damages and reasonable attorneys' fee reimbursement in private actions against violators of the act. For both the Sherman and Clayton Acts, the overwhelming majority of suits against violators have come from private party suits.

Questions

1. What is the maximum penalty that can be imposed for a criminal violation of the Sherman Act?
2. What are treble damages, and how are they relevant to the Sherman and Clayton Acts?
3. How does a court determine whether actions that may result in restraint of trade are illegal under the Sherman Act?
4. Give an example of a *per se* violation under the Sherman Act.
5. Do quantity discounts amount to illegal price discrimination under the Clayton Act?
6. Are all merger agreements subject to oversight by the FTC?
7. What are interlocking directorates?
8. When are directors and officers of corporations forbidden from working for or serving on the boards of competitors?
9. Who has jurisdiction with regard to enforcement of the Clayton Act?
10. What is the most common source of litigation with regard to violations of antitrust law to date?

Hypothetical Cases

1. Ines Inventor creates a new telecommunications device that she markets under the brand name Alter Ego. The device combines the functionality of a telephone, video player, micro tablet, and portable game machine in a slim package about the size and weight of a credit card. Because the device utilizes a version of Linux, the open-source operating system, it can run a wide range of applications and can be offered at a reduced cost. Six months after its launch, the device, which is aggressively priced at $199, gives Ines a 90% share of the cellular-phone market and transforms her startup company into a multibillion dollar behemoth that directly causes the demise of more than a dozen companies that cannot compete with the quality, features, or price of her new product.
    A. Assuming that Ines has a monopoly on the micro tablet and personal multifunction cell-phone market a year after the launch of her company, may she be successfully prosecuted for having established a monopoly under the Sherman Act?

B. Two companies that are put out of business because of the Alter Ego product bring civil suits against Ines claiming violations of the Sherman Act and asking for treble damages amounting to $100 billion. What result?

2. Assume the same facts in the last question, except that it costs Ines $250 to produce each of the devices, and she sells them for $199 for the first year after the launch of her company and then raises the wholesale price in the second year to $350. What result?

3. Office King, a national retailer of office equipment and supplies, offers computers and printers for sale, made by various third parties, at cost to business purchasers who agree to purchase all office supplies, including the toner, paper, and recordable media exclusively for a period of three years from Office King.
   A. Is this agreement permissible? Explain.
   B. Would your answer be the same if the office equipment were offered without a discount?

4. Carlos is the owner of a small business that specializes in refurbishing and selling used laptops for under $200 each. His business has been doing well, and he decides to expand his operation by purchasing ten similar small businesses from around the country and consolidating them under his brand name of "Under $200 Laptops, Inc."
   A. Assuming that all of the businesses purchased by Carlos were closely held corporations and that he purchased the entire voting shares for these and that the total assets of each business were under $10 million, would these purchases require FTC notification?
   B. Given the niche market in which Carlos operates, if the acquisitions leave him with 70% of the laptop refurbishing and resale market and if he had a 5% interest in that market prior to the acquisitions, is Carlos likely to be in violation of the Sherman or Clayton Acts?
   C. If Carlos provides used laptops to schools at cost, is Carlos guilty of illegal price discrimination under the Clayton Act?

Ethics and the Law

The restrictions on individuals serving as officers or board members of two or more competitors is intended to preclude the potential for concerted action that undermines free competition among companies that are supposed to be competitors. These restrictions, however, are limited to relatively large companies with aggregate capital in excess of $15.3 million as of this writing. And even in cases in which both companies meet the triggering amount, directors may serve if the competitive sales (e.g., sales involving areas in which companies are in direct competition) between the companies are less than $1,525,300, or, if greater than that, where the competitive sales are less than 2% of one corporation's total sales or less than 4% of the total sales in each corporation. This leaves a great deal of room for potential conflict in industries that are not dominated by large corporations, and allows for potential conflict of interest issues for directors and officers who owe fiduciary responsibilities to companies whose interests may be in opposition—whether or not they meet the triggering criteria for violation of the Clayton Act. Should interlocking directorates and interlocking executives be allowed in any publicly traded company? Is it consistent with the fiduciary responsibilities that directors and officers owe their corporations and the corporation's shareholders that we allow such key individuals to serve "multiple masters," regardless of a potential conflict with antitrust laws? Do these individuals not owe the corporations they serve the totality of their effort by the nature of the positions they agree to undertake? What do you think?

Unit VII—Cases for Further Study

NICOLE BAKER, PLAINTIFF, v. COUNTY OF NORTHUMBERLAND, DEFENDANT

4:14-CV-00076

UNITED STATES DISTRICT COURT FOR THE MIDDLE DISTRICT OF PENNSYLVANIA

October 29, 2014, Decided
October 29, 2014, Filed
[Case excerpt]

I. Background

Plaintiff, a female, was employed by Defendant in the Northumberland County Sheriff's Office as a deputy sheriff from March 2010 until her position was eliminated on April 23, 2012. She alleges that during her time as a deputy sheriff she was subjected to various instances of workplace discrimination and disparate treatment based on her gender. She alleges, for example, that she was not permitted to call off work during her probationary period, when at least one other male deputy was permitted to do so, that she was written up for punching in a few minutes late while other male employees did not receive such discipline for similar conduct, that Defendant would make rules after Plaintiff would perform a task the way the other deputies would perform the task, and that she was the only deputy not assigned to courtroom work for a 2010 murder trial. Furthermore, Plaintiff alleges that Defendant did not take reports from Plaintiff seriously, such as when she found a high dosage narcotic pill on a fellow deputy's desk and when another male deputy physically removed Plaintiff's hands from an individual she was trying to restrain. Finally, Plaintiff alleges that the male employees did not speak to her for two consecutive weeks in February 2012.

On April 23, 2012, Plaintiff was informed that the Northumberland County commissioners eliminated one deputy sheriff position; the position terminated was hers, despite the fact that there were three less senior male deputies who retained their positions. Plaintiff was not informed why they cut her position over that of any other deputy.

Following her termination, on October 19, 2012, Plaintiff filed a complaint with the PHRC, which was cross filed with the EEOC. This complaint was served on Defendant on January 16, 2013. On February 15, 2013, a male deputy sheriff, Daniel Zettlemoyer, resigned from his employment with Defendant and on February 19, 2013, Defendant hired another male, James Souder, to fill the open position. At no time did Defendant make an effort to recall Plaintiff to fill the open deputy position. Defendant further failed to reply to Plaintiff's request for an explanation as to why she was not recalled from her layoff status for the open position.

In her Complaint, Plaintiff asserts three claims against Defendant. Count I is a claim of sexual discrimination in violation of Title VII and the PHRA for Defendant's actions in terminating Plaintiff's position over that of any other deputies; Count II is a claim of retaliation in violation of Title VII and the PHRA for failing to rehire Plaintiff when a position opened because of her PHRC and EEOC activity; and Count III is asexual discrimination claim [footnote omitted] in violation of Title VII and the PHRA for their actions in failing to rehire Plaintiff when the position opened.

On March 19, 2014, Defendant filed a Motion to Dismiss Plaintiff's Complaint for failure to state a claim under Federal Rule of Procedure 12(b)(6). (ECF No. 7). Defendant first argues that Plaintiff's request for punitive damages must be dismissed because punitive damages are not available to a Plaintiff in an action against a municipal defendant under both Title VII and the PHRA. Defendant next argues that Counts I, II, and III should be dismissed under Federal Rule of Civil Procedure 12(b)(6) for failure to state a claim upon which relief can be granted. This matter is now ripe for disposition.

II. Discussion

A. Motion to Dismiss Standard

When considering a motion to dismiss under Federal Rule of Civil Procedure 12(b)(6), a court must view all allegations stated in the complaint as true and construe all inferences in the light most favorable to plaintiff. *Hishon v. King & Spalding,* 467 U.S. 69, 73, 104 S. Ct. 2229, 81 L. Ed. 2d 59 (1984); *Kost v. Kozakiewicz, 1 F.3d 176, 183 (3d Cir. 1993).* However, "the tenet that a court must accept as true all of the [factual] allegations contained in the complaint is inapplicable to legal conclusions." *Ashcroft v. Iqbal,* 556 U.S. 662, 678, 129 S. Ct. 1937, 173 L. Ed. 2d 868 (2009) (internal citations omitted). In ruling on such a motion, the court primarily considers the allegations of the pleading, but is not required to consider legal conclusions alleged in the complaint. *Kost,* 1 F.3d at 183. "Threadbare recitals of the elements of a cause of action, supported by mere conclusory statements, do not suffice." *Iqbal,* 556 U.S. at 678. At the motion to dismiss stage, the court considers whether plaintiff is entitled to offer evidence to support the allegations in the complaint. *Maio v. Aetna, Inc.,* 221 F.3d 472, 482 (3d Cir. 2000).

A complaint should only be dismissed if, accepting as true all of the allegations in the amended complaint, plaintiff has not pled enough facts to state a claim to relief that is plausible on its face. *Bell Atlantic Corp. v. Twombly,* 550 U.S. 544, 561, 127 S. Ct. 1955, 167 L. Ed. 2d 929 (2007). "Determining whether a complaint states a plausible claim for relief will . . . be a context-specific task that requires the reviewing court to draw on its judicial experience and common sense." *Iqbal,* 556 U.S. at 663–664.

"In considering a Rule 12(b)(6) motion, we must be mindful that federal courts require notice pleading, as opposed to the heightened standard of fact pleading." *Hellmann v. Kercher,* No. 07-1373, 2008 U.S. Dist. LEXIS 37207, 2008 WL 1969311 at * 3 (W.D. Pa. May 5, 2008) (Lancaster, J.). Federal Rule of Civil Procedure 8 "requires only a 'short and plain statement of the claim showing that the pleader is entitled to relief,' in order to 'give the defendant fair notice of what the . . . claim is and the grounds on which it rests,'" *Bell Atlantic Corp. v. Twombly,* 550 U.S. at 554 (*quoting Conley v. Gibson, 355* U.S. 41, 47, 78 S. Ct. 99, 2 L. Ed. 2d 80 (1957)). However, even under this lower notice pleading standard, a plaintiff must do more than recite the elements of a cause of action, and then make a blanket assertion of an entitlement to relief. *See Hellmann,* 2008 U.S. Dist. LEXIS 37207, 2008 WL 1969311 at *3. Instead, a plaintiff must make a factual showing of his entitlement to relief by alleging sufficient facts that, when taken as true, suggest the required elements of a particular legal theory. *See Twombly,* 550 U.S. at 561. "[W]here the well-pleaded facts do not permit the court to infer more than the mere possibility of misconduct, the complaint has alleged—but it has not "shown"—"that the pleader is entitled to relief." *Iqbal,* 556 U.S. at 679 (quoting Fed. R. Civ. P. 8(a)).

The failure-to-state-a-claim standard of Rule 12(b)(6) "streamlines litigation by dispensing with needless discovery and factfinding." *Neitzke v. Williams,* 490 U.S. 319, 326-27, 109 S. Ct. 1827, 104 L. Ed. 2d 338 *(1989).* A court may dismiss a claim under Rule 12(b)(6) where there is a "dispositive issue of law." Id. at 326. If it is beyond a doubt that the non-moving party can prove no set of facts in support of its allegations, then a claim must be dismissed "without regard to whether it is based on an outlandish legal theory or on a close but ultimately unavailing one." *Id.* at 327.

B. Availability of Punitive Damages

Defendant first requests that the Court dismiss Plaintiff's demand for punitive damages, arguing that punitive damages are not available under Title VII or the PHRA as against municipal defendants. Plaintiff agrees with this proposition and concurs in the dismissal of her request for punitive damages.

Defendant is correct in asserting that a Court may not reward punitive damages against a municipal defendant under Title VII. See 42 U.S.C. § 1981a(b)(1) ("A complaining party may recover punitive damages under this section against a respondent (other than a government, government agency or political subdivision). . .); *see also Evans v. Port Authority of N.Y.* and *N.J.,* 273 F.3d 346, 356–57 (3d Cir. 2001) (punitive damages are unavailable in Title VII suits against municipalities or quasi-governmental agencies).

Punitive damages are similarly not available under the PHRA. *See Hoy v. Angelone,* 554 Pa. 134, 720 A.2d 745, 749 (Pa. 1998) ("While punitive damages also serve to deter, simply put, we do not consider punitive damages to be consistent with the remedial nature of the Act. We believe that when interpreted in the context of contemplated affirmative action, the phrase 'any other legal or equitable relief' does not include punitive damages."); *see also Glickstein v. Neshaminy School Dist.,* No. 96-6236, 1999 U.S. Dist. LEXIS 727, 1999 WL 58578, at *20 (E.D.Pa. Jan. 26, 1999) (applying *Hoy* in a federal forum). As such, because the Defendant in this action is a municipal defendant, punitive damages are not available and all requests for punitive damages in Plaintiff's Complaint are dismissed.

C. Count I Sexual Discrimination

Defendant next alleges that Count I of Plaintiff's Complaint should be dismissed for failure to state a claim for which relief can be granted under Federal Rule of Civil Procedure 12(b)(6). Defendant appears to argue that Plaintiff has failed to assert a claim for sexual discrimination because she has not adequately pled an adverse employment action and because she has failed to plead any information in her Complaint which would tend to demonstrate an inference of gender discrimination. Moreover, Defendant argues that Plaintiff's Complaint is merely a formulaic recitation of the elements of a cause of action, which is insufficient to survive a motion to dismiss.

Under Title VII, "[i]t shall be an unlawful employment practice for an employer: (1) to fail or refuse to hire or to discharge any individual, or otherwise to discriminate against any individual with respect to his compensation, terms, conditions, or privileges of employment, because of such individual's race, color, religion, sex, or national origin. . . ." 42 U.S.C. § 2000e-2. To establish a prima facie case of sexual discrimination under Title VII, a plaintiff must demonstrate that: (1) she is a member of a protected class; (2) she was qualified for the position; (3) she suffered an adverse employment action; and (4) the action occurred under circumstances that could give rise to an inference of intentional discrimination. *See Makky v. Chertoff,* 541 F.3d 205, 214 (3d Cir. 2008). The elements of a sex discrimination claim under the PHRA are analogous to those under Title VII. *See Goosby v. Johnson & Johnson Medical, Inc.,* 228 F.3d 313, 317 n.3 (3d Cir. 2000) ("The analysis required for adjudicating Goosby's claim under PHRA is identical to a Title VII inquiry.").

In the case at bar, Plaintiff has pled a plausible claim under both Title VII and the PHRA. She has alleged that she is a female, a member of a protected class. Additionally, she has indirectly but adequately argued that she is qualified for the position from which she was terminated. Plaintiff's Complaint explicitly alleges that "[p]rior to [her] termination, she fully and competently performed the duties of her job." Additionally, she alleges that she worked for Defendant for over two years, allowing the Court to infer that she was qualified to perform her job for the purposes of deciding the present Motion to Dismiss. *See Bellamy v. Waterfront Square Condominiums,* No. 12-6618, 2013 U.S. Dist. LEXIS 21926, 2013 WL 607848, at * 3 n.2 (E.D.Pa. Feb. 19, 2013).

Furthermore, the Plaintiff has adequately alleged that she has suffered an adverse employment action. Regardless of whether her allegations of disparate treatment are sufficient to satisfy the third prong of the inquiry, Plaintiff has pled that her position was terminated as a result of Defendant's discrimination, and it is well-settled that termination constitutes an adverse employment action for the purposes of Title VII. *See Mandel v. M&Q Packaging Corp.,* 706 F.3d 157, 165 (3d Cir. 2013). Finally, Plaintiff has alleged more than enough facts from which the Court can infer intentional discrimination on the part of Defendant, including previous disparate treatment by the Defendant which the Plaintiff alleges was motivated by her gender, as well as the termination of her position despite the existence of three less senior deputy positions filled by males. Therefore, Plaintiff has sufficiently and plausibly pled a cause of action in Count I for sexual discrimination under both Title VII and the PHRA.

D. Count II Retaliation

Defendant next alleges that Plaintiff's claim for retaliation should be dismissed because Plaintiff has failed to plead any facts which would demonstrate the required causal connection between her alleged protected activity and the adverse employment action.

Section 704(a) of Title VII forbids an employer from discriminating against an employee "because he has opposed any practice made an unlawful employment practice by this subchapter, or because he has made a charge, testified, assisted, or participated in any manner in an investigation . . . under this subchapter." 42 U.S.C. § 2000e-3(a). Similarly, under the PHRA it is unlawful for an employer "to discriminate in any manner against any individual because such individual has opposed any practice forbidden by this act, or because such individual has made a charge . . . under this act." 43 P.S. § 955(d).

In order to establish a prima facie case of retaliation under Title VII, a plaintiff must demonstrate that (1) she was engaged in protected activity; (2) she suffered an adverse employment action subsequent to or contemporaneously with such activity; and (3) there is a causal link between the protected activity and the adverse activity. *See Woodson v. Scott Paper Co.,* 109 F.3d, 913, 920 (3d Cir. 1997). The elements of a retaliation claim under the PHRA are analogous to those under Title VII. *See Hussein v. UPMC Mercy Hosp.,* 466 Fed.Appx. 108, 111 (3d Cir. 2012).

In the case at bar, Plaintiff has alleged that she filed a complaint with the PHRC and the EEOC, which is protected activity under the afore-mentioned statutes. Further, she has alleged that she suffered an adverse employment action after the filing of her complaint; namely, that Defendant did not recall or rehire her from her layoff status when another deputy sheriff resigned from his position. Finally, she has demonstrated sufficient causal evidence between the filing of her complaint and Defendant's failure to hire her for the open position. Specifically, at this early stage in the litigation, Plaintiff explicitly alleges that the Defendant's failure or refusal to recall or rehire her "for the open Deputy Sheriff's position was retaliation for her previously filed discrimination complaint." This is sufficient to plead to claim for relief that would survive a motion to dismiss. *See Twombly,* 550 U.S. at 554 (explaining that Federal Rule of Civil Procedure 8 "requires only a 'short and plain statement of the claim showing that the pleader is entitled to relief,' in order to 'give the defendant fair notice of what the . . . claim is and the grounds on which it rests.'").

E. Count III Sexual Discrimination

Finally, Defendant alleges that Plaintiff's remaining claim should also be dismissed for failure to state a claim under Rule 12(b)(6). Though Plaintiff titles Count III as a retaliation claim, she admits that the heading was merely a typographical error and she is actually stating another claim for sexual discrimination based on the failure of the Defendant to rehire her when a deputy sheriff position opened. Defendant argues that Plaintiff has not pled a claim under

Count III because she has failed to plead both that she was qualified for the position as well as the existence of any facts supporting an inference of discrimination.

In order to state a claim for sexual discrimination here under Title VII and the PHRA, Plaintiff must plead the same elements as is required for Count I. *See infra* Part II.C. Specifically, Plaintiff must demonstrate that: (1) she is a member of a protected class; (2) she was qualified for the position; (3) she suffered an adverse employment action; and (4) the action occurred under circumstances that could give rise to an inference of intentional discrimination. *See Makky,* 541 F.3d at 214.

As previously stated, Plaintiff has alleged that she is a female and that she was qualified for the position for which she was not hired, by way of her competency at her previous deputy position and her years of experience in that job. Furthermore, failure to hire constitutes an adverse employment action under controlling law. *See Mandel,* 706 F.3d at 165. Finally, taken as a whole, Plaintiff's alleged facts are sufficient to support an inference of intentional discrimination, including, as in Count I, previous disparate treatment by the Defendant which the Plaintiff alleges was motivated by her gender, as well as the termination of her position despite the continued existence of three less senior deputy positions filled by males. As such, Plaintiff has plausibly pled a claim for sexual discrimination in Count III under both Title VII and the PHRA. However, for the sake of clarity the Plaintiff is directed to amend the heading of Count III to allege sexual discrimination rather than retaliation.

III. Conclusion

Defendant's Motion to Dismiss is granted in part and denied in part. Plaintiff's request for punitive damages is dismissed. Moreover, Plaintiff is directed to amend her Complaint to clarify that Count III is alleging a claim based on gender discrimination, rather than retaliation. Because this Court is granting Plaintiff leave to amend only to correct this minute typographical error, Defendant is not entitled to renew its motion to dismiss after Plaintiff files her amended complaint.

BY THE COURT:
/s/ Matthew W. Brann
Matthew W. Brann
United States District Judge

Optional Assignments

1. Brief the preceding abbreviated version of the case in a one- to two-page, single-spaced brief (with double spaces between paragraphs) that contains the following four sections: (1) The basic facts of the case [Facts]; (2) The legal issue the court is being asked to decide [Issue]; (3) The holding of the court (how it decides the legal issue before it) [Holding]; and (4) The rationale the court uses to support its decision [Rationale]. If your instructor asks you to brief the case, he will give you additional instructions.

2. Do you agree with the court's decision? Explain.

SUPREME COURT OF THE UNITED STATES

No. 12–416

FEDERAL TRADE COMMISSION, PETITIONER v. ACTAVIS, INC., ET AL.

ON WRIT OF CERTIORARI TO THE UNITED STATES COURT OF APPEALS FOR THE ELEVENTH CIRCUIT

570 U.S. ____ (2013)

[June 17, 2013]

[Excerpted decision]

JUSTICE BREYER delivered the opinion of the Court. Company A sues Company B for patent infringement. The two companies settle under terms that require (1) Company B, the claimed infringer, not to produce the patented product until the patent's term expires, and (2) Company A, the patentee, to pay B many millions of dollars. Because the settlement requires the patentee to pay the alleged infringer, rather than the other way around, this kind of settlement agreement is often called a "reverse payment" settlement agreement. And the basic question here is whether such an agreement can sometimes unreasonably diminish competition in violation of the antitrust laws. See, *e.g.,* 15 U. S. C. § 1 (Sherman Act prohibition of "restraint[s] of trade or commerce"). Cf. *Palmer* v. *BRG of Ga., Inc.*, 498 U.S. 46 (1990) (*per curiam*) (invalidating agreement not to compete).

In this case, the Eleventh Circuit dismissed a Federal Trade Commission (FTC) complaint claiming that a particular reverse payment settlement agreement violated the antitrust laws. In doing so, the Circuit stated that a reverse payment settlement agreement generally is "immune from antitrust attack so long as its anticompetitive effects fall within the scope of the exclusionary potential of the patent." *FTC* v. *Watson Pharmaceuticals, Inc.*, 677 F. 3d 1298, 1312 (2012). And since the alleged infringer's promise not to enter the patentee's market expired before the patent's term ended, the Circuit found the agreement legal and dismissed the FTC complaint. *Id.,* at 1315. In our view, however, reverse payment settlements such as the agreement alleged in the complaint before us can sometimes violate the antitrust laws. We consequently hold that the Eleventh Circuit should have allowed the FTC's lawsuit to proceed.

I A

Apparently most if not all reverse payment settlement agreements arise in the context of pharmaceutical drug regulation, and specifically in the context of suits brought under statutory provisions allowing a generic drug manufacturer (seeking speedy marketing approval) to challenge the validity of a patent owned by an already-approved brand-name drug owner. See Brief for Petitioner 29; 12 P. Areeda & H. Hovenkamp, Antitrust Law 2046, p. 338 (3d ed. 2012) (hereinafter Areeda); Hovenkamp, Sensible Antitrust Rules for Pharmaceutical Competition, 39 U.S. F. L. Rev. 11, 24 (2004). We consequently describe four key features of the relevant drug-regulatory frame work established by the Drug Price Competition and Patent Term Restoration Act of 1984, 98 Stat. 1585, as amended. That Act is commonly known as the Hatch-Waxman Act.

First, a drug manufacturer, wishing to market a new prescription drug, must submit a New Drug Application to the federal Food and Drug Administration (FDA) and undergo a long, comprehensive, and costly testing process, after which, if successful, the manufacturer will receive marketing approval from the FDA. See 21 U. S. C. § 355(b)(1) (requiring, among other things, "full reports of investigations" into safety and effectiveness; "a full list of the articles used as components"; and a "full description" of how the drug is manufactured, processed, and packed).

Second, once the FDA has approved a brand-name drug for marketing, a manufacturer of a generic drug can obtain similar marketing approval through use of abbreviated procedures. The Hatch-Waxman Act permits a generic manufacturer to file an Abbreviated New Drug Application specifying that the generic has the "same active ingredients as," and is "biologically equivalent" to, the already approved brand-name drug. *Caraco Pharmaceutical Laboratories, Ltd.* v. *Novo Nordisk A/S*, 566 U.S., (2012) (slip op., at 2) (citing 21 U. S. C. §§ 355(j)(2)(A)(ii), (iv)). In this way the generic manufacturer can obtain approval while avoiding the "costly and time-consuming studies" needed to obtain approval "for a pioneer drug." See *Eli Lilly & Co.* v. *Medtronic, Inc.*, 496 U.S. 661, 676 (1990). The Hatch-Waxman process, by allowing the generic to piggy-back on the pioneer's approval efforts, "speed[s] the introduction of low-cost generic drugs to market," *Caraco, supra*, at ___ (slip op., at 2), thereby furthering drug competition.

Third, the Hatch-Waxman Act sets forth special procedures for identifying, and resolving, related patent disputes. It requires the pioneer brand-name manufacturer to list in its New Drug Application the "number and the expiration date" of any relevant patent. See 21 U. S. C. § 355(b)(1). And it requires the generic manufacturer in its Abbreviated New Drug Application to "assure the FDA" that the generic "will not infringe" the brand-name's patents. See *Caraco, supra,* at ___ (slip op., at 3).

The generic can provide this assurance in one of several ways. See 21 U. S. C. § 355(j)(2)(A)(vii). It can certify that the brand-name manufacturer has not listed any relevant patents. It can certify that any relevant patents have expired. It can request approval to market beginning when any still-in-force patents expire. Or, it can certify that any listed, relevant patent "is invalid or will not be infringed by the manufacture, use, or sale" of the drug described in the Abbreviated New Drug Application. See § 355(j)(2)(A)(vii)(IV). Taking this last-mentioned route (called the "paragraph IV" route), automatically counts as patent infringement, see 35 U. S. C. § 271(e)(2)(A) (2006 ed., Supp. V), and often "means provoking litigation." *Caraco, supra,* at (slip op., at 5). If the brand-name patentee brings an infringement suit within 45 days, the FDA then must withhold approving the generic, usually for a 30-month period, while the parties litigate patent validity (or infringement) in court. If the courts decide the matter within that period, the FDA follows that determination; if they do not, the FDA may go forward and give approval to market the generic product. See 21 U. S. C. § 355(j)(5)(B)(iii).

Fourth, Hatch-Waxman provides a special incentive for a generic to be the first to file an Abbreviated New Drug Application taking the paragraph IV route. That applicant will enjoy a period of 180 days of exclusivity (from the first commercial marketing of its drug). See § 355(j)(5)(B)(iv) (establishing exclusivity period). During that period of exclusivity, no other generic can compete with the brand-name drug. If the first-to-file generic manufacturer can overcome any patent obstacle and bring the generic to market, this

180-day period of exclusivity can prove valuable, possibly "worth several hundred million dollars." Hemphill, Paying for Delay: Pharmaceutical Patent Settlement as a Regulatory Design Problem, 81 N. Y. U. L. Rev. 1553, 1579 (2006). Indeed, the Generic Pharmaceutical Association said in 2006 that the "'vast majority of potential profits for a generic drug manufacturer materialize during the 180-day exclusivity period.'" Brief for Petitioner 6 (quoting statement). The 180-day exclusivity period, however, can belong only to the first generic to file. Should that first-to-file generic forfeit the exclusivity right in one of the ways specified by statute, no other generic can obtain it. See § 355(j)(5)(D).

B

1

In 1999, Solvay Pharmaceuticals, a respondent here, filed a New Drug Application for a brand-name drug called AndroGel. The FDA approved the application in 2000. In 2003, Solvay obtained a relevant patent and disclosed that fact to the FDA, 677 F. 3d, at 1308, as Hatch-Waxman requires. See § 355(c)(2) (requiring, in addition, that FDA must publish new patent information upon submission).

Later the same year another respondent, Actavis, Inc. (then known as Watson Pharmaceuticals), filed an Abbreviated New Drug Application for a generic drug modeled after AndroGel. Subsequently, Paddock Laboratories, also a respondent, separately filed an Abbreviated New Drug Application for its own generic product. Both Actavis and Paddock certified under paragraph IV that Solvay's listed patent was invalid and their drugs did not infringe it. A fourth manufacturer, Par Pharmaceutical, likewise a respondent, did not file an application of its own but joined forces with Paddock, agreeing to share the patent litigation costs in return for a share of profits if Paddock obtained approval for its generic drug.

Solvay initiated paragraph IV patent litigation against Actavis and Paddock. Thirty months later the FDA approved Actavis' first-to-file generic product, but, in 2006, the patent-litigation parties all settled. Under the terms of the settlement Actavis agreed that it would not bring its generic to market until August 31, 2015, 65 months before Solvay's patent expired (unless someone else marketed a generic sooner). Actavis also agreed to promote AndroGel to urologists. The other generic manufacturers made roughly similar promises. And Solvay agreed to pay millions of dollars to each generic—$12 million in total to Paddock; $60 million in total to Par; and an estimated $19–$30 million annually, for nine years, to Actavis. See App. 46, 49–50, Complaint 66, 77. The companies described these payments as compensation for other services the generics promised to perform, but the FTC contends the other services had little value. According to the FTC the true point of the payments was to compensate the generics for agreeing not to compete against AndroGel until 2015. See *id.*, at 50–53, Complaint 81–85.

2

On January 29, 2009, the FTC filed this lawsuit against all the settling parties, namely, Solvay, Actavis, Paddock, and Par. The FTC's complaint (as since amended) alleged that respondents violated § 5 of the Federal Trade Commission Act, 15 U.S. C. § 45, by unlawfully agreeing "to share in Solvay's monopoly profits, abandon their patent challenges, and refrain from launching their low-cost generic products to compete with AndroGel for nine years." App. 29, Complaint 5. See generally *FTC v. Indiana Federation of Dentists*, 476 U.S. 447, 454 (1986) (Section 5 "encompass[es] . . . practices that violate the Sherman Act and the other antitrust laws"). The District Court held that these allegations did not set forth an antitrust law violation. *In re Androgel Antitrust Litigation (No. II)*, 687 F. Supp. 2d 1371, 1379 (ND Ga. 2010). It accordingly dismissed the FTC's complaint. The FTC appealed.

The Court of Appeals for the Eleventh Circuit affirmed the District Court. It wrote that "absent sham litigation or fraud in obtaining the patent, a reverse payment settlement is immune from antitrust attack so long as its anticompetitive effects fall within the scope of the exclusionary potential of the patent." 677 F. 3d, at 1312. The court recognized that "antitrust laws typically prohibit agreements where one company pays a potential competitor not to enter the market." *Id.*, at 1307 (citing *Valley Drug Co. v. Geneva Pharmaceuticals, Inc.*, 344 F. 3d 1294, 1304 (CA11 2003)). See also *Palmer*, 498 U.S., at 50 (agreement to divide territorial markets held "unlawful on its face"). But, the court found that "reverse payment settlements of patent litigation presen[t] atypical cases because one of the parties owns a patent." 677 F. 3d, at 1307 (internal quotation marks and second alteration omitted). Patent holders have a "lawful right to exclude others from the market," *ibid.* (internal quotation marks omitted); thus a patent "conveys the right to cripple competition." *Id.*, at 1310 (internal quotation marks omitted). The court recognized that, if the parties to this sort of case do not settle, a court might declare the patent invalid. *Id.*, at 1305. But, in light of the public policy favoring settlement of disputes (among other considerations) it held that the courts could not require the parties to continue to litigate in order to avoid antitrust liability. *Id.*, at 1313–1314.

The FTC sought certiorari. Because different courts have reached different conclusions about the application of the antitrust laws to Hatch-Waxman-related patent settlements, we granted the FTC's petition. Compare, *e.g., id.*, at 1312 (case below) (settlements generally "immune from antitrust attack"); *In re Ciprofloxacin Hydrochloride Antitrust Litigation*, 544 F. 3d 1323, 1332–1337 (CA Fed. 2008) (similar); *In re Tamoxifen Citrate Antitrust Litigation*, 466 F. 3d 187, 212–213 (CA2 2006) (similar), with *In re K-Dur Antitrust Litigation*, 686 F. 3d 197, 214–218 (CA3 2012) (settlements presumptively unlawful).

II A

Solvay's patent, if valid and infringed, might have permitted it to charge drug prices sufficient to recoup the reverse settlement payments it agreed to make to its potential generic competitors. And we are willing to take this fact as evidence that the agreement's "anticompetitive effects fall within the scope of the exclusionary potential of the patent." 677 F. 3d, at 1312. But we do not agree that that fact, or characterization, can immunize the agreement from antitrust attack.

For one thing, to refer, as the Circuit referred, simply to what the holder of a valid patent could do does not by itself answer the antitrust question. The patent here may or may not be valid, and may or may not be infringed. "[A] *valid* patent excludes all except its owner from the use of the protected process or product," *United States* v. *Line Material Co.*, 333 U.S. 287, 308 (1948) (emphasis added). And that exclusion may permit the patent owner to charge a higher-than-competitive price for the patented product. But an *invalidated* patent carries with it no such right. And even a valid patent confers no right to exclude products or processes that do not actually infringe. The paragraph IV litigation in this case put the patent's validity at issue, as well as its actual preclusive scope. The parties' settlement ended that litigation. The FTC alleges that in substance, the plaintiff agreed to pay the defendants many millions of dollars to stay out of its market, even though the defendants did not have any claim that the plaintiff was liable to them for damages. That form of settlement is unusual. And, for reasons discussed in Part II–B, *infra*, there is reason for concern that settlements taking this form tend to have significant adverse effects on competition. Given these factors, it would be incongruous to determine antitrust legality by measuring the settlement's anticompetitive effects solely against patent law policy, rather than by measuring them against procompetitive antitrust policies as well. And indeed, contrary to the Circuit's view that the only pertinent question is whether "the settlement agreement . . . fall[s] within" the legitimate "scope" of the patent's "exclusionary potential," 677 F. 3d, at 1309, 1312, this Court has indicated that patent and antitrust policies are both relevant in determining the "scope of the patent monopoly"—and consequently antitrust law immunity—that is conferred by a patent.

Thus, the Court in *Line Material* explained that "the improper use of [a patent] monopoly," is "invalid" under the antitrust laws and resolved the antitrust question in that case by seeking an accommodation "between the lawful restraint on trade of the patent monopoly and the illegal restraint prohibited broadly by the Sherman Act." 333 U.S., at 310. To strike that balance, the Court asked questions such as whether "the patent statute specifically gives a right" to restrain competition in the manner challenged; and whether "competition is impeded to a greater degree" by the restraint at issue than other restraints previously approved as reasonable. *Id.*, at 311. See also *United States* v. *United States Gypsum Co.*, 333 U.S. 364, 390–391 (1948) (courts must "balance the privileges of [the patent holder] and its licensees under the patent grants with the prohibitions of the Sherman Act against combinations and attempts to monopolize"); *Walker Process Equipment, Inc.* v. *Food Machinery & Chemical Corp.*, 382 U.S. 172, 174 (1965) ("[E]nforcement of a patent procured by fraud" may violate the Sherman Act). In short, rather than measure the length or amount of a restriction solely against the length of the patent's term or its earning potential, as the Court of Appeals apparently did here, this Court answered the antitrust question by considering traditional antitrust factors such as likely anticompetitive effects, redeeming virtues, market power, and potentially offsetting legal considerations present in the circumstances, such as here those related to patents. See Part II–B, *infra*. Whether a particular restraint lies "beyond the limits of the patent monopoly" is a *conclusion* that flows from that analysis and not, as THE CHIEF JUSTICE suggests, its starting point. *Post*, at 3, 8 (dissenting opinion).

For another thing, this Court's precedents make clear that patent-related settlement agreements can sometimes violate the antitrust laws. In *United States* v. *Singer Mfg. Co.*, 374 U.S. 174 (1963), for example, two sewing machine companies possessed competing patent claims; a third company sought a patent under circumstances where doing so might lead to the disclosure of information that would invalidate the other two firms' patents. All three firms settled their patent-related disagreements while assigning the broadest claims to the firm best able to enforce the patent against yet other potential competitors. *Id.*, at 190–192. The Court did not examine whether, on the assumption that all three patents were valid, patent law would have allowed the patents' holders to do the same. Rather, emphasizing that the Sherman Act "imposes strict limitations on the concerted activities in which patent owners may lawfully engage," *id.*, at 197, it held that the agreements, although settling patent disputes, violated the antitrust laws. *Id.*, at 195, 197. And that, in important part, was because "the public interest in granting patent monopolies" exists only to the extent that "the public is given a novel and useful invention" in "consideration for its grant." *Id.*, at 199 (White, J., concurring). See also *United States* v. *New Wrinkle, Inc.*, 342 U.S. 371, 378 (1952) (applying antitrust scrutiny to patent settlement); *Standard Oil Co. (Indiana)* v. *United States*, 283 U.S. 163 (1931) (same). Similarly, both within the settlement context and without, the Court has struck down overly restrictive patent licensing agreements—irrespective of whether those agreements produced supra-patent-permitted revenues. We concede that in *United States* v. *General Elec. Co.*, 272 U.S. 476, 489 (1926), the Court permitted a single patentee to grant to a single licensee a license containing a minimum resale price requirement. But in *Line Material, supra*, at 308, 310–311, the Court held that the antitrust laws forbid a group of patentees, each owning one or more patents, to cross-license each other, and, in doing so, to insist that each licensee maintain retail prices set collectively by the patent holders. The Court was willing to presume that the single-patentee practice approved in *General Electric* was a "reasonable restraint" that "accords with the patent monopoly granted by the patent law," 333 U.S., at 312, but declined to extend that conclusion to multiple-patentee agreements: "As the Sherman Act prohibits agreements to fix prices, any arrangement between patentees runs afoul of that prohibition and is outside the patent monopoly." *Ibid.* In *New Wrinkle*, 342 U.S., at 378, the Court held roughly the same, this time in respect to a similar arrangement in settlement of a litigation between two patentees, each of which contended that its own patent gave it the exclusive right to control production. That one or the other company (we may presume) was right about its patent did not lead the Court to confer antitrust immunity. Far from it, the agreement was found to violate the Sherman Act. *Id.,* at 380.

Finally in *Standard Oil Co. (Indiana)*, the Court upheld cross-licensing agreements among patentees that settled actual and impending patent litigation, 283 U.S., at 168, which agreements set royalty rates to be charged third parties for a license to practice all the patents at issue (and which divided resulting revenues). But, in doing so, Justice Brandeis, writing for the Court, warned that such an arrangement would have violated the Sherman Act had the patent holders thereby "dominate[d]" the industry and "curtail[ed] the manufacture and supply of an unpatented product." *Id.,* at 174. These cases do not simply ask whether a hypothetically valid patent's holder would be able to charge, *e.g.*, the high prices that the challenged patent-related term allowed. Rather, they seek to accommodate patent and antitrust policies, finding challenged terms and conditions unlawful unless patent law policy offsets the antitrust law policy strongly favoring competition.

Thus, contrary to the dissent's suggestion, *post*, at 4–6, there is nothing novel about our approach. What *does* appear novel are the dissent's suggestions that a patent holder may simply "pa[y] a competitor to respect its patent" and quit its patent invalidity or noninfringement claim without any antitrust scrutiny whatever, *post*, at 3, and that "such settlements . . . are a well-known feature of intellectual property litigation," *post*, at 10. Closer examination casts doubt on these claims. The dissent does not identify any patent statute that it understands to grant such a right to a patentee, whether expressly or by fair implication. It would be difficult to reconcile the proposed right with the patent-related policy of eliminating unwarranted patent grants so the public will not "continually be required to pay tribute to would-be monopolists without need or justification." *Lear, Inc.* v. *Adkins*, 395 U.S. 653, 670 (1969). And the authorities cited for this proposition (none from this Court, and none an antitrust case) are not on point. Some of them say that when Company A sues Company B for patent infringement and demands, say, $100 million in damages, it is not uncommon for B (the defendant) to pay A (the plaintiff) some amount less than the full demand as part of the settlement—$40 million, for example. See Schildkraut, Patent-Splitting Settlements and the Reverse Payment Fallacy, 71 Antitrust L. J. 1033, 1046 (2004) (suggesting that this hypothetical settlement includes "an implicit net payment" from A to B of $60 million—*i.e.,* the amount of the settlement discount). The Court cited authorities also indicate that if B has a counterclaim for damages against A, the original infringement plaintiff, A might end up paying B to settle B's counterclaim. Cf. *Metro-Goldwyn Mayer, Inc.* v. *007 Safety Prods., Inc.,* 183 F. 3d 10, 13 (CA1 1999) (describing trademark dispute and settlement). Insofar as the dissent urges that settlements taking these commonplace forms have not been thought for that reason alone subject to antitrust liability, we agree, and do not intend to alter that understanding. But the dissent appears also to suggest that reverse payment settlements—*e.g.*, in which A, the plaintiff, pays money to defendant B purely so B will give up the patent fight—should be viewed for antitrust purposes in the same light as these familiar settlement forms. See *post,* at 9–10. We cannot agree. In the traditional examples cited above, a party with a claim (or counterclaim) for damages receives a sum equal to or less than the value of its claim. In reverse payment settlements, in contrast, a party with no claim for damages (something that is usually true of a paragraph IV litigation defendant) walks away with money simply so it will stay away from the patentee's market. That, we think, is something quite different. Cf. *Verizon Communications, Inc.* v. *Law Offices of Curtis V. Trinko, LLP,* 540 U.S. 398, 408 (2004) ("[C]ollusion" is "the supreme evil of antitrust").

Finally, the Hatch-Waxman Act itself does not embody a statutory policy that supports the Eleventh Circuit's view. Rather, the general procompetitive thrust of the statute, its specific provisions facilitating challenges to a patent's validity, see Part I–A, *supra*, and its later-added provisions requiring parties to a patent dispute triggered by a paragraph IV filing to report settlement terms to the FTC and the Antitrust Division of the Department of Justice, all suggest the contrary. See §§ 1112–1113, 117 Stat. 2461–2462. Those interested in legislative history may also wish to examine the statements of individual Members of Congress condemning reverse payment settlements in advance of the 2003 amendments. See, *e.g.*, 148 Cong. Rec. 14437 (2002) (remarks of Sen. Hatch) ("It was and is very clear that the [Hatch-Waxman Act] was not designed to allow deals between brand and generic companies to delay competition"); 146 Cong. Rec. 18774 (2000) (remarks of Rep. Waxman) (introducing bill to deter companies from "strik[ing] collusive agreements to trade multimillion dollar payoffs by the brand company for delays in the introduction of lower cost, generic alternatives").

B

The Eleventh Circuit's conclusion finds some degree of support in a general legal policy favoring the settlement of disputes. 677 F. 3d, at 1313–1314. See also *Schering-Plough Corp.* v. *FTC*, 402 F. 3d 1056, 1074–1075 (2005) (same); *In re Tamoxifen Citrate*, 466 F. 3d, at 202 (noting public's "'strong interest in settlement'" of complex and expensive cases). The Circuit's related underlying practical concern consists of its fear that antitrust scrutiny of a reverse payment agreement would require the parties to litigate the validity of the patent in order to demonstrate what would have happened to competition in the absence of the settlement. Any such litigation will prove time consuming, complex, and expensive. The antitrust game, the Circuit may believe, would not be worth that litigation candle.

We recognize the value of settlements and the patent litigation problem. But we nonetheless conclude that this patent-related factor should not determine the result here. Rather, five sets of considerations lead us to conclude that the FTC should have been given the opportunity to prove its antitrust claim.

First, the specific restraint at issue has the "potential for genuine adverse effects on competition." *Indiana Federation of Dentists*, 476 U.S., at 460–461 (citing 7 Areeda 1511, at 429 (1986)). The payment in effect amounts to a purchase by the patentee of the exclusive right to sell its product, a right it already claims but would lose if the patent litigation were to continue and the patent were held invalid or not infringed by the generic product. Suppose, for example, that the exclusive right to sell produces $50 million in supracompetitive profits per year for the patentee. And suppose further that the patent has 10 more years to run. Continued litigation, if it results in patent invalidation or a finding of noninfringement, could cost the patentee $500 million in lost revenues, a sum that then would flow in large part to consumers in the form of lower prices. We concede that settlement on terms permitting the patent challenger to enter the market before the patent expires would also bring about competition, again to the consumer's benefit. But settlement on the terms said by the FTC to be at issue here—payment in return for staying out of the market—simply keeps prices at patentee-set levels, potentially producing the full patent-related $500 million monopoly return while dividing that return between the challenged patentee and the patent challenger. The patentee and the challenger gain; the consumer loses. Indeed, there are indications that patentees sometimes pay a generic challenger a sum even larger than what the generic would gain in profits if it won the paragraph IV litigation and entered the market. See Hemphill, 81 N. Y. U. L. Rev., at 1581. See also Brief for 118 Law, Economics, and Business Professors et al. as *Amici Curiae* 25 (estimating that this is true of the settlement challenged here). The rationale behind a payment of this size cannot in every case be supported by traditional settlement considerations. The payment may instead provide strong evidence that the patentee seeks to induce the generic challenger to abandon its claim with a share of its monopoly profits that would otherwise be lost in the competitive one might ask, as a practical matter would the parties be able to enter into such an anticompetitive agreement? Would not a high reverse payment signal to other potential challengers that the patentee lacks confidence in its patent, thereby provoking additional challenges, perhaps too many for the patentee to "buy off?" Two special features of Hatch-Waxman mean that the answer to this question is "not necessarily so." First, under Hatch-Waxman only the first challenger gains the special advantage of 180 days of an exclusive right to sell a generic version of the brand-name product. See Part I–A, *supra*. And as noted, that right has proved valuable—indeed, it can be worth several hundred million dollars. See Hemphill, *supra*, at 1579; Brief for Petitioner 6. Subsequent challengers cannot secure that exclusivity period, and thus stand to win significantly less than the first if they bring a successful paragraph IV challenge. That is, if subsequent litigation results in invalidation of the patent, or a ruling that the patent is not infringed, that litigation victory will free not just the challenger to compete, but all other potential competitors too (once they obtain FDA approval). The potential reward available to a subsequent challenger being significantly less, the patentee's payment to the initial challenger (in return for not pressing the patent challenge) will not necessarily provoke subsequent challenges. Second, a generic that files a paragraph IV after learning that the first filer has settled will (if sued by the brand-name) have to wait out a stay period of (roughly) 30 months before the FDA may approve its application, just as the first filer did. See 21 U. S. C. § 355(j)(5)(B)(iii). These features together mean that a reverse payment settlement with the first filer (or, as in this case, *all* of the initial filers) "removes from consideration the most motivated challenger, and the one closest to introducing competition." Hemphill, *supra*, at 1586. The dissent may doubt these provisions matter, *post*, at 15–17, but scholars in the field tell us that "where only one party owns a patent, it is virtually unheard of outside of pharmaceuticals for that party to pay an accused infringer to settle the lawsuit." 1 H. Hovenkamp, M. Janis, M. Lemley, & C. Leslie, IP and Antitrust § 15.3, p. 15–45, n. 161 (2d ed. Supp. 2011). It may well be that Hatch-Waxman's unique regulatory framework, including the special advantage that the 180-day exclusivity period gives to first filers, does much to explain why in this context, but not others, the patentee's ordinary incentives to resist paying off challengers (*i.e.,* the fear of provoking myriad other challengers) appear to be more frequently overcome. See 12 Areeda 2046, at 341 (3d ed. 2010) (noting that these provisions, no doubt unintentionally, have created special incentives for collusion).

Second, these anticompetitive consequences will at least sometimes prove unjustified. See 7 *id.*, 1504, at 410–415 (3d ed. 2010); *California Dental Assn.* v. *FTC*, 526 U.S., 756, 786–787 (1999) (BREYER, J., concurring in part and dissenting in part). As the FTC admits, offsetting or redeeming virtues are sometimes present. Brief for Petitioner 37–39. The reverse payment, for example, may amount to no more than a rough approximation of the litigation expenses saved through the settlement. That payment may reflect compensation for other services that the generic has promised to perform—such as distributing the patented item or helping to develop a market for that item. There may be other justifications. Where a reverse payment reflects traditional settlement considerations, such as avoided litigation costs or fair value for services, there is not the same concern that a patentee is using its monopoly profits to avoid the risk of patent invalidation or a finding of noninfringement. In such cases, the parties may have provided for a reverse payment without having sought or brought about the anticompetitive consequences we mentioned above. But that possibility does not justify dismissing the FTC's complaint. An antitrust defendant may show in the antitrust proceeding that legitimate justifications are present, thereby explaining the presence of the challenged term and showing the lawfulness of that term under the rule of reason. See, *e.g., Indiana Federation of Dentists, supra,* at 459; 7 Areeda 1504a–1504b, at 401–404 (3d ed. 2010).

Third, where a reverse payment threatens to work unjustified anticompetitive harm, the patentee likely possesses the power to bring that harm about in practice. See *id.,* 1503, at 392–393. At least, the "size of the payment from a branded drug manufacturer to a prospective generic is itself a strong indicator of power"—namely, the power to charge prices higher than the competitive level. 12 *id.*, 2046, at 351. An important patent itself helps to assure such power. Neither is a firm without that power likely to pay "large sums" to induce "others to stay out of its market." *Ibid.* In any event, the Commission has referred to studies showing that reverse payment agreements are associated with the presence of higher-than competitive profits—a strong indication of market power. See Brief for Petitioner 45.

Fourth, an antitrust action is likely to prove more feasible administratively than the Eleventh Circuit believed. The Circuit's holding does avoid the need to litigate the patent's validity (and also, any question of infringement). But to do so, it throws the baby out with the bath water, and there is no need to take that drastic step. That is because it is normally not necessary to litigate patent validity to answer the antitrust question (unless, perhaps, to determine whether the patent litigation is a sham, see 677 F. 3d, at 1312). An unexplained large reverse payment itself would normally suggest that the patentee has serious doubts about the patent's survival. And that fact, in turn, suggests that the payment's objective is to maintain supracompetitive prices to be shared among the patentee and the challenger rather than face what might have been a competitive market—the very anticompetitive consequence that underlies the claim of antitrust unlawfulness. The owner of a particularly valuable patent might contend, of course, that even a small risk of invalidity justifies a large payment. But, be that as it may, the payment (if otherwise unexplained) likely seeks to prevent the risk of competition. And, as we have said, that consequence constitutes the relevant anticompetitive harm. In a word, the size of the unexplained reverse payment can provide a workable surrogate for a patent's weakness, all without forcing a court to conduct a detailed exploration of the validity of the patent itself. 12 Areeda 2046, at 350–352.

Fifth, the fact that a large, unjustified reverse payment risks antitrust liability does not prevent litigating parties from settling their lawsuit. They may, as in other industries, settle in other ways, for example, by allowing the generic manufacturer to enter the patentee's market prior to the patent's expiration, without the patentee paying the challenger to stay out prior to that point. Although the parties may have reasons to prefer settlements that include reverse payments, the relevant antitrust question is: What are those reasons? If the basic reason is a desire to maintain and to share patent-generated monopoly profits, then, in the absence of some other justification, the antitrust laws are likely to forbid the arrangement.

In sum, a reverse payment, where large and unjustified, can bring with it the risk of significant anticompetitive effects; one who makes such a payment may be unable to explain and to justify it; such a firm or individual may well possess market power derived from the patent; a court, by examining the size of the payment, may well be able to assess its likely anticompetitive effects along with its potential justifications without litigating the validity of the patent; and parties may well find ways to settle patent disputes without the use of reverse payments. In our view, these considerations, taken together, outweigh the single strong consideration—the desirability of settlements—that led the Eleventh Circuit to provide near-automatic antitrust immunity to reverse payment settlements.

III

The FTC urges us to hold that reverse payment settlement agreements are presumptively unlawful and that courts reviewing such agreements should proceed via a "quick look" approach, rather than applying a "rule of reason."

See *California Dental*, 526 U.S., at 775, n. 12 ("Quick-look analysis in effect" shifts to "a defendant the burden to show empirical evidence of procompetitive effects"); 7 Areeda 1508, at 435–440 (3d ed. 2010). We decline to do so. In *California Dental*, we held (unanimously) that abandonment of the "rule of reason" in favor of presumptive rules (or a "quick-look" approach) is appropriate only where "an observer with even a rudimentary understanding of economics could conclude that the arrangements in question would have an anticompetitive effect on customers and markets." 526 U.S., at 770; *id.*, at 781 (BREYER, J., concurring in part and dissenting in part). We do not believe that reverse payment settlements, in the context we here discuss, meet this criterion.

That is because the likelihood of a reverse payment bringing about anticompetitive effects depends upon its size, its scale in relation to the payor's anticipated future litigation costs, its independence from other services for which it might represent payment, and the lack of any other convincing justification. The existence and degree of any anticompetitive consequence may also vary as among industries. These complexities lead us to conclude that the FTC must prove its case as in other rule-of-reason cases. To say this is not to require the courts to insist, contrary to what we have said, that the Commission need litigate the patent's validity, empirically demonstrate the virtues or vices of the patent system, present every possible supporting fact or refute every possible pro-defense theory.

As a leading antitrust scholar has pointed out, "'[t]here is always something of a sliding scale in appraising reasonableness,'" and as such "'the quality of proof required should vary with the circumstances.'" *California Dental*, *supra*, at 780 (quoting with approval 7 Areeda 1507, at 402 (1986)). As in other areas of law, trial courts can structure antitrust litigation so as to avoid, on the one hand, the use of antitrust theories too abbreviated to permit proper analysis, and, on the other, consideration of every possible fact or theory irrespective of the minimal light it may shed on the basic question—that of the presence of significant unjustified anticompetitive consequences. See 7 *id.*, 1508c, at 438–440. We therefore leave to the lower courts the structuring of the present rule-of-reason antitrust litigation. We reverse the judgment of the Eleventh Circuit. And we remand the case for further proceedings consistent with this opinion.

It is so ordered.

JUSTICE ALITO took no part in the consideration or decision of this case.
CHIEF JUSTICE ROBERTS, with whom JUSTICE SCALIA
and JUSTICE THOMAS join, dissenting.
[The dissenting opinion is omitted here but can be accessed along with the court's full opinion at http://www.supremecourt.gov/opinions/12pdf/12-416_m5n0.pdf].

Optional Assignments

1. Brief the preceding abbreviated version of the case in a one- to two-page, single-spaced brief (with double spaces between paragraphs) that contains the following four sections: (1) The basic facts of the case [Facts]; (2) The legal issue the court is being asked to decide [Issue]; (3) The holding of the court (how it decides the legal issue before it) [Holding]; and (4) The rationale the court uses to support its decision [Rationale]. If your instructor asks you to brief the case, he will give you additional instructions.

2. Read the dissenting opinion written by Chief Justice Roberts and joined by Justices Scalia and Thomas by accessing the entire opinion excerpted above at http://www.supremecourt.gov/opinions/12pdf/12-416_m5n0.pdf. Which opinion do you find more persuasive? Why?

UNIT 8

BUSINESS ORGANIZATIONS

Lukas Gojda/Shutterstock

CHAPTER 41
Sole Proprietorship

CHAPTER 42
Partnership

CHAPTER 43
Limited Partnership

CHAPTER 44
Corporations

CHAPTER 45
Limited Liability Companies

Introduction

One of the first decisions that anyone seeking to establish a new business must make is how to organize the business. The most common types of business organizations include sole proprietorships, partnerships, limited partnerships, corporations, and limited liability companies. As we will see in this unit, each type of business organization offers certain benefits as well as drawbacks that should be carefully weighed before deciding which form is best suited to the new business. The requirements for starting a business under each of the available forms of business organization vary widely. For example, individuals who start a business under their own name alone or in traditional partnerships will not typically be required to contend with any organizational formalities, whereas those who wish to organize a new business as a limited partnership, corporation, or limited liability company will need to strictly follow the requirements of their states' limited partnership, corporation, or limited liability company acts. In this unit, we will explore the most common forms of business organization to understand their fundamental makeup and examine the benefits and liabilities of structuring a business under each distinct form of business organization.

Sole Proprietorship

CHAPTER 41

Chapter Outline

Formation of the Sole Proprietorship

Benefits of the Sole Proprietorship

Liabilities of the Sole Proprietorship

Property Status of the Sole Proprietorship

Termination of the Sole Proprietorship

The oldest and simplest form of business organization is the sole proprietorship. Under this form of business organization, the owner of a business personally operates the business herself and is solely responsible for all aspects of the enterprise.

Formation of the Sole Proprietorship

The greatest benefit of the sole proprietorship form of business organization is that no formalities are required for its formation. A person wishing to go into business for himself in a business that carries his own name can start the enterprise at any time without the need to seek state or local approval. Of course, if the business is one that the state chooses to regulate to protect the safety, health, or welfare of the general public, then the sole proprietorship must meet whatever licensing criteria the state sets for the operation of such a business. For example, only a person who has been duly admitted to a state's bar may go into the business of practicing law in the state, and only persons who can obtain a liquor license may sell liquor. Likewise, if the business will be involved in the sale of goods or the providing of services subject to a state or local sales tax, the sole proprietor will need to fulfill the state's requirements for collecting and forwarding the required tax to the appropriate state or local agency. As long as the enterprise complies with all state and federal regulations applicable to all business concerns, the sole proprietorship needs no additional formalities for its formation.

Persons who wish to do business under an assumed name must apply for a permit from the appropriate county or state office in their state (typically the county clerk in every county in which they wish to do business) and pay a nominal fee for the privilege of doing business under a trade name. The primary purpose of this requirement is to prevent different persons from doing business under the same name in the same area when consumer confusion might ensue, and to have on record the names and addresses of the owners of these businesses so that they may be readily found and held accountable for the civil or criminal transgressions of the business, should the need arise. Thus, Rick Carpenter generally needs no special permission to start a carpentry business under the name Rick Carpenter or Rick Carpenter's Carpentry Service, but he would need to get what is commonly termed a *Doing Business As* (D.B.A.) certificate from the appropriate office(s) in his state if he wants to call his business Good Homes Carpentry, Expert Carpentry Works, or any other assumed name.

Benefits of the Sole Proprietorship

As previously noted, the greatest benefit of the sole proprietorship is that it requires no formalities for its inception. As a result, a person can begin doing business as a sole proprietorship at a moment's notice. Contrast this with limited partnerships, corporations, and limited liability companies that, as we will discuss in later chapters, require the drafting and filing of specific forms with appropriate state agencies before the business can get off the ground—a process that requires both time and money to complete.

Another benefit of the sole proprietorship form of business organization is that the proprietor need not share decision making with others for his business and can thus make business decisions quickly. Partnerships and corporations, on the other hand, require the reaching of a consensus and, in the case of corporations, the meeting of sometimes onerous formalities before some major business decisions (such as the sale of substantial portions of the assets of the business or the acquisition of business property) can be made; these processes can interfere with the smooth operation of some businesses and make the instituting of major changes a slow and often tedious process.

Just as important as the autonomy that the sole proprietorship permits the business owner is the freedom from liability for the negligent acts or bad business decisions of others. General partners in a partnership are deemed to be agents of the partnership and of one another under the common law of partnership, and directors and officers of a corporation are deemed to be agents of the corporation they serve. Under the law of agency, as we saw in Chapter 35, principals can be bound by the authorized acts of their agents and are liable for the negligent acts of their agents committed during the course of the agency. Thus, partners in a partnership can be held liable for contracts entered into on behalf of the partnership by any other partner as well as for the negligent acts of any partner that injures a third party. Likewise, a corporation can be held liable for the authorized acts of its officers and directors, as well as their negligence. A sole proprietor, however, need never worry about being responsible for the bad judgment, negligence, or bad faith of a joint owner; she is responsible only for her own acts and for the acts of any subordinate employees she hires.

There are also some financial advantages for the sole proprietorship in terms of tax savings and lower administrative costs. Unlike most corporations, the sole proprietorship does not pay federal, state, or local income taxes as a business entity; all income earned by the business is taxed as simple income to the owner. Because bookkeeping and legal formalities for the business are simplified, the administrative costs are usually lower than for other forms of business organization; for example, there is often less need for legal and accounting services for a sole proprietorship when compared with other business organizations.

Liabilities of the Sole Proprietorship

While many benefits are rooted in the simplicity of the sole proprietorship, a number of tangible liabilities also stem from this form of business organization. Chief among these is the unlimited personal liability of the sole proprietor for all debts incurred by the business. The sole proprietorship is not recognized as a separate entity from its owner; as a consequence, the debts of the business are deemed to be the *personal* debts of the owner, and the sole proprietor has unlimited personal liability for all the debts, contractual obligations, and legal judgments incurred by the business. If the business fails, its owner not only can lose the capital invested in the business but also faces the prospect of having business debts satisfied out of her other personal assets if the business assets are insufficient to cover business debts. Consequently, the business failure of a sole proprietorship can mean bankruptcy for the sole proprietor.

Another downside of the sole proprietorship is that the owner must rely solely on his own assets and expertise in running the business. While the business owner need not share profits or consult with others on business decisions, neither can he count on others to lend their expertise, share business losses, or shoulder part of the responsibilities for the daily operation of the business. Such assistance can be hired in the form of employees, but individuals who draw a salary are seldom as committed to the enterprise or as motivated to ensure its success as those whose fortunes are tied directly to the success or failure of the business. And the lack of co-owners of a business enterprise can be a particularly important drawback when the business owner needs to raise capital for expansion or to cover extraordinary expenses of the business.

Property Status of the Sole Proprietorship

A sole proprietorship is considered personal property. As such, it can be transferred in whole or in part at any time by its owner through sale or through an *inter vivos* or testamentary gift. If a business concern that is organized as a sole proprietorship is sold or otherwise transferred by its owner, its nature can change depending on both the terms or its transfer and the wishes of the new business owners. A sole proprietorship transferred to a single person who continues to run the business as a sole proprietor, for example, retains its previous status, whereas one transferred to two or more persons as joint owners becomes a partnership. A sole proprietorship can also be reorganized as a corporation if its new owner so desires. The type of business organization can also be changed by a present owner by reorganizing the business from a sole proprietorship to a partnership, corporation, or any other form of business organization recognized by the state.

Termination of the Sole Proprietorship

Just as there are no formalities for starting a sole proprietorship, there are none for ending one. The sole proprietorship can terminate as a business concern at any time at the will of its owner, or it can end by operation of law upon the death, incapacity, or bankruptcy of the owner. When the business ends, its owner will remain personally liable for completing any outstanding contracts and for meeting any other business obligations of the business. If the business ends due to the death or incapacity of its owner, the owner's estate or guardian will be responsible for paying creditors out of estate funds.

Questions

1. What are the common types of business organization available?
2. What is the simplest form of business organization?
3. What formalities are necessary for the formation of a sole proprietorship?
4. What are the basic benefits of doing business as a sole proprietorship?
5. What is the greatest drawback of the sole proprietorship?
6. Is it easier or harder to raise capital as a sole proprietorship than it is as a partnership? Explain.
7. What is the property status of a sole proprietorship, and how can a sole proprietorship be transferred?
8. What are the formalities for terminating a sole proprietorship?
9. What is the owner's liability for business debts upon the termination of a sole proprietorship?
10. What is the effect of the owner's death or incapacity on the liabilities of a sole proprietorship?

Hypothetical Cases

1. Robert Nussbaum, a talented college student with a wonderful voice, would like to start his own business selling self-published audiobooks that he will produce himself by reading from works of fiction in the public domain, digitally recording these on his computer, and burning them on CDs. He intends to sell his custom collections on eBay, Amazon, and through his web page and will advertise his collections as *Robert Nussbaum's Classic Audiobooks*.
   A. Will Robert be in violation of the law if he starts doing business without first seeking a permit from the state?
   B. Can Robert name his business *Classic Audiobook Productions* without getting a state permit?

2. Assume the same facts as in the last case. If Robert's state has a sales tax that applies to the sale of audio and music compact discs, can he go into business without informing the state if he believes that most of the sales will come from out of state?
3. Sandra Singh, a house painter, decides to go into business for herself as an independent contractor. She prints up flyers advertising the availability of her services, has letterhead printed with the name of *Sandra Singh's Paint Works*, and places a small ad in her local newspaper announcing the opening of her new business. After several days, calls start coming in and she contracts her services to several private homeowners and general contractors. She soon earns a reputation for her reasonable fees and professional work, and her business experiences tremendous growth in a short period of time.
   A. Assuming her net income for the first year is $100,000, will she have to pay any business income tax under the facts given?
   B. Given the fact that her business is successful, should Sandra be concerned about her potential liability if the business fails?
   C. After five years in business, Sandra has managed to increase her income to $300,000 per year. She has also purchased a new home, a small boat, and various other personal assets with a total value in excess of $1,000,000. The assets of her business, however, amount only to $10,000 in office equipment. If she is sued for $1,000,000 for negligently causing severe property damage and personal injuries to a client when scaffolding from her last job collapsed, what is her potential personal liability?
4. Assume the same facts as in the last question.
   A. If Sandra wants to incorporate her business in order to protect herself against the threat of unlimited personal liability, may she do so?
   B. If Sandra wants to sell her business and retire after ten years, may she do so?
   C. Sandra decides to leave her business to her favorite nephew, Upinder, and daughter, Samantha, after her death. When she dies, what will the nature of the business be after it passes to her relatives?

Partnership

CHAPTER 42

The Model Partnership Act, a model statute proposed by the National Conference of Commissioners on Uniform State Laws (NCCUSL) for adoption by all states, defines a partnership as "an association of two or more persons to carry on as co-owners a business for profit…" [§ 102 (11) Model Partnership Act of 1997 as amended in 2013]. Any time that two or more individuals are engaged in a business as co-owners with the intent to make a profit, a partnership arises automatically and the rights and responsibilities of each partner will be dictated by the law of partnership in the state that the partnership is formed.

Chapter Outline

Model Partnership Act

Formation of a Partnership

Relationship of Partners to the Partnership and to One Another

Agency Rights and Duties of Partners

Contractual Rights and Duties of Partners

Limitations on Partners' Ability to Define Their Rights and Obligations as Partners

Limitation on Partners' Right of Compensation

Partners' Capital Contributions

Admission of New Partners

Partners' Right to Inspect Partnership's Books

Partners' Liability for Partnership Debt

Purported Partners

Partners' Property Rights

Partner's Dissociation

Dissolution of a Partnership and Winding Up

Notice to Third Parties upon Dissolution

Model Partnership Act

All states except Louisiana adopted the Uniform Partnership Act of 1914 (UPA) promulgated by the National Conference of Commissioners on Uniform State Laws (NCCUSL). The UPA has undergone five revisions to date, with the first revision promulgated in 1992 by the NCCUSL and the last in 1997 (with amendments in 2013). The act is commonly referred to as the Revised Model Partnership Act (RUPA) followed by the year of the revised version referenced [e.g., RUPA (1992), (1993), (1994), (1996), or (1997)]. As of this writing, 38 states, Washington D.C., and the U.S. Virgin Islands have adopted the act with the 2013 amendments. Twelve states and the Commonwealth of Puerto Rico have not adopted the newest version of the act to date. All sections of the UPA quoted in the materials that follow are from RUPA (1997) with the 2013 amendments.

Generally speaking, the original Model Partnership Act largely codified the common law of partnership, which itself originally developed based on the common law of agency and contracts. The various revised versions of the model act have also made significant changes to the common law of partnership in an effort to have the law reflect modern business practices. Even in states that have adopted the latest version of the Model Partnership Act, some differences exist because state legislatures do not always adopt model acts in their entirety and courts do not always interpret even identical acts in precisely the same way from state to state.

Formation of a Partnership

Like the sole proprietorship, the partnership form of business organization does not require specific formalities for its formation. Oral and written agreements to enter into a partnership are generally equally binding. A partnership can also arise by operation of law even absent a specific agreement. Any voluntary association by two or more persons to conduct a business for profit as joint owners automatically results in the creation of a partnership by operation of law, whether or not the joint owners specifically intended it.

If two or more persons go into a business for profit together without making specific provisions for the type of business organization the business will take, a partnership automatically results, and the rights and responsibilities of the parties are dictated by the law of partnership. In most cases, however, persons wishing to go into business together will execute a formal partnership agreement, which is a contract that details the rights and obligations of each party. (See Figure 42.1 for a sample partnership agreement.)

Relationship of Partners to the Partnership and to One Another

The contractual provisions contained in the partnership agreement define the relationship between partners in a partnership and the rights and responsibilities they owe to one another. In the absence of a partnership agreement, or in cases in which the partnership agreement fails to define key rights and responsibilities of the partners, the state's common law of partnership and, where applicable, the state's partnership act will define these rights and obligations. The law of agency also plays a key role in defining the partnership relationship.

Agency Rights and Duties of Partners

Partners are agents of the partnership and of each other when they act within the scope of their authority. As such, they bind the partnership to any contracts they enter into on the partnership's behalf within the regular course of business. As is true of all agents, partners owe fiduciary duties to the partnership and to each other. As co-owners of the business, partners also have the interests of principals in the enterprise; since each partner is both an agent and a principal of the partnership, each partner also owes every other partner the duties of a fiduciary. As such, partners must place partnership interests above their own personal gain and must execute their duties as partners with the utmost good faith.

The general duties owed by agents to their principals that we discussed in Chapter 37 apply to each partner in the partnership. Thus, partners owe the partnership and one another not merely the duty of loyalty, but also the duties of obedience (they must carry out the rightful requests of the majority of the partners), the duty to exercise reasonable care and diligence in the exercise of their partnership duties, the duty to notify the partnership of any facts learned that are relevant to the partnership, and the duty to make an accounting to the partnership of any benefits derived from conducting partnership business as well as any expenses incurred on the partnership's behalf. By the same token, the partnership owes each individual partner the duty of reimbursement and indemnification, as well as the duty of cooperation.

Contractual Rights and Duties of Partners

Partners are generally free to control the nature of their relationship to one another and the precise reciprocal duties they owe one another and the partnership through the partnership agreement as long as they do not violate the law or the public policy of the states in which they do business. In the absence of provisions to the contrary in the partnership agreement, partners have an equal right to manage the business and to share in the profits of the business. The mere fact that one partner makes a greater capital contribution to the partnership will not give that partner a greater voice in the management of the business or a greater share in its profits unless it is otherwise provided in the partnership agreement. Unless the partnership agreement provides otherwise, partners must share in the losses of the business in accordance with the share of profits they receive from it. Thus, if partners share profits equally, they will also share losses equally, but if a formula is adopted for the unequal allocation of profits among the partners, the same formula will apply to the sharing of losses between the partners unless they agree otherwise.

PARTNERSHIP AGREEMENT

AGREEMENT made July 4, 2016 between Wendy Uhlinger of 100 Bucolic Dr., Slippery Rock, PA 16057-1014 and Enrique Garcia of 10 Country St., Newton, NJ 07860.

1. **NAME AND BUSINESS.** The parties hereby form a partnership under the name of W&E Computer Consulting to engage in the business of providing general computer consulting services and computer hardware and software sales. The principal office of the business shall be in One Technology Drive, Middletown, NY 10940.
2. **TERM.** The partnership shall begin on August 4, 2016 and shall continue until terminated as herein provided.
3. **CAPITAL.** The capital of the partnership shall be contributed in cash by the partners as follows: $50,000 (Fifty thousand dollars) by each partner.
   A separate capital account shall be maintained for each partner. Neither partner shall withdraw any part of his capital account. Upon the demand of either partner, the capital accounts of the partners shall be maintained at all times in the proportions in which the partners share in the profits and losses of the partnership.
4. **PROFIT AND LOSS.** The net profits of the partnership shall be divided equally between the partners and the net losses shall be borne equally by them. A separate income account shall be maintained for each partner. Partnership profits and losses shall be charged or credited to the separate income account of each partner. If a partner has no credit balance in his income account, losses shall be charged to his capital account.
5. **SALARIES AND DRAWINGS.** Neither partner shall receive any salary for services rendered to the partnership. Each partner may, from time to time, withdraw the credit balance in his income account.
6. **INTEREST.** No interest shall be paid on the initial contributions to the capital of the partnership or on any subsequent contributions of capital.
7. **MANAGEMENT DUTIES AND RESTRICTIONS.** The partners shall have equal rights in the management of the partnership business, and each partner shall devote his entire time to the conduct of the business. Without the consent of the other partner neither partner shall on behalf of the partnership borrow or lend or make, deliver, or accept any commercial paper, or execute any mortgage, security agreement, bond, or lease, or purchase or contract to purchase, or sell or contract to sell any property for or of the partnership other than the type of property bought and sold in the regular course of its business.
8. **BANKING.** All funds of the partnership shall be deposited in its name in such checking account or accounts as shall be designated by the partners. All withdrawals therefrom are to be made upon checks signed by either partner.
9. **BOOKS.** The partnership books shall be maintained at the principal office of the partnership, and each partner shall at all times have access thereto. The books shall be kept on a fiscal year basis, commencing August 1 and ending July 31, and shall be closed and balanced at the end of each fiscal year. An audit shall be made as of the closing date.
10. **VOLUNTARY TERMINATION.** The partnership may be dissolved at any time by agreement of the partners, in which event the partners shall proceed with reasonable promptness to liquidate the business of the partnership. The partnership name shall be sold with the other assets of the business. The assets of the partnership business shall be used and distributed in the following order: (a) to pay or provide for the payment of all partnership liabilities and liquidating expenses and obligations; (b) to equalize the income accounts of the partners; (c) to discharge the balance of the income accounts of the partners; (d) to equalize the capital accounts of the partners; and (e) to discharge the balance of the capital accounts of the partners.
11. **DEATH.** Upon the death of either partner, the surviving partner shall have the right either to purchase the interest of the decedent in the partnership or to terminate and liquidate the partnership business. If the surviving partner elects to purchase the decedent's interest, he shall serve notice in writing of such election, within three months after the death of the decedent, upon the executor or administrator of the decedent, or, if at the time of such election no legal representative has been appointed, upon any one of the known legal heirs of the decedent at the last-known address of such heir.
    (a) If the surviving partner elects to purchase the interest of the decedent in the partnership, the purchase price shall be equal to the decedent's capital account as at the date of his death plus the decedent's income account as at the end of the prior fiscal year, increased by his share of partnership profits or decreased by his share of partnership losses for the period from the beginning of the fiscal year in which his death occurred until the end of the calendar month in which his death occurred, and decreased by withdrawals charged to his income account during such period. No allowance shall be made for goodwill, trade name, patents, or other intangible assets, except as those assets have been reflected on the partnership books immediately prior to the decedent's death; but the survivor shall nevertheless be entitled to use the trade name of the partnership.
    (b) Except as herein otherwise stated, the procedure as to liquidation and distribution of the assets of the partnership business shall be the same as stated in paragraph 10 with reference to voluntary termination.
12. **ARBITRATION.** Any controversy or claim arising out of or relating to this Agreement, or the breach hereof, shall be settled by arbitration in accordance with the rules, then obtaining, of the American Arbitration Association, and judgment upon the award rendered may be entered in any court having jurisdiction thereof.

In witness whereof the parties have signed this Agreement.

Wendy Uhlinger

Enrique Garcia

FIGURE 42.1 Sample Partnership Agreement.

Limitations on Partners' Ability to Define Their Rights and Obligations as Partners

As previously noted, partners are generally free to define their obligations to each other and to the partnership in the partnership agreement. The MPA recognizes this common law principle in Section 105 (a) (1), which provides that the partnership agreement governs "relations among the partners as partners and between the partners and the partnership."

Section 105 (c) prohibits partners from engaging in certain activities that include unreasonably restricting the right of partners to access partnership books and records, eliminating the duty of loyalty (though partners may define what types of activities are not considered a violation of the duty of loyalty, as long as these are reasonable), eliminating the duty of care or the obligation of good faith owed by each partner to the partnership, or restricting the rights of third parties under the act.

Limitation on Partners' Right of Compensation

Unless otherwise agreed, partners serve without compensation for their services beyond the distribution of partnership profits to which they are entitled. A partner is entitled to reasonable compensation, however, for winding up the business after the dissolution of the partnership [RUPA (1997) § 401(j)].

Partners' Capital Contributions

Each partner is entitled to repayment of the capital contributions (cash and/or property) made to the partnership upon death or withdrawal from the partnership or upon the dissolution of the partnership. Payments or advances to the partnership by any partner above and beyond the agreed-upon initial capital contribution will earn interest for the partner as of the date it is made.

Admission of New Partners

Admission of new partners into an existing partnership agreement can be made only with the unanimous consent of all partners [RUPA (1997) § 402 (c)].

Partners' Right to Inspect Partnership's Books

Every partner has the right to inspect the books of the partnership at any time. The books must be kept at the principal office of the partnership and made available to every partner at all times for inspection and copying. RUPA (1997) Section 408 (b) also provides the right to a partner's agents and attorneys and to former partners, their agents, and attorneys pertaining to the period during which they were partners.

Partners' Liability for Partnership Debt

Partners are jointly and severally liable for all partnership debts. This means that partners can be sued individually or together by any person to whom the partnership owes a debt, including debts that arise from contracts, tort liability, or liability to the state and federal governments for taxes or fees connected to the running of the business. Thus, each partner is subject to unlimited personal liability for partnership debts. If a single partner is sued by a creditor, the partner must fully discharge the debt out of her personal assets and would then be able to seek reimbursement from the other partners for their individual share of the liability. If the other partners are insolvent, however, the partner could be left with no recourse.

New partners admitted to an existing partnership are liable only for partnership debts incurred after they join the partnership, and partners who dissociate themselves from the partnership are liable only for debts incurred up to the time of their dissociation but not after.

Purported Partners

In our discussion of agency in Chapter 37, we saw that if a principal misleads a third party into believing that a person who is not an agent is in fact the principal's agent, then the principal will be unable to disavow acts of the purported agent if the third party relies on the purported agent's misrepresentations and suffers some tangible loss as a consequence. The result in such circumstances is a purported agency by estoppel as the principal is prevented from denying the existence of the agency or the lack of authority of the purported agent when he is sued by an innocent third party who justifiably relied on the existence of the agency because of the principal's misrepresentation. The same principle applies at common law to partnerships where partners can be prevented from denying a purported partner's partnership status if the partners allow an innocent third party to mistakenly and justifiably believe that a nonpartner is a partner. In such cases, a partnership by estoppel exists, and the partners are prevented (estopped) from denying the nonpartner's partnership status with regard to any innocent third person who justifiably relied on the misrepresentation. The RUPA (1997) addresses the liability of purported partners in Section 308 (a), which reads in part: "If a person, by words or conduct, purports to be a partner, or consents to being represented by another as a partner . . . the purported partner is liable to a person to whom the representation is made, if that person, relying on the representation, enters into a transaction with the actual or purported partnership."

In such circumstances, partners in a partnership are also liable for the purported agent's actions as if the person were in fact a partner. If all partners in the partnership consent to the representation, all partners are bound by it; but if fewer than all of the partners of the existing partnership consent to the representation, only those partners who consented to the misrepresentation are jointly and severally liable to innocent third parties who relied on the misrepresentation in dealing with the purported partner [RUPA (1997) § 308 (b)]. Under the common law, UPA, and RUPA, it is clear that statements by a purported partner himself will not bind the partners in a partnership unless made publicly in their presence and with the apparent consent of the partners. The following examples will illustrate:

- Adam tells Betty that he is a partner of Charlene and David. Betty believes him and enters into a contract with Adam to sell the partnership of Adam, Charlene, and David $1,000,000 worth of office supplies and equipment. The contract will not bind Charlene or David because Adam's statements were not made in their presence or with their acquiescence. Only Adam is liable under this contract.
- Adam tells Betty that he is a partner of Charlene and David in Charlene's presence, and Charlene does not dispute the statement. Betty later enters into a contract with Adam to sell the partnership of Adam, Charlene, and David $1,000,000 worth of office supplies and equipment. The contract will bind Charlene but not David because Adam's statements were not made in David's presence or with his acquiescence. Only Adam and Charlene are liable under this contract.
- Adam tells Betty that he is a partner of Charlene and David in the presence of both Charlene and David, who do not dispute the statement. Betty later enters into a contract with Adam to sell the partnership of Adam, Charlene, and David $1,000,000 worth of office supplies and equipment. The contract will bind Charlene and David (as well as Adam) because the misrepresentation was made in their presence, and neither one of them objected to it.

Partners' Property Rights

At common law and under the UPA, each partner is a co-owner of partnership property and holds such property as a *tenant in partnership* with all other partners. Tenancy in partnership gives partners the right to possess all partnership property, be it real or personal, jointly with all other partners for partnership purposes only. A partner may not possess any partnership property for any other purpose without the consent of all other partners. Unlike other property interests, a tenancy in partnership is nonassignable other than through a transfer agreed to by all partners. Likewise, a partner's right to partnership property is not attachable by personal creditors of the partner; it is only subject to attachment by creditors of the *partnership*. Upon the death or incompetence of a partner, personal and real property held by him as a partner in partnership automatically vests in the surviving partners. (The estate of the deceased or incompetent partner is, of course, paid the value of the partner's share.)

The RUPA (1997) abolishes the concept of partners as tenants in partnership and holds that a "partner is not a co-owner of partnership property and has no interest in partnership property which can be transferred, either voluntarily or involuntarily" [RUPA (1997) § 501]. This change in the UPA is one of many related to a significant departure from a long-standing common law principle that a partnership is not an entity apart from its owners. For the first time, RUPA (1997) Section 201 (a) states that a "partnership is an entity distinct from its partners" and brings the partnership form of business organization in line with other forms of business organization that are creatures of statute such as the limited partnership, corporation, and limited liability company.

Absent provisions to the contrary in the partnership agreement, partners may not use partnership property for other than partnership business.

Partner's Dissociation

A partner may be dissociated from the partnership in a number of voluntary and involuntary ways. Section 601 of the RUPA (1997) codifies ten distinct ways in which a partner may be dissociated from the partnership. These include the following:

1. The partner expressing the will to dissociate himself from the partnership in a partnership at will;
2. The happening of an event agreed upon by the partners in the partnership agreement to cause a partner's dissociation;
3. The partner's expulsion pursuant to the partnership agreement;
4. The partner's expulsion by unanimous vote of the partners under any of the following circumstances;
   - it is unlawful to carry on the partnership business with that partner;
   - there has been a transfer of all or substantially all of that partner's transferable interest in the partnership, other than a transfer for security purposes, or a court order charging the partner's interest, which has not been foreclosed;
   - within 90 days after the partnership notifies a corporate partner that it will be expelled because it has filed a certificate of dissolution or the equivalent, its charter has been revoked, or its right to conduct business has been suspended by the jurisdiction of its incorporation, there is no revocation of the certificate of dissolution or no reinstatement of its charter or its right to conduct business; or
   - a partnership that is a partner has been dissolved and its business is being wound up;
5. On application by the partnership or another partner, the partner's expulsion by judicial determination because of the following reasons:
   - the partner engaged in wrongful conduct that adversely and materially affected the partnership business;
   - the partner willfully or persistently committed a material breach of the partnership agreement or of a duty owed to the partnership or the other partners;
   - the partner engaged in conduct relating to the partnership business that makes it not reasonably practicable to carry on the business in partnership with the partner;
6. The partner's becoming a debtor in bankruptcy, executing an assignment for the benefit of creditors, seeking, consenting to, or acquiescing in the appointment of a trustee, receiver, or liquidator of that partner or of all or substantially all of that partner's property;
7. In the case of a partner who is an individual, the partner's death, the appointment of a guardian or general conservator for the partner, or a judicial determination that

the partner has otherwise become incapable of performing the partner's duties under the partnership agreement;
8. In the case of a partner that is a trust or is acting as a partner by virtue of being a trustee of a trust, distribution of the trust's entire transferable interest in the partnership;
9. In the case of a partner that is an estate or is acting as a partner by virtue of being a personal representative of an estate, distribution of the estate's entire transferable interest in the partnership; or
10. Termination of a partner who is not an individual, partnership, corporation, trust, or estate (the dissolution of a limited liability company that is a partner, for example).

In addition to the preceding, dissociation of partners can also occur when the partnership terminates because of a merger, an interest exchange, a conversion, domestication or when the partnership dissolves and completes winding up [§ 601 (11)-(15) RUPA (1997)].

Dissolution of a Partnership and Winding Up

A partnership can end at any time for a number of reasons, including by the mutual agreement of the parties, the withdrawal of any one partner, or the expiration of a preset time period for the partnership's duration. Where there is no agreement to the contrary, partnerships are deemed to be voluntary and subject to dissolution at any time by the will of any one partner. Even in cases in which partners agree not to dissolve the partnership for a specific period of time, any one partner may still cause the partnership to dissolve by voluntarily withdrawing from it. If this happens, the withdrawing partner may be liable to the other partners for breach of contract, but the partnership will nevertheless be dissolved.

A partnership at will can also end by operation of law by the death or decreed insanity of a partner, or by a partner's bankruptcy. In addition, a partnership can be dissolved if a court decrees that any one partner is otherwise incapable of carrying out partnership duties (such as through illness or other disability), if a partner is found to be guilty of misconduct that prejudices the carrying out of the partnership business, or if the business can be carried out only at a loss.

Under the RUPA (1997), a partnership that is set up for a set term or to complete a particular purpose can be dissolved in one of three ways:

1. If within 90 days of a partner's dissociation (by death, voluntary or involuntary withdrawal) at least half of the remaining partners express the will to wind up the business [RUPA (1997) § 801(2) (A)];
2. By the express will of all partners to wind up the business [RUPA (1997) § 801(2) (B)];
3. By the expiration of the term or the completion of the event [RUPA (1997) § 801(2) (C)].

After dissolution, a partnership enters the winding-up period. During this time, the partners may continue to carry out business that is reasonably necessary to complete existing contracts that are in progress and to otherwise bring the business affairs to an orderly close. Upon dissolution of a partnership, partners lose the authority to bind the partnership to new contracts. If a partner enters into new contracts on behalf of the partnership during the winding-up period, the partnership and other partners will not be bound by such contracts; rather, the partner acting without express authority will be personally liable on these contracts in the same way as any agent who exceeds his actual authority.

Even after dissolution and winding up, partners retain unlimited personal liability for partnership debts. If the assets of a dissolved partnership are insufficient to cover partnership debts, creditors of the partnership can sue partners individually or jointly for any shortfall.

Notice to Third Parties upon Dissolution

Because partners are agents of the partnership, when a partnership is dissolved other than by operation of law (such as by the death or bankruptcy of a partner), partners still have apparent authority to bind the partnership with respect to persons who had previously extended credit to the partnership or known of its existence. For this reason, it is essential that notice be given to such persons that the partnership has been dissolved. Until such notice is received, persons who knew of the partnership's existence or who had extended credit to the partnership in the past may still enter into binding contracts with the partnership through any of its partners. To effectively revoke partners' apparent authority to bind the partnership to new contracts, persons who have previously extended credit to the partnership must be personally notified of the partnership's dissolution by any reasonable means (e.g., by letter, telephone, telegraph, or in person). If such notification is mailed, it is effective when it is received (even if it is never read). Notification to persons who might have known of the existence of the partnership but had not extended credit to it previously is sufficient if it is published in a newspaper of general circulation in the area or areas where the partnership did business.

Questions

1. Define the term *partnership*.
2. What specific requirements are there to the formation of a partnership?
3. What is the importance of the law of agency to the law of partnership?
4. What duties do partners owe the partnership?
5. What duties are owed all partners by the partnership?
6. In the absence of agreement to the contrary, how are profits in a partnership shared? What about expenses?
7. Partners may generally unilaterally bind the partnership to contracts they enter into with third parties on the partnership's behalf in the regular course of business. But some types of acts require unanimous assent by all partners in a partnership. What are they?
8. Can new members be admitted to an existing partnership? If so, how? What liability do such members have with respect to the debts of the partnership incurred before they joined it?
9. What is the liability of partners for partnership debt?
10. What types of activities can a partnership engage in during the winding-up period?

Hypothetical Cases

1. Alma, Barbara, and Chandler, three college students, decide it would be a good idea to provide research and word processing services for other students at State U for a fee. They advertise their business in the college newspaper under the name *Alma, Barbara, and Chandler Research and Writing Services*. Alma contributes $250 in cash toward the venture, while Barbara provides an old computer system with word processing software and Chandler provides a laser printer. The friends do not discuss the nature of the business and do not enter into any type of written or oral agreement relating to the business; they merely begin working together in the hope of earning enough money to defray the latest in a series of tuition increases at their college over the past few years and the high cost of college textbooks.
   A. What is the nature of the business?
   B. Assume that the value of the students' contribution to the business is as follows: Alma $250, Barbara $1,250, and Chandler $750. How will the profits of the business be distributed?
   C. How will business losses be shared?
   D. How would losses be shared if the friends had agreed that Alma was to receive 20% of the profits, Barbara 50%, and Chandler 30%?

2. Assume the same facts as in the previous question.
   A. If the friends had agreed in writing that they would work at the business throughout their college careers and Chandler quits the business after an unsuccessful semester, what will the effect on the business organization be? What can Alma and Barbara do if they are unwilling to dissolve the arrangement?
   B. Assuming that a partnership exists here, who owns the equipment given over to the business? May the partners take their equipment home with them for their own use as a matter of right over holidays and weekends if they choose to do so? Explain fully.

3. Harry and Harriet enter into an agreement to start an antique dealership business as equal partners. Harry agrees to make a $50,000 capital contribution to the business, and Harriet agrees to provide a commercial building that she has inherited worth $150,000 as her capital contribution. The agreement between the partners specifically states that business profits and losses will be shared equally. After successfully running the business for a number of years, the partners decide they would like to hire someone to manage the daily operation of the business for them. They hire Helen as the general manager of the business. Although Helen

is not a part owner of the business, her salary will be based on a share of the business profits. And, although all fundamental business decisions are made by Harry and Harriet, they often ask her advice before implementing new policies.
   A. Is Helen a partner? Explain fully.
   B. If the business goes bankrupt and after dissolution its debts exceed its assets by $200,000, what will the responsibility of Harry, Harriet, and Helen be with regard to the debts?
   C. Assume that after dissolution, the debts of the business exceed its assets by $100,000 and that Harry is insolvent, but Harriet has personal assets (including her family home) in excess of $100,000. How much of the debt could creditors ask Harriet to bear? Explain.
4. Evelyn and Bill open a used car dealership together. Evelyn makes a capital contribution of $100,000 to the business, and Bill, who has no money to contribute but who has a great deal of business sense and a willingness to work hard, agrees to manage all affairs of the business. No contract is entered into by the two who are long-time friends and implicitly trust each other.
   A. Is Bill entitled to receive a salary for his services? Explain.
   B. If the business is slow in getting off the ground, may Bill work part time for another auto dealership without Evelyn's consent in order to pay his rent? Explain.
   C. Assume that the venture is successful and, ten years later, Evelyn dies. What will the effect of her death be on the business?
   D. If the business is worth $1,000,000 at the time of Evelyn's death, how will the proceeds from the sale of the business be distributed between Evelyn's estate and Bill?
   E. After Evelyn's death, what exactly must Bill do in terms of the business?

Limited Partnership

CHAPTER 43

Chapter Outline

Formation of a Limited Partnership

Admission of New Partners

Rights and Obligations of General and Limited Partners

Sharing of Profits and Losses

Withdrawal by General and Limited Partners

Assignment of Partnership Interest

Dissolution of a Limited Partnership

Foreign Limited Partnership

Right of Limited Partners to Bring Derivative Actions

A limited partnership is a type of partnership made up of one or more general partners, who manage the business and have unlimited personal liability for partnership debts, and one or more limited partners, who contribute capital to the business and share in its profits but whose liability for partnership obligations is limited to the extent of their investment in the business.

Unlike the sole proprietorship and partnership forms of business organization that were recognized at common law, the limited partnership is a creation of statute. As such, a limited partnership can be created only in accordance with the specific requirements of a state's Limited Partnership Act. With the exception of Louisiana, all states, Washington D.C., and the U.S. Virgin Islands have adopted the 1916 and 1976 Uniform Limited Partnership Act (ULPA) versions promulgated by the National Conference of Commissioners on Uniform State Laws (NCCUSL). The newest version of the ULPA was promulgated by NCCUSL in 2001 (last amended in 2013) and has been adopted by 19 states and the District of Columbia as of this writing. In this chapter, we will concentrate on the 1976 version of the ULPA as amended in 1985 as it represents the law in the majority of jurisdictions. For the sake of simplicity, the act will be referenced simply as the ULPA from this point on. As always, keep in mind that the law in the individual states may vary and is always subject to change.

The limited partnership form of business organization was primarily created to address one of the worst shortcomings of the traditional partnership form: the unlimited personal liability of all partners for financial obligations incurred by the partnership. While such liability of partners protects the general public against losses when dealing with a partnership, the unlimited personal liability can have a negative effect on the willingness of individuals to become partners. What the limited partnership form of business organization accomplishes is the creation of a special class of partner who is merely an investor and does not become involved in the actual running of the business, while retaining unlimited personal liability for the traditional general partner(s) of the business. As an investor, the limited partner is in a position similar to that of a shareholder in a corporation and places the money invested in the partnership through her capital contribution at risk in the event that the enterprise fails, but is insulated from personal liability beyond the extent of her investment in the business.

Formation of a Limited Partnership

To form a limited partnership, a certificate of limited partnership needs to be executed and filed with the appropriate state office (usually the office of the secretary of state). ULPA Section 201 sets out the requirements for the information that must be contained in the certificate of limited partnership as follows:

1. The name of the limited partnership;
2. The address of the office and the name and address of the agent for service of process required to be maintained by Section 104;
3. The name and the business address of each general partner;
4. The latest date upon which the limited partnership is to dissolve; and
5. Any other matters the general partners determine to include therein.

The limited partnership is formed at the time of the filing of the certificate of limited partnership in the office of the secretary of state or at any later time specified in the certificate of limited partnership as long as the requirements for filing are substantially complied with.

As should be apparent from these requirements, the main purpose of requiring the limited partnership certificate to be executed and filed is to give notice to the general public of the existence of the partnership and the identity of its general partners since they will ultimately retain unlimited personal liability for partnership debt. Likewise, the requirement that an agent be named for service of process is intended to facilitate suing the partnership by clearly identifying the name and address of a person in the state authorized to receive service of process (e.g., notice that a lawsuit is instituted) on behalf of the partnership.

Once a certificate of limited partnership is filed, it can be amended by duly notifying the secretary of state of any desired changes. Amendments to the certificate are mandatory and must be made within 30 days after the admission or withdrawal of a general partner or the continuation of the business after the happening of an event that requires its dissolution, such as the withdrawal of a general partner.

Admission of New Partners

A person may become a limited partner at the time of the original formation of the limited partnership or "at any later time specified in the records of the limited partnership for becoming a limited partner" [ULPA § 301 (a) (2)]. After the original filing of the certificate with the secretary of state, a limited partner may be admitted as provided for in the partnership agreement or, if no provision is made in the agreement, by the unanimous consent of all partners. Section 401 also allows for the admission of general partners after the filing of the original certificate of limited partnership as provided in writing in the partnership agreement or with the written consent of all partners.

Rights and Obligations of General and Limited Partners

The rights and obligations of general partners in a limited partnership are similar to those of partners in a traditional partnership. General partners are co-owners of the business who owe the business the fiduciary duties of agents and who share in the management and in the profits of the business, as well as in its debts. Limited partners, on the other hand, share only in the profits of the business and are liable for its debts only up to the limit of their capital investment. They are prohibited from participating in the control of the business. ULPA Section 303 states that if a limited partner participates in the control of the business, he will be "liable to persons who transact business with the limited partnership reasonably believing, based upon the limited partner's conduct, that the limited partner is a general partner."

If a limited partner participates in the management of the business; he can lose his special status and be subject to unlimited liability for the debts of the business to persons who believe the limited partner to be a general partner because of his involvement in the management of the business. In other words, a limited partner who becomes involved in the management of the business is estopped from denying he is a general partner with regard to persons who might have reasonably believed him to be a general partner because of his involvement in managing the business. In addition, a limited partner who allows her name to be used in the name of the partnership will be liable as a general partner to any person who extends credit to the partnership without actual knowledge that the partner so named is a limited partner.

Despite the prohibition on limited partners managing the partnership, limited partners *can* be granted the right to vote along with general partners on some partnership matters by express provision in the limited partnership agreement. Voting on any of the following does not constitute participating in managing of the business under ULPA Section 303(b) (6):

   i. The dissolution and winding up of the limited partnership;
  ii. The sale, exchange, lease, mortgage, pledge, or other transfer of all or substantially all of the assets of the limited partnership;
 iii. The incurrence of indebtedness by the limited partnership other than in the ordinary course of its business;
  iv. A change in the nature of the business;
   v. The admission or removal of a general partner;
  vi. The admission or removal of a limited partner;
 vii. A transaction involving an actual or potential conflict of interest between a general partner and the limited partnership or the limited partners;
viii. An amendment to the partnership agreement or certificate of limited partnership; or
  ix. Matters related to the business of the limited partnership not otherwise enumerated in this subsection, which the partnership agreement states in writing may be subject to the approval or disapproval of limited partners.

In most states, corporations are allowed to be general or limited partners in limited partnerships. When corporations are involved as partners, the liability of the corporation for partnership debts will encompass either all assets of the corporation (if the corporation is a general partner) or the capital invested in the partnership (if the corporation is a limited partner). As you will see in the next chapter, the corporate shareholders (the owners of the corporation) in either case will be insulated from personal liability beyond their investment in the corporation.

Sharing of Profits and Losses

Section 503 of the ULPA states that unless the partnership agreement states otherwise, "profits and losses shall be allocated on the basis of the value, as stated in the partnership records required to be kept pursuant to Section 105, of the contributions made by each partner to the extent they have been received by the partnership and have not been returned." This is in contrast to the common law presumption in a general partnership that profits and losses are to be shared equally among partners unless the partnership agreement states otherwise.

Withdrawal by General and Limited Partners

A general partner may withdraw from a limited partnership at any time by giving written notice to the other partners. If the partnership agreement prohibits withdrawal, a general partner may still withdraw but will be in breach of the partnership contract and can be sued for damages by the other partners. Upon the withdrawal of a general partner, the partnership will be dissolved unless the partnership agreement makes provisions for continuation by the remaining partners in such an event.

Limited partners may also withdraw at any time upon the happening of events noted in the partnership agreement, or at any time by giving not less than six months' prior written notice of their intention to all partners. If the limited partner's right to withdraw is limited in the partnership contract and the limited partner withdraws in violation of such a contract, then the withdrawing partner may be liable for breach of contract damages. The withdrawal of a limited partner will not automatically dissolve the partnership unless the limited partnership agreement so provides.

Assignment of Partnership Interest

General and limited partnership interests are personal property that may be freely assigned in whole or in part in absence of an agreement to the contrary. Assignment of a partnership interest will not cause dissolution of the partnership. If a limited partnership interest is assigned, the assignee can become a limited partner of the business with all rights and responsibilities of the assignor limited partner and the limited partner. Assignees of a general partner's interest in a limited partnership do not become partners but are entitled to receive all the benefits that accrue to the assignor general partner. The assignor general partner will retain unlimited liability for business losses of the partnership and will still be responsible to render services to the partnership and retain unlimited personal liability. To put it another way, only the economic rights of a general partner may be assigned (or attached by creditors), but not the duties of the general partner.

Dissolution of a Limited Partnership

Under ULPA Section 801, a limited partnership will be dissolved under any of the following circumstances:

1. At the time specified in the certificate of limited partnership;
2. Upon the happening of events specified in writing in the partnership agreement;
3. The written consent of all partners;
4. An event of withdrawal of a general partner unless at the time there is at least one other general partner and the written provisions of the partnership agreement permit the business of the limited partnership to be carried on by the remaining general partner and that partner does so, but the limited partnership is not dissolved and is not required to be wound up by reason of any event of withdrawal if, within 90 days after the withdrawal, all partners agree in writing to continue the business of the limited partnership and to the appointment of one or more additional general partners if necessary or desired; or
5. Entry of a decree of judicial dissolution [e.g., if a court finds that it is reasonably impractical to carry out the business in conformity with the terms of the limited partnership agreement].

Foreign Limited Partnership

A limited partnership is considered a *domestic limited partnership* when doing business in the state in which it is organized and a *foreign limited partnership* in every other state. Foreign limited partnerships must register with the appropriate office in every state they wish to do business (generally the secretary of state's office) and pay the requisite fees before doing business in any state other than the one in which they are organized. To register as a foreign limited partnership, a general partner must submit a form in duplicate to the secretary of state of every state the partnership wishes to do business in (other than the state in which it is organized). ULPA Section 902 requires the following information to be provided in the application for registration to the secretary of state:

1. The name of the foreign limited partnership and, if different, the name under which it proposes to register and transact business in this state;
2. The state and date of its formation;
3. The name and address of any agent for service of process on the foreign limited partnership whom the foreign limited partnership elects to appoint;

4. A statement that the secretary of state is appointed the agent of the foreign limited partnership for service of process if no agent has been appointed under paragraph (3);
5. The address of the office required to be maintained in the state of its organization by the laws of that state or, if not so required, of the principal office of the foreign limited partnership;
6. The name and business address of each general partner; and
7. The address of the office at which is kept a list of the names and addresses of the limited partners and their capital contributions, together with an undertaking by the foreign limited partnership to keep those records until the foreign limited partnership's registration in this State is cancelled or withdrawn.

The registration requirements just stated are meant to protect the citizens of the state in the event that they have claims against a foreign limited partnership by making it easy to sue both the partnership and its individual members. In addition, the registration fee is a source of income for states. If an application to register as a foreign limited partnership is properly completed and accompanied by the appropriate fee (which varies from state to state), the secretary of state issues a certificate of registration to transact business to the applicant, returning a copy of the application to the applicant and keeping one on file.

In the event that a foreign limited partnership does business in a state without filing the required certificate, ULPA Section 907 provides that the partnership will not be allowed to bring any lawsuit in the state seeking civil relief for alleged breaches in contract or torts committed against it until it completes the registration process. It can, however, enter into valid contracts notwithstanding the failure to register, and can also be sued by third parties in the state's courts.

Right of Limited Partners to Bring Derivative Actions

Like shareholders of a corporation, limited partners in a partnership have the right to bring derivative actions on behalf of the limited partnership if the general partners refuse to do so. A derivative action is an action by a limited partner to enforce a partnership cause of action against third parties that the general partners are unwilling to enforce themselves.

ULPA Section 1004 provides that if a derivative action by a limited partner on behalf of the partnership is successful, a court has the power to award reasonable costs, including attorneys' fees, to the limited partner bringing the lawsuit on the partnership's behalf. Any recovery beyond the costs of litigating the case is then turned over to the partnership.

A derivative action can be brought only by a limited partner while he is still a partner for any action that accrued after he was admitted as a partner to the limited partnership. To bring a derivative action, the limited partner must show that the general partners have been unwilling to bring the action themselves on behalf of the limited partnership and that they are unlikely to do so on their own.

Questions

1. What is a limited partnership?
2. Did limited partnerships exist at common law?
3. How is a limited partnership formed?
4. What information must be contained in the certificate of limited partnership?
5. What is the basic difference between a limited partner and a general partner in a partnership?
6. May a corporation be a limited or general partner in most states?
7. If the partnership agreement is silent as to the withdrawal of members, what is the effect of a general partner withdrawing from the partnership? What is the effect of a limited partner withdrawing?
8. What are the circumstances upon which a limited partnership will be dissolved?
9. Define foreign and domestic limited partnerships.
10. May foreign limited partnerships do business in states other than the one they were organized in? If so, do they need to follow any specific procedures before they can do business?

Hypothetical Cases

1. Tom, Dick, and Harriet start a new tax preparation and financial planning business together. Their state does not require any special licensing for such businesses, and, since the three partners are good friends, they do not draw up any specific agreement relating to the business. They do, however, verbally agree that all profits of the business are to be shared equally, and so are all losses, except that Harriet will be responsible only up to the extent of her capital contribution in the business. They further agree that Harriet will not have any direct role in the management of the business but rather will be an investor.
   A. What form of business organization do the friends have? Explain.
   B. Is Harriet a limited partner, since that is obviously the role that the parties intended for her to play in the business?
   C. Assume that Harriet had invested $50,000 in the business, while Tom and Dick had invested $5,000 each in the venture. What is each party's potential liability should the business fail?
2. Abel, Betty, and Charlene want to purchase a bookstore to compete with the campus bookstore in their university. They believe that they can make a nifty profit by instituting a 10% markup on everything they sell—including the used books they buy back from students at a fair price. They are afraid, though, of the unlimited liability posed by the partnership form of business organization and would like to minimize their risk.
   A. Can they set up a limited partnership where all three are limited partners? Explain.
   B. If one of the three entrepreneurs volunteers to be a general partner provided that business insurance is purchased to cover any potential liability, could the business be set up as a limited partnership?
3. Assume the same facts as in the previous case. Further assume that the business is set up as a limited partnership and is very successful. After a year in business, a problem arises with one of their suppliers, which fails to ship a large order in time for the beginning of the semester, costing the business thousands of dollars in lost profits. If Abel and Betty refuse to sue the supplier, who is a relative of Abel and a very close friend of Betty, what can Charlene, the limited partner, do?
4. Dominick, Jerry, and Joan are partners in a general partnership involving a lucrative used automobile dealership in Northern Pennsylvania. Because of the success of their business, they want to expand their operations to New York and New Jersey, opening two new dealerships in those states.
   A. Can they reorganize the general partnership into a limited partnership to attract new investors?
   B. What requirements would have to be met by the limited partnership before it could start doing business in New York or New Jersey?

Corporations

CHAPTER 44

Chapter Outline

Corporate Formation
Articles of Incorporation
Corporate Name
Corporate Existence
Defective Incorporation
Promoters' Liability for Preincorporation Contracts
First Organizational Meeting of the Corporation
Management of the Corporation
Shareholders' Derivative Actions
Classification of Corporations
The Corporation as an Entity
Piercing the Corporate Veil
Chapter S Corporations

Like the limited partnership, the corporate form of business organization owes its existence to statutory law. New York was the first state to enact a corporate statute, in 1811, with other states following soon thereafter. Today, every state has enacted a business corporation statute, with about two-thirds of the states basing their business corporation law on the Model Business Corporation Act (MBCA) promulgated by the American Bar Association and adopted by its Committee on Corporate Laws of the Section of Business Law with the support of the American Bar Foundation. The MBCA was last revised in 2007 with proposed amendments through 2014. As of this writing, 30 states have adopted a version of the MBCA as the basis of their corporate law. For this chapter, we will refer to the MBCA 2002 version, which is the most widely adopted version. As always, keep in mind that even in states adopting the same model act, there can be minor differences in the law. Also keep in mind that a sizable number of jurisdictions do not base their business corporation act on the MBCA, so significant differences can exist among these state acts.

In this chapter, we will first concentrate on how a corporation is created and managed and then explore the unique nature of the corporate entity and explore its advantages and disadvantages over the partnership and sole proprietorship forms of business organization.

Corporate Formation

As is the case with limited partnerships, corporations are creatures of statute that owe their existence to the state statutes that make them possible (the state's Limited Partnership Act and Business Corporation Act, respectively). Therefore, corporations can be formed only by compliance with the relevant state statute that makes the corporate form of business organization possible.

Articles of Incorporation

Under the current Model Business Corporation Act [MBCA (2002)] on which most state business corporation law is based, the corporation's incorporators must deliver to the state's secretary of state corporate articles of incorporation, which *must* contain the following information [MBCA (2002) § 2.02 (a)]:

- The name for the corporation;
- The number of shares of stock that the corporation is authorized to issue;
- The address of the corporation's initial registered office and its initial registered agent at that office; and
- The name and address of each incorporator.

In addition to the preceding mandatory minimum information, articles of incorporation *may* also contain some or all of the following types of information [MBCA (2002) § 2.02 (b)]:

- The names and addresses of the individuals who are to serve as the initial directors;
- Provisions regarding the corporate purpose of the corporation, its management, and regulation; limits on powers of the corporation or its board of directors and its shareholders; the par value of its authorized shares or classes of shares; and the imposition of personal liability on shareholders for the debts of the corporation to a specified extent and under specified conditions;
- Any provision that under this act is required or permitted to be set forth in the bylaws;
- A provision eliminating or limiting the liability of a director to the corporation or its shareholders for money damages for any action taken, or any failure to take any action, as a director (with specified exception for actions taken in violation of law or fiduciary duties);
- Provisions for indemnifying directors for actions taken as a director (with certain exceptions, such as violations of criminal law or fiduciary responsibility to the corporation).

As you can see, the articles of incorporation have similar requirements to the certificate of limited partnership, and the required information serves a similar purpose: to give notice to the public at large of the existence of the corporation and to provide an agent on whom process can be served by anyone seeking to initiate legal action against the corporation.

Corporate Name

Incorporators must meet two requirements in selecting a corporate name. First, with few exceptions, the name may not currently be in use by another corporation in the same state. Second, the corporate name must include one of the following words in its title: *corporation, incorporated, company, limited*, or one of the following abbreviations for such words: *Corp., Inc., Co.,* or *Ltd.*

Corporate Existence

Under the MBCA (2002), a corporation's existence begins as soon as the articles of incorporation are filed by the secretary of state, unless the articles of incorporation state a later date for the beginning of the corporate existence. Articles of incorporation that meet the statutory criteria and are accompanied by the appropriate filing fee are stamped by the secretary of state and filed upon their receipt. A stamped copy of the articles of incorporation is then returned to the corporate office, along with a stamped receipt for the paid filing fee. If there is a defect in the articles of incorporation submitted for filing, the secretary of state rejects them without filing and returns the documents with a written explanation of the defect.

Defective Incorporation

A corporation that has been formed in strict compliance with a state's Business Corporation Act is said to be a *de jure* corporation, or a corporation by virtue of law. When the incorporators file articles of incorporation that do not meet all the requirements of the state's Business Corporation Act, a *de jure* corporation cannot be formed. Nevertheless, if a good-faith effort has been made to comply with the act and the proposed corporation qualifies for corporate status under the state's laws, the business enterprise can be considered a *de facto* corporation, or a corporation in fact, and treated as a valid corporation. For a corporation to qualify as a *de facto* corporation, its incorporators must have made a good-faith effort to comply with the state's Business Corporation Act, the business concern must be otherwise eligible for corporate status, and the business must be in operation as a corporation when the defect in its application is discovered. *De facto* corporate status typically results when necessary information is negligently omitted from the articles of incorporation, such as by omitting an incorporator's address or providing an incorrect name for the registered agent.

In states that adhere to the MBCA (2002), there can be no *de facto* corporations, since all corporations classify as *de jure* as soon as the secretary of state accepts the articles of incorporation. Errors can simply be corrected once discovered after filing in such states, and the certificate is returned without acceptance or filing (thus, the corporation does not come into existence) if the error is discovered by the secretary of state.

Promoters' Liability for Preincorporation Contracts

Before a corporation is formed, one or more persons are usually involved in obtaining stock subscriptions from investors and in laying the groundwork for the creation of the corporation. In assisting the new business enterprise get off the ground, promoters enter into contracts with third parties on behalf of the corporation that they are attempting to form. Because promoters act on behalf of a nonexistent entity when they begin their work on the corporation's behalf, they are not held to be agents of the corporation; a corporation that is not yet in existence cannot be a principal and, thus, cannot consent to the agency. This means that promoters are *personally* liable for any contracts they enter into on the future corporation's behalf before the corporation comes into existence. In most instances, this does not present a problem for promoters because the new corporation ratifies any contracts promoters enter into on its behalf at the first meeting of the board of directors as a matter of course, thus taking the promoters off the hook with regard to liability for such contracts. Nevertheless, there is an element of risk for promoters when they carry out their preincorporation duties, since there is no guarantee that the board of directors of the company will ratify the promoters' contracts on the corporation's behalf. In fact, the corporation may never even be formed. In such cases, promoters can find themselves in the very uncomfortable position of retaining personal liability for contracts entered into on the corporation's behalf and monies extended on behalf of the corporation for such necessary preincorporation activities as hiring lawyers, accountants, and other professionals to assist in getting the corporation off the ground, paying filing fees, and arranging commercial leases or employment contracts while the entity is still in its preincorporation embryonic stage.

Once the promoters' initial groundwork for the corporation is completed, the promoters must select one or more persons to act as incorporators (or the promoters can act as incorporators themselves). The incorporator has the responsibility of filing the articles of incorporation with the secretary of state and calling the first organizational meeting for the new corporation once it is formed. In most states, the secretary of state issues a certificate of incorporation signaling the birth of the new company after accepting and filing the articles of incorporation submitted by the incorporators. MBCA (2002), however, does not require the issuance of a certificate of incorporation, but rather states that a corporation is formed as soon as the secretary of state accepts and files the articles of incorporation.

First Organizational Meeting of the Corporation

If the corporation's directors are named in the articles of incorporation, an organizational meeting is called by a majority of the directors. The primary purpose of this meeting is the appointment of corporate officers and adoption of the corporate *bylaws*—the internal rules governing the operation of the corporation. During this first meeting, the directors also typically ratify any contracts that the promoters enter into on the corporation's behalf.

In the event that the directors are not listed in the articles of incorporation, the majority of the incorporators call the organizational meeting. At this meeting, the first order of business is the appointment of directors by the incorporators. Once appointed, the directors appoint the corporate officers, adopt the corporate bylaws, and ratify the incorporator's preincorporation contracts on the corporation's behalf.

Management of the Corporation

The owners of a corporation are its shareholders. Each shareholder owns a part of the corporation equal to the number of shares owned divided by the total number of shares issued and outstanding. As an example, if a corporation has 1,000 shares issued and outstanding and a shareholder owns 100 of those shares, she would own a one-tenth interest in the corporation.

Despite being the corporation's owners, shareholders do not have the right to directly participate in the management of the company, as is the case with limited partners in a limited partnership. Corporate shareholders can only indirectly participate in the corporation's management by exercising their right to vote to elect directors to the board of directors at annual shareholders' meetings. The responsibility for managing the corporation falls to the directors, who in turn hire corporate officers to implement their policies and manage the day-to-day operation of the corporate enterprise.

Corporate Directors

Directors have a fiduciary responsibility to the corporations they serve. As such, they must exercise their responsibilities in good faith and use reasonable care in their efforts to further the best interest of the corporation. Directors are personally liable to the corporation if they breach these duties.

In addition to the right to vote for directors at annual shareholders' meetings, shareholders can also remove directors by calling a meeting for that purpose at any time and then voting them out of office. The articles of incorporation can require that removal be only for cause; if the articles of incorporation are silent as to removal of directors, then they can be removed with or without cause (e.g., with or without a valid reason).

The term of the first board of directors named in the articles of incorporation or by the incorporators expires at the first shareholder's meeting. After this initial term, the articles of incorporation can provide for staggered terms for board of directors members. Section 8.06 of the MBCA (2002) provides that the articles of incorporation can specify that the board can be elected in two or three staggered groups that are as nearly equal in number as possible. If such a scheme is selected, the board members in the first group would serve for one year, the ones in the second for two years, and the ones in the third for three years.

Corporate Officers

Corporate officers are appointed by the board of directors and serve at the pleasure of the board. The specific duties of corporate officers can be set out in the corporate bylaws or prescribed by the board of directors. The board of directors, acting in a manner consistent with the corporate bylaws, can also appoint an officer to prescribe the duties of other officers. Like directors, officers serve in a fiduciary capacity and must also exercise their responsibilities in good faith using reasonable care, and must make a good-faith effort to further the best interest of the corporation.

The precise number and titles of corporate officers can be spelled out in the corporate bylaws, but every corporation must have an officer whose duty it is to keep records of directors' and shareholders' meetings and to authenticate records of the corporation (e.g., a secretary). Under Section 8.40 (d) of the MBCA (2002), a single person can act in various capacities as officer, so it is possible to have one officer who acts as president and secretary of the corporation. Some states, though, require there be at least two corporate officers in every corporation (e.g., a president and a secretary) even if a single shareholder owns all of the corporation's stock.

Shareholders' Derivative Actions

Directors and officers of a corporation have the responsibility to manage and further the interests of the corporations they serve. When shareholders believe that corporate actions have damaged the corporation or when management refuses to enforce the rights of the corporation in civil proceedings against third parties, one or more shareholders can seek to bring a derivative action on behalf of the corporation to recover civil damages.

Before a shareholder can begin derivative action on behalf of the corporation, the corporation must be given notice and the opportunity to entertain the shareholder's demand. [UBCL (2002) Section 7.42 (2) requires 90 days to pass from the date that the shareholder gives notice, or the corporation rejects the demand, before the derivative action can commence.] If a corporation begins an inquiry into the allegations of the complaint, a court can stay the action for a time period it deems appropriate to allow the corporation to investigate and possibly address the substance of the complaint. If the derivative action continues and is successful, any proceeds obtained in the proceedings go to the corporation on whose behalf the suit was brought by the shareholder(s).

After the completion of a derivative action, a court can order the corporation to reimburse the reasonable costs of the suit, including attorneys' fees, to the shareholder(s) who brought the derivative action if the proceedings result in a substantial benefit to the corporation.

Classification of Corporations

Corporations are commonly classified in accordance with their purpose, the nature of their activities, and their ownership.

Public and Private Corporations

The corporate form serves both private and public interests equally well. Public corporations are organized by federal, state, or local governments to carry out necessary public services. Municipalities, such as cities and towns, are often organized as public corporations, as are companies entrusted with the administration of public services. Private corporations, on the other hand, are organized by private individuals to carry out private business.

Profit and Nonprofit Corporations

Corporations can be created for profit and nonprofit purposes. Public corporations are by nature nonprofit, since their purpose is not to make money but rather to advance the public good in some way. Private corporations, on the other hand, can be either profit or nonprofit, depending on their purpose. A nonprofit corporation is one that is organized for the purpose of achieving some artistic, humanitarian, or philanthropic purpose or rendering some public service, as opposed to a traditional business organized to make a profit. Like Chapter S corporations discussed later, nonprofit corporations are exempt from having to pay federal income taxes (as well as state and local income taxes in states that assess these).

Domestic, Foreign, and Alien Corporations

Corporations are classified as domestic, foreign, or alien depending on where they were organized and where they do business. Like limited partnerships, corporations are deemed to be domestic when they do business in the state where they were incorporated and are considered foreign corporations in all other states. Corporations organized under the laws of another country are considered alien corporations when they do business anywhere in the United States. As is true of limited partnerships, corporations wishing to transact business in a state other than that of their incorporation must register with the secretary of state of each such state. The address of a registered office in the state and the name and address of a registered agent of the corporation for the state must be provided to the secretary of state as part of the registration process and accompanied by the appropriate fee required by each state.

Closely Held and Publicly Traded Corporations

A closely held corporation is one whose shares are not traded to the general public in any stock exchange. Such corporations are usually (but not always) small companies owned by a few investors. A publicly traded company, on the other hand, is one whose shares are traded in any stock exchange.

Professional Corporations

Professional corporations are for-profit corporations organized to provide a professional service. Physicians, lawyers, architects, accountants, and engineers are but a few of the professions whose members commonly form professional corporations. A professional corporation must have the words *Professional Corporation* or the letters *P.C.* following the corporate name instead of the normal words or abbreviations appended to corporate names (e.g., *Corp.*, *Inc.*, *Co.*, or *Ltd.*).

The Corporation as an Entity

Unlike sole proprietorships and traditional common law general partnerships, a corporation is viewed as a separate entity from its owners. The law grants a corporation status as an *artificial being* much like a person for most purposes. This means that the corporation has certain rights and responsibilities not traditionally enjoyed by other business organizations. As an artificial being, a corporation has the right to own property in its own name, borrow or lend money, sue and be sued. It also is entitled to the protection of most laws, the same as natural persons. On the other hand, like a natural person, a corporation must pay taxes (although at a lesser rate than individuals) and can be found guilty of crimes if the punishment is a fine (obviously, a corporation can't be put in prison). In addition, a corporation can be set up to enjoy perpetual existence, unlike sole proprietorships and partnerships which, unless provisions to the contrary are made in the partnership agreement, are dissolved upon the death or incapacity of the sole proprietor or of a general partner.

Because a corporation is deemed to be an entity separate from its owners, the owners of a corporation (its stockholders) are *not* personally liable for corporate debts beyond their investment in the company. All that a shareholder risks in purchasing a share of stock is the money paid for its purchase. The limited liability offered by a corporation to its owners is its greatest appeal. On the other hand, stockholders pay a premium for this protection. As already noted, corporations pay taxes in their own right, including federal income taxes (as well as state income taxes, where applicable). This means that the profits of the corporation are subject to double taxation: the corporation pays income taxes on corporate profits, and then the shareholders pay personal income taxes on corporate profits distributed to them as dividends.

Piercing the Corporate Veil

If shareholders are to enjoy the limited liability offered by the corporate form of business organization, it is crucial that the separate entity status of the corporation be maintained. Failure to meet the formalities required of a corporation can result in a court ignoring the corporate entity and holding its owners subject to unlimited personal liability for all corporate debt. A court will pierce the corporate veil in instances where a corporation is created to defraud creditors, where corporate funds or property are not kept separate from those of its shareholders, or when required formalities (such as the keeping of minutes of directors' and shareholders' meetings) are not met.

Chapter S Corporations

The greatest disadvantage of organizing a business as a corporation is the double taxation to which corporate profits are subject. The Internal Revenue Code (IRC), however, grants a tax exemption to small business corporations. Under IRC Section 1361(a) (1), an S corporation is defined as follows for any tax year: "a small business corporation for which an election under section 1362(a) is in effect for such year." Corporations subject to taxation that do not elect S corporation status are referred to as C corporations under IRC Section 1361(a) (2). To qualify as a Subchapter S *small business corporation* and enjoy the benefit of tax exemption, a corporation under IRC Section 1361(b) (1) may *not*

- Have more than 100 shareholders;
- Have as a shareholder a person [other than an estate, a trust described in Subsection (c) (2), or an organization described in subsection (c) (6)] who is not an individual;
- Have a nonresident alien as a shareholder; and
- Have more than one class of stock (but voting and nonvoting classifications within a class of stock are permitted).

Financial institutions and insurance companies are generally ineligible for S corporation status. Subchapter S corporations are permitted to have wholly owned subsidiaries as long as the corporation owns 100% of the subsidiary S corporation's stock.

Undistributed corporate income must be treated as taxable income to the shareholders (such income is not treated as taxable income in a regular C corporation until it is actually distributed to shareholders such as by cash dividends), and shareholders are allowed to deduct net operating losses from their gross income. (Shareholders in a standard corporation may not take such deductions.)

The purpose of Subchapter S is to allow relatively small, closely held businesses that would otherwise be organized as partnerships or limited partnerships to take advantage of the corporate form of business organization without being subjected to double taxation. Since Subchapter S corporations were first recognized, the trend has been to expand the eligibility requirements, at least as related to the maximum number of allowed shareholders, which has been incrementally increased over the past two decades from 15 to 100. Some states require corporations to file for Subchapter S treatment with the state as well as with the federal government, and federal tax exempt status does not automatically guarantee that a given state or city may not tax the corporation or apply different standards for income tax exemption under state and local law.

Questions

1. What information must be contained in a corporation's articles of incorporation?
2. What are the requirements to which the selection of a corporate name must conform?
3. Under the Model Business Corporation Act, when does a corporation's existence begin?
4. Define the terms *de jure corporation* and *de facto corporation*.
5. Is a corporation responsible for the preincorporation contracts of its promoters once it comes into existence? Explain.
6. Are promoters agents of the corporation? Explain.
7. What is the primary purpose of holding a corporation's first organizational meeting?
8. Who owns a corporation and who manages it?
9. What is the difference between a domestic, a foreign, and an alien corporation?
10. What are the basic benefits that a corporation enjoys over some other forms of business organization because of its status as a legal entity in the eyes of the law?
11. What are the basic liabilities that a corporation faces above those of other traditional business organizations due to its status as an entity?
12. What does the term *piercing the corporate veil* mean?
13. What requirements must a business meet before it can file as a Subchapter S corporation?
14. What is the main benefit of Subchapter S status?

Hypothetical Cases

1. Marlene, Charlene, and Phillip wish to start a band. They call their group *MCP* (Musically Challenged Persons) and begin booking gigs at local parties. Worried about the potential liability to which they may be subjected as a partnership, the three friends agree to incorporate their business. They sign an agreement that states *we the undersigned hereby establish the MCP Corporation, an entertainment company devoted to filling the needs of musically challenged audiences everywhere.* Each person then signs the agreement.
   A. Is a corporation formed by the agreement? Explain.
   B. Under these facts, what type of business organization is involved?
   C. Assume for the moment that a *de jure* corporation is not formed under the facts given. Is a *de facto* corporation formed? Explain.

2. Assume the same facts as in the previous question.
   A. What procedure should the three artistic entrepreneurs follow in order to incorporate their business?
   B. If the requirements for incorporation are met, when will the corporation actually be formed if the state in question follows the Model Business Corporation Act?
   C. If the three friends want to expressly provide in the articles of incorporation a prohibition against playing country or rap music, may they do so? Explain.

3. Able and Betty are directors of XYZ Corporation, a company involved in the petrochemical business. Both are also major stockholders of the company and serve on other corporations' boards of directors. Betty is also XYZ's President and Chief Executive Officer.
   A. Are Able and Betty legally able to serve as board members of a corporation in which they are also shareholders?
   B. If ExxonMobil would like Betty to also serve on its board of directors, may she do so? Explain.
   C. If Able would like to accept an offer to join the board of a large charitable organization and a food services company, may he do so?

4. Cathy, an electrical contractor, sets up a corporation in which she is the sole stockholder and president. Her husband, Claude, is the secretary and both she and her husband serve on the corporation's board of directors as its only two members. Cathy, who was a sole proprietor before incorporating her company, continues to run her business exactly as before. She pays company debts out of her personal checking account and deposits all checks payable to the company in her personal checking account. In addition, she does not consult her husband on any business decisions or hold regular meetings of the board of directors. She does, however, hold yearly stockholder's meetings and votes to re-elect herself and her husband as directors; her husband dutifully records the minutes of these meetings.
   A. Does the fact that there is only one shareholder invalidate this corporation?
   B. If the corporation becomes insolvent, will Cathy be sheltered against personal liability from the debts of the corporation? Explain fully.
   C. Assume that Cathy and Claude run the corporation as a bona-fide organization, keeping proper records of all necessary meetings and carefully avoiding the commingling of corporate and private funds. How would you classify this corporation in the state that it is organized and in which Cathy does business?

5. José, Karen, and Lenny are partners in a very successful restaurant business in New Jersey. José is a citizen of Mexico who is a legal resident alien in the U.S. Karen is a Canadian National who lives in Toronto, Canada, but travels frequently to the U.S. on business. Lenny is an American citizen who lives in Elizabeth, New Jersey. The partners have recently decided that they would like to expand their business to numerous other sites in the state and would like to incorporate to lessen their personal liability risks.
   A. May the partners opt to file as a Subchapter S corporation? Explain fully.
   B. What is the downside of creating a standard corporation for the partners?

Limited Liability Companies

CHAPTER 45

The first Limited Liability Act in the U.S. was adopted by the state of Wyoming in 1977. Eleven years later, the Internal Revenue Service paved the way for the widespread adoption of this form of business organization by other states in holding that limited liability companies would be treated as partnerships and exempt from federal income taxes [Rev. Rul. 88-76, 1988-2 C.B. 360]. Today, all states and Washington D.C. recognize limited liability companies in some form.

The limited liability company (LLC) can be an ideal form of business organization for small businesses of all types. It provides the favorable tax treatment of a partnership with the protection against unlimited liability of the corporate form of business organization for its owners, along with a flexible management structure that dispenses with some of the formalities required of corporations, such as the need for annual shareholders' meetings. In addition, under IRS rules the LLC can elect to be treated as a sole proprietorship, partnership, Subchapter S, or a C (traditional) corporation, providing maximum flexibility for federal income tax avoidance while retaining the protection against unlimited liability for its members (owners).

Although the limited liability company form of business organization can be very attractive for many small businesses, it is not without its shortfalls. Many states levy a franchise tax on this form of business organization similar to that which corporations need to pay as the price for their limited liability. And the entire income derived by a member of an LLC is treated as ordinary earned income, which is subject to FICA, unlike the income earned in most partnerships where only the income derived as wages is typically subject to FICA taxation.

The National Conference of Commissioners on Uniform State Laws (NCCUSL) promulgated the Uniform Limited Liability Company Act (ULLCA) in 1995. In 2006, the NCCUSL promulgated a revised version of the act as the Revised Uniform Limited Liability Company Act [RULLCA (2006)]. The act was last amended in 2013. In this chapter, we will explore some of the common features of limited liability companies largely by following the example of the RULLCA (2006), but keep in mind that there is still very significant variation in the actual adopted versions of the limited liability company statutes from state to state. Only 14 states and the District of Columbia have adopted RULLCA (2006), and legislation for its adoption has been introduced in two others as of this writing. Thus, while there are clear similarities in the limited liability company statutes among the states, a clear unified law has yet to emerge, and many significant differences remain among these statutes for this relatively new form of business organization adopted from the original European and Latin American models.

Chapter Outline

Purpose and Duration of a Limited Liability Company
Entity Status
Name of LLC
Operating Agreement
Formation of an LLC
Annual Report
Agency Power of Members
Liabilities of Members and Managers
Admission of New Members
Management
Transferable Interest
Dissociation
Dissolution and Winding Up

Purpose and Duration of a Limited Liability Company

A limited liability company (LLC) can generally be set up to conduct any lawful activity. Unless state law prevents it, an LLC may be set up for both profit and not-for-profit purposes, as well as to conduct any business activity regulated by the state, including professional practices in law, medicine, and accounting. Some states, however, impose different standards for professional limited liability companies (PLLC) that vary from state to state. Like a corporation, an LLC can have perpetual existence, or it can be set up to have a limited duration.

Entity Status

An LLC enjoys entity status apart from its owners and may own property, sue or be sued in its own name, and has "the power to do all things necessary or convenient to carry on its activities" [§ 105 RULLCA (2006)]. However, not all states recognize the entity status of the LLC.

Name of LLC

To identify itself as a business organization with limited liability and distinguish the business from other limited liability forms of ownership, the limited liability company must append to its business name one of the following variants: *limited liability company, limited company,* or the abbreviations *L.L.C., LLC, L.C., LC,* or *Ltd. Co.*

Operating Agreement

The LLC operating agreement governs the relations among the members of the LLC as well as the relationship between individual members and the LLC itself. The operating agreement can spell out the rights and responsibilities of managers, the business activities permitted of the enterprise, and the means for amending the operating agreement.

Formation of an LLC

One or more persons may act as organizers for the LLC by signing and delivering for filing to the secretary of state (or other official designated by the state) a certificate of organization containing the following information:

- The name of the limited liability company;
- The street and mailing addresses of the initial designated office and the name, street and mailing addresses of the initial agent for service of process of the company; and
- If the company will have no members when the secretary of state files the certificate, a statement to that effect [§ 201(b) (1-3) RULLCA (2006)].

In addition to the required information, the certificate of organization may contain additional information that is not inconsistent with state law. Unless the certificate calls for a later effective date, the LLC is formed when the secretary of state files the certificate and the company has at least one member.

Annual Report

Every year in the state in which an LLC is organized and in every state in which it does business as a foreign LLC, it must deliver to the secretary of state for filing a report that states the company's name, address, and the name and address of its agent for service of process in the state. Foreign LLCs must also identify in the report the state of their formation and any alternate name in use by the company outside of the state.

Agency Power of Members

Unlike traditional partnerships in which partners are agents of the partnership and have the authority to bind the partnership as they transact business with third parties, members of an LLC are not considered its agents and cannot bind the LLC in contracts with third parties. To empower a member with agency powers, the LLC needs to deliver a statement of authority to the secretary of state that specifies the specific authority of a member to transact business on behalf of the LLC. Under RULLCA (2006) Section 302(a), a statement of authority must include the following:

- The name of the company and the street and mailing addresses of its designated office;
- The authority, or limitations on the authority, of all persons holding specific positions in the company to transfer realty held in the name of the company, enter into other transactions on behalf of, or otherwise act for or bind, the company.

To revoke or amend the authority of any individual in a statement of authority filed by the secretary of state, the LLC must deliver an amendment or cancellation of authority certificate to the secretary of state for filing. A person named in a grant of authority filed by the secretary of state may deny her authority by delivering a statement of denial to the secretary of state for filing.

Liabilities of Members and Managers

Members and managers of the LLC do not bear personal liability for debts or other obligations of the company; these are the sole liability of the LLC. Under Section 304(b) of the RULLCA (2006), failure to observe formalities in the management or activities of an LLC is not grounds for imposing personal liability on members or managers for company debts, obligations, or liability. Thus, there is no analogue to "piercing the corporate veil" to reach the personal assets of members or managers in the LLC form of business organization.

Admission of New Members

New members may be admitted to an LLC as provided for in the operating agreement or by the unanimous consent of all members if no provision is made for new membership in the operating agreement.

Management

An LLC may be professionally managed or managed by its members. Unless the operating agreement expressly provides that the company will be professionally managed, the assumption is that it will be managed by its members, with each member having the right to participate in the management of the company as in a general partnership. In a professionally managed LLC, certain matters require the consent of all members. These include transfers of company assets not in the regular course of business, approval of merger agreements, and the amendment of the operating agreement. In a member-managed LLC, each member owes the company fiduciary responsibilities similar to those owed by partners in a general partnership and the officers and directors of a corporation. These include the duty of loyalty, the duty not to compete with the company, the duty of reasonable care in carrying out company business, and the duty to render an accounting.

Transferable Interest

As is true of partnership interests, members of an LLC may transfer their financial interests in the company but not the right and responsibility to participate in its management if the LLC is member-managed.

Dissociation

As is the case with partnerships, the member of an LLC may dissociate himself from the company at any time even if the operating agreement prohibits the dissociation, but a member is liable for breach of contract damages for wrongful dissociation. Dissociation may also occur for various other reasons, including the happening of an event provided for in the operating agreement, and by unanimous consent of other members when a member can no longer legally be a member of the company (e.g., a lawyer who is disbarred can no longer legally be a member of a law practice set up as an LLC and would be dissociated by unanimous vote of the other members) or when a member voluntarily transfers his entire interest in the LLC.

Dissolution and Winding Up

A limited liability company is dissolved, and its activities must be wound up upon any of the following events under RULLCA (2006) Section 701:

- An event or circumstance that under the operating agreement causes dissolution;
- The unanimous consent the members;
- The passage of 90 consecutive days during which the company has no members;
- The entry by a court with appropriate jurisdiction of an order dissolving the company on the grounds that:
    - The conduct of all or substantially all of the company's activities is unlawful;
    - It is not reasonably practicable to carry on the company's activities in conformity with the certificate of organization and the operating agreement; or
    - The managers or those members in control of the company have acted, are acting, or will act in a manner that is illegal or fraudulent or have acted or are acting in a manner that is oppressive and was, is, or will be directly harmful to the applicant.

Questions

1. What types of businesses are best suited to the LLC form of business organization?
2. What are the most attractive features of an LLC for many businesses?
3. Name two shortfalls of the LLC form of ownership over a traditional partnership or sole proprietorship?
4. How many jurisdictions have adopted the Uniform Limited Liability Company Act of 1996?
5. What types of business may an LLC conduct?
6. May a not-for-profit company be set up as an LLC?
7. Do all states treat an LLC as an entity apart from its owners/members?
8. What types of companies need to file an annual report with the secretary of state, and what information must it contain?
9. Are the members of an LLC generally considered to be agents for the business with the power to bind the LLC to contracts with third parties?
10. Are members' interests in an LLC transferable?

Hypothetical Cases

1. Vickie, Wendy, and Xena are attorneys interested in starting a law practice together in their state. The three are friends who have graduated from law school and passed their state's bar exam within the past two years. Each can make a maximum capital contribution of $20,000 by borrowing from supportive parents or other family members at a reasonable interest rate with a payback period of at least ten years. None of them has any significant assets beyond their training and license to practice law, and each intends to carry a minimum of $1,000,000 malpractice insurance. Based on these facts, answer the following questions.
    A. What form of business organization would you recommend for the venture?
    B. If the friends opt to start out as a traditional general partnership, may they convert it to an LLC or PLLC if their state recognizes both forms of business organization?

2. Assume the same facts as in the previous question. Further assume that the three attorneys opt to organize their practice as an LLC under the laws of their state.
   A. If a client trips on a loose rug in Vickie's office and falls, breaking a leg and chipping three teeth during a consultation to discuss a slip and fall case at a local supermarket, what is the liability of Vickie, Wendy, and Xena if the client successfully sues their LLC for $1,000,000 in damages and the business's liability insurance covers a maximum of $100,000 per occurrence?
   B. During an interview with a prospective client, Xena loses her cool and punches the man on the nose after he laughs about having pistol-whipped an elderly man for not turning over his wallet fast enough. The man later sues Xena for assault and wins a $500,000 judgment against her for the cost of his medical bills to reconstruct his broken nose and for pain and suffering. Is the LLC liable for paying this judgment? Are Vickie and Wendy personally liable for this judgment if Xena is unable to pay it?

3. Tom, Dick, and Harriet form an LLC in their state but do not enter into an operating agreement for the business.
   A. What will the management structure be for the business?
   B. May Alfonse become a member of this LLC a year later? If so, what is the procedure for having him become a new member?

4. Duane, Elsa, and Fran are three retired entrepreneurs who would like to provide free business consulting services to startup companies in economically depressed areas of their state as a public service.
   A. If protection from personal liability from their activities is their major concern and if they wish to establish a not-for-profit organization, what business organization model(s) would you recommend?
   B. What initials must be appended to the business name if it is possible to organize the business as an LLC?

Ethics and the Law

In the past 40 years, a clear trend has emerged in favor of expanding the ability of businesses to limit the personal liability of owners while avoiding the dual taxation of the traditional corporate form of business organization. Limited partnerships and their variants, the significant expansion of subchapter S business eligibility to increasingly larger businesses (e.g., the gradual increase in the limit of maximum number of owners from 15 to 100 over a 20-year period), and the popularity of limited liability companies have resulted. As a consequence, some very substantial businesses are exempt from corporate income taxes, while their owners still enjoy the safety of limited personal liability in the case of business failure that allows entrepreneurs to fail and fail again with limited risk to their own personal wealth. As the cost of business failure is invariably passed on to investors, consumers, borrowers, and tax payers, the question may fairly be asked who should bear the ultimate responsibility for business failure? Is it wise or just to allow business owners to insulate themselves from the consequences of their actions? What do you think?

Unit VIII — Cases for Further Study

IN THE UNITED STATES DISTRICT COURT FOR THE EASTERN DISTRICT OF PENNSYLVANIA
SUGARTOWN WORLDWIDE LLC v. KENNETH LINN SHANKS AND JAMES MICHAEL GLOVER
NO. 14-5063
MEMORANDUM
March 24, 2015
[EXCERPT OPINION]*

Kearney, J

Holding a $5,970,390.75 default judgment against non-party and judgment-proof Outlook International Limited ("Outlook") on an unpaid guaranty, judgment creditor Sugartown Worldwide LLC ("Sugartown") now seeks to hold Outlook's two individual principals liable for the default judgment. Sugartown seeks to pierce Outlook's corporate veil, collect damages and impose a receiver and a constructive trust arising from Defendants' alleged fraud, unjust enrichment, transfers violating the Pennsylvania Uniform Fraudulent Transfer Act ("PUFTA") and breach of fiduciary duty. Nobody disputes Outlook's guaranty liability. Facing a creative creditor's complaint after execution discovery, we now consider the extent this Court should allow Sugartown to set aside Outlook's corporate form or pursue Outlook's two owners through separate tort theories to collect on an unpaid judgment.

In his motion to dismiss, Outlook principal and defendant James Michael Glover ("Glover") argues that this Court lacks personal jurisdiction over him as he has been living in China on a resident visa at all material times and has never travelled to, or done business in, Pennsylvania. He also argues that Sugartown cannot use tort theories to transfer liability for Outlook's judgment to him as a matter of law. [Footnote omitted.]

We find that this Court lacks personal jurisdiction over Glover on the fraud in the inducement/common law conspiracy claim (Count II) and unjust enrichment claim (Count III). On a motion to dismiss standard, Sugartown may proceed into discovery against both Defendants under theories of fraudulent transfer (Count IV) and breach of fiduciary duty (Count V). In the accompanying Order, we grant Glover's motion to dismiss the "piercing the corporate veil" claim (Count I) without prejudice as it is not a cause of action and has not been sufficiently plead and dismiss any claim for a constructive trust or a receiver for assets under Count IV now held by non-party Outlook Sge or other non-party alleged transferees of some of Outlook's assets.

I. Facts Plausibly Alleged Regarding the Judgment

Sugartown owns Lilly Pulitzer trademarks, service marks and other intellectual property rights. (ECF Doc. No. 1, Compl., ¶ 7.) In January 2010, Sugartown and HFI Brand, Inc. ("HFI") entered into a license agreement (the "Agreement") allowing HFI to use the trademarks on certain furniture and related products. (Id. ¶¶ 8, 10.) In exchange, HFI agreed to make royalty payments to Sugartown. (Id. ¶ 10.) Sugartown asked HFI to secure a guaranty for the royalties. (Id. ¶¶ 8, 10.) Outlook agreed to guaranty (the "Guaranty") the royalty payments. (Id. ¶ 8.)

Defendant Shanks admitted that by early 2011, he knew that HFI would probably default and Outlook would be liable on the Guaranty. (Id. ¶ 29). Thereafter, Shanks admits that Outlook paid approximately $5.5 million to its

---

*The entire opinion is available at https://www.paed.uscourts.gov/documents/opinions/15D0236P.pdf (Last accessed February 5, 2016).

subsidiaries and other companies owned and controlled by Glover and him as "marketing" and "consultancy" fees. (*Id.* ¶ 30.)

At some unknown point in 2011, Outlook paid $500,000 to Shanks and Glover as "director's fees". (*Id.* ¶ 34.)

Glover and Shanks formed non-party Outlook Sge in March 2012 based in Singapore. (*Id.* ¶ 35.) Shanks and Glover own Outlook Sge and are its only board members. (*Id.*) Outlook Sge delivers many of the same services as Outlook. (*Id.* ¶ 36.) In July 2012, Outlook sold "most of its assets, including Outlook's various office assets and Outlook's subsidiary companies, to Outlook Sge." (*Id.* ¶ 37.) Sugartown alleges Shanks and Glover sold these assets to Outlook Sge for inadequate consideration or no consideration at all to avoid an impending payment to Sugartown. (*Id.* ¶ 39.)

By October 2012, HFI breached the Agreement by failing to pay over $5,850,000 in royalties. (*Id.*) On November 30, 2012, Sugartown sued HFI and Outlook in this Court. HFI and Outlook failed to answer. On March 19, 2013, the Honorable John R. Padova entered default judgment against Outlook for $5,970,390.75. (*Id.* ¶ 25; Ex. B.). After discovery in aid of execution, Sugartown filed this action.

Ii. Analysis

* * *

i. Sugartown cannot presently state a claim for piercing the corporate veil

Under Pennsylvania law, the corporate form may be disregarded "whenever justice or public policy demand and when the rights of innocent parties are not prejudiced nor the theory of the corporate entity rendered useless." *Ashley v. Ashley*, 482 Pa. 228, 393 A.2d 637, 641 (Pa. 1978). However, there is a strong presumption against piercing the veil. *See Lumax Indus., Inc. v. Aultman*, 543 Pa. 38, 669 A.2d 893, 895 (1995). "Piercing the corporate veil is admittedly an extraordinary remedy preserved for cases involving exceptional circumstances." *Village at Camelback Prop. Owners Ass'n, Inc. v. Carr*, 371 Pa. Super. 452, 538 A.2d 528, 533 (Pa. Super. Ct. 1988). "[T]he standard a party must meet to persuade a court to pierce the corporate veil is a stringent one." *Accurso v. Infra-Red Servs., Inc.*, 23 F. Supp. 3d 494, 509 (E.D. Pa. 2014) (citing *Pearson v. Component Tech. Corp.*, 247 F.3d 471, 485 (3d Cir. 2001) ("Such a burden is notoriously difficult for plaintiffs to meet.")).

While there appears to be no "clear test or well settled rule in Pennsylvania" as to when the corporate veil may be pierced, courts weigh certain relevant factors. *Fletcher-Harlee Corp. v. Szymanski*, 936 A.2d 87, 95 (Pa. Super. Ct. 2007) (citations omitted). These factors include "undercapitalization, failure to adhere to corporate formalities, substantial intermingling of corporate and personal affairs and the use of the corporate form to perpetrate a fraud." *Lumax Indus., Inc. v. Aultman*, 543 Pa. 38, 669 A.2d 893, 895 (1995). "These factors are not exhaustive, nor is every element required for a finding of liability; however, the situation must present 'an element of injustice or fundamental unfairness.'" *Siematic Mobelwerke GmbH & Co. KG v. Siematic Corp.*, 643 F. Supp. 2d 675, 695 (E.D. Pa. 2009) (quoting *Trustees, Nat. Elevator Indus. Pension v. Lutyk*, 332 F.3d 188, 194 (3d Cir. 2003)).

"Piercing the corporate veil is not an independent cause of action, but it is an equitable remedy that may be imposed by the court to "redress[] a wrong by the expedient of ignoring the legal fiction that a corporation's existence is separate from that of its owner." *Siematic*, 643 F. Supp. 2d at 694 (citation omitted) (alteration in original).

Here, Sugartown frames this equitable remedy as a cause of action. On this ground alone, Count I is dismissed. Looking to the substance, Sugartown's pleading to pierce Outlook's corporate veil runs the spectrum of theories. Sugartown alleges that Outlook was grossly undercapitalized, that Glover and Shanks disregarded corporate formalities, substantially intermingled personal and corporate affairs, misused the corporate form to perpetrate a fraud, and that the other Outlook entities were merely a fiction.

Aside from labels, conclusions and a formulaic recitation of factors, the Complaint is devoid of any factual allegations that can support piercing the veil based on disregarding corporate formalities and substantially intermingling personal and corporate affairs. The Complaint contains no facts regarding these factors. Sugartown also fails to state a claim for undercapitalization. Gross undercapitalization is of particular importance in a veil-piercing analysis. *See Trustees, Nat. Elevator Indus. Pension Lutyk*, 140 F. Supp. 2d 447, 458 (E.D. Pa. 2001). The Complaint lacks the requisite factual support that Outlook was undercapitalized. Sugartown does not allege that Outlook was undercapitalized at any relevant time until after the transfers. Outlook was sufficiently capitalized to make payments of approximately $5.5 million dollars to its subsidiaries in the years 2010 and 2011. (ECF Doc. No. 13, Pl.'s Mot., Ex. A part 5, 3.) The majority of the Complaint outlines Defendants' alleged self-dealing transfers for little or no consideration as Outlook's fiduciaries. Sugartown argues that Shanks' and Glover's fraudulent and fiduciary misconduct abused the corporate form to perpetrate a fraud. Sugartown asserts that when it was clear that HFI was going to default on the Agreement, Shanks and Glover, as Outlook's fiduciaries, conspired to strip it of assets. (ECF Doc. No. 1, Compl., ¶¶ 28–29.) Specifically, Shanks and Glover authorized payment of over $5,000,000 to the various Outlook subsidiaries. (*Id.* ¶ 30.) In March 2012, Shanks and Glover formed Outlook Sge, of which they were co-owners and the only board members. (*Id.* ¶ 35.) Then, in July 2012, prior to receiving Sugartown's notice of default, Shanks and Glover, as Outlook directors, authorized the sale of most of its assets to Outlook Sge. (Id. ¶¶ 37–39.) Sugartown further alleges that Glover and Shanks transferred these assets to Outlook Sge without receiving adequate consideration. (Id. ¶ 38–39.)

These specific facts create a plausible claim that, at a minimum, Outlook engaged in fraudulent transfers creating individual liability for Shanks and Glover. However, there is no other fact on the present record to warrant setting aside Outlook's corporate veil. There are no "specific, unusual circumstances" that call for an exception to the "general rule that the corporate entity should be recognized and upheld." *Official Committee of Unsecured Creditors v. R.F. Lafferty & Co., Inc.*, 267 F.3d 340, 353 (3d Cir. 2001). There are no pled facts that Glover and Shanks ignored corporate formalities or financial independence to affect these transfers. Self-dealing, fraudulent transfers and fiduciary misconduct do not alone "abuse the corporate form"; if so, every claim for breach of the duty of loyalty or fraudulent transfer by a controlling principal would create a risk of setting aside the corporate veil. The exception would otherwise swallow the rule.

As we hold below that Sugartown may proceed on its fraudulent transfer and fiduciary duty claims, it may find additional evidence of abuse of Outlook's corporate form. Accordingly, we dismiss Count I without prejudice.

* * *

Order

* * *

2. Defendant's Motion to Dismiss for Failure to State a Claim is DENIED in part and GRANTED in part:
   a. Defendant's Motion is GRANTED as to Count I (piercing the corporate veil). . . .

Optional Assignments

1. Brief the preceding abbreviated version of the case in a one- to two-page, single-spaced brief (with double spaces between paragraphs) that contains the following four sections: (1) The basic facts of the case [Facts]; (2) The legal issue the court is being asked to decide [Issue]; (3) The holding of the court (how it decides the legal issue before it) [Holding]; and (4) The rationale the court uses to support its decision [Rationale]. If your instructor asks you to brief the case, she will give you additional instructions.

2. The court dismisses the claim of piercing the corporate veil without prejudice, which means that the plaintiff is free to raise it again in a new lawsuit if it can provide sufficient additional evidence to sustain the claim—something it did not do in the case before the court. What type of new evidence will the plaintiff need to prevail if it decides to institute a new suit in an attempt to pierce the corporate veil?

IN THE SUPREME COURT OF THE STATE OF NEVADA

IN RE: CAY CLUBS

No. 58176

December 4, 2014

OPINION [Excerpted]

By the Court, SAITTA, J.

* * *

Facts and Procedural History

Based on the purchasers' evidence and allegations below, Cay Clubs appears to be a business that developed and sold condominiums at a resort called Las Vegas Cay Club. As indicated in the purchasers' allegations and Aeder's deposition testimony, Aeder created and managed the JDI entities, which extended financial support for the development of Cay Clubs' properties. The purchasers alleged that they entered into purchase agreements for Las Vegas Cay Club condominiums and engaged in related transactions with Flamingo Palms Villas, LLC, which Cay Clubs allegedly created and controlled. According to their allegations and supporting affidavits, the purchasers engaged in these transactions (1) after reviewing marketing materials, which advertised that Las Vegas Cay Club would be improved and developed into a luxury resort and which represented a partnership between Cay Clubs and the JDI entities; and (2) on the belief that the partnership relationship between Cay Clubs and the JDI entities provided the experience and financial wherewithal to develop the advertised luxury resort.

Believing that Cay Clubs disingenuously abandoned the plan to improve Las Vegas Cay Club and fraudulently took the purchasers' money, the purchasers filed suit against approximately 40 defendants, including Cay Clubs, Aeder, and the JDI entities. The claims included, but were not limited to, fraudulent misrepresentation, securities violations, deceptive trade practices, civil conspiracy, and fraudulent conveyances of money. Additionally, the purchasers pleaded that the JDI entities and Aeder were liable under NRS 87.160(1), Nevada's partnership-by-estoppel statute, for the wrongdoings of Cay Clubs.

After answering the complaint, Aeder and the JDI entities filed a motion for summary judgment. They contended that there was an absence of evidence to support the complaint and that the parol evidence rule and the purchase agreements prevented the purchasers from relying on evidence of representations of a partnership. They maintained that NRS 87.160(1) did not apply to the purchasers' tort-based claims because the statute imposed liability only for claims sounding in contract. They also argued that the statute did not apply to any of the claims because it conditioned liability on the extension of financial credit, which was not extended by the purchasers. Moreover, they maintained that NRS 87.160(1) could not be used to impose liability against Aeder and the JDI entities because the purchasers transacted solely with Flamingo Palms Villas and not with the purported partnership between Cay Clubs, Aeder, and the JDI entities on which their partnership-by-estoppel claim was based.

The purchasers opposed the motion. Submitting additional evidence in support of their complaint, they argued that issues of fact remained with respect to Aeder's and the JDI entities' liability, especially with respect to their liability under NRS 87.160(1). We reserve a more detailed discussion of the purchasers' evidence for our analysis of whether genuine issues of material fact remained with respect to Aeder's and the JDI entities' liability under NRS 87.160(1).

After a hearing, the district court granted the motion for summary judgment in favor of the JDI entities and Aeder upon finding that no genuine issues of material fact remained as to their liability for any of the asserted claims, including the partnership-by-estoppel claim under NRS 87.160(1). In so doing, it specifically noted that a "reference to a 'strategic partner'" in the marketing materials was insufficient for partnership by estoppel.

The order granting summary judgment was later certified as final under NRCP 54(b). In addition, the district court awarded costs to the JDI entities and Aeder. These consolidated appeals followed. A panel of this court issued an opinion affirming in part, reversing in part, and remanding a district court order granting summary judgment. After the panel denied the JDI entities' petition for rehearing, the JDI entities petitioned for reconsideration.

DISCUSSION The parties' argument on appeal

The parties dispute whether the district court erred in granting summary judgment in favor of Aeder and the JDI entities regarding their liability as putative partners with Cay Clubs under NRS 87.160(1). Modeled after section 16 of the 1914 version of the Uniform Partnership Act (UPA), NRS 87.160(1) codifies the common law partnership-by-estoppel doctrine. See 1931 Nev. Stat., ch. 74, § 1, at 112, 116; see also Facit-Addo, Inc. v. Davis Fin. Corp., 653 P.2d 356, 359-60 (Ariz. Ct. App. 1982) (providing that Arizona's partnership-by-estoppel statute—which is substantially identical to NRS 87.160(1)—codifies the partnership-by-estoppel doctrine). As long as other conditions are met, NRS 87.160(1) provides that a person may incur partnership liability where there is a holding out of that person as a partner, with the consent of that person being held out, and another person gives credit to the purported partnership upon believing in the representation:

> *When a person, by words spoken or written or by conduct, represents himself or herself, or consents to another representing him or her to any one, as a partner in an existing partnership or with one or more persons not actual partners, the person is liable to any such person to whom such representation has been made who has, on the faith of such representation, given credit to the actual or apparent partnership, and if the person has made such representation or consented to its being made in a public manner the person is liable to such person, whether the representation has or has not been made or communicated to such person so giving credit by or with the knowledge of the apparent partner making the representation or consenting to its being made.* (Emphases added.)

The parties offer different interpretations of this statute. In so doing, they disagree on the meaning of "partnership," what type of consent must be manifested for liability under the statute, and the meaning of "given credit." Aeder and the JDI entities maintain that NRS 87.160(1) requires a reasonable reliance on the representation of a partnership. They also dispute the statute's applicability to claims that do not sound in contract. Under dissimilar interpretations of NRS 87.160(1), the parties necessarily disagree over whether genuine issues of material fact precluded the district court's grant of summary judgment with respect to Aeder's and the JDI entities' liability under NRS 87.160(1).

Prior to this appeal, this court lacked the chance to address in any significant depth the partnership-by-estoppel doctrine or NRS 87.160(1)'s meaning. We do so now.

Because the arguments concern issues of statutory interpretation and the grant of a summary judgment, we engage in de novo review of the matters raised on appeal. Cromer v. Wilson, 126 Nev. 106, 109, 225 P.3d 788, 790 (2010).

NRS 87.160(1)'s meaning

In interpreting NRS 87.160(1), our ultimate goal is to effectuate the Legislature's intent. Cromer, 126 Nev. at 109, 225 P.3d at 790. We interpret a clear and unambiguous statute pursuant to its plain meaning by reading it as a whole and giving effect to each word and phrase. Davis v. Beling, 128 Nev. _, _, 278 P.3d 501, 508 (2012). We do not look to other sources, such as legislative history, unless a statutory ambiguity requires us to look beyond the statute's language to discern the legislative intent. State, Div. of Ins. v. State Farm Mut. Auto. Ins. Co., 116 Nev. 290, 294, 995 P.2d 482, 485 (2000). Moreover, our interpretation of NRS 87.160(1) is guided by the following rules that the Legislature set out: (1) the law of estoppel applies to NRS 87.160(1), (2) this court is not to apply "[t]he rule that statutes in derogation of the common law are to be strictly construed," and (3) the statutory scheme that contains NRS 87.160(1) "must be interpreted and construed as to effectuate its general purpose to make uniform the law of those states which enact it." NRS 87.040(1)-(2), (4).

The term "partnership" in NRS 87.160(1)

When arguing about the absence or presence of genuine issues of material fact, the parties implicitly raise an issue about the meaning of the statute's term "partnership." They appear to disagree about what type of relationship must be represented for partnership by estoppel: a partnership or a less formal but collaborative profit-oriented relationship, such as a joint venture. Their arguments about the nature of the purported relationship between Cay Clubs, Aeder, and the JDI entities urge us to answer whether partnership by estoppel can be found under NRS 87.160(1) when the subject of the actionable representation is a joint venture rather than a partnership.

Joint ventures and partnerships are similar but not identical. Hook v. Giuricich, 108 Nev. 29, 31, 823 P.2d 294, 296 (1992). "[A] partnership is an association of two or more persons to carry on as co-owners a business for profit. . . ." NRS 87;060(1). A joint venture is a similar collaboration for profit, but the collaboration is limited to a specific business objective rather than an ongoing business. Hook, 108 Nev. at 31, 823 P.2d at 296. Despite the distinction, Nevada caselaw provides that the principles of partnership law apply to joint ventures. Radaker v. Scott, 109 Nev. 653, 658, 855 P.2d 1037, 1040 (1993). Other jurisdictions have concluded the same, and they have applied the partnership-by-estoppel doctrine to impose liability for the representation of a joint venture. See, e.g., Daynard v. Ness, Motley, Loadholt, Richardson & Poole, P.A., 290 F.3d 42, 56 (1st Cir. 2002) (indicating that partnership by estoppel applies to joint ventures); John's, Inc. v. Island Garden Ctr. of Nassau, Inc., 269 N.Y.S.2d 231, 236 (Dist. Ct. 1966) (concluding that the rules that apply to partnerships, including partnership by estoppel, apply to joint ventures), aff'd sub nom. C.J. Zonneveld & Sons, Inc. v. Island Garden Ctr., Inc., 280 N.Y.S.2d 34, 34 (App. Term 1967); Allan Constr. Co. v. Parker Bros. & Co., 535 S.W.2d 751, 754-55 (Tex. Civ. App. 1976) (applying partnership by estoppel to conclude that a party was liable as a joint venturer). Likewise, we conclude that the partnership-by-estoppel doctrine, as defined by NRS 87.160(1), applies where the subject of the representation is a joint venture rather than a partnership.

The term "consents" in NRS 87.160(1)

Partnership by estoppel may arise where a party, "by words spoken or written or by conduct, represents himself or herself, or consents to another representing him or her to any one, as a partner . . . with one or more persons not actual partners." NRS 87.160(1). As to the term "consents," the parties disagree over the extent to which NRS 87.160(1) requires a manifestation of consent. Whereas Aeder and the JDI entities argue as though the statute requires an explicit communication of consent, the purchasers argue that consent may be found where it can be implied from one's conduct.

Consent may be "express[ed]" by words or "implied" by conduct. Black's Law Dictionary 323 (8th ed. 2004). Also, the comment to the UPA rule on which NRS 87.160(1) is based explains consent by directing the reader to caselaw which provides that consent may be implied when the facts make the implied conclusion reasonable. Unif. P'ship Act § 16, 6 U.L.A. 661-62 cmt. (1914) (explaining consent by citing to Morgan v. Farrel, 20 A. 614, 615-16 (1890) (indicating that consent may be reasonably implied)); see also Anderson Hay & Grain Co. v. Dunn, 467 P.2d 5, 7 (N.M. 1970) (concluding that the consent to being represented as a partner may be implied by conduct if the conduct would lead a reasonable person to that conclusion). Thus, we conclude that consent under NRS 87.160(1) may be manifested either by one's express words or one's conduct from which consent can be reasonably implied.

The phrase "given credit" in NRS 87.160(1)

The parties disagree on the type of credit that must be extended for partnership by estoppel. The purchasers contend that NRS 87.160(1)'s phrase "given credit" means a claimant's belief in and detrimental reliance on the representation of a partnership's existence. Aeder and the JDI entities respond that this statutory language conditions partnership liability on the extension of financial credit to the purported partnership.

"Credit" has been defined as the "[b]elief" or "trust" in another person, the "availability of funds . . . under a letter of credit," or the "ability to borrow money." Black's Law

Dictionary 396 (8th ed. 2004). Hence, because it lends itself to more than one reasonable interpretation, the term "credit" presents an ambiguity that invites us to refer to other authorities to resolve the statute's meaning. See State Farm, 116 Nev. At 294, 995 P.2d at 485. Unfortunately, NRS 87.160(1) lacks legislative history that addresses the meaning of "given credit." However, because the Legislature directed this court to construe NRS 87.160(1) in uniformity with other jurisdictions that have adopted the UPA, we look to other jurisdictions for guidance. See NRS 87.040(4).

Aeder and the JDI entities direct this court to one salient authority, Bertin Steel Processing, Inc. v. U.S. Steel Corp., No. 1:02 CV 1669, 2005 WL 2205332, at *14 (N.D. Ohio Sept. 6, 2005), wherein the phrase "given credit" was limited to financial credit. But numerous Aeder and the JDI entities also rely on the following authorities and unpublished decisions for their contention that the phrase "given credit" is limited to the extension of financial credit, but they overlook that none of these authorities expressly articulates such a limited definition of 1947A. Jurisdictions have either rejected that limited reading of the phrase or have read "given credit" to mean giving credence to a representation of a partnership by detrimentally relying on the representation. These authorities indicate that the phrase "given credit" is one that is reasonably understood as not being limited to the extension of financial credit.

In arguing that the phrase "given credit" only concerns extension of financial credit, Aeder and the JDI entities emphasize that the revised 1997 version of the UPA replaced the phrase "given credit" with "enter[] into a transaction." Unif. P'ship Act § 308(a), 6 U.L.A. 128 (1997). They contend that this revision expands the UPA's partnership-by-estoppel language to matters that do not involve financial credit, such that NRS 87.160(1)—which was based on the pre-1997 version of the UPA—must be construed to apply only to matters that involve financial credit. However, a comment to this revision suggests otherwise, as it explains that the revised language "continues the basic principles of partnership by estoppel from UPA Section 16." Unif. P'ship Act § 308(a), 6 U.L.A. 128, 129 cmt. (1997) Thus, the revision does not expand but, instead, clarifies and continues the partnership-by-estoppel principles that the drafters attempted to encapsulate. See id. Additionally, it provides indicia of the drafters' understanding that the partnership-by-estoppel doctrine applies to matters beyond those that implicate the extension of financial credit. See Id.

To adopt Aeder's and the JDI entities' construction of the phrase "given credit" would severely limit who could utilize the partnership-by-estoppel doctrine. Under their interpretation, NRS 87.160(1) would only benefit claimants with the financial resources and expertise to extend financial credit to a purported partnership. There are claimants beyond this cohort that face the risk of incurring an actionable injury because of the representation of a purported partnership. See, e.g., Sitchenko, 512 F. Supp. at 760-62. Thus, we do not read NRS 87.160(1)'s phrase "given credit" to only mean the extension of financial credit. Rather, as it appears in NRS 87.160(1), "given credit" means giving credence to the representation of a partnership by detrimentally relying on the representation, which may include, but is not limited to, the act of extending financial credit to the purported partnership or venture.

However, although there need not be an extension of credit for the partnership-by-estoppel doctrine to apply, there must nonetheless be a transaction between the claimants and the purported partnership. This transaction requirement is illustrated by the 1997 version of the UPA, which replaces "given credit" with "enter[ ] into a transaction." As stated above, the revised language of the 1997 version of the UPA merely clarifies and continues the partnership-by-estoppel principles encapsulated in previous versions of the UPA, on which NRS 87.160(1) was based. See Unif. P'ship Act § 308(a), 6 U.L.A. 128, 129 cmt. (1997). Thus, NRS 87.160(1) requires a transaction between the claimants and the purported partnership for the claimants to have "given credit" under the statute. The existence of or nature of any transaction between the purchasers and the purported partnership is a factual question to be resolved by the court below.

We now turn to a prerequisite for partnership by estoppel that is not explicitly stated in NRS 87.160(1). Generally, jurisdictions provide that the partnership-by-estoppel doctrine conditions liability on the plaintiff having reasonably relied on the representation of partnership, which often involves an exercise of due diligence to ascertain the facts. See, e.g., Bragg v. Johnson, 229 A.2d 497, 498 (Del. Super. Ct. 1966) (providing that plaintiff must have reasonably believed in the existence of a partnership to prevail on a partnership-by-estoppel claim); Anfenson v. Banks, 163 N.W. 608, 620-21 (Iowa 1917) (collecting cases where the common law definition of partnership by estoppel included the requirement of an exercise of due diligence to know the truth regarding the existence of a partnership); Gamble Robinson Co. v. Carousel Props., 688 P.2d 283, 288 (Mont. 1984) (explaining Montana's partnership-by-estoppel statute—which resembles NRS 87.160(1)—and concluding that it requires one to have reasonably relied on the representation of a partnership by making a reasonable inquiry about the representation's veracity); Wis. Tel. Co. v. Lehmann, 80 N.W.2d 267, 270 (Wis. 1957) (indicating that the reliance on the representation of a partnership must be reasonable for partnership by estoppel). Because Nevada caselaw lacks a significant discussion of the partnership-by-estoppel doctrine, it has not addressed the reasonable reliance requirement that other jurisdictions uphold.

However, the Legislature has provided that the law of estoppel applies to NRS 87.160(1). NRS 87.040(2).

Moreover, in a similar matter, we extended equitable estoppel's reasonable reliance requirement to a party's claim that the apparent authority of an agent was the basis for forming a contract. Great Am. Ins. Co. v. Gen. Builders, Inc., 113 Nev. 346, 352, 934 P.2d 257, 261 (1997). Likewise, we conclude that the reasonable reliance requirement, including the performance of due diligence to learn the veracity of the representation of partnership, that other jurisdictions impose for partnership by estoppel is one that NRS 87.160(1) includes as well. As indicated by its language, NRS 87.160(1) seeks to afford relief to those who incur an injury upon believing and detrimentally relying on the representation of a partnership. Without the reasonable reliance requirement, the partnership-by-estoppel doctrine would lack an objective limitation to prevent it from being abused by people who knew, or reasonably should have known, that the representation of the partnership or joint venture was untrue. This factual determination remains to be considered on remand.

NRS 87.160(1)'s applicability to claims that do not sound in contract

The parties disagree about whether partnership-by-estoppel liability under NRS 87.160(1) may be imposed where the claim for which that theory of liability is pleaded does not sound in contract. Aeder and the JDI entities argue that NRS 87.160(1) imposes partnership liability only for causes of action that sound in contract. The purchasers respond that the statute imposes liability for any cause of action that conditions liability on the reliance upon the representation of a partnership.

In a partnership, the partners are jointly and severally liable for injuries caused by a partner's actions within the ordinary course of the partnership's business or with the authority of other partners. NRS 87.130; NRS 87.150(1). This liability extends to tortious acts such as fraud. See Radaker v. Scott, 109 Nev. 653, 658, 660, 855 P.2d 1037, 1040, 1041 (1993) (providing that in the context of a joint venture-governed by the laws of partnerships—a joint venturer is liable for another joint venturer's fraudulent act that is completed within the scope of the joint venture's enterprise). We recognize that even though the partnership-by-estoppel doctrine provides for the same liability that would arise from a partnership, which would include tort liability, other jurisdictions have concluded that the doctrine only imposes liability under claims that sound in contract. See, e.g., Roethke v. Sanger, 68 S.W.3d 352, 360 (Ky. 2001) (providing in dicta that its partnership-by-estoppel statute only provides for contractual liability); Pruitt v. Fetty, 134 S.E.2d 713, 717 (W.Va. 1964) (concluding the same).

Generally, the premise relied on for concluding that the partnership-by-estoppel doctrine is limited to contract claims is that the doctrine's reliance element exists in contractual matters, in which a party relies on the existence of a partnership in entering into a contract, but does not exist in tortious matters, in which a victim often does not rely on a partnership's existence in sustaining an injury. See Pruitt, 134 S.E.2d at 717; see also Thomas Erickson, Recent Decision, 55 Mich. L. Rev. 1190, 1191 (1957) (noting that the reliance element for partnership by estoppel is often present in contract-based causes of action). This premise is poor, as reliance on a partnership or joint venture's existence may arise in claims that do not sound in contract. See Erickson, supra, at 1191 (concluding that partnership by estoppel applies to "tort actions involving reliance"). For example, "[i]n cases of fraud or misrepresentation, where one is induced to buy from those misrepresenting, . . . relying on their holding out of a partnership, he [or she] may sue them as partners and hold them estopped to deny the relation." Id.; see also Frye v. Anderson, 80 N.W.2d 593, 603 (Minn. 1957) (determining that the partnership-by-estoppel doctrine is applicable to tort-based causes of action).

Accordingly, we conclude that the application of NRS 87.160(1) does not turn on whether the cause of action sounds in contract. Instead, it turns on whether the claim implicates the reliance element that is required for partnership by estoppel. Thus, NRS 87.160(1) applies to the purchasers' claims that are based on their reliance upon the representations of a partnership or a joint venture and are not limited to contract claims.

A review of our determinations about NRS 87.160(1)'s meaning

Thus, to review, NRS 87.160(1)—Nevada's partnership-by-estoppel statute—imposes partnership liability on a party where, with the party's "consent[]," there is a representation that the party is a "partner," and another party has "given credit" to the purported "partnership." Partnership by estoppel may arise under this statute where the subject of the representation is a joint venture. Consent to the representation may be reasonably implied from one's conduct. The phrase "given credit" does not limit the statute's application to matters where financial credit is extended to the purported partnership or joint venture; rather, the phrase concerns the credence that is given to the representation when one detrimentally relies on it in conducting a transaction with the purported partnership, which may but is not required to include the extension of financial credit. The claimant who seeks to prevail on a partnership-by-estoppel claim must have reasonably relied on the representation of a partnership or joint venture, which entails the effort to learn the veracity of the representation. Finally, NRS 87.160(1) may impose partnership liability with respect to claims that implicate the reliance element that is required for partnership by estoppel, and such claims are not limited to those sounding in contract.

The summary judgment in favor of Aeder and the JDI entities

Having clarified NRS 87.160(1)'s meaning, we now consider whether genuine issues of material fact remained with respect to Aeder's and the JDI entities' liability under NRS 87.160(1).

The purchasers contend that Aeder and the JDI entities did not show the absence of genuine issues of material fact with respect to their liability under NRS 87.160(1) when they moved for summary judgment. The purchasers assert that their evidence revealed that they relied on and gave credence to a purported partnership between Cay Clubs, Aeder, and the JDI entities when purchasing condominiums and engaging in related transactions on their reasonable belief that the purported partnership provided the financial strength to create the advertised luxury resort. Further, they contend that the evidence showed that Aeder and the JDI entities consented to the representation of a partnership with Cay Clubs. Last, they argue that the district court placed undue emphasis on the word "strategic" in concluding that the marketing materials' use of the phrase "strategic partnership" was insufficient for establishing partnership-by-estoppel liability.

Aeder and the JDI entities respond that the parol evidence rule barred the purchasers from relying on their evidence of a purported partnership because the purchase agreements contained an integration clause and identified Flamingo Palms Villas, and not a partnership, as the seller of the Las Vegas Cay Club condominiums. They also argue that the purchasers did not give any credit to the purported partnership between Cay Clubs, Aeder, and the JDI entities because the purchasers' transactions and agreements were with Flamingo Palms Villas, which was not represented as being in a partnership with anyone.

In determining whether the district court erred in granting summary judgment, we resolve whether genuine issues of material fact remained with respect to partnership by estoppel under NRS 87.160(1), such that "a rational trier of fact could return a verdict for the nonmoving party." Wood v. Safeway, Inc., 121 Nev. 724, 731, 121 P.3d 1026, 1031 (2005). The party who moves for summary judgment has the burden of showing the absence of genuine issues of material fact. Cuzze v. Univ. & Cmty. Coll. Sys. of Nev., 123 Nev. 598, 602, 172 P.3d 131, 134 (2007). If that party lacks the burden of persuasion at trial, he or she may satisfy this burden by pointing to "'an absence of evidence to support the nonmoving party's case.'" Id. at 602-03, 172 P.3d at 134 (quoting Celotex Corp. v. Catrett, 477 U.S. 317, 325 (1986)). Generally, to defeat the motion for summary judgment, the nonmoving party must submit admissible evidence to show a genuine issue of material fact. Id. at 603, 172 P.3d at 134. But when a party does not object to the inadmissibility of evidence below, the issue is waived and otherwise inadmissible evidence can be considered. See Whalen v. State, 100 Nev. 192, 195-96, 679 P.2d 248, 250 (1984) (considering otherwise inadmissible evidence with respect to a summary judgment because the issue of admissibility was waived for lack of an objection).

The parol evidence rule and the purchasers' evidence

Aeder and the JDI entities argue that no admissible evidence was proffered to contest their motion for summary judgment because the evidence on which the purchasers relied was barred by the parol evidence rule. The parol evidence rule precludes the admission of extrinsic "evidence that would change the contract terms when the terms of a written agreement are clear, definite, and unambiguous." Ringle v. Bruton, 120 Nev. 82, 91, 86 P.3d 1032, 1037 (2004). It applies only when the contracting parties agree that the written agreement is the "final statement of the agreement." 11 Richard A. Lord, Williston on Contracts § 33:14 (4th ed. 2012). The rule does not bar extrinsic evidence that is offered to explain matters on which the contract is silent "so long as the evidence does not contradict the [agreement's] terms." Ringle, 120 Nev. At 91, 86 P.3d at 1037. For example, in a matter regarding partnership by estoppel, the Minnesota Supreme Court held that the parol evidence rule did not bar extrinsic evidence to help resolve uncertainties about a partnership's existence when the contract did not address a partnership or preclude its possibility. Blumberg v. Palm, 56 N.W.2d 412, 415-16 (Minn. 1953).

Aeder and the JDI entities rely on the following language of a purchase agreement in asserting that the parol evidence rule barred the purchasers' evidence for partnership by estoppel:

This Agreement, such documents and all addenda and exhibits attached hereto reflect the entire and exclusive agreement of the Parties regarding the construction of the Residence, the purchase and sale of the Property, representations, warranties and duties of Seller related to the Property and the materials and workmanship used in construction of the Property. No salesperson, agent or employee of Seller has the authority to make any representations that contradict or alter any terms of this Agreement. . . . Except as expressly set forth in this Agreement and such documents, Buyer has not relied upon any representations . . . with respect to any aspect of the Property. This Agreement is intended by Buyer and Seller as the final expression and the complete and exclusive statement of their agreement . . . , and any prior or contemporaneous oral or written agreements or understandings which may contradict, explain or supplement these terms are hereby superseded. . . .

This language suggests the intent to integrate the purchase agreement. Although the language provides that the purchasers did not rely on any representations about the "Property," this language on which Aeder and the JDI entities rely for their parol evidence argument was silent about a partnership. Thus, the parol evidence rule did not prohibit evidence regarding the representations of a partnership or a joint venture.

The genuine issues of material fact

Although some of the purchasers' evidence may have been inadmissible if objected to, Aeder and the JDI entities made no objections about the admissibility of the evidence beyond their assertion of the parol evidence rule. Thus, all of the evidence before the district court can be considered for determining whether genuine issues of material fact remained. See Whalen, 100 Nev. at 195-96, 679 P.2d at 250.

When moving for summary judgment, Aeder and the JDI entities averred that there was an absence of evidence for the purchasers' partnership-by-estoppel claim. At that time, the purchasers had not yet proffered evidence of actual representations of a partnership or joint venture. As a result, Aeder and the JDI entities satisfied their initial burden of showing the absence of genuine issues of material fact. But in contesting the motion, the purchasers submitted additional evidence that demonstrated genuine issues of material fact.

The purchasers submitted evidence of Cay Clubs' marketing materials. These materials included Cay Clubs' website, which stated that Cay Clubs was "a partnership of . . . professionals" and that its "strategic partner[s]" included the JDI entities. The marketing materials described the relationship with the JDI entities as a "partnership in excellence," identified the JDI entities as part of Cay Clubs' development team, and often used JDI Realty's logo alongside Cay Clubs' logo. Although the district court determined that a single use of the term "strategic" undermined the partnership-by-estoppel theory of liability, the multiple representations of a profit-oriented relationship between Cay Clubs and the JDI entities created a genuine issue of material fact as to whether these marketing materials represented a partnership, or at least a joint venture, between them.

The purchasers' evidence also established a genuine issue of material fact about whether JDI consented to the representations of a partnership or joint venture. In a deposition, Aeder stated that he reviewed Cay Clubs' marketing materials and did not doubt, but could not recall, that a reference was made to the JDI entities. Aeder also declared that he was the manager for the JDI entities. Hence, there was evidence of Aeder's potential knowledge of any actionable representations. There was also evidence which indicated that Aeder, through his LLCs, had supported Cay Clubs' development of other properties in the past and with respect to Las Vegas Cay Club. Therefore, there was evidence of a working relationship between Cay Clubs and Aeder and thus evidence of the same between Cay Clubs and Aeder's JDI entities. Accordingly, the totality of the evidence, especially the evidence of Aeder's knowledge of the marketing materials and his history of using his LLCs to extend support to Cay Clubs, indicated a genuine issue of material fact about whether Aeder, on behalf of the JDI entities, permitted Cay Clubs to make the actionable representations in the marketing materials.

With respect to the credit given to any actionable representations, multiple purchasers submitted affidavits wherein they stated that they relied on the representations of a partnership when purchasing their condominiums and engaging in related transactions with Cay Clubs. In those affidavits, they stated their beliefs that the partnership with the JDI entities provided the financial strength and experience to manage their money and perform the promised improvements to their property. Aeder and the JDI entities contend that the purchasers did not give any credit to the purported partnership between Cay Clubs and the JDI entities because the purchasers only transacted with Flamingo Palms Villas. However, the purchasers submitted to the district court an auditor's report that indicated that Cay Clubs appeared to be made of various LLCs that were created for each of its properties. Moreover, the district court had before it a deed of trust that related to a Las Vegas Cay Club property that was signed by the Flamingo Palms Villas' manager, who was identified in other documents as forming and being involved in other Cay Clubs properties. Thus, the evidence indicates that there remains a genuine issue of material fact as to whether credit was given to the purported partnership when the purchasers transacted with Flamingo Palms Villas, an entity that appeared to be one of many LLCs that made up Cay Clubs, and therefore whether the JDI entities may be held liable as Cay Club partners. The various parties' relationships and representations, if any, must be determined on remand.

As to the reasonable reliance requirement for partnership by estoppel, the evidence indicated a genuine issue of material fact about the purchasers' reasonable reliance on the representations of the relationship between Cay Clubs and the JDI entities. The marketing materials repeatedly emphasized a profit-oriented relationship between the two. Moreover, the affidavits of multiple purchasers provided that they attended sales and marketing presentations where such representations were made and that their belief in such representations was reinforced when reviewing marketing materials and Cay Clubs' website. Hence, the evidence established the indicia of an effort to follow up on the representations of a partnership or joint venture between the JDI entities and Cay Club.

Accordingly, the district court erred in granting summary judgment to the JDI entities with respect to their liability under NRS 87.160(1). Under this statute, the JDI entities may be liable as partners for the wrongdoings of others that are raised in the purchasers' claims that implicate their purported reasonable reliance on the representations of a partnership or joint venture between Cay

Clubs and the JDI entities. However, as to Aeder's liability under partnership by estoppel, the purchasers' briefing and analysis have only directed this court to evidence of partnership by estoppel with respect to the JDI entities. They have not analyzed or directed this court to evidence of representations of a partnership or joint venture with Aeder. Therefore, absent an analysis of such evidence, we conclude that the district court did not err in granting summary judgment in Aeder's favor regarding his liability under NRS 87.160(1).

Conclusion

Because of the genuine issues of material fact above, the district court erred in granting summary judgment to the JDI entities with regard to their liability under the partnership-by-estoppel doctrine that NRS 87.160(1) codifies. We conclude that partnership by estoppel may be found under NRS 87.160(1) where the subject of the actionable representation is a partnership or a joint venture, that the consent required for partnership by estoppel can be express or implied from one's conduct, that the statute's phrase "given credit" means giving credence to the representation by detrimentally relying on it to engage in a transaction with the purported partnership, and that the claimant who seeks to prevail on the partnership-by-estoppel claim must have reasonably relied on the representation of partnership or joint venture. Moreover, we conclude that NRS 87.160(1) may impose partnership liability with respect to claims that implicate the reliance element that is required for partnership by estoppel—such claims are not limited to causes of action that sound in contract.

Therefore, we reverse the order granting summary judgment in favor of the JDI entities with respect to their liability under NRS 87.160(1) and remand this matter to the district court for further proceedings that are consistent with this opinion. In addition, we reverse the award of costs that was predicated on the grant of summary judgment to the JDI entities. We have considered the remaining contentions on appeal and conclude that they lack merit.

Optional Assignments

1. Brief the preceding abbreviated version of the case in a one- to two-page, single-spaced brief (with double spaces between paragraphs) that contains the following four sections: (1) The basic facts of the case [Facts]; (2) The legal issue the court is being asked to decide [Issue]; (3) The holding of the court (how it decides the legal issue before it) [Holding]; and (4) The rationale the court uses to support its decision [Rationale]. If your instructor asks you to brief the case, he will give you additional instructions.

2. Discuss whether you agree or disagree with the opinion of the court.

U.S. Constitution

APPENDIX A

We the People of the United States, in Order to form a more perfect Union, establish Justice, insure domestic Tranquility, provide for the common defence, promote the general Welfare, and secure the Blessings of Liberty to ourselves and our Posterity, do ordain and establish this Constitution for the United States of America.

Article I

Section. 1. All legislative Powers herein granted shall be vested in a Congress of the United States, which shall consist of a Senate and House of Representatives.

Section. 2. The House of Representatives shall be composed of Members chosen every second Year by the People of the several States, and the Electors in each State shall have the Qualifications requisite for Electors of the most numerous Branch of the State Legislature.

No Person shall be a Representative who shall not have attained to the Age of twenty five Years, and been seven Years a Citizen of the United States, and who shall not, when elected, be an Inhabitant of that State in which he shall be chosen.

Representatives and direct Taxes shall be apportioned among the several States which may be included within this Union, according to their respective Numbers, which shall be determined by adding to the whole Number of free Persons, including those bound to Service for a Term of Years, and excluding Indians not taxed, three fifths of all other Persons [Modified by the 14th Amendment]. The actual Enumeration shall be made within three Years after the first Meeting of the Congress of the United States, and within every subsequent Term of ten Years, in such Manner as they shall by Law direct. The Number of Representatives shall not exceed one for every thirty Thousand, but each State shall have at Least one Representative; and until such enumeration shall be made, the State of New Hampshire shall be entitled to chuse three, Massachusetts eight, Rhode-Island and Providence Plantations one, Connecticut five, New-York six, New Jersey four, Pennsylvania eight, Delaware one, Maryland six, Virginia ten, North Carolina five, South Carolina five, and Georgia three.

When vacancies happen in the Representation from any State, the Executive Authority thereof shall issue Writs of Election to fill such Vacancies.

The House of Representatives shall chuse their Speaker and other Officers; and shall have the sole Power of Impeachment.

Section. 3. The Senate of the United States shall be composed of two Senators from each State, chosen by the Legislature thereof [Modified by the 17th Amendment], for six Years; and each Senator shall have one Vote.

Immediately after they shall be assembled in Consequence of the first Election, they shall be divided as equally as may be into three Classes. The Seats of the Senators of the first Class shall be vacated at the Expiration of the second Year, of the second Class at the Expiration of the fourth Year, and of the third Class at the Expiration of the sixth Year, so that one third may be chosen every second Year; and if Vacancies happen by Resignation, or otherwise, during the Recess of the Legislature of any State, the Executive thereof may make temporary Appointments until the next Meeting of the Legislature, which shall then fill such Vacancies [Modified by the 17th Amendment].

No Person shall be a Senator who shall not have attained to the Age of thirty Years, and been nine Years a Citizen of the United States, and who shall not, when elected, be an Inhabitant of that State for which he shall be chosen.

The Vice President of the United States shall be President of the Senate, but shall have no Vote, unless they be equally divided.

The Senate shall chuse their other Officers, and also a President pro tempore, in the Absence of the Vice President, or when he shall exercise the Office of President of the United States.

The Senate shall have the sole Power to try all Impeachments. When sitting for that Purpose, they shall be on Oath or Affirmation. When the President of the United States is tried, the Chief Justice shall preside: And no Person shall be convicted without the Concurrence of two thirds of the Members present.

Judgment in Cases of Impeachment shall not extend further than to removal from Office, and disqualification to hold and enjoy any Office of honor, Trust or Profit under the United States: but the Party convicted shall nevertheless be liable and subject to Indictment, Trial, Judgment and Punishment, according to Law.

Section. 4. The Times, Places and Manner of holding Elections for Senators and Representatives, shall be prescribed in each State by the Legislature thereof; but the Congress may at any time by Law make or alter such Regulations, except as to the Places of chusing Senators.

The Congress shall assemble at least once in every Year, and such Meeting shall be on the first Monday in December [Modified by the 20th Amendment], unless they shall by Law appoint a different Day.

Section. 5. Each House shall be the Judge of the Elections, Returns and Qualifications of its own Members, and a Majority of each shall constitute a Quorum to do Business; but a smaller Number may adjourn from day to day, and may be authorized to compel the Attendance of absent Members, in such Manner, and under such Penalties as each House may provide.

Each House may determine the Rules of its Proceedings, punish its Members for disorderly Behaviour, and, with the Concurrence of two thirds, expel a Member.

Each House shall keep a Journal of its Proceedings, and from time to time publish the same, excepting such Parts as may in their Judgment require Secrecy; and the Yeas and Nays of the Members of either House on any question shall, at the Desire of one fifth of those Present, be entered on the Journal.

Neither House, during the Session of Congress, shall, without the Consent of the other, adjourn for more than three days, nor to any other Place than that in which the two Houses shall be sitting.

Section. 6. The Senators and Representatives shall receive a Compensation for their Services, to be ascertained by Law, and paid out of the Treasury of the United States. They shall in all Cases, except Treason, Felony and Breach of the Peace, be privileged from Arrest during their Attendance at the Session of their respective Houses, and in going to and returning from the same; and for any Speech or Debate in either House, they shall not be questioned in any other Place.

No Senator or Representative shall, during the Time for which he was elected, be appointed to any civil Office under the Authority of the United States, which shall have been created, or the Emoluments whereof shall have been encreased during such time; and no Person holding any Office under the United States, shall be a Member of either House during his Continuance in Office.

Section. 7. All Bills for raising Revenue shall originate in the House of Representatives; but the Senate may propose or concur with Amendments as on other Bills.

Every Bill which shall have passed the House of Representatives and the Senate, shall, before it become a Law, be presented to the President of the United States; If he approve he shall sign it, but if not he shall return it, with his Objections to that House in which it shall have originated, who shall enter the Objections at large on their Journal, and proceed to reconsider it. If after such Reconsideration two thirds of that House shall agree to pass the Bill, it shall be sent, together with the Objections, to the other House, by which it shall likewise be reconsidered, and if approved by two thirds of that House, it shall become a Law. But in all such Cases the Votes of both Houses shall be determined by yeas and Nays, and the Names of the Persons voting for and against the Bill shall be entered on the Journal of each House respectively. If any Bill shall not be returned by the President within ten Days (Sundays excepted) after it shall have been presented to him, the Same shall be a Law, in like Manner as if he had signed it, unless the Congress by their Adjournment prevent its Return, in which Case it shall not be a Law.

Every Order, Resolution, or Vote to which the Concurrence of the Senate and House of Representatives may be necessary (except on a question of Adjournment) shall be presented to the President of the United States; and before the Same shall take Effect, shall be approved by him, or being disapproved by him, shall be repassed by two thirds of the Senate and House of Representatives, according to the Rules and Limitations prescribed in the Case of a Bill.

Section. 8. The Congress shall have Power To lay and collect Taxes, Duties, Imposts and Excises, to pay the Debts and provide for the common Defence and general Welfare of the United States; but all Duties, Imposts and Excises shall be uniform throughout the United States;

- To borrow Money on the credit of the United States;
- To regulate Commerce with foreign Nations, and among the several States, and with the Indian Tribes;
- To establish an uniform Rule of Naturalization, and uniform Laws on the subject of Bankruptcies throughout the United States;
- To coin Money, regulate the Value thereof, and of foreign Coin, and fix the Standard of Weights and Measures;
- To provide for the Punishment of counterfeiting the Securities and current Coin of the United States;
- To establish Post Offices and post Roads;
- To promote the Progress of Science and useful Arts, by securing for limited Times to Authors and Inventors the exclusive Right to their respective Writings and Discoveries;
- To constitute Tribunals inferior to the supreme Court;
- To define and punish Piracies and Felonies committed on the high Seas, and Offences against the Law of Nations;
- To declare War, grant Letters of Marque and Reprisal, and make Rules concerning Captures on Land and Water;
- To raise and support Armies, but no Appropriation of Money to that Use shall be for a longer Term than two Years;
- To provide and maintain a Navy;
- To make Rules for the Government and Regulation of the land and naval Forces;
- To provide for calling forth the Militia to execute the Laws of the Union, suppress Insurrections and repel Invasions;
- To provide for organizing, arming, and disciplining, the Militia, and for governing such Part of them as may be employed in the Service of the United States, reserving to the States respectively, the Appointment of the Officers, and the Authority of training the Militia according to the discipline prescribed by Congress;
- To exercise exclusive Legislation in all Cases whatsoever, over such District (not exceeding ten Miles square) as may, by Cession of particular States, and the Acceptance of Congress, become the Seat of the Government of the United States, and to exercise like Authority over all Places purchased by the Consent of the Legislature of

the State in which the Same shall be, for the Erection of Forts, Magazines, Arsenals, dock-Yards, and other needful Buildings;—And

To make all Laws which shall be necessary and proper for carrying into Execution the foregoing Powers, and all other Powers vested by this Constitution in the Government of the United States, or in any Department or Officer thereof.

Section. 9. The Migration or Importation of such Persons as any of the States now existing shall think proper to admit, shall not be prohibited by the Congress prior to the Year one thousand eight hundred and eight, but a Tax or duty may be imposed on such Importation, not exceeding ten dollars for each Person.

The Privilege of the Writ of Habeas Corpus shall not be suspended, unless when in Cases of Rebellion or Invasion the public Safety may require it.

No Bill of Attainder or ex post facto Law shall be passed.

No Capitation, or other direct, Tax shall be laid, unless in Proportion to the Census or Enumeration herein before directed to be taken.

No Tax or Duty shall be laid on Articles exported from any State.

No Preference shall be given by any Regulation of Commerce or Revenue to the Ports of one State over those of another; nor shall Vessels bound to, or from, one State, be obliged to enter, clear, or pay Duties in another.

No Money shall be drawn from the Treasury, but in Consequence of Appropriations made by Law; and a regular Statement and Account of the Receipts and Expenditures of all public Money shall be published from time to time.

No Title of Nobility shall be granted by the United States: And no Person holding any Office of Profit or Trust under them, shall, without the Consent of the Congress, accept of any present, Emolument, Office, or Title, of any kind whatever, from any King, Prince, or foreign State.

Section. 10. No State shall enter into any Treaty, Alliance, or Confederation; grant Letters of Marque and Reprisal; coin Money; emit Bills of Credit; make any Thing but gold and silver Coin a Tender in Payment of Debts; pass any Bill of Attainder, ex post facto Law, or Law impairing the Obligation of Contracts, or grant any Title of Nobility.

No State shall, without the Consent of the Congress, lay any Imposts or Duties on Imports or Exports, except what may be absolutely necessary for executing its inspection Laws; and the net Produce of all Duties and Imposts, laid by any State on Imports or Exports, shall be for the Use of the Treasury of the United States; and all such Laws shall be subject to the Revision and Controul of the Congress.

No State shall, without the Consent of Congress, lay any Duty of Tonnage, keep Troops, or Ships of War in time of Peace, enter into any Agreement or Compact with another State, or with a foreign Power, or engage in War, unless actually invaded, or in such imminent Danger as will not admit of delay.

Article II

Section. 1. The executive Power shall be vested in a President of the United States of America. He shall hold his Office during the Term of four Years, and, together with the Vice President, chosen for the same Term, be elected, as follows:

Each State shall appoint, in such Manner as the Legislature thereof may direct, a Number of Electors, equal to the whole Number of Senators and Representatives to which the State may be entitled in the Congress: but no Senator or Representative, or Person holding an Office of Trust or Profit under the United States, shall be appointed an Elector.

The Electors shall meet in their respective States, and vote by Ballot for two Persons, of whom one at least shall not be an Inhabitant of the same State with themselves. And they shall make a List of all the Persons voted for, and of the Number of Votes for each; which List they shall sign and certify, and transmit sealed to the Seat of the Government of the United States, directed to the President of the Senate. The President of the Senate shall, in the Presence of the Senate and House of Representatives, open all the Certificates, and the Votes shall then be counted. The Person having the greatest Number of Votes shall be the

President, if such Number be a Majority of the whole Number of Electors appointed; and if there be more than one who have such Majority, and have an equal Number of Votes, then the House of Representatives shall immediately chuse by Ballot one of them for President; and if no Person have a Majority, then from the five highest on the List the said House shall in like Manner chuse the President. But in chusing the President, the Votes shall be taken by States, the Representation from each State having one Vote; a quorum for this Purpose shall consist of a Member or Members from two thirds of the States, and a Majority of all the States shall be necessary to a Choice. In every Case, after the Choice of the President, the Person having the greatest Number of Votes of the Electors shall be the Vice President. But if there should remain two or more who have equal Votes, the Senate shall chuse from them by Ballot the Vice President [Modified by the 12th Amendment].

The Congress may determine the Time of chusing the Electors, and the Day on which they shall give their Votes; which Day shall be the same throughout the United States.

No Person except a natural born Citizen, or a Citizen of the United States, at the time of the Adoption of this Constitution, shall be eligible to the Office of President; neither shall any Person be eligible to that Office who shall not have attained to the Age of thirty five Years, and been fourteen Years a Resident within the United States.

In Case of the Removal of the President from Office, or of his Death, Resignation, or Inability to discharge the Powers and Duties of the said Office, the Same shall devolve on the Vice President, and the Congress may by Law provide for the Case of Removal, Death, Resignation or Inability, both of the President and Vice President, declaring what Officer shall then act as President, and such Officer shall act accordingly, until the Disability be removed, or a President shall be elected [Modified by the 25th Amendment].

The President shall, at stated Times, receive for his Services, a Compensation, which shall neither be increased nor diminished during the Period for which he shall have been elected, and he shall not receive within that Period any other Emolument from the United States, or any of them.

Before he enter on the Execution of his Office, he shall take the following Oath or Affirmation:—"I do solemnly swear (or affirm) that I will faithfully execute the Office of President of the United States, and will to the best of my Ability, preserve, protect and defend the Constitution of the United States."

Section. 2. The President shall be Commander in Chief of the Army and Navy of the United States, and of the Militia of the several States, when called into the actual Service of the United States; he may require the Opinion, in writing, of the principal Officer in each of the executive Departments, upon any Subject relating to the Duties of their respective Offices, and he shall have Power to grant Reprieves and Pardons for Offences against the United States, except in Cases of Impeachment.

He shall have Power, by and with the Advice and Consent of the Senate, to make Treaties, provided two thirds of the Senators present concur; and he shall nominate, and by and with the Advice and Consent of the Senate, shall appoint Ambassadors, other public Ministers and Consuls, Judges of the supreme Court, and all other Officers of the United States, whose Appointments are not herein otherwise provided for, and which shall be established by Law: but the Congress may by Law vest the Appointment of such inferior Officers, as they think proper, in the President alone, in the Courts of Law, or in the Heads of Departments.

The President shall have Power to fill up all Vacancies that may happen during the Recess of the Senate, by granting Commissions which shall expire at the End of their next Session.

Section. 3. He shall from time to time give to the Congress Information of the State of the Union, and recommend to their Consideration such Measures as he shall judge necessary and expedient; he may, on extraordinary Occasions, convene both Houses, or either of them, and in Case of Disagreement between them, with Respect to the Time of Adjournment, he may adjourn them to such Time as he shall think proper; he shall receive Ambassadors and other public Ministers; he shall take Care that the Laws be faithfully executed, and shall Commission all the Officers of the United States.

Section. 4. The President, Vice President and all civil Officers of the United States, shall be removed from Office on Impeachment for, and Conviction of, Treason, Bribery, or other high Crimes and Misdemeanors.

Article III

Section. 1. The judicial Power of the United States shall be vested in one supreme Court, and in such inferior Courts as the Congress may from time to time ordain and establish. The Judges, both of the supreme and inferior Courts, shall hold their Offices during good Behaviour, and shall, at stated Times, receive for their Services a Compensation, which shall not be diminished during their Continuance in Office.

Section. 2. The judicial Power shall extend to all Cases, in Law and Equity, arising under this Constitution, the Laws of the United States, and Treaties made, or which shall be made, under their Authority;—to all Cases affecting Ambassadors, other public Ministers and Consuls;—to all Cases of admiralty and maritime Jurisdiction;—to Controversies to which the United States shall be a Party;—to Controversies between two or more States;—between a State and Citizens of another State [Modified by the 11th Amendment];—between Citizens of different States;—between Citizens of the same State claiming Lands under Grants of different States, and between a State, or the Citizens thereof, and foreign States, Citizens or Subjects.

In all Cases affecting Ambassadors, other public Ministers and Consuls, and those in which a State shall be Party, the supreme Court shall have original Jurisdiction. In all the other Cases before mentioned, the supreme Court shall have appellate Jurisdiction, both as to Law and Fact, with such Exceptions, and under such Regulations as the Congress shall make.

The Trial of all Crimes, except in Cases of Impeachment, shall be by Jury; and such Trial shall be held in the State where the said Crimes shall have been committed; but when not committed within any State, the Trial shall be at such Place or Places as the Congress may by Law have directed.

Section. 3. Treason against the United States shall consist only in levying War against them, or in adhering to their Enemies, giving them Aid and Comfort. No Person shall be convicted of Treason unless on the Testimony of two Witnesses to the same overt Act, or on Confession in open Court.

The Congress shall have Power to declare the Punishment of Treason, but no Attainder of Treason shall work Corruption of Blood, or Forfeiture except during the Life of the Person attainted.

Article IV

Section. 1. Full Faith and Credit shall be given in each State to the public Acts, Records, and judicial Proceedings of every other State. And the Congress may by general Laws prescribe the Manner in which such Acts, Records and Proceedings shall be proved, and the Effect thereof.

Section. 2. The Citizens of each State shall be entitled to all Privileges and Immunities of Citizens in the several States.

A Person charged in any State with Treason, Felony, or other Crime, who shall flee from Justice, and be found in another State, shall on Demand of the executive Authority of the State from which he fled, be delivered up, to be removed to the State having Jurisdiction of the Crime.

No Person held to Service or Labour in one State, under the Laws thereof, escaping into another, shall, in Consequence of any Law or Regulation therein, be discharged from such Service or Labour, but shall be delivered up on Claim of the Party to whom such Service or Labour may be due [Modified by the 13th Amendment].

Section. 3. New States may be admitted by the Congress into this Union; but no new State shall be formed or erected within the Jurisdiction of any other State; nor any State be formed by the Junction of two or more States, or Parts of States, without the Consent of the Legislatures of the States concerned as well as of the Congress.

The Congress shall have Power to dispose of and make all needful Rules and Regulations respecting the Territory or other Property belonging to the United States; and nothing in this Constitution shall be so construed as to Prejudice any Claims of the United States, or of any particular State.

Section. 4. The United States shall guarantee to every State in this Union a Republican Form of Government, and shall protect each of them against Invasion; and on Application of the Legislature, or of the Executive (when the Legislature cannot be convened), against domestic Violence.

Article V

The Congress, whenever two thirds of both Houses shall deem it necessary, shall propose Amendments to this Constitution, or, on the Application of the Legislatures of two thirds of the several States, shall call a Convention for proposing Amendments, which, in either Case, shall be valid to all Intents and Purposes, as Part of this Constitution, when ratified by the Legislatures of three fourths of the several States, or by Conventions in three fourths thereof, as the one or the other Mode of Ratification may be proposed by the Congress; Provided that no Amendment which may be made prior to the Year One thousand eight hundred and eight shall in any Manner affect the first and fourth Clauses in the Ninth Section of the first Article; and that no State, without its Consent, shall be deprived of its equal Suffrage in the Senate.

Article VI

All Debts contracted and Engagements entered into, before the Adoption of this Constitution, shall be as valid against the United States under this Constitution, as under the Confederation.

This Constitution, and the Laws of the United States which shall be made in Pursuance thereof; and all Treaties made, or which shall be made, under the Authority of the United States, shall be the supreme Law of the Land; and the Judges in every State shall be bound thereby, any Thing in the Constitution or Laws of any State to the Contrary notwithstanding.

The Senators and Representatives before mentioned, and the Members of the several State Legislatures, and all executive and judicial Officers, both of the United States and of the several States, shall be bound by Oath or Affirmation, to support this Constitution; but no religious Test shall ever be required as a Qualification to any Office or public Trust under the United States.

Article VII

The Ratification of the Conventions of nine States, shall be sufficient for the Establishment of this Constitution between the States so ratifying the Same.

Amendment I

Congress shall make no law respecting an establishment of religion, or prohibiting the free exercise thereof; or abridging the freedom of speech, or of the press; or the right of the people peaceably to assemble, and to petition the Government for a redress of grievances.

Amendment II

A well regulated Militia, being necessary to the security of a free State, the right of the people to keep and bear Arms, shall not be infringed.

Amendment III

No Soldier shall, in time of peace be quartered in any house, without the consent of the Owner, nor in time of war, but in a manner to be prescribed by law.

Amendment IV

The right of the people to be secure in their persons, houses, papers, and effects, against unreasonable searches and seizures, shall not be violated, and no Warrants shall issue, but upon probable cause, supported by Oath or affirmation, and particularly describing the place to be searched, and the persons or things to be seized.

Amendment V

No person shall be held to answer for a capital, or otherwise infamous crime, unless on a presentment or indictment of a Grand Jury, except in cases arising in the land or naval forces, or in the Militia, when in actual service in time of War or public danger; nor shall any person be subject for the same offence to be twice put in jeopardy of life or limb; nor shall be compelled in any criminal case to be a witness against himself, nor be deprived of life, liberty, or property, without due process of law; nor shall private property be taken for public use, without just compensation.

Amendment VI

In all criminal prosecutions, the accused shall enjoy the right to a speedy and public trial, by an impartial jury of the State and district wherein the crime shall have been committed, which district shall have been previously ascertained by law, and to be informed of the nature and cause of the accusation; to be confronted with the witnesses against him; to have compulsory process for obtaining witnesses in his favor, and to have the Assistance of Counsel for his defence.

Amendment VII

In Suits at common law, where the value in controversy shall exceed twenty dollars, the right of trial by jury shall be preserved, and no fact tried by a jury, shall be otherwise re-examined in any Court of the United States, than according to the rules of the common law.

Amendment VIII

Excessive bail shall not be required, nor excessive fines imposed, nor cruel and unusual punishments inflicted.

Amendment IX

The enumeration in the Constitution, of certain rights, shall not be construed to deny or disparage others retained by the people.

Amendment X

The powers not delegated to the United States by the Constitution, nor prohibited by it to the States, are reserved to the States respectively, or to the people.

Amendment XI

[Ratified 1798]

The Judicial power of the United States shall not be construed to extend to any suit in law or equity, commenced or prosecuted against one of the United States by Citizens of another State, or by Citizens or Subjects of any Foreign State.

Amendment XII

[Ratified 1804]

The Electors shall meet in their respective states, and vote by ballot for President and Vice-President, one of whom, at least, shall not be an inhabitant of the same state with themselves; they shall name in their ballots the person voted for as President, and in distinct ballots the person voted for as Vice-President, and they shall make distinct lists of all persons voted for as President, and of all persons voted for as Vice-President, and of the number of votes for each, which lists they shall sign and certify, and transmit sealed to the seat of the government of the United States, directed to the President of the Senate;—The President of the Senate shall, in the presence of the Senate and House of Representatives, open all the certificates and the votes shall then be counted;—The person having the greatest number of votes for President, shall be the President, if such number be a majority of the whole number of Electors appointed; and if no person have such majority, then from the persons having the highest numbers not exceeding three on the list of those voted for as President, the House of Representatives shall choose immediately, by ballot, the President. But in choosing the President, the votes shall be taken by states, the representation from each state having one vote; a quorum for this purpose shall consist of a member or members from two-thirds of the states, and a majority of all the states shall be necessary to a choice. And if the House of Representatives shall not choose a President whenever the right of choice shall devolve upon them, before the fourth day of March next following, then the Vice-President shall act as President, as in the case of the death or other constitutional disability of the President.—The person having the greatest number of votes as Vice-President, shall be the Vice-President, if such number be a majority of the whole number of Electors appointed, and if no person have a majority, then from the two highest numbers on the list, the Senate shall choose the Vice-President; a quorum for the purpose shall consist of two-thirds of the whole number of Senators, and a majority of the whole number shall be necessary to a choice. But no person constitutionally ineligible to the office of President shall be eligible to that of Vice-President of the United States.

Amendment XIII

[Ratified 1865]

Section. 1. Neither slavery nor involuntary servitude, except as a punishment for crime whereof the party shall have been duly convicted, shall exist within the United States, or any place subject to their jurisdiction.

Section. 2. Congress shall have power to enforce this article by appropriate legislation.

Amendment XIV

[Ratified 1868]

Section. 1. All persons born or naturalized in the United States, and subject to the jurisdiction thereof, are citizens of the United States and of the State wherein they reside. No State shall make or enforce any law which shall abridge the privileges or immunities of citizens of the United States; nor shall any State deprive any person of life, liberty, or property, without due process of law; nor deny to any person within its jurisdiction the equal protection of the laws.

Section. 2. Representatives shall be apportioned among the several States according to their respective numbers, counting the whole number of persons in each State, excluding Indians not taxed. But when the right to vote at any election for the choice of electors for President and Vice President of the United States, Representatives in Congress, the Executive and Judicial officers of a State, or the members of the Legislature thereof, is denied to any of the male inhabitants of such State, being twenty-one years of age, and citizens of the United States, or in any way abridged, except for participation in rebellion, or other crime, the basis of representation therein shall be reduced in the proportion which the number of such male citizens shall bear to the whole number of male citizens twenty-one years of age in such State.

Section. 3. No person shall be a Senator or Representative in Congress, or elector of President and Vice President, or hold any office, civil or military, under the United States, or under any State, who, having previously taken an oath, as a member of Congress, or as an officer of the United States, or as a member of any State legislature, or as an executive or judicial officer of any State, to support the Constitution of the United States, shall have engaged in insurrection or rebellion against the same, or given aid or comfort to the enemies thereof. But Congress may by a vote of two-thirds of each House, remove such disability.

Section. 4. The validity of the public debt of the United States, authorized by law, including debts incurred for payment of pensions and bounties for services in suppressing insurrection or rebellion, shall not be questioned. But neither the United States nor any State shall assume or pay any debt or obligation incurred in aid of insurrection or rebellion against the United States, or any claim for the loss or emancipation of any slave; but all such debts, obligations and claims shall be held illegal and void.

Section. 5. The Congress shall have power to enforce, by appropriate legislation, the provisions of this article.

Amendment XV

[Ratified 1870]

Section. 1. The right of citizens of the United States to vote shall not be denied or abridged by the United States or by any State on account of race, color, or previous condition of servitude.

Section. 2. The Congress shall have power to enforce this article by appropriate legislation.

Amendment XVI

[Ratified 1913]

The Congress shall have power to lay and collect taxes on incomes, from whatever source derived, without apportionment among the several States, and without regard to any census or enumeration.

Amendment XVII

[Ratified 1913]

The Senate of the United States shall be composed of two Senators from each State, elected by the people thereof, for six years; and each Senator shall have one vote. The electors in each State shall have the qualifications requisite for electors of the most numerous branch of the State legislatures.

When vacancies happen in the representation of any State in the Senate, the executive authority of such State shall issue writs of election to fill such vacancies: Provided, That the legislature of any State may empower the executive thereof to make temporary appointments until the people fill the vacancies by election as the legislature may direct.

This amendment shall not be so construed as to affect the election or term of any Senator chosen before it becomes valid as part of the Constitution.

Amendment XVIII

[Ratified 1919; Repealed 1933]

Section. 1. After one year from the ratification of this article the manufacture, sale, or transportation of intoxicating liquors within, the importation thereof into, or the exportation thereof from the United States and all territory subject to the jurisdiction thereof for beverage purposes is hereby prohibited.

Section. 2. The Congress and the several States shall have concurrent power to enforce this article by appropriate legislation.

Section. 3. This article shall be inoperative unless it shall have been ratified as an amendment to the Constitution by the legislatures of the several States, as provided in the Constitution, within seven years from the date of the submission hereof to the States by the Congress.

Amendment XIX

[Ratified 1920]

The right of citizens of the United States to vote shall not be denied or abridged by the United States or by any State on account of sex.

Congress shall have power to enforce this article by appropriate legislation.

Amendment XX

[Ratified 1933]

Section. 1. The terms of the President and Vice President shall end at noon on the 20th day of January, and the terms of Senators and Representatives at noon on the 3d day of January, of the years in which such terms would have ended if this article had not been ratified; and the terms of their successors shall then begin.

Section. 2. The Congress shall assemble at least once in every year, and such meeting shall begin at noon on the 3d day of January, unless they shall by law appoint a different day.

Section. 3. If, at the time fixed for the beginning of the term of the President, the President elect shall have died, the Vice President elect shall become President. If a President shall not have been chosen before the time fixed for the beginning of his term, or if the President elect shall have failed to qualify, then the Vice President elect shall act as President until a President shall have qualified; and the Congress may by law provide for the case wherein neither a President elect nor a Vice President elect shall have qualified, declaring who shall then act as President, or the manner in which one who is to act shall be selected, and such person shall act accordingly until a President or Vice President shall have qualified.

Section. 4. The Congress may by law provide for the case of the death of any of the persons from whom the House of Representatives may choose a President whenever the right of choice shall have devolved upon them, and for the case of the death of any of the persons from whom the Senate may choose a Vice President whenever the right of choice shall have devolved upon them.

Section. 5. Sections 1 and 2 shall take effect on the 15th day of October following the ratification of this article.

Section. 6. This article shall be inoperative unless it shall have been ratified as an amendment to the Constitution by the legislatures of three-fourths of the several States within seven years from the date of its submission.

Amendment XXI

[Ratified 1933]

Section. 1. The eighteenth article of amendment to the Constitution of the United States is hereby repealed.

Section. 2. The transportation or importation into any State, Territory, or possession of the United States for delivery or use therein of intoxicating liquors, in violation of the laws thereof, is hereby prohibited.

Section. 3. This article shall be inoperative unless it shall have been ratified as an amendment to the Constitution by conventions in the several States, as provided in the Constitution, within seven years from the date of the submission hereof to the States by the Congress.

Amendment XXII

[Ratified 1951]

Section. 1. No person shall be elected to the office of the President more than twice, and no person who has held the office of President, or acted as President, for more than two years of a term to which some other person was elected President shall be elected to the office of the President more than once. But this Article shall not apply to any person holding the office of President when this Article was proposed by the Congress, and shall not prevent any person who may be holding the office of President, or acting as President, during the term within which this Article becomes operative from holding the office of President or acting as President during the remainder of such term.

Section. 2. This article shall be inoperative unless it shall have been ratified as an amendment to the Constitution by the legislatures of three-fourths of the several States within seven years from the date of its submission to the States by the Congress.

Amendment XXIII

[Ratified 1961]

Section. 1. The District constituting the seat of Government of the United States shall appoint in such manner as the Congress may direct:

A number of electors of President and Vice President equal to the whole number of Senators and Representatives in Congress to which the District would be entitled if it were a State, but in no event more than the least populous State; they shall be in addition to those appointed by the States, but they shall be considered, for the purposes of the election of President and Vice President, to be electors appointed by a State; and they shall meet in the District and perform such duties as provided by the twelfth article of amendment.

Section. 2. The Congress shall have power to enforce this article by appropriate legislation.

Amendment XXIV

[Ratified 1964]

Section. 1. The right of citizens of the United States to vote in any primary or other election for President or Vice President, for electors for President or Vice President, or for Senator or Representative in Congress, shall not be denied or abridged by the United States or any State by reason of failure to pay any poll tax or other tax.

Section. 2. The Congress shall have power to enforce this article by appropriate legislation.

Amendment XXV

[Ratified 1967]

Section. 1. In case of the removal of the President from office or of his death or resignation, the Vice President shall become President.

Section. 2. Whenever there is a vacancy in the office of the Vice President, the President shall nominate a Vice President who shall take office upon confirmation by a majority vote of both Houses of Congress.

Section. 3. Whenever the President transmits to the President pro tempore of the Senate and the Speaker of the House of Representatives his written declaration that he is unable to discharge the powers and duties of his office, and until he transmits to them a written declaration to the contrary, such powers and duties shall be discharged by the Vice President as Acting President.

Section. 4. Whenever the Vice President and a majority of either the principal officers of the executive departments or of such other body as Congress may by law provide, transmit to the President pro tempore of the Senate and the Speaker of the House of Representatives their written declaration that the President is unable to discharge the powers and duties of his office, the Vice President shall immediately assume the powers and duties of the office as Acting President.

Thereafter, when the President transmits to the President pro tempore of the Senate and the Speaker of the House of Representatives his written declaration that no inability exists, he shall resume the powers and duties of his office unless the Vice President and a majority of either the principal officers of the executive department or of such other body as Congress may by law provide, transmit within four days to the President pro tempore of the Senate and the Speaker of the House of Representatives their written declaration that the President is unable to discharge the powers and duties of his office. Thereupon Congress shall decide the issue, assembling within forty-eight hours for that purpose if not in session. If the Congress, within twenty-one days after receipt of the latter written declaration, or, if Congress is not in session, within twenty-one days after Congress is required to assemble, determines by two-thirds vote of both Houses that the President is unable to discharge the powers and duties of his office, the Vice President shall continue to discharge the same as Acting President; otherwise, the President shall resume the powers and duties of his office.

Amendment XXVI

[Ratified 1971]

Section. 1. The right of citizens of the United States, who are eighteen years of age or older, to vote shall not be denied or abridged by the United States or by any State on account of age.

Section. 2. The Congress shall have power to enforce this article by appropriate legislation.

Amendment XXVII

[Ratified 1992]

No law, varying the compensation for the services of the Senators and Representatives, shall take effect, until an election of Representatives shall have intervened.

Uniform Commercial Code (UCC)

APPENDIX B

(Articles 2, 3, and 9 as adopted by the States of Florida, California, and Illinois, respectively)

Introduction

The Uniform Commercial Code is one of many model statutes drafted by the National Conference of Commissioners on Uniform State Laws (NCCUSL). Information about the organization, all model acts, and the legislative history of state adoptions of the UCC and all NCCUSL model acts, including the Uniform Commercial Code, is available at the NCCUSL web page at http://www.uniformlaws.org/. For purposes of illustration, enacted versions of Articles 2, 3, and 9 are included in this appendix for reference purposes. Please note that in adopting the various articles of the UCC, state legislatures have often revised the language proposed by the NCCUSL in code sections. Though these revisions tend to be minor, some significant variations can be found in the states' UCC statutes, so the law is not identical in its final adopted form in all states.

Uniform Commercial Code Article 2 as adopted in the State of Florida

CHAPTER 672

UNIFORM COMMERCIAL CODE: SALES

ARTICLE 2

[Please Note: The numbering scheme of the Uniform Commercial Code has been changed in Florida to conform to the state's numbering scheme used in other chapters of the Florida statutes. To translate the Florida numbering scheme to the Code's original numbering scheme, replace the first three digits before the decimal point in each section with the Code article number and change the decimal point to a hyphen. The digits following the decimal point coincide with the original Code section numbers. For example, Florida's § 672.101 is the same as Code § 2-201, § 672.102 is the same as Code § 2-102 and so forth.]

PART I

SHORT TITLE, GENERAL CONSTRUCTION, AND SUBJECT MATTER

(ss. 672.101–672.107)

PART II

FORM, FORMATION, AND READJUSTMENT OF CONTRACT

(ss. 672.201–672.210)

PART III

GENERAL OBLIGATION AND CONSTRUCTION OF CONTRACT

(ss. 672.301–672.328)

PART IV

TITLE, CREDITORS, AND GOOD FAITH PURCHASERS

(ss. 672.401–672.403)

PART V

PERFORMANCE

(ss. 672.501–672.515)

PART VI

BREACH, REPUDIATION, AND EXCUSE

(ss. 672.601–672.616)

PART VII

REMEDIES

(ss. 672.701–672.724)

PART I
SHORT TITLE, GENERAL CONSTRUCTION, AND SUBJECT MATTER

672.101 Short title.

672.102 Scope; certain security and other transactions excluded from this chapter.

672.103 Definitions and index of definitions.

672.104 Definitions: "merchant"; "between merchants"; "financing agency."

672.105 Definitions: transferability; "goods"; "future" goods; "lot"; "commercial unit."

672.106 Definitions: "contract"; "agreement"; "contract for sale"; "sale"; "present sale"; "conforming" to contract; "termination"; "cancellation."

672.107 Goods to be severed from realty; recording.

672.101 Short title.—Chapter 672 shall be known and may be cited as the "Uniform Commercial Code—Sales."

672.102 Scope; certain security and other transactions excluded from this chapter.—Unless the context otherwise requires, this chapter applies to transactions in goods; it does not apply to any transaction which although in the form of an unconditional contract to sell or present sale is intended to operate only as a security transaction nor does this chapter impair or repeal any statute regulating sales to consumers, farmers or other specified classes of buyers.

672.103 Definitions and index of definitions.—

(1) In this chapter unless the context otherwise requires:

(a) "Buyer" means a person who buys or contracts to buy goods.

(b) "Good faith" in the case of a merchant means honesty in fact and the observance of reasonable commercial standards of fair dealing in the trade.

(c) "Receipt" of goods means taking physical possession of them.

(d) "Seller" means a person who sells or contracts to sell goods.

(2) Other definitions applying to this chapter, or to specified parts thereof, and the sections in which they appear are:

"Acceptance," s. 672.606.

"Banker's credit," s. 672.325.

"Between merchants," s. 672.104.

"Cancellation," s. 672.106(4).

"Commercial unit," s. 672.105.

"Confirmed credit," s. 672.325.

"Conforming to contract," s. 672.106.

"Contract for sale," s. 672.106.

"Cover," s. 672.712.

"Entrusting," s. 672.403.

"Financing agency," s. 672.104.

"Future goods," s. 672.105.

"Goods," s. 672.105.

"Identification," s. 672.501.

"Installment contract," s. 672.612.

"Letter of credit," s. 672.325.

"Lot," s. 672.105.

"Merchant," s. 672.104.

"Overseas," s. 672.323.

"Person in position of seller," s. 672.707.

"Present sale," s. 672.106.

"Sale," s. 672.106.

"Sale on approval," s. 672.326.

"Sale or return," s. 672.326.

"Termination," s. 672.106.

(3) The following definitions in other chapters apply to this chapter:

"Check," s. 673.1041.

"Consignee," s. 677.102.

"Consignor," s. 677.102.

"Consumer goods," s. 679.1021.

"Control," s. 677.106.

"Dishonor," s. 673.5021.

"Draft," s. 673.1041.

(4) In addition chapter 671 contains general definitions and principles of construction and interpretation applicable throughout this chapter.

672.104 Definitions: "merchant"; "between merchants"; "financing agency."—

(1) "Merchant" means a person who deals in goods of the kind or otherwise by occupation holds himself or herself out as having knowledge or skill peculiar to the practices or goods involved in the transaction or to whom such knowledge or skill may be attributed by his or her employment of an agent or broker or other intermediary who by occupation holds himself or herself out as having such knowledge or skill.

(2) "Financing agency" means a bank, finance company or other person who in the ordinary course of business makes advances against goods or documents of title or who by arrangement with either the seller or the buyer intervenes in ordinary course to make or collect payment due or claimed under the contract for sale, as by purchasing or paying the seller's draft or making advances against it or by merely taking it for collection whether or not documents of title accompany or are associated with the draft. "Financing agency" includes also a bank or other person who similarly intervenes between persons who are in the position of seller and buyer in respect to the goods (s. 672.707).

(3) "Between merchants" means in any transaction with respect to which both parties are chargeable with the knowledge or skill of merchants.

672.105 Definitions: transferability; "goods"; "future" goods; "lot"; "commercial unit."—

(1) "Goods" means all things (including specially manufactured goods) which are movable at the time of identification to the contract for sale other than the money in which the price is to be paid, investment securities (chapter 678) and things in action. "Goods" also includes the unborn young of animals and growing crops and other identified things attached to realty as described in the section on goods to be severed from realty (s. 672.107).

(2) Goods must be both existing and identified before any interest in them can pass. Goods which are not both existing and identified are "future" goods. A purported present sale of future goods or of any interest therein operates as a contract to sell.

(3) There may be a sale of a part interest in existing identified goods.

(4) An undivided share in an identified bulk of fungible goods is sufficiently identified to be sold although the quantity of the bulk is not determined. Any agreed proportion of such a bulk or any quantity thereof agreed upon by number, weight or other measure may to the extent of the seller's interest in the bulk be sold to the buyer who then becomes an owner in common.

(5) "Lot" means a parcel or a single article which is the subject matter of a separate sale or delivery, whether or not it is sufficient to perform the contract.

(6) "Commercial unit" means such a unit of goods as by commercial usage is a single whole for purposes of sale and division of which materially impairs its character or value on the market or in use. A commercial unit may be a single article (as a machine) or a set of articles (as a suite of furniture or an assortment of sizes) or a quantity (as a bale, gross, or carload) or any other unit treated in use or in the relevant market as a single whole.

672.106 Definitions: "contract"; "agreement"; "contract for sale"; "sale"; "present sale"; "conforming" to contract; "termination"; "cancellation."—

(1) In this chapter unless the context otherwise requires "contract" and "agreement" are limited to those relating to the present or future sale of goods. "Contract for sale" includes both a present sale of goods and a contract to sell goods at a future time. A "sale" consists in the passing of title from the seller to the buyer for a price (s. 672.401). A "present sale" means a sale which is accomplished by the making of the contract.

(2) Goods or conduct including any part of a performance are "conforming" or conform to the contract when they are in accordance with the obligations under the contract.

(3) "Termination" occurs when either party pursuant to a power created by agreement or law puts an end to the contract otherwise than for its breach. On termination, all obligations which are still executory on both sides are discharged but any right based on prior breach or performance survives.

(4) "Cancellation" occurs when either party puts an end to the contract for breach by the other and its effect is the same as that of "termination" except that the canceling party also retains any remedy for breach of the whole contract or any unperformed balance.

672.107 Goods to be severed from realty; recording.—

(1) A contract for the sale of minerals or the like (including oil and gas) or a structure or its materials to be removed from realty is a contract for the sale of goods within this chapter if they are to be severed by the seller, but until severance a purported present sale thereof which is not effective as a transfer of an interest in land is effective only as a contract to sell.

(2) A contract for the sale apart from the land of growing crops or other things attached to realty and capable of severance without material harm thereto but not described in subsection (1) or of timber to be cut is a contract for the sale of goods within this chapter whether the subject matter is to be severed by the buyer or by the seller even though it forms part of the realty at the time of contracting, and the parties can by identification effect a present sale before severance.

(3) The provisions of this section are subject to any third-party rights provided by the law relating to realty records, and the contract for sale may be executed and recorded as a document transferring an interest in land and shall then constitute notice to third parties of the buyer's rights under the contract for sale.

PART II

FORM, FORMATION, AND READJUSTMENT OF CONTRACT

672.201 Formal requirements; statute of frauds.

672.202 Final written expression; parol or extrinsic evidence.

672.203 Seals inoperative.

672.204 Formation in general.

672.205 Firm offers.

672.206 Offer and acceptance in formation of contract.

672.207 Additional terms in acceptance or confirmation.

672.208 Course of performance or practical construction.

672.209 Modification, rescission, and waiver.

672.210 Delegation of performance; assignment of rights.

672.201 Formal requirements; statute of frauds.—

(1) Except as otherwise provided in this section a contract for the sale of goods for the price of $500 or more is not enforceable by way of action or defense unless there is some writing sufficient to indicate that a contract for sale has been made between the parties and signed by the party against whom enforcement is sought or by his or her authorized agent or broker. A writing is not insufficient because it omits or incorrectly states a term agreed upon but the contract is not enforceable under this paragraph beyond the quantity of goods shown in such writing.

(2) Between merchants if within a reasonable time a writing in confirmation of the contract and sufficient against the sender is received and the party receiving it has reason to know its contents, it satisfies the requirements of subsection (1) against such party unless written notice of objection to its contents is given within 10 days after it is received.

(3) A contract which does not satisfy the requirements of subsection (1) but which is valid in other respects is enforceable:

(a) If the goods are to be specially manufactured for the buyer and are not suitable for sale to others in the ordinary course of the seller's business and the seller, before notice of repudiation is received and under circumstances which reasonably indicate that the goods are for the buyer, has made either a substantial beginning of their manufacture or commitments for their procurement; or

(b) If the party against whom enforcement is sought admits in his or her pleading, testimony or otherwise in court that a contract for sale was made, but the contract is not enforceable under this provision beyond the quantity of goods admitted; or

(c) With respect to goods for which payment has been made and accepted or which have been received and accepted (s. 672.606).

672.202 Final written expression; parol or extrinsic evidence.—Terms with respect to which the confirmatory memoranda of the parties agree or which are otherwise set forth in a writing intended by the parties as a final expression of their agreement with respect to such terms as are included therein may not be contradicted by evidence of any prior agreement or of a contemporaneous oral agreement but may be explained or supplemented:

(1) By course of dealing or usage of trade (s. 671.205) or by course of performance (s. 672.208); and

(2) By evidence of consistent additional terms unless the court finds the writing to have been intended also as a complete and exclusive statement of the terms of the agreement.

672.203 Seals inoperative.—The affixing of a seal to a writing evidencing a contract for sale or an offer to buy or sell goods does not constitute the writing a sealed instrument and the law with respect to sealed instruments does not apply to such a contract or offer.

672.204 Formation in general.—

(1) A contract for sale of goods may be made in any manner sufficient to show agreement, including conduct by both parties which recognizes the existence of such a contract.

(2) An agreement sufficient to constitute a contract for sale may be found even though the moment of its making is undetermined.

(3) Even though one or more terms are left open a contract for sale does not fail for indefiniteness if the parties have intended to make a contract and there is a reasonably certain basis for giving an appropriate remedy.

672.205 Firm offers.—An offer by a merchant to buy or sell goods in a signed writing which by its terms gives assurance that it will be held open is not revocable, for lack of consideration, during the time stated or if no time is stated for a reasonable time, but in no event may such period of irrevocability exceed 3 months; but any such term of assurance on a form supplied by the offeree must be separately signed by the offeror.

672.206 Offer and acceptance in formation of contract.—

(1) Unless otherwise unambiguously indicated by the language or circumstances:

(a) An offer to make a contract shall be construed as inviting acceptance in any manner and by any medium reasonable in the circumstances;

(b) An order or other offer to buy goods for prompt or current shipment shall be construed as inviting acceptance either by a prompt promise to ship or by the prompt or current shipment of conforming or nonconforming goods, but such a shipment of nonconforming goods does not constitute an acceptance if the seller seasonably notifies the buyer that the shipment is offered only as an accommodation to the buyer.

(2) Where the beginning of a requested performance is a reasonable mode of acceptance an offeror who is not notified of acceptance within a reasonable time may treat the offer as having lapsed before acceptance.

672.207 Additional terms in acceptance or confirmation.—

(1) A definite and seasonable expression of acceptance or a written confirmation which is sent within a reasonable time operates as an acceptance even though it states

terms additional to or different from those offered or agreed upon, unless acceptance is expressly made conditional on assent to the additional or different terms.

(2) The additional terms are to be construed as proposals for addition to the contract. Between merchants such terms become part of the contract unless:

(a) The offer expressly limits acceptance to the terms of the offer;

(b) They materially alter it; or

(c) Notification of objection to them has already been given or is given within a reasonable time after notice of them is received.

(3) Conduct by both parties which recognizes the existence of a contract is sufficient to establish a contract for sale although the writings of the parties do not otherwise establish a contract. In such case the terms of the particular contract consist of those terms on which the writings of the parties agree, together with any supplementary terms incorporated under any other provisions of this code.

672.208 Course of performance or practical construction.—

(1) Where the contract for sale involves repeated occasions for performance by either party with knowledge of the nature of the performance and opportunity for objection to it by the other, any course of performance accepted or acquiesced in without objection shall be relevant to determine the meaning of the agreement.

(2) The express terms of the agreement and any such course of performance, as well as any course of dealing and usage of trade, shall be construed whenever reasonable as consistent with each other; but when such construction is unreasonable, express terms shall control course of performance and course of performance shall control both course of dealing and usage of trade (s. 671.205).

(3) Subject to the provisions of the next section on modification and waiver, such course of performance shall be relevant to show a waiver or modification of any term inconsistent with such course of performance.

672.209 Modification, rescission, and waiver.—

(1) An agreement modifying a contract within this chapter needs no consideration to be binding.

(2) A signed agreement which excludes modification or rescission except by a signed writing cannot be otherwise modified or rescinded, but except as between merchants such a requirement on a form supplied by the merchant must be separately signed by the other party.

(3) The requirements of the statute of frauds section of this chapter (s. 672.201) must be satisfied if the contract as modified is within its provisions.

(4) Although an attempt at modification or rescission does not satisfy the requirements of subsection (2) or (3) it can operate as a waiver.

(5) A party who has made a waiver affecting an executory portion of the contract may retract the waiver by reasonable notification received by the other party that strict performance will be required of any term waived, unless the retraction would be unjust in view of a material change of position in reliance on the waiver.

672.210 Delegation of performance; assignment of rights.—

(1) A party may perform her or his duty through a delegate unless otherwise agreed or unless the other party has a substantial interest in having her or his original promisor perform or control the acts required by the contract. No delegation of performance relieves the party delegating of any duty to perform or any liability for breach.

(2) Except as otherwise provided in s. 679.4061, unless otherwise agreed all rights of either seller or buyer can be assigned except where the assignment would materially change the duty of the other party, or increase materially the burden or risk imposed on her or him by her or his contract, or impair materially her or his chance of obtaining return performance. A right to damages for breach of the whole contract or a right arising out of the assignor's due performance of her or his entire obligation can be assigned despite agreement otherwise.

(3) The creation, attachment, perfection, or enforcement of a security interest in the seller's interest under a contract is not a transfer that materially changes the duty of or increases materially the burden or risk imposed on the buyer or impairs materially the buyer's chance of obtaining return performance within the purview of subsection (2) unless, and then only to the extent that, enforcement actually results in a delegation of material performance of the seller. Even in that event, the creation, attachment, perfection, and enforcement of the security interest remain effective, but the seller is liable to the buyer for damages caused by the delegation to the extent that the damages could not reasonably be prevented by the buyer. A court having jurisdiction may grant other appropriate relief, including cancellation of the contract for sale or an injunction against enforcement of the security interest or consummation of the enforcement.

(4) Unless the circumstances indicate the contrary a prohibition of assignment of "the contract" is to be construed as barring only the delegation to the assignee of the assignor's performance.

(5) An assignment of "the contract" or of "all my rights under the contract" or an assignment in similar general terms is an assignment of rights and unless the language or the circumstances (as in an assignment for security) indicate the contrary, it is a delegation of performance of the duties of the assignor and its acceptance by the assignee constitutes a promise by her or him to perform those duties. This promise is enforceable by either the assignor or the other party to the original contract.

(6) The other party may treat any assignment which delegates performance as creating reasonable grounds for insecurity and may without prejudice to her or his rights against the assignor demand assurances from the assignee (s. 672.609).

PART III

GENERAL OBLIGATION AND CONSTRUCTION OF CONTRACT

672.301 General obligations of parties.

672.302 Unconscionable contract or clause.

672.303 Allocation or division of risks.

672.304 Price payable in money, goods, realty, or otherwise.

672.305 Open price term.

672.306 Output, requirements, and exclusive dealings.

672.307 Delivery in single lot or several lots.

672.308 Absence of specified place for delivery.

672.309 Absence of specific time provisions; notice of termination.

672.310 Open time for payment or running of credit; authority to ship under reservation.

672.311 Options and cooperation respecting performance.

672.312 Warranty of title and against infringement; buyer's obligation against infringement.

672.313 Express warranties by affirmation, promise, description, sample.

672.314 Implied warranty; merchantability; usage of trade.

672.315 Implied warranty; fitness for particular purpose.

672.316 Exclusion or modification of warranties.

672.317 Cumulation and conflict of warranties express or implied.

672.318 Third-party beneficiaries of warranties express or implied.

672.319 "F.O.B." and "F.A.S." terms.

672.320 "C.I.F." and "C. & F." terms.

672.321 C.I.F. or C. & F.; "net landed weights"; "payment on arrival"; warranty of condition on arrival.

672.322 Delivery "ex-ship."

672.323 Form of bill of lading required in overseas shipment; "overseas."

672.324 "No arrival, no sale" term.

672.325 "Letter of credit" term; "confirmed credit."

672.326 Sale on approval and sale or return; rights of creditors.

672.327 Special incidents of sale on approval and sale or return.

672.328 Sale by auction.

672.301 General obligations of parties.—The obligation of the seller is to transfer and deliver and that of the buyer is to accept and pay in accordance with the contract.

672.302 Unconscionable contract or clause.—

(1) If the court as a matter of law finds the contract or any clause of the contract to have been unconscionable at the time it was made the court may refuse to enforce the contract, or it may enforce the remainder of the contract without the unconscionable clause, or it may so limit the application of any unconscionable clause as to avoid any unconscionable result.

(2) When it is claimed or appears to the court that the contract or any clause thereof may be unconscionable the parties shall be afforded a reasonable opportunity to present evidence as to its commercial setting, purpose and effect to aid the court in making the determination.

672.303 Allocation or division of risks.—Where this chapter allocates a risk or a burden as between the parties "unless otherwise agreed," the agreement may not only shift the allocation but may also divide the risk or burden.

672.304 Price payable in money, goods, realty, or otherwise.—

(1) The price can be made payable in money or otherwise. If it is payable in whole or in part in goods each party is a seller of the goods which he or she is to transfer.

(2) Even though all or part of the price is payable in an interest in realty the transfer of the goods and the seller's obligations with reference to them are subject to this chapter, but not the transfer of the interest in realty or the transferor's obligations in connection therewith.

672.305 Open price term.—

(1) The parties if they so intend can conclude a contract for sale even though the price is not settled. In such a case the price is a reasonable price at the time for delivery if:

(a) Nothing is said as to price; or

(b) The price is left to be agreed by the parties and they fail to agree; or

(c) The price is to be fixed in terms of some agreed market or other standard as set or recorded by a third person or agency and it is not so set or recorded.

(2) A price to be fixed by the seller or by the buyer means a price for her or him to fix in good faith.

(3) When a price left to be fixed otherwise than by agreement of the parties fails to be fixed through fault of one party the other may at her or his option treat the contract as canceled or herself or himself fix a reasonable price.

(4) Where, however, the parties intend not to be bound unless the price be fixed or agreed and it is not fixed or agreed there is no contract. In such a case the buyer must return any goods already received or if unable so to do must pay their reasonable value at the time of delivery and the seller must return any portion of the price paid on account.

672.306   Output, requirements, and exclusive dealings.—

(1) A term which measures the quantity by the output of the seller or the requirements of the buyer means such actual output or requirements as may occur in good faith, except that no quantity unreasonably disproportionate to any stated estimate or in the absence of a stated estimate to any normal or otherwise comparable prior output or requirements may be tendered or demanded.

(2) A lawful agreement by either the seller or the buyer for exclusive dealing in the kind of goods concerned imposes unless otherwise agreed an obligation by the seller to use best efforts to supply the goods and by the buyer to use best efforts to promote their sale.

672.307   Delivery in single lot or several lots.—Unless otherwise agreed all goods called for by a contract for sale must be tendered in a single delivery and payment is due only on such tender but where the circumstances give either party the right to make or demand delivery in lots the price if it can be apportioned may be demanded for each lot.

672.308   Absence of specified place for delivery.—Unless otherwise agreed:

(1) The place for delivery of goods is the seller's place of business or if the seller has none his or her residence; but

(2) In a contract for sale of identified goods which to the knowledge of the parties at the time of contracting are in some other place, that place is the place for their delivery; and

(3) Documents of title may be delivered through customary banking channels.

672.309   Absence of specific time provisions; notice of termination.—

(1) The time for shipment or delivery or any other action under a contract if not provided in this chapter or agreed upon shall be a reasonable time.

(2) Where the contract provides for successive performances but is indefinite in duration it is valid for a reasonable time but unless otherwise agreed may be terminated at any time by either party.

(3) Termination of a contract by one party except on the happening of an agreed event requires that reasonable notification be received by the other party and an agreement dispensing with notification is invalid if its operation would be unconscionable.

672.310   Open time for payment or running of credit; authority to ship under reservation.—Unless otherwise agreed:

(1) Payment is due at the time and place at which the buyer is to receive the goods even though the place of shipment is the place of delivery; and

(2) If the seller is authorized to send the goods she or he may ship them under reservation, and may tender the documents of title, but the buyer may inspect the goods after their arrival before payment is due unless such inspection is inconsistent with the terms of the contract (s. 672.513); and

(3) If delivery is authorized and made by way of documents of title otherwise than by subsection (2) then payment is due regardless of where the goods are to be received at the time and place at which the buyer is to receive delivery of the tangible documents or at the time the buyer is to receive delivery of the electronic documents and at the seller's place of business or, if none, the seller's residence; and

(4) Where the seller is required or authorized to ship the goods on credit the credit period runs from the time of shipment but postdating the invoice or delaying its dispatch will correspondingly delay the starting of the credit period.

672.311 Options and cooperation respecting performance.—

(1) An agreement for sale which is otherwise sufficiently definite (s. 672.204(3)) to be a contract is not made invalid by the fact that it leaves particulars of performance to be specified by one of the parties. Any such specification must be made in good faith and within limits set by commercial reasonableness.

(2) Unless otherwise agreed specifications relating to assortment of the goods are at the buyer's option and except as otherwise provided in s. 672.319(1)(c) and (3) specifications or arrangements relating to shipment are at the seller's option.

(3) Where such specification would materially affect the other party's performance but is not seasonably made or where one party's cooperation is necessary to the agreed performance of the other but is not seasonably forthcoming, the other party in addition to all other remedies:

(a) Is excused for any resulting delay in his or her own performance; and

(b) May also either proceed to perform in any reasonable manner or after the time for a material part of his or her own performance treat the failure to specify or to cooperate as a breach by failure to deliver or accept the goods.

672.312 Warranty of title and against infringement; buyer's obligation against infringement.—

(1) Subject to subsection (2) there is in a contract for sale a warranty by the seller that:

(a) The title conveyed shall be good, and its transfer rightful; and

(b) The goods shall be delivered free from any security interest or other lien or encumbrance of which the buyer at the time of contracting has no knowledge.

(2) A warranty under subsection (1) will be excluded or modified only by specific language or by circumstances which give the buyer reason to know that the person selling does not claim title in herself or himself or that the seller is purporting to sell only such right or title as she or he or a third person may have.

(3) Unless otherwise agreed a seller who is a merchant regularly dealing in goods of the kind warrants that the goods shall be delivered free of the rightful claim of any third person by way of infringement or the like but a buyer who furnishes specifications to the seller must hold the seller harmless against any such claim which arises out of compliance with the specifications.

672.313 Express warranties by affirmation, promise, description, sample.—

(1) Express warranties by the seller are created as follows:

(a) Any affirmation of fact or promise made by the seller to the buyer which relates to the goods and becomes part of the basis of the bargain creates an express warranty that the goods shall conform to the affirmation or promise.

(b) Any description of the goods which is made part of the basis of the bargain creates an express warranty that the goods shall conform to the description.

(c) Any sample or model which is made part of the basis of the bargain creates an express warranty that the whole of the goods shall conform to the sample or model.

(2) It is not necessary to the creation of an express warranty that the seller use formal words such as "warrant" or "guarantee" or that the seller have a specific intention to make a warranty, but an affirmation merely of the value of the goods or a statement purporting to be merely the seller's opinion or commendation of the goods does not create a warranty.

672.314   Implied warranty; merchantability; usage of trade.—

(1) Unless excluded or modified (s. 672.316), a warranty that the goods shall be merchantable is implied in a contract for their sale if the seller is a merchant with respect to goods of that kind. Under this section the serving for value of food or drink to be consumed either on the premises or elsewhere is a sale.

(2) Goods to be merchantable must be at least such as:

(a) Pass without objection in the trade under the contract description; and

(b) In the case of fungible goods, are of fair average quality within the description; and

(c) Are fit for the ordinary purposes for which such goods are used; and

(d) Run, within the variations permitted by the agreement, of even kind, quality and quantity within each unit and among all units involved; and

(e) Are adequately contained, packaged, and labeled as the agreement may require; and

(f) Conform to the promises or affirmations of fact made on the container or label if any.

(3) Unless excluded or modified (s. 672.316) other implied warranties may arise from course of dealing or usage of trade.

672.315   Implied warranty; fitness for particular purpose.—Where the seller at the time of contracting has reason to know any particular purpose for which the goods are required and that the buyer is relying on the seller's skill or judgment to select or furnish suitable goods, there is unless excluded or modified under the next section an implied warranty that the goods shall be fit for such purpose.

672.316   Exclusion or modification of warranties.—

(1) Words or conduct relevant to the creation of an express warranty and words or conduct tending to negate or limit warranty shall be construed wherever reasonable as consistent with each other; but, subject to the provisions of this chapter on parol or extrinsic evidence (s. 672.202), negation or limitation is inoperative to the extent that such construction is unreasonable.

(2) Subject to subsection (3), to exclude or modify the implied warranty of merchantability or any part of it, the language must mention merchantability and in case of a writing must be conspicuous; and, to exclude or modify any implied warranty of fitness, the exclusion must be by a writing and conspicuous. Language to exclude all implied warranties of fitness is sufficient if it states, for example, that "There are no warranties which extend beyond the description on the face hereof."

(3) Notwithstanding subsection (2):

(a) Unless the circumstances indicate otherwise, all implied warranties are excluded by expressions like "as is" or "with all faults" or other language which in common understanding calls the buyer's attention to the exclusion of warranties and makes plain that there is no implied warranty; and

(b) When the buyer before entering into the contract has examined the goods or the sample or model as fully as he or she desired or has refused to examine the goods, there is no implied warranty with regard to defects which an examination ought in the circumstances to have revealed to him or her; and

(c) An implied warranty can also be excluded or modified by a course of dealing or course of performance or usage of trade.

(d) In a transaction involving the sale of cattle or hogs, there is no implied warranty that the cattle or hogs are free from sickness or disease. However, no exemption applies in cases where the seller knowingly sells cattle or hogs that are diseased.

(4) Remedies for breach of warranty can be limited in accordance with the provisions of this chapter on liquidation or limitation of damages and on contractual modification of remedy (ss. 672.718 and 672.719).

(5) The procurement, processing, storage, distribution, or use of whole blood, plasma, blood products, and blood derivatives for the purpose of injecting or transfusing the same, or any of them, into the human body for any purpose whatsoever is declared to be the rendering of a service by any person participating therein and does not constitute a sale, whether or not any consideration is given therefor; and the implied warranties of merchantability and fitness for a particular purpose are not applicable.

(6) The procurement, processing, testing, storing, or providing of human tissue and organs for human transplant, by an institution qualified for such purposes, is the rendering of a service; and such service does not constitute the sale of goods or products to which implied warranties of merchantability or fitness for a particular purpose are applicable. No implied warranties exist as to defects which cannot be detected, removed, or prevented by reasonable use of available scientific procedures or techniques.

672.317 Cumulation and conflict of warranties express or implied.—Warranties whether express or implied shall be construed as consistent with each other and as cumulative, but if such construction is unreasonable the intention of the parties shall determine which warranty is dominant. In ascertaining that intention the following rules apply:

(1) Exact or technical specifications displace an inconsistent sample or model or general language of description.

(2) A sample from an existing bulk displaces inconsistent general language of description.

(3) Express warranties displace inconsistent implied warranties other than an implied warranty of fitness for a particular purpose.

672.318 Third-party beneficiaries of warranties express or implied.—A seller's warranty whether express or implied extends to any natural person who is in the family or household of his or her buyer, who is a guest in his or her home or who is an employee, servant or agent of his or her buyer if it is reasonable to expect that such person may use, consume or be affected by the goods and who is injured in person by breach of the warranty. A seller may not exclude nor limit the operation of this section.

672.319 "F.O.B." and "F.A.S." terms.—

(1) Unless otherwise agreed the term "F.O.B." (which means "free on board") at a named place, even though used only in connection with the stated price, is a delivery term under which:

(a) When the term is "F.O.B. the place of shipment," the seller must at that place ship the goods in the manner provided in this chapter (s. 672.504) and bear the expense and risk of putting them into the possession of the carrier; or

(b) When the term is "F.O.B. the place of destination," the seller must at her or his own expense and risk transport the goods to that place and there tender delivery of them in the manner provided in this chapter (s. 672.503);

(c) When under either (a) or (b) the term is also "F.O.B. vessel, car or other vehicle," the seller must in addition at her or his own expense and risk load the goods on board.

If the term is "F.O.B. vessel" the buyer must name the vessel and in an appropriate case the seller must comply with the provisions of this chapter on the form of bill of lading (s. 672.323).

(2) Unless otherwise agreed the term "F.A.S. vessel" (which means "free alongside") at a named port, even though used only in connection with the stated price, is a delivery term under which the seller must:

(a) At her or his own expense and risk deliver the goods alongside the vessel in the manner usual in that port or on a dock designated and provided by the buyer; and

(b) Obtain and tender a receipt for the goods in exchange for which the carrier is under a duty to issue a bill of lading.

(3) Unless otherwise agreed in any case falling within subsection (1)(a) or (c) or subsection (2) the buyer must seasonably give any needed instructions for making delivery, including when the term is "F.A.S." or "F.O.B. the loading berth of the vessel" and in an appropriate case its name and sailing date. The seller may treat the failure of needed instructions as a failure of cooperation under this chapter (s. 672.311). The seller may also at her or his option move the goods in any reasonable manner preparatory to delivery or shipment.

(4) Under the term "F.O.B. vessel" or "F.A.S." unless otherwise agreed the buyer must make payment against tender of the required documents and the seller may not tender nor the buyer demand delivery of the goods in substitution for the documents.

672.320 "C.I.F." and "C. & F." terms.—

(1) The term "C.I.F." means that the price includes in a lump sum the cost of the goods and the insurance and freight to the named destination. The term "C. & F." or "C.F." means that the price so includes cost and freight to the named destination.

(2) Unless otherwise agreed and even though used only in connection with the stated price and destination, the term C.I.F. destination or its equivalent requires the seller at his or her own expense and risk to:

(a) Put the goods into the possession of a carrier at the port for shipment and obtain a negotiable bill or bills of lading covering the entire transportation to the named destination; and

(b) Load the goods and obtain a receipt from the carrier (which may be contained in the bill of lading) showing that the freight has been paid or provided for; and

(c) Obtain a policy or certificate of insurance, including any war risk insurance, of a kind and on terms then-current at the port of shipment in the usual amount, in the currency of the contract, shown to cover the same goods covered by the bill of lading and providing for payment of loss to the order of the buyer or for the account of whom it may concern; but the seller may add to the price the amount of the premium for any such war risk insurance; and

(d) Prepare an invoice of the goods and procure any other documents required to effect shipment or to comply with the contract; and

(e) Forward and tender with commercial promptness all the documents in due form and with any indorsement necessary to perfect the buyer's rights.

(3) Unless otherwise agreed the term C. & F. or its equivalent has the same effect and imposes upon the seller the same obligations and risks as a C.I.F. term except the obligation as to insurance.

(4) Under the term C.I.F. or C. & F. unless otherwise agreed the buyer must make payment against tender of the required documents and the seller may not tender nor the buyer demand delivery of the goods in substitution for the documents.

672.321 C.I.F. or C. & F.; "net landed weights"; "payment on arrival"; warranty of condition on arrival.—Under a contract containing a term C.I.F. or C. & F.:

(1) Where the price is based on or is to be adjusted according to "net landed weights," "delivered weights," "out turn" quantity or quality or the like, unless otherwise agreed the seller must reasonably estimate the price. The payment due on tender of the documents called for by the contract is the amount so estimated, but after final adjustment of the price a settlement must be made with commercial promptness.

(2) An agreement described in subsection (1) or any warranty of quality or condition of the goods on arrival places upon the seller the risk of ordinary deterioration, shrinkage and the like in transportation but has no effect on the place or time of identification to the contract for sale or delivery or on the passing of the risk of loss.

(3) Unless otherwise agreed where the contract provides for payment on or after arrival of the goods the seller must before payment allow such preliminary inspection as is feasible; but if the goods are lost delivery of the documents and payment are due when the goods should have arrived.

672.322 Delivery "ex-ship."—

(1) Unless otherwise agreed a term for delivery of goods "ex-ship" (which means from the carrying vessel) or in equivalent language is not restricted to a particular ship and requires delivery from a ship which has reached a place at the named port of destination where goods of the kind are usually discharged.

(2) Under such a term unless otherwise agreed:

(a) The seller must discharge all liens arising out of the carriage and furnish the buyer with a direction which puts the carrier under a duty to deliver the goods; and

(b) The risk of loss does not pass to the buyer until the goods leave the ship's tackle or are otherwise properly unloaded.

672.323 Form of bill of lading required in overseas shipment; "overseas."—

(1) Where the contract contemplates overseas shipment and contains a term "C.I.F." or "C. & F. or F.O.B. vessel," the seller unless otherwise agreed shall obtain a negotiable bill of lading stating that the goods have been loaded in board or, in the case of a term "C.I.F." or "C. & F.," received for shipment.

(2) Where in a case within subsection (1) a tangible bill of lading has been issued in a set of parts, unless otherwise agreed if the documents are not to be sent from abroad the buyer may demand tender of the full set; otherwise only one part of the bill of lading need be tendered. Even if the agreement expressly requires a full set:

(a) Due tender of a single part is acceptable within the provisions of this chapter on cure of improper delivery (s. 672.508(1)); and

(b) Even though the full set is demanded, if the documents are sent from abroad the person tendering an incomplete set may nevertheless require payment upon furnishing an indemnity which the buyer in good faith deems adequate.

(3) A shipment by water or by air or a contract contemplating such shipment is "overseas" insofar as by usage of trade or agreement it is subject to the commercial, financing or shipping practices characteristic of international deepwater commerce.

672.324 "No arrival, no sale" term.—Under a term "no arrival, no sale" or terms of like meaning, unless otherwise agreed:

(1) The seller must properly ship conforming goods and if they arrive by any means the seller must tender them on arrival but she or he assumes no obligation that the goods will arrive unless she or he has caused the nonarrival; and

(2) Where without fault of the seller the goods are in part lost or have so deteriorated as no longer to conform to the contract or arrive after the contract time, the buyer may proceed as if there had been casualty to identified goods (s. 672.613).

672.325 "Letter of credit" term; "confirmed credit."—

(1) Failure of the buyer seasonably to furnish an agreed letter of credit is a breach of the contract for sale.

(2) The delivery to seller of a proper letter of credit suspends the buyer's obligation to pay. If the letter of credit is dishonored, the seller may on seasonable notification to the buyer require payment directly from him or her.

(3) Unless otherwise agreed the term "letter of credit" or "banker's credit" in a contract for sale means an irrevocable credit issued by a financing agency of good repute and, where the shipment is overseas, of good international repute. The term "confirmed credit" means that the credit must also carry the direct obligation of such an agency which does business in the seller's financial market.

672.326 Sale on approval and sale or return; rights of creditors.—

(1) Unless otherwise agreed, if delivered goods may be returned by the buyer even though they conform to the contract, the transaction is:

(a) A "sale on approval" if the goods are delivered primarily for use, and

(b) A "sale or return" if the goods are delivered primarily for resale.

(2) Goods held on approval are not subject to the claims of the buyer's creditors until acceptance; goods held on sale or return are subject to such claims while in the buyer's possession.

(3) Any "or return" term of a contract for sale is to be treated as a separate contract for sale within the statute of frauds section of this chapter (s. 672.201) and as contradicting the sale aspect of the contract within the provisions of this chapter on parol or extrinsic evidence (s. 672.202).

672.327 Special incidents of sale on approval and sale or return.—

(1) Under a sale on approval unless otherwise agreed:

(a) Although the goods are identified to the contract the risk of loss and the title do not pass to the buyer until acceptance; and

(b) Use of the goods consistent with the purpose of trial is not acceptance but failure seasonably to notify the seller of election to return the goods is acceptance, and if the goods conform to the contract acceptance of any part is acceptance of the whole; and

(c) After due notification of election to return, the return is at the seller's risk and expense but a merchant buyer must follow any reasonable instructions.

(2) Under a sale or return unless otherwise agreed:

(a) The option to return extends to the whole or any commercial unit of the goods while in substantially their original condition, but must be exercised seasonably; and

(b) The return is at the buyer's risk and expense.

672.328 Sale by auction.—

(1) In a sale by auction if goods are put up in lots each lot is the subject of a separate sale.

(2) A sale by auction is complete when the auctioneer so announces by the fall of the hammer or in other customary manner. Where a bid is made while the hammer is falling in acceptance of a prior bid the auctioneer may in his or her discretion reopen the bidding or declare the goods sold under the bid on which the hammer was falling.

(3) Such a sale is with reserve unless the goods are in explicit terms put up without reserve. In an auction with reserve the auctioneer may withdraw the goods at any time until he or she announces completion of the sale. In an auction without reserve, after the auctioneer calls for bids on an article or lot, that article or lot cannot be withdrawn unless no bid is made within a reasonable time. In either case a bidder may retract his or her bid until the auctioneer's announcement of completion of the sale, but a bidder's retraction does not revive any previous bid.

(4) If the auctioneer knowingly receives a bid on the seller's behalf or the seller makes or procures such a bid, and notice has not been given that liberty for such bidding is reserved, the buyer may at his or her option avoid the sale or take the goods at the price of the last good faith bid prior to the completion of the sale. This subsection shall not apply to any bid at a forced sale.

PART IV

TITLE, CREDITORS, AND GOOD FAITH PURCHASERS

672.401 Passing of title; reservation for security; limited application of this section.

672.402 Rights of seller's creditors against sold goods.

672.403 Power to transfer; good faith purchase of goods; "entrusting."

672.401 Passing of title; reservation for security; limited application of this section.—Each provision of this chapter with regard to the rights, obligations and remedies of the seller, the buyer, purchasers or other third parties applies irrespective of title to the goods except where the provision refers to such title. Insofar as situations are not covered by the other provisions of this chapter and matters concerning title become material the following rules apply:

(1) Title to goods cannot pass under a contract for sale prior to their identification to the contract (s. 672.501), and unless otherwise explicitly agreed the buyer acquires by their identification a special property as limited by this code. Any retention or reservation by the seller of the title (property) in goods shipped or delivered to the buyer is limited in effect to a reservation of a security interest. Subject to these provisions and to the provisions of the chapter on secured transactions (chapter 679), title to goods passes from the seller to the buyer in any manner and on any conditions explicitly agreed on by the parties.

(2) Unless otherwise explicitly agreed title passes to the buyer at the time and place at which the seller completes her or his performance with reference to the physical delivery of the goods, despite any reservation of a security interest and even though a document of title is to be delivered at a different time or place; and in particular and despite any reservation of a security interest by the bill of lading:

(a) If the contract requires or authorizes the seller to send the goods to the buyer but does not require him or her to deliver them at destination, title passes to the buyer at the time and place of shipment; but

(b) If the contract requires delivery at destination, title passes on tender there.

(3) Unless otherwise explicitly agreed where delivery is to be made without moving the goods:

(a) If the seller is to deliver a tangible document of title, title passes at the time when and the place where he or she delivers such documents and if the seller is to deliver an electronic document of title, title passes when the seller delivers the document; or

(b) If the goods are at the time of contracting already identified and no documents of title are to be delivered, title passes at the time and place of contracting.

(4) A rejection or other refusal by the buyer to receive or retain the goods, whether or not justified, or a justified revocation of acceptance revests title to the goods in the seller. Such revesting occurs by operation of law and is not a "sale."

672.402 Rights of seller's creditors against sold goods.—

(1) Except as provided in subsections (2) and (3), rights of unsecured creditors of the seller with respect to goods which have been identified to a contract for sale are subject to the buyer's rights to recover the goods under this chapter (ss. 672.502 and 672.716).

(2) A creditor of the seller may treat a sale or an identification of goods to a contract for sale as void if as against him or her a retention of possession by the seller is fraudulent under any rule of law of the state where the goods are situated, except that retention of possession in good faith and current course of trade by a merchant-seller for a commercially reasonable time after a sale or identification is not fraudulent.

(3) Nothing in this chapter shall be deemed to impair the rights of creditors of the seller:

(a) Under the provisions of the chapter on secured transactions (chapter 679); or

(b) Where identification to the contract or delivery is made not in current course of trade but in satisfaction of or as security for a preexisting claim for money, security or the like and is made under circumstances which under any rule of law of the state where the goods are situated would apart from this chapter constitute the transaction a fraudulent transfer or voidable preference.

672.403 Power to transfer; good faith purchase of goods; "entrusting."—

(1) A purchaser of goods acquires all title which her or his transferor had or had power to transfer except that a purchaser of a limited interest acquires rights only to the extent of the interest purchased. A person with voidable title has power to transfer a good title to a good faith purchaser for value. When goods have been delivered under a transaction of purchase the purchaser has such power even though:

(a) The transferor was deceived as to the identity of the purchaser, or

(b) The delivery was in exchange for a check which is later dishonored, or

(c) It was agreed that the transaction was to be a "cash sale," or

(d) The delivery was procured through fraud punishable as larcenous under the criminal law.

(2) Any entrusting of possession of goods to a merchant who deals in goods of that kind gives the merchant power to transfer all rights of the entruster to a buyer in ordinary course of business.

(3) "Entrusting" includes any delivery and any acquiescence in retention of possession regardless of any condition expressed between the parties to the delivery or acquiescence and regardless of whether the procurement of the entrusting or the possessor's disposition of the goods have been such as to be larcenous under the criminal law.

(4) The rights of other purchasers of goods and of lien creditors are governed by the chapters on secured transactions (chapter 679) and documents of title (chapter 677).

PART V
PERFORMANCE

672.501 Insurable interest in goods; manner of identification of goods.

672.502 Buyer's right to goods on seller's repudiation, failure to deliver, or insolvency.

672.503 Manner of seller's tender of delivery.

672.504 Shipment by seller.

672.505 Seller's shipment under reservation.

672.506 Rights of financing agency.

672.507 Effect of seller's tender; delivery on condition.

672.508 Cure by seller of improper tender or delivery; replacement.

672.509 Risk of loss in the absence of breach.

672.510 Effect of breach on risk of loss.

672.511 Tender of payment by buyer; payment by check.

672.512 Payment by buyer before inspection.

672.513 Buyer's right to inspection of goods.

672.514 When documents deliverable on acceptance; when on payment.

672.515 Preserving evidence of goods in dispute.

672.501 Insurable interest in goods; manner of identification of goods.—

(1) The buyer obtains a special property and an insurable interest in goods by identification of existing goods as goods to which the contract refers even though the goods so identified are nonconforming and the buyer has an option to return or reject them. Such identification can be made at any time and in any manner explicitly agreed to by the parties. In the absence of explicit agreement identification occurs:

(a) When the contract is made if it is for the sale of goods already existing and identified;

(b) If the contract is for the sale of future goods other than those described in paragraph (c), when goods are shipped, marked or otherwise designated by the seller as goods to which the contract refers;

(c) When the crops are planted or otherwise become growing crops or the young are conceived if the contract is for the sale of unborn young to be born within 12 months after contracting or for the sale of crops to be harvested within 12 months or the next normal harvest season after contracting whichever is longer.

(2) The seller retains an insurable interest in goods so long as title to or any security interest in the goods remains in him or her and where the identification is by the seller alone he or she may until default or insolvency or notification to the buyer that the identification is final substitute other goods for those identified.

(3) Nothing in this section impairs any insurable interest recognized under any other statute or rule of law.

672.502 Buyer's right to goods on seller's repudiation, failure to deliver, or insolvency.—

(1) Subject to subsections (2) and (3), and even though the goods have not been shipped, a buyer who has paid a part or all of the price of goods in which she or he has a special property under the provisions of the immediately preceding section may on making and keeping good a tender of any unpaid portion of their price recover them from the seller if:

(a) In the case of goods bought for personal, family, or household purposes, the seller repudiates or fails to deliver as required by the contract; or

(b) In all cases, the seller becomes insolvent within ten days after receipt of the first installment on their price.

(2) The buyer's right to recover the goods under paragraph (1)(a) vests upon acquisition of a special property, even if the seller has not then repudiated or failed to deliver.

(3) If the identification creating her or his special property has been made by the buyer she or he acquires the right to recover the goods only if they conform to the contract for sale.

672.503 Manner of seller's tender of delivery.—

(1) Tender of delivery requires that the seller put and hold conforming goods at the buyer's disposition and give the buyer any notification reasonably necessary to enable him or her to take delivery. The manner, time and place for tender are determined by the agreement and this chapter, and in particular:

(a) Tender must be at a reasonable hour, and if it is of goods they must be kept available for the period reasonably necessary to enable the buyer to take possession; but

(b) Unless otherwise agreed the buyer must furnish facilities reasonably suited to the receipt of the goods.

(2) Where the case is within the next section respecting shipment tender requires that the seller comply with its provisions.

(3) Where the seller is required to deliver at a particular destination tender requires that he or she comply with subsection (1) and also in any appropriate case tender documents as described in subsections (4) and (5) of this section.

(4) Where goods are in the possession of a bailee and are to be delivered without being moved:

(a) Tender requires that the seller either tender a negotiable document of title covering such goods or procure acknowledgment by the bailee of the buyer's right to possession of the goods; but

(b) Tender to the buyer of a nonnegotiable document of title or of a record directing the bailee to deliver is sufficient tender unless the buyer seasonably objects, and, except as otherwise provided in chapter 679, receipt by the bailee of notification of the buyer's rights fixes those rights as against the bailee and all third persons; but risk of loss of the goods and of any failure by the bailee to honor the nonnegotiable document of title or to obey the direction remains on the seller until the buyer has had a reasonable time to present the document or direction, and a refusal by the bailee to honor the document or to obey the direction defeats the tender.

(5) Where the contract requires the seller to deliver documents:

(a) He or she shall tender all such documents in correct form, except as provided in this chapter with respect to bills of lading in a set (s. 672.323(2)); and

(b) Tender through customary banking channels is sufficient and dishonor of a draft accompanying or associated with the documents constitutes nonacceptance or rejection.

672.504 Shipment by seller.—Where the seller is required or authorized to send the goods to the buyer and the contract does not require her or him to deliver them at a particular destination, then unless otherwise agreed the seller must:

(1) Put the goods in the possession of such a carrier and make such a contract for their transportation as may be reasonable having regard to the nature of the goods and other circumstances of the case; and

(2) Obtain and promptly deliver or tender in due form any document necessary to enable the buyer to obtain possession of the goods or otherwise required by the agreement or by usage of trade; and

(3) Promptly notify the buyer of the shipment.

Failure to notify the buyer under subsection (3) or to make a proper contract under subsection (1) is a ground for rejection only if material delay or loss ensues.

672.505 Seller's shipment under reservation.—

(1) Where the seller has identified goods to the contract by or before shipment:

(a) His or her procurement of a negotiable bill of lading to his or her own order or otherwise reserves in him or her a security interest in the goods. His or her procurement of the bill to the order of a financing agency or of the buyer indicates in addition only the seller's expectation of transferring that interest to the person named.

(b) A nonnegotiable bill of lading to himself or herself or his or her nominee reserves possession of the goods as security but except in a case of conditional delivery (s. 672.507(2)) a nonnegotiable bill of lading naming the buyer as consignee reserves no security interest even though the seller retains possession or control of the bill of lading.

(2) When shipment by the seller with reservation of a security interest is in violation of the contract for sale it constitutes an improper contract for transportation within the preceding section but impairs neither the rights given to the buyer by shipment and identification of the goods to the contract nor the seller's powers as a holder of a negotiable document of title.

672.506 Rights of financing agency.—

(1) A financing agency by paying or purchasing for value a draft which relates to a shipment of goods acquires to the extent of the payment or purchase and in addition to its own rights under the draft and any document of title securing it any rights of the shipper in the goods including the right to stop delivery and the shipper's right to have the draft honored by the buyer.

(2) The right to reimbursement of a financing agency which has in good faith honored or purchased the draft under commitment to or authority from the buyer is not impaired by subsequent discovery of defects with reference to any relevant document which was apparently regular.

672.507 Effect of seller's tender; delivery on condition.—

(1) Tender of delivery is a condition to the buyer's duty to accept the goods and, unless otherwise agreed, to the buyer's duty to pay for them. Tender entitles the seller to acceptance of the goods and to payment according to the contract.

(2) Where payment is due and demanded on the delivery to the buyer of goods or documents of title, the buyer's right as against the seller to retain or dispose of them is conditional upon her or his making the payment due.

672.508 Cure by seller of improper tender or delivery; replacement.—

(1) Where any tender or delivery by the seller is rejected because nonconforming and the time for performance has not yet expired, the seller may seasonably notify the buyer of his or her intention to cure and may then within the contract time make a conforming delivery.

(2) Where the buyer rejects a nonconforming tender which the seller had reasonable grounds to believe would be acceptable with or without money allowance the seller may if he or she seasonably notifies the buyer have a further reasonable time to substitute a conforming tender.

672.509 Risk of loss in the absence of breach.—

(1) Where the contract requires or authorizes the seller to ship the goods by carrier:

(a) If it does not require her or him to deliver them at a particular destination, the risk of loss passes to the buyer when the goods are duly delivered to the carrier even though the shipment is under reservation (s. 672.505); but

(b) If it does require her or him to deliver them at a particular destination and the goods are there duly tendered while in the possession of the carrier, the risk of loss passes to the buyer when the goods are there duly so tendered as to enable the buyer to take delivery.

(2) Where the goods are held by a bailee to be delivered without being moved, the risk of loss passes to the buyer:

(a) On her or his receipt of possession or control of a negotiable document of title covering the goods; or

(b) On acknowledgment by the bailee of the buyer's right to possession of the goods; or

(c) After her or his receipt of possession or control of a nonnegotiable document of title or other direction to deliver in a record, as provided in s. 672.503(4)(b).

(3) In any case not within subsection (1) or (2), the risk of loss passes to the buyer on her or his receipt of the goods if the seller is a merchant; otherwise the risk passes to the buyer on tender of delivery.

(4) The provisions of this section are subject to contrary agreement of the parties and to the provisions of this chapter on sale on approval (s. 672.327) and on effect of breach on risk of loss (s. 672.510).

672.510 Effect of breach on risk of loss.—

(1) Where a tender or delivery of goods so fails to conform to the contract as to give a right of rejection the risk of their loss remains on the seller until cure or acceptance.

(2) Where the buyer rightfully revokes acceptance he or she may to the extent of any deficiency in his or her effective insurance coverage treat the risk of loss as having rested on the seller from the beginning.

(3) Where the buyer as to conforming goods already identified to the contract for sale repudiates or is otherwise in breach before risk of their loss has passed to him or her, the seller may to the extent of any deficiency in his or her effective insurance coverage treat the risk of loss as resting on the buyer for a commercially reasonable time.

672.511 Tender of payment by buyer; payment by check.—

(1) Unless otherwise agreed tender of payment is a condition to the seller's duty to tender and complete any delivery.

(2) Tender of payment is sufficient when made by any means or in any manner current in the ordinary course of business unless the seller demands payment in legal tender and gives any extension of time reasonably necessary to procure it.

(3) Subject to the provisions of this code on the effect of an instrument on an obligation (s. 673.3101), payment by check is conditional and is defeated as between the parties by dishonor of the check on due presentment.

672.512 Payment by buyer before inspection.—

(1) Where the contract requires payment before inspection nonconformity of the goods does not excuse the buyer from so making payment unless:

(a) The nonconformity appears without inspection; or

(b) Despite tender of the required documents the circumstances would justify injunction against honor under the provisions of s. 675.109(2).

(2) Payment pursuant to subsection (1) does not constitute an acceptance of goods or impair the buyer's right to inspect or any of her or his remedies.

672.513 Buyer's right to inspection of goods.—

(1) Unless otherwise agreed and subject to subsection (3), where goods are tendered or delivered or identified to the contract for sale, the buyer has a right before payment or acceptance to inspect them at any reasonable place and time and in any reasonable manner. When the seller is required or authorized to send the goods to the buyer, the inspection may be after their arrival.

(2) Expenses of inspection must be borne by the buyer but may be recovered from the seller if the goods do not conform and are rejected.

(3) Unless otherwise agreed and subject to the provisions of this chapter on C.I.F. contracts (s. 672.321(3)), the buyer is not entitled to inspect the goods before payment of the price when the contract provides:

(a) For delivery "C.O.D." or on other like terms; or

(b) For payment against documents of title, except where such payment is due only after the goods are to become available for inspection.

(4) A place or method of inspection fixed by the parties is presumed to be exclusive but unless otherwise expressly agreed it does not postpone identification or shift the place for delivery or for passing the risk of loss. If compliance becomes impossible, inspection shall be as provided in this section unless the place or method fixed was clearly intended as an indispensable condition failure of which avoids the contract.

672.514 When documents deliverable on acceptance; when on payment.—Unless otherwise agreed documents against which a draft is drawn are to be delivered to the drawee on acceptance of the draft if it is payable more than 3 days after presentment; otherwise, only on payment.

672.515 Preserving evidence of goods in dispute.—In furtherance of the adjustment of any claim or dispute:

(1) Either party on reasonable notification to the other and for the purpose of ascertaining the facts and preserving evidence has the right to inspect, test and sample the goods including such of them as may be in the possession or control of the other; and

(2) The parties may agree to a third-party inspection or survey to determine the conformity or condition of the goods and may agree that the findings shall be binding upon them in any subsequent litigation or adjustment.

PART VI

BREACH, REPUDIATION, AND EXCUSE

672.601 Buyer's rights on improper delivery.

672.602 Manner and effect of rightful rejection.

672.603 Merchant buyer's duties as to rightfully rejected goods.

672.604 Buyer's options as to salvage of rightfully rejected goods.

672.605 Waiver of buyer's objections by failure to particularize.

672.606 What constitutes acceptance of goods.

672.607 Effect of acceptance; notice of breach; burden of establishing breach after acceptance; notice of claim or litigation to person answerable over.

672.608 Revocation of acceptance in whole or in part.

672.609 Right to adequate assurance of performance.

672.610 Anticipatory repudiation.

672.611 Retraction of anticipatory repudiation.

672.612 "Installment contract"; breach.

672.613 Casualty to identified goods.

672.614 Substituted performance.

672.615 Excuse by failure of presupposed conditions.

672.616 Procedure on notice claiming excuse.

672.601 Buyer's rights on improper delivery.—Subject to the provisions of this chapter on breach in installment contracts (s. 672.612) and unless otherwise agreed under the sections on contractual limitations of remedy (ss. 672.718 and 672.719), if the goods or the tender of delivery fail in any respect to conform to the contract, the buyer may:

(1) Reject the whole; or

(2) Accept the whole; or

(3) Accept any commercial unit or units and reject the rest.

672.602 Manner and effect of rightful rejection.—

(1) Rejection of goods must be within a reasonable time after their delivery or tender. It is ineffective unless the buyer seasonably notifies the seller.

(2) Subject to the provisions of the two following sections on rejected goods (ss. 672.603 and 672.604):

(a) After rejection any exercise of ownership by the buyer with respect to any commercial unit is wrongful as against the seller; and

(b) If the buyer has before rejection taken physical possession of goods in which he or she does not have a security interest under the provisions of this chapter (s. 672.711(3)), the buyer is under a duty after rejection to hold them with reasonable care at the seller's disposition for a time sufficient to permit the seller to remove them; but

(c) The buyer has no further obligations with regard to goods rightfully rejected.

(3) The seller's rights with respect to goods wrongfully rejected are governed by the provisions of this chapter on seller's remedies in general (s. 672.703).

672.603 Merchant buyer's duties as to rightfully rejected goods.—

(1) Subject to any security interest in the buyer (s. 672.711(3)) when the seller has no agent or place of business at the market of rejection a merchant buyer is under a duty after rejection of goods in her or his possession or control to follow any reasonable instructions received from the seller with respect to the goods and in the absence of such instructions to make reasonable efforts to sell them for the seller's account if they are perishable or threaten to decline in value speedily. Instructions are not reasonable if on demand indemnity for expenses is not forthcoming.

(2) When the buyer sells goods under subsection (1), she or he is entitled to reimbursement from the seller or out of the proceeds for reasonable expenses of caring for and selling them, and if the expenses include no selling commission then to such commission as is usual in the trade or if there is none to a reasonable sum not exceeding 10 percent on the gross proceeds.

(3) In complying with this section the buyer is held only to good faith and good faith conduct hereunder is neither acceptance nor conversion nor the basis of an action for damages.

672.604 Buyer's options as to salvage of rightfully rejected goods.—Subject to the provisions of the immediately preceding section on perishables if the seller gives no instructions within a reasonable time after notification of rejection the buyer may store the rejected goods for the seller's account or reship them to him or her or resell them for the seller's account with reimbursement as provided in the preceding section. Such action is not acceptance or conversion.

672.605 Waiver of buyer's objections by failure to particularize.—

(1) The buyer's failure to state in connection with rejection a particular defect which is ascertainable by reasonable inspection precludes the buyer from relying on the unstated defect to justify rejection or to establish breach:

(a) Where the seller could have cured it if stated seasonably; or

(b) Between merchants when the seller has after rejection made a request in writing for a full and final written statement of all defects on which the buyer proposes to rely.

(2) Payment against documents made without reservation of rights precludes recovery of the payment for defects apparent in the documents.

672.606 What constitutes acceptance of goods.—

(1) Acceptance of goods occurs when the buyer:

(a) After a reasonable opportunity to inspect the goods signifies to the seller that the goods are conforming or that the buyer will take or retain them in spite of their nonconformity; or

(b) Fails to make an effective rejection (s. 672.602(1)), but such acceptance does not occur until the buyer has had a reasonable opportunity to inspect them; or

(c) Does any act inconsistent with the seller's ownership; but if such act is wrongful as against the seller it is an acceptance only if ratified by her or him.

(2) Acceptance of a part of any commercial unit is acceptance of that entire unit.

672.607 Effect of acceptance; notice of breach; burden of establishing breach after acceptance; notice of claim or litigation to person answerable over.—

(1) The buyer must pay at the contract rate for any goods accepted.

(2) Acceptance of goods by the buyer precludes rejection of the goods accepted and if made with knowledge of a nonconformity cannot be revoked because of it unless the acceptance was on the reasonable assumption that the nonconformity would be seasonably cured but acceptance does not of itself impair any other remedy provided by this chapter for nonconformity.

(3) Where a tender has been accepted:

(a) The buyer must within a reasonable time after he or she discovers or should have discovered any breach notify the seller of breach or be barred from any remedy; and

(b) If the claim is one for infringement or the like (s. 672.312(3)) and the buyer is sued as a result of such a breach he or she must so notify the seller within a reasonable time after he or she receives notice of the litigation or be barred from any remedy over for liability established by the litigation.

(4) The burden is on the buyer to establish any breach with respect to the goods accepted.

(5) Where the buyer is sued for breach of a warranty or other obligation for which his or her seller is answerable over:

(a) The buyer may give his or her seller written notice of the litigation. If the notice states that the seller may come in and defend and that if the seller does not do so he or she will be bound in any action against him or her by his or her buyer by any determination of fact common to the two litigations, then unless the seller after seasonable receipt of the notice does come in and defend he or she is so bound.

(b) If the claim is one for infringement or the like (s. 672.312(3)) the original seller may demand in writing that his or her buyer turn over to him or her control of the litigation including settlement or else be barred from any remedy over and if he or she also agrees to bear all expense and to satisfy any adverse judgment, then unless the buyer after seasonable receipt of the demand does turn over control the buyer is so barred.

(6) The provisions of subsections (3), (4) and (5) apply to any obligation of a buyer to hold the seller harmless against infringement or the like (s. 672.312(3)).

672.608 Revocation of acceptance in whole or in part.—

(1) The buyer may revoke her or his acceptance of a lot or commercial unit whose nonconformity substantially impairs its value to her or him if she or he has accepted it:

(a) On the reasonable assumption that its nonconformity would be cured and it has not been seasonably cured; or

(b) Without discovery of such nonconformity if her or his acceptance was reasonably induced either by the difficulty of discovery before acceptance or by the seller's assurances.

(2) Revocation of acceptance must occur within a reasonable time after the buyer discovers or should have discovered the ground for it and before any substantial change in condition of the goods which is not caused by their own defects. It is not effective until the buyer notifies the seller of it.

(3) A buyer who so revokes has the same rights and duties with regard to the goods involved as if she or he had rejected them.

672.609 Right to adequate assurance of performance.—

(1) A contract for sale imposes an obligation on each party that the other's expectation of receiving due performance will not be impaired. When reasonable grounds for insecurity arise with respect to the performance of either party the other may in writing demand adequate assurance of due performance and until he or she receives such assurance may if commercially reasonable suspend any performance for which he or she has not already received the agreed return.

(2) Between merchants the reasonableness of grounds for insecurity and the adequacy of any assurance offered shall be determined according to commercial standards.

(3) Acceptance of any improper delivery or payment does not prejudice the aggrieved party's right to demand adequate assurance of future performance.

(4) After receipt of a justified demand failure to provide within a reasonable time not exceeding 30 days such assurance of due performance as is adequate under the circumstances of the particular case is a repudiation of the contract.

672.610 Anticipatory repudiation.—When either party repudiates the contract with respect to a performance not yet due the loss of which will substantially impair the value of the contract to the other, the aggrieved party may:

(1) For a commercially reasonable time await performance by the repudiating party; or

(2) Resort to any remedy for breach (s. 672.703 or s. 672.711), even though the aggrieved party has notified the repudiating party that she or he would await the latter's performance and has urged retraction; and

(3) In either case suspend her or his own performance or proceed in accordance with the provisions of this chapter on the seller's right to identify goods to the contract notwithstanding breach or to salvage unfinished goods (s. 672.704).

672.611 Retraction of anticipatory repudiation.—

(1) Until the repudiating party's next performance is due he or she can retract his or her repudiation unless the aggrieved party has since the repudiation canceled or materially changed position or otherwise indicated that he or she considers the repudiation final.

(2) Retraction may be by any method which clearly indicates to the aggrieved party that the repudiating party intends to perform, but must include any assurance justifiably demanded under the provisions of this chapter (s. 672.609).

(3) Retraction reinstates the repudiating party's rights under the contract with due excuse and allowance to the aggrieved party for any delay occasioned by the repudiation.

672.612 "Installment contract"; breach.—

(1) An "installment contract" is one which requires or authorizes the delivery of goods in separate lots to be separately accepted, even though the contract contains a clause "each delivery is a separate contract" or its equivalent.

(2) The buyer may reject any installment which is nonconforming if the nonconformity substantially impairs the value of that installment and cannot be cured or if the nonconformity is a defect in the required documents; but if the nonconformity does not fall within subsection (3) and the seller gives adequate assurance of its cure the buyer must accept that installment.

(3) Whenever nonconformity or default with respect to one or more installments substantially impairs the value of the whole contract there is a breach of the whole. But the aggrieved party reinstates the contract if she or he accepts a nonconforming installment without seasonably notifying of cancellation or if she or he brings an action with respect only to past installments or demands performance as to future installments.

672.613 Casualty to identified goods.—Where the contract requires for its performance goods identified when the contract is made, and the goods suffer casualty without fault of either party before the risk of loss passes to the buyer, or in a proper case under a "no arrival, no sale" term (s. 672.324) then:

(1) If the loss is total the contract is avoided; and

(2) If the loss is partial or the goods have so deteriorated as no longer to conform to the contract the buyer may nevertheless demand inspection and at his or her option either treat the contract as avoided or accept the goods with due allowance from the contract price for the deterioration or the deficiency in quantity but without further right against the seller.

672.614 Substituted performance.—

(1) Where without fault of either party the agreed berthing, loading, or unloading facilities fail or an agreed type of carrier becomes unavailable or the agreed manner of delivery otherwise becomes commercially impracticable but a commercially reasonable substitute is available, such substitute performance must be tendered and accepted.

(2) If the agreed means or manner of payment fails because of domestic or foreign governmental regulation, the seller may withhold or stop delivery unless the buyer provides a means or manner of payment which is commercially a substantial equivalent. If delivery has already been taken, payment by the means or in the manner provided by the regulation discharges the buyer's obligation unless the regulation is discriminatory, oppressive or predatory.

672.615 Excuse by failure of presupposed conditions.—Except so far as a seller may have assumed a greater obligation and subject to the preceding section on substituted performance:

(1) Delay in delivery or nondelivery in whole or in part by a seller who complies with subsections (2) and (3) is not a breach of her or his duty under a contract for sale if performance as agreed has been made impracticable by the occurrence of a contingency the nonoccurrence of which was a basic assumption on which the contract was made or by compliance in good faith with any applicable foreign or domestic governmental regulation or order whether or not it later proves to be invalid.

(2) Where the causes mentioned in subsection (1) affect only a part of the seller's capacity to perform, the seller must allocate production and deliveries among her or his customers but may at her or his option include regular customers not then under contract as well as the seller's own requirements for further manufacture. The seller may so allocate in any manner which is fair and reasonable.

(3) The seller must notify the buyer seasonably that there will be delay or nondelivery and, when allocation is required under subsection (2), of the estimated quota thus made available for the buyer.

672.616 Procedure on notice claiming excuse.—

(1) Where the buyer receives notification of a material or indefinite delay or an allocation justified under the preceding section he or she may by written notification to the seller as to any delivery concerned, and where the prospective deficiency substantially impairs the value of the whole contract under the provisions of this chapter relating to breach of installment contracts (s. 672.612), then also as to the whole:

(a) Terminate and thereby discharge any unexecuted portion of the contract; or

(b) Modify the contract by agreeing to take his or her available quota in substitution.

(2) If after receipt of such notification from the seller the buyer fails so to modify the contract within a reasonable time not exceeding 30 days the contract lapses with respect to any deliveries affected.

(3) The provisions of this section may not be negated by agreement except in so far as the seller has assumed a greater obligation under the preceding section.

PART VII

REMEDIES

672.701 Remedies for breach of collateral contracts not impaired.

672.702 Seller's remedies on discovery of buyer's insolvency.

672.703 Seller's remedies in general.

672.704 Seller's right to identify goods to the contract notwithstanding breach or to salvage unfinished goods.

672.705 Seller's stoppage of delivery in transit or otherwise.

672.706 Seller's resale including contract for resale.

672.707 "Person in the position of a seller."

672.708 Seller's damages for nonacceptance or repudiation.

672.709 Action for the price.

672.710 Seller's incidental damages.

672.711 Buyer's remedies in general; buyer's security interest in rejected goods.

672.712 "Cover"; buyer's procurement of substitute goods.

672.713 Buyer's damages for nondelivery or repudiation.

672.714 Buyer's damages for breach in regard to accepted goods.

672.715 Buyer's incidental and consequential damages.

672.716 Buyer's right to specific performance or replevin.

672.717 Deduction of damages from the price.

672.718 Liquidation or limitation of damages; deposits.

672.719 Contractual modification or limitation of remedy.

672.720 Effect of "cancellation" or "rescission" on claims for antecedent breach.

672.721 Remedies for fraud.

672.722 Who can sue third parties for injury to goods.

672.723 Proof of market price; time and place.

672.724 Admissibility of market quotations.

672.701 Remedies for breach of collateral contracts not impaired.—Remedies for breach of any obligation or promise collateral or ancillary to a contract for sale are not impaired by the provisions of this chapter.

672.702 Seller's remedies on discovery of buyer's insolvency.—

(1) Where the seller discovers the buyer to be insolvent the seller may refuse delivery except for cash including payment for all goods theretofore delivered under the contract, and stop delivery under this chapter (s. 672.705).

(2) Where the seller discovers that the buyer has received goods on credit while insolvent the seller may reclaim the goods upon demand made within 10 days after the receipt, but if misrepresentation of solvency has been made to the particular seller in writing within 3 months before delivery the 10-day limitation does not apply. Except as provided in this subsection the seller may not base a right to reclaim goods on the buyer's fraudulent or innocent misrepresentation of solvency or of intent to pay.

(3) The seller's right to reclaim under subsection (2) is subject to the rights of a buyer in ordinary course or other good faith purchaser under this chapter (s. 672.403). Successful reclamation of goods excludes all other remedies with respect to them.

672.703 Seller's remedies in general.—Where the buyer wrongfully rejects or revokes acceptance of goods or fails to make a payment due on or before delivery or repudiates with respect to a part or the whole, then with respect to any goods directly affected and, if the breach is of the whole contract (s. 672.612), then also with respect to the whole undelivered balance, the aggrieved seller may:

(1) Withhold delivery of such goods;

(2) Stop delivery by any bailee as hereafter provided (s. 672.705);

(3) Proceed under the next section respecting goods still unidentified to the contract;

(4) Resell and recover damages as hereafter provided (s. 672.706);

(5) Recover damages for nonacceptance (s. 672.708) or in a proper case the price (s. 672.709);

(6) Cancel.

672.704 Seller's right to identify goods to the contract notwithstanding breach or to salvage unfinished goods.—

(1) An aggrieved seller under the preceding section may:

(a) Identify to the contract conforming goods not already identified if at the time the seller learned of the breach they are in her or his possession or control;

(b) Treat as the subject of resale goods which have demonstrably been intended for the particular contract even though those goods are unfinished.

(2) Where the goods are unfinished an aggrieved seller may in the exercise of reasonable commercial judgment for the purposes of avoiding loss and of effective realization

either complete the manufacture and wholly identify the goods to the contract or cease manufacture and resell for scrap or salvage value or proceed in any other reasonable manner.

672.705 Seller's stoppage of delivery in transit or otherwise.—

(1) The seller may stop delivery of goods in the possession of a carrier or other bailee when he or she discovers the buyer to be insolvent (s. 672.702) and may stop delivery of carload, truckload, planeload or larger shipments of express or freight when the buyer repudiates or fails to make a payment due before delivery or if for any other reason the seller has a right to withhold or reclaim the goods.

(2) As against such buyer the seller may stop delivery until:

(a) Receipt of the goods by the buyer; or

(b) Acknowledgment to the buyer by any bailee of the goods except a carrier that the bailee holds the goods for the buyer; or

(c) Such acknowledgment to the buyer by a carrier by reshipment or as a warehouse; or

(d) Negotiation to the buyer of any negotiable document of title covering the goods.

(3)(a) To stop delivery the seller shall so notify as to enable the bailee by reasonable diligence to prevent delivery of the goods.

(b) After such notification the bailee shall hold and deliver the goods according to the directions of the seller but the seller is liable to the bailee for any ensuing charges or damages.

(c) If a negotiable document of title has been issued for goods the bailee is not obliged to obey a notification to stop until surrender of possession or control of the document.

(d) A carrier who has issued a nonnegotiable bill of lading is not obliged to obey a notification to stop received from a person other than the consignor.

672.706 Seller's resale including contract for resale.—

(1) Under the conditions stated in s. 672.703 on seller's remedies, the seller may resell the goods concerned or the undelivered balance thereof. Where the resale is made in good faith and in a commercially reasonable manner the seller may recover the difference between the resale price and the contract price together with any incidental damages allowed under the provisions of this chapter (s. 672.710), but less expenses saved in consequence of the buyer's breach.

(2) Except as otherwise provided in subsection (3) or unless otherwise agreed resale may be at public or private sale including sale by way of one or more contracts to sell or of identification to an existing contract of the seller. Sale may be as a unit or in parcels and at any time and place and on any terms but every aspect of the sale including the method, manner, time, place and terms must be commercially reasonable. The resale must be reasonably identified as referring to the broken contract, but it is not necessary that the goods be in existence or that any or all of them have been identified to the contract before the breach.

(3) Where the resale is at private sale the seller must give the buyer reasonable notification of her or his intention to resell.

(4) Where the resale is at public sale:

(a) Only identified goods can be sold except where there is a recognized market for a public sale of futures in goods of the kind; and

(b) It must be made at a usual place or market for public sale if one is reasonably available and except in the case of goods which are perishable or threaten to decline in value speedily the seller must give the buyer reasonable notice of the time and place of the resale; and

(c) If the goods are not to be within the view of those attending the sale the notification of sale must state the place where the goods are located and provide for their reasonable inspection by prospective bidders; and

(d) The seller may buy.

(5) A purchaser who buys in good faith at a resale takes the goods free of any rights of the original buyer even though the seller fails to comply with one or more of the requirements of this section.

(6) The seller is not accountable to the buyer for any profit made on any resale. A person in the position of a seller (s. 672.707) or a buyer who has rightfully rejected or justifiably revoked acceptance must account for any excess over the amount of her or his security interest, as hereinafter defined (s. 672.711(3)).

672.707 "Person in the position of a seller."—

(1) A "person in the position of a seller" includes as against a principal an agent who has paid or become responsible for the price of goods on behalf of his or her principal or anyone who otherwise holds a security interest or other right in goods similar to that of a seller.

(2) A person in the position of a seller may as provided in this chapter withhold or stop delivery (s. 672.705) and resell (s. 672.706) and recover incidental damages (s. 672.710).

672.708 Seller's damages for nonacceptance or repudiation.—

(1) Subject to subsection (2) and to the provisions of this chapter with respect to proof of market price (s. 672.723), the measure of damages for nonacceptance or repudiation by the buyer is the difference between the market price at the time and place for tender and the unpaid contract price together with any incidental damages provided in this chapter (s. 672.710), but less expenses saved in consequence of the buyer's breach.

(2) If the measure of damages provided in subsection (1) is inadequate to put the seller in as good a position as performance would have done then the measure of damages is the profit (including reasonable overhead) which the seller would have made from full performance by the buyer, together with any incidental damages provided in this chapter (s. 672.710), due allowance for costs reasonably incurred and due credit for payments or proceeds of resale.

672.709 Action for the price.—

(1) When the buyer fails to pay the price as it becomes due the seller may recover, together with any incidental damages under the next section, the price:

(a) Of goods accepted or of conforming goods lost or damaged within a commercially reasonable time after risk of their loss has passed to the buyer; and

(b) Of goods identified to the contract if the seller is unable after reasonable effort to resell them at a reasonable price or the circumstances reasonably indicate that such effort will be unavailing.

(2) Where the seller sues for the price she or he must hold for the buyer any goods which have been identified to the contract and are still in her or his control except that if resale becomes possible the seller may resell them at any time prior to the collection of the judgment. The net proceeds of any such resale must be credited to the buyer and payment of the judgment entitles her or him to any goods not resold.

(3) After the buyer has wrongfully rejected or revoked acceptance of the goods or has failed to make a payment due or has repudiated (s. 672.610), a seller who is held not

entitled to the price under this section shall nevertheless be awarded damages for nonacceptance under the preceding section.

672.710 Seller's incidental damages.—Incidental damages to an aggrieved seller include any commercially reasonable charges, expenses or commissions incurred in stopping delivery, in the transportation, care and custody of goods after the buyer's breach, in connection with return or resale of the goods or otherwise resulting from the breach.

672.711 Buyer's remedies in general; buyer's security interest in rejected goods.—

(1) Where the seller fails to make delivery or repudiates or the buyer rightfully rejects or justifiably revokes acceptance then with respect to any goods involved, and with respect to the whole if the breach goes to the whole contract (s. 672.612), the buyer may cancel and whether or not he or she has done so may in addition to recovering so much of the price as has been paid:

(a) "Cover" and have damages under the next section as to all the goods affected whether or not they have been identified to the contract; or

(b) Recover damages for nondelivery as provided in this chapter (s. 672.713).

(2) Where the seller fails to deliver or repudiates the buyer may also:

(a) If the goods have been identified recover them as provided in this chapter (s. 672.502); or

(b) In a proper case obtain specific performance or replevy the goods as provided in this chapter (s. 672.716).

(3) On rightful rejection or justifiable revocation of acceptance a buyer has a security interest in goods in his or her possession or control for any payments made on their price and any expenses reasonably incurred in their inspection, receipt, transportation, care and custody and may hold such goods and resell them in like manner as an aggrieved seller (s. 672.706).

672.712 "Cover"; buyer's procurement of substitute goods.—

(1) After a breach within the preceding section the buyer may "cover" by making in good faith and without unreasonable delay any reasonable purchase of or contract to purchase goods in substitution for those due from the seller.

(2) The buyer may recover from the seller as damages the difference between the cost of cover and the contract price together with any incidental or consequential damages as hereinafter defined (s. 672.715), but less expenses saved in consequence of the seller's breach.

(3) Failure of the buyer to effect cover within this section does not bar her or him from any other remedy.

672.713 Buyer's damages for nondelivery or repudiation.—

(1) Subject to the provisions of this chapter with respect to proof of market price (s. 672.723), the measure of damages for nondelivery or repudiation by the seller is the difference between the market price at the time when the buyer learned of the breach and the contract price together with any incidental and consequential damages provided in this chapter (s. 672.715), but less expenses saved in consequence of the seller's breach.

(2) Market price is to be determined as of the place for tender or, in cases of rejection after arrival or revocation of acceptance, as of the place of arrival.

672.714 Buyer's damages for breach in regard to accepted goods.—

(1) Where the buyer has accepted goods and given notification (s. 672.607(3)) he or she may recover as damages for any nonconformity of tender the loss resulting in the

ordinary course of events from the seller's breach as determined in any manner which is reasonable.

(2) The measure of damages for breach of warranty is the difference at the time and place of acceptance between the value of the goods accepted and the value they would have had if they had been as warranted, unless special circumstances show proximate damages of a different amount.

(3) In a proper case any incidental and consequential damages under the next section may also be recovered.

672.715 Buyer's incidental and consequential damages.—

(1) Incidental damages resulting from the seller's breach include expenses reasonably incurred in inspection, receipt, transportation and care and custody of goods rightfully rejected, any commercially reasonable charges, expenses or commissions in connection with effecting cover and any other reasonable expense incident to the delay or other breach.

(2) Consequential damages resulting from the seller's breach include:

(a) Any loss resulting from general or particular requirements and needs of which the seller at the time of contracting had reason to know and which could not reasonably be prevented by cover or otherwise; and

(b) Injury to person or property proximately resulting from any breach of warranty.

672.716 Buyer's right to specific performance or replevin.—

(1) Specific performance may be decreed where the goods are unique or in other proper circumstances.

(2) The decree for specific performance may include such terms and conditions as to payment of the price, damages, or other relief as the court may deem just.

(3) The buyer has a right of replevin for goods identified to the contract if after reasonable effort she or he is unable to effect cover for such goods or the circumstances reasonably indicate that such effort will be unavailing or if the goods have been shipped under reservation and satisfaction of the security interest in them has been made or tendered. In the case of goods bought for personal, family, or household purposes, the buyer's right of replevin vests upon acquisition of a special property, even if the seller had not then repudiated or failed to deliver.

672.717 Deduction of damages from the price.—The buyer on notifying the seller of her or his intention to do so may deduct all or any part of the damages resulting from any breach of the contract from any part of the price still due under the same contract.

672.718 Liquidation or limitation of damages; deposits.—

(1) Damages for breach by either party may be liquidated in the agreement but only at an amount which is reasonable in the light of the anticipated or actual harm caused by the breach, the difficulties of proof of loss, and the inconvenience or nonfeasibility of otherwise obtaining an adequate remedy. A term fixing unreasonably large liquidated damages is void as a penalty.

(2) Where the seller justifiably withholds delivery of goods because of the buyer's breach, the buyer is entitled to restitution of any amount by which the sum of his or her payments exceeds:

(a) The amount to which the seller is entitled by virtue of terms liquidating the seller's damages in accordance with subsection (1), or

(b) In the absence of such terms, 20 percent of the value of the total performance for which the buyer is obligated under the contract or $500, whichever is smaller.

(3) The buyer's right to restitution under subsection (2) is subject to offset to the extent that the seller establishes:

(a) A right to recover damages under the provisions of this chapter other than subsection (1), and

(b) The amount or value of any benefits received by the buyer directly or indirectly by reason of the contract.

(4) Where a seller has received payment in goods their reasonable value or the proceeds of their resale shall be treated as payments for the purposes of subsection (2); but if the seller has notice of the buyer's breach before reselling goods received in part performance, his or her resale is subject to the conditions laid down in this chapter on resale by an aggrieved seller (s. 672.706).

672.719 Contractual modification or limitation of remedy.—

(1) Subject to the provisions of subsections (2) and (3) of this section and of the preceding section on liquidation and limitation of damages:

(a) The agreement may provide for remedies in addition to or in substitution for those provided in this chapter and may limit or alter the measure of damages recoverable under this chapter, as by limiting the buyer's remedies to return of the goods and repayment of the price or to repair and replacement of nonconforming goods or parts; and

(b) Resort to a remedy as provided is optional unless the remedy is expressly agreed to be exclusive, in which case it is the sole remedy.

(2) Where circumstances cause an exclusive or limited remedy to fail of its essential purpose, remedy may be had as provided in this code.

(3) Consequential damages may be limited or excluded unless the limitation or exclusion is unconscionable. Limitation of consequential damages for injury to the person in the case of consumer goods is prima facie unconscionable but limitation of damages where the loss is commercial is not.

672.720 Effect of "cancellation" or "rescission" on claims for antecedent breach.— Unless the contrary intention clearly appears, expressions of "cancellation" or "rescission" of the contract or the like shall not be construed as a renunciation or discharge of any claim in damages for an antecedent breach.

672.721 Remedies for fraud.—Remedies for material misrepresentation or fraud include all remedies available under this chapter for nonfraudulent breach. Neither rescission or a claim for rescission of the contract for sale nor rejection or return of the goods shall bar or be deemed inconsistent with a claim for damages or other remedy.

672.722 Who can sue third parties for injury to goods.—Where a third party so deals with goods which have been identified to a contract for sale as to cause actionable injury to a party to that contract:

(1) A right of action against the third party is in either party to the contract for sale who has title to or a security interest or a special property or an insurable interest in the goods; and if the goods have been destroyed or converted a right of action is also in the party who either bore the risk of loss under the contract for sale or has since the injury assumed that risk as against the other;

(2) If at the time of the injury the party plaintiff did not bear the risk of loss as against the other party to the contract for sale and there is no arrangement between them for disposition of the recovery, her or his suit or settlement is, subject to her or his own interest, as a fiduciary for the other party to the contact;

(3) Either party may with the consent of the other sue for the benefit of whom it may concern.

672.723 Proof of market price; time and place.—

(1) If an action based on anticipatory repudiation comes to trial before the time for performance with respect to some or all of the goods, any damages based on market price (s. 672.708 or s. 672.713) shall be determined according to the price of such goods prevailing at the time when the aggrieved party learned of the repudiation.

(2) If evidence of a price prevailing at the times or places described in this chapter is not readily available the price prevailing within any reasonable time before or after the time described or at any other place which in commercial judgment or under usage of trade would serve as a reasonable substitute for the one described may be used, making any proper allowance for the cost of transporting the goods to or from such other place.

(3) Evidence of a relevant price prevailing at a time or place other than the one described in this chapter offered by one party is not admissible unless and until he or she has given the other party such notice as the court finds sufficient to prevent unfair surprise.

672.724 Admissibility of market quotations.—Whenever the prevailing price or value of any goods regularly bought and sold in any established commodity market is in issue, reports in official publications or trade journals or in newspapers or periodicals of general circulation published as the reports of such market shall be admissible in evidence. The circumstances of the preparation of such a report may be shown to affect its weight but not its admissibility.

Uniform Commercial Code Article 3 as adopted in the State of California

CHAPTER 1.

GENERAL PROVISIONS AND DEFINITIONS

3101. This division may be cited as Uniform Commercial Code—Negotiable Instruments.

3102. (a) This division applies to negotiable instruments. It does not apply to money, to payment orders governed by Division 11 (commencing with Section 11101), or to securities governed by Division 8 (commencing with Section 8101).

(b) If there is conflict between this division and Division 4 (commencing with Section 4101) or Division 9 (commencing with Section 9101), Divisions 4 and 9 govern.

(c) Regulations of the Board of Governors of the Federal Reserve System and operating circulars of the Federal Reserve Banks supersede any inconsistent provision of this division to the extent of the inconsistency.

3103. (a) In this division:

(1) "Acceptor" means a drawee who has accepted a draft.

(2) "Drawee" means a person ordered in a draft to make payment.

(3) "Drawer" means a person who signs or is identified in a draft as a person ordering payment.

(4) [Reserved]

(5) "Maker" means a person who signs or is identified in a note as a person undertaking to pay.

(6) "Order" means a written instruction to pay money signed by the person giving the instruction. The instruction may be addressed to any person, including the person giving the instruction, or to one or more persons jointly or in the alternative but not in succession. An authorization to pay is not an order unless the person authorized to pay is also instructed to pay.

(7) "Ordinary care" in the case of a person engaged in business means observance of reasonable commercial standards, prevailing in the area in which the person is located, with respect to the business in which the person is engaged. In the case of a bank that takes an instrument for processing for collection or payment by automated means, reasonable commercial standards do not require the bank to examine the instrument if the failure to examine does not violate the bank's prescribed procedures and the bank's procedures do not vary unreasonably from general banking usage not disapproved by this division or Division 4 (commencing with Section 4101).

(8) "Party" means a party to an instrument.

(9) "Promise" means a written undertaking to pay money signed by the person undertaking to pay. An acknowledgment of an obligation by the obligor is not a promise unless the obligor also undertakes to pay the obligation.

(10) "Prove" with respect to a fact means to meet the burden of establishing the fact (paragraph (8) of subdivision (b) of Section 1201).

(11) "Remitter" means a person who purchases an instrument from its issuer if the instrument is payable to an identified person other than the purchaser.

(b) Other definitions applying to this division and the sections in which they appear are:

"Acceptance"	Section 3409
"Accommodated party"	Section 3419
"Accommodation party"	Section 3419
"Alteration"	Section 3407
"Anomalous endorsement"	Section 3205
"Blank endorsement"	Section 3205
"Cashier's check"	Section 3104

"Certificate of deposit"	Section 3104
"Certified check"	Section 3409
"Check"	Section 3104
"Consideration"	Section 3303
"Demand Draft"	Section 3104
"Draft"	Section 3104
"Holder in due course"	Section 3302
"Incomplete instrument"	Section 3115
"Indorsement"	Section 3204
"Indorser"	Section 3204
"Instrument"	Section 3104
"Issue"	Section 3105
"Issuer"	Section 3105
"Negotiable instrument"	Section 3104
"Negotiation"	Section 3201
"Note"	Section 3104
"Payable at a definite time"	Section 3108
"Payable on demand"	Section 3108
"Payable to bearer"	Section 3109
"Payable to order"	Section 3109
"Payment"	Section 3602
"Person entitled to enforce"	Section 3301
"Presentment"	Section 3501
"Reacquisition"	Section 3207
"Special indorsement"	Section 3205
"Teller's check"	Section 3104
"Transfer of instrument"	Section 3203
"Traveler's check"	Section 3104
"Value"	Section 3303

(c) The following definitions in other divisions apply to this division:

"Bank"	Section 4105
"Banking day"	Section 4104
"Clearinghouse"	Section 4104
"Collecting bank"	Section 4105
"Depositary bank"	Section 4105
"Documentary draft"	Section 4104
"Intermediary bank"	Section 4105
"Item"	Section 4104
"Payor bank"	Section 4105
"Suspends payments"	Section 4104

(d) In addition, Division 1 (commencing with Section 1101) contains general definitions and principles of construction and interpretation applicable throughout this division.

3104. (a) Except as provided in subdivisions (c) and (d), "negotiable instrument" means an unconditional promise or order to pay a fixed amount of money, with or without interest or other charges described in the promise or order, if it is all of the following:

(1) Is payable to bearer or to order at the time it is issued or first comes into possession of a holder.

(2) Is payable on demand or at a definite time.

(3) Does not state any other undertaking or instruction by the person promising or ordering payment to do any act in addition to the payment of money, but the promise or order may contain (i) an undertaking or power to give, maintain, or protect collateral to secure payment, (ii) an authorization or power to the holder to confess judgment or realize

on or dispose of collateral, or (iii) a waiver of the benefit of any law intended for the advantage or protection of an obligor.

(b) "Instrument" means a negotiable instrument.

(c) An order that meets all of the requirements of subdivision (a), except paragraph (1), and otherwise falls within the definition of "check" in subdivision (f) is a negotiable instrument and a check.

(d) A promise or order other than a check is not an instrument if, at the time it is issued or first comes into possession of a holder, it contains a conspicuous statement, however expressed, to the effect that the promise or order is not negotiable or is not an instrument governed by this division.

(e) An instrument is a "note" if it is a promise and is a "draft" if it is an order. If an instrument falls within the definition of both "note" and "draft," a person entitled to enforce the instrument may treat it as either.

(f) "Check" means (1) a draft, other than a documentary draft, payable on demand and drawn on a bank, (2) a cashier's check or teller's check, or (3) a demand draft. An instrument may be a check even though it is described on its face by another term, such as "money order."

(g) "Cashier's check" means a draft with respect to which the drawer and drawee are the same bank or branches of the same bank.

(h) "Teller's check" means a draft drawn by a bank (1) on another bank, or (2) payable at or through a bank.

(i) "Traveler's check" means an instrument that (1) is payable on demand, (2) is drawn on or payable at or through a bank, (3) is designated by the term "traveler's check" or by a substantially similar term, and (4) requires, as a condition to payment, a countersignature by a person whose specimen signature appears on the instrument.

(j) "Certificate of deposit" means an instrument containing an acknowledgment by a bank that a sum of money has been received by the bank and a promise by the bank to repay the sum of money. A certificate of deposit is a note of the bank.

(k) "Demand draft" means a writing not signed by a customer that is created by a third party under the purported authority of the customer for the purpose of charging the customer's account with a bank. A demand draft shall contain the customer's account number and may contain any or all of the following:

(1) The customer's printed or typewritten name.

(2) A notation that the customer authorized the draft.

(3) The statement "No Signature Required" or words to that effect.

A demand draft shall not include a check purportedly drawn by and bearing the signature of a fiduciary, as defined in paragraph (1) of subdivision (a) of Section 3307.

3105. (a) "Issue" means the first delivery of an instrument by the maker or drawer, whether to a holder or nonholder, for the purpose of giving rights on the instrument to any person.

(b) An unissued instrument, or an unissued incomplete instrument that is completed, is binding on the maker or drawer, but nonissuance is a defense. An instrument that is conditionally issued or is issued for a special purpose is binding on the maker or drawer, but failure of the condition or special purpose to be fulfilled is a defense.

(c) "Issuer" applies to issued and unissued instruments and means a maker or drawer of an instrument.

3106. (a) Except as provided in this section, for the purposes of subdivision (a) of Section 3104, a promise or order is unconditional unless it states (1) an express condition to payment, (2) that the promise or order is subject to or governed by another writing, or (3) that rights or obligations with respect to the promise or order are stated in another writing. A reference to another writing does not of itself make the promise or order conditional.

(b) A promise or order is not made conditional (1) by a reference to another writing for a statement of rights with respect to collateral, prepayment, or acceleration, or (2) because payment is limited to resort to a particular fund or source.

(c) If a promise or order requires, as a condition to payment, a countersignature by a person whose specimen signature appears on the promise or order, the condition does not make the promise or order conditional for the purposes of subdivision (a) of Section 3104. If the person whose specimen signature appears on an instrument fails to countersign the instrument, the failure to countersign is a defense to the obligation of the issuer, but the failure does not prevent a transferee of the instrument from becoming a holder of the instrument.

(d) If a promise or order at the time it is issued or first comes into possession of a holder contains a statement, required by applicable statutory or administrative law, to the effect that the rights of a holder or transferee are subject to claims or defenses that the issuer could assert against the original payee, the promise or order is not thereby made conditional for the purposes of subdivision (a) of Section 3104; but if the promise or order is an instrument, there cannot be a holder in due course of the instrument.

3107. Unless the instrument otherwise provides, an instrument that states the amount payable in foreign money may be paid in the foreign money or in an equivalent amount in dollars calculated by using the current bank-offered spot rate at the place of payment for the purchase of dollars on the day on which the instrument is paid.

3108. (a) A promise or order is "payable on demand" if it (1) states that it is payable on demand or at sight, or otherwise indicates that it is payable at the will of the holder, or (2) does not state any time of payment.

(b) A promise or order is "payable at a definite time" if it is payable on elapse of a definite period of time after sight or acceptance or at a fixed date or dates or at a time or times readily ascertainable at the time the promise or order is issued, subject to rights of (1) prepayment, (2) acceleration, (3) extension at the option of the holder, or (4) extension to a further definite time at the option of the maker or acceptor or automatically upon or after a specified act or event.

(c) If an instrument, payable at a fixed date, is also payable upon demand made before the fixed date, the instrument is payable on demand until the fixed date and, if demand for payment is not made before that date, becomes payable at a definite time on the fixed date.

3109. (a) A promise or order is payable to bearer if it is any of the following:
(1) States that it is payable to bearer or to the order of bearer or otherwise indicates that the person in possession of the promise or order is entitled to payment.
(2) Does not state a payee.
(3) States that it is payable to or to the order of cash or otherwise indicates that it is not payable to an identified person.

(b) A promise or order that is not payable to bearer is payable to order if it is payable (1) to the order of an identified person or (2) to an identified person or order. A promise or order that is payable to order is payable to the identified person.

(c) An instrument payable to bearer may become payable to an identified person if it is specially indorsed pursuant to subdivision (a) of Section 3205. An instrument payable to an identified person may become payable to bearer if it is indorsed in blank pursuant to subdivision (b) of Section 3205.

3110. (a) The person to whom an instrument is initially payable is determined by the intent of the person, whether or not authorized, signing as, or in the name or behalf of, the issuer of the instrument. The instrument is payable to the person intended by the signer even if that person is identified in the instrument by a name or other identification that is not that of the intended person. If more than one person signs in the name or behalf of the issuer of an instrument and all the signers do not intend the same person as payee, the instrument is payable to any person intended by one or more of the signers.

(b) If the signature of the issuer of an instrument is made by automated means, such as a check-writing machine, the payee of the instrument is determined by the intent of the person who supplied the name or identification of the payee, whether or not authorized to do so.

(c) A person to whom an instrument is payable may be identified in any way, including by name, identifying number, office, or account number. For the purpose of determining the holder of an instrument, the following rules apply:

(1) If an instrument is payable to an account and the account is identified only by number, the instrument is payable to the person to whom the account is payable. If an instrument is payable to an account identified by number and by the name of a person, the instrument is payable to the named person, whether or not that person is the owner of the account identified by number.

(2) If an instrument is payable to:

(A) A trust, an estate, or a person described as trustee or representative of a trust or estate, the instrument is payable to the trustee, the representative, or a successor of either, whether or not the beneficiary or estate is also named.

(B) A person described as agent or similar representative of a named or identified person, the instrument is payable to the represented person, the representative, or a successor of the representative.

(C) A fund or organization that is not a legal entity, the instrument is payable to a representative of the members of the fund or organization.

(D) An office or to a person described as holding an office, the instrument is payable to the named person, the incumbent of the office, or a successor to the incumbent.

(d) If an instrument is payable to two or more persons alternatively, it is payable to any of them and may be negotiated, discharged, or enforced by any or all of them in possession of the instrument. If an instrument is payable to two or more persons not alternatively, it is payable to all of them and may be negotiated, discharged, or enforced only by all of them. If an instrument payable to two or more persons is ambiguous as to whether it is payable to the persons alternatively, the instrument is payable to the persons alternatively.

3111. Except as otherwise provided for items in Division 4 (commencing with Section 4101), an instrument is payable at the place of payment stated in the instrument. If no place of payment is stated, an instrument is payable at the address of the drawee or maker stated in the instrument. If no address is stated, the place of payment is the place of business of the drawee or maker. If a drawee or maker has more than one place of business, the place of payment is any place of business of the drawee or maker chosen by the person entitled to enforce the instrument. If the drawee or maker has no place of business, the place of payment is the residence of the drawee or maker.

3112. (a) Unless otherwise provided in the instrument, (1) an instrument is not payable with interest, and (2) interest on an interest-bearing instrument is payable from the date of the instrument.

(b) Interest may be stated in an instrument as a fixed or variable amount of money or it may be expressed as a fixed or variable rate or rates. The amount or rate of interest may be stated or described in the instrument in any manner and may require reference to information not contained in the instrument. If an instrument provides for interest, but the amount of interest payable cannot be ascertained from the description, interest is payable at the judgment rate in effect at the place of payment of the instrument and at the time interest first accrues.

3113. (a) An instrument may be antedated or postdated. The date stated determines the time of payment if the instrument is payable at a fixed period after date. Except as provided in subdivision (c) of Section 4401, an instrument payable on demand is not payable before the date of the instrument.

(b) If an instrument is undated, its date is the date of its issue or, in the case of an unissued instrument, the date it first comes into possession of a holder.

3114. If an instrument contains contradictory terms, typewritten terms prevail over printed terms, handwritten terms prevail over both, and words prevail over numbers.

3115. (a) "Incomplete instrument" means a signed writing, whether or not issued by the signer, the contents of which show at the time of signing that it is incomplete but that the signer intended it to be completed by the addition of words or numbers.

(b) Subject to subdivision (c), if an incomplete instrument is an instrument under Section 3104, it may be enforced according to its terms if it is not completed, or according to its terms as augmented by completion. If an incomplete instrument is not an instrument under Section 3104, but, after completion, the requirements of Section 3104 are met, the instrument may be enforced according to its terms as augmented by completion.

(c) If words or numbers are added to an incomplete instrument without authority of the signer, there is an alteration of the incomplete instrument under Section 3407.

(d) The burden of establishing that words or numbers were added to an incomplete instrument without authority of the signer is on the person asserting the lack of authority.

3116. (a) Except as otherwise provided in the instrument, two or more persons who have the same liability on an instrument as makers, drawers, acceptors, indorsers who indorse as joint payees, or anomalous indorsers are jointly and severally liable in the capacity in which they sign.

(b) Except as provided in subdivision (e) of Section 3419 or by agreement of the affected parties, a party having joint and several liability who pays the instrument is entitled to receive from any party having the same joint and several liability contribution in accordance with applicable law.

(c) Discharge of one party having joint and several liability by a person entitled to enforce the instrument does not affect the right under subdivision (b) of a party having the same joint and several liability to receive contribution from the party discharged.

3117. Subject to applicable law regarding exclusion of proof of contemporaneous or previous agreements, the obligation of a party to an instrument to pay the instrument may be modified, supplemented, or nullified by a separate agreement of the obligor and a person entitled to enforce the instrument, if the instrument is issued or the obligation is incurred in reliance on the agreement or as part of the same transaction giving rise to the agreement. To the extent an obligation is modified, supplemented, or nullified by an agreement under this section, the agreement is a defense to the obligation.

3118. (a) Except as provided in subdivision (e), an action to enforce the obligation of a party to pay a note payable at a definite time shall be commenced within six years after the due date or dates stated in the note or, if a due date is accelerated, within six years after the accelerated due date.

(b) Except as provided in subdivision (d) or (e), if demand for payment is made to the maker of a note payable on demand, an action to enforce the obligation of a party to pay the note shall be commenced within six years after the demand. If no demand for payment is made to the maker, an action to enforce the note is barred if neither principal nor interest on the note has been paid for a continuous period of 10 years.

(c) Except as provided in subdivision (d), an action to enforce the obligation of a party to an unaccepted draft to pay the draft shall be commenced within three years after dishonor of the draft or 10 years after the date of the draft, whichever period expires first.

(d) An action to enforce the obligation of the acceptor of a certified check or the issuer of a teller's check, cashier's check, or traveler's check shall be commenced within three years after demand for payment is made to the acceptor or issuer, as the case may be.

(e) An action to enforce the obligation of a party to a certificate of deposit to pay the instrument shall be commenced within six years after demand for payment is made to the maker, but if the instrument states a due date and the maker is not required to pay before that date, the six-year period begins when a demand for payment is in effect and the due date has passed.

(f) An action to enforce the obligation of a party to pay an accepted draft, other than a certified check, shall be commenced (1) within six years after the due date or dates stated in the draft or acceptance if the obligation of the acceptor is payable at a definite time, or (2) within six years after the date of the acceptance if the obligation of the acceptor is payable on demand.

(g) Unless governed by other law regarding claims for indemnity or contribution, an action (1) for conversion of an instrument, for money had and received, or like action based on conversion, (2) for breach of warranty, or (3) to enforce an obligation, duty, or right arising under this division and not governed by this section shall be commenced within three years after the cause of action accrues.

3119. In an action for breach of an obligation for which a third person is answerable over pursuant to this division or Division 4 (commencing with Section 4101), the defendant may give the third person written notice of the litigation, and the person notified may then give similar notice to any other person who is answerable over.

If the notice states (1) that the person notified may come in and defend and (2) that failure to do so will bind the person notified in an action later brought by the person giving the notice as to any determination of fact common to the two litigations, the person notified is so bound unless after seasonable receipt of the notice the person notified does come in and defend.

CHAPTER 2.

NEGOTIATION, TRANSFER, AND INDORSEMENT

3201. (a) "Negotiation" means a transfer of possession, whether voluntary or involuntary, of an instrument by a person other than the issuer to a person who thereby becomes its holder.

(b) Except for negotiation by a remitter, if an instrument is payable to an identified person, negotiation requires transfer of possession of the instrument and its indorsement by the holder. If an instrument is payable to bearer, it may be negotiated by transfer of possession alone.

3202. (a) Negotiation is effective even if obtained (1) from an infant, a corporation exceeding its powers, or a person without capacity, (2) by fraud, duress, or mistake, or (3) in breach of duty or as part of an illegal transaction.

(b) To the extent permitted by other law, negotiation may be rescinded or may be subject to other remedies, but those remedies may not be asserted against a subsequent holder in due course or a person paying the instrument in good faith and without knowledge of facts that are a basis for rescission or other remedy.

3203. (a) An instrument is transferred when it is delivered by a person other than its issuer for the purpose of giving to the person receiving delivery the right to enforce the instrument.

(b) Transfer of an instrument, whether or not the transfer is a negotiation, vests in the transferee any right of the transferor to enforce the instrument, including any right as a holder in due course, but the transferee cannot acquire rights of a holder in due course by a transfer, directly or indirectly, from a holder in due course if the transferee engaged in fraud or illegality affecting the instrument.

(c) Unless otherwise agreed, if an instrument is transferred for value and the transferee does not become a holder because of lack of indorsement by the transferor, the transferee has a specifically enforceable right to the unqualified indorsement of the transferor, but negotiation of the instrument does not occur until the indorsement is made.

(d) If a transferor purports to transfer less than the entire instrument, negotiation of the instrument does not occur. The transferee obtains no rights under this division and has only the rights of a partial assignee.

3204. (a) "Indorsement" means a signature, other than that of a signer as maker, drawer, or acceptor, that alone or accompanied by other words is made on an instrument for the purpose of (1) negotiating the instrument, (2) restricting payment of the instrument, or (3) incurring indorser's liability on the instrument, but regardless of the intent of the signer, a signature and its accompanying words is an indorsement unless the accompanying words, terms of the instrument, place of the signature, or other circumstances unambiguously indicate that the signature was made for a purpose other than indorsement. For the purpose of determining whether a signature is made on an instrument, a paper affixed to the instrument is a part of the instrument.

(b) "Indorser" means a person who makes an indorsement.

(c) For the purpose of determining whether the transferee of an instrument is a holder, an indorsement that transfers a security interest in the instrument is effective as an unqualified indorsement of the instrument.

(d) If an instrument is payable to a holder under a name that is not the name of the holder, indorsement may be made by the holder in the name stated in the instrument or in the holder's name or both, but signature in both names may be required by a person paying or taking the instrument for value or collection.

3205. (a) If an indorsement is made by the holder of an instrument, whether payable to an identified person or payable to bearer, and the indorsement identifies a person to whom it makes the instrument payable, it is a "special indorsement." When specially indorsed, an instrument becomes payable to the identified person and may be negotiated only by the indorsement of that person. The principles stated in Section 3110 apply to special indorsements.

(b) If an indorsement is made by the holder of an instrument and it is not a special indorsement, it is a "blank indorsement." When indorsed in blank, an instrument becomes payable to bearer and may be negotiated by transfer of possession alone until specially indorsed.

(c) The holder may convert a blank indorsement that consists only of a signature into a special indorsement by writing, above the signature of the indorser, words identifying the person to whom the instrument is made payable.

(d) "Anomalous indorsement" means an indorsement made by a person who is not the holder of the instrument. An anomalous indorsement does not affect the manner in which the instrument may be negotiated.

3206. (a) An indorsement limiting payment to a particular person or otherwise prohibiting further transfer or negotiation of the instrument is not effective to prevent further transfer or negotiation of the instrument.

(b) An indorsement stating a condition to the right of the indorsee to receive payment does not affect the right of the indorsee to enforce the instrument. A person paying the instrument or taking it for value or collection may disregard the condition, and the rights and liabilities of that person are not affected by whether the condition has been fulfilled.

(c) If an instrument bears an indorsement (i) described in subdivision (b) of Section 4201, or (ii) in blank or to a particular bank using the words "for deposit," "for collection," or other words indicating a purpose of having the instrument collected by a bank for the indorser or for a particular account, the following rules apply:

(1) A person, other than a bank, who purchases the instrument when so indorsed converts the instrument unless the amount paid for the instrument is received by the indorser or applied consistently with the indorsement.

(2) A depositary bank that purchases the instrument or takes it for collection when so indorsed converts the instrument unless the amount paid by the bank with respect to the instrument is received by the indorser or applied consistently with the indorsement.

(3) A payor bank that is also the depositary bank or that takes the instrument for immediate payment over the counter from a person other than a collecting bank converts the instrument unless the proceeds of the instrument are received by the indorser or applied consistently with the indorsement.

(4) Except as otherwise provided in paragraph (3), a payor bank or intermediary bank may disregard the indorsement and is not liable if the proceeds of the instrument are not received by the indorser or applied consistently with the indorsement.

(d) Except for an indorsement covered by subdivision (c), if an instrument bears an indorsement using words to the effect that payment is to be made to the indorsee as agent, trustee, or other fiduciary for the benefit of the indorser or another person, the following rules apply:

(1) Unless there is notice of breach of fiduciary duty as provided in Section 3307, a person who purchases the instrument from the indorsee or takes the instrument from the

indorsee for collection or payment may pay the proceeds of payment or the value given for the instrument to the indorsee without regard to whether the indorsee violates a fiduciary duty to the indorser.

(2) A subsequent transferee of the instrument or person who pays the instrument is neither given notice nor otherwise affected by the restriction in the indorsement unless the transferee or payor knows that the fiduciary dealt with the instrument or its proceeds in breach of fiduciary duty.

(e) The presence on an instrument of an indorsement to which this section applies does not prevent a purchaser of the instrument from becoming a holder in due course of the instrument unless the purchaser is a converter under subdivision (c) or has notice or knowledge of breach of fiduciary duty as stated in subdivision (d).

(f) In an action to enforce the obligation of a party to pay the instrument, the obligor has a defense if payment would violate an indorsement to which this section applies and the payment is not permitted by this section.

3207. Reacquisition of an instrument occurs if it is transferred to a former holder, by negotiation or otherwise. A former holder who reacquires the instrument may cancel indorsements made after the reacquirer first became a holder of the instrument. If the cancellation causes the instrument to be payable to the reacquirer or to bearer, the reacquirer may negotiate the instrument. An indorser whose indorsement is canceled is discharged, and the discharge is effective against any subsequent holder.

CHAPTER 3.

ENFORCEMENT OF INSTRUMENTS

3301. "Person entitled to enforce" an instrument means (a) the holder of the instrument, (b) a nonholder in possession of the instrument who has the rights of a holder, or (c) a person not in possession of the instrument who is entitled to enforce the instrument pursuant to Section 3309 or subdivision (d) of Section 3418. A person may be a person entitled to enforce the instrument even though the person is not the owner of the instrument or is in wrongful possession of the instrument.

3302. (a) Subject to subdivision (c) and subdivision (d) of Section 3106, "holder in due course" means the holder of an instrument if both of the following apply:

(1) The instrument when issued or negotiated to the holder does not bear such apparent evidence of forgery or alteration or is not otherwise so irregular or incomplete as to call into question its authenticity.

(2) The holder took the instrument (A) for value, (B) in good faith, (C) without notice that the instrument is overdue or has been dishonored or that there is an uncured default with respect to payment of another instrument issued as part of the same series, (D) without notice that the instrument contains an unauthorized signature or has been altered, (E) without notice of any claim to the instrument described in Section 3306, and (F) without notice that any party has a defense or claim in recoupment described in subdivision (a) of Section 3305.

(b) Notice of discharge of a party, other than discharge in an insolvency proceeding, is not notice of a defense under subdivision (a), but discharge is effective against a person who became a holder in due course with notice of the discharge. Public filing or recording of a document does not of itself constitute notice of a defense, claim in recoupment, or claim to the instrument.

(c) Except to the extent a transferor or predecessor in interest has rights as a holder in due course, a person does not acquire rights of a holder in due course of an instrument taken (1) by legal process or by purchase in an execution, bankruptcy, or creditor's sale or similar proceeding, (2) by purchase as part of a bulk transaction not in ordinary course of business of the transferor, or (3) as the successor in interest to an estate or other organization.

(d) If, under paragraph (1) of subdivision (a) of Section 3303, the promise of performance that is the consideration for an instrument has been partially performed, the holder may assert rights as a holder in due course of the instrument only to the fraction of the amount payable under the instrument equal to the value of the partial performance divided by the value of the promised performance.

(e) If (1) the person entitled to enforce an instrument has only a security interest in the instrument and (2) the person obliged to pay the instrument has a defense, claim in recoupment, or claim to the instrument that may be asserted against the person who granted the security interest, the person entitled to enforce the instrument may assert rights as a holder in due course only to an amount payable under the instrument which, at the time of enforcement of the instrument, does not exceed the amount of the unpaid obligation secured.

(f) To be effective, notice shall be received at a time and in a manner that gives a reasonable opportunity to act on it.

(g) This section is subject to any law limiting status as a holder in due course in particular classes of transactions.

3303. (a) An instrument is issued or transferred for value if any of the following apply:

(1) The instrument is issued or transferred for a promise of performance, to the extent the promise has been performed.

(2) The transferee acquires a security interest or other lien in the instrument other than a lien obtained by judicial proceeding.

(3) The instrument is issued or transferred as payment of, or as security for, an antecedent claim against any person, whether or not the claim is due.

(4) The instrument is issued or transferred in exchange for a negotiable instrument.

(5) The instrument is issued or transferred in exchange for the incurring of an irrevocable obligation to a third party by the person taking the instrument.

(b) "Consideration" means any consideration sufficient to support a simple contract. The drawer or maker of an instrument has a defense if the instrument is issued without consideration. If an instrument is issued for a promise of performance, the issuer has a defense to the extent performance of the promise is due and the promise has not been performed. If an instrument is issued for value as stated in subdivision (a), the instrument is also issued for consideration.

3304. (a) An instrument payable on demand becomes overdue at the earliest of the following times:

(1) On the day after the day demand for payment is duly made.

(2) If the instrument is a check, 90 days after its date.

(3) If the instrument is not a check, when the instrument has been outstanding for a period of time after its date which is unreasonably long under the circumstances of the particular case in light of the nature of the instrument and usage of the trade.

(b) With respect to an instrument payable at a definite time the following rules apply:

(1) If the principal is payable in installments and a due date has not been accelerated, the instrument becomes overdue upon default under the instrument for nonpayment of an installment, and the instrument remains overdue until the default is cured.

(2) If the principal is not payable in installments and the due date has not been accelerated, the instrument becomes overdue on the day after the due date.

(3) If a due date with respect to principal has been accelerated, the instrument becomes overdue on the day after the accelerated due date.

(c) Unless the due date of principal has been accelerated, an instrument does not become overdue if there is default in payment of interest but no default in payment of principal.

3305. (a) Except as stated in subdivision (b), the right to enforce the obligation of a party to pay an instrument is subject to all of the following:

(1) A defense of the obligor based on (A) infancy of the obligor to the extent it is a defense to a simple contract, (B) duress, lack of legal capacity, or illegality of the transaction which, under other law, nullifies the obligation of the obligor, (C) fraud that induced

the obligor to sign the instrument with neither knowledge nor reasonable opportunity to learn of its character or its essential terms, or (D) discharge of the obligor in insolvency proceedings.

(2) A defense of the obligor stated in another section of this division or a defense of the obligor that would be available if the person entitled to enforce the instrument were enforcing a right to payment under a simple contract.

(3) A claim in recoupment of the obligor against the original payee of the instrument if the claim arose from the transaction that gave rise to the instrument; but the claim of the obligor may be asserted against a transferee of the instrument only to reduce the amount owing on the instrument at the time the action is brought.

(b) The right of a holder in due course to enforce the obligation of a party to pay the instrument is subject to defenses of the obligor stated in paragraph (1) of subdivision (a), but is not subject to defenses of the obligor stated in paragraph (2) of subdivision (a) or claims in recoupment stated in paragraph (3) of subdivision (a) against a person other than the holder.

(c) Except as stated in subdivision (d), in an action to enforce the obligation of a party to pay the instrument, the obligor may not assert against the person entitled to enforce the instrument a defense, claim in recoupment, or claim to the instrument (Section 3306) of another person, but the other person's claim to the instrument may be asserted by the obligor if the other person is joined in the action and personally asserts the claim against the person entitled to enforce the instrument. An obligor is not obliged to pay the instrument if the person seeking enforcement of the instrument does not have rights of a holder in due course and the obligor proves that the instrument is a lost or stolen instrument.

(d) In an action to enforce the obligation of an accommodation party to pay an instrument, the accommodation party may assert against the person entitled to enforce the instrument any defense or claim in recoupment under subdivision (a) that the accommodated party could assert against the person entitled to enforce the instrument, except the defenses of discharge in insolvency proceedings, infancy, and lack of legal capacity.

3306. A person taking an instrument, other than a person having rights of a holder in due course, is subject to a claim of a property or possessory right in the instrument or its proceeds, including a claim to rescind a negotiation and to recover the instrument or its proceeds. A person having rights of a holder in due course takes free of the claim to the instrument.

3307. (a) In this section:

(1) "Fiduciary" means an agent, trustee, partner, corporate officer or director, limited liability company manager, or other representative owing a fiduciary duty with respect to an instrument.

(2) "Represented person" means the principal, beneficiary, partnership, corporation, limited liability company, or other person to whom the duty stated in paragraph (1) is owed.

(b) If (i) an instrument is taken from a fiduciary for payment or collection or for value, (ii) the taker has knowledge of the fiduciary status of the fiduciary, and (iii) the represented person makes a claim to the instrument or its proceeds on the basis that the transaction of the fiduciary is a breach of fiduciary duty, the following rules apply:

(1) Notice of breach of fiduciary duty by the fiduciary is notice of the claim of the represented person.

(2) In the case of an instrument payable to the represented person or the fiduciary as such, the taker has notice of the breach of fiduciary duty if the instrument is (A) taken in payment of or as security for a debt known by the taker to be the personal debt of the fiduciary, (B) taken in a transaction known by the taker to be for the personal benefit of the fiduciary, or (C) deposited to an account other than an account of the fiduciary, as such, or an account of the represented person.

(3) If an instrument is issued by the represented person or the fiduciary as such, and made payable to the fiduciary personally, the taker does not have notice of the breach of fiduciary duty unless the taker knows of the breach of fiduciary duty.

(4) If an instrument is issued by the represented person or the fiduciary as such, to the taker as payee, the taker has notice of the breach of fiduciary duty if the instrument is (A) taken in payment of or as security for a debt known by the taker to be the personal debt of the fiduciary, (B) taken in a transaction known by the taker to be for the personal benefit of the fiduciary, or (C) deposited to an account other than an account of the fiduciary, as such, or an account of the represented person.

3308. (a) In an action with respect to an instrument, the authenticity of, and authority to make, each signature on the instrument is admitted unless specifically denied in the pleadings. If the validity of a signature is denied in the pleadings, the burden of establishing validity is on the person claiming validity, but the signature is presumed to be authentic and authorized unless the action is to enforce the liability of the purported signer and the signer is dead or incompetent at the time of trial of the issue of validity of the signature. If an action to enforce the instrument is brought against a person as the undisclosed principal of a person who signed the instrument as a party to the instrument, the plaintiff has the burden of establishing that the defendant is liable on the instrument as a represented person under subdivision (a) of Section 3402.

(b) If the validity of signatures is admitted or proved and there is compliance with subdivision (a), a plaintiff producing the instrument is entitled to payment if the plaintiff proves entitlement to enforce the instrument under Section 3301, unless the defendant proves a defense or claim in recoupment. If a defense or claim in recoupment is proved, the right to payment of the plaintiff is subject to the defense or claim, except to the extent the plaintiff proves that the plaintiff has rights of a holder in due course which are not subject to the defense or claim.

3309. (a) A person not in possession of an instrument is entitled to enforce the instrument if (1) the person was in possession of the instrument and entitled to enforce it when loss of possession occurred, (2) the loss of possession was not the result of a transfer by the person or a lawful seizure, and (3) the person cannot reasonably obtain possession of the instrument because the instrument was destroyed, its whereabouts cannot be determined, or it is in the wrongful possession of an unknown person or a person that cannot be found or is not amenable to service of process.

(b) A person seeking enforcement of an instrument under subdivision (a) shall prove the terms of the instrument and the person's right to enforce the instrument. If that proof is made, Section 3308 applies to the case as if the person seeking enforcement had produced the instrument. The court may not enter judgment in favor of the person seeking enforcement unless it finds that the person required to pay the instrument is adequately protected against loss that might occur by reason of a claim by another person to enforce the instrument. Adequate protection may be provided by any reasonable means.

3310. (a) Unless otherwise agreed, if a certified check, cashier's check, or teller's check is taken for an obligation, the obligation is discharged to the same extent discharge would result if an amount of money equal to the amount of the instrument were taken in payment of the obligation. Discharge of the obligation does not affect any liability that the obligor may have as an indorser of the instrument.

(b) Unless otherwise agreed and except as provided in subdivision (a), if a note or an uncertified check is taken for an obligation, the obligation is suspended to the same extent the obligation would be discharged if an amount of money equal to the amount of the instrument were taken, and the following rules apply:

(1) In the case of an uncertified check, suspension of the obligation continues until dishonor of the check or until it is paid or certified. Payment or certification of the check results in discharge of the obligation to the extent of the amount of the check.

(2) In the case of a note, suspension of the obligation continues until dishonor of the note or until it is paid. Payment of the note results in discharge of the obligation to the extent of the payment.

(3) Except as provided in paragraph (4), if the check or note is dishonored and the obligee of the obligation for which the instrument was taken is the person entitled to enforce

the instrument, the obligee may enforce either the instrument or the obligation. In the case of an instrument of a third person which is negotiated to the obligee by the obligor, discharge of the obligor on the instrument also discharges the obligation.

(4) If the person entitled to enforce the instrument taken for an obligation is a person other than the obligee, the obligee may not enforce the obligation to the extent the obligation is suspended. If the obligee is the person entitled to enforce the instrument but no longer has possession of it because it was lost, stolen, or destroyed, the obligation may not be enforced to the extent of the amount payable on the instrument, and to that extent the obligee's rights against the obligor are limited to enforcement of the instrument.

(c) If an instrument other than one described in subdivision (a) or (b) is taken for an obligation, the effect is (1) that stated in subdivision (a) if the instrument is one on which a bank is liable as maker or acceptor, or (2) that stated in subdivision (b) in any other case.

3311. (a) If a person against whom a claim is asserted proves that (1) that person in good faith tendered an instrument to the claimant as full satisfaction of the claim, (2) the amount of the claim was unliquidated or subject to a bona fide dispute, and (3) the claimant obtained payment of the instrument, the following subdivisions apply.

(b) Unless subdivision (c) applies, the claim is discharged if the person against whom the claim is asserted proves that the instrument or an accompanying written communication contained a conspicuous statement to the effect that the instrument was tendered as full satisfaction of the claim.

(c) Subject to subdivision (d), a claim is not discharged under subdivision (b) if either of the following applies:

(1) The claimant, if an organization, proves that (A) within a reasonable time before the tender, the claimant sent a conspicuous statement to the person against whom the claim is asserted that communications concerning disputed debts, including an instrument tendered as full satisfaction of a debt, are to be sent to a designated person, office, or place, and (B) the instrument or accompanying communication was not received by that designated person, office, or place.

(2) The claimant, whether or not an organization, proves that within 90 days after payment of the instrument, the claimant tendered repayment of the amount of the instrument to the person against whom the claim is asserted. This paragraph does not apply if the claimant is an organization that sent a statement complying with subparagraph (A) of paragraph (1).

(d) A claim is discharged if the person against whom the claim is asserted proves that within a reasonable time before collection of the instrument was initiated, the claimant, or an agent of the claimant having direct responsibility with respect to the disputed obligation, knew that the instrument was tendered in full satisfaction of the claim.

3312. (a) In this section:

(1) "Check" means a cashier's check, teller's check, or certified check.

(2) "Claimant" means a person who claims the right to receive the amount of a cashier's check, teller's check, or certified check that was lost, destroyed, or stolen.

(3) "Declaration of loss" means a written statement, made under penalty of perjury, to the effect that (i) the declarer lost possession of a check, (ii) the declarer is the drawer or payee of the check, in the case of a certified check, or the remitter or payee of the check, in the case of a cashier's check or teller's check, (iii) the loss of possession was not the result of a transfer by the declarer or a lawful seizure, and (iv) the declarer cannot reasonably obtain possession of the check because the check was destroyed, its whereabouts cannot be determined, or it is in the wrongful possession of an unknown person or a person that cannot be found or is not amenable to service of process.

(4) "Obligated bank" means the issuer of a cashier's check or teller's check or the acceptor of a certified check.

(b) A claimant may assert a claim to the amount of a check by a communication to the obligated bank describing the check with reasonable certainty and requesting payment of the amount of the check, if (i) the claimant is the drawer or payee of a certified check or the remitter or payee of a cashier's check or teller's check, (ii) the communication contains or is accompanied by a declaration of loss of the claimant with respect to the check, (iii) the communication is received at a time and in a manner affording the bank a reasonable time to act on it before the check is paid, and (iv) the claimant provides reasonable identification if requested by the obligated bank. Delivery of a declaration of loss is a warranty of the truth of the statements made in the declaration. The warranty is made to the obligated bank and any person entitled to enforce the check. If a claim is asserted in compliance with this subdivision, the following rules apply:

(1) The claim becomes enforceable at the later of (i) the time the claim is asserted, or (ii) the 90th day following the date of the check, in the case of a cashier's check or teller's check, or the 90th day following the date of the acceptance, in the case of a certified check.

(2) Until the claim becomes enforceable, it has no legal effect and the obligated bank may pay the check or, in the case of a teller's check, may permit the drawee to pay the check. Payment to a person entitled to enforce the check discharges all liability of the obligated bank with respect to the check.

(3) If the claim becomes enforceable before the check is presented for payment, the obligated bank is not obliged to pay the check.

(4) When the claim becomes enforceable, the obligated bank becomes obliged to pay the amount of the check to the claimant if payment of the check has not been made to a person entitled to enforce the check. Subject to paragraph (1) of subdivision (a) of Section 4302, payment to the claimant discharges all liability of the obligated bank with respect to the check.

(c) If the obligated bank pays the amount of a check to a claimant under paragraph (4) of subdivision (b) and, after the claim became enforceable, the check is presented for payment by a person having rights of a holder in due course, the claimant is obliged to (i) refund the payment to the obligated bank if the check is paid, or (ii) pay the amount of the check to the person having rights of a holder in due course if the check is dishonored.

(d) If a claimant has the right to assert a claim under subdivision (b) and is also a person entitled to enforce a cashier's check, teller's check, or certified check which is lost, destroyed, or stolen, the claimant may assert rights with respect to the check either under this section or Section 3309.

CHAPTER 4.

LIABILITY OF PARTIES

3401. (a) A person is not liable on an instrument unless (1) the person signed the instrument, or (2) the person is represented by an agent or representative who signed the instrument and the signature is binding on the represented person under Section 3402.

(b) A signature may be made (1) manually or by means of a device or machine, and (2) by the use of any name, including a trade or assumed name, or by a word, mark, or symbol executed or adopted by a person with present intention to authenticate a writing.

3402. (a) If a person acting, or purporting to act, as a representative signs an instrument by signing either the name of the represented person or the name of the signer, the represented person is bound by the signature to the same extent the represented person would be bound if the signature were on a simple contract. If the represented person is bound, the signature of the representative is the "authorized signature of the represented person" and the represented person is liable on the instrument, whether or not identified in the instrument.

(b) If a representative signs the name of the representative to an instrument and the signature is an authorized signature of the represented person, the following rules apply:

(1) If the form of the signature shows unambiguously that the signature is made on behalf of the represented person who is identified in the instrument, the representative is not liable on the instrument.

(2) Subject to subdivision (c), if (A) the form of the signature does not show unambiguously that the signature is made in a representative capacity or (B) the represented person

is not identified in the instrument, the representative is liable on the instrument to a holder in due course that took the instrument without notice that the representative was not intended to be liable on the instrument. With respect to any other person, the representative is liable on the instrument unless the representative proves that the original parties did not intend the representative to be liable on the instrument.

(c) If a representative signs the name of the representative as drawer of a check without indication of the representative status and the check is payable from an account of the represented person who is identified on the check, the signer is not liable on the check if the signature is an authorized signature of the represented person.

3403. (a) Unless otherwise provided in this division or Division 4 (commencing with Section 4101), an unauthorized signature is ineffective except as the signature of the unauthorized signer in favor of a person who in good faith pays the instrument or takes it for value. An unauthorized signature may be ratified for all purposes of this division.

(b) If the signature of more than one person is required to constitute the authorized signature of an organization, the signature of the organization is unauthorized if one of the required signatures is lacking.

(c) The civil or criminal liability of a person who makes an unauthorized signature is not affected by any provision of this division which makes the unauthorized signature effective for the purposes of this division.

3404. (a) If an impostor, by use of the mails or otherwise, induces the issuer of an instrument to issue the instrument to the impostor, or to a person acting in concert with the impostor, by impersonating the payee of the instrument or a person authorized to act for the payee, an indorsement of the instrument by any person in the name of the payee is effective as the indorsement of the payee in favor of a person who, in good faith, pays the instrument or takes it for value or for collection.

(b) If (i) a person whose intent determines to whom an instrument is payable (subdivision (a) or (b) of Section 3110) does not intend the person identified as payee to have any interest in the instrument, or (ii) the person identified as payee of an instrument is a fictitious person, the following rules apply until the instrument is negotiated by special indorsement:

(1) Any person in possession of the instrument is its holder.

(2) An indorsement by any person in the name of the payee stated in the instrument is effective as the indorsement of the payee in favor of a person who, in good faith, pays the instrument or takes it for value or for collection.

(c) Under subdivision (a) or (b), an indorsement is made in the name of a payee if (1) it is made in a name substantially similar to that of the payee or (2) the instrument, whether or not indorsed, is deposited in a depositary bank to an account in a name substantially similar to that of the payee.

(d) With respect to an instrument to which subdivision (a) or (b) applies, if a person paying the instrument or taking it for value or for collection fails to exercise ordinary care in paying or taking the instrument and that failure contributes to loss resulting from payment of the instrument, the person bearing the loss may recover from the person failing to exercise ordinary care to the extent the failure to exercise ordinary care contributed to the loss.

3405. (a) In this section:

(1) "Employee" includes an independent contractor and employee of an independent contractor retained by the employer.

(2) "Fraudulent indorsement" means (A) in the case of an instrument payable to the employer, a forged indorsement purporting to be that of the employer, or (B) in the case of an instrument with respect to which the employer is the issuer, a forged indorsement purporting to be that of the person identified as payee.

(3) "Responsibility" with respect to instruments means authority (A) to sign or indorse instruments on behalf of the employer, (B) to process instruments received by the

employer for bookkeeping purposes, for deposit to an account, or for other disposition, (C) to prepare or process instruments for issue in the name of the employer, (D) to supply information determining the names or addresses of payees of instruments to be issued in the name of the employer, (E) to control the disposition of instruments to be issued in the name of the employer, or (F) to act otherwise with respect to instruments in a responsible capacity. "Responsibility" does not include authority that merely allows an employee to have access to instruments or blank or incomplete instrument forms that are being stored or transported or are part of incoming or outgoing mail, or similar access.

(b) For the purpose of determining the rights and liabilities of a person who, in good faith, pays an instrument or takes it for value or for collection, if an employer entrusted an employee with responsibility with respect to the instrument and the employee or a person acting in concert with the employee makes a fraudulent indorsement of the instrument, the indorsement is effective as the indorsement of the person to whom the instrument is payable if it is made in the name of that person. If the person paying the instrument or taking it for value or for collection fails to exercise ordinary care in paying or taking the instrument and that failure contributes to loss resulting from the fraud, the person bearing the loss may recover from the person failing to exercise ordinary care to the extent the failure to exercise ordinary care contributed to the loss.

(c) Under subdivision (b), an indorsement is made in the name of the person to whom an instrument is payable if (1) it is made in a name substantially similar to the name of that person or (2) the instrument, whether or not indorsed, is deposited in a depositary bank to an account in a name substantially similar to the name of that person.

3406. (a) A person whose failure to exercise ordinary care contributes to an alteration of an instrument or to the making of a forged signature on an instrument is precluded from asserting the alteration or the forgery against a person who, in good faith, pays the instrument or takes it for value or for collection.

(b) Under subdivision (a), if the person asserting the preclusion fails to exercise ordinary care in paying or taking the instrument and that failure contributes to loss, the loss is allocated between the person precluded and the person asserting the preclusion according to the extent to which the failure of each to exercise ordinary care contributed to the loss.

(c) Under subdivision (a), the burden of proving failure to exercise ordinary care is on the person asserting the preclusion. Under subdivision (b), the burden of proving failure to exercise ordinary care is on the person precluded.

3407. (a) "Alteration" means (1) an unauthorized change in an instrument that purports to modify in any respect the obligation of a party, or (2) an unauthorized addition of words or numbers or other change to an incomplete instrument relating to the obligation of a party.

(b) Except as provided in subdivision (c), an alteration fraudulently made discharges a party whose obligation is affected by the alteration unless that party assents or is precluded from asserting the alteration. No other alteration discharges a party, and the instrument may be enforced according to its original terms.

(c) A payor bank or drawee paying a fraudulently altered instrument or a person taking it for value, in good faith and without notice of the alteration, may enforce rights with respect to the instrument (1) according to its original terms, or (2) in the case of an incomplete instrument altered by unauthorized completion, according to its terms as completed.

3408. A check or other draft does not of itself operate as an assignment of funds in the hands of the drawee available for its payment, and the drawee is not liable on the instrument until the drawee accepts it.

3409. (a) "Acceptance" means the drawee's signed agreement to pay a draft as presented. It shall be written on the draft and may consist of the drawee's signature alone. Acceptance may be made at any time and becomes effective when notification pursuant to instructions is given or the accepted draft is delivered for the purpose of giving rights on the acceptance to any person.

(b) A draft may be accepted although it has not been signed by the drawer, is otherwise incomplete, is overdue, or has been dishonored.

(c) If a draft is payable at a fixed period after sight and the acceptor fails to date the acceptance, the holder may complete the acceptance by supplying a date in good faith.

(d) "Certified check" means a check accepted by the bank on which it is drawn. Acceptance may be made as stated in subdivision (a) or by a writing on the check which indicates that the check is certified. The drawee of a check has no obligation to certify the check, and refusal to certify is not dishonor of the check.

3410. (a) If the terms of a drawee's acceptance vary from the terms of the draft as presented, the holder may refuse the acceptance and treat the draft as dishonored. In that case, the drawee may cancel the acceptance.

(b) The terms of a draft are not varied by an acceptance to pay at a particular bank or place in the United States, unless the acceptance states that the draft is to be paid only at that bank or place.

(c) If the holder assents to an acceptance varying the terms of a draft, the obligation of each drawer and indorser that does not expressly assent to the acceptance is discharged.

3411. (a) In this section, "obligated bank" means the acceptor of a certified check or the issuer of a cashier's check or teller's check bought from the issuer.

(b) If the obligated bank wrongfully (1) refuses to pay a cashier's check or certified check, (2) stops payment of a teller's check, or (3) refuses to pay a dishonored teller's check, the person asserting the right to enforce the check is entitled to compensation for expenses and loss of interest resulting from the nonpayment and may recover consequential damages if the obligated bank refuses to pay after receiving notice of particular circumstances giving rise to the damages.

(c) Expenses or consequential damages under subdivision (b) are not recoverable if the refusal of the obligated bank to pay occurs because (1) the bank suspends payments, (2) the obligated bank asserts a claim or defense of the bank that it has reasonable grounds to believe is available against the person entitled to enforce the instrument, (3) the obligated bank has a reasonable doubt whether the person demanding payment is the person entitled to enforce the instrument, or (4) payment is prohibited by law.

3412. The issuer of a note or cashier's check or other draft drawn on the drawer is obliged to pay the instrument (a) according to its terms at the time it was issued or, if not issued, at the time it first came into possession of a holder, or (b) if the issuer signed an incomplete instrument, according to its terms when completed, to the extent stated in Sections 3115 and 3407. The obligation is owed to a person entitled to enforce the instrument or to an indorser who paid the instrument under Section 3415.

3413. (a) The acceptor of a draft is obliged to pay the draft (1) according to its terms at the time it was accepted, even though the acceptance states that the draft is payable "as originally drawn" or equivalent terms, (2) if the acceptance varies the terms of the draft, according to the terms of the draft as varied, or (3) if the acceptance is of a draft that is an incomplete instrument, according to its terms when completed, to the extent stated in Sections 3115 and 3407. The obligation is owed to a person entitled to enforce the draft or to the drawer or an indorser who paid the draft under Section 3414 or 3415.

(b) If the certification of a check or other acceptance of a draft states the amount certified or accepted, the obligation of the acceptor is that amount. If (1) the certification or acceptance does not state an amount, (2) the amount of the instrument is subsequently raised, and (3) the instrument is then negotiated to a holder in due course, the obligation of the acceptor is the amount of the instrument at the time it was taken by the holder in due course.

3414. (a) This section does not apply to cashier's checks or other drafts drawn on the drawer.

(b) If an unaccepted draft is dishonored, the drawer is obliged to pay the draft (1) according to its terms at the time it was issued or, if not issued, at the time it first came into possession of a holder, or (2) if the drawer signed an incomplete instrument, according to its terms when completed, to the extent stated in Sections 3115 and 3407. The obligation is owed to a person entitled to enforce the draft or to an indorser who paid the draft under Section 3415.

(c) If a draft is accepted by a bank, the drawer is discharged, regardless of when or by whom acceptance was obtained.

(d) If a draft is accepted and the acceptor is not a bank, the obligation of the drawer to pay the draft if the draft is dishonored by the acceptor is the same as the obligation of an indorser under subdivisions (a) and (c) of Section 3415.

(e) If a draft states that it is drawn "without recourse" or otherwise disclaims liability of the drawer to pay the draft, the drawer is not liable under subdivision (b) to pay the draft if the draft is not a check. A disclaimer of the liability stated in subdivision (b) is not effective if the draft is a check.

(f) If (1) a check is not presented for payment or given to a depositary bank for collection within 30 days after its date, (2) the drawee suspends payments after expiration of the 30-day period without paying the check, and (3) because of the suspension of payments, the drawer is deprived of funds maintained with the drawee to cover payment of the check, the drawer to the extent deprived of funds may discharge its obligation to pay the check by assigning to the person entitled to enforce the check the rights of the drawer against the drawee with respect to the funds.

3415. (a) Subject to subdivisions (b), (c), and (d) and to subdivision (d) of Section 3419, if an instrument is dishonored, an indorser is obliged to pay the amount due on the instrument (1) according to the terms of the instrument at the time it was indorsed, or (2) if the indorser indorsed an incomplete instrument, according to its terms when completed, to the extent stated in Sections 3115 and 3407. The obligation of the indorser is owed to a person entitled to enforce the instrument or to a subsequent indorser who paid the instrument under this section.

(b) If an indorsement states that it is made "without recourse" or otherwise disclaims liability of the indorser, the indorser is not liable under subdivision (a) to pay the instrument.

(c) If notice of dishonor of an instrument is required by Section 3503 and notice of dishonor complying with that section is not given to an indorser, the liability of the indorser under subdivision (a) is discharged.

(d) If a draft is accepted by a bank after an indorsement is made, the liability of the indorser under subdivision (a) is discharged.

(e) If an indorser of a check is liable under subdivision (a) and the check is not presented for payment, or given to a depositary bank for collection, within 30 days after the day the indorsement was made, the liability of the indorser under subdivision (a) is discharged.

3416. (a) A person who transfers an instrument for consideration warrants all of the following to the transferee and, if the transfer is by indorsement, to any subsequent transferee:

(1) The warrantor is a person entitled to enforce the instrument.

(2) All signatures on the instrument are authentic and authorized.

(3) The instrument has not been altered.

(4) The instrument is not subject to a defense or claim in recoupment of any party which can be asserted against the warrantor.

(5) The warrantor has no knowledge of any insolvency proceeding commenced with respect to the maker or acceptor or, in the case of an unaccepted draft, the drawer.

(6) If the instrument is a demand draft, creation of the instrument according to the terms on its face was authorized by the person identified as drawer.

(b) A person to whom the warranties under subdivision (a) are made and who took the instrument in good faith may recover from the warrantor as damages for breach of warranty an amount equal to the loss suffered as a result of the breach, but not more than the amount of the instrument plus expenses and loss of interest incurred as a result of the breach.

(c) The warranties stated in subdivision (a) cannot be disclaimed with respect to checks. Unless notice of a claim for breach of warranty is given to the warrantor within 30 days after the claimant has reason to know of the breach and the identity of the warrantor, the liability of the warrantor under subdivision (b) is discharged to the extent of any loss caused by the delay in giving notice of the claim.

(d) A cause of action for breach of warranty under this section accrues when the claimant has reason to know of the breach.

(e) If the warranty in paragraph (6) of subdivision (a) is not given by a transferor under applicable conflict of law rules, then the warranty is not given to that transferor when that transferor is a transferee.

3417. (a) If an unaccepted draft is presented to the drawee for payment or acceptance and the drawee pays or accepts the draft, (i) the person obtaining payment or acceptance, at the time of presentment, and (ii) a previous transferor of the draft, at the time of transfer, warrant all of the following to the drawee making payment or accepting the draft in good faith:

(1) The warrantor is, or was, at the time the warrantor transferred the draft, a person entitled to enforce the draft or authorized to obtain payment or acceptance of the draft on behalf of a person entitled to enforce the draft.

(2) The draft has not been altered.

(3) The warrantor has no knowledge that the signature of the drawer of the draft is unauthorized.

(4) If the draft is a demand draft, creation of the demand draft according to the terms on its face was authorized by the person identified as drawer.

(b) A drawee making payment may recover from any warrantor damages for breach of warranty equal to the amount paid by the drawee less the amount the drawee received or is entitled to receive from the drawer because of the payment. In addition, the drawee is entitled to compensation for expenses and loss of interest resulting from the breach. The right of the drawee to recover damages under this subdivision is not affected by any failure of the drawee to exercise ordinary care in making payment. If the drawee accepts the draft, breach of warranty is a defense to the obligation of the acceptor. If the acceptor makes payment with respect to the draft, the acceptor is entitled to recover from any warrantor for breach of warranty the amounts stated in this subdivision.

(c) If a drawee asserts a claim for breach of warranty under subdivision (a) based on an unauthorized indorsement of the draft or an alteration of the draft, the warrantor may defend by proving that the indorsement is effective under Section 3404 or 3405 or the drawer is precluded under Section 3406 or 4406 from asserting against the drawee the unauthorized indorsement or alteration.

(d) If (i) a dishonored draft is presented for payment to the drawer or an indorser or (ii) any other instrument is presented for payment to a party obliged to pay the instrument, and (iii) payment is received, the following rules apply:

(1) The person obtaining payment and a prior transferor of the instrument warrant to the person making payment in good faith that the warrantor is, or was, at the time the warrantor transferred the instrument, a person entitled to enforce the instrument or authorized to obtain payment on behalf of a person entitled to enforce the instrument.

(2) The person making payment may recover from any warrantor for breach of warranty an amount equal to the amount paid plus expenses and loss of interest resulting from the breach.

(e) The warranties stated in subdivisions (a) and (d) cannot be disclaimed with respect to checks. Unless notice of a claim for breach of warranty is given to the warrantor within 30 days after the claimant has reason to know of the breach and the identity of the warrantor, the liability of the warrantor under subdivision (b) or (d) is discharged to the extent of any loss caused by the delay in giving notice of the claim.

(f) A cause of action for breach of warranty under this section accrues when the claimant has reason to know of the breach.

(g) A demand draft is a check, as provided in subdivision (f) of Section 3104.

(h) If the warranty in paragraph (4) of subdivision (a) is not given by a transferor under applicable conflict of law rules, then the warranty is not given to that transferor when that transferor is a transferee.

3418. (a) Except as provided in subdivision (c), if the drawee of a draft pays or accepts the draft and the drawee acted on the mistaken belief that (1) payment of the draft had not been stopped pursuant to Section 4403 or (2) the signature of the drawer of the draft was authorized, the drawee may recover the amount of the draft from the person to whom or for whose benefit payment was made or, in the case of acceptance, may revoke the acceptance. Rights of the drawee under this subdivision are not affected by failure of the drawee to exercise ordinary care in paying or accepting the draft.

(b) Except as provided in subdivision (c), if an instrument has been paid or accepted by mistake and the case is not covered by subdivision (a), the person paying or accepting may, to the extent permitted by the law governing mistake and restitution, (1) recover the payment from the person to whom or for whose benefit payment was made or (2) in the case of acceptance, may revoke the acceptance.

(c) The remedies provided by subdivision (a) or (b) may not be asserted against a person who took the instrument in good faith and for value or who in good faith changed position in reliance on the payment or acceptance. This subdivision does not limit remedies provided by Section 3417 or 4407.

(d) Notwithstanding Section 4215, if an instrument is paid or accepted by mistake and the payor or acceptor recovers payment or revokes acceptance under subdivision (a) or (b), the instrument is deemed not to have been paid or accepted and is treated as dishonored, and the person from whom payment is recovered has rights as a person entitled to enforce the dishonored instrument.

3419. (a) If an instrument is issued for value given for the benefit of a party to the instrument ("accommodated party") and another party to the instrument ("accommodation party") signs the instrument for the purpose of incurring liability on the instrument without being a direct beneficiary of the value given for the instrument, the instrument is signed by the accommodation party "for accommodation."

(b) An accommodation party may sign the instrument as maker, drawer, acceptor, or indorser and, subject to subdivision (d), is obliged to pay the instrument in the capacity in which the accommodation party signs. The obligation of an accommodation party may be enforced notwithstanding any statute of frauds and whether or not the accommodation party receives consideration for the accommodation.

(c) A person signing an instrument is presumed to be an accommodation party and there is notice that the instrument is signed for accommodation if the signature is an anomalous indorsement or is accompanied by words indicating that the signer is acting as surety or guarantor with respect to the obligation of another party to the instrument. Except as provided in Section 3605, the obligation of an accommodation party to pay the instrument is not affected by the fact that the person enforcing the obligation had notice when the instrument was taken by that person that the accommodation party signed the instrument for accommodation.

(d) If the signature of a party to an instrument is accompanied by words indicating unambiguously that the party is guaranteeing collection rather than payment of the obligation of another party to the instrument, the signer is obliged to pay the amount due on the instrument to a person entitled to enforce the instrument only if (1) execution of judgment against the other party has been returned unsatisfied, (2) the other party is insolvent or in an insolvency proceeding, (3) the other party cannot be served with process, or (4) it is otherwise apparent that payment cannot be obtained from the other party.

(e) An accommodation party who pays the instrument is entitled to reimbursement from the accommodated party and is entitled to enforce the instrument against the accommodated party. An accommodated party who pays the instrument has no right of recourse against, and is not entitled to contribution from, an accommodation party.

3420. (a) The law applicable to conversion of personal property applies to instruments. An instrument is also converted if it is taken by transfer, other than a negotiation, from a person not entitled to enforce the instrument or a bank makes or obtains payment with respect to the instrument for a person not entitled to enforce the instrument or receive payment. An action for conversion of an instrument may not be brought by (1) the issuer or acceptor of the instrument or (2) a payee or indorsee who did not receive delivery of the instrument either directly or through delivery to an agent or a copayee.

(b) In an action under subdivision (a), the measure of liability is presumed to be the amount payable on the instrument, but recovery may not exceed the amount of the plaintiff's interest in the instrument.

(c) A representative, other than a depositary bank, who has in good faith dealt with an instrument or its proceeds on behalf of one who was not the person entitled to enforce the instrument is not liable in conversion to that person beyond the amount of any proceeds that it has not paid out.

CHAPTER 5.

DISHONOR

3501. (a) "Presentment" means a demand made by or on behalf of a person entitled to enforce an instrument (1) to pay the instrument made to the drawee or a party obliged to pay the instrument or, in the case of a note or accepted draft payable at a bank, to the bank, or (2) to accept a draft made to the drawee.

(b) The following rules are subject to Division 4 (commencing with Section 4101), agreement of the parties, and clearinghouse rules and the like:

(1) Presentment may be made at the place of payment of the instrument and shall be made at the place of payment if the instrument is payable at a bank in the United States; may be made by any commercially reasonable means, including an oral, written, or electronic communication; is effective when the demand for payment or acceptance is received by the person to whom presentment is made; and is effective if made to any one of two or more makers, acceptors, drawees, or other payors.

(2) Upon demand of the person to whom presentment is made, the person making presentment shall (A) exhibit the instrument, (B) give reasonable identification and, if presentment is made on behalf of another person, reasonable evidence of authority to do so, and (C) sign a receipt on the instrument for any payment made or surrender the instrument if full payment is made.

(3) Without dishonoring the instrument, the party to whom presentment is made may (A) return the instrument for lack of a necessary indorsement, or (B) refuse payment or acceptance for failure of the presentment to comply with the terms of the instrument, an agreement of the parties, or other applicable law or rule.

(4) The party to whom presentment is made may treat presentment as occurring on the next business day after the day of presentment if the party to whom presentment is made has established a cutoff hour not earlier than 2 p.m. for the receipt and processing of instruments presented for payment or acceptance and presentment is made after the cutoff hour.

3502. (a) Dishonor of a note is governed by the following rules:

(1) If the note is payable on demand, the note is dishonored if presentment is duly made to the maker and the note is not paid on the day of presentment.

(2) If the note is not payable on demand and is payable at or through a bank or the terms of the note require presentment, the note is dishonored if presentment is duly made and the note is not paid on the day it becomes payable or the day of presentment, whichever is later.

(3) If the note is not payable on demand and paragraph (2) does not apply, the note is dishonored if it is not paid on the day it becomes payable.

(b) Dishonor of an unaccepted draft other than a documentary draft is governed by the following rules:

(1) If a check is duly presented for payment to the payor bank otherwise than for immediate payment over the counter, the check is dishonored if the payor bank makes timely return of the check or sends timely notice of dishonor or nonpayment under Section 4301 or 4302, or becomes accountable for the amount of the check under Section 4302.

(2) If a draft is payable on demand and paragraph (1) does not apply, the draft is dishonored if presentment for payment is duly made to the drawee and the draft is not paid on the day of presentment.

(3) If a draft is payable on a date stated in the draft, the draft is dishonored if (A) presentment for payment is duly made to the drawee and payment is not made on the day the draft becomes payable or the day of presentment, whichever is later, or (B) presentment for acceptance is duly made before the day the draft becomes payable and the draft is not accepted on the day of presentment.

(4) If a draft is payable on elapse of a period of time after sight or acceptance, the draft is dishonored if presentment for acceptance is duly made and the draft is not accepted on the day of presentment.

(c) Dishonor of an unaccepted documentary draft occurs according to the rules stated in paragraphs (2), (3), and (4) of subdivision (b), except that payment or acceptance may be delayed without dishonor until no later than the close of the third business day of the drawee following the day on which payment or acceptance is required by those paragraphs.

(d) Dishonor of an accepted draft is governed by the following rules:

(1) If the draft is payable on demand, the draft is dishonored if presentment for payment is duly made to the acceptor and the draft is not paid on the day of presentment.

(2) If the draft is not payable on demand, the draft is dishonored if presentment for payment is duly made to the acceptor and payment is not made on the day it becomes payable or the day of presentment, whichever is later.

(e) In any case in which presentment is otherwise required for dishonor under this section and presentment is excused under Section 3504, dishonor occurs without presentment if the instrument is not duly accepted or paid.

(f) If a draft is dishonored because timely acceptance of the draft was not made and the person entitled to demand acceptance consents to a late acceptance, from the time of acceptance the draft is treated as never having been dishonored.

3503. (a) The obligation of an indorser stated in subdivision (a) of Section 3415 and the obligation of a drawer stated in subdivision (d) of Section 3414 may not be enforced unless (1) the indorser or drawer is given notice of dishonor of the instrument complying with this section or (2) notice of dishonor is excused under subdivision (b) of Section 3504.

(b) Notice of dishonor may be given by any person; may be given by any commercially reasonable means, including an oral, written, or electronic communication; and is sufficient if it reasonably identifies the instrument and indicates that the instrument has been dishonored or has not been paid or accepted. Return of an instrument given to a bank for collection is sufficient notice of dishonor.

(c) Subject to subdivision (c) of Section 3504, with respect to an instrument taken for collection by a collecting bank, notice of dishonor shall be given (1) by the bank before midnight of the next banking day following the banking day on which the bank receives notice of dishonor of the instrument, or (2) by any other person within 30 days following the day on which the person receives notice of dishonor. With respect to any other instrument, notice of dishonor shall be given within 30 days following the day on which dishonor occurs.

3504. (a) Presentment for payment or acceptance of an instrument is excused if (1) the person entitled to present the instrument cannot with reasonable diligence make presentment, (2) the maker or acceptor has repudiated an obligation to pay the instrument or is dead or in insolvency proceedings, (3) by the terms of the instrument presentment is not necessary to enforce the obligation of indorsers or the drawer, (4) the drawer or indorser whose obligation is being enforced has waived presentment or otherwise has no reason to expect or right to require that the instrument be paid or accepted, or (5) the drawer instructed the drawee not to pay or accept the draft or the drawee was not obligated to the drawer to pay the draft.

(b) Notice of dishonor is excused if (1) by the terms of the instrument notice of dishonor is not necessary to enforce the obligation of a party to pay the instrument, or (2) the party whose obligation is being enforced waived notice of dishonor. A waiver of presentment is also a waiver of notice of dishonor.

(c) Delay in giving notice of dishonor is excused if the delay was caused by circumstances beyond the control of the person giving the notice and the person giving the notice exercised reasonable diligence after the cause of the delay ceased to operate.

3505. (a) The following are admissible as evidence and create a presumption of dishonor and of any notice of dishonor stated:

(1) A document regular in form as provided in subdivision (b) which purports to be a protest.

(2) A purported stamp or writing of the drawee, payor bank, or presenting bank on or accompanying the instrument stating that acceptance or payment has been refused unless reasons for the refusal are stated and the reasons are not consistent with dishonor.

(3) A book or record of the drawee, payor bank, or collecting bank, kept in the usual course of business that shows dishonor, even if there is no evidence of who made the entry.

(b) A protest is a certificate of dishonor made by a United States consul or vice consul, or a notary public during the course and scope of employment with a financial institution or other person authorized to administer oaths by the laws of any other state, government, or country in the place where dishonor occurs. It may be made upon information satisfactory to that person. The protest shall identify the instrument and certify either that presentment has been made or, if not made, the reason why it was not made, and that the instrument has been dishonored by nonacceptance or nonpayment. The protest may also certify that notice of dishonor has been given to some or all parties.

PART 6. [CHAPTER 6.]
DISCHARGE AND PAYMENT

3601. (a) The obligation of a party to pay the instrument is discharged as stated in this division or by an act or agreement with the party which would discharge an obligation to pay money under a simple contract.

(b) Discharge of the obligation of a party is not effective against a person acquiring rights of a holder in due course of the instrument without notice of the discharge.

3602. (a) Subject to subdivision (b), an instrument is paid to the extent payment is made (1) by or on behalf of a party obliged to pay the instrument, and (2) to a person entitled to enforce the instrument. To the extent of the payment, the obligation of the party obliged to pay the instrument is discharged even though payment is made with knowledge of a claim to the instrument under Section 3306 by another person.

(b) The obligation of a party to pay the instrument is not discharged under subdivision (a) if either of the following applies:

(1) A claim to the instrument under Section 3306 is enforceable against the party receiving payment and (A) payment is made with knowledge by the payor that payment is prohibited by injunction or similar process of a court of competent jurisdiction, or (B) in the case of an instrument other than a cashier's check, teller's check, or certified check, the party making payment accepted, from the person having a claim to the instrument, indemnity against loss resulting from refusal to pay the person entitled to enforce the instrument.

(2) The person making payment knows that the instrument is a stolen instrument and pays a person it knows is in wrongful possession of the instrument.

3603. (a) If tender of payment of an obligation to pay an instrument is made to a person entitled to enforce the instrument, the effect of tender is governed by principles of law applicable to tender of payment under a simple contract.

(b) If tender of payment of an obligation to pay an instrument is made to a person entitled to enforce the instrument and the tender is refused, there is discharge, to the extent of the amount of the tender, of the obligation of an indorser or accommodation party having a right of recourse with respect to the obligation to which the tender relates.

(c) If tender of payment of an amount due on an instrument is made to a person entitled to enforce the instrument, the obligation of the obligor to pay interest after the due date on the amount tendered is discharged. If presentment is required with respect to an instrument and the obligor is able and ready to pay on the due date at every place of payment stated in the instrument, the obligor is deemed to have made tender of payment on the due date to the person entitled to enforce the instrument.

3604. (a) A person entitled to enforce an instrument, with or without consideration, may discharge the obligation of a party to pay the instrument (1) by an intentional voluntary act, such as surrender of the instrument to the party, destruction, mutilation, or cancellation of the instrument, cancellation or striking out of the party's signature, or the addition of words to the instrument indicating discharge, or (2) by agreeing not to sue or otherwise renouncing rights against the party by a signed writing.

(b) Cancellation or striking out of an indorsement pursuant to subdivision (a) does not affect the status and rights of a party derived from the indorsement.

3605. (a) In this section, the term "indorser" includes a drawer having the obligation described in subdivision (d) of Section 3414.

(b) Discharge, under Section 3604, of the obligation of a party to pay an instrument does not discharge the obligation of an indorser or accommodation party having a right of recourse against the discharged party.

(c) If a person entitled to enforce an instrument agrees, with or without consideration, to an extension of the due date of the obligation of a party to pay the instrument, the extension discharges an indorser or accommodation party having a right of recourse against the party whose obligation is extended to the extent the indorser or accommodation party proves that the extension caused loss to the indorser or accommodation party with respect to the right of recourse.

(d) If a person entitled to enforce an instrument agrees, with or without consideration, to a material modification of the obligation of a party other than an extension of the due date, the modification discharges the obligation of an indorser or accommodation party having a right of recourse against the person whose obligation is modified to the extent the modification causes loss to the indorser or accommodation party with respect to the right of recourse. The loss suffered by the indorser or accommodation party as a result of the modification is equal to the amount of the right of recourse unless the person enforcing the instrument proves that no loss was caused by the modification or that the loss caused by the modification was an amount less than the amount of the right of recourse.

(e) If the obligation of a party to pay an instrument is secured by an interest in collateral and a person entitled to enforce the instrument impairs the value of the interest in collateral, the obligation of an indorser or accommodation party having a right of recourse against the obligor is discharged to the extent of the impairment. The value of an interest in collateral is impaired to the extent (1) the value of the interest is reduced to an amount less than the amount of the right of recourse of the party asserting discharge, or (2) the reduction in value of the interest causes an increase in the amount by which the amount of the right of recourse exceeds the value of the interest. The burden of proving impairment is on the party asserting discharge.

(f) If the obligation of a party is secured by an interest in collateral not provided by an accommodation party and a person entitled to enforce the instrument impairs the value of the interest in collateral, the obligation of any party who is jointly and severally liable with respect to the secured obligation is discharged to the extent the impairment causes the party asserting discharge to pay more than that party would have been obliged to pay, taking into account rights of contribution, if impairment had not occurred. If the party asserting discharge is an accommodation party not entitled to discharge under subdivision (e), the party is deemed to have a right to contribution based on joint and several liability rather than a right to reimbursement. The burden of proving impairment is on the party asserting discharge.

(g) Under subdivision (e) or (f), impairing value of an interest in collateral includes (1) failure to obtain or maintain perfection or recordation of the interest in collateral, (2) release of collateral without substitution of collateral of equal value, (3) failure to perform a duty to preserve the value of collateral owed, under Division 9 (commencing with Section 9101) or other law, to a debtor or surety or other person secondarily liable, or (4) failure to comply with applicable law in disposing of collateral.

(h) An accommodation party is not discharged under subdivision (c), (d), or (e) unless the person entitled to enforce the instrument knows of the accommodation or has notice under subdivision (c) of Section 3419 that the instrument was signed for accommodation.

(i) A party is not discharged under this section if (1) the party asserting discharge consents to the event or conduct that is the basis of the discharge, or (2) the instrument or a separate agreement of the party provides for waiver of discharge under this section either specifically or by general language indicating that parties waive defenses based on suretyship or impairment of collateral.

Uniform Commercial Code Article 9 as adopted in the State of Illinois

COMMERCIAL CODE
(810 ILCS 5/) Uniform Commercial Code.
  (810 ILCS 5/Art. 9 heading)
ARTICLE 9
SECURED TRANSACTIONS
  (810 ILCS 5/Art. 9 Pt. 1 heading)
PART 1. GENERAL PROVISIONS

  (810 ILCS 5/Art. 9 Pt. 1 Sub. 1 heading)
SUBPART 1. SHORT TITLE, DEFINITIONS, AND GENERAL CONCEPTS

  (810 ILCS 5/9-101) (from Ch. 26, par. 9-101)
  Sec. 9-101. Short title. This Article may be cited as Uniform Commercial Code - Secured Transactions.
  (Source: P.A. 91-893, eff. 7-1-01.)

  (810 ILCS 5/9-102) (from Ch. 26, par. 9-102)
  Sec. 9-102. Definitions and index of definitions.
  (a) Article 9 definitions. In this Article:
  (1) "Accession" means goods that are physically united with other goods in such a manner that the identity of the original goods is not lost.
  (2) "Account", except as used in "account for", means a right to payment of a monetary obligation, whether or not earned by performance, (i) for property that has been or is to be sold, leased, licensed, assigned, or otherwise disposed of, (ii) for services rendered or to be rendered, (iii) for a policy of insurance issued or to be issued, (iv) for a secondary obligation incurred or to be incurred, (v) for energy provided or to be provided, (vi) for the use or hire of a vessel under a charter or other contract, (vii) arising out of the use of a credit or charge card or information contained on or for use with the card, or (viii) as winnings in a lottery or other game of chance operated or sponsored by a State, governmental unit of a State, or person licensed or authorized to operate the game by a State or governmental unit of a State. The term includes health-care-insurance receivables. The term does not include (i) rights to payment evidenced by chattel paper or an instrument, (ii) commercial tort claims, (iii) deposit accounts, (iv) investment property, (v) letter-of-credit rights or letters of credit, or (vi) rights to payment for money or funds advanced or sold, other than rights arising out of the use of a credit or charge card or information contained on or for use with the card.
  (3) "Account debtor" means a person obligated on an account, chattel paper, or general intangible. The term does not include persons obligated to pay a negotiable instrument, even if the instrument constitutes part of chattel paper.
  (4) "Accounting", except as used in "accounting for", means a record:
  (A) authenticated by a secured party;
  (B) indicating the aggregate unpaid secured obligations as of a date not more than 35 days earlier or 35 days later than the date of the record; and
  (C) identifying the components of the obligations in reasonable detail.
  (5) "Agricultural lien" means an interest, other than a security interest, in farm products:
  (A) which secures payment or performance of an obligation for goods or services furnished in connection with a debtor's farming operation;
  (B) which is created by statute in favor of a person that in the ordinary course of its business furnished goods or services to a debtor in connection with a debtor's farming operation; and
  (C) whose effectiveness does not depend on the person's possession of the personal property.

(6) "As-extracted collateral" means:

(A) oil, gas, or other minerals that are subject to a security interest that:

(i) is created by a debtor having an interest in the minerals before extraction; and

(ii) attaches to the minerals as extracted;

or

(B) accounts arising out of the sale at the wellhead or minehead of oil, gas, or other minerals in which the debtor had an interest before extraction.

(7) "Authenticate" means:

(A) to sign; or

(B) to execute or otherwise adopt a symbol, or encrypt or similarly process a record in whole or in part, with the present intent of the authenticating person to identify the person and adopt or accept a record.

(8) "Bank" means an organization that is engaged in the business of banking. The term includes savings banks, savings and loan associations, credit unions, and trust companies.

(9) "Cash proceeds" means proceeds that are money, checks, deposit accounts, or the like.

(10) "Certificate of title" means a certificate of title with respect to which a statute provides for the security interest in question to be indicated on the certificate as a condition or result of the security interest's obtaining priority over the rights of a lien creditor with respect to the collateral.

(11) "Chattel paper" means a record or records that evidence both a monetary obligation and a security interest in specific goods, a security interest in specific goods and software used in the goods, a security interest in specific goods and license of software used in the goods, a lease of specific goods, or a lease of specified goods and a license of software used in the goods. In this paragraph, "monetary obligation" means a monetary obligation secured by the goods or owed under a lease of the goods and includes a monetary obligation with respect to software used in the goods. The term does not include (i) charters or other contracts involving the use or hire of a vessel or (ii) records that evidence a right to payment arising out of the use of a credit or charge card or information contained on or for use with the card. If a transaction is evidenced by records that include an instrument or series of instruments, the group of records taken together constitutes chattel paper.

(12) "Collateral" means the property subject to a security interest or agricultural lien. The term includes:

(A) proceeds to which a security interest attaches;

(B) accounts, chattel paper, payment intangibles, and promissory notes that have been sold; and

(C) goods that are the subject of a consignment.

(13) "Commercial tort claim" means a claim arising in tort with respect to which:

(A) the claimant is an organization; or

(B) the claimant is an individual and the claim:

(i) arose in the course of the claimant's business or profession; and

(ii) does not include damages arising out of personal injury to or the death of an individual.

(14) "Commodity account" means an account maintained by a commodity intermediary in which a commodity contract is carried for a commodity customer.

(15) "Commodity contract" means a commodity futures contract, an option on a commodity futures contract, a commodity option, or another contract if the contract or option is:

(A) traded on or subject to the rules of a board of trade that has been designated as a contract market for such a contract pursuant to federal commodities laws; or

(B) traded on a foreign commodity board of trade, exchange, or market, and is carried on the books of a commodity intermediary for a commodity customer.

(16) "Commodity customer" means a person for which a commodity intermediary carries a commodity contract on its books.

(17) "Commodity intermediary" means a person that:

(A) is registered as a futures commission merchant under federal commodities law; or

(B) in the ordinary course of its business provides clearance or settlement services for a board of trade that has been designated as a contract market pursuant to federal commodities law.

(18) "Communicate" means:

(A) to send a written or other tangible record;

(B) to transmit a record by any means agreed upon by the persons sending and receiving the record; or

(C) in the case of transmission of a record to or by a filing office, to transmit a record by any means prescribed by filing-office rule.

(19) "Consignee" means a merchant to which goods are delivered in a consignment.

(20) "Consignment" means a transaction, regardless of its form, in which a person delivers goods to a merchant for the purpose of sale and:

(A) the merchant:

(i) deals in goods of that kind under a name other than the name of the person making delivery;

(ii) is not an auctioneer; and

(iii) is not generally known by its creditors to be substantially engaged in selling the goods of others;

(B) with respect to each delivery, the aggregate value of the goods is $1,000 or more at the time of delivery;

(C) the goods are not consumer goods immediately before delivery; and

(D) the transaction does not create a security interest that secures an obligation.

(21) "Consignor" means a person that delivers goods to a consignee in a consignment.

(22) "Consumer debtor" means a debtor in a consumer transaction.

(23) "Consumer goods" means goods that are used or bought for use primarily for personal, family, or household purposes.

(24) "Consumer-goods transaction" means a consumer transaction in which:

(A) an individual incurs an obligation primarily for personal, family, or household purposes; and

(B) a security interest in consumer goods secures the obligation.

(25) "Consumer obligor" means an obligor who is an individual and who incurred the obligation as part of a transaction entered into primarily for personal, family, or household purposes.

(26) "Consumer transaction" means a transaction in which (i) an individual incurs an obligation primarily for personal, family, or household purposes, (ii) a security interest secures the obligation, and (iii) the collateral is held or acquired primarily for personal, family, or household purposes. The term includes consumer-goods transactions.

(27) "Continuation statement" means an amendment of a financing statement which:

(A) identifies, by its file number, the initial financing statement to which it relates; and

(B) indicates that it is a continuation statement for, or that it is filed to continue the effectiveness of, the identified financing statement.

(28) "Debtor" means:

(A) a person having an interest, other than a security interest or other lien, in the collateral, whether or not the person is an obligor;

(B) a seller of accounts, chattel paper, payment intangibles, or promissory notes; or

(C) a consignee.

(29) "Deposit account" means a demand, time, savings, passbook, nonnegotiable certificates of deposit, uncertificated certificates of deposit, nontransferrable certificates of deposit, or similar account maintained with a bank. The term does not include investment property or accounts evidenced by an instrument.

(30) "Document" means a document of title or a receipt of the type described in Section 7-201(b).

(31) "Electronic chattel paper" means chattel paper evidenced by a record or records consisting of information stored in an electronic medium.

(32) "Encumbrance" means a right, other than an ownership interest, in real property. The term includes mortgages and other liens on real property.

(33) "Equipment" means goods other than inventory, farm products, or consumer goods.

(34) "Farm products" means goods, other than standing timber, with respect to which the debtor is engaged in a farming operation and which are:

(A) crops grown, growing, or to be grown, including:

(i) crops produced on trees, vines, and bushes; and

(ii) aquatic goods produced in aquacultural operations;

(B) livestock, born or unborn, including aquatic goods produced in aquacultural operations;

(C) supplies used or produced in a farming operation; or

(D) products of crops or livestock in their unmanufactured states.

(35) "Farming operation" means raising, cultivating, propagating, fattening, grazing, or any other farming, livestock, or aquacultural operation.

(36) "File number" means the number assigned to an initial financing statement pursuant to Section 9-519(a).

(37) "Filing office" means an office designated in Section 9-501 as the place to file a financing statement.

(38) "Filing-office rule" means a rule adopted pursuant to Section 9-526.

(39) "Financing statement" means a record or records composed of an initial financing statement and any filed record relating to the initial financing statement.

(40) "Fixture filing" means the filing of a financing statement covering goods that are or are to become fixtures and satisfying Section 9-502(a) and (b). The term includes the filing of a financing statement covering goods of a transmitting utility which are or are to become fixtures.

(41) "Fixtures" means goods that have become so related to particular real property that an interest in them arises under real property law.

(42) "General intangible" means any personal property, including things in action, other than accounts, chattel paper, commercial tort claims, deposit accounts, documents, goods, instruments, investment property, letter-of-credit rights, letters of credit, money, and oil, gas, or other minerals before extraction. The term includes payment intangibles and software.

(43) "Good faith" means honesty in fact and the observance of reasonable commercial standards of fair dealing.

(44) "Goods" means all things that are movable when a security interest attaches. The term includes (i) fixtures, (ii) standing timber that is to be cut and removed under a conveyance or contract for sale, (iii) the unborn young of animals, (iv) crops grown, growing, or to be grown, even if the crops are produced on trees, vines, or bushes, and (v) manufactured homes. The term also includes a computer program embedded in goods and any supporting information provided in connection with a transaction relating to the program if (i) the program is associated with the goods in such a manner that it customarily is considered part of the goods, or (ii) by becoming the owner of the goods, a person acquires a right to use the program in connection with the goods. The term does not include a computer program embedded in goods that consist solely of the medium in which the program is embedded. The term also does not include accounts, chattel paper, commercial tort claims, deposit accounts, documents, general intangibles, instruments, investment property, letter-of-credit rights, letters of credit, money, or oil, gas, or other minerals before extraction.

(45) "Governmental unit" means a subdivision, agency, department, county, parish, municipality, or other unit of the government of the United States, a State, or a foreign country. The term includes an organization having a separate corporate existence if the organization is eligible to issue debt on which interest is exempt from income taxation under the laws of the United States.

(46) "Health-care-insurance receivable" means an interest in or claim under a policy of insurance which is a right to payment of a monetary obligation for health-care goods or services provided.

(47) "Instrument" means a negotiable instrument or any other writing that evidences a right to the payment of a monetary obligation, is not itself a security agreement or lease, and is of a type that in ordinary course of business is transferred by delivery with any necessary indorsement or assignment. The term does not include (i) investment property, (ii) letters of credit, (iii) nonnegotiable certificates of deposit, (iv) uncertificated certificates of deposit, (v) nontransferrable certificates of deposit, or (vi) writings that evidence a right to payment arising out of the use of a credit or charge card or information contained on or for use with the card.

(48) "Inventory" means goods, other than farm products, which:

(A) are leased by a person as lessor;

(B) are held by a person for sale or lease or to be furnished under a contract of service;

(C) are furnished by a person under a contract of service; or

(D) consist of raw materials, work in process, or materials used or consumed in a business.

(49) "Investment property" means a security, whether certificated or uncertificated, security entitlement, securities account, commodity contract, or commodity account.

(50) "Jurisdiction of organization", with respect to a registered organization, means the jurisdiction under whose law the organization is organized.

(51) "Letter-of-credit right" means a right to payment or performance under a letter of credit, whether or not the beneficiary has demanded or is at the time entitled to demand payment or performance. The term does not include the right of a beneficiary to demand payment or performance under a letter of credit.

(52) "Lien creditor" means:

(A) a creditor that has acquired a lien on the property involved by attachment, levy, or the like;

(B) an assignee for benefit of creditors from the time of assignment;

(C) a trustee in bankruptcy from the date of the filing of the petition; or

(D) a receiver in equity from the time of appointment.

(53) "Manufactured home" means a structure, transportable in one or more sections, which, in the traveling mode, is eight body feet or more in width or 40 body feet or more in length, or, when erected on site, is 320 or more square feet, and which is built on a permanent chassis and designed to be used as a dwelling with or without a permanent foundation when connected to the required utilities, and includes the plumbing, heating, air-conditioning, and electrical systems contained therein. The term includes any structure that meets all of the requirements of this paragraph except the size requirements and with respect to which the manufacturer voluntarily files a certification required by the United States Secretary of Housing and Urban Development and complies with the standards established under Title 42 of the United States Code.

(54) "Manufactured-home transaction" means a secured transaction:

(A) that creates a purchase-money security interest in a manufactured home, other than a manufactured home held as inventory; or

(B) in which a manufactured home, other than a manufactured home held as inventory, is the primary collateral.

(55) "Mortgage" means a consensual interest in real property, including fixtures, which secures payment or performance of an obligation.

(56) "New debtor" means a person that becomes bound as debtor under Section 9-203(d) by a security agreement previously entered into by another person.

(57) "New value" means (i) money, (ii) money's worth in property, services, or new credit, or (iii) release by a transferee of an interest in property previously transferred to the transferee. The term does not include an obligation substituted for another obligation.

(58) "Noncash proceeds" means proceeds other than cash proceeds.

(59) "Obligor" means a person that, with respect to an obligation secured by a security interest in or an agricultural lien on the collateral, (i) owes payment or other performance of the obligation, (ii) has provided property other than the collateral to secure payment or

other performance of the obligation, or (iii) is otherwise accountable in whole or in part for payment or other performance of the obligation. The term does not include issuers or nominated persons under a letter of credit.

(60) "Original debtor", except as used in Section 9-310(c), means a person that, as debtor, entered into a security agreement to which a new debtor has become bound under Section 9-203(d).

(61) "Payment intangible" means a general intangible under which the account debtor's principal obligation is a monetary obligation.

(62) "Person related to", with respect to an individual, means:

(A) the spouse of the individual;

(B) a brother, brother-in-law, sister, or sister-in-law of the individual;

(C) an ancestor or lineal descendant of the individual or the individual's spouse; or

(D) any other relative, by blood or marriage, of the individual or the individual's spouse who shares the same home with the individual.

(63) "Person related to", with respect to an organization, means:

(A) a person directly or indirectly controlling, controlled by, or under common control with the organization;

(B) an officer or director of, or a person performing similar functions with respect to, the organization;

(C) an officer or director of, or a person performing similar functions with respect to, a person described in subparagraph (A);

(D) the spouse of an individual described in subparagraph (A), (B), or (C); or

(E) an individual who is related by blood or marriage to an individual described in subparagraph (A), (B), (C), or (D) and shares the same home with the individual.

(64) "Proceeds", except as used in Section 9-609(b), means the following property:

(A) whatever is acquired upon the sale, lease, license, exchange, or other disposition of collateral;

(B) whatever is collected on, or distributed on account of, collateral;

(C) rights arising out of collateral;

(D) to the extent of the value of collateral, claims arising out of the loss, nonconformity, or interference with the use of, defects or infringement of rights in, or damage to, the collateral; or

(E) to the extent of the value of collateral and to the extent payable to the debtor or the secured party, insurance payable by reason of the loss or nonconformity of, defects or infringement of rights in, or damage to, the collateral.

(65) "Promissory note" means an instrument that evidences a promise to pay a monetary obligation, does not evidence an order to pay, and does not contain an acknowledgment by a bank that the bank has received for deposit a sum of money or funds.

(66) "Proposal" means a record authenticated by a secured party which includes the terms on which the secured party is willing to accept collateral in full or partial satisfaction of the obligation it secures pursuant to Sections 9-620, 9-621, and 9-622.

(67) "Public-finance transaction" means a secured transaction in connection with which:

(A) debt securities are issued;

(B) all or a portion of the securities issued have an initial stated maturity of at least 20 years; and

(C) the debtor, obligor, secured party, account debtor or other person obligated on collateral, assignor or assignee of a secured obligation, or assignor or assignee of a security interest is a State or a governmental unit of a State.

(68) "Pursuant to commitment", with respect to an advance made or other value given by a secured party, means pursuant to the secured party's obligation, whether or not a subsequent event of default or other event not within the secured party's control has relieved or may relieve the secured party from its obligation.

(69) "Record", except as used in "for record", "of record", "record or legal title", and "record owner", means information that is inscribed on a tangible medium or which is stored in an electronic or other medium and is retrievable in perceivable form.

(70) "Registered organization" means an organization organized solely under the law of a single State or the United States and as to which the State or the United States must maintain a public record showing the organization to have been organized.

(71) "Secondary obligor" means an obligor to the extent that:

(A) the obligor's obligation is secondary; or

(B) the obligor has a right of recourse with respect to an obligation secured by collateral against the debtor, another obligor, or property of either.

(72) "Secured party" means:

(A) a person in whose favor a security interest is created or provided for under a security agreement, whether or not any obligation to be secured is outstanding;

(B) a person that holds an agricultural lien;

(C) a consignor;

(D) a person to which accounts, chattel paper, payment intangibles, or promissory notes have been sold;

(E) a trustee, indenture trustee, agent, collateral agent, or other representative in whose favor a security interest or agricultural lien is created or provided for; or

(F) a person that holds a security interest arising under Section 2-401, 2-505, 2-711(3), 2A-508(5), 4-210, or 5-118.

(73) "Security agreement" means an agreement that creates or provides for a security interest.

(74) "Send", in connection with a record or notification, means:

(A) to deposit in the mail, deliver for transmission, or transmit by any other usual means of communication, with postage or cost of transmission provided for, addressed to any address reasonable under the circumstances; or

(B) to cause the record or notification to be received within the time that it would have been received if properly sent under subparagraph (A).

(75) "Software" means a computer program and any supporting information provided in connection with a transaction relating to the program. The term does not include a computer program that is included in the definition of goods.

(76) "State" means a State of the United States, the District of Columbia, Puerto Rico, the United States Virgin Islands, or any territory or insular possession subject to the jurisdiction of the United States.

(77) "Supporting obligation" means a letter-of-credit right or secondary obligation that supports the payment or performance of an account, chattel paper, a document, a general intangible, an instrument, or investment property.

(78) "Tangible chattel paper" means chattel paper evidenced by a record or records consisting of information that is inscribed on a tangible medium.

(79) "Termination statement" means an amendment of a financing statement which:

(A) identifies, by its file number, the initial financing statement to which it relates; and

(B) indicates either that it is a termination statement or that the identified financing statement is no longer effective.

(80) "Transmitting utility" means a person primarily engaged in the business of:

(A) operating a railroad, subway, street railway, or trolley bus;

(B) transmitting communications electrically, electromagnetically, or by light;

(C) transmitting goods by pipeline or sewer; or

(D) transmitting or producing and transmitting electricity, steam, gas, or water.

(b) Definitions in other Articles. "Control" as provided in Section 7-106 and the following definitions in other Articles apply to this Article:

"Applicant"	Section 5-102
"Beneficiary"	Section 5-102
"Broker"	Section 8-102
"Certificated security"	Section 8-102
"Check"	Section 3-104
"Clearing corporation"	Section 8-102
"Contract for sale"	Section 2-106

"Customer"	Section 4-104
"Entitlement holder"	Section 8-102
"Financial asset"	Section 8-102
"Holder in due course"	Section 3-302
"Issuer" (with respect to a letter of credit or letter-of-credit right)	Section 5-102
"Issuer" (with respect to a security)	Section 8-201
"Issuer" (with respect to documents of title)	Section 7-102
"Lease"	Section 2A-103
"Lease agreement"	Section 2A-103
"Lease contract"	Section 2A-103
"Leasehold interest"	Section 2A-103
"Lessee"	Section 2A-103
"Lessee in ordinary course of business"	Section 2A-103
"Lessor"	Section 2A-103
"Lessor's residual interest"	Section 2A-103
"Letter of credit"	Section 5-102
"Merchant"	Section 2-104
"Negotiable instrument"	Section 3-104
"Nominated person"	Section 5-102
"Note"	Section 3-104
"Proceeds of a letter of credit"	Section 5-114
"Prove"	Section 3-103
"Sale"	Section 2-106
"Securities account"	Section 8-501
"Securities intermediary"	Section 8-102
"Security"	Section 8-102
"Security certificate"	Section 8-102
"Security entitlement"	Section 8-102
"Uncertificated security"	Section 8-102

(c) Article 1 definitions and principles. Article 1 contains general definitions and principles of construction and interpretation applicable throughout this Article.
(Source: P.A. 95-895, eff. 1-1-09.)

(810 ILCS 5/9-103) (from Ch. 26, par. 9-103)
Sec. 9-103. Purchase-money security interest; application of payments; burden of establishing.
(a) Definitions. In this Section:
(1) "purchase-money collateral" means goods or software that secures a purchase-money obligation incurred with respect to that collateral; and
(2) "purchase-money obligation" means an obligation of an obligor incurred as all or part of the price of the collateral or for value given to enable the debtor to acquire rights in or the use of the collateral if the value is in fact so used.
(b) Purchase-money security interest in goods. A security interest in goods is a purchase-money security interest:
(1) to the extent that the goods are purchase-money collateral with respect to that security interest;
(2) if the security interest is in inventory that is or was purchase-money collateral, also to the extent that the security interest secures a purchase-money obligation incurred with respect to other inventory in which the secured party holds or held a purchase-money security interest; and

(3) also to the extent that the security interest secures a purchase-money obligation incurred with respect to software in which the secured party holds or held a purchase-money security interest.

(c) Purchase-money security interest in software. A security interest in software is a purchase-money security interest to the extent that the security interest also secures a purchase-money obligation incurred with respect to goods in which the secured party holds or held a purchase-money security interest if:

(1) the debtor acquired its interest in the software in an integrated transaction in which it acquired an interest in the goods; and

(2) the debtor acquired its interest in the software for the principal purpose of using the software in the goods.

(d) Consignor's inventory purchase-money security interest. The security interest of a consignor in goods that are the subject of a consignment is a purchase-money security interest in inventory.

(e) Application of payment in non-consumer-goods transaction. In a transaction other than a consumer-goods transaction, if the extent to which a security interest is a purchase-money security interest depends on the application of a payment to a particular obligation, the payment must be applied:

(1) in accordance with any reasonable method of application to which the parties agree;

(2) in the absence of the parties' agreement to a reasonable method, in accordance with any intention of the obligor manifested at or before the time of payment; or

(3) in the absence of an agreement to a reasonable method and a timely manifestation of the obligor's intention, in the following order:

(A) to obligations that are not secured; and

(B) if more than one obligation is secured, to obligations secured by purchase-money security interests in the order in which those obligations were incurred.

(f) No loss of status of purchase-money security interest in non-consumer-goods transaction. In a transaction other than a consumer-goods transaction, a purchase-money security interest does not lose its status as such, even if:

(1) the purchase-money collateral also secures an obligation that is not a purchase-money obligation;

(2) collateral that is not purchase-money collateral also secures the purchase-money obligation; or

(3) the purchase-money obligation has been renewed, refinanced, consolidated, or restructured.

(g) Burden of proof in non-consumer-goods transaction. In a transaction other than a consumer-goods transaction, a secured party claiming a purchase-money security interest has the burden of establishing the extent to which the security interest is a purchase-money security interest.

(h) Non-consumer-goods transactions; no inference. The limitation of the rules in subsections (e), (f), and (g) to transactions other than consumer-goods transactions is intended to leave to the court the determination of the proper rules in consumer-goods transactions. The court may not infer from that limitation the nature of the proper rule in consumer-goods transactions and may continue to apply established approaches.

(Source: P.A. 91-893, eff. 7-1-01.)

(810 ILCS 5/9-104) (from Ch. 26, par. 9-104)

Sec. 9-104. Control of deposit account.

(a) Requirements for control. A secured party has control of a deposit account if:

(1) the secured party is the bank with which the deposit account is maintained;

(2) the debtor, secured party, and bank have agreed in an authenticated record that the bank will comply with instructions originated by the secured party directing disposition of the funds in the deposit account without further consent by the debtor; or

(3) the secured party becomes the bank's customer with respect to the deposit account.

(b) Debtor's right to direct disposition. A secured party that has satisfied subsection (a) has control, even if the debtor retains the right to direct the disposition of funds from the deposit account.
(Source: P.A. 91-893, eff. 7-1-01.)

(810 ILCS 5/9-105) (from Ch. 26, par. 9-105)
Sec. 9-105. Control of electronic chattel paper. A secured party has control of electronic chattel paper if the record or records comprising the chattel paper are created, stored, and assigned in such a manner that:
(1) a single authoritative copy of the record or records exists which is unique, identifiable and, except as otherwise provided in paragraphs (4), (5), and (6), unalterable;
(2) the authoritative copy identifies the secured party as the assignee of the record or records;
(3) the authoritative copy is communicated to and maintained by the secured party or its designated custodian;
(4) copies or revisions that add or change an identified assignee of the authoritative copy can be made only with the participation of the secured party;
(5) each copy of the authoritative copy and any copy of a copy is readily identifiable as a copy that is not the authoritative copy; and
(6) any revision of the authoritative copy is readily identifiable as an authorized or unauthorized revision.
(Source: P.A. 90-665, eff. 7-30-98; 91-893, eff. 7-1-01.)

(810 ILCS 5/9-106) (from Ch. 26, par. 9-106)
Sec. 9-106. Control of investment property.
(a) Control under Section 8-106. A person has control of a certificated security, uncertificated security, or security entitlement as provided in Section 8-106.
(b) Control of commodity contract. A secured party has control of a commodity contract if:
(1) the secured party is the commodity intermediary with which the commodity contract is carried; or
(2) the commodity customer, secured party, and commodity intermediary have agreed that the commodity intermediary will apply any value distributed on account of the commodity contract as directed by the secured party without further consent by the commodity customer.
(c) Effect of control of securities account or commodity account. A secured party having control of all security entitlements or commodity contracts carried in a securities account or commodity account has control over the securities account or commodity account.
(Source: P.A. 90-665, eff. 7-30-98; 91-893, eff. 7-1-01.)

(810 ILCS 5/9-107) (from Ch. 26, par. 9-107)
Sec. 9-107. Control of letter-of-credit right. A secured party has control of a letter-of-credit right to the extent of any right to payment or performance by the issuer or any nominated person if the issuer or nominated person has consented to an assignment of proceeds of the letter of credit under Section 5-114(c) or otherwise applicable law or practice.
(Source: P.A. 91-893, eff. 7-1-01.)

(810 ILCS 5/9-107.1)
Sec. 9-107.1. Control of Beneficial Interest in Illinois Land Trust.
(a) Requirements for Control. A secured party has control of the beneficial interest in an Illinois land trust if:
(1) the secured party shall have transmitted to the trustee for the trust a record authenticated by the debtor that contains a collateral assignment by the debtor of, or the grant of a security interest in, a beneficial interest in the trust; and
(2) in an authenticated record, the trustee for the trust has accepted the collateral assignment or security agreement.

(b) Debtor's right to direct disposition and proceeds. A secured party that has satisfied subsection (a) has control, even if the debtor retains, subject to the terms and conditions of the collateral assignment or security agreement, the power of direction of the trustee and the right to receive the rents, income and profits thereof.
(Source: P.A. 92-234, eff. 1-1-02.)

(810 ILCS 5/9-108) (from Ch. 26, par. 9-108)
Sec. 9-108. Sufficiency of description.
(a) Sufficiency of description. Except as otherwise provided in subsections (c), (d), and (e), a description of personal or real property is sufficient, whether or not it is specific, if it reasonably identifies what is described.
(b) Examples of reasonable identification. Except as otherwise provided in subsection (d), a description of collateral reasonably identifies the collateral if it identifies the collateral by:
(1) specific listing;
(2) category;
(3) except as otherwise provided in subsection (e), a type of collateral defined in the Uniform Commercial Code;
(4) quantity;
(5) computational or allocational formula or procedure; or
(6) except as otherwise provided in subsection (c), any other method, if the identity of the collateral is objectively determinable.
(c) Supergeneric description not sufficient. A description of collateral as "all the debtor's assets" or "all the debtor's personal property" or using words of similar import does not reasonably identify the collateral.
(d) Investment property. Except as otherwise provided in subsection (e), a description of a security entitlement, securities account, or commodity account is sufficient if it describes:
(1) the collateral by those terms or as investment property; or
(2) the underlying financial asset or commodity contract.
(e) When description by type insufficient. A description only by type of collateral defined in the Uniform Commercial Code is an insufficient description of:
(1) a commercial tort claim; or
(2) in a consumer transaction, consumer goods, a security entitlement, a securities account, or a commodity account.
(Source: P.A. 91-893, eff. 7-1-01.)

(810 ILCS 5/Art. 9 Pt. 1 Sub. 2 heading)
SUBPART 2. APPLICABILITY OF ARTICLE

(810 ILCS 5/9-109) (from Ch. 26, par. 9-109)
Sec. 9-109. Scope.
(a) General scope of Article. Except as otherwise provided in subsections (c) and (d), this Article applies to:
(1) a transaction, regardless of its form, that creates a security interest in personal property or fixtures by contract;
(2) an agricultural lien;
(3) a sale of accounts, chattel paper, payment intangibles, or promissory notes;
(4) a consignment;
(5) a security interest arising under Section 2-401, 2-505, 2-711(3), or 2A-508(5), as provided in Section 9-110; and
(6) a security interest arising under Section 4-210 or 5-118.
(b) Security interest in secured obligation. The application of this Article to a security interest in a secured obligation is not affected by the fact that the obligation is itself secured by a transaction or interest to which this Article does not apply.
(c) Extent to which Article does not apply. This Article does not apply to the extent that:

(1) a statute, regulation, or treaty of the United States preempts this Article;

(2) another statute of this State expressly governs the creation, perfection, priority, or enforcement of a security interest created by this State or a governmental unit of this State;

(3) a statute of another State, a foreign country, or a governmental unit of another State or a foreign country, other than a statute generally applicable to security interests, expressly governs creation, perfection, priority, or enforcement of a security interest created by the State, country, or governmental unit;

(4) the rights of a transferee beneficiary or nominated person under a letter of credit are independent and superior under Section 5-114;

(5) this Article is in conflict with Section 205-410 of the Department of Agriculture Law of the Civil Administrative Code of Illinois or the Grain Code; or

(6) this Article is in conflict with Section 18-107 of the Public Utilities Act.

(d) Inapplicability of Article. This Article does not apply to:

(1) a landlord's lien;

(2) a lien, other than an agricultural lien, given by statute or other rule of law for services or materials, but Section 9-333 applies with respect to priority of the lien;

(3) an assignment of a claim for wages, salary, or other compensation of an employee;

(4) a sale of accounts, chattel paper, payment intangibles, or promissory notes as part of a sale of the business out of which they arose;

(5) an assignment of accounts, chattel paper, payment intangibles, or promissory notes which is for the purpose of collection only;

(6) an assignment of a right to payment under a contract to an assignee that is also obligated to perform under the contract;

(7) an assignment of a single account, payment intangible, or promissory note to an assignee in full or partial satisfaction of a preexisting indebtedness;

(8) a transfer of an interest in or an assignment of a claim under a policy of insurance, other than an assignment by or to a health-care provider of a health-care-insurance receivable and any subsequent assignment of the right to payment, but Sections 9-315 and 9-322 apply with respect to proceeds and priorities in proceeds;

(9) an assignment of a right represented by a judgment, other than a judgment taken on a right to payment that was collateral;

(10) a right of recoupment or set-off, but:

(A) Section 9-340 applies with respect to the effectiveness of rights of recoupment or set-off against deposit accounts; and

(B) Section 9-404 applies with respect to defenses or claims of an account debtor;

(11) the creation or transfer of an interest in or lien on real property, including a lease or rents thereunder, except to the extent that provision is made for:

(A) liens on real property in Sections 9-203 and 9-308;

(B) fixtures in Section 9-334;

(C) fixture filings in Sections 9-501, 9-502, 9-512, 9-516, and 9-519; and

(D) security agreements covering personal and real property in Section 9-604;

(12) an assignment of a claim arising in tort, other than a commercial tort claim, but Sections 9-315 and 9-322 apply with respect to proceeds and priorities in proceeds;

(13) a transfer by a government or governmental subdivision or agency;

(14) a claim or a right to receive compensation for injuries or sickness as described in Section 104(a)(1) or (2) of Title 26 of the United States Code, as amended from time to time; or

(15) a claim or right to receive benefits under a special needs trust as described in Section 1396p(d)(4) of Title 42 of the United States Code, as amended from time to time.
(Source: P.A. 91-893, eff. 7-1-01; 92-819, eff. 8-21-02.)

(810 ILCS 5/9-110) (from Ch. 26, par. 9-110)

Sec. 9-110. Security interests arising under Article 2 or 2A. A security interest arising under Section 2-401, 2-505, 2-711(3), or 2A-508(5) is subject to this Article. However, until the debtor obtains possession of the goods:

(1) the security interest is enforceable, even if Section 9-203(b)(3) has not been satisfied;

(2) filing is not required to perfect the security interest;
(3) the rights of the secured party after default by the debtor are governed by Article 2 or 2A; and
(4) the security interest has priority over a conflicting security interest created by the debtor.
(Source: P.A. 91-893, eff. 7-1-01.)

(810 ILCS 5/9-112) (from Ch. 26, par. 9-112)
Sec. 9-112. (Blank).
(Source: P.A. 91-893, eff. 7-1-01.)

(810 ILCS 5/9-113) (from Ch. 26, par. 9-113)
Sec. 9-113. (Blank).
(Source: P.A. 91-893, eff. 7-1-01.)

(810 ILCS 5/9-114) (from Ch. 26, par. 9-114)
Sec. 9-114. (Blank).
(Source: P.A. 91-893, eff. 7-1-01.)

(810 ILCS 5/9-115) (from Ch. 26, par. 9-115)
Sec. 9-115. (Blank).
(Source: P.A. 91-893, eff. 7-1-01.)

(810 ILCS 5/9-116)
Sec. 9-116. (Blank).
(Source: P.A. 91-893, eff. 7-1-01.)

(810 ILCS 5/9-150)
Sec. 9-150. (Blank).
(Source: P.A. 91-893, eff. 7-1-01.)

(810 ILCS 5/Art. 9 Pt. 2 heading)
PART 2. EFFECTIVENESS OF SECURITY AGREEMENT; ATTACHMENT OF SECURITY INTEREST; RIGHTS OF PARTIES TO SECURITY AGREEMENT

(810 ILCS 5/Art. 9 Pt. 2 Sub. 1 heading)
SUBPART 1. EFFECTIVENESS AND ATTACHMENT

(810 ILCS 5/9-201) (from Ch. 26, par. 9-201)
Sec. 9-201. General effectiveness of security agreement.
(a) General effectiveness. Except as otherwise provided in the Uniform Commercial Code, a security agreement is effective according to its terms between the parties, against purchasers of the collateral, and against creditors.
(b) Applicable consumer laws and other law. A transaction subject to this Article is subject to any applicable rule of law, statute, or regulation which establishes a different rule for consumers, including:
(1) the Retail Installment Sales Act;
(2) the Motor Vehicle Retail Installment Sales Act;
(3) Article II of Chapter 3 of the Illinois Vehicle Code;
(4) Article IIIB of the Boat Registration and Safety Act;
(5) the Pawnbroker Regulation Act;
(6) the Motor Vehicle Leasing Act;
(7) the Consumer Installment Loan Act; and
(8) the Consumer Deposit Security Act of 1987.
(c) Other applicable law controls. In case of conflict between this Article and a rule of law, statute, or regulation described in subsection (b), the rule of law, statute, or regulation controls. Failure to comply with a rule of law, statute, or regulation described in subsection (b) has only the effect such rule of law, statute, or regulation specifies.

(d) Further deference to other applicable law. This Article does not:

(1) validate any rate, charge, agreement, or practice that violates a rule of law, statute, or regulation described in subsection (b); or

(2) extend the application of the rule of law, statute, or regulation to a transaction not otherwise subject to it.

(Source: P.A. 91-893, eff. 7-1-01.)

(810 ILCS 5/9-202) (from Ch. 26, par. 9-202)

Sec. 9-202. Title to collateral immaterial. Except as otherwise provided with respect to consignments or sales of accounts, chattel paper, payment intangibles, or promissory notes, the provisions of this Article with regard to rights and obligations apply whether title to collateral is in the secured party or the debtor.

(Source: P.A. 91-893, eff. 7-1-01.)

(810 ILCS 5/9-203) (from Ch. 26, par. 9-203)

Sec. 9-203. Attachment and enforceability of security interest; proceeds; supporting obligations; formal requisites.

(a) Attachment. A security interest attaches to collateral when it becomes enforceable against the debtor with respect to the collateral, unless an agreement expressly postpones the time of attachment.

(b) Enforceability. Except as otherwise provided in subsections (c) through (i), a security interest is enforceable against the debtor and third parties with respect to the collateral only if:

(1) value has been given;

(2) the debtor has rights in the collateral or the power to transfer rights in the collateral to a secured party; and

(3) one of the following conditions is met:

(A) the debtor has authenticated a security agreement that provides a description of the collateral and, if the security interest covers timber to be cut, a description of the land concerned;

(B) the collateral is not a certificated security and is in the possession of the secured party under Section 9-313 pursuant to the debtor's security agreement;

(C) the collateral is a certificated security in registered form and the security certificate has been delivered to the secured party under Section 8-301 pursuant to the debtor's security agreement; or

(D) the collateral is deposit accounts, electronic chattel paper, investment property, letter-of-credit rights, or electronic documents, and the secured party has control under Section 7-106, 9-104, 9-105, 9-106, or 9-107 pursuant to the debtor's security agreement.

(c) Other UCC provisions. Subsection (b) is subject to Section 4-210 on the security interest of a collecting bank, Section 5-118 on the security interest of a letter-of-credit issuer or nominated person, Section 9-110 on a security interest arising under Article 2 or 2A, and Section 9-206 on security interests in investment property.

(d) When person becomes bound by another person's security agreement. A person becomes bound as debtor by a security agreement entered into by another person if, by operation of law other than this Article or by contract:

(1) the security agreement becomes effective to create a security interest in the person's property; or

(2) the person becomes generally obligated for the obligations of the other person, including the obligation secured under the security agreement, and acquires or succeeds to all or substantially all of the assets of the other person.

(e) Effect of new debtor becoming bound. If a new debtor becomes bound as debtor by a security agreement entered into by another person:

(1) the agreement satisfies subsection (b)(3) with respect to existing or after-acquired property of the new debtor to the extent the property is described in the agreement; and

(2) another agreement is not necessary to make a security interest in the property enforceable.

(f) Proceeds and supporting obligations. The attachment of a security interest in collateral gives the secured party the rights to proceeds provided by Section 9-315 and is also attachment of a security interest in a supporting obligation for the collateral.

(g) Lien securing right to payment. The attachment of a security interest in a right to payment or performance secured by a security interest or other lien on personal or real property is also attachment of a security interest in the security interest, mortgage, or other lien.

(h) Security entitlement carried in securities account. The attachment of a security interest in a securities account is also attachment of a security interest in the security entitlements carried in the securities account.

(i) Commodity contracts carried in commodity account. The attachment of a security interest in a commodity account is also attachment of a security interest in the commodity contracts carried in the commodity account.

(Source: P.A. 95-895, eff. 1-1-09.)

(810 ILCS 5/9-204) (from Ch. 26, par. 9-204)

Sec. 9-204. After-acquired property; future advances.

(a) After-acquired collateral. Except as otherwise provided in subsection (b), a security agreement may create or provide for a security interest in after-acquired collateral.

(b) When after-acquired property clause not effective. A security interest does not attach under a term constituting an after-acquired property clause to:

(1) consumer goods, other than an accession when given as additional security, unless the debtor acquires rights in them within 10 days after the secured party gives value; or

(2) a commercial tort claim.

(c) Future advances and other value. A security agreement may provide that collateral secures, or that accounts, chattel paper, payment intangibles, or promissory notes are sold in connection with, future advances or other value, whether or not the advances or value are given pursuant to commitment.

(Source: P.A. 91-893, eff. 7-1-01.)

(810 ILCS 5/9-205) (from Ch. 26, par. 9-205)

Sec. 9-205. Use or disposition of collateral permissible.

(a) When security interest not invalid or fraudulent. A security interest is not invalid or fraudulent against creditors solely because:

(1) the debtor has the right or ability to:

(A) use, commingle, or dispose of all or part of the collateral, including returned or repossessed goods;

(B) collect, compromise, enforce, or otherwise deal with collateral;

(C) accept the return of collateral or make repossessions; or

(D) use, commingle, or dispose of proceeds; or

(2) the secured party fails to require the debtor to account for proceeds or replace collateral.

(b) Requirements of possession not relaxed. This Section does not relax the requirements of possession if attachment, perfection, or enforcement of a security interest depends upon possession of the collateral by the secured party.

(Source: P.A. 91-893, eff. 7-1-01.)

(810 ILCS 5/9-205.1) (from Ch. 26, par. 9-205.1)

Sec. 9-205.1. Listing by debtor of purchasers or receivers of collateral. A secured party may require that the debtor include as part of the security agreement a list of persons to whom the debtor desires to sell or otherwise dispose of the collateral. The debtor shall not sell or otherwise dispose of the collateral to a person not included in that list unless the debtor has notified the secured party of his desire to sell or otherwise dispose of the collateral to such person at least 7 days prior to the sale or other disposition.

(Source: P.A. 91-893, eff. 7-1-01.)

(810 ILCS 5/9-206) (from Ch. 26, par. 9-206)
Sec. 9-206. Security interest arising in purchase or delivery of financial asset.
(a) Security interest when person buys through securities intermediary. A security interest in favor of a securities intermediary attaches to a person's security entitlement if:
(1) the person buys a financial asset through the securities intermediary in a transaction in which the person is obligated to pay the purchase price to the securities intermediary at the time of the purchase; and
(2) the securities intermediary credits the financial asset to the buyer's securities account before the buyer pays the securities intermediary.
(b) Security interest secures obligation to pay for financial asset. The security interest described in subsection (a) secures the person's obligation to pay for the financial asset.
(c) Security interest in payment against delivery transaction. A security interest in favor of a person that delivers a certificated security or other financial asset represented by a writing attaches to the security or other financial asset if:
(1) the security or other financial asset:
(A) in the ordinary course of business is transferred by delivery with any necessary indorsement or assignment; and
(B) is delivered under an agreement between persons in the business of dealing with such securities or financial assets; and
(2) the agreement calls for delivery against payment.
(d) Security interest secures obligation to pay for delivery. The security interest described in subsection (c) secures the obligation to make payment for the delivery.
(Source: P.A. 91-893, eff. 7-1-01.)

(810 ILCS 5/Art. 9 Pt. 2 Sub. 2 heading)
SUBPART 2. RIGHTS AND DUTIES

(810 ILCS 5/9-207) (from Ch. 26, par. 9-207)
Sec. 9-207. Rights and duties of secured party having possession or control of collateral.
(a) Duty of care when secured party in possession. Except as otherwise provided in subsection (d), a secured party shall use reasonable care in the custody and preservation of collateral in the secured party's possession. In the case of chattel paper or an instrument, reasonable care includes taking necessary steps to preserve rights against prior parties unless otherwise agreed.
(b) Expenses, risks, duties, and rights when secured party in possession. Except as otherwise provided in subsection (d), if a secured party has possession of collateral:
(1) reasonable expenses, including the cost of insurance and payment of taxes or other charges, incurred in the custody, preservation, use, or operation of the collateral are chargeable to the debtor and are secured by the collateral;
(2) the risk of accidental loss or damage is on the debtor to the extent of a deficiency in any effective insurance coverage;
(3) the secured party shall keep the collateral identifiable, but fungible collateral may be commingled; and
(4) the secured party may use or operate the collateral:
(A) for the purpose of preserving the collateral or its value;
(B) as permitted by an order of a court having competent jurisdiction; or
(C) except in the case of consumer goods, in the manner and to the extent agreed by the debtor.
(c) Duties and rights when secured party in possession or control. Except as otherwise provided in subsection (d), a secured party having possession of collateral or control of collateral under Section 7-106, 9-104, 9-105, 9-106, or 9-107:
(1) may hold as additional security any proceeds, except money or funds, received from the collateral;
(2) shall apply money or funds received from the collateral to reduce the secured obligation, unless remitted to the debtor; and

(3) may create a security interest in the collateral.

(d) Buyer of certain rights to payment. If the secured party is a buyer of accounts, chattel paper, payment intangibles, or promissory notes or a consignor:

(1) subsection (a) does not apply unless the secured party is entitled under an agreement:

(A) to charge back uncollected collateral; or

(B) otherwise to full or limited recourse against the debtor or a secondary obligor based on the nonpayment or other default of an account debtor or other obligor on the collateral; and

(2) subsections (b) and (c) do not apply.

(Source: P.A. 95-895, eff. 1-1-09.)

(810 ILCS 5/9-208) (from Ch. 26, par. 9-208)

Sec. 9-208. Additional duties of secured party having control of collateral.

(a) Applicability of Section. This Section applies to cases in which there is no outstanding secured obligation and the secured party is not committed to make advances, incur obligations, or otherwise give value.

(b) Duties of secured party after receiving demand from debtor. Within 10 days after receiving an authenticated demand by the debtor:

(1) a secured party having control of a deposit account under Section 9-104(a)(2) shall send to the bank with which the deposit account is maintained an authenticated statement that releases the bank from any further obligation to comply with instructions originated by the secured party;

(2) a secured party having control of a deposit account under Section 9-104(a)(3) shall:

(A) pay the debtor the balance on deposit in the deposit account; or

(B) transfer the balance on deposit into a deposit account in the debtor's name;

(3) a secured party, other than a buyer, having control of electronic chattel paper under Section 9-105 shall:

(A) communicate the authoritative copy of the electronic chattel paper to the debtor or its designated custodian;

(B) if the debtor designates a custodian that is the designated custodian with which the authoritative copy of the electronic chattel paper is maintained for the secured party, communicate to the custodian an authenticated record releasing the designated custodian from any further obligation to comply with instructions originated by the secured party and instructing the custodian to comply with instructions originated by the debtor; and

(C) take appropriate action to enable the debtor or its designated custodian to make copies of or revisions to the authoritative copy which add or change an identified assignee of the authoritative copy without the consent of the secured party;

(4) a secured party having control of investment property under Section 8-106(d)(2) or 9-106(b) shall send to the securities intermediary or commodity intermediary with which the security entitlement or commodity contract is maintained an authenticated record that releases the securities intermediary or commodity intermediary from any further obligation to comply with entitlement orders or directions originated by the secured party;

(5) a secured party having control of a letter-of-credit right under Section 9-107 shall send to each person having an unfulfilled obligation to pay or deliver proceeds of the letter of credit to the secured party an authenticated release from any further obligation to pay or deliver proceeds of the letter of credit to the secured party; and

(6) a secured party having control of an electronic document shall:

(A) give control of the electronic document to the debtor or its designated custodian;

(B) if the debtor designates a custodian that is the designated custodian with which the authoritative copy of the electronic document is maintained for the secured party, communicate to the custodian an authenticated record releasing the designated custodian from any further obligation to comply with instructions originated by the secured party and instructing the custodian to comply with instructions originated by the debtor; and

(C) take appropriate action to enable the debtor or its designated custodian to make copies of or revisions to the authoritative copy which add or change an identified assignee of the authoritative copy without the consent of the secured party.

(Source: P.A. 95-895, eff. 1-1-09.)

(810 ILCS 5/9-209)

Sec. 9-209. Duties of secured party if account debtor has been notified of assignment.

(a) Applicability of Section. Except as otherwise provided in subsection (c), this Section applies if:

(1) there is no outstanding secured obligation; and

(2) the secured party is not committed to make advances, incur obligations, or otherwise give value.

(b) Duties of secured party after receiving demand from debtor. Within 10 days after receiving an authenticated demand by the debtor, a secured party shall send to an account debtor that has received notification of an assignment to the secured party as assignee under Section 9-406(a) an authenticated record that releases the account debtor from any further obligation to the secured party.

(c) Inapplicability to sales. This Section does not apply to an assignment constituting the sale of an account, chattel paper, or payment intangible.

(Source: P.A. 91-893, eff. 7-1-01.)

(810 ILCS 5/9-210)

Sec. 9-210. Request for accounting; request regarding list of collateral or statement of account.

(a) Definitions. In this Section:

(1) "Request" means a record of a type described in paragraph (2), (3), or (4).

(2) "Request for an accounting" means a record authenticated by a debtor requesting that the recipient provide an accounting of the unpaid obligations secured by collateral and reasonably identifying the transaction or relationship that is the subject of the request.

(3) "Request regarding a list of collateral" means a record authenticated by a debtor requesting that the recipient approve or correct a list of what the debtor believes to be the collateral securing an obligation and reasonably identifying the transaction or relationship that is the subject of the request.

(4) "Request regarding a statement of account" means a record authenticated by a debtor requesting that the recipient approve or correct a statement indicating what the debtor believes to be the aggregate amount of unpaid obligations secured by collateral as of a specified date and reasonably identifying the transaction or relationship that is the subject of the request.

(b) Duty to respond to requests. Subject to subsections (c), (d), (e), and (f), a secured party, other than a buyer of accounts, chattel paper, payment intangibles, or promissory notes or a consignor, shall comply with a request within 14 days after receipt:

(1) in the case of a request for an accounting, by authenticating and sending to the debtor an accounting; and

(2) in the case of a request regarding a list of collateral or a request regarding a statement of account, by authenticating and sending to the debtor an approval or correction.

(c) Request regarding list of collateral; statement concerning type of collateral. A secured party that claims a security interest in all of a particular type of collateral owned by the debtor may comply with a request regarding a list of collateral by sending to the debtor an authenticated record including a statement to that effect within 14 days after receipt.

(d) Request regarding list of collateral; no interest claimed. A person that receives a request regarding a list of collateral, claims no interest in the collateral when it receives the request, and claimed an interest in the collateral at an earlier time shall comply with the request within 14 days after receipt by sending to the debtor an authenticated record:

(1) disclaiming any interest in the collateral; and

(2) if known to the recipient, providing the name and mailing address of any assignee of or successor to the recipient's interest in the collateral.

(e) Request for accounting or regarding statement of account; no interest in obligation claimed. A person that receives a request for an accounting or a request regarding a statement of account, claims no interest in the obligations when it receives the request, and claimed an interest in the obligations at an earlier time shall comply with the request within 14 days after receipt by sending to the debtor an authenticated record:

(1) disclaiming any interest in the obligations; and

(2) if known to the recipient, providing the name and mailing address of any assignee of or successor to the recipient's interest in the obligations.

(f) Charges for responses. A debtor is entitled without charge to one response to a request under this Section during any six-month period. The secured party may require payment of a charge not exceeding $25 for each additional response.

(Source: P.A. 91-893, eff. 7-1-01.)

(810 ILCS 5/Art. 9 Pt. 3 heading)
PART 3. PERFECTION AND PRIORITY

(810 ILCS 5/Art. 9 Pt. 3 Sub. 1 heading)
SUBPART 1. LAW GOVERNING PERFECTION AND PRIORITY

(810 ILCS 5/9-301) (from Ch. 26, par. 9-301)
Sec. 9-301. Law governing perfection and priority of security interests. Except as otherwise provided in Sections 9-303 through 9-306.1, the following rules determine the law governing perfection, the effect of perfection or nonperfection, and the priority of a security interest in collateral:

(1) Except as otherwise provided in this Section, while a debtor is located in a jurisdiction, the local law of that jurisdiction governs perfection, the effect of perfection or nonperfection, and the priority of a security interest in collateral.

(2) While collateral is located in a jurisdiction, the local law of that jurisdiction governs perfection, the effect of perfection or nonperfection, and the priority of a possessory security interest in that collateral.

(3) Except as otherwise provided in paragraph (4), while tangible negotiable documents, goods, instruments, money, or tangible chattel paper is located in a jurisdiction, the local law of that jurisdiction governs:

(A) perfection of a security interest in the goods by filing a fixture filing;

(B) perfection of a security interest in timber to be cut; and

(C) the effect of perfection or nonperfection and the priority of a nonpossessory security interest in the collateral.

(4) The local law of the jurisdiction in which the wellhead or minehead is located governs perfection, the effect of perfection or nonperfection, and the priority of a security interest in as-extracted collateral.

(Source: P.A. 95-895, eff. 1-1-09.)

(810 ILCS 5/9-302) (from Ch. 26, par. 9-302)
Sec. 9-302. Law governing perfection and priority of agricultural liens. While farm products are located in a jurisdiction, the local law of that jurisdiction governs perfection, the effect of perfection or nonperfection, and the priority of an agricultural lien on the farm products.

(Source: P.A. 90-665, eff. 7-30-98; 91-893, eff. 7-1-01.)

(810 ILCS 5/9-303) (from Ch. 26, par. 9-303)
Sec. 9-303. Law governing perfection and priority of security interests in goods covered by a certificate of title.

(a) Applicability of Section. This Section applies to goods covered by a certificate of title, even if there is no other relationship between the jurisdiction under whose certificate of title the goods are covered and the goods or the debtor.

(b) When goods covered by certificate of title. Goods become covered by a certificate of title when a valid application for the certificate of title and the applicable fee are delivered to the appropriate authority. Goods cease to be covered by a certificate of title at the earlier of the time the certificate of title ceases to be effective under the law of the issuing jurisdiction or the time the goods become covered subsequently by a certificate of title issued by another jurisdiction.

(c) Applicable law. The local law of the jurisdiction under whose certificate of title the goods are covered governs perfection, the effect of perfection or nonperfection, and the priority of a security interest in goods covered by a certificate of title from the time the goods become covered by the certificate of title until the goods cease to be covered by the certificate of title.
(Source: P.A. 91-893, eff. 7-1-01.)

(810 ILCS 5/9-304) (from Ch. 26, par. 9-304)
Sec. 9-304. Law governing perfection and priority of security interests in deposit accounts.
(a) Law of bank's jurisdiction governs. The local law of a bank's jurisdiction governs perfection, the effect of perfection or nonperfection, and the priority of a security interest in a deposit account maintained with that bank.
(b) Bank's jurisdiction. The following rules determine a bank's jurisdiction for purposes of this Part:
(1) If an agreement between the bank and the debtor governing the deposit account expressly provides that a particular jurisdiction is the bank's jurisdiction for purposes of this Part, this Article, or the Uniform Commercial Code, that jurisdiction is the bank's jurisdiction.
(2) If paragraph (1) does not apply and an agreement between the bank and its customer governing the deposit account expressly provides that the agreement is governed by the law of a particular jurisdiction, that jurisdiction is the bank's jurisdiction.
(3) If neither paragraph (1) nor paragraph (2) applies and an agreement between the bank and its customer governing the deposit account expressly provides that the deposit account is maintained at an office in a particular jurisdiction, that jurisdiction is the bank's jurisdiction.
(4) If none of the preceding paragraphs applies, the bank's jurisdiction is the jurisdiction in which the office identified in an account statement as the office serving the customer's account is located.
(5) If none of the preceding paragraphs applies, the bank's jurisdiction is the jurisdiction in which the chief executive office of the bank is located.
(Source: P.A. 91-893, eff. 7-1-01.)

(810 ILCS 5/9-305) (from Ch. 26, par. 9-305)
Sec. 9-305. Law governing perfection and priority of security interests in investment property.
(a) Governing law: general rules. Except as otherwise provided in subsection (c), the following rules apply:
(1) While a security certificate is located in a jurisdiction, the local law of that jurisdiction governs perfection, the effect of perfection or nonperfection, and the priority of a security interest in the certificated security represented thereby.
(2) The local law of the issuer's jurisdiction as specified in Section 8-110(d) governs perfection, the effect of perfection or nonperfection, and the priority of a security interest in an uncertificated security.
(3) The local law of the securities intermediary's jurisdiction as specified in Section 8-110(e) governs perfection, the effect of perfection or nonperfection, and the priority of a security interest in a security entitlement or securities account.
(4) The local law of the commodity intermediary's jurisdiction governs perfection, the effect of perfection or nonperfection, and the priority of a security interest in a commodity contract or commodity account.
(b) Commodity intermediary's jurisdiction. The following rules determine a commodity intermediary's jurisdiction for purposes of this Part:
(1) If an agreement between the commodity intermediary and commodity customer governing the commodity account expressly provides that a particular jurisdiction is the commodity intermediary's jurisdiction for purposes of this Part, this Article, or the Uniform Commercial Code, that jurisdiction is the commodity intermediary's jurisdiction.

(2) If paragraph (1) does not apply and an agreement between the commodity intermediary and commodity customer governing the commodity account expressly provides that the agreement is governed by the law of a particular jurisdiction, that jurisdiction is the commodity intermediary's jurisdiction.

(3) If neither paragraph (1) nor paragraph (2) applies and an agreement between the commodity intermediary and commodity customer governing the commodity account expressly provides that the commodity account is maintained at an office in a particular jurisdiction, that jurisdiction is the commodity intermediary's jurisdiction.

(4) If none of the preceding paragraphs applies, the commodity intermediary's jurisdiction is the jurisdiction in which the office identified in an account statement as the office serving the commodity customer's account is located.

(5) If none of the preceding paragraphs applies, the commodity intermediary's jurisdiction is the jurisdiction in which the chief executive office of the commodity intermediary is located.

(c) When perfection governed by law of jurisdiction where debtor located. The local law of the jurisdiction in which the debtor is located governs:

(1) perfection of a security interest in investment property by filing;

(2) automatic perfection of a security interest in investment property created by a broker or securities intermediary; and

(3) automatic perfection of a security interest in a commodity contract or commodity account created by a commodity intermediary.

(Source: P.A. 91-893, eff. 7-1-01.)

(810 ILCS 5/9-306) (from Ch. 26, par. 9-306)
Sec. 9-306. Law governing perfection and priority of security interests in letter-of-credit rights.

(a) Governing law: issuer's or nominated person's jurisdiction. Subject to subsection (c), the local law of the issuer's jurisdiction or a nominated person's jurisdiction governs perfection, the effect of perfection or nonperfection, and the priority of a security interest in a letter-of-credit right if the issuer's jurisdiction or nominated person's jurisdiction is a State.

(b) Issuer's or nominated person's jurisdiction. For purposes of this Part, an issuer's jurisdiction or nominated person's jurisdiction is the jurisdiction whose law governs the liability of the issuer or nominated person with respect to the letter-of-credit right as provided in Section 5-116.

(c) When Section not applicable. This Section does not apply to a security interest that is perfected only under Section 9-308(d).

(Source: P.A. 91-893, eff. 7-1-01.)

(810 ILCS 5/9-306.01) (from Ch. 26, par. 9-306.01)
Sec. 9-306.01. (Blank).
(Source: P.A. 91-893, eff. 7-1-01.)

(810 ILCS 5/9-306.02) (from Ch. 26, par. 9-306.02)
Sec. 9-306.02. (Blank).
(Source: P.A. 91-893, eff. 7-1-01.)

(810 ILCS 5/9-306.1)
Sec. 9-306.1. Law Governing Perfection and Priority of Collateral Assignments of Beneficial Interests in Illinois Land Trusts. The local law of the State of Illinois governs perfection, the effect of perfection or nonperfection, and the priority of a collateral assignment of, or other security interest in, a beneficial interest in an Illinois land trust. This Section implements the important interest of this State in matters associated with the administration of Illinois land trusts created for the principal purpose of owning an interest in Illinois land and the regulation of restrictions on the transfer of beneficial interests in, and of the power of appointments under, such trusts.

(Source: P.A. 92-234, eff. 1-1-02.)

(810 ILCS 5/9-307) (from Ch. 26, par. 9-307)

Sec. 9-307. Location of debtor.

(a) "Place of business." In this Section, "place of business" means a place where a debtor conducts its affairs.

(b) Debtor's location: general rules. Except as otherwise provided in this Section, the following rules determine a debtor's location:

(1) A debtor who is an individual is located at the individual's principal residence.

(2) A debtor that is an organization and has only one place of business is located at its place of business.

(3) A debtor that is an organization and has more than one place of business is located at its chief executive office.

(c) Limitation of applicability of subsection (b). Subsection (b) applies only if a debtor's residence, place of business, or chief executive office, as applicable, is located in a jurisdiction whose law generally requires information concerning the existence of a nonpossessory security interest to be made generally available in a filing, recording, or registration system as a condition or result of the security interest's obtaining priority over the rights of a lien creditor with respect to the collateral. If subsection (b) does not apply, the debtor is located in the District of Columbia.

(d) Continuation of location: cessation of existence, etc. A person that ceases to exist, have a residence, or have a place of business continues to be located in the jurisdiction specified by subsections (b) and (c).

(e) Location of registered organization organized under State law. A registered organization that is organized under the law of a State is located in that State.

(f) Location of registered organization organized under federal law; bank branches and agencies. Except as otherwise provided in subsection (i), a registered organization that is organized under the law of the United States and a branch or agency of a bank that is not organized under the law of the United States or a State are located:

(1) in the State that the law of the United States designates, if the law designates a State of location;

(2) in the State that the registered organization, branch, or agency designates, if the law of the United States authorizes the registered organization, branch, or agency to designate its State of location; or

(3) in the District of Columbia, if neither paragraph (1) nor paragraph (2) applies.

(g) Continuation of location: change in status of registered organization. A registered organization continues to be located in the jurisdiction specified by subsection (e) or (f) notwithstanding:

(1) the suspension, revocation, forfeiture, or lapse of the registered organization's status as such in its jurisdiction of organization; or

(2) the dissolution, winding up, or cancellation of the existence of the registered organization.

(h) Location of United States. The United States is located in the District of Columbia.

(i) Location of foreign bank branch or agency if licensed in only one State. A branch or agency of a bank that is not organized under the law of the United States or a State is located in the State in which the branch or agency is licensed, if all branches and agencies of the bank are licensed in only one State.

(j) Location of foreign air carrier. A foreign air carrier under the Federal Aviation Act of 1958, as amended, is located at the designated office of the agent upon which service of process may be made on behalf of the carrier.

(k) Section applies only to this Part. This Section applies only for purposes of this Part.

(Source: P.A. 91-357, eff. 7-29-99; 91-893, eff. 7-1-01.)

(810 ILCS 5/9-307.1) (from Ch. 26, par. 9-307.1)

Sec. 9-307.1. (Blank).

(Source: P.A. 91-893, eff. 7-1-01.)

(810 ILCS 5/9-307.2) (from Ch. 26, par. 9-307.2)
Sec. 9-307.2. (Blank).
(Source: P.A. 91-893, eff. 7-1-01.)

(810 ILCS 5/Art. 9 Pt. 3 Sub. 2 heading)
SUBPART 2. PERFECTION

(810 ILCS 5/9-308) (from Ch. 26, par. 9-308)
Sec. 9-308. When security interest or agricultural lien is perfected; continuity of perfection.

(a) Perfection of security interest. Except as otherwise provided in this Section and Section 9-309, a security interest is perfected if it has attached and all of the applicable requirements for perfection in Sections 9-310 through 9-316 have been satisfied. A security interest is perfected when it attaches if the applicable requirements are satisfied before the security interest attaches.

(b) Perfection of agricultural lien. An agricultural lien is perfected if it has become effective and all of the applicable requirements for perfection in Section 9-310 have been satisfied. An agricultural lien is perfected when it becomes effective if the applicable requirements are satisfied before the agricultural lien becomes effective.

(c) Continuous perfection; perfection by different methods. A security interest or agricultural lien is perfected continuously if it is originally perfected by one method under this Article and is later perfected by another method under this Article, without an intermediate period when it was unperfected.

(d) Supporting obligation. Perfection of a security interest in collateral also perfects a security interest in a supporting obligation for the collateral.

(e) Lien securing right to payment. Perfection of a security interest in a right to payment or performance also perfects a security interest in a security interest, mortgage, or other lien on personal or real property securing the right.

(f) Security entitlement carried in securities account. Perfection of a security interest in a securities account also perfects a security interest in the security entitlements carried in the securities account.

(g) Commodity contract carried in commodity account. Perfection of a security interest in a commodity account also perfects a security interest in the commodity contracts carried in the commodity account.
(Source: P.A. 91-893, eff. 7-1-01.)

(810 ILCS 5/9-309) (from Ch. 26, par. 9-309)
Sec. 9-309. Security interest perfected upon attachment. The following security interests are perfected when they attach:

(1) a purchase-money security interest in consumer goods, except as otherwise provided in Section 9-311(b) with respect to consumer goods that are subject to a statute or treaty described in Section 9-311(a);

(2) an assignment of accounts or payment intangibles which does not by itself or in conjunction with other assignments to the same assignee transfer a significant part of the assignor's outstanding accounts or payment intangibles;

(3) a sale of a payment intangible;

(4) a sale of a promissory note;

(5) a security interest created by the assignment of a health-care-insurance receivable to the provider of the health-care goods or services;

(6) a security interest arising under Section 2-401, 2-505, 2-711(3), or 2A-508(5), until the debtor obtains possession of the collateral;

(7) a security interest of a collecting bank arising under Section 4-210;

(8) a security interest of an issuer or nominated person arising under Section 5-118;

(9) a security interest arising in the delivery of a financial asset under Section 9-206(c);

(10) a security interest in investment property created by a broker or securities intermediary;

(11) a security interest in a commodity contract or a commodity account created by a commodity intermediary;

(12) an assignment for the benefit of all creditors of the transferor and subsequent transfers by the assignee thereunder; and

(13) a security interest created by an assignment of a beneficial interest in a decedent's estate.

(Source: P.A. 91-893, eff. 7-1-01.)

(810 ILCS 5/9-310) (from Ch. 26, par. 9-310)

Sec. 9-310. When filing required to perfect security interest or agricultural lien; security interests and agricultural liens to which filing provisions do not apply.

(a) General rule: perfection by filing. Except as otherwise provided in subsection (b) and Section 9-312(b), a financing statement must be filed to perfect all security interests and agricultural liens.

(b) Exceptions: filing not necessary. The filing of a financing statement is not necessary to perfect a security interest:

(1) that is perfected under Section 9-308(d), (e), (f), or (g);

(2) that is perfected under Section 9-309 when it attaches;

(3) in property subject to a statute, regulation, or treaty described in Section 9-311(a);

(4) in goods in possession of a bailee which is perfected under Section 9-312(d)(1) or (2);

(5) in certificated securities, documents, goods, or instruments which is perfected without filing, control, or possession under Section 9-312(e), (f), or (g);

(6) in collateral in the secured party's possession under Section 9-313;

(7) in a certificated security which is perfected by delivery of the security certificate to the secured party under Section 9-313;

(8) in deposit accounts, electronic chattel paper, electronic documents, investment property, letter-of-credit rights, or beneficial interests in Illinois land trusts which is perfected by control under Section 9-314;

(9) in proceeds which is perfected under Section 9-315; or

(10) that is perfected under Section 9-316.

(c) Assignment of perfected security interest. If a secured party assigns a perfected security interest or agricultural lien, a filing under this Article is not required to continue the perfected status of the security interest against creditors of and transferees from the original debtor.

(Source: P.A. 95-895, eff. 1-1-09.)

(810 ILCS 5/9-311) (from Ch. 26, par. 9-311)

Sec. 9-311. Perfection of security interests in property subject to certain statutes, regulations, and treaties.

(a) Security interest subject to other law. Except as otherwise provided in subsection (d), the filing of a financing statement is not necessary or effective to perfect a security interest in property subject to:

(1) a statute, regulation, or treaty of the United States whose requirements for a security interest's obtaining priority over the rights of a lien creditor with respect to the property preempt Section 9-310(a);

(2) the Illinois Vehicle Code or the Boat Registration and Safety Act; or

(3) a certificate-of-title statute of another jurisdiction which provides for a security interest to be indicated on the certificate as a condition or result of the security interest's obtaining priority over the rights of a lien creditor with respect to the property.

(b) Compliance with other law. Compliance with the requirements of a statute, regulation, or treaty described in subsection (a) for obtaining priority over the rights of a lien creditor is equivalent to the filing of a financing statement under this Article. Except as otherwise provided in subsection (d) and Sections 9-313 and 9-316(d) and (e) for goods covered by a certificate of title, a security interest in property subject to a statute, regulation, or treaty described in subsection (a) may be perfected only by compliance with those requirements, and a security interest so perfected remains perfected notwithstanding a change in the use or transfer of possession of the collateral.

(c) Duration and renewal of perfection. Except as otherwise provided in subsection (d) and Section 9-316(d) and (e), duration and renewal of perfection of a security interest perfected by compliance with the requirements prescribed by a statute, regulation, or treaty described in subsection (a) are governed by the statute, regulation, or treaty. In other respects, the security interest is subject to this Article.

(d) Inapplicability to certain inventory. During any period in which collateral subject to a statute specified in subsection (a)(2) is inventory held for sale or lease by a person or leased by that person as lessor and that person is in the business of selling or leasing goods of that kind, this Section does not apply to a security interest in that collateral created by that person as debtor.

(Source: P.A. 91-893, eff. 7-1-01.)

(810 ILCS 5/9-312) (from Ch. 26, par. 9-312)

Sec. 9-312. Perfection of security interests in chattel paper, deposit accounts, documents, goods covered by documents, instruments, investment property, letter-of-credit rights, and money; perfection by permissive filing; temporary perfection without filing or transfer of possession.

(a) Perfection by filing permitted. A security interest in chattel paper, negotiable documents, instruments, beneficial interests in Illinois land trusts, or investment property may be perfected by filing.

(b) Control or possession of certain collateral. Except as otherwise provided in Section 9-315(c) and (d) for proceeds:

(1) a security interest in a deposit account may be perfected only by control under Section 9-314;

(2) and except as otherwise provided in Section 9-308(d), a security interest in a letter-of-credit right may be perfected only by control under Section 9-314; and

(3) a security interest in money may be perfected only by the secured party's taking possession under Section 9-313.

(c) Goods covered by negotiable document. While goods are in the possession of a bailee that has issued a negotiable document covering the goods:

(1) a security interest in the goods may be perfected by perfecting a security interest in the document; and

(2) a security interest perfected in the document has priority over any security interest that becomes perfected in the goods by another method during that time.

(d) Goods covered by nonnegotiable document. While goods are in the possession of a bailee that has issued a nonnegotiable document covering the goods, a security interest in the goods may be perfected by:

(1) issuance of a document in the name of the secured party;

(2) the bailee's receipt of notification of the secured party's interest; or

(3) filing as to the goods.

(e) Temporary perfection: new value. A security interest in certificated securities, negotiable documents, or instruments is perfected without filing or the taking of possession or control for a period of 20 days from the time it attaches to the extent that it arises for new value given under an authenticated security agreement.

(f) Temporary perfection: goods or documents made available to debtor. A perfected security interest in a negotiable document or goods in possession of a bailee, other than one that has issued a negotiable document for the goods, remains perfected for 20 days without filing if the secured party makes available to the debtor the goods or documents representing the goods for the purpose of:

(1) ultimate sale or exchange; or

(2) loading, unloading, storing, shipping, transshipping, manufacturing, processing, or otherwise dealing with them in a manner preliminary to their sale or exchange.

(g) Temporary perfection: delivery of security certificate or instrument to debtor. A perfected security interest in a certificated security or instrument remains perfected for 20 days without filing if the secured party delivers the security certificate or instrument to the debtor for the purpose of:

(1) ultimate sale or exchange; or

(2) presentation, collection, enforcement, renewal, or registration of transfer.

(h) Expiration of temporary perfection. After the 20-day period specified in subsection (e), (f), or (g) expires, perfection depends upon compliance with this Article.

(Source: P.A. 95-895, eff. 1-1-09.)

(810 ILCS 5/9-313) (from Ch. 26, par. 9-313)

Sec. 9-313. When possession by or delivery to secured party perfects security interest without filing.

(a) Perfection by possession or delivery. Except as otherwise provided in subsection (b), a secured party may perfect a security interest in tangible negotiable documents, goods, instruments, money, or tangible chattel paper by taking possession of the collateral. A secured party may perfect a security interest in certificated securities by taking delivery of the certificated securities under Section 8-301.

(b) Goods covered by certificate of title. With respect to goods covered by a certificate of title issued by this State, a secured party may perfect a security interest in the goods by taking possession of the goods only in the circumstances described in Section 9-316(d).

(c) Collateral in possession of person other than debtor. With respect to collateral other than certificated securities and goods covered by a document, a secured party takes possession of collateral in the possession of a person other than the debtor, the secured party, or a lessee of the collateral from the debtor in the ordinary course of the debtor's business, when:

(1) the person in possession authenticates a record acknowledging that it holds possession of the collateral for the secured party's benefit; or

(2) the person takes possession of the collateral after having authenticated a record acknowledging that it will hold possession of collateral for the secured party's benefit.

(d) Time of perfection by possession; continuation of perfection. If perfection of a security interest depends upon possession of the collateral by a secured party, perfection occurs no earlier than the time the secured party takes possession and continues only while the secured party retains possession.

(e) Time of perfection by delivery; continuation of perfection. A security interest in a certificated security in registered form is perfected by delivery when delivery of the certificated security occurs under Section 8-301 and remains perfected by delivery until the debtor obtains possession of the security certificate.

(f) Acknowledgment not required. A person in possession of collateral is not required to acknowledge that it holds possession for a secured party's benefit.

(g) Effectiveness of acknowledgment; no duties or confirmation. If a person acknowledges that it holds possession for the secured party's benefit:

(1) the acknowledgment is effective under subsection (c) or Section 8-301(a), even if the acknowledgment violates the rights of a debtor; and

(2) unless the person otherwise agrees or law other than this Article otherwise provides, the person does not owe any duty to the secured party and is not required to confirm the acknowledgment to another person.

(h) Secured party's delivery to person other than debtor. A secured party having possession of collateral does not relinquish possession by delivering the collateral to a person other than the debtor or a lessee of the collateral from the debtor in the ordinary course of the debtor's business if the person was instructed before the delivery or is instructed contemporaneously with the delivery:

(1) to hold possession of the collateral for the secured party's benefit; or

(2) to redeliver the collateral to the secured party.

(i) Effect of delivery under subsection (h); no duties or confirmation. A secured party does not relinquish possession, even if a delivery under subsection (h) violates the rights of a debtor. A person to which collateral is delivered under subsection (h) does not owe any duty to the secured party and is not required to confirm the delivery to another person unless the person otherwise agrees or law other than this Article otherwise provides.

(Source: P.A. 95-895, eff. 1-1-09.)

(810 ILCS 5/9-314) (from Ch. 26, par. 9-314)
Sec. 9-314. Perfection by control.

(a) Perfection by control. A security interest in investment property, deposit accounts, electronic chattel paper, letter-of-credit rights, electronic documents, or beneficial interests in Illinois land trusts may be perfected by control of the collateral under Section 7-106, 9-104, 9-105, 9-106, 9-107, or 9-107.1.

(b) Specified collateral: time of perfection by control; continuation of perfection. A security interest in deposit accounts, electronic chattel paper, letter-of-credit rights, electronic documents, or beneficial interests in Illinois land trusts is perfected by control under Section 7-106, 9-104, 9-105, 9-107, or 9-107.1 when the secured party obtains control and remains perfected by control only while the secured party retains control.

(c) Investment property: time of perfection by control; continuation of perfection. A security interest in investment property is perfected by control under Section 9-106 from the time the secured party obtains control and remains perfected by control until:

(1) the secured party does not have control; and

(2) one of the following occurs:

(A) if the collateral is a certificated security, the debtor has or acquires possession of the security certificate;

(B) if the collateral is an uncertificated security, the issuer has registered or registers the debtor as the registered owner; or

(C) if the collateral is a security entitlement, the debtor is or becomes the entitlement holder.

(Source: P.A. 95-895, eff. 1-1-09.)

(810 ILCS 5/9-315) (from Ch. 26, par. 9-315)
Sec. 9-315. Secured party's rights on disposition of collateral and in proceeds.

(a) Disposition of collateral: continuation of security interest or agricultural lien; proceeds. Except as otherwise provided in this Article and in Section 2-403(2):

(1) a security interest or agricultural lien continues in collateral notwithstanding sale, lease, license, exchange, or other disposition thereof unless the secured party authorized the disposition free of the security interest or agricultural lien; and

(2) a security interest attaches to any identifiable proceeds of collateral.

(b) When commingled proceeds identifiable. Proceeds that are commingled with other property are identifiable proceeds:

(1) if the proceeds are goods, to the extent provided by Section 9-336; and

(2) if the proceeds are not goods, to the extent that the secured party identifies the proceeds by a method of tracing, including application of equitable principles, that is permitted under law other than this Article with respect to commingled property of the type involved.

(c) Perfection of security interest in proceeds. A security interest in proceeds is a perfected security interest if the security interest in the original collateral was perfected.

(d) Continuation of perfection. A perfected security interest in proceeds becomes unperfected on the 21st day after the security interest attaches to the proceeds unless:

(1) the following conditions are satisfied:

(A) a filed financing statement covers the original collateral;

(B) the proceeds are collateral in which a security interest may be perfected by filing in the office in which the financing statement has been filed; and

(C) the proceeds are not acquired with cash proceeds;

(2) the proceeds are identifiable cash proceeds; or

(3) the security interest in the proceeds is perfected other than under subsection (c) when the security interest attaches to the proceeds or within 20 days thereafter.

(e) When perfected security interest in proceeds becomes unperfected. If a filed financing statement covers the original collateral, a security interest in proceeds which remains perfected under subsection (d)(1) becomes unperfected at the later of:

(1) when the effectiveness of the filed financing statement lapses under Section 9-515 or is terminated under Section 9-513; or

(2) the 21st day after the security interest attaches to the proceeds.
(Source: P.A. 91-893, eff. 7-1-01.)

(810 ILCS 5/9-315.01)
Sec. 9-315.01. Debtor disposing of collateral and failing to pay secured party amount due under security agreement; penalties for violation.
(1) It is unlawful for a debtor under the terms of a security agreement (a) who has no right of sale or other disposition of the collateral or (b) who has a right of sale or other disposition of the collateral and is to account to the secured party for the proceeds of any sale or other disposition of the collateral, to sell or otherwise dispose of the collateral and willfully and wrongfully to fail to pay the secured party the amount of said proceeds due under the security agreement. Failure to pay such proceeds to the secured party within 10 days after the sale or other disposition of the collateral is prima facie evidence of a willful and wanton failure to pay.
(2) An individual convicted of a violation of this Section shall be guilty of a Class 3 felony.
(3) A corporation convicted of a violation of this Section shall be guilty of a business offense and shall be fined not less than $2,000 nor more than $10,000.
(4) In the event the debtor under the terms of a security agreement is a corporation or a partnership, any officer, director, manager, or managerial agent of the debtor who violates this Section or causes the debtor to violate this Section shall be guilty of a Class 3 felony.
(Source: P.A. 91-893, eff. 7-1-01.)

(810 ILCS 5/9-315.02)
Sec. 9-315.02. Disposal of collateral by debtor to persons other than those previously disclosed to secured party—penalties for violation—defense.
(1) Where, pursuant to Section 9-205.1, a secured party has required that before the debtor sells or otherwise disposes of collateral in the debtor's possession he disclose to the secured party the persons to whom he desires to sell or otherwise dispose of such collateral, it is unlawful for the debtor to sell or otherwise dispose of the collateral to a person other than a person so disclosed to the secured party.
(2) An individual convicted of a violation of this Section shall be guilty of a Class A misdemeanor.
(3) A corporation convicted of a violation of this Section shall be guilty of a business offense and shall be fined not less than $2,000 nor more than $10,000.
(4) In the event the debtor under the terms of a security agreement is a corporation or a partnership, any officer, director, manager, or managerial agent of the debtor who violates this Section or causes the debtor to violate this Section shall be guilty of a Class A misdemeanor.
(5) It is an affirmative defense to a prosecution for the violation of this Section that the debtor has paid to the secured party the proceeds from the sale or other disposition of the collateral within 10 days after such sale or disposition.
(Source: P.A. 91-893, eff. 7-1-01; 92-16, eff. 6-28-01.)

(810 ILCS 5/9-316) (from Ch. 26, par. 9-316)
Sec. 9-316. Continued perfection of security interest following change in governing law.
(a) General rule: effect on perfection of change in governing law. A security interest perfected pursuant to the law of the jurisdiction designated in Section 9-301(1) or 9-305(c) remains perfected until the earliest of:
(1) the time perfection would have ceased under the law of that jurisdiction;
(2) the expiration of four months after a change of the debtor's location to another jurisdiction; or
(3) the expiration of one year after a transfer of collateral to a person that thereby becomes a debtor and is located in another jurisdiction.
(b) Security interest perfected or unperfected under law of new jurisdiction. If a security interest described in subsection (a) becomes perfected under the law of the other jurisdiction before the earliest time or event described in that subsection, it

remains perfected thereafter. If the security interest does not become perfected under the law of the other jurisdiction before the earliest time or event, it becomes unperfected and is deemed never to have been perfected as against a purchaser of the collateral for value.

(c) Possessory security interest in collateral moved to new jurisdiction. A possessory security interest in collateral, other than goods covered by a certificate of title and as-extracted collateral consisting of goods, remains continuously perfected if:

(1) the collateral is located in one jurisdiction and subject to a security interest perfected under the law of that jurisdiction;

(2) thereafter the collateral is brought into another jurisdiction; and

(3) upon entry into the other jurisdiction, the security interest is perfected under the law of the other jurisdiction.

(d) Goods covered by certificate of title from this State. Except as otherwise provided in subsection (e), a security interest in goods covered by a certificate of title which is perfected by any method under the law of another jurisdiction when the goods become covered by a certificate of title from this State remains perfected until the security interest would have become unperfected under the law of the other jurisdiction had the goods not become so covered.

(e) When subsection (d) security interest becomes unperfected against purchasers. A security interest described in subsection (d) becomes unperfected as against a purchaser of the goods for value and is deemed never to have been perfected as against a purchaser of the goods for value if the applicable requirements for perfection under Section 9-311(b) or 9-313 are not satisfied before the earlier of:

(1) the time the security interest would have become unperfected under the law of the other jurisdiction had the goods not become covered by a certificate of title from this State; or

(2) the expiration of four months after the goods had become so covered.

(f) Change in jurisdiction of bank, issuer, nominated person, securities intermediary, or commodity intermediary. A security interest in deposit accounts, letter-of-credit rights, or investment property which is perfected under the law of the bank's jurisdiction, the issuer's jurisdiction, a nominated person's jurisdiction, the securities intermediary's jurisdiction, or the commodity intermediary's jurisdiction, as applicable, remains perfected until the earlier of:

(1) the time the security interest would have become unperfected under the law of that jurisdiction; or

(2) the expiration of four months after a change of the applicable jurisdiction to another jurisdiction.

(g) Subsection (f) security interest perfected or unperfected under law of new jurisdiction. If a security interest described in subsection (f) becomes perfected under the law of the other jurisdiction before the earlier of the time or the end of the period described in that subsection, it remains perfected thereafter. If the security interest does not become perfected under the law of the other jurisdiction before the earlier of that time or the end of that period, it becomes unperfected and is deemed never to have been perfected as against a purchaser of the collateral for value.

(Source: P.A. 91-893, eff. 7-1-01.)

(810 ILCS 5/Art. 9 Pt. 3 Sub. 3 heading)
SUBPART 3. PRIORITY

(810 ILCS 5/9-317) (from Ch. 26, par. 9-317)

Sec. 9-317. Interests that take priority over or take free of security interest or agricultural lien.

(a) Conflicting security interests and rights of lien creditors. A security interest or agricultural lien is subordinate to the rights of:

(1) a person entitled to priority under Section 9-322; and

(2) except as otherwise provided in subsection (e) or (f), a person that becomes a lien creditor before the earlier of the time:

(A) the security interest or agricultural lien is perfected; or

(B) one of the conditions specified in Section 9-203(b)(3) is met and a financing statement covering the collateral is filed.

(b) Buyers that receive delivery. Except as otherwise provided in subsection (e), a buyer, other than a secured party, of tangible chattel paper, tangible documents, goods, instruments, or a security certificate takes free of a security interest or agricultural lien if the buyer gives value and receives delivery of the collateral without knowledge of the security interest or agricultural lien and before it is perfected.

(c) Lessees that receive delivery. Except as otherwise provided in subsection (e), a lessee of goods takes free of a security interest or agricultural lien if the lessee gives value and receives delivery of the collateral without knowledge of the security interest or agricultural lien and before it is perfected.

(d) Licensees and buyers of certain collateral. A licensee of a general intangible or a buyer, other than a secured party, of accounts, electronic chattel paper, electronic documents, general intangibles, or investment property other than a certificated security takes free of a security interest if the licensee or buyer gives value without knowledge of the security interest and before it is perfected.

(e) Purchase-money security interest. Except as otherwise provided in Sections 9-320 and 9-321, if a person files a financing statement with respect to a purchase-money security interest before or within 20 days after the debtor receives delivery of the collateral, the security interest takes priority over the rights of a buyer, lessee, or lien creditor which arise between the time the security interest attaches and the time of filing.

(f) Public deposits. An unperfected security interest shall take priority over the rights of a lien creditor if (i) the lien creditor is a trustee or receiver of a bank or acting in furtherance of its supervisory authority over such bank and (ii) a security interest is granted by the bank to secure a deposit of public funds with the bank or a repurchase agreement with the bank pursuant to the Government Securities Act of 1986, as amended.

(Source: P.A. 95-895, eff. 1-1-09.)

(810 ILCS 5/9-318) (from Ch. 26, par. 9-318)

Sec. 9-318. No interest retained in right to payment that is sold; rights and title of seller of account or chattel paper with respect to creditors and purchasers.

(a) Seller retains no interest. A debtor that has sold an account, chattel paper, payment intangible, or promissory note does not retain a legal or equitable interest in the collateral sold.

(b) Deemed rights of debtor if buyer's security interest unperfected. For purposes of determining the rights of creditors of, and purchasers for value of an account or chattel paper from, a debtor that has sold an account or chattel paper, while the buyer's security interest is unperfected, the debtor is deemed to have rights and title to the account or chattel paper identical to those the debtor sold.

(Source: P.A. 91-893, eff. 7-1-01.)

(810 ILCS 5/9-319)

Sec. 9-319. Rights and title of consignee with respect to creditors and purchasers.

(a) Consignee has consignor's rights. Except as otherwise provided in subsection (b), for purposes of determining the rights of creditors of, and purchasers for value of goods from, a consignee, while the goods are in the possession of the consignee, the consignee is deemed to have rights and title to the goods identical to those the consignor had or had power to transfer.

(b) Applicability of other law. For purposes of determining the rights of a creditor of a consignee, law other than this Article determines the rights and title of a consignee while goods are in the consignee's possession if, under this Part, a perfected security interest held by the consignor would have priority over the rights of the creditor.

(Source: P.A. 91-893, eff. 7-1-01.)

(810 ILCS 5/9-320)
Sec. 9-320. Buyer of goods and farm products.

(a) Buyer in ordinary course of business. Except as otherwise provided in subsections (e) and (f), a buyer in the ordinary course of business takes free of a security interest created by the buyer's seller, even if the security interest is perfected and the buyer knows of its existence.

(b) Buyer of consumer goods. Except as otherwise provided in subsection (e), a buyer of goods from a person who used or bought the goods for use primarily for personal, family, or household purposes takes free of a security interest, even if perfected, if the buyer buys:

(1) without knowledge of the security interest;
(2) for value;
(3) primarily for the buyer's personal, family, or household purposes; and
(4) before the filing of a financing statement covering the goods.

(c) Effectiveness of filing for subsection (b). To the extent that it affects the priority of a security interest over a buyer of goods under subsection (b), the period of effectiveness of a filing made in the jurisdiction in which the seller is located is governed by Section 9-316(a) and (b).

(d) Buyer in ordinary course of business at wellhead or minehead. A buyer in ordinary course of business buying oil, gas, or other minerals at the wellhead or minehead or after extraction takes free of an interest arising out of an encumbrance.

(e) Possessory security interest not affected. Subsections (a) and (b) do not affect a security interest in goods in the possession of the secured party under Section 9-313.

(f) Buyer of farm products.

(1) A buyer of farm products takes subject to a security interest created by the seller if:

(A) within one year before the sale of the farm products, the buyer has received from the secured party or the seller written notice of the security interest organized according to farm products that:

(i) is an original or reproduced copy thereof;

(ii) contains: (a) the name and address of the secured party; (b) the name and address of the person indebted to the secured party; (c) the social security number of the debtor or, in the case of a debtor doing business other than as an individual, the Internal Revenue Service taxpayer identification number of such debtor; (d) a description of the farm products subject to the security interest created by the debtor, including the amount of such products where applicable, crop year, county, and a reasonable description of the property;

(iii) must be amended in writing, within 3 months, similarly signed and transmitted, to reflect material changes;

(iv) will lapse on either the expiration period of the statement or the transmission of a notice signed by the secured party that the statement has lapsed, whichever occurs first; and

(v) sets forth any payment obligations imposed on the buyer by the secured party as conditions for waiver or release of the security interest; and

(B) the buyer has failed to perform the payment obligations.

(2) For the purposes of this subsection (f), a buyer of farm products has received notice from the secured party or seller when written notice of the security interest is sent to the buyer by registered or certified mail.

(Source: P.A. 91-893, eff. 7-1-01.)

(810 ILCS 5/9-320.1)
Sec. 9-320.1. Liability of commission merchant or selling agent engaged in sale of livestock or other farm products to holder of security interest.

(a) A commission merchant or selling agent who sells a farm product for others shall be subject to a security interest created by the seller in such farm product if:

(1) within one year before the sale of the farm products, the buyer has received from the secured party or the seller written notice of the security interest organized according to farm products that:

(A) is an original or reproduced copy thereof;

(B) contains: (i) the name and address of the secured party; (ii) the name and address of the person indebted to the secured party; (iii) the social security number of the debtor or, in case of a debtor doing business other than as an individual, the Internal Revenue Service taxpayer identification number of such debtor; (iv) a description of the farm products subject to the security interest created by the debtor, including the amount of such products where applicable, crop year, county, and a reasonable description of the property;

(C) must be amended in writing, within 3 months, similarly signed and transmitted, to reflect material changes;

(D) will lapse on either the expiration period of the statement or the transmission of a notice signed by the secured party that the statement has lapsed, whichever occurs first; and

(E) sets forth any payment obligations imposed on the buyer by the secured party as conditions for waiver or release of the security interest; and

(2) the commission merchant or selling agent has failed to perform the payment obligations.

(b) For the purposes of this Section, a commission merchant or selling agent has received notice from the secured party or seller when written notice of the security interest is sent to the commission merchant or selling agent by registered or certified mail.

(Source: P.A. 91-893, eff. 7-1-01.)

(810 ILCS 5/9-320.2)

Sec. 9-320.2. Notice to seller of farm products. A commission merchant or selling agent who sells farm products for others, and any person buying farm products in the ordinary course of business from a person engaged in farming operations, shall post at each licensed location where the merchant, agent, or person buying farm products in the ordinary course of business does business a notice that shall read as follows:

"NOTICE TO SELLERS OF FARM PRODUCTS

It is a criminal offense to sell farm products subject to a security interest without making payment to the secured party. You should notify the purchaser if there is a security interest in the farm products you are selling."

The notice shall be posted in a conspicuous manner and shall be in contrasting type, large enough to be read from a distance of 10 feet.

(Source: P.A. 91-893, eff. 7-1-01.)

(810 ILCS 5/9-321)

Sec. 9-321. Licensee of general intangible and lessee of goods in ordinary course of business.

(a) "Licensee in ordinary course of business." In this Section, "licensee in ordinary course of business" means a person that becomes a licensee of a general intangible in good faith, without knowledge that the license violates the rights of another person in the general intangible, and in the ordinary course from a person in the business of licensing general intangibles of that kind. A person becomes a licensee in the ordinary course if the license to the person comports with the usual or customary practices in the kind of business in which the licensor is engaged or with the licensor's own usual or customary practices.

(b) Rights of licensee in ordinary course of business. A licensee in ordinary course of business takes its rights under a nonexclusive license free of a security interest in the general intangible created by the licensor, even if the security interest is perfected and the licensee knows of its existence.

(c) Rights of lessee in ordinary course of business. A lessee in ordinary course of business takes its leasehold interest free of a security interest in the goods created by the lessor, even if the security interest is perfected and the lessee knows of its existence.

(Source: P.A. 91-893, eff. 7-1-01.)

(810 ILCS 5/9-322)

Sec. 9-322. Priorities among conflicting security interests in and agricultural liens on same collateral.

(a) General priority rules. Except as otherwise provided in this Section, priority among conflicting security interests and agricultural liens in the same collateral is determined according to the following rules:

(1) Conflicting perfected security interests and agricultural liens rank according to priority in time of filing or perfection. Priority dates from the earlier of the time a filing covering the collateral is first made or the security interest or agricultural lien is first perfected, if there is no period thereafter when there is neither filing nor perfection.

(2) A perfected security interest or agricultural lien has priority over a conflicting unperfected security interest or agricultural lien.

(3) The first security interest or agricultural lien to attach or become effective has priority if conflicting security interests and agricultural liens are unperfected.

(b) Time of perfection: proceeds and supporting obligations. For the purposes of subsection (a)(1):

(1) the time of filing or perfection as to a security interest in collateral is also the time of filing or perfection as to a security interest in proceeds; and

(2) the time of filing or perfection as to a security interest in collateral supported by a supporting obligation is also the time of filing or perfection as to a security interest in the supporting obligation.

(c) Special priority rules: proceeds and supporting obligations. Except as otherwise provided in subsection (f), a security interest in collateral which qualifies for priority over a conflicting security interest under Section 9-327, 9-328, 9-329, 9-329.1, 9-330, or 9-331 also has priority over a conflicting security interest in:

(1) any supporting obligation for the collateral; and

(2) proceeds of the collateral if:

(A) the security interest in proceeds is perfected;

(B) the proceeds are cash proceeds or of the same type as the collateral; and

(C) in the case of proceeds that are proceeds of proceeds, all intervening proceeds are cash proceeds, proceeds of the same type as the collateral, or an account relating to the collateral.

(d) First-to-file priority rule for certain collateral. Subject to subsection (e) and except as otherwise provided in subsection (f), if a security interest in chattel paper, deposit accounts, negotiable documents, instruments, investment property, letter-of-credit rights, or beneficial interests in Illinois land trusts is perfected by a method other than filing, conflicting perfected security interests in proceeds of the collateral rank according to priority in time of filing.

(e) Applicability of subsection (d). Subsection (d) applies only if the proceeds of the collateral are not cash proceeds, chattel paper, negotiable documents, instruments, investment property, beneficial interests in Illinois land trusts, or letter-of-credit rights.

(f) Limitations on subsections (a) through (e). Subsections (a) through (e) are subject to:

(1) subsection (g) and the other provisions of this Part;

(2) Section 4-210 with respect to a security interest of a collecting bank;

(3) Section 5-118 with respect to a security interest of an issuer or nominated person; and

(4) Section 9-110 with respect to a security interest arising under Article 2 or 2A.

(g) Priority under agricultural lien statute. A perfected agricultural lien on collateral has priority over a conflicting security interest in or agricultural lien on the same collateral if the statute creating the agricultural lien so provides.

(Source: P.A. 91-893, eff. 7-1-01; 92-234, eff. 1-1-02.)

(810 ILCS 5/9-323)

Sec. 9-323. Future advances.

(a) When priority based on time of advance. Except as otherwise provided in subsection (c), for purposes of determining the priority of a perfected security interest under

Section 9-322(a)(1), perfection of the security interest dates from the time an advance is made to the extent that the security interest secures an advance that:

(1) is made while the security interest is perfected only:

(A) under Section 9-309 when it attaches; or

(B) temporarily under Section 9-312(e), (f), or (g); and

(2) is not made pursuant to a commitment entered into before or while the security interest is perfected by a method other than under Section 9-309 or 9-312(e), (f), or (g).

(b) Lien creditor. Except as otherwise provided in subsection (c), a security interest is subordinate to the rights of a person that becomes a lien creditor to the extent that the security interest secures an advance made more than 45 days after the person becomes a lien creditor unless the advance is made:

(1) without knowledge of the lien; or

(2) pursuant to a commitment entered into without knowledge of the lien.

(c) Buyer of receivables. Subsections (a) and (b) do not apply to a security interest held by a secured party that is a buyer of accounts, chattel paper, payment intangibles, or promissory notes or a consignor.

(d) Buyer of goods. Except as otherwise provided in subsection (e), a buyer of goods other than a buyer in ordinary course of business takes free of a security interest to the extent that it secures advances made after the earlier of:

(1) the time the secured party acquires knowledge of the buyer's purchase; or

(2) 45 days after the purchase.

(e) Advances made pursuant to commitment: priority of buyer of goods. Subsection (d) does not apply if the advance is made pursuant to a commitment entered into without knowledge of the buyer's purchase and before the expiration of the 45-day period.

(f) Lessee of goods. Except as otherwise provided in subsection (g), a lessee of goods, other than a lessee in ordinary course of business, takes the leasehold interest free of a security interest to the extent that it secures advances made after the earlier of:

(1) the time the secured party acquires knowledge of the lease; or

(2) 45 days after the lease contract becomes enforceable.

(g) Advances made pursuant to commitment: priority of lessee of goods. Subsection (f) does not apply if the advance is made pursuant to a commitment entered into without knowledge of the lease and before the expiration of the 45-day period.

(Source: P.A. 91-893, eff. 7-1-01.)

(810 ILCS 5/9-324)

Sec. 9-324. Priority of purchase-money security interests.

(a) General rule: purchase-money priority. Except as otherwise provided in subsection (g), a perfected purchase-money security interest in goods other than inventory or livestock has priority over a conflicting security interest in the same goods, and, except as otherwise provided in Section 9-327, a perfected security interest in its identifiable proceeds also has priority, if the purchase-money security interest is perfected when the debtor receives possession of the collateral or within 20 days thereafter.

(b) Inventory purchase-money priority. Subject to subsection (c) and except as otherwise provided in subsection (g), a perfected purchase-money security interest in inventory has priority over a conflicting security interest in the same inventory, has priority over a conflicting security interest in chattel paper or an instrument constituting proceeds of the inventory and in proceeds of the chattel paper, if so provided in Section 9-330, and, except as otherwise provided in Section 9-327, also has priority in identifiable cash proceeds of the inventory to the extent the identifiable cash proceeds are received on or before the delivery of the inventory to a buyer, if:

(1) the purchase-money security interest is perfected when the debtor receives possession of the inventory;

(2) the purchase-money secured party sends an authenticated notification to the holder of the conflicting security interest;

(3) the holder of the conflicting security interest receives the notification within five years before the debtor receives possession of the inventory; and

(4) the notification states that the person sending the notification has or expects to acquire a purchase-money security interest in inventory of the debtor and describes the inventory.

(c) Holders of conflicting inventory security interests to be notified. Subsections (b)(2) through (4) apply only if the holder of the conflicting security interest had filed a financing statement covering the same types of inventory:

(1) if the purchase-money security interest is perfected by filing, before the date of the filing; or

(2) if the purchase-money security interest is temporarily perfected without filing or possession under Section 9-312(f), before the beginning of the 20-day period thereunder.

(d) Livestock purchase-money priority. Subject to subsection (e) and except as otherwise provided in subsection (g), a perfected purchase-money security interest in livestock that are farm products has priority over a conflicting security interest in the same livestock, and, except as otherwise provided in Section 9-327, a perfected security interest in their identifiable proceeds and identifiable products in their unmanufactured states also has priority, if:

(1) the purchase-money security interest is perfected when the debtor receives possession of the livestock;

(2) the purchase-money secured party sends an authenticated notification to the holder of the conflicting security interest;

(3) the holder of the conflicting security interest receives the notification within six months before the debtor receives possession of the livestock; and

(4) the notification states that the person sending the notification has or expects to acquire a purchase-money security interest in livestock of the debtor and describes the livestock.

(e) Holders of conflicting livestock security interests to be notified. Subsections (d)(2) through (4) apply only if the holder of the conflicting security interest had filed a financing statement covering the same types of livestock:

(1) if the purchase-money security interest is perfected by filing, before the date of the filing; or

(2) if the purchase-money security interest is temporarily perfected without filing or possession under Section 9-312(f), before the beginning of the 20-day period thereunder.

(f) Software purchase-money priority. Except as otherwise provided in subsection (g), a perfected purchase-money security interest in software has priority over a conflicting security interest in the same collateral, and, except as otherwise provided in Section 9-327, a perfected security interest in its identifiable proceeds also has priority, to the extent that the purchase-money security interest in the goods in which the software was acquired for use has priority in the goods and proceeds of the goods under this Section.

(g) Conflicting purchase-money security interests. If more than one security interest qualifies for priority in the same collateral under subsection (a), (b), (d), or (f):

(1) a security interest securing an obligation incurred as all or part of the price of the collateral has priority over a security interest securing an obligation incurred for value given to enable the debtor to acquire rights in or the use of collateral; and

(2) in all other cases, Section 9-322(a) applies to the qualifying security interests.
(Source: P.A. 91-893, eff. 7-1-01.)

(810 ILCS 5/9-325)
Sec. 9-325. Priority of security interests in transferred collateral.

(a) Subordination of security interest in transferred collateral. Except as otherwise provided in subsection (b), a security interest created by a debtor is subordinate to a security interest in the same collateral created by another person if:

(1) the debtor acquired the collateral subject to the security interest created by the other person;

(2) the security interest created by the other person was perfected when the debtor acquired the collateral; and

(3) there is no period thereafter when the security interest is unperfected.

(b) Limitation of subsection (a) subordination. Subsection (a) subordinates a security interest only if the security interest:
  (1) otherwise would have priority solely under Section 9-322(a) or 9-324; or
  (2) arose solely under Section 2-711(3) or 2A-508(5).
  (Source: P.A. 91-893, eff. 7-1-01.)

(810 ILCS 5/9-326)
Sec. 9-326. Priority of security interests created by new debtor.
  (a) Subordination of security interest created by new debtor. Subject to subsection (b), a security interest created by a new debtor which is perfected by a filed financing statement that is effective solely under Section 9-508 in collateral in which a new debtor has or acquires rights is subordinate to a security interest in the same collateral which is perfected other than by a filed financing statement that is effective solely under Section 9-508.
  (b) Priority under other provisions; multiple original debtors. The other provisions of this Part determine the priority among conflicting security interests in the same collateral perfected by filed financing statements that are effective solely under Section 9-508. However, if the security agreements to which a new debtor became bound as debtor were not entered into by the same original debtor, the conflicting security interests rank according to priority in time of the new debtor's having become bound.
  (Source: P.A. 91-893, eff. 7-1-01.)

(810 ILCS 5/9-327)
Sec. 9-327. Priority of security interests in deposit account. The following rules govern priority among conflicting security interests in the same deposit account:
  (1) A security interest held by a secured party having control of the deposit account under Section 9-104 has priority over a conflicting security interest held by a secured party that does not have control.
  (2) Except as otherwise provided in paragraphs (3) and (4), security interests perfected by control under Section 9-314 rank according to priority in time of obtaining control.
  (3) Except as otherwise provided in paragraph (4), a security interest held by the bank with which the deposit account is maintained has priority over a conflicting security interest held by another secured party.
  (4) A security interest perfected by control under Section 9-104(a)(3) has priority over a security interest held by the bank with which the deposit account is maintained.
  (Source: P.A. 91-893, eff. 7-1-01.)

(810 ILCS 5/9-328)
Sec. 9-328. Priority of security interests in investment property. The following rules govern priority among conflicting security interests in the same investment property:
  (1) A security interest held by a secured party having control of investment property under Section 9-106 has priority over a security interest held by a secured party that does not have control of the investment property.
  (2) Except as otherwise provided in paragraphs (3) and (4), conflicting security interests held by secured parties each of which has control under Section 9-106 rank according to priority in time of:
    (A) if the collateral is a security, obtaining control;
    (B) if the collateral is a security entitlement carried in a securities account and:
      (i) if the secured party obtained control under Section 8-106(d)(1), the secured party's becoming the person for which the securities account is maintained;
      (ii) if the secured party obtained control under Section 8-106(d)(2), the securities intermediary's agreement to comply with the secured party's entitlement orders with respect to security entitlements carried or to be carried in the securities account; or
      (iii) if the secured party obtained control through another person under Section 8-106(d)(3), the time on which priority would be based under this paragraph if the other person were the secured party; or

(C) if the collateral is a commodity contract carried with a commodity intermediary, the satisfaction of the requirement for control specified in Section 9-106(b)(2) with respect to commodity contracts carried or to be carried with the commodity intermediary.

(3) A security interest held by a securities intermediary in a security entitlement or a securities account maintained with the securities intermediary has priority over a conflicting security interest held by another secured party.

(4) A security interest held by a commodity intermediary in a commodity contract or a commodity account maintained with the commodity intermediary has priority over a conflicting security interest held by another secured party.

(5) A security interest in a certificated security in registered form which is perfected by taking delivery under Section 9-313(a) and not by control under Section 9-314 has priority over a conflicting security interest perfected by a method other than control.

(6) Conflicting security interests created by a broker, securities intermediary, or commodity intermediary which are perfected without control under Section 9-106 rank equally.

(7) In all other cases, priority among conflicting security interests in investment property is governed by Sections 9-322 and 9-323.
(Source: P.A. 91-893, eff. 7-1-01.)

(810 ILCS 5/9-329)
Sec. 9-329. Priority of security interests in letter-of-credit right. The following rules govern priority among conflicting security interests in the same letter-of-credit right:
(1) A security interest held by a secured party having control of the letter-of-credit right under Section 9-107 has priority to the extent of its control over a conflicting security interest held by a secured party that does not have control.
(2) Security interests perfected by control under Section 9-314 rank according to priority in time of obtaining control.
(Source: P.A. 91-893, eff. 7-1-01.)

(810 ILCS 5/9-329.1)
Sec. 9-329.1. Priority of Security Interests in Beneficial Interest in an Illinois Land Trust. The following rules govern priority among conflicting security interests in the same beneficial interest in an Illinois land trust:
(1) A security interest held by a secured party having control of the beneficial interest under Section 9-107.1 has priority to the extent of its control over a conflicting security interest held by a secured party that does not have control.
(2) Security interests perfected by control under Section 9-314 rank according to priority in time of obtaining control.
(Source: P.A. 92-234, eff. 1-1-02.)

(810 ILCS 5/9-330)
Sec. 9-330. Priority of purchaser of chattel paper or instrument.
(a) Purchaser's priority: security interest claimed merely as proceeds. A purchaser of chattel paper has priority over a security interest in the chattel paper which is claimed merely as proceeds of inventory subject to a security interest if:
(1) in good faith and in the ordinary course of the purchaser's business, the purchaser gives new value and takes possession of the chattel paper or obtains control of the chattel paper under Section 9-105; and
(2) the chattel paper does not indicate that it has been assigned to an identified assignee other than the purchaser.
(b) Purchaser's priority: other security interests. A purchaser of chattel paper has priority over a security interest in the chattel paper which is claimed other than merely as proceeds of inventory subject to a security interest if the purchaser gives new value and takes possession of the chattel paper or obtains control of the chattel paper under Section 9-105 in good faith, in the ordinary course of the purchaser's business, and without knowledge that the purchase violates the rights of the secured party.

(c) Chattel paper purchaser's priority in proceeds. Except as otherwise provided in Section 9-327, a purchaser having priority in chattel paper under subsection (a) or (b) also has priority in proceeds of the chattel paper to the extent that:

(1) Section 9-322 provides for priority in the proceeds; or

(2) the proceeds consist of the specific goods covered by the chattel paper or cash proceeds of the specific goods, even if the purchaser's security interest in the proceeds is unperfected.

(d) Instrument purchaser's priority. Except as otherwise provided in Section 9-331(a), a purchaser of an instrument has priority over a security interest in the instrument perfected by a method other than possession if the purchaser gives value and takes possession of the instrument in good faith and without knowledge that the purchase violates the rights of the secured party.

(e) Holder of purchase-money security interest gives new value. For purposes of subsections (a) and (b), the holder of a purchase-money security interest in inventory gives new value for chattel paper constituting proceeds of the inventory.

(f) Indication of assignment gives knowledge. For purposes of subsections (b) and (d), if chattel paper or an instrument indicates that it has been assigned to an identified secured party other than the purchaser, a purchaser of the chattel paper or instrument has knowledge that the purchase violates the rights of the secured party.

(Source: P.A. 91-893, eff. 7-1-01.)

(810 ILCS 5/9-331)

Sec. 9-331. Priority of rights of purchasers of instruments, documents, and securities under other Articles; priority of interests in financial assets and security entitlements under Article 8.

(a) Rights under Articles 3, 7, and 8 not limited. This Article does not limit the rights of a holder in due course of a negotiable instrument, a holder to which a negotiable document of title has been duly negotiated, or a protected purchaser of a security. These holders or purchasers take priority over an earlier security interest, even if perfected, to the extent provided in Articles 3, 7, and 8.

(b) Protection under Article 8. This Article does not limit the rights of or impose liability on a person to the extent that the person is protected against the assertion of a claim under Article 8.

(c) Filing not notice. Filing under this Article does not constitute notice of a claim or defense to the holders, or purchasers, or persons described in subsections (a) and (b).

(Source: P.A. 91-893, eff. 7-1-01.)

(810 ILCS 5/9-332)

Sec. 9-332. Transfer of money; transfer of funds from deposit account.

(a) Transferee of money. A transferee of money takes the money free of a security interest unless the transferee acts in collusion with the debtor in violating the rights of the secured party.

(b) Transferee of funds from deposit account. A transferee of funds from a deposit account takes the funds free of a security interest in the deposit account unless the transferee acts in collusion with the debtor in violating the rights of the secured party.

(Source: P.A. 91-893, eff. 7-1-01.)

(810 ILCS 5/9-333)

Sec. 9-333. Priority of certain liens arising by operation of law.

(a) "Possessory lien." In this Section, "possessory lien" means an interest, other than a security interest or an agricultural lien:

(1) which secures payment or performance of an obligation for services or materials furnished with respect to goods by a person in the ordinary course of the person's business;

(2) which is created by statute or rule of law in favor of the person; and

(3) whose effectiveness depends on the person's possession of the goods.

(b) Priority of possessory lien. A possessory lien on goods has priority over a security interest in the goods unless the lien is created by a statute that expressly provides otherwise.
(Source: P.A. 91-893, eff. 7-1-01.)

(810 ILCS 5/9-334)
Sec. 9-334. Priority of security interests in fixtures and crops.
(a) Security interest in fixtures under this Article. A security interest under this Article may be created in goods that are fixtures or may continue in goods that become fixtures. A security interest does not exist under this Article in ordinary building materials incorporated into an improvement on land.
(b) Security interest in fixtures under real-property law. This Article does not prevent creation of an encumbrance upon fixtures under real property law.
(c) General rule: subordination of security interest in fixtures. In cases not governed by subsections (d) through (h), a security interest in fixtures is subordinate to a conflicting interest of an encumbrancer or owner of the related real property other than the debtor.
(d) Fixtures purchase-money priority. Except as otherwise provided in subsection (h), a perfected security interest in fixtures has priority over a conflicting interest of an encumbrancer or owner of the real property if the debtor has an interest of record in or is in possession of the real property and:
(1) the security interest is a purchase-money security interest;
(2) the interest of the encumbrancer or owner arises before the goods become fixtures; and
(3) the security interest is perfected by a fixture filing before the goods become fixtures or within 20 days thereafter.
(e) Priority of security interest in fixtures over interests in real property. A perfected security interest in fixtures has priority over a conflicting interest of an encumbrancer or owner of the real property if:
(1) the debtor has an interest of record in the real property or is in possession of the real property and the security interest:
(A) is perfected by a fixture filing before the interest of the encumbrancer or owner is of record; and
(B) has priority over any conflicting interest of a predecessor in title of the encumbrancer or owner;
(2) before the goods become fixtures, the security interest is perfected by any method permitted by this Article and the fixtures are readily removable:
(A) factory or office machines;
(B) equipment that is not primarily used or leased for use in the operation of the real property; or
(C) replacements of domestic appliances that are consumer goods;
(3) the conflicting interest is a lien on the real property obtained by legal or equitable proceedings after the security interest was perfected by any method permitted by this Article; or
(4) the security interest is:
(A) created in a manufactured home in a manufactured-home transaction; and
(B) perfected pursuant to a statute described in Section 9-311(a)(2).
(f) Priority based on consent, disclaimer, or right to remove. A security interest in fixtures, whether or not perfected, has priority over a conflicting interest of an encumbrancer or owner of the real property if:
(1) the encumbrancer or owner has, in an authenticated record, consented to the security interest or disclaimed an interest in the goods as fixtures; or
(2) the debtor has a right to remove the goods as against the encumbrancer or owner.
(g) Continuation of subsection (f)(2) priority. The priority of the security interest under subsection (f)(2) continues for a reasonable time if the debtor's right to remove the goods as against the encumbrancer or owner terminates.

(h) Priority of construction mortgage. A mortgage is a construction mortgage to the extent that it secures an obligation incurred for the construction of an improvement on land, including the acquisition cost of the land, if a recorded record of the mortgage so indicates. Except as otherwise provided in subsections (e) and (f), a security interest in fixtures is subordinate to a construction mortgage if a record of the mortgage is recorded before the goods become fixtures and the goods become fixtures before the completion of the construction. A mortgage has this priority to the same extent as a construction mortgage to the extent that it is given to refinance a construction mortgage.

(i) Priority of security interest in crops.

(1) Subject to Section 9-322(g), a perfected security interest in crops growing on real property has priority over:

(A) a conflicting interest of an encumbrancer or owner of the real property; and

(B) the rights of a holder of an obligation secured by a collateral assignment of beneficial interest in a land trust, including rights by virtue of an equitable lien.

(2) For purposes of this subsection:

(A) "Collateral assignment of beneficial interest" means any pledge or assignment of the beneficial interest in a land trust to a person to secure a debt to other obligation.

(B) "Land trust" means any trust arrangement under which the legal and equitable title to real estate is held by a trustee, the interest of the beneficiary of the trust is personal property, and the beneficiary or any person designated in writing by the beneficiary has (i) the exclusive power to direct or control the trustee in dealing with the title to the trust property, (ii) the exclusive control of the management, operation, renting, and selling of the trust property, and (iii) the exclusive right to the earnings, avails, and proceeds of trust property.

(Source: P.A. 91-893, eff. 7-1-01.)

(810 ILCS 5/9-335)

Sec. 9-335. Accessions.

(a) Creation of security interest in accession. A security interest may be created in an accession and continues in collateral that becomes an accession.

(b) Perfection of security interest. If a security interest is perfected when the collateral becomes an accession, the security interest remains perfected in the collateral.

(c) Priority of security interest. Except as otherwise provided in subsection (d), the other provisions of this Part determine the priority of a security interest in an accession.

(d) Compliance with certificate-of-title statute. A security interest in an accession is subordinate to a security interest in the whole which is perfected by compliance with the requirements of a certificate-of-title statute under Section 9-311(b).

(e) Removal of accession after default. After default, subject to Part 6, a secured party may remove an accession from other goods if the security interest in the accession has priority over the claims of every person having an interest in the whole.

(f) Reimbursement following removal. A secured party that removes an accession from other goods under subsection (e) shall promptly reimburse any holder of a security interest or other lien on, or owner of, the whole or of the other goods, other than the debtor, for the cost of repair of any physical injury to the whole or the other goods. The secured party need not reimburse the holder or owner for any diminution in value of the whole or the other goods caused by the absence of the accession removed or by any necessity for replacing it. A person entitled to reimbursement may refuse permission to remove until the secured party gives adequate assurance for the performance of the obligation to reimburse.

(Source: P.A. 91-893, eff. 7-1-01.)

(810 ILCS 5/9-336)

Sec. 9-336. Commingled goods.

(a) "Commingled goods." In this Section, "commingled goods" means goods that are physically united with other goods in such a manner that their identity is lost in a product or mass.

(b) No security interest in commingled goods as such. A security interest does not exist in commingled goods as such. However, a security interest may attach to a product or mass that results when goods become commingled goods.

(c) Attachment of security interest to product or mass. If collateral becomes commingled goods, a security interest attaches to the product or mass.

(d) Perfection of security interest. If a security interest in collateral is perfected before the collateral becomes commingled goods, the security interest that attaches to the product or mass under subsection (c) is perfected.

(e) Priority of security interest. Except as otherwise provided in subsection (f), the other provisions of this Part determine the priority of a security interest that attaches to the product or mass under subsection (c).

(f) Conflicting security interests in product or mass. If more than one security interest attaches to the product or mass under subsection (c), the following rules determine priority:

(1) A security interest that is perfected under subsection (d) has priority over a security interest that is unperfected at the time the collateral becomes commingled goods.

(2) If more than one security interest is perfected under subsection (d), the security interests rank equally in proportion to the value of the collateral at the time it became commingled goods.

(Source: P.A. 91-893, eff. 7-1-01.)

(810 ILCS 5/9-337)

Sec. 9-337. Priority of security interests in goods covered by certificate of title. If, while a security interest in goods is perfected by any method under the law of another jurisdiction, this State issues a certificate of title that does not show that the goods are subject to the security interest or contain a statement that they may be subject to security interests not shown on the certificate:

(1) a buyer of the goods, other than a person in the business of selling goods of that kind, takes free of the security interest if the buyer gives value and receives delivery of the goods after issuance of the certificate and without knowledge of the security interest; and

(2) the security interest is subordinate to a conflicting security interest in the goods that attaches, and is perfected under Section 9-311(b), after issuance of the certificate and without the conflicting secured party's knowledge of the security interest.

(Source: P.A. 91-893, eff. 7-1-01.)

(810 ILCS 5/9-338)

Sec. 9-338. Priority of security interest or agricultural lien perfected by filed financing statement providing certain incorrect information. If a security interest or agricultural lien is perfected by a filed financing statement providing information described in Section 9-516(b)(5) which is incorrect at the time the financing statement is filed:

(1) the security interest or agricultural lien is subordinate to a conflicting perfected security interest in the collateral to the extent that the holder of the conflicting security interest gives value in reasonable reliance upon the incorrect information; and

(2) a purchaser, other than a secured party, of the collateral takes free of the security interest or agricultural lien to the extent that, in reasonable reliance upon the incorrect information, the purchaser gives value and, in the case of tangible chattel paper, tangible documents, goods, instruments, or a security certificate, receives delivery of the collateral.

(Source: P.A. 95-895, eff. 1-1-09.)

(810 ILCS 5/9-339)

Sec. 9-339. Priority subject to subordination. This Article does not preclude subordination by agreement by a person entitled to priority.

(Source: P.A. 91-893, eff. 7-1-01.)

(810 ILCS 5/Art. 9 Pt. 3 Sub. 4 heading)
SUBPART 4. RIGHTS OF BANK

(810 ILCS 5/9-340)

Sec. 9-340. Effectiveness of right of recoupment or set-off against deposit account.

(a) Exercise of recoupment or set-off. Except as otherwise provided in subsection (c), a bank with which a deposit account is maintained may exercise any right of recoupment or set-off against a secured party that holds a security interest in the deposit account.

(b) Recoupment or set-off not affected by security interest. Except as otherwise provided in subsection (c), the application of this Article to a security interest in a deposit account does not affect a right of recoupment or set-off of the secured party as to a deposit account maintained with the secured party.

(c) When set-off ineffective. The exercise by a bank of a set-off against a deposit account is ineffective against a secured party that holds a security interest in the deposit account which is perfected by control under Section 9-104(a)(3), if the set-off is based on a claim against the debtor.

(Source: P.A. 91-893, eff. 7-1-01.)

(810 ILCS 5/9-341)

Sec. 9-341. Bank's rights and duties with respect to deposit account. Except as otherwise provided in Section 9-340(c), and unless the bank otherwise agrees in an authenticated record, a bank's rights and duties with respect to a deposit account maintained with the bank are not terminated, suspended, or modified by:

(1) the creation, attachment, or perfection of a security interest in the deposit account;
(2) the bank's knowledge of the security interest; or
(3) the bank's receipt of instructions from the secured party.

(Source: P.A. 91-893, eff. 7-1-01.)

(810 ILCS 5/9-342)

Sec. 9-342. Bank's right to refuse to enter into or disclose existence of control agreement. This Article does not require a bank to enter into an agreement of the kind described in Section 9-104(a)(2), even if its customer so requests or directs. A bank that has entered into such an agreement is not required to confirm the existence of the agreement to another person unless requested to do so by its customer.

(Source: P.A. 91-893, eff. 7-1-01.)

(810 ILCS 5/Art. 9 Pt. 4 heading)
PART 4. RIGHTS OF THIRD PARTIES

(810 ILCS 5/9-401) (from Ch. 26, par. 9-401)
Sec. 9-401. Alienability of debtor's rights.

(a) Other law governs alienability; exceptions. Except as otherwise provided in subsection (b) and Sections 9-406, 9-407, 9-408, and 9-409, whether a debtor's rights in collateral may be voluntarily or involuntarily transferred is governed by law other than this Article.

(b) Agreement does not prevent transfer. An agreement between the debtor and secured party which prohibits a transfer of the debtor's rights in collateral or makes the transfer a default does not prevent the transfer from taking effect.

(Source: P.A. 90-300, eff. 1-1-98; 91-893, eff. 7-1-01.)

(810 ILCS 5/9-401A)
Sec. 9-401A. (Blank).
(Source: P.A. 90-300, eff. 1-1-98; 91-893, eff. 7-1-01.)

(810 ILCS 5/9-402) (from Ch. 26, par. 9-402)
Sec. 9-402. Secured party not obligated on contract of debtor or in tort. The existence of a security interest, agricultural lien, or authority given to a debtor to dispose of or use collateral, without more, does not subject a secured party to liability in contract or tort for the debtor's acts or omissions.

(Source: P.A. 91-357, eff. 7-29-99; 91-893, eff. 7-1-01.)

(810 ILCS 5/9-403) (from Ch. 26, par. 9-403)
Sec. 9-403. Agreement not to assert defenses against assignee.
(a) "Value." In this Section, "value" has the meaning provided in Section 3-303(a).
(b) Agreement not to assert claim or defense. Except as otherwise provided in this Section, an agreement between an account debtor and an assignor not to assert against

an assignee any claim or defense that the account debtor may have against the assignor is enforceable by an assignee that takes an assignment:

(1) for value;

(2) in good faith;

(3) without notice of a claim of a property or possessory right to the property assigned; and

(4) without notice of a defense or claim in recoupment of the type that may be asserted against a person entitled to enforce a negotiable instrument under Section 3-305(a).

(c) When subsection (b) not applicable. Subsection (b) does not apply to defenses of a type that may be asserted against a holder in due course of a negotiable instrument under Section 3-305(b).

(d) Omission of required statement in consumer transaction. In a consumer transaction, if a record evidences the account debtor's obligation, law other than this Article requires that the record include a statement to the effect that the rights of an assignee are subject to claims or defenses that the account debtor could assert against the original obligee, and the record does not include such a statement:

(1) the record has the same effect as if the record included such a statement; and

(2) the account debtor may assert against an assignee those claims and defenses that would have been available if the record included such a statement.

(e) Rule for individual under other law. This Section is subject to law other than this Article which establishes a different rule for an account debtor who is an individual and who incurred the obligation primarily for personal, family, or household purposes.

(f) Other law not displaced. Except as otherwise provided in subsection (d), this Section does not displace law other than this Article which gives effect to an agreement by an account debtor not to assert a claim or defense against an assignee.

(Source: P.A. 90-300, eff. 1-1-98; 91-357, eff. 7-29-99; 91-893, eff. 7-1-01.)

(810 ILCS 5/9-404) (from Ch. 26, par. 9-404)

Sec. 9-404. Rights acquired by assignee; claims and defenses against assignee.

(a) Assignee's rights subject to terms, claims, and defenses; exceptions. Unless an account debtor has made an enforceable agreement not to assert defenses or claims, and subject to subsections (b) through (e), the rights of an assignee are subject to:

(1) all terms of the agreement between the account debtor and assignor and any defense or claim in recoupment arising from the transaction that gave rise to the contract; and

(2) any other defense or claim of the account debtor against the assignor which accrues before the account debtor receives a notification of the assignment authenticated by the assignor or the assignee.

(b) Account debtor's claim reduces amount owed to assignee. Subject to subsection (c) and except as otherwise provided in subsection (d), the claim of an account debtor against an assignor may be asserted against an assignee under subsection (a) only to reduce the amount the account debtor owes.

(c) Rule for individual under other law. This Section is subject to law other than this Article which establishes a different rule for an account debtor who is an individual and who incurred the obligation primarily for personal, family, or household purposes.

(d) Omission of required statement in consumer transaction. In a consumer transaction, if a record evidences the account debtor's obligation, law other than this Article requires that the record include a statement to the effect that the account debtor's recovery against an assignee with respect to claims and defenses against the assignor may not exceed amounts paid by the account debtor under the record, and the record does not include such a statement, the extent to which a claim of an account debtor against the assignor may be asserted against an assignee is determined as if the record included such a statement.

(e) Inapplicability to health-care-insurance receivable. This Section does not apply to an assignment of a health-care-insurance receivable.

(Source: P.A. 91-893, eff. 7-1-01.)

(810 ILCS 5/9-404.5)

Sec. 9-404.5. Termination statement; duties of filing officer.

(1) If a financing statement covering consumer goods is filed on or after July 1, 1973, then within one month or within 10 days following written demand by the debtor after there is no outstanding secured obligation and no commitment to make advances, incur obligations or otherwise give value, the secured party must file with each filing officer with whom the financing statement was filed, a termination statement to the effect that he no longer claims a security interest under the financing statement, which shall be identified by file number. In other cases whenever there is no outstanding secured obligation and no commitment to make advances, incur obligations or otherwise give value, the secured party must on written demand by the debtor send the debtor, for each filing officer with whom the financing statement was filed, a termination statement to the effect that he no longer claims a security interest under the financing statement, which shall be identified by file number. A termination statement signed by a person other than the secured party of record must be accompanied by a separate written statement of assignment signed by the secured party of record. If the affected secured party fails to file such a termination statement as required by this subsection, or to send such a termination statement within 10 days after proper demand therefor, he shall be liable to the debtor for $100 and in addition for any loss caused to the debtor by such failure.

(2) On presentation to the filing officer of such a termination statement he must note it in the index. If he has received the termination statement in duplicate, he shall return one copy of the termination statement to the secured party stamped to show the time of receipt thereof. If the filing officer has a microfilm or other photographic record of the financing statement, and of any related continuation statement, statement of assignment and statement of release, he may remove the originals from the files at any time after receipt of the termination statement, or if he has no such record, he may remove them from the files at any time after one year after receipt of the termination statement.

(3) If the termination statement is in the standard form prescribed by the Secretary of State, the uniform fee for filing and indexing the termination statement in the office of a county recorder shall be $5 and otherwise shall be $10, plus in each case an additional fee of $5 for each name more than one at each address listed against which the termination statement is required to be indexed.

(Source: P.A. 91-893, eff. 7-6-00.)

(810 ILCS 5/9-405) (from Ch. 26, par. 9-405)

Sec. 9-405. Modification of assigned contract.

(a) Effect of modification on assignee. A modification of or substitution for an assigned contract is effective against an assignee if made in good faith. The assignee acquires corresponding rights under the modified or substituted contract. The assignment may provide that the modification or substitution is a breach of contract by the assignor. This subsection is subject to subsections (b) through (d).

(b) Applicability of subsection (a). Subsection (a) applies to the extent that:

(1) the right to payment or a part thereof under an assigned contract has not been fully earned by performance; or

(2) the right to payment or a part thereof has been fully earned by performance and the account debtor has not received notification of the assignment under Section 9-406(a).

(c) Rule for individual under other law. This Section is subject to law other than this Article which establishes a different rule for an account debtor who is an individual and who incurred the obligation primarily for personal, family, or household purposes.

(d) Inapplicability to health-care-insurance receivable. This Section does not apply to an assignment of a health-care-insurance receivable.

(Source: P.A. 91-893, eff. 7-1-01.)

(810 ILCS 5/9-406) (from Ch. 26, par. 9-406)

Sec. 9-406. Discharge of account debtor; notification of assignment; identification and proof of assignment; restrictions on assignment of accounts, chattel paper, payment intangibles, and promissory notes ineffective.

(a) Discharge of account debtor; effect of notification. Subject to subsections (b) through (i), an account debtor on an account, chattel paper, or a payment intangible may discharge its obligation by paying the assignor until, but not after, the account debtor receives a notification, authenticated by the assignor or the assignee, that the amount due or to become due has been assigned and that payment is to be made to the assignee. After receipt of the notification, the account debtor may discharge its obligation by paying the assignee and may not discharge the obligation by paying the assignor.

(b) When notification ineffective. Subject to subsection (h), notification is ineffective under subsection (a):

(1) if it does not reasonably identify the rights assigned;

(2) to the extent that an agreement between an account debtor and a seller of a payment intangible limits the account debtor's duty to pay a person other than the seller and the limitation is effective under law other than this Article; or

(3) at the option of an account debtor, if the notification notifies the account debtor to make less than the full amount of any installment or other periodic payment to the assignee, even if:

(A) only a portion of the account, chattel paper, or payment intangible has been assigned to that assignee;

(B) a portion has been assigned to another assignee; or

(C) the account debtor knows that the assignment to that assignee is limited.

(c) Proof of assignment. Subject to subsection (h), if requested by the account debtor, an assignee shall seasonably furnish reasonable proof that the assignment has been made. Unless the assignee complies, the account debtor may discharge its obligation by paying the assignor, even if the account debtor has received a notification under subsection (a).

(d) Term restricting assignment generally ineffective. Except as otherwise provided in subsection (e) and Sections 2A-303 and 9-407, and subject to subsection (h), a term in an agreement between an account debtor and an assignor or in a promissory note is ineffective to the extent that it:

(1) prohibits, restricts, or requires the consent of the account debtor or person obligated on the promissory note to the assignment or transfer of, or the creation, attachment, perfection, or enforcement of a security interest in, the account, chattel paper, payment intangible, or promissory note; or

(2) provides that the assignment or transfer or the creation, attachment, perfection, or enforcement of the security interest may give rise to a default, breach, right of recoupment, claim, defense, termination, right of termination, or remedy under the account, chattel paper, payment intangible, or promissory note.

(e) Inapplicability of subsection (d) to certain sales. Subsection (d) does not apply to the sale of a payment intangible or promissory note.

(f) Legal restrictions on assignment generally ineffective. Except as otherwise provided in Sections 2A-303 and 9-407 and subject to subsections (h) and (i), a rule of law, statute, or regulation that prohibits, restricts, or requires the consent of a government, governmental body or official, or account debtor to the assignment or transfer of, or creation of a security interest in, an account or chattel paper is ineffective to the extent that the rule of law, statute, or regulation:

(1) prohibits, restricts, or requires the consent of the government, governmental body or official, or account debtor to the assignment or transfer of, or the creation, attachment, perfection, or enforcement of a security interest in the account or chattel paper; or

(2) provides that the assignment or transfer or the creation, attachment, perfection, or enforcement of the security interest may give rise to a default, breach, right of recoupment, claim, defense, termination, right of termination, or remedy under the account or chattel paper.

(g) Subsection (b)(3) not waivable. Subject to subsection (h), an account debtor may not waive or vary its option under subsection (b)(3).

(h) Rule for individual under other law. This Section is subject to law other than this Article which establishes a different rule for an account debtor who is an individual and who incurred the obligation primarily for personal, family, or household purposes.

(i) Inapplicability to health-care-insurance receivable. This Section does not apply to an assignment of a health-care-insurance receivable.
(Source: P.A. 91-893, eff. 7-1-01.)

(810 ILCS 5/9-407) (from Ch. 26, par. 9-407)
Sec. 9-407. Restrictions on creation or enforcement of security interest in leasehold interest or in lessor's residual interest.
(a) Term restricting assignment generally ineffective. Except as otherwise provided in subsection (b), a term in a lease agreement is ineffective to the extent that it:
(1) prohibits, restricts, or requires the consent of a party to the lease to the assignment or transfer or the creation, attachment, perfection, or enforcement of a security interest in an interest of a party under the lease contract or in the lessor's residual interest in the goods; or
(2) provides that the assignment or transfer or the creation, attachment, perfection, or enforcement of the security interest may give rise to a default, breach, right of recoupment, claim, defense, termination, right of termination, or remedy under the lease.
(b) Effectiveness of certain terms. Except as otherwise provided in Section 2A-303(7), a term described in subsection (a)(2) is effective to the extent that there is:
(1) a transfer by the lessee of the lessee's right of possession or use of the goods in violation of the term; or
(2) a delegation of a material performance of either party to the lease contract in violation of the term.
(c) Security interest not material impairment. The creation, attachment, perfection, or enforcement of a security interest in the lessor's interest under the lease contract or the lessor's residual interest in the goods is not a transfer that materially impairs the lessee's prospect of obtaining return performance or materially changes the duty of or materially increases the burden or risk imposed on the lessee within the purview of Section 2A-303(4) unless, and then only to the extent that, enforcement actually results in a delegation of material performance of the lessor.
(Source: P.A. 91-893, eff. 7-1-01.)

(810 ILCS 5/9-408) (from Ch. 26, par. 9-408)
Sec. 9-408. Restrictions on assignment of promissory notes, health-care-insurance receivables, and certain general intangibles ineffective.
(a) Term restricting assignment generally ineffective. Except as otherwise provided in subsection (b), a term in a promissory note or in an agreement between an account debtor and a debtor which relates to a health-care-insurance receivable or a general intangible, including a contract, permit, license, or franchise, and which term prohibits, restricts, or requires the consent of the person obligated on the promissory note or the account debtor to, the assignment or transfer of, or creation, attachment, or perfection of a security interest in, the promissory note, health-care-insurance receivable, or general intangible, is ineffective to the extent that the term:
(1) would impair the creation, attachment, or perfection of a security interest; or
(2) provides that the assignment or transfer or the creation, attachment, or perfection of the security interest may give rise to a default, breach, right of recoupment, claim, defense, termination, right of termination, or remedy under the promissory note, health-care-insurance receivable, or general intangible.
(b) Applicability of subsection (a) to sales of certain rights to payment. Subsection (a) applies to a security interest in a payment intangible or promissory note only if the security interest arises out of a sale of the payment intangible or promissory note.
(c) Legal restrictions on assignment generally ineffective. A rule of law, statute, or regulation that prohibits, restricts, or requires the consent of a government, governmental body or official, person obligated on a promissory note, or account debtor to the assignment or transfer of, or creation of a security interest in, a promissory note, health-care-insurance receivable, or general intangible, including a contract, permit, license, or franchise between an account debtor and a debtor, is ineffective to the extent that the rule of law, statute, or regulation:
(1) would impair the creation, attachment, or perfection of a security interest; or

(2) provides that the assignment or transfer or the creation, attachment, or perfection of the security interest may give rise to a default, breach, right of recoupment, claim, defense, termination, right of termination, or remedy under the promissory note, health-care-insurance receivable, or general intangible.

(d) Limitation on ineffectiveness under subsections (a) and (c). To the extent that a term in a promissory note or in an agreement between an account debtor and a debtor which relates to a health-care-insurance receivable or general intangible or a rule of law, statute, or regulation described in subsection (c) would be effective under law other than this Article but is ineffective under subsection (a) or (c), the creation, attachment, or perfection of a security interest in the promissory note, health-care-insurance receivable, or general intangible:

(1) is not enforceable against the person obligated on the promissory note or the account debtor;

(2) does not impose a duty or obligation on the person obligated on the promissory note or the account debtor;

(3) does not require the person obligated on the promissory note or the account debtor to recognize the security interest, pay or render performance to the secured party, or accept payment or performance from the secured party;

(4) does not entitle the secured party to use or assign the debtor's rights under the promissory note, health-care-insurance receivable, or general intangible, including any related information or materials furnished to the debtor in the transaction giving rise to the promissory note, health-care-insurance receivable, or general intangible;

(5) does not entitle the secured party to use, assign, possess, or have access to any trade secrets or confidential information of the person obligated on the promissory note or the account debtor; and

(6) does not entitle the secured party to enforce the security interest in the promissory note, health-care-insurance receivable, or general intangible.

(Source: P.A. 91-893, eff. 7-1-01.)

(810 ILCS 5/9-409)

Sec. 9-409. Restrictions on assignment of letter-of-credit rights ineffective.

(a) Term or law restricting assignment generally ineffective. A term in a letter of credit or a rule of law, statute, regulation, custom, or practice applicable to the letter of credit which prohibits, restricts, or requires the consent of an applicant, issuer, or nominated person to a beneficiary's assignment of or creation of a security interest in a letter-of-credit right is ineffective to the extent that the term or rule of law, statute, regulation, custom, or practice:

(1) would impair the creation, attachment, or perfection of a security interest in the letter-of-credit right; or

(2) provides that the assignment or the creation, attachment, or perfection of the security interest may give rise to a default, breach, right of recoupment, claim, defense, termination, right of termination, or remedy under the letter-of-credit right.

(b) Limitation on ineffectiveness under subsection (a). To the extent that a term in a letter of credit is ineffective under subsection (a) but would be effective under law other than this Article or a custom or practice applicable to the letter of credit, to the transfer of a right to draw or otherwise demand performance under the letter of credit, or to the assignment of a right to proceeds of the letter of credit, the creation, attachment, or perfection of a security interest in the letter-of-credit right:

(1) is not enforceable against the applicant, issuer, nominated person, or transferee beneficiary;

(2) imposes no duties or obligations on the applicant, issuer, nominated person, or transferee beneficiary; and

(3) does not require the applicant, issuer, nominated person, or transferee beneficiary to recognize the security interest, pay or render performance to the secured party, or accept payment or other performance from the secured party.

(Source: P.A. 91-893, eff. 7-1-01.)

(810 ILCS 5/9-410)
Sec. 9-410. (Blank).
(Source: P.A. 91-893, eff. 7-1-01.)

(810 ILCS 5/Art. 9 Pt. 5 heading)
PART 5. FILING

(810 ILCS 5/Art. 9 Pt. 5 Sub. 1 heading)
SUBPART 1. FILING OFFICE; CONTENTS AND EFFECTIVENESS OF FINANCING STATEMENT

(810 ILCS 5/9-501) (from Ch. 26, par. 9-501)
Sec. 9-501. Filing office.
(a) Filing offices. Except as otherwise provided in subsection (b), if the local law of this State governs perfection of a security interest or agricultural lien, the office in which to file a financing statement to perfect the security interest or agricultural lien is:
(1) the office designated for the filing or recording of a record of a mortgage on the related real property, if:
(A) the collateral is as-extracted collateral or timber to be cut; or
(B) the financing statement is filed as a fixture filing and the collateral is goods that are or are to become fixtures; or
(2) the office of the Secretary of State in all other cases, including a case in which the collateral is goods that are or are to become fixtures and the financing statement is not filed as a fixture filing.
(b) Filing office for transmitting utilities. The office in which to file a financing statement to perfect a security interest in collateral, including fixtures, of a transmitting utility is the office of the Secretary of State. The financing statement also constitutes a fixture filing as to the collateral indicated in the financing statement which is or is to become fixtures.
(Source: P.A. 91-357, eff. 7-29-99; 91-893, eff. 7-1-01.)

(810 ILCS 5/9-502) (from Ch. 26, par. 9-502)
Sec. 9-502. Contents of financing statement; record of mortgage as financing statement; time of filing financing statement.
(a) Sufficiency of financing statement. Subject to subsection (b), a financing statement is sufficient only if it:
(1) provides the name of the debtor;
(2) provides the name of the secured party or a representative of the secured party; and
(3) indicates the collateral covered by the financing statement.
(b) Real-property-related financing statements. Except as otherwise provided in Section 9-501(b), to be sufficient, a financing statement that covers as-extracted collateral or timber to be cut, or which is filed as a fixture filing and covers goods that are or are to become fixtures, must satisfy subsection (a) and also:
(1) indicate that it covers this type of collateral;
(2) indicate that it is to be filed in the real property records;
(3) provide a description of the real property to which the collateral is related sufficient to give constructive notice of a mortgage under the law of this State if the description were contained in a record of the mortgage of the real property; and
(4) if the debtor does not have an interest of record in the real property, provide the name of a record owner.
(c) Record of mortgage as financing statement. A record of a mortgage is effective, from the date of recording, as a financing statement filed as a fixture filing or as a financing statement covering as-extracted collateral or timber to be cut only if:
(1) the record indicates the goods or accounts that it covers;
(2) the goods are or are to become fixtures related to the real property described in the record or the collateral is related to the real property described in the record and is as-extracted collateral or timber to be cut;

(3) the record satisfies the requirements for a financing statement in this Section other than an indication that it is to be filed in the real property records; and

(4) the record is recorded.

(d) Filing before security agreement or attachment. A financing statement may be filed before a security agreement is made or a security interest otherwise attaches.

(Source: P.A. 91-893, eff. 7-1-01.)

(810 ILCS 5/9-503) (from Ch. 26, par. 9-503)

Sec. 9-503. Name of debtor and secured party.

(a) Sufficiency of debtor's name. A financing statement sufficiently provides the name of the debtor:

(1) if the debtor is a registered organization, only if the financing statement provides the name of the debtor indicated on the public record of the debtor's jurisdiction of organization which shows the debtor to have been organized;

(2) if the debtor is a decedent's estate, only if the financing statement provides the name of the decedent and indicates that the debtor is an estate;

(3) if the debtor is a trust or a trustee acting with respect to property held in trust, only if the financing statement:

(A) provides the name specified for the trust in its organic documents or, if no name is specified, provides the name of the settlor and additional information sufficient to distinguish the debtor from other trusts having one or more of the same settlors; and

(B) indicates, in the debtor's name or otherwise, that the debtor is a trust or is a trustee acting with respect to property held in trust; and

(4) in other cases:

(A) if the debtor has a name, only if it provides the individual or organizational name of the debtor; and

(B) if the debtor does not have a name, only if it provides the names of the partners, members, associates, or other persons comprising the debtor.

(b) Additional debtor-related information. A financing statement that provides the name of the debtor in accordance with subsection (a) is not rendered ineffective by the absence of:

(1) a trade name or other name of the debtor; or

(2) unless required under subsection (a)(4)(B), names of partners, members, associates, or other persons comprising the debtor.

(c) Debtor's trade name insufficient. A financing statement that provides only the debtor's trade name does not sufficiently provide the name of the debtor.

(d) Representative capacity. Failure to indicate the representative capacity of a secured party or representative of a secured party does not affect the sufficiency of a financing statement.

(e) Multiple debtors and secured parties. A financing statement may provide the name of more than one debtor and the name of more than one secured party.

(Source: P.A. 91-893, eff. 7-1-01.)

(810 ILCS 5/9-504) (from Ch. 26, par. 9-504)

Sec. 9-504. Indication of collateral. A financing statement sufficiently indicates the collateral that it covers if the financing statement provides:

(1) a description of the collateral pursuant to Section 9-108; or

(2) an indication that the financing statement covers all assets or all personal property.

(Source: P.A. 91-893, eff. 7-1-01.)

(810 ILCS 5/9-505) (from Ch. 26, par. 9-505)

Sec. 9-505. Filing and compliance with other statutes and treaties for consignments, leases, other bailments, and other transactions.

(a) Use of terms other than "debtor" and "secured party." A consignor, lessor, or other bailor of goods, a licensor, or a buyer of a payment intangible or promissory note may file a financing statement, or may comply with a statute or treaty described in Section

9-311(a), using the terms "consignor", "consignee", "lessor", "lessee", "bailor", "bailee", "licensor", "licensee", "owner", "registered owner", "buyer", "seller", or words of similar import, instead of the terms "secured party" and "debtor".

(b) Effect of financing statement under subsection (a). This part applies to the filing of a financing statement under subsection (a) and, as appropriate, to compliance that is equivalent to filing a financing statement under Section 9-311(b), but the filing or compliance is not of itself a factor in determining whether the collateral secures an obligation. If it is determined for another reason that the collateral secures an obligation, a security interest held by the consignor, lessor, bailor, licensor, owner, or buyer which attaches to the collateral is perfected by the filing or compliance.

(Source: P.A. 91-893, eff. 7-1-01.)

(810 ILCS 5/9-506) (from Ch. 26, par. 9-506)

Sec. 9-506. Effect of errors or omissions.

(a) Minor errors and omissions. A financing statement substantially satisfying the requirements of this Part is effective, even if it has minor errors or omissions, unless the errors or omissions make the financing statement seriously misleading.

(b) Financing statement seriously misleading. Except as otherwise provided in subsection (c), a financing statement that fails sufficiently to provide the name of the debtor in accordance with Section 9-503(a) is seriously misleading.

(c) Financing statement not seriously misleading. If a search of the records of the filing office under the debtor's correct name, using the filing office's standard search logic, if any, would disclose a financing statement that fails sufficiently to provide the name of the debtor in accordance with Section 9-503(a), the name provided does not make the financing statement seriously misleading.

(d) "Debtor's correct name." For purposes of Section 9-508(b), the "debtor's correct name" in subsection (c) means the correct name of the new debtor.

(Source: P.A. 91-893, eff. 7-1-01.)

(810 ILCS 5/9-507) (from Ch. 26, par. 9-507)

Sec. 9-507. Effect of certain events on effectiveness of financing statement.

(a) Disposition. A filed financing statement remains effective with respect to collateral that is sold, exchanged, leased, licensed, or otherwise disposed of and in which a security interest or agricultural lien continues, even if the secured party knows of or consents to the disposition.

(b) Information becoming seriously misleading. Except as otherwise provided in subsection (c) and Section 9-508, a financing statement is not rendered ineffective if, after the financing statement is filed, the information provided in the financing statement becomes seriously misleading under Section 9-506.

(c) Change in debtor's name. If a debtor so changes its name that a filed financing statement becomes seriously misleading under Section 9-506:

(1) the financing statement is effective to perfect a security interest in collateral acquired by the debtor before, or within four months after, the change; and

(2) the financing statement is not effective to perfect a security interest in collateral acquired by the debtor more than four months after the change, unless an amendment to the financing statement which renders the financing statement not seriously misleading is filed within four months after the change.

(Source: P.A. 90-214, eff. 7-25-97; 91-893, eff. 7-1-01.)

(810 ILCS 5/9-508)

Sec. 9-508. Effectiveness of financing statement if new debtor becomes bound by security agreement.

(a) Financing statement naming original debtor. Except as otherwise provided in this Section, a filed financing statement naming an original debtor is effective to perfect a security interest in collateral in which a new debtor has or acquires rights to the extent that the financing statement would have been effective had the original debtor acquired rights in the collateral.

(b) Financing statement becoming seriously misleading. If the difference between the name of the original debtor and that of the new debtor causes a filed financing statement that is effective under subsection (a) to be seriously misleading under Section 9-506:

(1) the financing statement is effective to perfect a security interest in collateral acquired by the new debtor before, and within four months after, the new debtor becomes bound under Section 9-203(d); and

(2) the financing statement is not effective to perfect a security interest in collateral acquired by the new debtor more than four months after the new debtor becomes bound under Section 9-203(d) unless an initial financing statement providing the name of the new debtor is filed before the expiration of that time.

(c) When Section not applicable. This Section does not apply to collateral as to which a filed financing statement remains effective against the new debtor under Section 9-507(a).
(Source: P.A. 91-893, eff. 7-1-01.)

(810 ILCS 5/9-509)
Sec. 9-509. Persons entitled to file a record.

(a) Person entitled to file record. A person may file an initial financing statement, amendment that adds collateral covered by a financing statement, or amendment that adds a debtor to a financing statement only if:

(1) the debtor authorizes the filing in an authenticated record or pursuant to subsection (b) or (c); or

(2) the person holds an agricultural lien that has become effective at the time of filing and the financing statement covers only collateral in which the person holds an agricultural lien.

(b) Security agreement as authorization. By authenticating or becoming bound as debtor by a security agreement, a debtor or new debtor authorizes the filing of an initial financing statement, and an amendment, covering:

(1) the collateral described in the security agreement; and

(2) property that becomes collateral under Section 9-315(a)(2), whether or not the security agreement expressly covers proceeds.

(c) Acquisition of collateral as authorization. By acquiring collateral in which a security interest or agricultural lien continues under Section 9-315(a)(1), a debtor authorizes the filing of an initial financing statement, and an amendment, covering the collateral and property that becomes collateral under Section 9-315(a)(2).

(d) Person entitled to file certain amendments. A person may file an amendment other than an amendment that adds collateral covered by a financing statement or an amendment that adds a debtor to a financing statement only if:

(1) the secured party of record authorizes the filing; or

(2) the amendment is a termination statement for a financing statement as to which the secured party of record has failed to file or send a termination statement as required by Section 9-513(a) or (c), the debtor authorizes the filing, and the termination statement indicates that the debtor authorized it to be filed.

(e) Multiple secured parties of record. If there is more than one secured party of record for a financing statement, each secured party of record may authorize the filing of an amendment under subsection (d).
(Source: P.A. 91-893, eff. 7-1-01.)

(810 ILCS 5/9-510)
Sec. 9-510. Effectiveness of filed record.

(a) Filed record effective if authorized. A filed record is effective only to the extent that it was filed by a person that may file it under Section 9-509.

(b) Authorization by one secured party of record. A record authorized by one secured party of record does not affect the financing statement with respect to another secured party of record.

(c) Continuation statement not timely filed. A continuation statement that is not filed within the six-month period prescribed by Section 9-515(d) is ineffective.
(Source: P.A. 91-893, eff. 7-1-01.)

(810 ILCS 5/9-511)
Sec. 9-511. Secured party of record.

(a) Secured party of record. A secured party of record with respect to a financing statement is a person whose name is provided as the name of the secured party or a representative of the secured party in an initial financing statement that has been filed. If an initial financing statement is filed under Section 9-514(a), the assignee named in the initial financing statement is the secured party of record with respect to the financing statement.

(b) Amendment naming secured party of record. If an amendment of a financing statement which provides the name of a person as a secured party or a representative of a secured party is filed, the person named in the amendment is a secured party of record. If an amendment is filed under Section 9-514(b), the assignee named in the amendment is a secured party of record.

(c) Amendment deleting secured party of record. A person remains a secured party of record until the filing of an amendment of the financing statement which deletes the person.

(Source: P.A. 91-893, eff. 7-1-01.)

(810 ILCS 5/9-512)
Sec. 9-512. Amendment of financing statement.

(a) Amendment of information in financing statement. Subject to Section 9-509, a person may add or delete collateral covered by, continue or terminate the effectiveness of, or, subject to subsection (e), otherwise amend the information provided in, a financing statement by filing an amendment that:

(1) identifies, by its file number, the initial financing statement to which the amendment relates; and

(2) if the amendment relates to an initial financing statement filed or recorded in a filing office described in Section 9-501(a)(1), provides the date and time that the initial financing statement was filed and the information specified in Section 9-502(b).

(b) Period of effectiveness not affected. Except as otherwise provided in Section 9-515, the filing of an amendment does not extend the period of effectiveness of the financing statement.

(c) Effectiveness of amendment adding collateral. A financing statement that is amended by an amendment that adds collateral is effective as to the added collateral only from the date of the filing of the amendment.

(d) Effectiveness of amendment adding debtor. A financing statement that is amended by an amendment that adds a debtor is effective as to the added debtor only from the date of the filing of the amendment.

(e) Certain amendments ineffective. An amendment is ineffective to the extent it:

(1) purports to delete all debtors and fails to provide the name of a debtor to be covered by the financing statement; or

(2) purports to delete all secured parties of record and fails to provide the name of a new secured party of record.

(Source: P.A. 91-893, eff. 7-1-01.)

(810 ILCS 5/9-513)
Sec. 9-513. Termination statement.

(a) Consumer goods. A secured party shall cause the secured party of record for a financing statement to file a termination statement for the financing statement if the financing statement covers consumer goods and:

(1) there is no obligation secured by the collateral covered by the financing statement and no commitment to make an advance, incur an obligation, or otherwise give value; or

(2) the debtor did not authorize the filing of the initial financing statement.

(b) Time for compliance with subsection (a). To comply with subsection (a), a secured party shall cause the secured party of record to file the termination statement:

(1) within one month after there is no obligation secured by the collateral covered by the financing statement and no commitment to make an advance, incur an obligation, or otherwise give value; or

(2) if earlier, within 20 days after the secured party receives an authenticated demand from a debtor.

(c) Other collateral. In cases not governed by subsection (a), within 20 days after a secured party receives an authenticated demand from a debtor, the secured party shall cause the secured party of record for a financing statement to send to the debtor a termination statement for the financing statement or file the termination statement in the filing office if:

(1) except in the case of a financing statement covering accounts or chattel paper that has been sold or goods that are the subject of a consignment, there is no obligation secured by the collateral covered by the financing statement and no commitment to make an advance, incur an obligation, or otherwise give value;

(2) the financing statement covers accounts or chattel paper that has been sold but as to which the account debtor or other person obligated has discharged its obligation;

(3) the financing statement covers goods that were the subject of a consignment to the debtor but are not in the debtor's possession; or

(4) the debtor did not authorize the filing of the initial financing statement.

(d) Effect of filing termination statement. Except as otherwise provided in Section 9-510, upon the filing of a termination statement with the filing office, the financing statement to which the termination statement relates ceases to be effective. Except as otherwise provided in Section 9-510, for purposes of Sections 9-519(g), 9-522(a), and 9-523(c) the filing with the filing office of a termination statement relating to a financing statement that indicates that the debtor is a transmitting utility also causes the effectiveness of the financing statement to lapse.

(Source: P.A. 91-893, eff. 7-1-01.)

(810 ILCS 5/9-514)

Sec. 9-514. Assignment of powers of secured party of record.

(a) Assignment reflected on initial financing statement. Except as otherwise provided in subsection (c), an initial financing statement may reflect an assignment of all of the secured party's power to authorize an amendment to the financing statement by providing the name and mailing address of the assignee as the name and address of the secured party.

(b) Assignment of filed financing statement. Except as otherwise provided in subsection (c), a secured party of record may assign of record all or part of its power to authorize an amendment to a financing statement by filing in the filing office an amendment of the financing statement which:

(1) identifies, by its file number, the initial financing statement to which it relates;

(2) provides the name of the assignor; and

(3) provides the name and mailing address of the assignee.

(c) Assignment of record of mortgage. An assignment of record of a security interest in a fixture covered by a record of a mortgage which is effective as a financing statement filed as a fixture filing under Section 9-502(c) may be made only by an assignment of record of the mortgage in the manner provided by law of this State other than the Uniform Commercial Code.

(Source: P.A. 91-893, eff. 7-1-01.)

(810 ILCS 5/9-515)

Sec. 9-515. Duration and effectiveness of financing statement; effect of lapsed financing statement.

(a) Five-year effectiveness. Except as otherwise provided in subsections (b), (e), (f), and (g), a filed financing statement is effective for a period of five years after the date of filing.

(b) Public-finance or manufactured-home transaction. Except as otherwise provided in subsections (e), (f), and (g), an initial financing statement filed in connection with a public-finance transaction or manufactured-home transaction is effective for a period of 30 years after the date of filing if it indicates that it is filed in connection with a public-finance transaction or manufactured-home transaction.

(c) Lapse and continuation of financing statement. The effectiveness of a filed financing statement lapses on the expiration of the period of its effectiveness unless before the lapse a continuation statement is filed pursuant to subsection (d). Upon lapse, a financing statement ceases to be effective and any security interest or agricultural lien that was perfected by the financing statement becomes unperfected, unless the security interest is perfected otherwise. If the security interest or agricultural lien becomes unperfected upon lapse, it is deemed never to have been perfected as against a purchaser of the collateral for value.

(d) When continuation statement may be filed. A continuation statement may be filed only within six months before the expiration of the five-year period specified in subsection (a) or the 30-year period specified in subsection (b), whichever is applicable.

(e) Effect of filing continuation statement. Except as otherwise provided in Section 9-510, upon timely filing of a continuation statement, the effectiveness of the initial financing statement continues for a period of five years commencing on the day on which the financing statement would have become ineffective in the absence of the filing. Upon the expiration of the five-year period, the financing statement lapses in the same manner as provided in subsection (c), unless, before the lapse, another continuation statement is filed pursuant to subsection (d). Succeeding continuation statements may be filed in the same manner to continue the effectiveness of the initial financing statement.

(f) Transmitting utility financing statement. If a debtor is a transmitting utility and a filed financing statement so indicates, the financing statement is effective until a termination statement is filed.

(g) Record of mortgage as financing statement. A record of a mortgage that is effective as a financing statement filed as a fixture filing under Section 9-502(c) remains effective as a financing statement filed as a fixture filing until the mortgage is released or satisfied of record or its effectiveness otherwise terminates as to the real property.

(Source: P.A. 91-893, eff. 7-1-01.)

(810 ILCS 5/9-516)
Sec. 9-516. What constitutes filing; effectiveness of filing.

(a) What constitutes filing. Except as otherwise provided in subsection (b), communication of a record to a filing office and tender of the filing fee or acceptance of the record by the filing office constitutes filing.

(b) Refusal to accept record; filing does not occur. Filing does not occur with respect to a record that a filing office refuses to accept because:

(1) the record is not communicated by a method or medium of communication authorized by the filing office;

(2) an amount equal to or greater than the applicable filing fee is not tendered;

(3) the filing office is unable to index the record because:

(A) in the case of an initial financing statement, the record does not provide a name for the debtor;

(B) in the case of an amendment or correction statement, the record:

(i) does not identify the initial financing statement as required by Section 9-512 or 9-518, as applicable; or

(ii) identifies an initial financing statement whose effectiveness has lapsed under Section 9-515;

(C) in the case of an initial financing statement that provides the name of a debtor identified as an individual or an amendment that provides a name of a debtor identified as an individual which was not previously provided in the financing statement to which the record relates, the record does not identify the debtor's last name;

(D) in the case of a record filed or recorded in the filing office described in Section 9-501(a)(1), the record does not provide a sufficient description of the real property to which it relates; or

(E) in the case of a record submitted to the filing office described in Section 9-501(b), the debtor does not meet the definition of a transmitting utility as described in Section 9-102(a)(80);

(3.5) in the case of an initial financing statement or an amendment, if the filing office believes in good faith that a document submitted for filing is being filed for the purpose of defrauding any person or harassing any person in the performance of duties as a public servant;

(4) in the case of an initial financing statement or an amendment that adds a secured party of record, the record does not provide a name and mailing address for the secured party of record;

(5) in the case of an initial financing statement or an amendment that provides a name of a debtor which was not previously provided in the financing statement to which the amendment relates, the record does not:

(A) provide a mailing address for the debtor;
(B) indicate whether the debtor is an individual or an organization; or
(C) if the financing statement indicates that the debtor is an organization, provide:
(i) a type of organization for the debtor;
(ii) a jurisdiction of organization for the debtor; or
(iii) an organizational identification number for the debtor or indicate that the debtor has none;

(6) in the case of an assignment reflected in an initial financing statement under Section 9-514(a) or an amendment filed under Section 9-514(b), the record does not provide a name and mailing address for the assignee; or

(7) in the case of a continuation statement, the record is not filed within the six-month period prescribed by Section 9-515(d).

(c) Rules applicable to subsection (b). For purposes of subsection (b):

(1) a record does not provide information if the filing office is unable to read or decipher the information; and

(2) a record that does not indicate that it is an amendment or identify an initial financing statement to which it relates, as required by Section 9-512, 9-514, or 9-518, is an initial financing statement.

(d) Refusal to accept record; record effective as filed record. A record that is communicated to the filing office with tender of the filing fee, but which the filing office refuses to accept for a reason other than one set forth in subsection (b), is effective as a filed record except as against a purchaser of the collateral which gives value in reasonable reliance upon the absence of the record from the files.

(e) The Secretary of State may refuse to accept a record for filing under subdivision (b)(3)(E) or (b)(3.5) only if the refusal is approved by the Department of Business Services of the Secretary of State and the General Counsel to the Secretary of State.

(Source: P.A. 95-446, eff. 1-1-08.)

(810 ILCS 5/9-517)

Sec. 9-517. Effect of indexing errors. The failure of the filing office to index a record correctly does not affect the effectiveness of the filed record.

(Source: P.A. 91-893, eff. 7-1-01.)

(810 ILCS 5/9-518)

Sec. 9-518. Claim concerning inaccurate or wrongfully filed record.

(a) Correction statement. A person may file in the filing office a correction statement with respect to a record indexed there under the person's name if the person believes that the record is inaccurate or was wrongfully filed.

(b) Sufficiency of correction statement. A correction statement must:

(1) identify the record to which it relates by:

(A) the file number assigned to the initial financing statement to which the record relates; and

(B) if the correction statement relates to a record filed or recorded in a filing office described in Section 9-501(a)(1), the date and time that the initial financing statement was filed and the information specified in Section 9-502(b);

(2) indicate that it is a correction statement; and

(3) provide the basis for the person's belief that the record is inaccurate and indicate the manner in which the person believes the record should be amended to cure any inaccuracy or provide the basis for the person's belief that the record was wrongfully filed.

(c) Record not affected by correction statement. The filing of a correction statement does not affect the effectiveness of an initial financing statement or other filed record.

(Source: P.A. 91-893, eff. 7-1-01.)

(810 ILCS 5/Art. 9 Pt. 5 Sub. 2 heading)
SUBPART 2. DUTIES AND OPERATION OF FILING OFFICE

(810 ILCS 5/9-519)
Sec. 9-519. Numbering, maintaining, and indexing records; communicating information provided in records.

(a) Filing office duties. For each record filed in a filing office, the filing office shall:

(1) assign a unique number to the filed record;

(2) create a record, which may be electronic, microfilm, or otherwise, that bears the number assigned to the filed record and the date and time of filing;

(3) maintain the filed record for public inspection; and

(4) index the filed record in accordance with subsections (c), (d), and (e).

(b) File number. A file number assigned after January 1, 2002, must include a digit that:

(1) is mathematically derived from or related to the other digits of the file number; and

(2) aids the filing office in determining whether a number communicated as the file number includes a single-digit or transpositional error.

(c) Indexing: general. Except as otherwise provided in subsections (d) and (e), the filing office shall:

(1) index an initial financing statement according to the name of the debtor and index all filed records relating to the initial financing statement in a manner that associates with one another an initial financing statement and all filed records relating to the initial financing statement; and

(2) index a record that provides a name of a debtor which was not previously provided in the financing statement to which the record relates also according to the name that was not previously provided.

(d) Indexing: real-property-related financing statement. If a financing statement is filed as a fixture filing or covers as-extracted collateral or timber to be cut, it must be filed for record and the filing office shall index it:

(1) under the names of the debtor and of each owner of record shown on the financing statement as if they were the mortgagors under a mortgage of the real property described; and

(2) to the extent that the law of this State provides for indexing of records of mortgages under the name of the mortgagee, under the name of the secured party as if the secured party were the mortgagee thereunder, or, if indexing is by description, as if the financing statement were a record of a mortgage of the real property described.

(e) Indexing: real-property-related assignment. If a financing statement is filed as a fixture filing or covers as-extracted collateral or timber to be cut, the filing office shall index an assignment filed under Section 9-514(a) or an amendment filed under Section 9-514(b):

(1) under the name of the assignor as grantor; and

(2) to the extent that the law of this State provides for indexing a record of the assignment of a mortgage under the name of the assignee, under the name of the assignee.

(f) Retrieval and association capability. The filing office shall maintain a capability:

(1) to retrieve a record by the name of the debtor and by the file number assigned to the initial financing statement to which the record relates; and

(2) to associate and retrieve with one another an initial financing statement and each filed record relating to the initial financing statement.

(g) Removal of debtor's name. The filing office may not remove a debtor's name from the index until one year after the effectiveness of a financing statement naming the debtor lapses under Section 9-515 with respect to all secured parties of record.

(h) Timeliness of filing office performance. The filing office shall perform the acts required by subsections (a) through (e) at the time and in the manner prescribed by filing-office rule, but not later than two business days after the filing office receives the record in question.

(i) Inapplicability to real-property-related filing office. Subsections (b) and (h) do not apply to a filing office described in Section 9-501(a)(1).

(j) Unless a statute on disposition of public records provides otherwise, if the filing officer has an electronic, microfilm, or other image record to be maintained of the financing statement, continuation statement, statement of assignment, statement of release, termination statement, or any other related document, he or she may remove and destroy the original paper submission.

(Source: P.A. 91-893, eff. 7-1-01; 92-33, eff. 7-1-01.)

(810 ILCS 5/9-520)
Sec. 9-520. Acceptance and refusal to accept record.

(a) Mandatory refusal to accept record. A filing office shall refuse to accept a record for filing for a reason set forth in Section 9-516(b) and may refuse to accept a record for filing only for a reason set forth in Section 9-516(b).

(b) Communication concerning refusal. If a filing office refuses to accept a record for filing, it shall communicate to the person that presented the record the fact of and reason for the refusal and the date and time the record would have been filed had the filing office accepted it. The communication must be made at the time and in the manner prescribed by filing-office rule, but in the case of a filing office described in Section 9-501(a)(2), in no event more than two business days after the filing office receives the record.

(c) When filed financing statement effective. A filed financing statement satisfying Section 9-502(a) and (b) is effective, even if the filing office is required to refuse to accept it for filing under subsection (a). However, Section 9-338 applies to a filed financing statement providing information described in Section 9-516(b)(5) which is incorrect at the time the financing statement is filed.

(d) Separate application to multiple debtors. If a record communicated to a filing office provides information that relates to more than one debtor, this Part applies as to each debtor separately.

(Source: P.A. 91-893, eff. 7-1-01.)

(810 ILCS 5/9-521)
Sec. 9-521. Uniform form of written financing statement and amendment.

(a) Initial financing statement form. A filing office that accepts written records may not refuse to accept a written initial financing statement in the form and format set forth in the final official text of the 1999 revisions to Article 9 of the Uniform Commercial Code promulgated by the American Law Institute and the National Conference of Commissioners on Uniform State Laws, except for a reason set forth in Section 9-516(b).

(b) Amendment form. A filing office that accepts written records may not refuse to accept a written record in the form and format set forth in the final official text of the 1999 revisions to Article 9 of the Uniform Commercial Code promulgated by the American Law Institute and the National Conference of Commissioners on Uniform State Laws, except for a reason set forth in Section 9-516(b).

(Source: P.A. 91-893, eff. 7-1-01.)

(810 ILCS 5/9-522)
Sec. 9-522. Maintenance and destruction of records.

(a) Post-lapse maintenance and retrieval of information. The filing office shall maintain a record of the information provided in a filed financing statement for at least one year after the effectiveness of the financing statement has lapsed under Section 9-515 with respect to all secured parties of record. The record must be retrievable by using the name of the debtor and:

(1) if the record was filed in the filing office described in Section 9-501(a)(1), by using the file number assigned to the initial financing statement to which the record relates and the date and time that the record was filed or recorded; or

(2) if the record was filed in the filing office described in Section 9-501(a)(2), by using the file number assigned to the initial financing statement to which the record relates.

(b) Destruction of written records. Except to the extent that a statute governing disposition of public records provides otherwise, the filing office immediately may destroy any written record evidencing a financing statement. However, if the filing office destroys a written record, it shall maintain another record of the financing statement which complies with subsection (a).

(Source: P.A. 91-893, eff. 7-1-01.)

(810 ILCS 5/9-523)
Sec. 9-523. Information from filing office; sale or license of records.

(a) Acknowledgment of filing written record. If a person that files a written record requests an acknowledgment of the filing, the filing office shall send to the person an image of the record showing the number assigned to the record pursuant to Section 9-519(a)(1) and the date and time of the filing of the record. However, if the person furnishes a copy of the record to the filing office, the filing office may instead:

(1) note upon the copy the number assigned to the record pursuant to Section 9-519(a)(1) and the date and time of the filing of the record; and

(2) send the copy to the person.

(b) Acknowledgment of filing other record. If a person files a record other than a written record, the filing office shall communicate to the person an acknowledgment that provides:

(1) the information in the record;

(2) the number assigned to the record pursuant to Section 9-519(a)(1); and

(3) the date and time of the filing of the record.

(c) Communication of requested information. The filing office shall communicate or otherwise make available in a record the following information to any person that requests it:

(1) whether there is on file on a date and time specified by the filing office, but not a date earlier than three business days before the filing office receives the request, any financing statement that:

(A) designates a particular debtor or, if the request so states, designates a particular debtor at the address specified in the request;

(B) has not lapsed under Section 9-515 with respect to all secured parties of record; and

(C) if the request so states, has lapsed under Section 9-515 and a record of which is maintained by the filing office under Section 9-522(a);

(2) the date and time of filing of each financing statement; and

(3) the information provided in each financing statement.

(d) Medium for communicating information. In complying with its duty under subsection (c), the filing office may communicate information in any medium. However, if requested, the filing office shall communicate information by issuing a record that can be admitted into evidence in the courts of this State without extrinsic evidence of its authenticity.

(e) Timeliness of filing office performance. The filing office shall perform the acts required by subsections (a) through (d) at the time and in the manner prescribed by filing-office rule, but in the case of a filing office described in Section 9-501(a)(2), not later than two business days after the filing office receives the request.

(f) Public availability of records. At least weekly, the Secretary of State shall offer to sell or license to the public on a nonexclusive basis, in bulk, copies of all records filed in it under this Part, in every medium from time to time available to the filing office.

(Source: P.A. 91-893, eff. 7-1-01.)

(810 ILCS 5/9-524)

Sec. 9-524. Delay by filing office. Delay by the filing office beyond a time limit prescribed by this Part is excused if:

(1) the delay is caused by interruption of communication or computer facilities, war, emergency conditions, failure of equipment, or other circumstances beyond control of the filing office; and

(2) the filing office exercises reasonable diligence under the circumstances.

(Source: P.A. 91-893, eff. 7-1-01.)

(810 ILCS 5/9-525)

Sec. 9-525. Fees.

(a) Initial financing statement or other record: general rule. Except as otherwise provided in subsection (e), the fee for filing and indexing a record under this Part, other than an initial financing statement of the kind described in subsection (b), is:

(1) $20 if the record is communicated in writing and consists of one or two pages;

(2) $20 if the record is communicated in writing and consists of more than two pages; and

(3) $20 if the record is communicated by another medium authorized by filing-office rule.

(b) Initial financing statement: public-finance and manufactured-housing transactions. Except as otherwise provided in subsection (e), the fee for filing and indexing an initial financing statement of the following kind is:

(1) $20 if the financing statement indicates that it is filed in connection with a public-finance transaction;

(2) $20 if the financing statement indicates that it is filed in connection with a manufactured-home transaction.

(c) Number of names. The number of names required to be indexed does not affect the amount of the fee in subsections (a) and (b).

(d) Response to information request. The fee for responding to a request for information from the filing office, including for issuing a certificate showing communicating whether there is on file any financing statement naming a particular debtor, is:

(1) $10 if the request is communicated in writing; and

(2) $10 if the request is communicated by another medium authorized by filing-office rule.

(e) Record of mortgage. This Section does not require a fee with respect to a record of a mortgage which is effective as a financing statement filed as a fixture filing or as a financing statement covering as-extracted collateral or timber to be cut under Section 9-502(c). However, the recording and satisfaction fees that otherwise would be applicable to the record of the mortgage apply.

(f) Of the total money collected for each filing with the Secretary of State of an original financing statement, amended statement, continuation, or assignment, or for a release of collateral, $12 of the filing fee shall be paid into the Secretary of State Special Services Fund. The remaining $8 shall be deposited into the General Revenue Fund in the State treasury.

(Source: P.A. 93-990, eff. 8-23-04.)

(810 ILCS 5/9-526)

Sec. 9-526. Filing-office rules.

(a) Adoption of filing-office rules. The Secretary of State shall adopt and publish rules to implement this Article. The filing-office rules must be:

(1) consistent with this Article; and

(2) adopted and published in accordance with the Illinois Administrative Procedure Act.

(b) Harmonization of rules. To keep the filing-office rules and practices of the filing office in harmony with the rules and practices of filing offices in other jurisdictions that enact substantially this Part, and to keep the technology used by the filing office compatible with the technology used by filing offices in other jurisdictions that enact substantially this Part, the Secretary of State, so far as is consistent with the purposes, policies, and provisions of this Article, in adopting, amending, and repealing filing-office rules, shall:

(1) consult with filing offices in other jurisdictions that enact substantially this Part; and

(2) consult the most recent version of the Model Rules promulgated by the International Association of Corporate Administrators or any successor organization; and

(3) take into consideration the rules and practices of, and the technology used by, filing offices in other jurisdictions that enact substantially this Part.

(Source: P.A. 91-893, eff. 7-1-01.)

(810 ILCS 5/9-527)

Sec. 9-527. Duty to report. The Secretary of State shall report annually to the Governor and Legislature on the operation of the filing office. The report must contain a statement of the extent to which:

(1) the filing-office rules are not in harmony with the rules of filing offices in other jurisdictions that enact substantially this Part and the reasons for these variations; and

(2) the filing-office rules are not in harmony with the most recent version of the Model Rules promulgated by the International Association of Corporate Administrators, or any successor organization, and the reasons for these variations.

(Source: P.A. 91-893, eff. 7-1-01.)

(810 ILCS 5/9-528)

Sec. 9-528. Liability of filing officer. Neither the filing officer nor any of the filing officer's employees or agents shall be subject to personal liability by reason of any error or omission in the performance of any duty under this Article except in the case of willful and wanton conduct.

(Source: P.A. 92-33, eff. 7-1-01.)

(810 ILCS 5/Art. 9 Pt. 6 heading)
PART 6. DEFAULT

(810 ILCS 5/Art. 9 Pt. 6 Sub. 1 heading)
SUBPART 1. DEFAULT AND ENFORCEMENT
OF SECURITY INTEREST

(810 ILCS 5/9-601)

Sec. 9-601. Rights after default; judicial enforcement; consignor or buyer of accounts, chattel paper, payment intangibles, or promissory notes.

(a) Rights of secured party after default. After default, a secured party has the rights provided in this Part and, except as otherwise provided in Section 9-602, those provided by agreement of the parties. A secured party:

(1) may reduce a claim to judgment, foreclose, or otherwise enforce the claim, security interest, or agricultural lien by any available judicial procedure; and

(2) if the collateral is documents, may proceed either as to the documents or as to the goods they cover.

(b) Rights and duties of secured party in possession or control. A secured party in possession of collateral or control of collateral under Section 7-106, 9-104, 9-105, 9-106, or 9-107 has the rights and duties provided in Section 9-207.

(c) Rights cumulative; simultaneous exercise. The rights under subsections (a) and (b) are cumulative and may be exercised simultaneously.

(d) Rights of debtor and obligor. Except as otherwise provided in subsection (g) and Section 9-605, after default, a debtor and an obligor have the rights provided in this Part and by agreement of the parties.

(e) Lien of levy after judgment. If a secured party has reduced its claim to judgment, the lien of any levy that may be made upon the collateral by virtue of a judgment relates back to the earliest of:

(1) the date of perfection of the security interest or agricultural lien in the collateral;

(2) the date of filing a financing statement covering the collateral; or

(3) any date specified in a statute under which the agricultural lien was created.

(f) Execution sale. A sale pursuant to a judgment is a foreclosure of the security interest or agricultural lien by judicial procedure within the meaning of this Section. A secured party may purchase at the sale and thereafter hold the collateral free of any other requirements of this Article.

(g) Consignor or buyer of certain rights to payment. Except as otherwise provided in Section 9-607(c), this Part imposes no duties upon a secured party that is a consignor or is a buyer of accounts, chattel paper, payment intangibles, or promissory notes.

(Source: P.A. 95-895, eff. 1-1-09.)

(810 ILCS 5/9-602)

Sec. 9-602. Waiver and variance of rights and duties. Except as otherwise provided in Section 9-624, to the extent that they give rights to a debtor or obligor and impose duties on a secured party, the debtor or obligor may not waive or vary the rules stated in the following listed Sections:

(1) Section 9-207(b)(4)(C), which deals with use and operation of the collateral by the secured party;

(2) Section 9-210, which deals with requests for an accounting and requests concerning a list of collateral and statement of account;

(3) Section 9-607(c), which deals with collection and enforcement of collateral;

(4) Sections 9-608(a) and 9-615(c) to the extent that they deal with application or payment of noncash proceeds of collection, enforcement, or disposition;

(5) Sections 9-608(a) and 9-615(d) to the extent that they require accounting for or payment of surplus proceeds of collateral;

(6) Section 9-609 to the extent that it imposes upon a secured party that takes possession of collateral without judicial process the duty to do so without breach of the peace;

(7) Sections 9-610(b), 9-611, 9-613, and 9-614, which deal with disposition of collateral;

(8) Section 9-615(f), which deals with calculation of a deficiency or surplus when a disposition is made to the secured party, a person related to the secured party, or a secondary obligor;

(9) Section 9-616, which deals with explanation of the calculation of a surplus or deficiency;

(10) Sections 9-620, 9-621, and 9-622, which deal with acceptance of collateral in satisfaction of obligation;

(11) Section 9-623, which deals with redemption of collateral;

(12) Section 9-624, which deals with permissible waivers; and

(13) Sections 9-625 and 9-626, which deal with the secured party's liability for failure to comply with this Article.

(Source: P.A. 91-893, eff. 7-1-01.)

(810 ILCS 5/9-603)

Sec. 9-603. Agreement on standards concerning rights and duties.

(a) Agreed standards. The parties may determine by agreement the standards measuring the fulfillment of the rights of a debtor or obligor and the duties of a secured party under a rule stated in Section 9-602 if the standards are not manifestly unreasonable.

(b) Agreed standards inapplicable to breach of peace. Subsection (a) does not apply to the duty under Section 9-609 to refrain from breaching the peace.

(Source: P.A. 91-893, eff. 7-1-01.)

(810 ILCS 5/9-604)

Sec. 9-604. Procedure if security agreement covers real property or fixtures.

(a) Enforcement: personal and real property. If a security agreement covers both personal and real property, a secured party may proceed:

(1) under this Part as to the personal property without prejudicing any rights with respect to the real property; or

(2) as to both the personal property and the real property in accordance with the rights with respect to the real property, in which case the other provisions of this Part do not apply.

(b) Enforcement: fixtures. Subject to subsection (c), if a security agreement covers goods that are or become fixtures, a secured party may proceed:

(1) under this Part; or

(2) in accordance with the rights with respect to real property, in which case the other provisions of this Part do not apply.

(c) Removal of fixtures. Subject to the other provisions of this Part, if a secured party holding a security interest in fixtures has priority over all owners and encumbrancers of the real property, the secured party, after default, may remove the collateral from the real property.

(d) Injury caused by removal. A secured party that removes collateral shall promptly reimburse any encumbrancer or owner of the real property, other than the debtor, for the cost of repair of any physical injury caused by the removal. The secured party need not reimburse the encumbrancer or owner for any diminution in value of the real property caused by the absence of the goods removed or by any necessity of replacing them. A person entitled to reimbursement may refuse permission to remove until the secured party gives adequate assurance for the performance of the obligation to reimburse.

(Source: P.A. 91-893, eff. 7-1-01.)

(810 ILCS 5/9-605)

Sec. 9-605. Unknown debtor or secondary obligor. A secured party does not owe a duty based on its status as secured party:

(1) to a person that is a debtor or obligor, unless the secured party knows:

(A) that the person is a debtor or obligor;

(B) the identity of the person; and

(C) how to communicate with the person; or

(2) to a secured party or lienholder that has filed a financing statement against a person, unless the secured party knows:

(A) that the person is a debtor; and

(B) the identity of the person.

(Source: P.A. 91-893, eff. 7-1-01.)

(810 ILCS 5/9-606)

Sec. 9-606. Time of default for agricultural lien. For purposes of this Part, a default occurs in connection with an agricultural lien at the time the secured party becomes entitled to enforce the lien in accordance with the statute under which it was created.

(Source: P.A. 91-893, eff. 7-1-01.)

(810 ILCS 5/9-607)

Sec. 9-607. Collection and enforcement by secured party.

(a) Collection and enforcement generally. If so agreed, and in any event after default, a secured party:

(1) may notify an account debtor or other person obligated on collateral to make payment or otherwise render performance to or for the benefit of the secured party;

(2) may take any proceeds to which the secured party is entitled under Section 9-315;

(3) may enforce the obligations of an account debtor or other person obligated on collateral and exercise the rights of the debtor with respect to the obligation of the account debtor or other person obligated on collateral to make payment or otherwise render performance to the debtor, and with respect to any property that secures the obligations of the account debtor or other person obligated on the collateral;

(4) if it holds a security interest in a deposit account perfected by control under Section 9-104(a)(1), may apply the balance of the deposit account to the obligation secured by the deposit account; and

(5) if it holds a security interest in a deposit account perfected by control under Section 9-104(a)(2) or (3), may instruct the bank to pay the balance of the deposit account to or for the benefit of the secured party.

(b) Nonjudicial enforcement of mortgage. If necessary to enable a secured party to exercise under subsection (a)(3) the right of a debtor to enforce a mortgage nonjudicially, the secured party may record in the office in which a record of the mortgage is recorded:

(1) a copy of the security agreement that creates or provides for a security interest in the obligation secured by the mortgage; and

(2) the secured party's sworn affidavit in recordable form stating that:

(A) a default has occurred; and

(B) the secured party is entitled to enforce the mortgage nonjudicially.

(c) Commercially reasonable collection and enforcement. A secured party shall proceed in a commercially reasonable manner if the secured party:

(1) undertakes to collect from or enforce an obligation of an account debtor or other person obligated on collateral; and

(2) is entitled to charge back uncollected collateral or otherwise to full or limited recourse against the debtor or a secondary obligor.

(d) Expenses of collection and enforcement. A secured party may deduct from the collections made pursuant to subsection (c) reasonable expenses of collection and enforcement, including reasonable attorney's fees and legal expenses incurred by the secured party.

(e) Duties to secured party not affected. This Section does not determine whether an account debtor, bank, or other person obligated on collateral owes a duty to a secured party.

(Source: P.A. 91-893, eff. 7-1-01.)

(810 ILCS 5/9-608)

Sec. 9-608. Application of proceeds of collection or enforcement; liability for deficiency and right to surplus.

(a) Application of proceeds, surplus, and deficiency if obligation secured. If a security interest or agricultural lien secures payment or performance of an obligation, the following rules apply:

(1) A secured party shall apply or pay over for application the cash proceeds of collection or enforcement under Section 9-607 in the following order to:

(A) the reasonable expenses of collection and enforcement and, to the extent provided for by agreement and not prohibited by law, reasonable attorney's fees and legal expenses incurred by the secured party;

(B) the satisfaction of obligations secured by the security interest or agricultural lien under which the collection or enforcement is made; and

(C) the satisfaction of obligations secured by any subordinate security interest in or other lien on the collateral subject to the security interest or agricultural lien under which the collection or enforcement is made if the secured party receives an authenticated demand for proceeds before distribution of the proceeds is completed.

(2) If requested by a secured party, a holder of a subordinate security interest or other lien shall furnish reasonable proof of the interest or lien within a reasonable time. Unless the holder complies, the secured party need not comply with the holder's demand under paragraph (1)(C).

(3) A secured party need not apply or pay over for application noncash proceeds of collection and enforcement under Section 9-607 unless the failure to do so would be commercially unreasonable. A secured party that applies or pays over for application noncash proceeds shall do so in a commercially reasonable manner.

(4) A secured party shall account to and pay a debtor for any surplus, and the obligor is liable for any deficiency.

(b) No surplus or deficiency in sales of certain rights to payment. If the underlying transaction is a sale of accounts, chattel paper, payment intangibles, or promissory notes, the debtor is not entitled to any surplus, and the obligor is not liable for any deficiency.

(Source: P.A. 91-893, eff. 7-1-01.)

(810 ILCS 5/9-609)

Sec. 9-609. Secured party's right to take possession after default.

(a) Possession; rendering equipment unusable; disposition on debtor's premises. After default, a secured party:

(1) may take possession of the collateral; and

(2) without removal, may render equipment unusable and dispose of collateral on a debtor's premises under Section 9-610.

(b) Judicial and nonjudicial process. A secured party may proceed under subsection (a):

(1) pursuant to judicial process; or

(2) without judicial process, if it proceeds without breach of the peace.

(c) Assembly of collateral. If so agreed, and in any event after default, a secured party may require the debtor to assemble the collateral and make it available to the secured party at a place to be designated by the secured party which is reasonably convenient to both parties.

(Source: P.A. 91-893, eff. 7-1-01.)

(810 ILCS 5/9-610)

Sec. 9-610. Disposition of collateral after default.

(a) Disposition after default. After default, a secured party may sell, lease, license, or otherwise dispose of any or all of the collateral in its present condition or following any commercially reasonable preparation or processing.

(b) Commercially reasonable disposition. Every aspect of a disposition of collateral, including the method, manner, time, place, and other terms, must be commercially reasonable. If commercially reasonable, a secured party may dispose of collateral by public or private proceedings, by one or more contracts, as a unit or in parcels, and at any time and place and on any terms.

(c) Purchase by secured party. A secured party may purchase collateral:

(1) at a public disposition; or

(2) at a private disposition only if the collateral is of a kind that is customarily sold on a recognized market or the subject of widely distributed standard price quotations.

(d) Warranties on disposition. A contract for sale, lease, license, or other disposition includes the warranties relating to title, possession, quiet enjoyment, and the like which by operation of law accompany a voluntary disposition of property of the kind subject to the contract.

(e) Disclaimer of warranties. A secured party may disclaim or modify warranties under subsection (d):

(1) in a manner that would be effective to disclaim or modify the warranties in a voluntary disposition of property of the kind subject to the contract of disposition; or

(2) by communicating to the purchaser a record evidencing the contract for disposition and including an express disclaimer or modification of the warranties.

(f) Record sufficient to disclaim warranties. A record is sufficient to disclaim warranties under subsection (e) if it indicates "There is no warranty relating to title, possession, quiet enjoyment, or the like in this disposition" or uses words of similar import.

(Source: P.A. 91-893, eff. 7-1-01.)

(810 ILCS 5/9-611)

Sec. 9-611. Notification before disposition of collateral.

(a) "Notification date." In this Section, "notification date" means the earlier of the date on which:

(1) a secured party sends to the debtor and any secondary obligor an authenticated notification of disposition; or

(2) the debtor and any secondary obligor waive the right to notification.

(b) Notification of disposition required. Except as otherwise provided in subsection (d), a secured party that disposes of collateral under Section 9-610 shall send to the persons specified in subsection (c) a reasonable authenticated notification of disposition.

(c) Persons to be notified. To comply with subsection (b), the secured party shall send an authenticated notification of disposition to:

(1) the debtor;

(2) any secondary obligor; and

(3) if the collateral is other than consumer goods:

(A) any other person from which the secured party has received, before the notification date, an authenticated notification of a claim of an interest in the collateral;

(B) any other secured party or lienholder that, 10 days before the notification date, held a security interest in or other lien on the collateral perfected by the filing of a financing statement that:

(i) identified the collateral;

(ii) was indexed under the debtor's name as of that date; and

(iii) was filed in the office in which to file a financing statement against the debtor covering the collateral as of that date; and

(C) any other secured party that, 10 days before the notification date, held a security interest in the collateral perfected by compliance with a statute, regulation, or treaty described in Section 9-311(a).

(d) Subsection (b) inapplicable: perishable collateral; recognized market. Subsection (b) does not apply if the collateral is perishable or threatens to decline speedily in value or is of a type customarily sold on a recognized market.

(e) Compliance with subsection (c)(3)(B). A secured party complies with the requirement for notification prescribed by subsection (c)(3)(B) if:

(1) not later than 20 days or earlier than 30 days before the notification date, the secured party requests, in a commercially reasonable manner, information concerning financing statements indexed under the debtor's name in the office indicated in subsection (c)(3)(B); and

(2) before the notification date, the secured party:

(A) did not receive a response to the request for information; or

(B) received a response to the request for information and sent an authenticated notification of disposition to each secured party or other lienholder named in that response whose financing statement covered the collateral.

(Source: P.A. 91-893, eff. 7-1-01.)

(810 ILCS 5/9-612)

Sec. 9-612. Timeliness of notification before disposition of collateral.

(a) Reasonable time is question of fact. Except as otherwise provided in subsection (b), whether a notification is sent within a reasonable time is a question of fact. The limitation of the rule in subsection (b) to transactions other than consumer-goods transactions is intended to leave to the court the determination of the proper rules in consumer-goods transactions. The court may not infer from that limitation the nature of the proper rule in consumer-goods transactions and may continue to apply established approaches.

(b) 10-day period sufficient in non-consumer transaction. In a transaction other than a consumer transaction, a notification of disposition sent after default and 10 days or more before the earliest time of disposition set forth in the notification is sent within a reasonable time before the disposition.

(Source: P.A. 91-893, eff. 7-1-01.)

(810 ILCS 5/9-613)

Sec. 9-613. Contents and form of notification before disposition of collateral: general. Except in a consumer-goods transaction, the following rules apply:

(1) The contents of a notification of disposition are sufficient if the notification:

(A) describes the debtor and the secured party;

(B) describes the collateral that is the subject of the intended disposition;

(C) states the method of intended disposition;

(D) states that the debtor is entitled to an accounting of the unpaid indebtedness and states the charge, if any, for an accounting; and

(E) states the time and place of a public disposition or the time after which any other disposition is to be made.

(2) Whether the contents of a notification that lacks any of the information specified in paragraph (1) are nevertheless sufficient is a question of fact.

(3) The contents of a notification providing substantially the information specified in paragraph (1) are sufficient, even if the notification is accompanied by or combined other notification or includes:

(A) information not specified by that paragraph; or

(B) minor errors that are not seriously misleading.

(4) A particular phrasing of the notification is not required.

(5) The following form of notification and the form appearing in Section 9-614(4), when completed, each provides sufficient information:

NOTIFICATION OF DISPOSITION OF COLLATERAL

To: .... (Name of debtor, obligor, or other person to which the notification is sent)

From: .... (Name, address, and telephone number of secured party)

Name of Debtor(s): .... (Include only if debtor(s) are not an addressee)

For a public disposition:

We will sell or lease or license, as applicable, the .... (describe collateral) to the highest qualified bidder in public as follows:

Day and Date: ....

Time: ....

Place: ....

For a private disposition:

We will sell (or lease or license, as applicable) the .... (describe collateral) privately sometime after .... (day and date).

You are entitled to an accounting of the unpaid indebtedness secured by the property that we intend to sell or lease or license, as applicable for a charge of $.................. You may request an accounting by calling us at .... (telephone number).

(Source: P.A. 91-893, eff. 7-1-01.)

(810 ILCS 5/9-614)

Sec. 9-614. Contents and form of notification before disposition of collateral: consumer-goods transaction. In a consumer-goods transaction, the following rules apply:

(1) A notification of disposition must provide the following information:

(A) the information specified in Section 9-613(1);

(B) a description of any liability for a deficiency of the person to which the notification is sent;

(C) a telephone number from which the amount that must be paid to the secured party to redeem the collateral under Section 9-623 is available; and

(D) a telephone number or mailing address from which additional information concerning the disposition and the obligation secured is available.

(2) A particular phrasing of the notification is not required.

(3) The contents of a notification providing substantially the information specified in paragraph (1) are sufficient, even if the notification:

(A) is accompanied by or combined with other notifications;

(B) includes information not specified by that paragraph; or

(C) includes minor errors that are not seriously misleading.

(4) The following form of notification, when completed, provides sufficient information:

.... (Name and address of secured party)

.... (Date)

NOTICE OF OUR PLAN TO SELL PROPERTY

....

(Name and address of any obligor who is also a debtor)

Subject: ....

(Identification of Transaction)

We have your .... (describe collateral), because you broke promises in our agreement.

For a public disposition:

We will sell .... (describe collateral) at public sale. A sale could include a lease or license. The sale will be held as follows:

Date: ....

Time: ....

Place: ....

You may attend the sale and bring bidders if you want.

For a private disposition:

We will sell .... (describe collateral) at private sale sometime after .... (date). A sale could include a lease or license.

The money that we get from the sale (after paying our costs) will reduce the amount you owe. If we get less money than you owe, you .... (will or will not, as applicable) still owe us the difference. If we get more money than you owe, you will get the extra money, unless we must pay it to someone else.

You can get the property back at any time before we sell it by paying us the full amount you owe (not just the past due payments), including our expenses. To learn the exact amount you must pay, call us at .... (telephone number).

If you want us to explain to you in writing how we have figured the amount that you owe us, you may call us at .... (telephone number) or write us at .... (secured party's address) and request a written explanation. We will charge you $ .... for the explanation if we sent you another written explanation of the amount you owe us within the last six months.

If you need more information about the sale call us at .... (telephone number) or write us at .... (secured party's address).

We are sending this notice to the following other people who have an interest .... (describe collateral) or who owe money under your agreement:

....

(Names of all other debtors and obligors, if any)

(5) A notification in the form of paragraph (4) is sufficient, even if it includes errors in information not required by paragraph (1).

(6) If a notification under this Section is not in the form of paragraph (4), law other than this Article determines the effect of including information not required by paragraph (1).
(Source: P.A. 91-893, eff. 7-1-01.)

(810 ILCS 5/9-615)
Sec. 9-615. Application of proceeds of disposition; liability for deficiency and right to surplus.
(a) Application of proceeds. A secured party shall apply or pay over for application the cash proceeds of disposition in the following order to:
(1) the reasonable expenses of retaking, holding, preparing for disposition, processing, and disposing, and, to the extent provided for by agreement and not prohibited by law, reasonable attorney's fees and legal expenses incurred by the secured party;
(2) the satisfaction of obligations secured by the security interest or agricultural lien under which the disposition is made;
(3) the satisfaction of obligations secured by any subordinate security interest in or other subordinate lien on the collateral if:
(A) the secured party receives from the holder of the subordinate security interest or other lien an authenticated demand for proceeds before distribution of the proceeds is completed; and
(B) in a case in which a consignor has an interest in the collateral, the subordinate security interest or other lien is senior to the interest of the consignor; and
(4) a secured party that is a consignor of the collateral if the secured party receives from the consignor an authenticated demand for proceeds before distribution of the proceeds is completed.
(b) Proof of subordinate interest. If requested by a secured party, a holder of a subordinate security interest or other lien shall furnish reasonable proof of the interest or lien within a reasonable time. Unless the holder does so, the secured party need not comply with the holder's demand under subsection (a)(3).
(c) Application of noncash proceeds. A secured party need not apply or pay over for application noncash proceeds of disposition under this Section unless the failure to do so would be commercially unreasonable. A secured party that applies or pays over for application noncash proceeds shall do so in a commercially reasonable manner.
(d) Surplus or deficiency if obligation secured. If the security interest under which a disposition is made secures payment or performance of an obligation, after making the payments and applications required by subsection (a) and permitted by subsection (c):
(1) unless subsection (a)(4) requires the secured party to apply or pay over cash proceeds to a consignor, the secured party shall account to and pay a debtor for any surplus; and
(2) the obligor is liable for any deficiency.
(e) No surplus or deficiency in sales of certain rights to payment. If the underlying transaction is a sale of accounts, chattel paper, payment intangibles, or promissory notes:
(1) the debtor is not entitled to any surplus; and
(2) the obligor is not liable for any deficiency.
(f) Calculation of surplus or deficiency in disposition to person related to secured party. The surplus or deficiency following a disposition is calculated based on the amount of proceeds that would have been realized in a disposition complying with this Part and described in subsection (f)(2) of this Section to a transferee other than the secured party, a person related to the secured party, or a secondary obligor if:
(1) the transferee in the disposition is the secured party, a person related to the secured party, or a secondary obligor; and
(2) the amount of proceeds of the disposition is significantly below the range of proceeds that would have been received from a complying disposition by a forced sale without reserve to a willing buyer other than the secured party, a person related to the secured party, or a secondary obligor.
(g) Cash proceeds received by junior secured party. A secured party that receives cash proceeds of a disposition in good faith and without knowledge that the receipt violates the

rights of the holder of a security interest or other lien that is not subordinate to the security interest or agricultural lien under which the disposition is made:

(1) takes the cash proceeds free of the security interest or other lien;

(2) is not obligated to apply the proceeds of the disposition to the satisfaction of obligations secured by the security interest or other lien; and

(3) is not obligated to account to or pay the holder of the security interest or other lien for any surplus.

(Source: P.A. 91-893, eff. 7-1-01.)

(810 ILCS 5/9-616)

Sec. 9-616. Explanation of calculation of surplus or deficiency.

(a) Definitions. In this Section:

(1) "Explanation" means a writing that:

(A) states whether a surplus or deficiency is owed and the amount of the surplus, if applicable;

(B) states, if applicable, that future debits, credits, charges, including additional credit service charges or interest, rebates, and expenses may affect the amount of the surplus or deficiency;

(C) provides a telephone number or mailing address from which the debtor or consumer obligor may obtain additional information concerning the transaction and from which such person may request the amount of the deficiency and further information regarding how the secured party calculated the surplus or deficiency; and

(D) at the sender's option, the information set forth in subsection (c).

(2) "Request" means a record:

(A) authenticated by a debtor or consumer obligor;

(B) requesting that the recipient provide information of how it calculated the surplus or deficiency; and

(C) sent after disposition of the collateral under Section 9-610.

(b) Explanation of calculation. In a consumer-goods transaction in which the debtor is entitled to a surplus or a consumer obligor is liable for a deficiency under Section 9-615, the secured party shall:

(1) send an explanation to the debtor or consumer obligor, as applicable, after the disposition and:

(A) before or when the secured party accounts to the debtor and pays any surplus or first makes written demand on the consumer obligor after the disposition for payment of the deficiency, other than in instances in which such demand is made by a third-party debt collector covered by the Fair Debt Collection Practices Act; and

(B) within 14 days after receipt of a request made by the debtor or consumer obligor within one year after the secured party has given an explanation under this Section or notice to such debtor or consumer obligor under Section 9-614 of this Article; or

(2) in the case of a consumer obligor who is liable for a deficiency, within 14 days after receipt of a request, send to the consumer obligor a record waiving the secured party's right to a deficiency.

(c) Required information for response to request. To comply with a request, the secured party must provide a response in writing which includes the following information:

(1) the aggregate amount of obligations secured by the security interest under which the disposition was made, and, if the amount reflects a rebate of unearned interest or credit service charge, an indication of that fact, calculated as of a specified date:

(A) if the secured party takes or receives possession of the collateral after default, not more than 35 days before the secured party takes or receives possession; or

(B) if the secured party takes or receives possession of the collateral before default or does not take possession of the collateral, not more than 35 days before the disposition;

(2) the amount of proceeds of the disposition;

(3) the aggregate amount of the obligations after deducting the amount of proceeds;

(4) the amount, in the aggregate or by type, and types of expenses, including expenses of retaking, holding, preparing for disposition, processing, and disposing of the collateral,

and attorney's fees secured by the collateral which are known to the secured party and relate to the current disposition;

(5) the amount, in the aggregate or by type, and types of credits, including rebates of interest or credit service charges, to which the obligor is known to be entitled and which are not reflected in the amount in paragraph (1); and

(6) the amount of the surplus or deficiency.

(d) Substantial compliance. A particular phrasing of the explanation or response to a request is not required. An explanation or a response to a request complying substantially with the requirements of this Section is sufficient even if it is:

(1) accompanied by or combined with other notifications;

(2) includes information not specified by this Section;

(3) includes minor errors that are not seriously misleading; or

(4) includes errors in information not required by this Section.

(e) Charges for responses. A debtor or consumer obligor is entitled without charge to one response to a request under this Section during any six-month period in which the secured party did not send to the debtor or consumer obligor an explanation pursuant to subsection (b)(1). The secured party may require payment of a charge not exceeding $25 for each additional response.

(Source: P.A. 91-893, eff. 7-1-01.)

(810 ILCS 5/9-617)

Sec. 9-617. Rights of transferee of collateral.

(a) Effects of disposition. A secured party's disposition of collateral after default:

(1) transfers to a transferee for value all of the debtor's rights in the collateral;

(2) discharges the security interest under which the disposition is made; and

(3) discharges any subordinate security interest or other subordinate lien.

(b) Rights of good-faith transferee. A transferee that acts in good faith takes free of the rights and interests described in subsection (a), even if the secured party fails to comply with this Article or the requirements of any judicial proceeding.

(c) Rights of other transferee. If a transferee does not take free of the rights and interests described in subsection (a), the transferee takes the collateral subject to:

(1) the debtor's rights in the collateral;

(2) the security interest or agricultural lien under which the disposition is made; and

(3) any other security interest or other lien.

(Source: P.A. 91-893, eff. 7-1-01.)

(810 ILCS 5/9-618)

Sec. 9-618. Rights and duties of certain secondary obligors.

(a) Rights and duties of secondary obligor. A secondary obligor acquires the rights and becomes obligated to perform the duties of the secured party after the secondary obligor:

(1) receives an assignment of a secured obligation from the secured party;

(2) receives a transfer of collateral from the secured party and agrees to accept the rights and assume the duties of the secured party; or

(3) is subrogated to the rights of a secured party with respect to collateral.

(b) Effect of assignment, transfer, or subrogation. An assignment, transfer, or subrogation described in subsection (a):

(1) is not a disposition of collateral under Section 9-610; and

(2) relieves the secured party of further duties under this Article.

(Source: P.A. 91-893, eff. 7-1-01.)

(810 ILCS 5/9-619)

Sec. 9-619. Transfer of record or legal title.

(a) "Transfer statement." In this Section, "transfer statement" means a record authenticated by a secured party stating:

(1) that the debtor has defaulted in connection with an obligation secured by specified collateral;

(2) that the secured party has exercised its post-default remedies with respect to the collateral;

(3) that, by reason of the exercise, a transferee has acquired the rights of the debtor in the collateral; and

(4) the name and mailing address of the secured party, debtor, and transferee.

(b) Effect of transfer statement. A transfer statement entitles the transferee to the transfer of record of all rights of the debtor in the collateral specified in the statement in any official filing, recording, registration, or certificate-of-title system covering the collateral. If a transfer statement is presented with the applicable fee and request form to the official or office responsible for maintaining the system, the official or office shall:

(1) accept the transfer statement;

(2) promptly amend its records to reflect the transfer; and

(3) if applicable, issue a new appropriate certificate of title in the name of the transferee.

(c) Transfer not a disposition; no relief of secured party's duties. A transfer of the record or legal title to collateral to a secured party under subsection (b) or otherwise is not of itself a disposition of collateral under this Article and does not of itself relieve the secured party of its duties under this Article.

(Source: P.A. 91-893, eff. 7-1-01.)

(810 ILCS 5/9-620)

Sec. 9-620. Acceptance of collateral in full or partial satisfaction of obligation; compulsory disposition of collateral.

(a) Conditions to acceptance in satisfaction. Except as otherwise provided in subsection (g), a secured party may accept collateral in full or partial satisfaction of the obligation it secures only if:

(1) the debtor consents to the acceptance under subsection (c);

(2) the secured party does not receive, within the time set forth in subsection (d), a notification of objection to the proposal authenticated by:

(A) a person to which the secured party was required to send a proposal under Section 9-621; or

(B) any other person, other than the debtor, holding an interest in the collateral subordinate to the security interest that is the subject of the proposal;

(3) if the collateral is consumer goods, the collateral is not in the possession of the debtor when the debtor consents to the acceptance; and

(4) subsection (e) does not require the secured party to dispose of the collateral or the debtor waives the requirement pursuant to Section 9-624.

(b) Purported acceptance ineffective. A purported or apparent acceptance of collateral under this Section is ineffective unless:

(1) the secured party consents to the acceptance in an authenticated record or sends a proposal to the debtor; and

(2) the conditions of subsection (a) are met.

(c) Debtor's consent. For purposes of this Section:

(1) a debtor consents to an acceptance of collateral in partial satisfaction of the obligation it secures only if the debtor agrees to the terms of the acceptance in a record authenticated after default; and

(2) a debtor consents to an acceptance of collateral in full satisfaction of the obligation it secures only if the debtor agrees to the terms of the acceptance in a record authenticated after default or the secured party:

(A) sends to the debtor after default a proposal that is unconditional or subject only to a condition that collateral not in the possession of the secured party be preserved or maintained;

(B) in the proposal, proposes to accept collateral in full satisfaction of the obligation it secures; and

(C) does not receive a notification of objection authenticated by the debtor within 20 days after the proposal is sent.

(d) Effectiveness of notification. To be effective under subsection (a)(2), a notification of objection must be received by the secured party:

(1) in the case of a person to which the proposal was sent pursuant to Section 9-621, within 20 days after notification was sent to that person; and

(2) in other cases:

(A) within 20 days after the last notification was sent pursuant to Section 9-621; or

(B) if a notification was not sent, before the debtor consents to the acceptance under subsection (c).

(e) Mandatory disposition of consumer goods. A secured party that has taken possession of collateral shall dispose of the collateral pursuant to Section 9-610 within the time specified in subsection (f) if:

(1) 60 percent of the cash price has been paid in the case of a purchase-money security interest in consumer goods; or

(2) 60 percent of the principal amount of the obligation secured has been paid in the case of a non-purchase-money security interest in consumer goods.

(f) Compliance with mandatory disposition requirement. To comply with subsection (e), the secured party shall dispose of the collateral:

(1) within 90 days after taking possession; or

(2) within any longer period to which the debtor and all secondary obligors have agreed in an agreement to that effect entered into and authenticated after default.

(g) No partial satisfaction in consumer transaction. In a consumer transaction, a secured party may not accept collateral in partial satisfaction of the obligation it secures.

(Source: P.A. 91-893, eff. 7-1-01.)

(810 ILCS 5/9-621)

Sec. 9-621. Notification of proposal to accept collateral.

(a) Persons to which proposal to be sent. A secured party that desires to accept collateral in full or partial satisfaction of the obligation it secures shall send its proposal to:

(1) any person from which the secured party has received, before the debtor consented to the acceptance, an authenticated notification of a claim of an interest in the collateral;

(2) any other secured party or lienholder that, 10 days before the debtor consented to the acceptance, held a security interest in or other lien on the collateral perfected by the filing of a financing statement that:

(A) identified the collateral;

(B) was indexed under the debtor's name as of that date; and

(C) was filed in the office or offices in which to file a financing statement against the debtor covering the collateral as of that date; and

(3) any other secured party that, 10 days before the debtor consented to the acceptance, held a security interest in the collateral perfected by compliance with a statute, regulation, or treaty described in Section 9-311(a).

(b) Proposal to be sent to secondary obligor in partial satisfaction. A secured party that desires to accept collateral in partial satisfaction of the obligation it secures shall send its proposal to any secondary obligor in addition to the persons described in subsection (a).

(Source: P.A. 91-893, eff. 7-1-01.)

(810 ILCS 5/9-622)

Sec. 9-622. Effect of acceptance of collateral.

(a) Effect of acceptance. A secured party's acceptance of collateral in full or partial satisfaction of the obligation it secures:

(1) discharges the obligation to the extent consented to by the debtor;

(2) transfers to the secured party all of a debtor's rights in the collateral;

(3) discharges the security interest or agricultural lien that is the subject of the debtor's consent and any subordinate security interest or other subordinate lien; and

(4) terminates any other subordinate interest.

(b) Discharge of subordinate interest notwithstanding noncompliance. A subordinate interest is discharged or terminated under subsection (a), even if the secured party fails to comply with this Article.
(Source: P.A. 91-893, eff. 7-1-01.)

(810 ILCS 5/9-623)
Sec. 9-623. Right to redeem collateral.
(a) Persons that may redeem. A debtor, any secondary obligor, or any other secured party or lienholder may redeem collateral.
(b) Requirements for redemption. To redeem collateral, a person shall tender:
(1) fulfillment of all obligations secured by the collateral; and
(2) the reasonable expenses and attorney's fees described in Section 9-615(a)(1).
(c) When redemption may occur. A redemption may occur at any time before a secured party:
(1) has collected collateral under Section 9-607;
(2) has disposed of collateral or entered into a contract for its disposition under Section 9-610; or
(3) has accepted collateral in full or partial satisfaction of the obligation it secures under Section 9-622.
(Source: P.A. 91-893, eff. 7-1-01.)

(810 ILCS 5/9-624)
Sec. 9-624. Waiver.
(a) Waiver of disposition notification. A debtor or secondary obligor may waive the right to notification of disposition of collateral under Section 9-611 only by an agreement to that effect entered into and authenticated after default.
(b) Waiver of mandatory disposition. A debtor may waive the right to require disposition of collateral under Section 9-620(e) only by an agreement to that effect entered into and authenticated after default.
(c) Waiver of redemption right. A debtor or secondary obligor may waive the right to redeem collateral under Section 9-623 only by an agreement to that effect entered into and authenticated after default.
(Source: P.A. 91-893, eff. 7-1-01.)

(810 ILCS 5/Art 9, P6, Sub 2 heading)

SUBPART 2. NONCOMPLIANCE WITH ARTICLE

(810 ILCS 5/9-625)
Sec. 9-625. Remedies for secured party's failure to comply with Article.
(a) Judicial orders concerning noncompliance. If it is established that a secured party is not proceeding in accordance with this Article, a court may order or restrain collection, enforcement, or disposition of collateral on appropriate terms and conditions.
(b) Damages for noncompliance. Subject to subsections (c), (d), and (f), a person is liable for damages in the amount of any loss caused by a failure to comply with this Article. Loss caused by a failure to comply with a request under Section 9-210 may include loss resulting from the debtor's inability to obtain, or increased costs of, alternative financing.
(c) Persons entitled to recover damages; statutory damages in consumer-goods transaction. Except as otherwise provided in Section 9-628:
(1) a person that, at the time of the failure, was a debtor, was an obligor, or held a security interest in or other lien on the collateral may recover in an individual action damages under subsection (b) for its loss; and
(2) if the collateral is consumer goods, a person that was a debtor or a secondary obligor at the time a secured party failed to comply with this Part may recover in an individual action for that failure in any event an amount not less than the credit service charge plus 10 percent of the principal amount of the obligation or the time-price differential plus 10 percent of the cash price.

(d) Recovery when deficiency eliminated or reduced. A debtor whose deficiency is eliminated under Section 9-626 may recover damages for the loss of any surplus. However, a debtor or secondary obligor whose deficiency is eliminated or reduced under Section 9-626 may not otherwise recover under subsection (b) for noncompliance with the provisions of this Part relating to collection, enforcement, disposition, or acceptance.

(e) Statutory damages: noncompliance with specified provisions. In addition to any damages recoverable under subsection (b), the debtor, consumer obligor, or person named as a debtor in a filed record, as applicable, may recover in an individual action $500 for each instance that a person:

(1) fails to comply with Section 9-208;

(2) fails to comply with Section 9-209;

(3) files a record that the person is not entitled to file under Section 9-509(a); or

(4) fails to cause the secured party of record to file or send a termination statement as required by Section 9-513(a) or (c).

(f) Statutory damages: noncompliance with Section 9-210. A debtor or consumer obligor may recover damages under subsection (b) and, in addition, may in an individual action recover $500 in each case from a person that, without reasonable cause, fails to comply with a request under Section 9-210. A recipient of a request under Section 9-210 which never claimed an interest in the collateral or obligations that are the subject of a request under that Section has a reasonable excuse for failure to comply with the request within the meaning of this subsection.

(g) Limitation of security interest: noncompliance with Section 9-210. If a secured party fails to comply with a request regarding a list of collateral or a statement of account under Section 9-210, the secured party may claim a security interest only as shown in the statement included in the request as against a person that is reasonably misled by the failure.

(Source: P.A. 91-893, eff. 7-1-01.)

(810 ILCS 5/9-626)

Sec. 9-626. Action in which deficiency or surplus is in issue; applicable rules if amount of deficiency or surplus is in issue. In an action in which the amount of a deficiency or surplus is in issue, the following rules apply:

(1) A secured party need not prove compliance with the provisions of this Part relating to collection, enforcement, disposition, or acceptance unless the debtor or a secondary obligor places the secured party's compliance in issue.

(2) If the secured party's compliance is placed in issue, the secured party has the burden of establishing that the collection, enforcement, disposition, or acceptance was conducted in accordance with this Part.

(3) Except as otherwise provided in Section 9-628, if a secured party fails to prove that the collection, enforcement, disposition, or acceptance was conducted in accordance with the provisions of this Part relating to collection, enforcement, disposition, or acceptance, the liability of a debtor or a secondary obligor for a deficiency is limited to an amount by which the sum of the secured obligation, expenses, and attorney's fees exceeds the greater of:

(A) the proceeds of the collection, enforcement, disposition, or acceptance; or

(B) the amount of proceeds that would have been realized had the noncomplying secured party proceeded in accordance with the provisions of this Part relating to collection, enforcement, disposition, or acceptance.

(4) For purposes of paragraph (3)(B), the amount of proceeds that would have been realized is equal to the sum of the secured obligation, expenses, and attorney's fees unless the secured party proves that the amount is less than that sum.

(5) If a deficiency or surplus is calculated under Section 9-615(f), the debtor or obligor has the burden of establishing that the amount of proceeds of the disposition is significantly below the range of prices that a complying disposition to a person other than the secured party, a person related to the secured party, or a secondary obligor would have brought.

(Source: P.A. 91-893, eff. 7-1-01.)

(810 ILCS 5/9-627)

Sec. 9-627. Determination of whether conduct was commercially reasonable.

(a) Greater amount obtainable under other circumstances; no preclusion of commercial reasonableness. The fact that a greater amount could have been obtained by a collection, enforcement, disposition, or acceptance at a different time or in a different method from that selected by the secured party is not of itself sufficient to preclude the secured party from establishing that the collection, enforcement, disposition, or acceptance was made in a commercially reasonable manner.

(b) Dispositions that are commercially reasonable. A disposition of collateral is made in a commercially reasonable manner if the disposition is made:

(1) in the usual manner on any recognized market;

(2) at the price current in any recognized market at the time of the disposition; or

(3) otherwise in conformity with reasonable commercial practices among dealers in the type of property that was the subject of the disposition.

(c) Approval by court or on behalf of creditors. A collection, enforcement, disposition, or acceptance is commercially reasonable if it has been approved:

(1) in a judicial proceeding;

(2) by a bona fide creditors' committee;

(3) by a representative of creditors; or

(4) by an assignee for the benefit of creditors.

(d) Approval under subsection (c) not necessary; absence of approval has no effect. Approval under subsection (c) need not be obtained, and lack of approval does not mean that the collection, enforcement, disposition, or acceptance is not commercially reasonable.

(Source: P.A. 91-893, eff. 7-1-01.)

(810 ILCS 5/9-628)

Sec. 9-628. Nonliability and limitation on liability of secured party; liability of secondary obligor.

(a) Limitation of liability to debtor or obligor. Unless a secured party knows that a person is a debtor or obligor, knows the identity of the person, and knows how to communicate with the person:

(1) the secured party is not liable to the person, or to a secured party or lienholder that has filed a financing statement against the person, for failure to comply with this Article; and

(2) the secured party's failure to comply with this Article does not affect the liability of the person for a deficiency.

(b) Limitation of liability to debtor, obligor, another secured party, or lienholder. A secured party is not liable because of its status as secured party:

(1) to a person that is a debtor or obligor, unless the secured party knows:

(A) that the person is a debtor or obligor;

(B) the identity of the person; and

(C) how to communicate with the person; or

(2) to a secured party or lienholder that has filed a financing statement against a person, unless the secured party knows:

(A) that the person is a debtor; and

(B) the identity of the person.

(c) Limitation of liability if reasonable belief that transaction not a consumer-goods transaction or consumer transaction. A secured party is not liable to any person, and a person's liability for a deficiency is not affected, because of any act or omission arising out of the secured party's reasonable belief that a transaction is not a consumer-goods transaction or a consumer transaction or that goods are not consumer goods, if the secured party's belief is based on its reasonable reliance on:

(1) a debtor's representation concerning the purpose for which collateral was to be used, acquired, or held; or

(2) an obligor's representation concerning the purpose for which a secured obligation was incurred.

(d) Limitation of liability for statutory damages. A secured party is not liable to any person under Section 9-625(c)(2) for its failure to comply with Section 9-616.

(e) Limitation of multiple liability for statutory damages. A secured party is not liable under Section 9-625(c)(2) more than once with respect to any one secured obligation.

(Source: P.A. 91-893, eff. 7-1-01.)

(810 ILCS 5/Art. 9 Pt. 7 heading)
PART 7. TRANSITION
(810 ILCS 5/9-701)
Sec. 9-701. Effective date. (See Section 99 of the Public Act adding this Section to this Act.)
(Source: P.A. 91-893, eff. 7-1-01.)

(810 ILCS 5/9-702)
Sec. 9-702. Savings clause.

(a) Pre-effective-date transactions or liens. Except as otherwise provided in this Part, this Act applies to a transaction or lien within its scope, even if the transaction or lien was entered into or created before the effective date of this amendatory Act of the 91st General Assembly.

(b) Continuing validity. Except as otherwise provided in subsection (c) and Sections 9-703 through 9-709:

(1) transactions and liens that were not governed by Article 9 as it existed before the effective date of this amendatory Act of the 91st General Assembly, were validly entered into or created before the effective date of this amendatory Act of the 91st General Assembly, and would be subject to this Act if they had been entered into or created after the effective date of this amendatory Act of the 91st General Assembly, and the rights, duties, and interests flowing from those transactions and liens remain valid after the effective date of this amendatory Act of the 91st General Assembly; and

(2) the transactions and liens may be terminated, completed, consummated, and enforced as required or permitted by this Act or by the law that otherwise would apply if this Act had not taken effect.

(c) Pre-effective-date proceedings. This amendatory Act of the 91st General Assembly does not affect an action, case, or proceeding commenced before the effective date of this amendatory Act of the 91st General Assembly.

(Source: P.A. 91-893, eff. 7-1-01.)

(810 ILCS 5/9-703)
Sec. 9-703. Security interest perfected before effective date.

(a) Continuing priority over lien creditor: perfection requirements satisfied. A security interest that is enforceable immediately before the effective date of this amendatory Act of the 91st General Assembly and would have priority over the rights of a person that becomes a lien creditor at that time is a perfected security interest under this Act if, on the effective date of this amendatory Act of the 91st General Assembly, the applicable requirements for enforceability and perfection under this Act are satisfied without further action.

(b) Continuing priority over lien creditor: perfection requirements not satisfied. Except as otherwise provided in Section 9-705, if, immediately before the effective date of this amendatory Act of the 91st General Assembly, a security interest is enforceable and would have priority over the rights of a person that becomes a lien creditor at that time, but the applicable requirements for enforceability or perfection under this Act are not satisfied on the effective date of this amendatory Act of the 91st General Assembly, the security interest:

(1) is a perfected security interest for one year after the effective date of this amendatory Act of the 91st General Assembly;

(2) remains enforceable thereafter only if the security interest becomes enforceable under Section 9-203 before the year expires; and

(3) remains perfected thereafter only if the applicable requirements for perfection under this Act are satisfied before the year expires.

(Source: P.A. 91-893, eff. 7-1-01.)

(810 ILCS 5/9-704)

Sec. 9-704. Security interest unperfected before effective date. A security interest that is enforceable immediately before the effective date of this amendatory Act of the 91st General Assembly but which would be subordinate to the rights of a person that becomes a lien creditor at that time:

(1) remains an enforceable security interest for one year after the effective date of this amendatory Act of the 91st General Assembly;

(2) remains enforceable thereafter if the security interest becomes enforceable under Section 9-203 on the effective date of this amendatory Act of the 91st General Assembly or within one year thereafter; and

(3) becomes perfected:

(A) without further action, on the effective date of this amendatory Act of the 91st General Assembly if the applicable requirements for perfection under this Act are satisfied before or at that time; or

(B) when the applicable requirements for perfection are satisfied if the requirements are satisfied after that time.

(Source: P.A. 91-893, eff. 7-1-01.)

(810 ILCS 5/9-705)

Sec. 9-705. Effectiveness of action taken before effective date.

(a) Pre-effective-date action; one-year perfection period unless reperfected. If action, other than the filing of a financing statement, is taken before the effective date of this amendatory Act of the 91st General Assembly and the action would have resulted in priority of a security interest over the rights of a person that becomes a lien creditor had the security interest become enforceable before the effective date of this amendatory Act of the 91st General Assembly, the action is effective to perfect a security interest that attaches under this Act within one year after the effective date of this amendatory Act of the 91st General Assembly. An attached security interest becomes unperfected one year after the effective date of this amendatory Act of the 91st General Assembly unless the security interest becomes a perfected security interest under this Act before the expiration of that period.

(b) Pre-effective-date filing. The filing of a financing statement before the effective date of this amendatory Act of the 91st General Assembly is effective to perfect a security interest to the extent the filing would satisfy the applicable requirements for perfection under this Act.

(c) Pre-effective-date filing in jurisdiction formerly governing perfection. This Act does not render ineffective an effective financing statement that, before the effective date of this amendatory Act of the 91st General Assembly, is filed and satisfies the applicable requirements for perfection under the law of the jurisdiction governing perfection as provided in Section 9-103 of the Uniform Commercial Code as it existed before the effective date of this amendatory Act of the 91st General Assembly. However, except as otherwise provided in subsections (d) and (e) and Section 9-706, the financing statement ceases to be effective at the earlier of:

(1) the time the financing statement would have ceased to be effective under the law of the jurisdiction in which it is filed; or

(2) June 30, 2006.

(d) Continuation statement. The filing of a continuation statement after the effective date of this amendatory Act of the 91st General Assembly does not continue the effectiveness of the financing statement filed before the effective date of this amendatory Act of the 91st General Assembly. However, upon the timely filing of a continuation statement after the effective date of this amendatory Act of the 91st General Assembly and in accordance with the law of the jurisdiction governing perfection as provided in Part 3, the effectiveness of a financing statement filed in the same office in that jurisdiction before the effective date of this amendatory Act of the 91st General Assembly continues for the period provided by the law of that jurisdiction.

(e) Application of subsection (c)(2) to transmitting utility financing statement. Subsection (c)(2) applies to a financing statement that, before the effective date of this amendatory Act of the 91st General Assembly, is filed against a transmitting utility and satisfies the applicable requirements for perfection under the law of the jurisdiction governing perfection as provided in Section 9-103, as that Section existed before the effective date of this amendatory Act of the 91st General Assembly, only to the extent that Part 3 provides that the law of a jurisdiction other than jurisdiction in which the financing statement is filed governs perfection of a security interest in collateral covered by the financing statement.

(f) Application of Part 5. A financing statement that includes a financing statement filed before the effective date of this amendatory Act of the 91st General Assembly and a continuation statement filed after the effective date of this amendatory Act of the 91st General Assembly is effective only to the extent that it satisfies the requirements of Part 5 for an initial financing statement.
(Source: P.A. 91-893, eff. 7-1-01.)

(810 ILCS 5/9-706)
Sec. 9-706. When initial financing statement suffices to continue effectiveness of financing statement.

(a) Initial financing statement in lieu of continuation statement. The filing of an initial financing statement in the office specified in Section 9-501 continues the effectiveness of a financing statement filed before the effective date of this amendatory Act of the 91st General Assembly if:

(1) the filing of an initial financing statement in that office would be effective to perfect a security interest under this Act;

(2) the pre-effective-date financing statement was filed in an office in another State or another office in this State; and

(3) the initial financing statement satisfies subsection (c).

(b) Period of continued effectiveness. The filing of an initial financing statement under subsection (a) continues the effectiveness of the pre-effective-date financing statement:

(1) if the initial financing statement is filed before the effective date of this amendatory Act of the 91st General Assembly, for the period provided in Section 9-403 of the Uniform Commercial Code as it existed before the effective date of this amendatory Act of the 91st General Assembly with respect to a financing statement; and

(2) if the initial financing statement is filed after the effective date of this amendatory Act of the 91st General Assembly, for the period provided in Section 9-515 with respect to an initial financing statement.

(c) Requirements for initial financing statement under subsection (a). To be effective for purposes of subsection (a), an initial financing statement must:

(1) satisfy the requirements of Part 5 for an initial financing statement;

(2) identify the pre-effective-date financing statement by indicating the office in which the financing statement was filed and providing the dates of filing and file numbers, if any, of the financing statement and of the most recent continuation statement filed with respect to the financing statement; and

(3) indicate that the pre-effective-date financing statement remains effective.
(Source: P.A. 91-893, eff. 7-1-01.)

(810 ILCS 5/9-707)
Sec. 9-707. Amendment of pre-effective-date financing statement.

(a) "Pre-effective-date financing statement". In this Section, "pre-effective-date financing statement" means a financing statement filed before the effective date of this amendatory Act of the 91st General Assembly.

(b) Applicable law. After the effective date of this amendatory Act of the 91st General Assembly, a person may add or delete collateral covered by, continue or terminate the effectiveness of, or otherwise amend the information provided in, a pre-effective-date financing statement only in accordance with the law of the jurisdiction governing perfection as provided in Part 3. However, the effectiveness of a pre-effective-date financing statement also may be terminated in accordance with the law of the jurisdiction in which the financing statement is filed.

(c) Method of amending: general rule. Except as otherwise provided in subsection (d), if the law of this State governs perfection of a security interest, the information in a pre-effective-date financing statement may be amended after the effective date of this amendatory Act of the 91st General Assembly only if:

(1) the pre-effective-date financing statement and an amendment are filed in the office specified in Section 9-501;

(2) an amendment is filed in the office specified in Section 9-501 concurrently with, or after the filing in that office of, an initial financing statement that satisfies Section 9-706(c); or

(3) an initial financing statement that provides the information as amended and satisfies Section 9-706(c) is filed in the office specified in Section 9-501.

(d) Method of amending: continuation. If the law of this State governs perfection of a security interest, the effectiveness of a pre-effective-date financing statement may be continued only under Section 9-705(d) and (f) or Section 9-706.

(e) Method of amending: additional termination rule. Whether or not the law of this State governs perfection of a security interest, the effectiveness of a pre-effective-date financing statement filed in this State may be terminated after the effective date of this amendatory Act of the 91st General Assembly by filing a termination statement in the office in which the pre-effective-date financing statement is filed, unless an initial financing statement that satisfies Section 9-706(c) has been filed in the office specified by the law of the jurisdiction governing perfection as provided in Part 3 as the office in which to file a financing statement.

(Source: P.A. 91-893, eff. 7-1-01.)

(810 ILCS 5/9-708)

Sec. 9-708. Persons entitled to file initial financing statement or continuation statement. A person may file an initial financing statement or a continuation statement under this Part if:

(1) the secured party of record authorizes the filing; and

(2) the filing is necessary under this Part:

(A) to continue the effectiveness of a financing statement filed before the effective date of this amendatory Act of the 91st General Assembly; or

(B) to perfect or continue the perfection of a security interest.

(Source: P.A. 91-893, eff. 7-1-01.)

(810 ILCS 5/9-709)

Sec. 9-709. Priority.

(a) Law governing priority. This Act determines the priority of conflicting claims to collateral. However, if the relative priorities of the claims were established before the effective date of this amendatory Act of the 91st General Assembly, Article 9 as it existed before the effective date of this amendatory Act of the 91st General Assembly determines priority.

(b) Priority if security interest becomes enforceable under Section 9-203. For purposes of Section 9-322(a), the priority of a security interest that becomes enforceable under Section 9-203 of this Act dates from the effective date of this amendatory Act of the 91st General Assembly if the security interest is perfected under this Act by the filing of a financing statement before the effective date of this amendatory Act of the 91st General Assembly which would not have been effective to perfect the security interest under Article 9 as it existed before the effective date of this amendatory Act of the 91st General Assembly. This subsection does not apply to conflicting security interests each of which is perfected by the filing of such a financing statement.

(Source: P.A. 91-893, eff. 7-1-01.)

(810 ILCS 5/9-710)

Sec. 9-710. Local-filing office responsibilities for filings under the Uniform Commercial Code prior to this amendatory Act of the 91st General Assembly.

(a) In this Section:

(1) "Local-filing office" means a filing office, other than the office of the Secretary of State, that is designated as the proper place to file a financing statement under Section 9-401(1) of the Uniform Commercial Code as in effect immediately before the effective date of this amendatory Act of the 91st General Assembly. The term applies only with respect to a record that covers a type of collateral as to which the filing office is designated in that Section as the proper place to file.

(2) "Former-Article-9 records" means:

(A) financing statements and other records that have been filed in a local-filing office before July 1, 2001, and that are, or upon processing and indexing will be, reflected in the index maintained, as of June 30, 2001, by the local-filing office for financing statements and other records filed in the local filing office before July 1, 2001.

(B) the index as of June 30, 2001.

(b) Except for a record terminating a former-Article-9 record, a local-filing office must not accept for filing a record presented after June 30, 2001, whether or not the record relates to a financing statement filed in the local-filing office before July 1, 2001. If the record terminating such former-Article-9 record statement is in the standard form prescribed by the Secretary of State, the uniform fee for filing and indexing the termination statement in the office of a county recorder shall be $5 and otherwise shall be $10, plus in each case an additional fee of $5 for each name more than one at each address listed against which the record is required to be indexed.

(c) Until July 1, 2001, each local-filing office must maintain all former-Article-9 records in accordance with the Uniform Commercial Code as in effect immediately before the effective date of this amendatory Act of the 91st General Assembly. A former-Article-9 record that is not reflected on the index maintained on June 30, 2001, by the local-filing office must be processed and indexed, and reflected on the index as of June 30, 2001, as soon as practicable but in any event no later than July 30, 2001.

(d) Until at least June 30, 2008, each local-filing office must respond to requests for information with respect to former-Article-9 records relating to a debtor and issue certificates, in accordance with the Uniform Commercial Code as in effect immediately before this amendatory Act of the 91st General Assembly. The fees charged for responding to requests for information relating to the debtor issuing the certificates with respect to former-Article-9 records must be the fees in effect under the Uniform Commercial Code as in effect immediately before the effective date of this amendatory Act of the 91st General Assembly on June 30, 2001, unless a different fee is later set by the local filing office. However, the different fee must not exceed $10 for responding to a request for information relating to a debtor or $10 for issuing a certificate.

(e) After June 30, 2008, each local-filing office may remove and destroy, in accordance with any then applicable record retention law of this State, all former-Article-9 records, including the related index.

(f) This Section does not apply, with respect to financing statements and other records, to a filing office in which mortgages or records of mortgages on real property are required to be filed or recorded if:

(1) the collateral is timber to be cut or as-extracted collateral, or

(2) the record is or relates to a financing statement filed as a fixture filing and the collateral is goods that are or are to become fixtures.

(Source: P.A. 91-893, eff. 7-1-01.)

(810 ILCS 5/Art. 9 Pt. 99 heading)
PART 99. (BLANK)

(810 ILCS 5/9-9901) (from Ch. 26, par. 9-9901)
Sec. 9-9901. (Blank).
(Source: P.A. 91-893, eff. 7-1-01.)

(810 ILCS 5/9-9902) (from Ch. 26, par. 9-9902)
Sec. 9-9902. (Blank).
(Source: P.A. 91-893, eff. 7-1-01.)

Index

abandoned property, 222
abortion, privacy rights, 16
ACA (Patient Protection and Affordable Care Act), 268, 328
acceptance, 83–84, 142
acceptor, 168
accessibility, ADA regulations, 328
accession, acquisition of personal property through, 224–225
accommodation party, 168, 183
accommodations, ADA regulations, 327
accounting, 308, 334
accrual, 143
accused persons, rights of, 16
acquisition, Clayton Act, 339
Act for the Prevention of Frauds and Perjuries, 107
action for the price, 162
adjustment of debts, 207–212
administrative agencies
    administrative law and, 35
    business regulation, 32–33
    executive agencies, 36
    federal agencies, 35–36
    limits on, 37
    state agencies, 36
administrative law. *See also* administrative agencies
    Administrative Procedure Act, 35, 36–37
    executive agencies, 36
    federal agencies, 35–36
    overview, 8–9
    state agencies, 36
Administrative Procedure Act, 35, 36–37
administrators, statute of frauds, 109
adoption, Family and Medical Leave Act, 326–327
adversarial system, 9
adverse possession, title through, 253–254
advertising, service mark, 231
affirmative defenses, 47
affirmative easements, 246–247
age
    of consent, 43
    contractual capacity and, 94–95
    criminal intent and, 49–50
    discrimination, 324
    wills and, 274
Age Discrimination in Employment Act, 324
agency
    agent's apparent authority, 304–305
    agent's authority, 304
    agent's authorized contracts, 309–310
    agent's duties, 307–308
    agent's unauthorized contracts, 308
    creation of, 303–304
    employer–employee relations, 319–320
    by estoppel, 305
    liability of agents for contracts, 308
    in LLCs, 385
    overview, 303
    in partnerships, 360
    principal's duties, 306–307
    principal's liability for agent's torts, 308–309
    purported partners, 363
    termination of, 306
agents
    agency duties, 307–308
    apparent authority of, 304–305
    authority of, 304
    authorized contracts, 309–310
    unauthorized contracts, 308
aggravated assault, 42
aiding and abetting, 46
air rights, 45
alibi, 47
alien corporations, 379–380
allonge, 176
American Bar Association, 375
American Bar Foundation, 375
American law
    as adversarial system, 9
    complexity of, 8–9
    overview, 1–2
    sources of, 5–9
American Law Institute, 39, 49, 167
Americans with Disabilities Act, 6, 327–328
anarchists, 31
animals
    strict liability, 69
    title to by possession, 221–222
annual report, LLCs, 384
annual shareholders' meetings, 378
anomalous indorsements, 176
antedating, 172
anticipatory repudiation, 152
Antitrust Division, 339, 340
antitrust regulation, 33, 321
appeals
    state courts, 26–27
    U.S. District Courts, 24–25
    U.S. Supreme Court, 23, 25, 27
appellant, 27
appellate jurisdiction, 23
appropriation, person's name or likeness, 57
appurtenant easements, 247
Aquinas, St. Thomas, 1, 30
arson, 43
Arthur Andersen, 33
Article I, U.S. Constitution, 11–12, 13
Article III, U.S. Constitution, 21–22, 23, 24
Article V, U.S. Constitution, 6
Article VI, U.S. Constitution, 5–6
Article 2 (UCC), 139–144, 147–153, 155–158, 414–448. *See also* sales and lease contracts
Article 3 (UCC), 167–173, 449–473. *See also* commercial paper
Article 9 (UCC), 187–190, 474–554. *See also* secured transactions
articles of incorporation, 375–376
artificial beings, corporations as, 380
assault, 42, 56–57
assembly, right to, 13–14

assignee, 114
assignment, partnership interest, 372
assignor, 114
Assistant Attorney General in Charge of the Antitrust Division, 339, 340
assumption of risk, 68
attachment, personal property exempt from, 203–205
attempted crimes, 47
auction sales, UCC, 143
authorized contracts, agents, 309–310
Ayres v. Burnett, 132–135

bad checks, crime of issuing, 45
bail, protection against excessive, 16
bailee, 151, 237–240
bailments
    constructive, 240
    defined, 237
    mutual benefit, 238–239
    overview, 237–240
    rights and duties in, 239–240
    for the sole benefit of the bailee, 238
    for the sole benefit of the bailor, 237–238
    special, 240
bailors, 237–240
Baker v. County of Northumberland, 342–345
bankruptcy
    Chapter 7 liquidation, 201–205
    Chapter 11 reorganization, 205–207
    Chapter 13 adjustment of debts, 207–212
    common law, 201
    overview, 201
Bankruptcy Abuse Prevention and Consumer Protection Act (BAPCPA), 201, 212
Bankruptcy Act, 203, 205
bankruptcy decree, 202–203
BAPCPA (Bankruptcy Abuse Prevention and Consumer Protection Act), 201, 212
bargained-for exchange, 87
base fee, 244
battery, 56
bearer, 168
bearer instrument, 175
beneficiary, 281
benefit plans, 325–326
Bentham, Jeremy, 30
bequest, 274
Berne Convention for the Protection of Literary and Artistic Works, 233
beyond a reasonable doubt, 15, 47–48
bilateral contracts, 79, 87, 113–114
Bill of Rights, 13–18
Blackstone, William, 1
blank indorsements, 176
blue sky laws, 334
board of directors, 378
Bonaparte, Napoleon, 3
books, right to inspect, 362
boycotts, 321

555

breach of contract
  anticipatory repudiation, 152
  common law, 152
  discharge and, 122
  remedies for, 123–127. *See also* remedies
  rental agreement, 262–263
  sales and lease contracts, 161–165
breach of duty
  sales and lease contracts, 147–153
  tort liability, 55–56
breaking and entering, 44
bribery, 33, 45–46
burden of proof, 15, 47
Bureau of Indian Affairs, 36
burglary, 44
business contracts, minors, 95
Business Corporation Act, 376
business liability insurance, 268
business organizations
  corporations, 375–381
  limited liability companies, 383–386
  limited partnerships, 369–373
  overview, 353
  partnerships, 359–366
  sole proprietorships, 355–357
business regulation
  employment relations, 319–328
  federal antitrust law, 337–340
  federal securities acts, 331–334
  overview, 317
  regulatory environment, 32–33
business relationships, tort of interference with, 60
buyers
  remedies for breach of contract, 162–164, 164–165
  right to inspect goods, 151
  rights on improper delivery, 151–152
  rights to rightfully rejected goods, 152
bylaws, 377–378

C corporations, 381
cancellation, insurance contracts, 267
capacity, 93–95, 274
capital contribution, 362, 369
carelessness, 65–66
case studies
  Ayres v. Burnett, 132–135
  Baker v. County of Northumberland, 342–345
  Dernier & Dernier V. U.S. Bank National Ass'n., 195–198
  Douglass v. Pflueger Hawaii, 130–132
  Federal Trade Commission v. Actavis, 345–352
  In Re: Cay Clubs, 390–397
  In the Matter of the Estate of Burton, 296–299
  Kelo et al. v. City of New London, 289–293
  Law v. Siegel, 214–217
  Maeder Brothers Quality Wood Pellets v. Hammond Drives & Equipment, 192–195
  Obergefell v. Hodges, 71–73
  Regions Bank v. Maroone Chevrolet, 312–315
  Schoenholz v. Hinzman, 293–296
  Sugartown Worldwide v. Shanks and Glover, 388–390
  Walker v. Texas Division, Sons of Confederate Veterans, 73–74
categorical imperatives, 30
Central Intelligence Agency, 36
certificate of deposit, 169
certification marks, 231
Chapter 7 liquidation, 201–205
Chapter 11 reorganization, 205–207
Chapter 13 adjustment of debts, 207–212
Chapter S corporations, 379, 381
charitable trust, 282
chattel paper, 187
checks, 45, 169
children, 277, 326–327. *See also* minors

Cicero, 1
CISG (Contracts for the International Sale of Goods), 143–144
citizens, U.S. jurisdiction, 17–18
civil law systems, 3–4, 32
civil offenses
  burden of proof, 15
  right to jury trial, 16
  securities sanctions, 333–334
  Sherman Act, 338
  U.S. District Courts, 24
Civil Rights Act, 323–324
class A–C misdemeanors, 41
Clayton Act, 103, 104, 321, 339–340
closed shop agreements, 321
closely held corporations, 380
Code of Hammurabi, 3
codes of ethics, 33
codicil, 274
collateral, 188
collective bargaining, 321
collective marks, 231
color, as suspect classification, 7
Commerce Clause, 12–13, 35, 317
commercial bribery, 46
commercial impracticability, discharge through, 120–121
commercial lease, example, 261
commercial paper
  form of negotiable instruments, 168
  general rules for, 172–173
  indorsement, 175–177
  liabilities of parties to, 181–183
  negotiation of, 175
  overview, 167
  parties to, 168, 181–184
  presentment and notice of dishonor, 184
  requirements for negotiability, 170–171
  rights of a holder, 177
  rights of a holder in due course, 177–178
  transfer of, 175
  types of negotiable instruments, 168–170
  warranties on presentment and transfer, 183
commercial speech, 14
committee of creditors, 205
Committee on Corporate Laws of the Section of Business Law, 375
common carrier, shipment by, 148, 240
common law
  arson, 43
  breach of contract, 152
  burglary, 44
  contracts for sale and lease of goods, 139–144
  criminal law and, 39
  curtsey, 277
  debt and bankruptcy, 201
  dower, 244–245, 277
  engagement rings, 226
  ethical principles and, 32
  infancy, 50
  marital rape, 43
  mirror image rule, 82–83
  nuisance torts, 61–62
  overview, 4–5
  partnerships, 360
  personal property, 221
  privity of contract, 158
  property rights, 45
  tortious interference, 60
Communism, 31
comparative negligence, 67–68
compensation of agent duty, 307
compensatory damages, 62, 123–125
competition, restraint of trade, 103–104
concurrent ownership, real property, 254–255
conditional indorsements, 176

confidentiality, public disclosure of private facts, 58
confirmation, Chapter 13 payment plan, 211
Congress. *See* U.S. Congress
consent
  age and, 43, 94–95
  battery and, 56
  termination of agency by, 306
consequential damages, 124–125, 163
consideration
  additional terms in, UCC, 142
  illusory promises, 88–89
  offer revocation, 82
  overview, 87–88
  past consideration, 89
  pre-existing duty, 89–90
consignee, 188
consignment sales, 148–149, 148, 187, 188
consignor, 188
Consolidated Omnibus Budget Reconciliation Act, 325–326
conspiracy, 47
constitutional law, 5–6, 11–19. *See also* U.S. Constitution
constructive bailments, 240
constructive trusts, 282, 287
Consumer Price Index, 203
consumer protection, 33
contempt of court, 60
contingent reversionary interest, 246
contraception, privacy rights and, 16
contract law/contracts
  acceptance, 83–84
  assignment to third-party beneficiaries, 113–116
  authorized, agents, 309–310
  breach of, 119–122
  capacity, 93–95
  classification of, 78–80
  common law, 158
  consideration, 87–90
  criteria for valid, 77
  discharge, 119–122
  employer–employee relations, 320
  fraud and, 59–60
  genuine assent, 97–100
  insurance, 265–268
  lease of goods. *See* sales and lease contracts
  legality, 103–105
  liability for agents for contracts entered into on principal's behalf, 308
  mirror image rule, 82–83
  novation, 115
  offer, 81–83
  overview, 75, 77–78
  partnerships, 360, 371–372
  performance, 122
  personal liability of promoters, 377
  privity of contracts, 158
  remedies for breach of, 123–127. *See also* remedies
  sale of goods. *See* sales and lease contracts
  statute of frauds, 107–110
  tortious interference, 60
  unauthorized, agents, 308
  unconscionable, 104–105, 142–143
contract of sale, deeds, 252
Contracts for the International Sale of Goods (CISG), 143–144
contractual liability, commercial paper, 182–183
contradictory terms, negotiable instruments, 173
contributory negligence, 66–67
conversion, 61
copyright, 230–231, 233
Copyright Act, 231
corporations
  articles of incorporation, 375–376
  Chapter S, 381

classification of, 379–380
corporate bylaws, 377–378
corporate directors, 378
corporate existence, 376
corporate name, 376
corporate officers, 378
corporate scandals, 33
defective incorporation, 376–377
as entities, 380
first organizational meeting, 377–378
formation of, 375
management, 377
overview, 375
piercing the corporate veil, 380
promoter liability for preincorporation contracts, 377
regulation of business environment, 33
shareholder derivative actions, 379
stock acquisition, Clayton Act, 339
Corpus Juris Civilis, 3
cost, insurance, and freight (C.I.F.), 148
cost and freight (C. & F.), 148, 148
cost of curing the defect damages, 124
counsel, right to, 15–16
counteroffer, 83
course of dealing, UCC, 141
course of performance, UCC, 141
court system
  federal, 23–25
  jurisdiction, 21–23
  overview, 21
  state, 25–27
cover, substitute goods, 163
credit agreements, usurious contracts, 104
credit card fraud, 45
credit counseling, bankruptcy, 212
creditors, 205, 209–211
crime(s)
  against judicial process, 45–46
  against persons, 41–43
  against property, 43–45
  aiding in the commission of, 46
  attempted, 47
  classification of, 41
  contracts and, 103
  elements of, 39–41
  specific, 41–46
  strict liability, 40
  torts vs., 55
criminal act or omission, 39–40, 47–48
criminal conspiracy, 47
criminal intent, 39–40, 47–48, 49–50
criminal law
  attempted crimes and criminal conspiracy, 47
  classification of crimes, 41
  common law and, 39
  defenses to criminal liability, 47–51
  elements of a crime, 39–41
  ethical principles and, 32
  overview, 39
  securities sanctions, 333–334
  specific crimes, 41–46
  tort law vs., 55
criminal mischief, 44
criminal offenses
  burden of proof, 15
  defenses to criminal liability, 47–51
  Sixth Amendment rights, 16
  U.S. District Courts, 24
criminal trespass, 44
cruel and unusual punishment, 15–16
curtesy, 245, 277

damages
  breach of accepted goods, 163
  compensatory, 123–125
  consequential, 163
  deduction of from price of goods, 164
  incidental, 162, 163
  infringement of a registered mark, 232
  liquidation of, 164
  mitigation of, 127
  nonacceptance or repudiation of goods, 162
  nondelivery or repudiation of goods, 163
  worker injuries, 325
dangerous activities, strict liability, 68, 69
dangerous animals, strict liability, 69
D.C. Circuit courts, 23
de facto corporations, 376–377
de jure corporations, 376
deadly force, 51
debt(s)
  of another, statute of frauds, 109
  bankruptcy and, 201–212
  Chapter 13 adjustment of, 207–212
  common law, 201
  in LLCs, 385
  in partnerships, 362
  in sole proprietorships, 356
debtor, 188
decedent, 271
deed, transfer by, 251
defamation, 58–59
default, secured transactions, 190
defective incorporation, 376–377
defective performance, 124
defense of others, 50
defense of property, 51
defenses
  to criminal liability, 47–51
  to negligence, 66–68
delegatee, 114–115
delegation, 114
delegator, 114–115
delivery, goods, 147, 149–153, 161
democratic governments, 31–32
deontology, 30
derivative actions, 373, 379
Dernier & Dernier v. U.S. Bank National Ass'n., 195–198
design defects, product liability, 69
determinable fee, 244
devise, 274
Digital Millennium Copyright Act, 231
directorates, Clayton Act, 340
directors, corporate, 340, 378
disabled individuals, ADA regulations, 327–328
discharge
  Chapter 13 payment plan, 211
  contracts, 119–122
disclosure
  principals, 309–310
  securities, 333
discrimination, 323–324, 327–328
disinheritance, wills, 277
disparagement, 59
dissociation
  limited liability companies, 386
  partnerships, 364–365
dissolution
  limited liability companies, 386
  limited partnerships, 372
  partnerships, 365–366
distributee, 273
District of Columbia v. Heller, 7, 14
dividends, 380
divorce, will revocation, 276–277. *See also* marital law
domestic animals, strict liability, 69
domestic corporations, 379–380
domestic limited partnership, 372
double jeopardy, protection against, 15
double taxation, 380, 381

Douglass v. Pflueger Hawaii, 130–132
dower, 244–245, 277
draft, 169
drawee, 168, 183
drawer, 168, 183
due care, 308
due diligence, 333
due process clause, 16
due process of law, 15–16
duration. *See* time frames
duress, 98, 274
Durham Rule, 48
duty of care, 65–66
duty of cooperation, 147–148, 307
duty of loyalty, 307
duty of obedience, 308
duty of reimbursement and indemnification, 307
duty to act, 40, 55–56
duty to communicate relevant information to the principal, 308
duty to compensate agent, 307
duty to exercise due care in agency business, 308
duty to render an accounting, 308

E. A. Westermarck, 31
easement appurtenant, 247
easement in gross, 247
easements, 246–247
EDGAR (Electronic Data Gathering Analysis and Retrieval) database, 333
Eight Amendment, 16
Eighteenth Amendment, 6
email, offer acceptance, 83–84
emancipated minors, contractual capacity, 95
embezzlement, 45
emergency situations, trespass to land, 60–61
eminent domain, 16, 252–253
emotional distress, intentional infliction of, 57
employees/employers. *See* employment relations
employment relations
  ADA, 327–328
  Affordable Healthcare Act, 328
  age discrimination, 324
  agency law, 319–320
  contract law, 320
  discrimination, 323–324
  ethical behavior and, 33
  federal legislation affecting, 323–328
  health and safety regulations, 325
  labor-management relations, 320–321
  liability of principal for agent's torts, 308–309. *See also* agency
  medical leave, 326–327
  overview, 319
  pension plans, 325–326
  sexual harassment, 324
  unemployment benefits, 325
  workers' compensation, 325
Employment Retirement Income Security Act (ERISA), 325–326
engagement rings, 225, 226
England, law system, 4–5, 39. *See also* common law
Enron, 33, 334
entity status, 380, 384
entrapment, 51
Environmental Protection Agency, 36
equal dignities rule, 304
Equal Employment Opportunity Commission, 36, 323, 324, 327
equal protection clause, 13, 16, 18
equitable remedies, 62, 125–126
ERISA (Employment Retirement Income Security Act), 325–326
estate for years, 245
estates, statute of frauds, 109
estates in land, 243

estoppel, 305, 363
ethical absolutism, 30, 31
ethical philosophies, 29–31
ethical relativism, 31, 32
ethics
    ethical philosophies, 29–31
    overview, 29
    problem areas, 32
    public policy and, 31–32
    regulatory environment of business, 32–33
examiner, bankruptcy, 205–206
excessive bail, 15–16
exclusive dealing contracts, 339
execution, fraud in, 99–100
executive agencies, 36
executor, 109, 271
executrix, 271
express contracts, 78
express grant, easement by, 247
express trusts, 281, 282
express warranties, 155–156
extortion, 45–46

Fair Labor Standards Act, 321–322
fair use, copyright, 230–231
false imprisonment, 43, 57
false light, 58
false statements, 58–59
Family and Medical Leave Act, 326–327
family courts, 26
Fascism, 31
federal agencies, 35–36. *See also* administrative agencies
Federal Aviation Administration, 8, 36
Federal Bureau of Investigation, 36
Federal Circuit courts, 23
Federal Communications Commission, 8, 36
Federal Copyright Act, 230
federal court system 21–23, 23–25
federal government
    administrative agencies of. *See* administrative agencies
    administrative law, 8–9
    antitrust law, 337–340
    Bill of Rights protections, 18
    business regulation, 317. *See also* business regulation
    debt of, 17
    eminent domain, 252–253
    employees of, constitutional protections, 18–19
    employment legislation, 323–328
    labor-management relations regulation, 320–321
    limitations on powers of, 12, 13, 16, 17
    minimum wage regulation, 321–322
    powers granted by Constitution, 6
    privacy rights and, 16
    regulation of business environment, 32–33
    scope of constitutional protections, 18–19
    securities regulation, 331–334
    statutory law, 6–8
Federal Register, 37, 203
federal securities acts, 331–334
Federal Trade Commission (FTC), 8, 36, 339, 340
Federal Trade Commission, v. Actavis, 345–352
fee simple absolute, 244
felonies, 41
feudal system, 4–5
FICA taxation, 383
fiduciary relationship, 100, 281
Fifth Amendment, 15–16, 252–253
financial statements, SOX regulations, 334
financing statement, 188, 189
First Amendment, 13–14, 18–19
first-degree felonies, 41
fitness for purpose, warranty of, 157
fixtures, 188, 189

fleeing suspect, 15
forbearance, 87–88
foreign corporations, 33, 379–380
foreign limited partnerships, 372–373
foreseeable harm, 65–66
forgery, 45
formal contracts, 80
Fourteenth Amendment, 13, 16, 17–18
Fourth Amendment, 14–15
franchise tax, 383
Frankfurter, Felix, 1
fraud
    in contracts, 98–100
    credit card, 45
    tort of, 59–60
    wills, 274
fraud in the execution, 99–100
fraud in the inducement, 98–99
free alongside a vessel (F.A.S.) shipping, 148, 150–151
free on board (F.O.B.) shipping, 148, 150–151
freedom of speech, religion, and assembly, 13–14, 18–19
freehold estates, 244–245
frustration of purpose, discharge through, 121
FTC (Federal Trade Commission), 8, 36, 339, 340
fully disclosed principals, 309
future gifts, wills as, 271
future interests, real property, 245–246
future performance, unilateral contracts, 79–80

gambling contracts, 104
gap creditor, 203
general partners, 370–371
general trial courts, 26
genuine assent
    contracts, 93–95
    duress, 98
    fraud in the execution, 99–100
    fraud in the inducement, 98–99
    mutual mistake, 97–98
    overview, 97
    undue influence, 100
gift(s)
    acquisition of personal property through, 225–226
    causa mortis, 226
    future, wills as, 271. *See also* wills
Goldman, Ron, 15
good faith, contracts, 88–89
Good Samaritans, 50
goods
    accepted, damage for breach, 163
    action for the price, 162
    buyer's right to inspect, 151
    casualty to identified, 152–153
    deduction of damage from price of, 164
    delivery, 147, 149, 153, 161
    description of, 155–156
    express statement or promise about, 155
    insurable interest on, 149
    lease of. *See* sales and lease contracts
    nonacceptance or repudiation, 162
    nonconformity, 151–152
    nondelivery or repudiation of, 163
    passing of title to, 149
    rejected, security interest in, 163
    return of, 148–149
    right to resell, 162
    rightfully rejected, 152
    sale of. *See* sales and lease contracts
    sample or model, 156
    shipment of, 147–148, 150–151, 152–153, 240
    substitute, 163
    UCC definition of, 139–140
    unfinished, right to salvage, 161
government, forms of, 31–32
government, U.S. *See* federal government

grand jury indictment, right to, 15
grantee, 244, 251
grantor, 251
Great Britain, common law system, 5. *See also* common law
Griswold v. Connecticut, 16
guarantor, 168, 183

health and safety regulations, 325
health benefit plans, 325–326
health insurance, 268, 326, 328
Health Insurance Portability and Accountability Act (HIPAA), 326
holder in due course (HDC), 177–178
holders' rights, commercial paper, 177–178
holographic wills, 276
homicide, 41–42
hospitality industry, 240
hot pursuit, 15
Hume v. U.S., 143

illegal activity, contracts and, 87–88, 103, 120
illusory promises, 88–89
immunity, privilege against self-incrimination, 15
impartial jury, right to, 15–16
implied in fact contracts, 79
implied warranties, 156–157
impossibility of performance, 120
in personam jurisdiction, 21
in rem jurisdiction, 21
In the Matter of the Estate of Burton, 296–299
incidental beneficiaries, 116
incidental damages, 124, 162, 163
income taxes, 380, 383
incompetents, contracts, 93–94
incomplete negotiable instruments, 172–173
incorporation
    Bill of Rights, 13
    defective, 376–377
indemnification, duty of, 307
independent contractors, 308–309, 319–320
independent federal agencies, 35–36
individual rights, 13–18, 18–19
indorsee, 168
indorsement, 175–177
indorser, 168, 183
inducement, 59–60, 98–99
infancy, 49–50
influence peddling, 46
infringement, warranty against, 156–157
injunction(s)
    breach of contract, 126
    nuisance torts, 62
    trespass to land, 60
    union boycotts, 321
    union strikes, 322–323
innkeepers, 240
insanity defense, 48–49
insurable interest, 149, 266
insurance contracts, 265–268
intangible property, 219–220, 223–224, 229, 243
intellectual property
    copyrights, 230–231
    international arena, 232–233
    overview, 229
    patents, 229–230
    remedies for infringement of rights, 232
    service marks, collective marks, and certification marks, 231
    trade secrets, 232
    trademarks, 231
intended beneficiaries, 115–116
intended use, product liability, 69
intentional infliction of emotional distress, 57
intentional misrepresentation, 59–60

intentional torts
    against persons, 56–60
    against property, 60–62
    breach of duty and tort liability, 55–56
    overview, 55
inter vivos gifts, 225, 252
inter vivos trusts, 282
interest
    future, 245–246
    insurable, 149, 266
    real property, transfer of, 251–256
    remainder, 246
    reversionary, 245–246
    usurious contracts, 104
interference with business relationships, 60
interference with contract rights, 60
interim trustee, bankruptcy, 202
intermediate courts of appeals, 26–27
Internal Revenue Code (IRC), 6, 381
Internal Revenue Service, 37, 383
international law
    foreign corporations, 33, 379–380
    foreign limited partnerships, 372–373
    intellectual property, 232–233
    sale of goods, 143–144
interstate commerce, 6, 103–104
Interstate Commerce Commission, 36
intestacy, 273, 277, 278
intestacy statute, 273
intestate, 273
intestate succession, 273
intoxication, 49, 94
intrusion into seclusion, 57–58
invasion of privacy, 57–58
involuntary intoxication, 49
IRC (Internal Revenue Code), 6, 381
irresistible impulse test, 48
irrevocable trusts, 282–284, 285–286
issue, 273

joint tenancy, 254–255
Judicial Conference of the United States, 203
judicial process, crimes against, 45–46
judicial review, 7–8
jurisdiction, 21–23
jury trial, right to, 15–16
justice of the peace courts, 26
Justinian Code, 3
Justinian I, 3

Kant, Immanuel, 30
Kelo v. City of New London, 16, 289–293
kidnapping, 42–43
King v. Burwell, 268
King's Court, 4
Kropotkin, Peter, 31

labor law, 33, 319, 320–321. *See also* employment relations
Labor Management Relations Act, 322–323
Labor Management Reporting and Disclosure Act, 323
labor organization, antitrust law, 339
land. *See also* real estate; real property
    eminent domain, 16, 252–253
    nonpossessory interests in, 246
    nuisance torts, 61–62
    tort of trespass to, 60–61
    trespassing, 243
    use restrictions, 255–256
    zoning, 62, 255–256
landlord-tenant relationship
    creation of, 259
    landlord's remedies for breach, 262–263
    overview, 259
    tenant's remedies upon breach, 263
    tenant's rights and responsibilities, 262

    termination of, 259
    unlawful termination of, 259–262
Landrum–Griffin Act, 323
lapse, insurance contracts, 267
larceny, 45
Law v. Siegel, 214–217
lawyers, in United States, 8–9
leaders, ethical behavior and, 33
leases, goods. *See* sales and lease contracts
leases, landlord-tenant relationship, 259–263
legal age, wills, 274
legal capacity, wills, 274
legal precedent, common law system, 5
legal remedies. *See* remedies
legal value, 87
legality, of contracts, 103–105
lessees, 164–165
lessors, 161–162, 164–165
liability
    of agents for contracts on principal's behalf, 308
    commercial paper, 181–183
    corporations, 380
    limited partnerships, 371
    LLCs, 383, 385
    of principal for agent's torts, 308–309
    of promoters for preincorporation contracts, 377
    product, 69
    sole proprietorships, 356–357
    strict, 68–69
liability insurance contracts, 268
libel, 58–59
licenses, as real property, 248
life estate, 244
life insurance contracts, 267
Limited Liability Act, 383
limited liability companies
    admission of new members, 385
    agency powers, 385
    annual report, 384
    dissociation, 386
    dissolution and winding up, 386
    entity status, 384
    formation of, 384
    liability of members and managers, 385
    management, 385
    name, 384
    operating agreement, 384
    overview, 383
    purpose and duration of, 384
    transferable interest, 385
limited partners, 370–371
Limited Partnership Act, 369
limited partnerships
    admission of new partners, 370
    assignment of partnership interest, 372
    dissolution of, 372
    foreign, 372–373
    formation of, 370
    overview, 369
    right to bring derivative actions, 373
    rights and obligations of partners, 370–371
    sharing of profits and losses, 371
    withdrawal by general and limited partners, 371–372
liquidated damages, 125, 164
liquidation, Chapter 7, 201–205
loss of the bargain damages, 123–124
lost property, 222, 223
loyalty, duty of, 307

M'Naughten Rule, 48
Madrid Protocol, 233, 234
Maeder Brothers Quality Wood Pellets v. Hammond Drives & Equipment, 192–195
mailbox rule, 83–84
majority rule, 32

maker, 168, 183
malice aforethought, 41–42
malpractice insurance, 268
management
    corporations, 377
    ethical behavior and, 33
    limited liability companies, 385
mandatory retirement, 324
manslaughter, 42
manufacturing, acquisition of personal property through, 223–224
manufacturing defects, 69
Marbury v. Madison, 7
marriage law
    consideration, statute of frauds, 109–110
    curtesy, 245, 277
    dower, 244–245, 277
    engagement rings, 225, 226
    marital rape, 43
    will disinheritance of spouses, 277
    will revocation, 276–277
Marshall, John, 7–8
Marx, Karl, 30
Marxism, 31
material errors, 24–25
material fact, 59–60
material misrepresentation, 59–60
Matter of Totten, 284
maximum hours provisions, 321–322
MBCA (Model Business Corporation Act), 375–376, 377, 378
means test, bankruptcy, 212
media, torts involving, 58–59
Medicaid, 268
medical leave, 326–327
Medicare, 268
member-managed LLCs, 385
mental illness
    contractual capacity and, 93–94
    criminal liability and, 48–49
merchantability, warranty of, 157
merchants, 139
mergers, notification of, 339
Middle East, 31
Mill, John Stuart, 30
minimum wage, 321–322
minors
    business contracts, 95
    contractual capacity, 94–95
    infancy and, 50
    wills, 274
mirror image rule, 82–83
misdemeanors, 41
mislaid property, 222
misrepresentation, intentional, 99
mitigation of damages, 127
Model Business Corporation Act (MBCA), 375–376, 377, 378
model goods, 156
Model Partnership Act, 359
Model Penal Act, 42
Model Penal Code, 39, 43, 44, 47, 49
model Penal Code Test, 49
modified comparative negligence, 67–68
monopolies, 103–104, 337–338
moral relativism, 32
morality, 30–31
murder, 41–42
mutual benefit bailments, 238–239
mutual mistake, 97–98

NAFTA (North American Free Trade Agreement), 2, 6
name
    corporate, 376
    LLCs, 384

Napoleonic Code, 3–4
National Conference of Commissioners on Uniform State Laws (NCCUSL), 167, 187, 359, 369, 383
National Federation of Independent Business v. Sebelius, 268
National Labor Relations Act, 321, 322, 323
National Labor Relations Board (NLRB), 8, 321
national origin, as suspect classification, 7
natural person, 158
NCCUSL (National Conference of Commissioners on Uniform State Laws), 167, 187, 359, 369, 383
necessary and proper clause, 13
negative easements, 247
negligence
    defenses to, 66–68
    liability of principal for agent's torts, 308–309
    malpractice insurance, 268
    overview, 65–66
negligent homicide, 42
negotiability, requirements for, 170–171
negotiable instruments, 80, 168–170, 175–178. *See also* commercial paper
negotiation, commercial paper, 175
New Hampshire Rule, 48
nihilism, 31
Ninth Amendment, 16
NLRB (National Labor Relations Board), 8, 321
No Electronic Theft Act, 231
noise ordinances, 62
nominal damages, 125
nonacceptance, goods, 162
nonconforming use, 256
nonconformity, goods, 151–152
nondomestic animals, strict liability, 69
nonfreehold estates, 245
nonpossessory interests, land, 246
nonprofit corporations, 379
Norris La Guardia Act, 321
North American Free Trade Agreement (NAFTA), 2, 6
not-for-profit LLCs, 384
notes, 169–170
notice of dishonor, 184
notice of revocation, 82
notice of termination, 147
notice recording acts, 253
notice to third parties upon dissolution, 365–366
novation, 115, 121–122
Nuclear Regulatory Commission, 8, 36
nuncupative wills, 276

Obama, Barack, 268
Obamacare, 268
obedience, duty of, 308
Obergefell v. Hodges, 16, 71–73
obligations, negotiable instruments, 171
obligees, 79, 113
obligors, 79, 113
obstruction of justice, 46
Occupational Safety and Health Act, 325
Occupational Safety and Health Administration, 325
offer, 81–83, 142
offeree, 78, 81
offeror, 78, 81
officers, corporate, 340, 378
operating agreement, LLCs, 384
operation of law, termination of agency by, 306
organizational meetings, 377–378
original jurisdiction, 23
output contracts, 88–89
overtime pay, 322
ownership interest
    commercial paper, 175
    real property, 243–244
ownership rights, trusts, 281. *See also* trusts

paid leave, 326–327
Parliament, 5, 8, 107
parol evidence, 140
parol evidence rule, 140–141
partially disclosed principles, 309–310
parties, commercial paper, 168
partnerships
    admission of new partners, 362
    agency rights and duties, 360
    capital contributions of partners, 362
    common law, 360
    contractual rights and duties, 360
    debt liability, 362
    dissociation, 364–365
    dissolution and winding up, 365
    by estoppel, 363
    formation of, 359–360
    limitations on partner rights, 362
    Model Partnership Act, 359
    notice to third parties upon dissolution, 365–366
    overview, 359
    partner relationships, 260
    property rights, 363–364
    purported partners, 363
    right to inspect books, 362
    sample partnership agreement, 361
past consideration, 89
patents, 229–230 233
Patient Protection and Affordable Care Act (ACA), 268, 328
payable on demand, 172
payable requirements, negotiable instruments, 172, 173
payee, 168
payment plan, Chapter 13 reorganization, 211
PCAOB (Public Company Accounting Oversight Board), 334
pension plans, 325–326
per capita, wills, 273
per stirpes, 273–274
perfection, security interest, 189
performance
    commercial impracticability of, 120–121
    discharge through, 119
    duration beyond one year, 108
    impossibility of, 120
    sales and lease contracts, 147–153
    specific, buyer's right to, 163
    substituted, 153
periodic tenancy, 245, 259
perjury, 46
perpetual existence, corporations, 380
personal jurisdiction, 21–23
personal liability
    corporate directors, 378
    corporations, 380
    general partnerships, 371
    LLCs, 383, 385
    of promoters, 377
    piercing the corporate veil, 380
    shareholders, 380
personal property
    bailments, 237–240
    bankruptcy valuation, 212
    common law, 221
    contracts for the sale of, 109
    debtor, exempt from attachment, 203–205
    defined, 219 220
    insurance contracts, 267
    liability insurance contracts, 268
    overview, 221
    sale and lease of goods, UCC, 139–144
    secured transactions, 187–190
    title to through accession, 224–225
    title to through gift, 225–226
    title to through manufacturing, 223–224

title to through possession, 221–222
title to through purchase, 222–223
wills. *See* wills
persons
    appropriation of name or likeness of, 57
    crimes against, 41–43
    defamation of, 58–59
    intentional torts against, 56–60
pets, strict liability, 69
philosophies, ethical, 29–31
piercing the corporate veil, 380
plain sight, 14–15
Plato, 30
PLLCs (professional limited liability companies), 384
police powers, state governments, 12
possession, acquisition of personal property through, 221–222
possibility of a reverter, 246
postdating, 172
post-effective period, 332
power of attorney, 304
predatory trade practices, 103–104
pre-existing duty, 89–90
prefiling period, 332
preincorporation contracts, promoter liability for, 377
premerger notification, 339
preponderance of the evidence, 47
presentment, commercial paper, 184
presentment warranties, commercial paper, 183
president
    administrative agencies and, 35, 36
    Fourteenth Amendment provisions and, 17
    statutory law and, 6
price, 103–104, 162, 164, 339
price discrimination, 339
price fixing, 103–104
primary sources of law, 8
principals
    agency duties, 306–307
    liability for agent's torts, 308–309
priority order, creditor claims, 209–211
privacy
    invasion of as tort, 57–58
    private actions, constitutional protections, 18–19
    right to, 16
private corporations, 379
private facts, public disclosure of, 58
private land use restrictions, 255–256
private nuisance, 62
private trust, 282
privileges and immunities clause, 18
probable cause, 14–15
procedural due process, 15–16
product liability, 69
products. *See also* goods
    disparagement, 59
    misuse of, 68, 69
    strict liability, 69
    unsafe, 33
professional corporations, 380
professional limited liability companies (PLLCs), 384
profits
    corporations, 379, 380, 381
    limited partnerships, 371
    LLCs, 384
profits à prendre, 247, 248
prohibition, 6
promise
    express warranties, 155
    negotiable instruments, 171
    defined, 79
    illusory, 88–89

promisors, 79
promoters, liability for preincorporation contracts, 377
property. *See also* intellectual property; personal property; real property
   contracts transferring interest in, 108–109
   crimes against, 43–45
   defense of, 51
   eminent domain and, 16
   intentional torts against, 60–62
   overview, 219–220
property insurance contracts, 267
property rights. *See also* intellectual property; personal property; real property
   criminal trespass, 44–45
   nuisance torts, 61–62
   partnerships, 363–364
   trespass to land, 60–61
property status, sole proprietorships, 357
proximate cause, 65–66
proxy solicitations, 333
Public Company Accounting Oversight Board (PCAOB), 334
Public Company Accounting Reform and Investor Protection Act, 334
public corporations, 379
public disclosure of private facts, 58
public figure, defamation, 58–59
public land use restrictions, 255–256
public nuisance, 62
public officials, 46
public places, ADA regulations, 328
public policy
   contracts contrary to, 104–105
   ethics and, 31–32
public records, tampering with, 46
public trial, right to, 16
publication requirement, wills, 275–276
publications, torts involving, 58–59
publicly traded corporations, 380
purchase, acquisition of personal property through, 222–223
pure comparative negligence, 67–68
purported partners, 363

qualified fee, 244
quasi contract, 126
questions of fact, 24–25
quitclaim deed, 251–252

race, as suspect classification, 7
race-notice recording acts, 253
race recording acts, 253
rape, 43
rational basis test, 12
rational relationship test, 6–7
real estate. *See also* land; real property
   contract for transfer of interest, 108–109
   eminent domain, 252–253
   as real property, 243
   trespass to land, 60–61
real property
   concurrent ownership, 254–255
   contracts transferring interest in, 108–109
   creation and transfer of interests in, 251–256
   defined, 219–220
   easements, 246–247
   estates in land, 243
   freehold estates, 244–245
   future interests, 245–246
   insurance contracts, 267
   landlord-tenant relationship, 259–263
   liability insurance contracts, 268
   licenses, 248
   nonfreehold estates, 245
   nonpossessory interests in land, 246

overview, 243
profits à prendre, 247, 248
wills. *See* wills
reasonable care
   mutual benefit bailments, 239
   negligence torts, 65–66
reasonable doubt, 47–48
reasonable investigation, securities sanctions, 333
reasonable person standard, 65–66
receiving stolen property, 45
reckless endangerment, 42
recognizances, formal contracts, 80
recording statutes, deeds, 253
Regions Bank v. Maroone Chevrolet, 312–315
registration statement, securities, 331–332
Regulations A and D, Securities Act of 1933, 332—333
regulatory environment, business, 32–33
Rehabilitation Act, 327
reimbursement, duty of, 307
rejected goods, security interest in, 163
release, discharge through, 121
relevant information, duty to communicate to the principal, 308
religion
   as suspect classification, 7
   First Amendment rights, 13–14
   religious fundamentalism, 30, 31
remainder interest, 246
remedies
   breach of contract, 123–125
   breach of rental agreement, 262–263
   contractual modification or limitation of, 164
   election of, 126–127
   equitable, 125–126
   infringement of a registered mark, 232
   infringement of intellectual property rights, 232
   legal, 123–125
   mitigation of damages, 127
   overview, 123
   sales and lease contracts, 161–165
   self-help, 263
rental agreement, breach of, 262–263
reorganization, Chapter 11, 205–207
reorganization plan, 207
replevin, 163
repudiation, goods, 162, 163
requirements contracts, 88–89
rescinded contracts, 93
reselling, right to, 162
reservation, easement by, 247
residential lease, example, 260
respondents, 27
Restatements of Law, 8
restraint of trade, 103–104, 338
restrictive indorsements, 176–177
resulting trusts, 281, 287
retirement, mandatory, 324
retirement plans, 325–326
return of goods, 148–149
reversible errors, 25, 27
reversionary interest, 245–246
Revised Model Partnership Act (RUPA), 359, 362, 363, 364, 365
Revised Uniform Limited Liability Company Act (RULLCA), 383, 384, 385, 386
revocable trusts, 282–284, 285–286
revocation
   offer, 82
   real property licenses, 248
   wills, 276–277
rights of holders, commercial paper, 177–178
rights, bailments, 239–240
risk, assumption of, 68
risk of loss, shipment of goods, 148, 149, 150–151
robbery, 45

Roe v. Wade, 16
Roman Empire, 3, 4
rule of reason test, 338
rulemaking, 37
Rules 147, 504, 505, and 506, Securities Act of 1933, 332–333
RULLCA (Revised Uniform Limited Liability Company Act), 383, 384, 385, 386
RUPA (Revised Model Partnership Act), 359, 362, 363, 364, 365

safety regulations, 33, 325
sale of goods
   statute of frauds, 109
   UCC, 107, 121
sale on approval, 148–149
sales and lease contracts
   applicability of UCC, 139–140
   Articles 2 and 2A of UCC, 139–144, 147–153, 155–158
   breach of duty, 147–153
   Clayton Act prohibitions, 339
   contract formation, 141–143
   formal requirements and rules of construction, 140
   inapplicability of seals, 141
   international contracts, 143–144
   overview, 139
   parol evidence rule, 140–141
   performance, 147–153
   remedies for breach of, 161–165
   rights and duties of parties, 147–153
   sales of $500 or more, 140
   statue of frauds, 140
   statute of limitations for breach of, 164
   warranties, 155–158
salvage, unfinished goods, 161
same-sex marriage, 16
sample goods, 156
sanctions, Securities Act of 1933, 333
Sarbanes–Oxley Act (SOX), 334
Schoenholz v. Hinzman, 293–296
seals, inapplicability of, 141
search warrants, 14–15
searches, 14–15
SEC v. W. J. Howey Co., 331
seclusion, intrusion into, 57–58
Second Amendment, 7, 14
second-degree felonies, 41
secondary sources of law, 8
Secret Service, 36
Secretary of Labor, 325
Section 24, Securities Act of 1933, 333
Sections 10(b), 18, and 32, Securities Exchange Act of 1934, 333–334
Sections 302, 806, and 906, Sarbanes–Oxley Act (SOX), 334
secured party, 188
secured transactions
   applicability of Article 9, 187
   creation of security interest, 188–189
   default, 190
   duration of perfected security interest, 189–190
   overview, 187
   perfection of security interest, 189
   priorities among conflicting interests, 190
   terminology, 188
Securities Act of 1933, 331–333
Securities and Exchange Commission (SEC), 8, 36, 331–332, 333
Securities Exchange Act of 1934, 333–334
securities
   exempt from registration, 332–333
   federal regulations, 33, 331–334
   registration, 331–332
   state regulations, 334

security agreement, 188
security interest
    creation of, 188–189
    duration of perfected, 189–190
    perfection, 189
    priorities among conflicting interests, 190
    rejected goods, 163
seizures, 14–15
self-defense, 47, 50
self-help remedy, 262
self-incrimination, privilege against, 15
sellers
    general rules affecting, 164–165
    remedies for breach of contract, 161–162
    shipment by 150
    tender of delivery, 149–150
service marks, 231
services, disparagement, 59
Seventh Amendment, 16
sex, as suspect classification, 7
sex discrimination, 324
sexual harassment, 324
sexual orientation discrimination, 324
shareholders
    Chapter S corporations, 381
    derivative actions, 379
    as owners, 378
shares, corporate, 378
Sherman Antitrust Act, 103, 337–338
shipment, goods, 147–148, 150–151, 152–153, 240
shoplifting, 43
signature liability, 181–182
signatures, commercial paper, 181–182
signed writing
    insurance contracts, 266
    negotiable instruments, 169–170
    statute of frauds, 108, 140
    wills, 275
simple assault, 42
simple contracts, 80
Simpson, Nicole Brown, 15
Simpson, O. J., 15
Sixth Amendment, 16
slander, 58–59
slavery, 18
small claims courts, 25–26
Social Security Act, 325
Social Security Administration, 36
sole proprietorships
    benefits of, 356
    formation of, 355
    liabilities of, 356–357
    property status, 357
    termination of, 357
SOX (Sarbanes–Oxley Act), 334
special bailments, 240
special indorsements, 176
specialized courts
    federal, 23–24
    state, 25–26
specific performance
    buyer's right to, 163
    remedies, 125
    unilateral contracts, 79–80
speech, constitutional protections, 13–14, 18–19
speedy public trial, right to, 15–16
spouses, 277, 326–327. See also marriage law
standard of care, negligence torts, 65–66
Standard Oil Co. v. U.S., 338
stare decisis, 5
state agencies, 36
state court system, 21–23, 25–27
state governments
    administrative agencies, 36
    administrative law, 8–9
    Bill of Rights protections, 18

constitutional amendment process, 6
duty to act and, 56
eminent domain powers, 16, 252–253
incorporation of Bill of Rights, 13
limits on powers of, 16, 17
nuisance torts, 61–62
police powers of, 12
powers granted by Constitution, 6
regulation of business environment, 32–33
and right to bear arms, 14
scope of constitutional protections, 18–19
securities regulation, 334
statutory law, 6–8
zoning regulations, 255–256
state supreme courts, 27
statute of frauds
    debt of another, 109
    executors and administrators, 109
    insurance contracts, 266
    marriage consideration, 109–110
    overview, 107
    performance beyond one year, 108
    sale of goods for $500 or more, 109
    signed writing, 108
    transfer in real estate interest, 108–109
    UCC, 140
statute of limitations
    breach of sales and lease contracts, 164
    commercial paper, 173
    contracts for sales, 143
statutory law, 6–8
statutory rape, 43
stock acquisition, Clayton Act, 339
strict liability crimes, 40
strict scrutiny test, 7, 14
strikes, 321, 322–323
Subchapter S corporations, 381
subject matter jurisdiction, 21–23
subleasing of goods, 140
substantial performance, discharge through, 119
substantive due process, 15–16
substitute goods, procurement of, 163
substituted performance, 153
subsurface rights, 45
sum certain, negotiable instruments, 171
supernumeraries, wills, 275
surrogate courts, 26
suspect classification, 7

Taft–Hartley Act, 322–323
tampering, public records, 46
tangible loss, 59–60
tangible property, 219–220, 229, 243
tax exemptions, 381
tax penalty, lack of health insurance, 268, 328
telegraph, offer acceptance, 83–84
tenancy
    in common, 254
    by the entirety, 254
    landlord-tenant relationship, 259–263
    real property, 254–255
    at will, 245, 259
tenant in partnership, 363–364
tenants. See landlord-tenant relationship; tenancy
tender of delivery, 149–150
Tenth Amendment, 17
term life insurance contracts, 267
termination
    agency, 306
    landlord-tenant relationship, 259
    notice of, 147
    sole proprietorships, 357
    trusts, 287
terms, of contracts, 108
testamentary gifts, 226 252
testamentary trusts, 282, 286

testator, 271
testatrix, 271
testimony, privilege against self-incrimination, 15
theft of services, 45
theocracies, 31
Third Amendment, 14
third-degree felonies, 41
third-party beneficiaries
    assignment of contracts to, 113–116
    of warranties, 158
threats
    assault and, 56–57
    duress, 98
tie-in sales arrangements, 339
time frames
    bankruptcy, 212
    board of directors, 378
    copyright, 230
    corporations, 380
    delivery of goods, 147
    expiration of agency, 305
    LLC duration, 384
    negotiable instruments, 172
    offer revocation, 82
    patents, 229–230
    perfected security interest, 189–190
    real property ownership interests, 243–244
    terms of contract, 108
    trademarks, 231
title
    gaining through adverse possession, 253–254
    gaining through eminent domain, 252–253
    gaining through *inter vivos* gifts, 252
    gaining through testamentary gifts, 252
    to goods, passing, 149
    to personal property, acquiring, 221–226
    warranty of, 156–157
Title VII, Civil Rights Act, 323–324
Titles I and III, ADA, 327, 328
tombstone ads, 332
tort law
    breach of duty to act, 55–56
    contracts and, 103
    criminal law vs., 55
    intentional torts, 55–62
    negligence, 65–68
    principal's liability for agent's torts, 308–309
    strict liability, 68–69
    torts vs. crimes, 55
tortious interference, 60
totalitarian regimes, 31
trade, restraint of, 103–104
trade secrets, 232
trademarks, 231, 234
traffic courts, 26
transactions. See secured transactions
transfer
    commercial paper, 175, 183
    by deed, 251
    LLC interest, 385
    real estate interest, 108–109
    real property interests, 251–256
transfer warranties, 183
transferee, 175
transferor, 175
treaties, 6
treble damages, 232, 338
trespass, 44–45
trespass to land, 60–61, 243
trial, bankruptcy, 202
trial by jury, right to, 15–16
trial courts, 26
trier of fact, 24
Trotten trusts, 284
trust corpus, 281
trust settlor, 281

trustees, 281, 282
trustees, bankruptcy, 202, 206
trusts
    defined, 281
    constructive, 282, 287
    express, 281, 282
    irrevocable and revocable, 282–284, 285–286
    overview, 281–282
    resulting, 281, 287
    termination of, 287
    testamentary, 282, 286
    Trotten, 284
    trustee rights, responsibilities, and requirements, 282
Turgenev, Ivan, 31
Twelve Tables of Roman law, 3
Twenty-First Amendment, 6
Tyco International, 334

UCC. *See* Uniform Commercial Code (UCC)
ULLCA (Uniform Limited Liability Company Act), 383
ULPA (Uniform Limited Partnership Act), 369, 370, 371, 372, 373
ultrahazardous activities, 68
unauthorized contracts, agents, 308
unauthorized signatures, 182
unconditional promise, 171
unconscionable contracts, 104–105, 142–143
undisclosed principals, 310
undue influence, 100, 274
unemployment benefits, 325
unequivocal offer/promise, 81–82, 83
unfair competition, 337–338
unfinished goods, right to salvage, 161
Uniform Commercial Code (UCC)
    Article 2. *See* sales and lease contracts
    Article 3. *See* commercial paper
    Article 9. *See* secured transactions
    commercial impracticability, 121
    commercial paper, 167–173, 175–178, 181–184
    formal contracts, 80
    illusory promises, 88–89
    mitigation of damages, 127
    overview, 137
    pre-existing duty, 89
    sales and lease contracts. *See* sales and lease contracts
    statute of frauds, 107, 109, 140
    statute of limitations, 164
    text of, 413–554
    warranties, 155–158
Uniform Limited Liability Company Act (ULLCA), 383
Uniform Limited Partnership Act (ULPA), 369, 370, 371, 372, 373
Uniform Partnership Act of 1914 (UPA), 359, 363
unilateral contracts, 79, 84
union agreements, 321, 322
unions, 320–323
United Nations, 143–144, 233
United States. *See also under U.S.*
    complexity of legal system, 8–9
    jurisdiction of, 17–18
    lawyers in, 8–9
    sources of American law, 5–9

Universal Copyright Convention, 233
universal life insurance contracts, 267
unlawful termination, landlord-tenant relationship, 259–262
unreasonable searches and seizures, 14–15
UPA (Uniform Partnership Act of 1914 (UPA), 359, 363
U.S. Attorney General, 327
U.S. Bankruptcy Code, 201, 212
U.S. Claims Court, 23
U.S. Congress
    administrative agencies and, 35–36
    administrative law and, 8
    bankruptcy regulations, 201
    Commerce Clause, 12–13, 317
    constitutional amendment process, 6
    employment legislation, 323
    Fourteenth Amendment provisions, 17–18
    health insurance regulation, 268
    intellectual property regulation, 229
    interstate commerce regulation, 35
    judicial review and, 8
    regulatory powers of, 11–12
    statutory law and, 6–8
U.S. Constitution. *See also specific amendments*
    Article I, 11–12, 13
    Article III, 21–22, 23, 24
    Article V, 6
    Article VI, 5–6
    bankruptcy and, 201
    Bill of Rights, 13–18
    Commerce Clause, 12–13
    constitutional amendment process, 6
    eminent domain, 252–253
    intellectual property rights, 229
    jurisdiction and, 21–23
    as supreme law of the land, 5–6
    text of, 399–411
U.S. Copyright Office, 229, 230
U.S. Court of International Trade, 23
U.S. Department of Justice, 333, 339, 340
U.S. Department of Labor, 322, 325, 326
U.S. District Courts, 24
U.S. District Courts of Appeal, 24–25
U.S. Food and Drug Administration, 36
U.S. House of Representatives, 6
U.S. House of Representatives Judiciary Committee Report 109-031, 212
U.S. Immigration and Customs Enforcement, 36
U.S. Patent and Trademark Office, 229, 230, 231
U.S. Securities and Exchange Commission (SEC), 8, 36, 331–332, 333
U.S. Senate, 6, 17
U.S. Supreme Court
    on ACA, 268
    appeals, 23, 25, 27
    on Commerce Clause, 35, 317
    on due process protections, 16
    in federal court system, 25
    on Fourteenth Amendment, 18
    interpretation of Constitution, 6, 13
    jurisdiction, 23
    overview, 25
    power of judicial review, 7–8
    on restraint of trade, 338
    on right to bear arms, 7, 14
    on securities investments, 331

U.S. Tax Court, 23
U.S. Trustees, 205, 212
usage of trade, UCC, 141
use of force, 50, 51
usurious contracts, 104
utilitarianism, 30

valid offer, requirements, 81–82
value, legal, 87
variance, zoning, 256
violations, 41
vital interest, 7
voice mail, offer acceptance, 83–84
voluntary intoxication, 49
voting rights, 17–18

W. G. Sumner, 31
Wagner Act, 321, 322, 323
waiting period, 332
Walker v. Texas Division, Sons of Confederate Veterans, 73–74
warranties
    exclusion or modification of, 157
    express, 155–156
    implied, 156–157
    sales and lease contracts, 155–158
    third-party beneficiaries of, 158
warrants, 14–15
warranty deed, 251
warranty of fitness for purpose, 157
warranty of merchantability, 157
warranty of title, 156–157
whole life insurance contracts, 267
widows/widowers, 244–245, 277
wild animals, 69, 221–222
William I, 4
wills
    disinheritance of spouses and children, 277
    holographic and nuncupative, 276
    intestacy, 277, 278
    overview, 271–274
    requirement of valid, 274–276
    revocation of, 276–277
    sample will, 272–273
winding up
    LLCs, 386
    partnerships, 365
WIPO (World Intellectual Property Organization), 233, 234
withdrawal, partner, 371–372
witnesses
    right to subpoena, 16
    wills, 275
women, voting rights, 18
workers' compensation, 325
worker's compensation insurance, 268
World Intellectual Property Organization (WIPO), 233, 234
WorldCom, 33, 334
Writs of Certiorari, 25

yellow dog contracts, 321

zoning, 62, 255–256